Do We Know Jesus?

Do We Know Jesus?

Daily Insights for the Mind and Soul

Adolf Schlatter

translated by
Andreas Köstenberger
Robert Yarbrough

Do We Know Jesus?

© 2005 by Kregel Publications, a division of Kregel, Inc., P.O. Box 2607, Grand Rapids, MI 49501.

Translated by Andreas J. Köstenberger and Robert W. Yarbrough

All rights reserved. No part of this book may be reproduced, stored in a retrieval system, or transmitted in any form or by any means—electronic, mechanical, photocopy, recording, or otherwise—without written permission of the publisher, except for brief quotations in printed reviews.

This translation taken from *Kennen wir Jesus?* © 4th edition 1980 by special arrangement with Calwer Verlag.

Library of Congress Cataloging-in-Publication Data
Schlatter, Adolf von, 1852-1938.
    [Kennen wir Jesus? English]
    Do we know Jesus? : daily insights for the mind and soul / by Adolf
Schlatter ; translated by Andreas J. Köstenberger and Robert W. Yarbrough.
    p. cm.
    Includes index.
    1. Devotional exercises. 2. Devotional calendars. I. Title.
BV4832.3.S3513 2005   242'.2--dc22   2005011577

    ISBN 0-8254-3667-2

Printed in the United States of America

1 2 3 4 5 / 09 08 07 06 05

Contents

Translators' Preface 17
Preface to the First Edition 19
Preface to the Second Edition 20
Foreword to the Fourth Edition 21

Section 1: The New Word of God

January 1:	God's Rule Is Proclaimed	34
January 2:	The God and Father of Jesus	35
January 3:	"Christ": What Does This Mean?	37
January 4:	Jesus' Aim Is the Salvation of Man	38
January 5:	Away with the Old Thoughts	39
January 6:	Jesus' Gift Is That We Believe in God	41
January 7:	The Baptism of Repentance for the Forgiveness of Sins	42
January 8:	What Is a Sacrament?	44
January 9:	Two Kinds of Judaism	45
January 10:	Why Do We Confess Our Sins?	46
January 11:	Why Does God Forgive?	48
January 12:	Christ Forgives Through His Death	49
January 13:	Holy Wrath	50
January 14:	Love Awakens	51
January 15:	Worthless Repentance	53
January 16:	Acknowledging God as God	54
January 17:	The Elimination of All That Does Not Bear Fruit	55
January 18:	The Christ Baptizes with the Spirit	57

Section 2: The Son of God Appears on the Scene

January 19:	Even the Christ Was Baptized	60
January 20:	Conceived by the Spirit of God	61
January 21:	The Spirit Becomes Visible and God's Call Audible	62
January 22:	The Lamb of God	63
January 23:	The Freedom Purchased with Blood	65
January 24:	The Difference Between the Two Messengers of God	66

Section 3: Jesus Gathers His Disciples

January 25:	The Nature of Discipleship	70
January 26:	The Disciples Will Not Lack Anything	71
January 27:	The Goal of Discipleship	73
January 28:	The Disciples' First Encounters with Jesus	74
January 29:	God's Building Gets Underway	76
January 30:	The Son of Man	77
January 31:	The Christ in the Midst of Angels	79
February 1:	The Angels of the Little Ones	80
February 2:	Small the Beginning, Great the Outcome	81

Section 4: Jesus Renounces His Home

February 3:	Separated from His Mother, United with His Father	84
February 4:	God Removes John the Baptist	86
February 5:	No Worship of the Ruler of the World	87
February 6:	The Healing Power of the Word	88
February 7:	Giving Thanks for God's Word	90
February 8:	The End of Poverty	91
February 9:	Those in Bondage Are Set Free	93
February 10:	Can One Who Is Like Us Be Believed?	94
February 11:	Selfish Desires Are Not from God	95
February 12:	Jesus' Renunciation of the Wisdom of the World and Its Rulers	96
February 13:	Faith Liberates from Self-Will	98
February 14:	Faith Waits for God's Command	99
February 15:	God Does Not Reveal Himself Solely to the Jews	100
February 16:	God Has No Favorites	102
February 17:	God's Love Is Free from Selfishness	103

Section 5: Jesus Stirs Faith

February 18:	Faith Receives an Answer	106
February 19:	Faith in God Is Born	107
February 20:	Faith Is Righteousness	108
February 21:	Faith Brings Security	110
February 22:	Jesus' Commitment to the Jews	111
February 23:	The Message Is Believed	113

CONTENTS

February 24:	What Makes Righteous Is Faith, Not Works	114
February 25:	Jesus, the Atypical Jew	116
February 26:	Kindness Has Appeared	117

Section 6: All Are Given Access to Jesus

February 27:	Revelation or Blasphemy?	120
February 28:	It Is Easier to Forgive than to Heal	121
February 29:	Open Access to Jesus	123
March 1:	The New Thing Tax Collectors Learned from Jesus	125
March 2:	Jesus' Will Is Love	126
March 3:	The Commandment's Goal	128
March 4:	God Is Not Pleased with Sacrifice	129
March 5:	Jerusalem's Sacrifices Are Futile	130
March 6:	God's Creative Mercy	132
March 7:	The Call Is Issued to Sinners	133
March 8:	The Greater Righteousness	135
March 9:	God's Greater Word	136
March 10:	God's Indestructible Scriptures	137
March 11:	Hating Only One's Enemy	139
March 12:	Love Has No End	140
March 13:	The Heart Cannot Change	141
March 14:	Jesus' Mercy Toward the Righteous	142
March 15:	The Light Load	144
March 16:	The End of Selfishness	145
March 17:	Forbearing Love	146
March 18:	Fellowship with Jesus Brings Joy and Suffering	148
March 19:	Tears of Joy	149
March 20:	The Joy That Is Always Available	151
March 21:	Ready to Suffer	152
March 22:	The Liberty of Jesus' Followers	153
March 23:	Guard What You Have Received	155
March 24:	Freedom That Turns into Calamity	156
March 25:	The Free Slaves of God	157
March 26:	God Does Nothing Halfway	159

Section 7: The Law Does Not Place Any Constraints on Jesus

March 27:	Imaginary Sin That Is No Sin	162
March 28:	Jesus' Followers Don't Sin	164
March 29:	It Is Impossible to Sin While Being in the Presence of Jesus	165
March 30:	Where Does God Live?	166
March 31:	The Lord of the Sabbath	168
April 1:	Doing What Is Right Can Never Be Sin	170
April 2:	Jesus Must Die on Account of the Sanctity of the Sabbath	171
April 3:	Is Jesus Dangerous?	173
April 4:	Be Glad Now!	174

Section 8: Jesus' Word Creates the New Person

April 5:	Jesus Speaks in Vain	178
April 6:	The New and Greater Repentance	179
April 7:	The New and Greater Wisdom	180
April 8:	Insurmountable Resistance	182
April 9:	The Word Is One with God	183
April 10:	No Root, No Fruit	184
April 11:	The Word Prepares Us for the Time to Come	186
April 12:	Either the World or God	187
April 13:	Wealth Is Deceitful	189
April 14:	God Is the Owner, We Are His Administrators	190
April 15:	Must Wealth Be People's Ruin?	192
April 16:	How Does God Reward the One Who Honors Him?	193
April 17:	The Word Gives Birth to the Congregation	194
April 18:	Jesus' Legacy	196
April 19:	Jesus' Possessions Are Increasing	197
April 20:	The Invisible Church	198
April 21:	Jesus Remains Incomprehensible to the Jews	200
April 22:	Everyone Must Be Told the Word	202
April 23:	The Pure Community Is Not Yet Called into Being	204
April 24:	As Long as Jesus Is in the World, He Does Not Judge	205

April 25:	Only a Few Are Called	207
April 26:	The Number Is Small and the End Regal	208
April 27:	God Shows Those Who Are Lowly What He Does	210
April 28:	Great Things Come from Small Things	211
April 29:	Unable to Pray	213
April 30:	The Prayer God Desires	214
May 1:	God Works in Secret	216
May 2:	There Is Such a Thing as Sinful Prayer	217

Section 9: Jesus Brings Purity

May 3:	Human Traditions Are in Conflict with the Divine Commandment	220
May 4:	Tradition Separates People from Jesus	222
May 5:	Are There Christian Rabbinic Regulations?	223
May 6:	What Nature Brings Forth Is Pure	224
May 7:	Jesus Calls the Pure in Heart	226
May 8:	God Also Created What Is Within Man	227
May 9:	All Are Sinners; No One Is Unclean	229
May 10:	Truth Purifies the Soul	230
May 11:	The Free Person Can Enjoy or Abstain	231
May 12:	Faith Purifies	233
May 13:	Either Everything Is Pure, or Everything Is Impure	234
May 14:	Honor for Everyone!	235
May 15:	When Do We Enjoy Our Possessions the Most?	237
May 16:	Away from God	239
May 17:	Back to God	240
May 18:	What Happens with the One Who Comes to Jesus?	242
May 19:	Jesus Invites the Loveless Righteous Ones in Vain	243
May 20:	Jesus Fulfills Isaiah's Declaration	245
May 21:	Jerusalem Resembles the Son Who Only Appears to Be Obedient	247

Section 10: The Christ Calls His Messengers

May 22:	Jesus the Christ	252

May 23:	Peter Speaks God's Word	253
May 24:	Peter's Mother-in-Law Also Served Jesus	255
May 25:	Jesus Will Establish His Community	256
May 26:	Jesus Predicts the Resurrection	257
May 27:	The Gatekeeper of God's Kingdom	258
May 28:	Peter Chooses for Himself the Ministry of the Word	259
May 29:	The Apostle Speaks the Liberating Word	260
May 30:	The Apostle Speaks the Word That Binds	262
May 31:	There Are Hearers of the Word Who Die and Hearers Who Are Raised to Life	263
June 1:	The Disciple Is Not Allowed to Judge	264
June 2:	Forgiveness Knows No Bounds	266
June 3:	The Limits of Forgiveness	268

Section 11: Jesus' Demise Becomes Evident

June 4:	Jesus Must Go to Jerusalem	272
June 5:	Trust in Jerusalem Is Misplaced	273
June 6:	Jesus Must Suffer Many Things	275
June 7:	Jesus Must Be Killed	276
June 8:	Jesus Must Rise	278
June 9:	Peter Thinks He Knows Better than God	279
June 10:	Renouncing Human Plans	281
June 11:	The Disciple's Sole Duty	282
June 12:	Who Is Worthy of Him?	283
June 13:	Self-Denial	285
June 14:	The Battle Is Fought with Unequal Weapons	286
June 15:	The One Who Is Good Is the Victor	287
June 16:	Jesus Does Not Derive His Power from the World	289
June 17:	Jesus' Disciples Are Not Like the Prophets	290
June 18:	There Is Only One Danger	291
June 19:	Love Is the End of Fear	292
June 20:	Save Yourselves!	294
June 21:	Free of Charge	295
June 22:	Jesus Does Not Make Beggars Out of His Disciples	296

June 23:	Jesus Rewards Every Good Deed	298
June 24:	What Does the Disciple See in Nature?	299
June 25:	Those of Little Faith	300
June 26:	Cares Are Cast on God	302
June 27:	The Believer Calls upon the Almighty	303

Section 12: Jesus Alone Is the Judge

June 28:	Jesus Will Pronounce the Verdict upon the Disciples	306
June 29:	The Coming Settling of Accounts	307
June 30:	Paul Brings to the Lord What He Has Acquired	308
July 1:	That Which Is Hidden Will Be Judged	310
July 2:	The Pure Church Arises Only After Judgment	311
July 3:	It Is Not the Disciples Who Produce the Pure Church	313
July 4:	Why Are We Called to Render a Verdict?	314
July 5:	The Christian Honors Even the Unjust Ruler	316
July 6:	When Does the Bible Unite Us?	317
July 7:	Christianity Is More than Correct Doctrine	318
July 8:	Without Rights of Citizenship for Jesus' Sake	320
July 9:	Everybody Agrees: It's Good to Do Good	321
July 10:	The Christian Honors the Emperor	323
July 11:	When Does Condemnation by the State Become an Honor?	324
July 12:	God Appoints Those Who Rule	325
July 13:	The Divine Mandate of Rulers	327
July 14:	The Worker Obeys His Master	328
July 15:	Roman Judgment in Keeping with God's Command	330
July 16:	The Disciples Are Ready for Victory	331
July 17:	Jesus Extends the Cup to His Disciples	332
July 18:	God Has Ordained What Lies Ahead	334
July 19:	The Disciples Become Like a Child	335
July 20:	Those Who Serve Are Great	337
July 21:	Jesus' Path into Death Is Service	338
July 22:	The Disciples Are Invulnerable	340
July 23:	Abiding Joy	341

Section 13: Jesus Reveals Himself to Jerusalem

July 24:	The Disciples Want to Die with Jesus	344
July 25:	Hosanna!	345
July 26:	What Was Promised to Jerusalem?	346
July 27:	Out of Zion Comes Peace	348
July 28:	The Words About Jerusalem Are Fulfilled	349
July 29:	God's Word Remains in Force	350
July 30:	Jesus Suffers	351
July 31:	God Gives Up His Vineyard	352
August 1:	Who Should Be Honored: the Jew or God?	354
August 2:	The Outcome of the Battle	356
August 3:	The Proud Boast of the Jew	357
August 4:	The Plight of the Jew	359
August 5:	Bear Fruit or Be Cut Down	360
August 6:	God's Love Becomes Visible in Jesus' Cross	361
August 7:	The Work of Grace from the Work of Wrath	363
August 8:	The Advocate of Those Who Fall	364
August 9:	The Gift of the Murdered One Is Eternal Life	365
August 10:	Love Does Not Cut and Run	366
August 11:	The Condemnation of Jesus Is Invalid	368
August 12:	Jesus Brings His Word into the Temple	369
August 13:	The Temple Is Defiled	370
August 14:	The Temple Worshiper Acceptable to God	371
August 15:	The Law Prescribes the Love of God	373
August 16:	Love with a Whole Heart	374
August 17:	The Sons, the Laborers, the Guests of God	376
August 18:	Jerusalem's Politicians Miscalculate	378
August 19:	Is Jesus a Freedom Fighter?	379
August 20:	When Is the Jew Loyal to Caesar?	381
August 21:	Jesus Is No Enemy of Caesar	382
August 22:	What Happens to That Which Belongs to God?	383
August 23:	The Sign of the Christ Is the Sword	384
August 24:	The One Who Overcomes the World	386
August 25:	The Victor over Satan	387
August 26:	Peter Saved from the Tempter	388
August 27:	Jesus Powerfully Transforms Human Lapse	389

Contents

13

August 28:	Faith Is the Victory	390
August 29:	Jesus Dies in Peace	391
August 30:	Jesus Is David's Lord	392
August 31:	Nothing Remains of the Temple	394
September 1:	Temples Everywhere Fade Away	395
September 2:	The Disciples Exercise Persistent Prayer	396
September 3:	The New Prayer Arises Through the Spirit and the Truth	398
September 4:	We Have the Right to Pray for Every Person	399
September 5:	Jesus Makes the Spirit of Truth His Disciples' Advocate	401
September 6:	It Is Not Yet the End	402
September 7:	Jesus' Words Do Not Pass Away	404
September 8:	Jesus Prophesies for This Generation	405
September 9:	There Are Disciples Who Will Not Die	407
September 10:	God Has Promised a New Heaven and a New Earth	408

Section 14: Jesus Receives the Cross

September 11:	Jesus Celebrates Easter by His Death	412
September 12:	Jesus Is Honored Beyond Measure	413
September 13:	Jesus Is Always Ready to Forgive	414
September 14:	Jesus Cleanses the Clean	416
September 15:	Sinners Become Righteous Through Faith	417
September 16:	Did Jesus Make His Disciples Perfect?	418
September 17:	The Apostolic Prince Is Judged	420
September 18:	Those Who Get Drunk on Hope Lose Hope	421
September 19:	Jesus Establishes the New Covenant	423
September 20:	Jesus Gives to His Disciples His Body and His Blood	424
September 21:	Jesus' Flesh Nourishes, Jesus' Blood Quenches	426
September 22:	Jesus' Saving Power Stems from the Spirit	427
September 23:	Jesus Invokes the Omnipotence of Grace	428
September 24:	The Disciples Can Bear No Temptation	430
September 25:	Jesus Protects the Disciples	431
September 26:	The Rulers of the World Prepare Death for Jesus	432
September 27:	Where Did the Jews Seek Jesus' Guilt?	434

September 28:	The High Priest Expresses Horror	435
September 29:	The High Priest Finally Recognizes What Jesus Was	436
September 30:	Jesus Confesses Peter	438
October 1:	Jesus Receives Peter's Confession of His Love	439
October 2:	Paul Cannot Deny Jesus	440
October 3:	Jesus Dies as the King of the Jews	442
October 4:	No Roman Puts Up with a Jewish King	443
October 5:	Behold the Man!	444
October 6:	Jesus Was Reckoned Among the Transgressors	445
October 7:	Jesus Suffered Guiltlessly	446
October 8:	Jesus Does Not Call for Elijah	447
October 9:	Jesus Promises Paradise	448
October 10:	The Just One Suffers for the Unjust	450
October 11:	Jesus Becomes the Church's Example	451
October 12:	Jesus Affirms His Mother	452
October 13:	The Mother of the Christ Must Suffer	454
October 14:	A Grave Is Found for Jesus' Body	455

Section 15: Jesus Reveals Eternal Life

October 15:	The Slain Christ Is the One Who Lives Eternally	458
October 16:	John Believes in the Empty Grave of Jesus	459
October 17:	The Resurrected One Is the One Promised by Scripture	460
October 18:	Jesus Quiets Mary's Longing for His Bodily Presence	462
October 19:	Jesus Rescues the Disbelieving Disciple	464
October 20:	Faith Arises Without Seeing	465
October 21:	Jesus' Resurrection Is the Rebirth of Man	466
October 22:	Our Life Is Guarded for Us in Heaven	467
October 23:	The Light of Life Has Appeared	469
October 24:	The Word of Life Creates Radiant People	470
October 25:	The New Creation	471

Section 16: Jesus Becomes the Lord of the New Community

October 26:	The One Community	474
October 27:	Whoever Believes in Jesus Remains in Him	475

October 28:	Who Are the Ones Who Belong to Jesus?	476
October 29:	The Firstfruit of the Harvest Is the Spirit	477
October 30:	The Powers That Create the Church	479
October 31:	Jesus' Unbounded Authority	480
November 1:	The Sending of the Disciples to All Peoples	481
November 2:	The Presence of the Christ with Even a Few	483
November 3:	The Apostle Is Obligated to All	484
November 4:	What Must a Guest of the King Do?	485
November 5:	The Message of Jesus: First to the Jew	487
November 6:	There Is Only One Saving Name	488
November 7:	The Same Blood Gives Life to All	489
November 8:	The Jews and the Pagans Are Called	490
November 9:	Jesus Prayed for the Unity of His Disciples	492
November 10:	The Jews Are Enemies and Beloved at the Same Time	493
November 11:	Paul: A Jew Among Jews and a Greek Among Greeks	495
November 12:	The Church Arises Through Baptism	496
November 13:	Baptism Comes from the Triune God	498
November 14:	The Ethiopian Is Baptized en Route	499
November 15:	Those Buried in Baptism Rise Again	501
November 16:	The Jailer Is Baptized in Prison	502
November 17:	Baptism Makes the Conscience Clean	504
November 18:	The Disciples Teach the Commands of Jesus	505
November 19:	Free for Fellowship	506
November 20:	The Law Attains Force	508
November 21:	Those Who Believe Are Willing and Active	509
November 22:	Our Willing and Working Are God's Work	511
November 23:	Great Purposes	512
November 24:	Powerless Faith Is Good for Nothing	514
November 25:	Love Determines the Actions of Believers	515
November 26:	Love Arrives at the Proper Resolve	517
November 27:	Faith Makes Love Strong	518
November 28:	The New Temple Is Built	519
November 29:	The Congregation Proclaims God's Mighty Acts	521
November 30:	God's Witnesses Speak	522

December 1:	The Church Is the Body of Christ	523
December 2:	The Truth Is Entrusted to the Church	525
December 3:	Mythmakers Are Not Believers	526
December 4:	What We Do Is Stewardship	527
December 5:	The Believer's Body Is Offered to God	529
December 6:	Through the Body Arises Praise to God	530
December 7:	God's Word Is Spoken in the Church	531
December 8:	The Old Testament Is Read Publicly	533
December 9:	We Are Admonished and Instructed	534
December 10:	The Old Testament Leads to Faith in Jesus	536
December 11:	The Old and the New Are God's Gift	537
December 12:	We Hope in God's Appearing	539
December 13:	God Has Patience	540
December 14:	How Does Man Become Free from the Workings of the Evil One?	541
December 15:	The One Who Believes Is Not Judged	543
December 16:	The Unpardonable Sin	544
December 17:	The World Ceases to Be Worthy of Love	545
December 18:	The New Order of Our Lives	547
December 19:	The Eyes of the Heart See What Is Promised	549
December 20:	God Shows the Christ to All	550
December 21:	The Rulers of This World Pass Away	552
December 22:	Christ Hands over Lordship to God	553
December 23:	The Marvel of Honoring God	554
December 24:	Jesus' Humanity Renders Him Visible	556
December 25:	The Vindication of Jesus Is the Spirit	557
December 26:	In the World There Are Those Who Believe on Jesus	559
December 27:	Jesus Has Glory	560
December 28:	The One Who Rejects Jesus Does Not Know What He Is Doing	561
December 29:	Attack or Assistance?	563
December 30:	That Which Abides	564
December 31:	What Is Left for Us Without Jesus?	566
	Scripture Index	569

Translators' Preface

Adolf Schlatter's was a life well lived. When he put pen to paper and wrote what turned out to be his final work, *Do We Know Jesus?* he could look back on a remarkable career that spanned half a century of teaching and writing. Born in Switzerland in 1852, Schlatter had already written nine full-scale commentaries and major works on New Testament theology, systematics, ethics, and philosophy, as well as more popular pieces such as his ten-volume New Testament expositions called *Erläuterungen Zum Neuen Testament.* Yet what occupied Schlatter's attention during the final few months of his long and satisfying career? It was the quest of knowing *Jesus.*

What does knowing Jesus entail? For Schlatter, it meant knowing Jesus *historically,* as the first-century Jew who was heralded by John the Baptist as the promised Christ and who walked the earth much like a Jewish rabbi, teaching his disciples and challenging the religious establishment of his day. For Schlatter, knowing Jesus historically was possible through careful listening to the text of the Gospels and through establishing plausible connecting lines between causes (such as Jesus' messianic claims or his amazing deeds) and effects (most notably the cross).

Schlatter's quest to know Jesus more deeply and fully through the Gospels coincided historically with the rise of Nazi Germany under Adolf Hitler. Not unlike Luke, who in his gospel contrasts Jesus—the Savior ushering in God's kingdom—to the Roman emperor Augustus—who was credited with ushering in a golden age of peace and worldly prosperity—Schlatter presents Jesus, the Christ, Savior, and king, against the ominous backdrop of Adolf Hitler, the self-styled *Führer* (leader), who rallied the German masses in a quest for worldwide domination that would entail the extermination of millions of Jews.

In the mercy of God, Schlatter would not live to see the final outcome of Hitler's final solution. But the present volume, *Do We Know Jesus?* leaves no doubt that he was keenly aware of the storm clouds brewing over the German nation and that his allegiance belonged once and for all to Jesus, his *Führer* and Lord. For this reason, *Do We Know Jesus?* must be seen not only as a miniature theology of Jesus and the Gospels in form of daily readings (so much more than a "devotional") but also as providing a fascinating glimpse of a major defining moment in twentieth-century history, the dawn of the Second World War with its earth-shattering racial, national, and deeply personal effects.

Do We Know Jesus? is one of only a few of Schlatter's writings that have been translated into English. The difficulty of providing a readable rendition of Schlatter's material is well known and need not be rehearsed here. It is our hope as translators that this work will serve its purpose of focusing not on Adolf Schlatter, and much less on those who translated the volume, but on *Jesus* himself. In the original German, the title is posed in the form of a question: "Do we know Jesus?" One can reasonably surmise that Schlatter's answer to his own query was "No," or at least "Not nearly as well as we ought."

It is a telling testimony to Schlatter's own humility that he included himself in this indictment. Because he felt that even he, who had devoted a long life to the study of Jesus, was in need of greater firsthand knowledge of his Lord and Savior, Schlatter embarked on this quest of knowing Jesus as his final, testamentary, even prophetic, journey. Not that Schlatter would have considered himself to have arrived; like Paul, he knew that he had not. But even at age eighty-five, Schlatter strove to know Jesus better, and challenged others—including you and us—to join him in this quest. As you read this book, may you get to know Jesus better and grow in your relationship with him.

ANDREAS J. KÖSTENBERGER
ROBERT W. YARBROUGH

Preface to the First Edition

Do we know Jesus? If we no longer know him, we no longer know ourselves. For in our ancestral line, he is at work with unrivaled power. Compared to him, what is a Hildebrand become one with his sword, or a Krimhild burning with passionate lust? The condition of our inner lives and of our national community proves that the things Jesus built into this world are both present and at work among us. This is not obscured even by the numerous antichrists among us. For precisely when they, with blazing wrath, seek to suppress any memory of Jesus, their thoughts and intentions are inevitably shaped by the One they combat as their enemy.

But it was not this thought that caused me to take up my pen one last time. I do not write to increase knowledge of our national psyche. Rather, I am moved by the questions, Can Jesus offer us more than what we already possess in our national and ecclesial community? Are not his gifts richer than what we currently call our own? No one who knows the New Testament will fail to answer these questions in the affirmative. For the distance separating New Testament history from our own experience is all too plain. Is it our inevitable destiny to languish spiritually? Do we have no choice but to succumb to the things that impede our ability to think and act and that impoverish our fellowship? Genuine resolve that is able to raise us to a higher level can arise only from unmitigated perception. This is why everyone who participates in our national and ecclesial community should earnestly ask himself the question, Do we know Jesus?

This conversation with Jesus was divided into small sections because it is therapeutic for us to use a quiet portion of each day to listen to Jesus. But this should not prevent anyone from reading this volume more quickly. It will be readily apparent to the reader that the individual parts make up a unified whole.

ADOLF SCHLATTER
1937

Preface to the Second Edition

This book is my father's legacy in a special way. It is the last of his works, on which he labored until past his eighty-fifth birthday. He was driven by the glowing desire to show Jesus to our nation once again—to Christendom, which should know him, and to those who perhaps do not know him owing to the neglect of Christendom, so that together we may in him grasp God's gift with renewed gratitude.

A second edition quickly became necessary. For this second edition, it was still my father who divided the individual reflections into small segments for greater ease of understanding. Then he read the proofs until the very last pages. It was the final work that the one who had grown tired carried out with utmost exertion of energy and with trembling hand. Before the print had been completed, God's call reached my father on May 19, which led him from faith to sight, to that complete knowing which the apostle extols in 1 Corinthians 13:12.

THEODOR SCHLATTER
EARLY JUNE 1938

Foreword to the Fourth Edition

Adolf Schlatter wrote many books, both weighty tomes and thin volumes. They were—and still are—read by many. They made a particularly strong impact on those readers who had experienced Schlatter personally as a passionate professor and authentic Christian. The recollection of his manner of presentation and the appreciation of his lifelong concerns apparently helped people to understand Schlatter. His life with all its strains, struggles, failures, and influence shed light on his ideas. For his way of speaking and writing was peculiarly condensed and in its brevity frequently appears Delphic. This, of course, was already alleged during his lifetime. He also took this criticism to heart. Even after the completion of his final volume, he confessed to me that he had striven hard for a more intelligible presentation. But, he conceded, he had not succeeded; he had to write as he was able.

Now his final book is released in this new edition, the book he considered to be his legacy, the book by which he sought to take part in the spiritual crisis of the year 1937. Is it possible to help the reader of 1980? If so, this can be done solely by a glimpse of his life or, better still, by a snapshot of this year of struggle, 1937. I was in close contact with him particularly during this time and knew what his concerns and hopes were. Thus I attempt to provide such help for the reader.

Do we know Jesus? The intended answer is, "If we know him at all, we don't know him well enough." The distance between the living history that the New Testament presents and our own life experiences is all too great. We languish spiritually. Is this an inevitable fate? By no means. For what Jesus offers is much more than what we currently possess. Schlatter himself expressed such thoughts in 1937 in his preface. He added, "Genuine resolve that is able to raise us to a higher level can arise only from unmitigated perception. This is why everyone who participates in our national and ecclesial community should earnestly ask himself the question, Do we know Jesus?"

The picture of Jesus can be distorted through the dust of familiarity. We may be apathetic in our efforts to grasp the precise nature of the events surrounding Jesus in politics, society, and religion. The picture of Jesus can also be disfigured through hateful propaganda. While Schlatter was writing, people were preparing for the convention of the National Socialist Party in Nuremberg. This event was designed to be "a convention of honor." In keeping with unconditional commitment to the *Führer* and the ethnic German self-consciousness proclaimed by Rosenberg, the event was planned to launch an attack on Christianity. But the preparation for the expansion of Germany into the Greater German Reich (which subsequently took place in 1938) turned out to be a more important priority for Hitler. Thus, the major attack on the church was not launched, with a view toward vital territorial concerns. It can be seen in many portions of his book that Schlatter kept an eye on the long-standing slander of Christians and their message.

In order to impart a true knowledge of Jesus, Schlatter invites us to take a "walk through one year in conversation with him."[1] We should not discard the expression "conversation with him" too quickly, as if the *Herr Professor's* lectures were, after all, only in the form of monologues, providing us with 366 scholarly minitreatises—nothing more. The one who listens more closely discovers quickly how often the objections and doubts of Schlatter's contemporaries are taken into consideration.

The "walk through one year" is envisioned as the chronological reading of one portion a day, taking an average of four minutes. This proposal may strike us as odd. For books that need to be read slowly may be viewed as boring. Moreover, I must confess that I myself never took Schlatter's advice. In the fall of 1937 I read with great appetite and in one sitting. In the following forty-three years, I frequently consulted daily portions as the course of my work allowed. And now I have read the book again in the period of one week.

Nevertheless, Schlatter's counsel is sound. Many among us, especially those involved in busy careers, have little time, and the "quiet portion of our day," of which Schlatter speaks in his preface, may often turn out to be exceedingly short. What is more, every section is so condensed that it is hard to "digest" a series of daily readings. They may have the effect of an overdose of heart medication, which, when taken appropriately, sustains a person's life.

In contrast with an earlier book, entitled *Andachten* (Devotionals) by Schlatter, *Kennen wir Jesus?* is not a devotional work. It seeks to provide reliable information, to impart indispensable knowledge for understanding and following Jesus. I liken it to one of those magnificent mosaics in Ravenna in which hundreds of small pieces are combined into a picture that shines unaltered through the ages. This is how this book on Jesus should be read. Who would want to break 100 or 200 pieces out of an ancient mosaic composed of 366 pieces? For the book in its entirety to have maximum impact upon us, we need a certain amount of energy and discipline.

The material is divided into sixteen major sections. In each case, they are gathered under a major heading, which—with one exception—constitutes a full sentence, such as "Jesus Renounces His Home," "Jesus Brings Purity," "The Christ Calls His Messengers," "Jesus Alone Is the Judge." These major sections comprise between six and sixty-seven individual units and thus vary considerably in scope. The conceptual flow of the book follows the traditional course of the history of Jesus' life, from the call to repentance issued by John the Baptist and Jesus' ministry in his home region, to the resolve to press for decision in Jerusalem and to his passion, resurrection, and the formation of a new community. The scriptural texts for a given day, too, differ considerably in length, from a single phrase to twenty-eight lines. Every passage is condensed in a heading. Here I am astonished again and again by the accuracy with which Schlatter's formulations, in their simplicity and timelessness, capture the essence of the biblical statement. A few examples: "'Christ': What Does This Mean?"; "Two Kinds of Judaism"; "Separated from His Mother, United with His Father"; "Imaginary Sin That Is No Sin"; "The Free Person Can Enjoy or Abstain"; "Jesus Is No Enemy of Caesar"; "Love Arrives at the Proper Resolve."

There are also entire clusters of interpretation, such as of 1 Timothy 3:16 or Matthew 16:13–19 and Matthew 28:18–20. At times a particular text constitutes the point of departure for a discussion of an issue that takes several days to unfold. What is interesting in this regard is which further texts are brought in from the Epistles and which further dimensions come into view. Among the Gospels, the evangelist Matthew is dominant, as is always the case in Schlatter. Among the Epistles, it is Romans, 1 Peter, and the letters to Timothy and Titus that receive most thorough coverage. Schlatter's practical orientation is evidenced by unexpected "rabbit trails" in the discussion of a major theme. Thus, the monumental statements regarding Jesus' conversation with Peter (May 23–27) include a helpful discussion of aspects of similarity and dissimilarity between female and male service in the church (May 24, "Peter's Mother-in-Law Also Served Jesus"). Schlatter was heartened by the fact that it was this very concern— Does this fit into the present context?—that drew the first response. He took it as a good omen for his final work.

This brings us to the course of Schlatter's life. Schlatter was also a preacher and counselor. He delivered lectures and passionate contributions to the discussion of various topics in the church. But foremost of all he was professor of theology, a scholar, and a writer. In his seven years as lecturer in Berne (1881–1888), he worked out the basic parameters for his theological work. The years as professor in Greifswald (1888–1893) and Berlin (1893–1898), as well as the first years of his long tenure in Tübingen (1898–1938), primarily served the purpose of tedious research in the areas of the language of the New Testament and of the documents of Jewish tradition before and after the birth of Christ. In the twenty years from 1906 to 1926, he stood at the pinnacle of his scholarly stature and published a theological interpretation of the history of modern philosophy, a history of Israel, a two-volume theology of the New Testament, a dogmatic theology, a volume on ethics, and a history of early Christianity. In retirement he still held lectures for eight years, for a total of one hundred semesters. During this period he repeatedly wrote about his life and his aims. But when he was seventy-five years old, a new field of fruitful labor opened up. Now he wrote great scholarly commentaries—interpretations of Scripture that presupposed the knowledge of Greek and Hebrew—on the four Gospels, the three longest Pauline epistles, the Pastorals, James, and 1 Peter.

Anyone who could watch him at that time could not help but notice how he always appeared tired at the conclusion of a given commentary. He only revived when friends showed him another scholarly challenge. As soon as he was convinced of it, he began to write.

Why did he not put down his pen after he had finished his final commentary at the age of eighty-four? What caused him "to take up my pen one last time"? Where did he—at age eighty-five—find the strength for his last extensive work? He viewed himself as the "debtor" of the German people. For he believed that he knew the gospel. What moved him was the condition of our nation in the year 1936, the internal state of Christendom in this troubled and agitated Germany. Anyone who came to him had to give a thorough account of contemporary events. Anything that could help Schlatter diagnose our situation was important to him. And he asked himself the urgent questions, What does this have to do with God? What does Jesus offer for this situation? Do we already know him?

On May 23, 1938, the day of Schlatter's funeral, Friedrich von Bodelschwingh, the son of the founder of Bethel, said at a commemorative event,

> I was deeply moved by the last statement Schlatter himself wrote for me. It was a brief dedication in his final work, *Kennen wir Jesus?* It read, "I wrote it for the sake of our nation." And when I visited him for the last time, our entire conversation went along the same lines. The old man had the limitation and the advantage that he no longer experienced public life and the ecclesiastical struggle as thoroughly in every detail and immediacy as we have to, or have the privilege to. All the more did he see the big picture, and I was honored to follow the train of thought of the old man who was preparing to die. What resonated was that he, the Swiss, grew more and more in his love for the German people. All the connections and formulations we could have construed for ourselves during the last few years did not exist for him. Rather, from his deep love and his eternal perspective with which he observed the encounter between church and state, he derived an expansiveness, a flexibility, a liberty, a revolutionary strength vis-à-vis our church's attitude that continues to haunt and challenge me.

A man in his eighty-fifth year of life, who owing to his physical weakness can hardly embark on a car ride for a trip to the country; who depends on others to tell him what happens "out there"; a Swiss who identifies with the German fate; a Christian who establishes for the Hitler-led nation the diagnosis that it will, apart from Jesus, involve itself in crippling self-contradiction; a teacher of the church who does not trust his church, even the confessing church, to reveal the living God today in its formations and formulations—it was such a man who overcame all tiredness, overwhelmed by love, and took up his pen in order to write this book.

His love for Jesus the Christ gave him the expansiveness and flexibility that Bodelschwingh sensed. Schlatter considered the picture of Jesus that conventional ecclesiastical methods were able to provide to be too dogmatic and one-sided. What others were saying about Jesus appeared to him to be determined by questions that had been posed in the past. Schlatter always feared the academic; he loved to call it "scholasticism." Scholastically oriented groups and persons are in danger of dealing only with biblical texts that served as guides for the ancient teachers and are discussed in their writings. But this issues in a selection that results in impoverishment. Scripture itself is richer. If one's scholastic spectacles are laid aside—which always requires conscious effort—new dimensions underlying biblical events come to the fore. These dynamics, in turn, have the potential of addressing contemporary issues. The reader of this work today should pay attention to which scenes are selected from Jesus' life, which emphases are set by Schlatter, which individual aspects he develops with often surprising thoroughness. His interest and involvement in the German destiny is readily apparent.

The Question of "Nature"

The question of the significance of "nature" for our common existence was raised. In the Germany of Schlatter's day, the National Socialist worldview engendered a degree of propaganda for the German people's natural right to territory, size of population, economic and military might, physical vigor, genetic health, and "racial purity" that would be unimaginable in our day. This provoked an important aspect of Schlatter's lifework. In his final book, Schlatter thus gives extensive coverage to God's activity in nature, Christians' divinely ordained role in nature, and the significance of communities that are conditioned by nature and serve natural development. He also portrays the conflict between people's natural desires and the countervailing will of God, furnishing impressive proof that solely the spirit of Christian love residing in the believer attains to the divinely willed rule over the demands of what is natural.

This topic's importance for Schlatter can already be seen from a comment he made in the fall of 1933. When National Socialist aims and common ground seized young people in particular, he was alert in both commonality and difference. In view of this challenge, he said, "Doubtless it is good that someone seeks to attract young people with a hand that is stronger than that of a pastor. But dressage in order to create racists? The care and feeding of the German beast? No! And I hope to find much support for this *no!*

among our people. The current movement shows a dual thrust: a natural one, toward health and vigor—which can be our ally—but also a naturalistic one: now we have arrived at godlessness."

A few weeks before his death, Schlatter's legacy was once more the subject of discussion between him and a younger friend. At the end of the conversation the visitor remarked that he often encountered the verdict that Schlatter was the father of German Christians. This impression had arisen in certain quarters, even though Schlatter at no time had regard for "German Christians," who were for him a pale representation of the National Socialist Party and with whom serious dialogue was therefore impossible. Schlatter's reply is telling: "Yes, in one thing I have always been ahead of my colleagues: in serious dialogue with opposing views. While my colleagues always found enemies in idealists or others with whom they did battle, the one with whom I was to talk stood before me always as a human being rooted in nature. To him I was sent with the gift of Jesus. Only then does our conversation take on a completely sincere and merciful character. This you can see one last time in my final book, *Kennen wir Jesus?*"

Finally, one more quote, from Pastor Friedrich Graeber of Essen, who exercised decisive influence on the young Gustav Heinemann.[2] He said, likewise on May 23, 1938,

> Schlatter wanted the church to address the people for whom it exists. This is what he advocated unyieldingly and in submission to the Lord Christ. This is what he called the church to do, and this is the purpose for which he wrote his great work, *Kennen wir Jesus?* In it he first of all wanted to help adults accurately instruct the young about Jesus. But in writing this book he also had, beyond this, young people in mind. In correspondence during the last few months of the past year he briefly discussed with me the question of whether it was still possible to accomplish religious instruction today with Reformation catechesis. His answer was a resounding "No," for the following reason: "In this way you do not yet provide young people with the nourishment they need from the New Testament today." . . . Where, in Schlatter's view, should our Christian instruction today begin? The catechism Schlatter envisioned must first of all show pupils (who come to the instruction of the church from instruction in schools) the natural community in which they are placed: this is the way family, school,

nation, and country operate. But then they must be shown the church that they now approach for the purpose of religious instruction, a different community, God's people in distinction from the nation. This must constitute the point of departure for a new catechism.

Aimed at Action

At another point, too, Schlatter showed himself profoundly moved by Christians' situations in the Third Reich. In October 1933 he pronounced the diagnosis that Germany's "new leaders" were devoted to the primacy of the will and of action while failing to give adequate attention to intellectual and emotional aspects. This is what we should pay attention to in regard to Jesus.

> The people who fashion our national community do not come from the classroom but from the battlefield. Our church's condition is no longer that which prevailed during the time of the Reformation. . . . When Melanchthon talked to Roman Catholic theologians, their question was, "What do you Protestants teach?" And his answer consisted in the formulation of various doctrinal statements. It is childish to criticize this. Our task is not to scrutinize what happened but to perceive what should be done. We are no longer speaking with learned scholars. We do not gain a hearing among enlightened Germans by promising to preserve confessions and to teach our nation. They demand, "What do you Christians want? We want our national community!" They assess a person by his will and demand the exercise of all his strength. We should be glad that the church's dialogue with our nation is lifted out of the circumstances of the Reformation period. It is no longer our task to explain old catechisms, liturgies, and textbooks; this is not the church's treasure. The church's true treasure is that it remains with us in the communion of the Spirit. Because the love of God gives us fellowship with the Spirit through the grace of Christ, the church will never be embarrassed when it is asked, "What do you want?"

In the following years, Schlatter did not change his mind on this topic, which was so vital for him. The entire book *Kennen wir Jesus?* is pervaded by the question, Do we know that Jesus' word and work always aims at his disciples' actions? With Jesus there is no passive listening or cheap grace. In this, Schlatter and Dietrich Bonhoeffer concurred. Jesus does not merely provide us with new insights regarding man and God. He creates a new man and awakens him to a new work. Why was Jesus' passion necessary to spur Christians to action? This question is taken up carefully. It is possible to circumvent one's need for action in a Pharisaic, national-idealistic, even Christian manner, while at the same time instilling in others, and proclaiming to them, what is good. Schlatter's book does not tire in exposing this dichotomy between talk and action, in combating cowardly cover-ups of this rift, and in pointing the way to truth and freedom.

God and "Caesar"

What should a Christian do in a country where commands are no longer derived from a divine mandate, where total submission is demanded, whose leader allows—in fact desires—that he be deified and who spreads the illusion that his worldview is the final, definitive word on the issue?

The answer given in our book is unambiguous. If a contradiction arises between God's commandment and that of "Caesar," the Christian must do God's will. In this case he must fear those in power. He must be prepared to suffer. Directives issued by the government may derive from godless, merely human desires. They may even stem from diabolical sources and turn into an attack on Christ and his work.

Schlatter carefully demonstrates that state, government, and power should and can serve human justice and well-being. As long as this is at least approximately the case, a Christian is called to participate in national life and to contribute to the well-being of all. No government and no instance of the state must assume absolute powers. The Christian knows that all people in authority, even those who forget this, are only human. Therefore he can and will pray for them. But every act of "homage" is performed under one condition. For no oath can induce the Christian to take away honor from God, to whom it is due, and to transfer it to man, to whom it is not due.

It was announced passionately in 1937 that Hitler's state would make Germany great and that the new worldview would overcome selfishness through a sense for the common good. Schlatter repeatedly addresses this claim. Read how he predicts the demise of that community in which the law of national preservation is proclaimed!

Schlatter's book can be viewed as a single attempt to spell out in the twentieth century what is meant by the word *Christian*. It is outright exciting to observe how he, in so doing, depicts the essence of what is anti-Christian as well. In his preface he speaks of the "numerous antichrists among us." They, too, attest to Jesus' greatness: "For precisely when they, with blazing wrath, seek to suppress any memory of Jesus, their thoughts and intentions are inevitably shaped by the One they combat as their enemy."

It is clear that this conflict remained current in certain places and became important in others. As Christians in South Africa ask how Bonhoeffer's witness can be applied to their situation, Christians' political conduct can orient itself at Schlatter's careful exegesis in places such as South Korea, Latin America, and in East as well as West Germany.

Jewish Character

As a final distinctive of this book, we may cite its Jewish character. It goes without saying that the Jewish question receives extensive treatment. Knowing Jesus means knowing him in his historical context, in close relationship with the traditions of his people, in his conflict with many influential religious leaders of his day, as well as in his fateful significance for the further spiritual and thus also external path of his nation. Schlatter was competent to present these complex issues. It is no surprise that he follows the theological views of the first Evangelist. Because this Evangelist probably wrote his gospel only six decades after Jesus' ministry, he has unusual perspective on the Jewish question, but he also has a combative tendency that can be explained by his wrestling with contemporary Judaism. Schlatter's interpretation of the Matthean texts seems to me to be masterful and on-target. Nevertheless, a certain focus on the theological tendency of the first Evangelist is plainly evident. From our critical contemporary perspective—four decades after the extermination of large portions of European Jewry—one might wish, of course, that the hope for Israel expressed in Romans would receive more extensive coverage.

Schlatter's statements on the Jewish question leave one with feelings of ambiguity. On the one hand, one is troubled by generalizations such as the expression *the Jew* and similar phrases. Here we miss today a sign of solidarity between the Christians of 1937 and the hard-pressed German Jews. We should remember in this regard that Schlatter probably had few direct relationships with Jews and that there stood in close proximity to his apartment a synagogue, whose destruction on November 9, 1938, however, he did not live to see. It is also evident that Schlatter did not possess the charisma of prophecy in this matter, which someone like Bonhoeffer had, but rather the gift of interpretation. Thus one must declare from our contemporary vantage point that Schlatter did not free himself from traditional views regarding the relationship between synagogue and church, views whose connection with European Christian anti-Semitism can no longer be overlooked. I would also not view as critically as Schlatter the development of Judaism after the separation of church and synagogue. One may recall once again that the first Evangelist painted the future of Judaism in the bleakest colors.

This is the one side. On the other, one can only be grateful for the clarity and profundity of Schlatter's interpretation of the new element given by Jesus to his people and humanity, and of his apprehension of the conflict with the heirs of the old covenant who moved toward the Talmud and were confirmed in their resolve even further through their encounter with Jesus.

At a time of Christian-Jewish dialogue—in which we are in our necessary efforts compelled to thoroughgoing restitution vis-à-vis Jewish theology and religion, including even content criticism of the apostolic witness—Schlatter's voice is of great value, if one does not shrink back from the aforementioned needed correction.

The new release of *Kennen wir Jesus?* is to be welcomed for the following reasons:

1. The book provides us with rich information about Jesus. All the important facets of his life are clearly treated. Less well-known aspects of Jesus' time and details of his message take on significance. The full relevance of Jesus for us and all time is discussed in plain language and freed from conventional scholarly jargon.
2. The book provides us with precise information about Jesus that has matured over many years of scholarly research. Every statement of the New Testament is placed in its historical context. The uniquely historical dimension of the words of the first witnesses of Jesus takes on significance for a message relevant for all. Historical elements are never eliminated but remain transparent throughout. The New Testament authors retain their personality. At the same time,

attention is drawn to the unity and common ground of their ministry in the work of the Holy Spirit.

3. The book provides pastoral counsel regarding Jesus. It envisions a particular readership, namely, the young generation of 1937, which was stirred and confused by National Socialism—they as well as their spiritual leaders, their hopes, motives, disappointments, and doubts. It relates the historical hours of early Christianity to the historical hours shortly before the outbreak of the Second World War. Jesus throws light on this chaotic time; the ominous hour is illumined by the gospel. We learn by example what it means to address the gospel to people in the midst of a spiritual crisis.

4. Contemporary reading of the book provides a glimpse of the incongruities that are inevitable when one allows oneself to be impacted by such pastoral proclamation more than forty years after it was originally given. Times change; errors and omissions come to light and make us modest. The historical gap of four decades ensures that people become small while God appears great. The one who truly has heard will be able to lay the book aside in the assurance that Jesus Christ is the same yesterday, today, and forever (Heb. 13:8).

HANS STROH, 1980

---

[1] *Translators' note:* The full title of the present volume is *Kennen Wir Jesus? Ein Gang durch ein Jahr im Gespräch mit Ihm* ("Do We Know Jesus? A Walk Through One Year in Conversation with Him").

[2] *Translators' note:* Heinemann later served as president of Germany from 1969 to 1974.

Section 1

THE NEW WORD OF GOD

God's Rule Is Proclaimed
January 1

John the Baptist proclaims in the Judean desert, "The dominion of heaven is near."
—MATTHEW 3:1–2

However we translate the core term of the message that John proclaimed to the Jews—"rule of God," "dominion of heaven," "domain of God," "domain of the heavens," "kingdom of God," "kingdom of the heavens"— God's promised activity is compared with the activity of a king.

A kingdom arises when the national community is in danger of disintegrating, either from enemies who attack it from the outside and seek to destroy it (except for a remnant that they intend to enslave), or from inner strife that weakens the community to such an extent that it can no longer safeguard its members' lives. The purpose of the royal office is therefore to provide security and unity for the community.

When the Jews were promised God's kingly activity, they were being told that they could not procure security for themselves. No one could have been deceived about this at that time. The Jewish community was choked by the pressure placed on it by powerful nations, and this pressure not only brought about political subjection but also corrupted the nation's entire fabric of life. The desire to become like the other nations was overwhelming, but this would inevitably lead to internal disintegration. When selfish desire rules a person, the community is ruptured. Parties are formed that fight for their convictions and seek to destroy each other, and the selfish quest for the essentials of life results in the accumulation of great wealth. This, in turn, goes hand in hand with the abject impoverishment of that segment of the population that seeks to bring forth food from the land by its own hard labor.

The strong bond of unity that characterized the Jews from their very beginning resisted corruption. This unifying force was the Law, which provided the Jews with not only national unity but also their knowledge of God and the promise of his grace. At the same time, the Law gave the Jews their nation and their religion. Nevertheless, it was unable to create the unified community that was protected from decay. In view of God, the Law raised the difficult question of when it was fulfilled. For the great achievements of obedience were offset by transgressions no less severe. This, in turn, brought public conditions into an irremediable, all too apparent conflict with the Law.

If God's regal activity was now being announced, this promised not only a new establishment of the ethnic community but also a new revelation of God. This revelation will take the place of the Law, which up to that point had reigned supreme. In its place a new word of God will be issued to the people. It will be a word of judgment, bringing an end to all influences that resist God and corrupt the community. But the community is preserved not merely by the manifestation of divine power. The word by which God will act as king toward his people is a gracious word proclaiming peace—peace with God in the place of godlessness, and peace among people in place of the corrupting power of selfishness.

Everyone who proclaims the rule of God affirms that God does not place our security into our own hands or expect us to save ourselves; we are not able to do so. God himself is the one who saves us. His good work heals our evil works. His righteousness provides the remedy for our unrighteousness. His truth sets us free from our lies and illusions, and his creating power is stronger than death. The new word of God will therefore launch an unfathomably great enterprise, renewing the life of the people and the life of every individual.

The God and Father of Jesus
January 2

Jesus answered, "I praise you, Father,
Lord of heaven and earth."
—Matthew 11:25

Jesus proclaims God's rule because it is the salvation of mankind. What does Jesus have in mind when he speaks of "God"? He uses two expressions. To begin with, God is his Father, from whom he has life, receiving from him his thoughts and desires. Thus he speaks God's word and accomplishes God's work.

Yet the expression Jesus uses to describe his fellowship with God is not fully adequate to convey what God is for him. A second term is necessary:

"the Lord of heaven and earth." God is Lord of heaven and earth because he has made them and preserves them. This is how Jesus describes the relationship with God of every living thing; the one to whom everything, heavenly or earthly, is subjected is his Father, the one through whom and for whom he lives.

By ruling over all of creation, God reveals his greatness. The distance separating man from him is exposed. God is the Distant One, concealed from the human eye, not subject to man's will, independent of people's activity. God's fatherhood, on the other hand, in whose power Jesus lives as his Son, reveals God's grace. By it he is the one who is present among people, who talks to them, works for them, and gives them life. As Lord of heaven and earth, he is the Omnipresent One. As the Father of his Son, he is the one who is present here and now.

Nevertheless, both statements regarding God refer to the One, and are inseparable. This lends glory to the divine sonship enjoyed by Jesus, uniting him with the Lord of heaven and earth. This constitutes the Son as the one to whom all things are entrusted. Moreover, sonship completes universal lordship because it translates subordination to God into a unity of will with that subordination. The Son is not merely subject to God like everything else. Rather, he is the one who obeys God and lives by his obedience to the Father's will.

These two designations of God correspond to the two words of God received by mankind. The Lord of heaven and earth is the ruler. When he speaks to his creatures, his word is authoritative, binding law for them. The word by which the Son comes to mankind, on the other hand, is the message of God's grace, which announces what God does and gives. Yet both words proceed from the one. Because whoever comes to the Son of God is led to the one who owns heaven and earth, everyone who hears the message of God's grace also receives his commandment.

The Son of God is God's slave too, because he completely belongs to God as a slave belongs to his master. And just as a slave serves his master—exclusively and fully—so the Son serves the Father alone. For it is by renouncing that very life—by which the creature exalts itself to the same level as the Creator, and opposes him —that we enter God's kingdom.

"Christ": What Does This Mean?
January 3

The angel said to them: "Do not fear. For behold,
I proclaim to you great joy, which will be for all the people.
For today is born for you the Savior, that is, Christ the Lord,
in the city of David."
—LUKE 2:10–11

At that time all in Palestine were moved by an immeasurably great hope: they expected "the Christ." The righteous prayed for his coming, and the rulers feared his appearing. The priests who administered the temple called for him. But the shepherds, too, who led their herds of sheep through the desert, expected salvation from his advent.

The Christ? Who is he? He is called the Anointed One because he has been installed in the royal office by the will of God and possesses lordship by the commission of God. This lordship is given to him so that he may be the Savior. He fends off all calamities and serves as the protector of his people. From him they receive their security. He is born "for you." The kingdom exists for the sake of the people, and because they are in danger, the Savior is sent to them. He comes for the entire nation, for the people are a unity. Life is transferred from one person to another. Moreover, their unified thoughts and actions provide a common bond and history.

On Palestinian soil this joint experience was uniquely profound. There existed a divine word that was spoken to all, that made God's will known to all, and that gave to all a common goal to which the Christ would lead them. This, however, did not unify the people. Rather, it divided them into parties that treated each other with hostility. There were devout and godless men, righteous ones and transgressors, scribes and ignorant people. Yet the One who received the royal commission validates it by coming for all. He speaks to all, seeks to liberate all from what corrupts them, and wants to unite all through his rule.

This glorious calling, however, is at the same time fraught with danger. For rulers are already on the scene, and these are inevitably his enemies. When Jesus was born, Herod was king in Jerusalem, a ruler by virtue of his will to power. Herod knew no other law than passionately inflamed selfish ambition. His power was grounded in terror, with hundreds murdered in his prisons. He was the persecutor of him who is Lord by God's commission, and of all those who confessed that Lord, came to him for help, and brought him their gifts. Nevertheless, the message about the Christ is joy. For the Christ knows no fear. His anointing means that he goes about his work in peace. For he enjoys God's protection.

Jesus' Aim Is the Salvation of Man
January 4

You are guarded by God's power through faith for salvation, which is ready to be revealed in the last time.
—1 Peter 1:5

What is the end to which Jesus leads us? Whoever is kept by God because he believes in him is given salvation. We cannot reproduce the apostolic word with a single one of our words. *Salvation!* This is an essential part of Jesus' promise. The processes that destroy life vanish through him. What currently attacks and corrupts us is gone, and the danger constantly arising from what we are and do is repulsed. This, among other things, removes from our existence anything that presently characterizes our experience and controls our conduct.

But the apostolic word draws our attention not merely to Christ's bringing our pitiable state to an end because he is the messenger of divine grace. For through salvation, which comes to us with the gift of divine grace, he drives away the misery we create for ourselves. God's favor remedies what we produce in error and failure. Righteousness saves us from our sins, and truth heals our delusion and unbelief. We are led out of darkness by being visited by the light, and we are freed from prison by receiving our acquittal. The One who must die is saved by resurrection, and our godlessness dissipates because God reveals himself to us.

Luther called God's promise to us "the blessedness," pointing to the gift by which sin and shame, misery and death come to an end. But our word *blessedness* lacks certain connotations, making it unfit to replace the apostolic word. The first thing that comes to mind is the healing of our emotions, which assail us through passion or suffering. But whatever incites our emotions, be it fear, pain, restlessness, or impatience, will disappear because our entire existence is promised renewal.

This comprehensive healing is already present in the will of God and in the completed work of Christ. But it is not yet made part of our history and perspective. Its revelation is reserved for the end of time and will bring an end to present history. Does it have an end? That it has a beginning is certain, although it remains a complete mystery to us. Will its result be universal death and destruction? No one who believes in Jesus affirms this, nor does anyone who listens to the consciousness he is granted. For he knows that he is created not to perish but to know his Creator, created so that his Creator may become his Father. Then the saving blessedness that brings all misery to an end will come to light.

Away with the Old Thoughts
January 5

Jesus began to proclaim,
"Repent! For the dominion of heaven is near."
—Matthew 4:17

New ideas, new goals, new desires, new actions—this demand was the clear result of Jesus' coming to men. His existence testified that God's rule was near and that God's work was done, by which he brought people to their divinely desired goal. This, however, revolutionizes our entire outlook. Not a single thought is left untouched. To be sure, the message transmitted to our senses by nature remains intact. Man is not removed from nature. The sun still shines for him, for he is not transformed into a bodiless spirit. Over this sensual portion of our mental state we have no control. We cannot obtain it when our senses fail, nor can we reject what nature shows us through them. But through this experience and knowledge, we are given material that we process internally. We transform our perceptions into a whole, evaluate what happens to us, and create images by which we stimulate our desires and set aims for it. It is this aspect of our outlook that Jesus' command addresses when he says: Away with your thoughts! We use different words for it: worldview, philosophy, theology, morality, politics. These terms convey the different ways in which our mental faculties operate.

But these differences never invalidate Jesus' command, which demands from us new thoughts and a new will. Yet our thoughts and wills become new solely as we renounce our old thoughts and shed our old desires. What is new does not merely supplement the old; it replaces it. This lends profound seriousness to the demand "Renew your thoughts," and this is what ecclesial language had in view when it called what Jesus desires "repentance." But this word does not express the essential element in what Jesus is after: the transformation of our conduct.

We express thereby that we keenly experience the battle in which Jesus' call places us, because he calls our thoughts and desires reprehensible. This battle affects our innermost lives and at the same time has far-reaching consequences for our dealings with one another. In this battle, even thoughts that are dear to us come under divine condemnation, and we must judge as reprehensible aspirations to which we have, up to that point, devoted our entire lives. Nor is the process a matter of gradual change, such as occurs in general culture where a first discovery leads to a second one. On the contrary, Jesus demands a decision and thus brings about division. This is inevitable because God's kingdom is not a supplement or continuation of our natural existence. Our relationship with God is now ordered by God's gracious will, and this revolutionizes our condition.

The disciples provide a graphic example of the nature of such repentance. When they considered their participation in God's plan, they thought of God's law, and when they looked at the outcome of their lives, they assumed that their end would be death. As long as they sought God's gift to them in the Law, they looked for righteousness in themselves. But now they long for God's kingdom and righteousness, knowing that his kingdom is not characterized by the demanding God who calls people to work, but rather that it takes place through the revelation of his grace. Thus they live on account of what God produces from them, and they know that God's kingdom brings about God's eternal fellowship with them, granting them eternal life. Everything became new in the disciples. They were elevated to the liberty of faith, to which is given forgiveness of sins, and they were liberated from resigning themselves to death. This was a complete "turnaround."

Jesus' Gift Is That We Believe in God
January 6

Jesus proclaimed the saving message of God and said,
"The time is fulfilled; the rule of God is near.
Repent and believe on account of the gospel."
—MARK 1:14–15

When God's kingdom comes, our perspective is completely transformed. What is more, the scope of our activity, the realm of our vocation, and the content of our obligations are completely renewed. This is why Jesus commands us: Let your thoughts go; they are old. Surrender your intentions; they are worthless. Desist from your undertakings; they render you guilty.

Yet the proclamation of God's rule, which gives rise to Jesus' call to repentance, is a promise that transcends everything we know and experience. It was transcendent not merely when Jesus began his ministry but also when he rose from the dead and when the church was gathered. And it remains transcendent regardless of what happens with the church. What then? What are we to do while waiting for God's kingdom? God's work is accompanied by his word. God's communion with Jesus, which granted Jesus divine sonship, made him the herald of a message, and this message is a saving message. For God's rule takes place by his revealing his grace toward us. This grace, in turn, installs Jesus in his kingly office in order that he may bring to us the gift of divine grace. But when a divine message comes to us, and a salvific message at that, we are called to faith.

Thus the new essence that enters into the natural realm of man through Jesus is identified: man now believes in God. The stance we take toward Jesus' message decides whether we relate to God in a believing or unbelieving manner. When his word enters us and becomes our possession, we believe. But then we do not merely believe a truth or a teaching; rather, we believe in the One whose word it is, whose will it tells us, and whose work it promises to us. Because Jesus' word speaks to us about God and his grace, the faith he effects in us is faith in God.

Does anything change in us when our disposition becomes faith? Does anything change in a family when the husband trusts the wife, the wife trusts the husband, the children trust the parents, and the parents trust the children? Did anything change in our nation when we trusted in our *Führer*? Does our worldview change when we trust in God? Oh yes! Everything changes. Unbelief, ill will, and suspicion result in a combative attitude toward everything that comes our way: Be careful; you are being taken advantage of. You have enemies surrounding you, a nature that kills you, people who abuse you for their own selfish gain, a treacherous fate that deals with you harshly.

All of this is exorcised from our soul when it learns to believe, once it has been seized by the gospel. Now it is open to God's counsel and able to listen to his word. Now it is also open toward other people who are told the same salvific message. It makes all the difference in the world whether a person is open or closed, open not merely toward irresistible nature but toward the operation of the Spirit, who gives us life from within. Therefore, Jesus' great salvific act is that he induces us human beings to believe in God.

The Baptism of Repentance for the Forgiveness of Sins
January 7

John proclaimed a baptism of repentance for the forgiveness of sins.
—Mark 1:4

God's royal work takes place among his people and prepares for him a community that belongs to him. This community arose in conjunction with what had happened earlier (that is, in Judaism) but was not a mere continuation of these events. A new beginning sets off what takes place now from what already existed, and the newness of this beginning is manifest for all in their call to baptism. The reason they are to wait for God's kingdom with assured hope is that baptism is administered to them. The new arises through the demise of the old, and the impure is removed. What now is beginning is imparted to those who have been made pure.

But how does an impure person become pure, or a guilty person righteous? How does a godless person enter into fellowship with God? The divine word turns him away from his blind thoughts by which he justified and defended his impure longings, and it shows him God's will. What is more, God now frees him from the dilemma he has created for himself by his sinning. God does not act as an avenger and does not determine a person's destiny according to his sins. God does not allow him to experience how greatly he has violated God's law. What is reprehensible in him is not a factor in God's dealings with him. Because God acts in his own grace toward him, he cancels his guilt. The first thing by which God's kingdom comes, therefore, is the forgiveness of sins, the liberation from the condemnation we incur through our guilt, the joyful message of God's grace.

Such was not an unintelligible concept for the Jews, and for those alive today it can appear unintelligible only to those who are not conscious of their dependence on God but rather want to be in charge of their own lives. But this is a dangerous maiming of human consciousness. For the notions are deeply embedded in us that we did not create ourselves but are creatures made by our Creator, and that the creature's conduct is subject to the verdict of him from whom it has received everything that it is. The moment, however, that we inquire regarding the relationship between our wills and actions and the will of our Creator, we are given a realization of sin, however incomplete and distorted by our self-love it may be. Moreover, we recognize in Jesus' message—that our sins no longer separate us from God—the message of salvation.

The offer of forgiveness also reveals to us the boundless magnitude of divine grace. When sins do not separate us from it, then there is nothing that separates us from it. All other distinctions vanish in comparison to what sin perpetrates. No other characteristic given to us by nature strips us of honor and right. Man becomes dishonored and disenfranchised only through unrighteousness and lies. His godlessness renders him worthy of death before God. But now it no longer separates him from God, because God forgives his sins. This beginning brought about a sense of the immeasurably great things that were to follow and of how wonderfully God's glory was to be revealed.

What Is a Sacrament?
January 8

John said to all:
"I baptize you with water in order that you might repent."
—Matthew 3:11

Can it be that Jesus' ministry begins with a childish fantasy? Many of us do without baptism and get along just fine. What is so important about water? We would indeed be fantasizing if we thought that forgiveness of sins consisted in baptism and were contained in water. Was the Jordan able to wash away what had taken place in Judaism? Can water undo what has happened and break the chains that bind man internally, chains that he is unable to break even when he tries to shake them off? Can water bend the will of man, and—more importantly—can it bend the will of God? Does it possess the magical power to transform wrath into grace? If a Jew, when undergoing the washing prescribed by the Law after touching a dead object, thought the water had cleansed him and had washed away what clung to his body, this, too, was a childish hope. Yet it was still far more reasonable than the expectation that undergoing baptism effected the forgiveness of sins.

But John did not allow anyone to chide baptism as useless. For he powerfully confirmed his message by concluding it with the offer of baptism. Because we can speak only in metaphors, we create images by the way we illustrate or act, even when we want the message to be strong. The Baptist strongly instilled in everyone whom he baptized the necessity of listening to his message. The recipient of baptism was told this message not merely as information but in order that he might obey the message, because it was to be fulfilled in him. Do you believe the message told to you? This question was addressed to everyone who was enjoined by the Baptist to dip under in the Jordan, because he had proclaimed the forgiveness of sins.

Yet a metaphor never contains more than the message it is designed to illustrate and render more effective. This is why the Baptist said: I baptize you with water. But if you receive nothing but a washing with water, you will not be helped. This will not bring an end to your guilt or provide you with a share in God's kingdom. You can desire the mere cleansing with water only if you care about nothing but the image, severing it from the message that is given to you together with this image.

Baptism is the forgiveness of sins because it presents us with the gracious word of God. If the word is muted in baptism, it becomes one of the many empty sacraments humanity has produced in its religious efforts. From the very beginning, therefore, baptism was not a silent event. The gracious word of God that called the baptized person into his kingdom was issued to him, and he answered the divine word by acknowledging his guilt and by reiterating in faith what he had been told by the grace of God. If baptism is administered on the basis of the divine word, we are also told that God's words are not empty words. God's word is effective. Thus we know how it is possible for there to be forgiveness of sins and how it takes place. It occurs because God's gracious word is realized in us.

Two Kinds of Judaism
January 9

*It is not the children of the flesh who are God's children,
but the children of the promise.*
—ROMANS 9:8

Through baptism, Judaism was divided into two camps. There were those who rejected baptism because they lacked confidence in the Baptist and were not attracted to the kingdom of God he proclaimed. Whoever was able to live all his days in glory and joy did not desire a kingdom that made him God's subject, and whoever was content with his daily worship and congratulated himself on his religious achievements did not long for something that was new and uncertain. But the fact that a portion of the people submitted to baptism meant that a new people of God was being extracted from the existing people of God—a new people whose unity and community were grounded in the divine word and no longer in natural descent. This separation was intensified and made irreversible by everything that took place as a result of the preaching of baptism: the rejection of Jesus, the disciples' confession of the Crucified One, and the gathering of Christian congregations in many Greek cities, congregations in which Jews and Gentiles were united with one another but were hated and persecuted by the synagogues.

Was this God's will? Was participation in his grace really not tied to natural phenomena? The Jew zealously insisted that he had been given the promise because he was a Jew. Yet he thereby expunged from his history the greatest and most significant event and forgot how Abraham was the starting point for the forming of the nation. There were two kinds of sons of Abraham and two kinds of sons of Isaac. This was so because it was not merely the natural process (by which men become fathers and women mothers) that led to the formation of God's people. Natural procreation is, of course, indispensable for the genesis of a people of God. Yet although natural life is the prerequisite for what we obtain in our dealings with God, it is insufficient to produce children of God.

This requires God's own activity, his will to love. God's love, in turn, is the source of the promise, which exercises creative power in generating the life God gives to that which has come about through natural processes. God is greater than nature, and his will is different from natural desire. Therefore there are children of nature who are nothing but creatures of nature, and there are children of nature who are made God's children through God's election and grace. This activity of God mightily impacts human history and began with the baptism that opened access to God's kingdom.

Why Do We Confess Our Sins?
January 10

If we say we have no sin, we deceive ourselves and do not have the truth in us. If we say we have not sinned, we make God a liar, and his word is not in us.

—1 John 1:8, 10

If our *Führer* commanded me, "You must not acknowledge that you are a sinner. You are a useful member of the nation only if you are honorable," this is how I would respond: "This command cannot be obeyed. For if I obeyed it, I would be dishonorable. In that case I would be a liar."

But is it, then, not true that confession of sin amounts to loss of honor? When we talk about our sinning, we acknowledge that we did what we should not have done and did not do what we should have done. We said what we should not have said and did not say what we should have said. We did not think about things that we should have thought about, neither about God's sovereign majesty nor about the sanctity of community that obligates us to give to others what belongs to them. Instead, we thought about many things and made many plans that were driven by nothing but our selfishness. It would be a long discourse indeed if we gave an account of our sinfulness, and it is evident that it could never bring us praise or honor. Whoever sins must condemn himself, and others are obligated to do the same toward him.

Is this not an unbearable situation? Where is there still room for community among us? What becomes of a marriage if the husband considers his wife to be a sinner and vice versa? How can there be a national community, and how can there be the brotherhood that Jesus promises us when we all must condemn ourselves as sinners? Dishonorable men must hide. The only kind of existence available to them is loneliness.

What compels us to persist in this awful situation without thinking of escape? The truth. We are not spinning yarns when we acknowledge that we have sinned: we do, in fact, sin, and when we deny it we sin once again, with completely disastrous and shameful results. The apostle confronts us with God's testimony in order that we may not be cowards and resort to lies.

When God's word has reached us, we know that we are sinners not merely because God's word admonishes and punishes us, but precisely as it reveals to us his gracious will and shows us how to act according to his will. Now our eyes are opened to the gulf between our actual conduct and what it should be. This gulf, in turn, is not so vast because we lack the ability or opportunity to do good. Rather, we are robbed of honor and life because we ourselves contradict what is true, right, and good before God.

Moreover, we are not able to say, unfortunately, that at some point in the past certain things happened that are reprehensible but are mere accidents of the past. The apostle calls this self-deception. "We have sin," he says. For we are forever responsible for the things we have done. This has issued in an indebtedness no one can remove from himself. Is our condition therefore without remedy? It is a hopeless situation for us humans, but not for God, not for the one who has forgiven us our sins.

Why Does God Forgive?
January 11

When we confess our sins, he is faithful and just to forgive us
our sins and to cleanse us from all unrighteousness.
—1 JOHN 1:9

God's royal activity began with the forgiveness of sins, for forgiveness is the deed of a king, the manifestation of his authority and incomparable honor. By forgiving, he demonstrates his faithfulness and righteousness toward us. Is it not part of the royal office to be shield and shelter and to keep us from corrupting influences? And what corrupts us more thoroughly than our sinning, by which we become death's slave?

Why then do we say among our people that forgiveness is something reprehensible, a violation of justice, because the guilty person is not treated the way he deserves? Why do we object to forgiveness as the mere pretense that sin does not exist when, in fact, sin pollutes and corrupts everything with unfettered power? Whoever speaks in these terms thinks merely of human forgiveness: the forgiveness of the coward who closes his eyes because he is frightened by reality; the forgiveness of the one who is powerless and who tolerates evil because he cannot keep it from happening; the forgiveness of the guilty person who forgoes justice because it is justice that condemns him.

But when a person is called to baptism, the issue is not human forgiveness. Rather, it is God's lordship that is proclaimed, and this lordship, in turn, manifests itself in forgiveness. God is able to remove the sting from our sin so that it cannot corrupt us. He is able to restore broken justice so that it produces renewed and now inseparable communion. And he is able to make shine the truth that we have trampled underfoot, so that we are placed in its light. He can transform our godless deeds, by which we dishonor God's name, into reasonable worship that brings him glory. God alone can do this. For forgiving is a creative act that makes a new beginning in our lives. God does so because he is faithful and just.

The Creator of our lives stands with us in his faithfulness. He heals us. And because he loves justice, he puts an end to our unrighteousness and invests his righteousness with the victorious power that makes righteousness dwell in us and that transforms our conduct toward God and others. This is what was promised to those who were willing to be baptized. Yet when they were baptized, they did not see how the promise was going to be fulfilled; this is what they waited for.

Christ Forgives Through His Death
January 12

This is the blood of the covenant, which is shed on account of many for the forgiveness of sins.
—Matthew 26:28

At the beginning of Jesus' ministry stands baptism, which is to be desired because it promises the forgiveness of sins. At the end of his life stands his death, the shedding of his blood, which gave him authority to forgive many their sins. Jesus' entire ministry is controlled by a uniform will. From beginning to end, he served the same gracious will of God, and with his final act he acknowledged and confirmed his first. Not to take revenge, not to judge, not to perish, but to forgive—this was the goal the Baptist called him out of Nazareth to fulfill. And it was once again his will when he took up his cross.

Just as baptism took place in the name of the King of Kings, who will manifest his rule, so also his death was the act of the Christ, which he accomplishes in the power of his royal commission. The grace that shields man, that protects him from himself and sets him free from all corrupting influences, glorifies the One into whose hands everything has been given by the Father. He was prepared to die not because he considered sin to be invincible or because he was resigned to it in the face of his powerlessness. Rather, he faced death because by death he would overcome sin.

But what is accomplished in all of this by his blood? Who can forgive? Who pardons in truth? The One who is faithful and just. He was faithful when he did not spare his blood, and he was just when he bore the verdict of God that lay upon man. The One who can deny himself and who stands apart from all evil reaped the cross through his confession before Caiaphas and Pilate. Yet he did not seek peace from them. The One who is light and who has no darkness in him, the One who expels every lie was the truth before his judges, and in the face of this truth their devotion and righteousness turned into a lie. The One who is love, who brings about communion and does not allow hatred to work unrighteousness, transformed his death into the manifestation of divine love. Apart from this God would not be the one who forgives nor Jesus the one who acquired for himself the authority to forgive in God's name.

Yet his blood reveals precisely that he had no fellowship with sinners and did not enter into union with godlessness or wickedness. He accomplished this by allowing himself to be condemned by sinners and by permitting himself to be rejected from their community as the One who has no right to live and no place in the holy congregation. By confessing God rather than pledging allegiance to the world—which he did by shedding his blood—he transformed his fellowship with sinners into the forgiveness of their sins.

Holy Wrath
January 13

Brood of vipers!
—Matthew 3:7; 12:34

Can one say such things in God's name? Were those who proclaimed forgiveness permitted to speak this way to those they sought to win and draw into their fellowship? "Your nature is like what a snake passes on to its brood" means "You are not merely corrupt yourselves; you also corrupt the people. You must be avoided as one avoids a snake." *Brood of vipers!* This is a declaration of war in no uncertain terms. It is not directed to the tax collectors and sinners, who were moved solely by natural desires, but pronounces judgment upon the "righteous" and the community's leaders. It removes from them everything that is their source of pride. The condemnation cast upon them is an utter reproach.

But why is this harsh assessment part of the ministry of the messengers of God's grace? Is there still room in them for wrath beside love? Do they show us God's character and will, even through this? It was not schizophrenic of the Baptist to strip the "righteous" of all honor and hope while at the same time offering them baptism. Rather, his attack on them and his outreach to them had the same source. For in both instances he obeyed the truth.

Both are truth: the weapon of divine wrath that judges us, and the weapon of divine love that draws us to it. What is a verdict worth if it is devoid of truth? It is but tyranny, able to subjugate us but unable to make us honor it. But when truth becomes our judge and shows us what is reprehensible, we fall silent before our just judge. What is love without truth? It is selfishness in disguise, which does not truly want to help and which offers fellowship to us only to the degree considered beneficial by those who extend it. But when love comes to us in the light of truth, we are truly those who are loved and called to fellowship. Then the Giver has given himself to us and has himself searched for us.

God's will is neither divided nor inconsistent. For everything God does to us—whether he is for us or against us, whether he reins us in or sets us free, whether he lets us die or brings us to life—everything issues from truth. And because there was truth in the wrath and love of the Baptist and Jesus, they neither wavered, nor lessened love through wrath, nor drove away wrath through loving. What gave them the power to do this was their faith in the omnipotence of grace.

The Baptist recoiled from what he saw in the "righteous." Still, he offered them baptism. Concerning the rich, Jesus said that a camel could not go through the eye of the needle; nor could a rich person enter God's kingdom. But he maintained that nothing was impossible with God. God's grace has creative power. Whoever knows this does not avoid confessing sin and does not turn a deaf ear to people's misery. But by the same token God does not vanish from sight when a person is revealed for who he really is. Both are placed into that person's field of vision: the truth concerning man and the truth of God. And he is comforted by the assurance that grace is omnipotent.

Love Awakens
January 14

And the crowd asked him, "What should we do?" But John answered, "Whoever has two tunics, share with the one who has none; and whoever has food should do the same."
—Luke 3:10–11

Was the Baptist dreaming? Did he see people only in an artificial light that blurred their natural traits? Someone has no tunic: why should I care?

I have two and am persecuted. How should this result in an obligation toward the one who lacks? I can eat my fill, but someone else cannot. Everyone has as much as he is able to grab for himself. If people had obeyed the Baptist, the entire economy would have collapsed, even though it was grounded in the Law.

The Law commanded, "Thou shalt not steal," thereby placing people's possessions under God's protection. Yet the Baptist did not stand in conflict with the Law. He did not command, "Demand what you do not have from the one who has." What he said was rather: You who have, give! This was a new commandment, even though all lived in the national community. What is expressed by the word *nation* was energetically pursued in Judaism. After all, they would not have longed for God's kingdom and come to the Baptist in droves to receive baptism if they had not realized that no one can live outside the national community. But inside the national community selfish desire was the passion that determined everyone's conduct. To the extent that the community proved beneficial, everyone accepted it. But the boundary that selfish desire draws between me and others remains intact. The Baptist, however, demanded that those who had subjected themselves to God's rule not push their neighbor away or put him on a lower level than themselves. Rather, another person's needs must be judged as important as one's own.

God's rule removes the boundaries that separate people from each other. Whoever is brought to God is also brought to other people. The nation whose king is God establishes perfect communion among its members. But this communion has not yet come into being when it is held together merely by the Law; rather, it arises when love shapes the community. The love commandment became the community's controlling principle through the proclamation of the rule of God. This took place in harmony with the Law that forbade the Jews to esteem their neighbor less than they esteemed themselves. And yet it was evident that the entire fabric of the Jewish nation was renewed when love was generated in the community united through baptism.

Worthless Repentance
January 15

Bring fruit worthy of repentance.
—Matthew 3:8

There were baptisms that did not free a person from God's condemning verdict, and there were new ideas that did not change a person's conduct. There was a forgiveness of sins in which an individual remained a sinner. This is indicated by those who despised baptism and did not believe in the possibility of repentance. "You baptize the people," they said, "but it does not change them, and when you rouse them through your call to repentance, this may issue in a movement similar to the one the Baptist spawned among the Jews. But waves subside quickly, and in the end everything will return to the place where it started." Is this strange? On the contrary! The way we see it, such is to be expected.

The new element injected into us through God's word first engages our minds. Then, when it is spoken into us in firm faith and strong love, we may be strongly moved by the appeal to refrain from what is sinful and to open ourselves up to what is God's. Then new ideas may be stirred in us. This, however, is no different from what the Law was able to achieve. The Law provides man with two aspects: an external one, by which he claims to be a servant of God, and an internal one, by which he obeys his own selfish will. God's new word opposes this schizophrenic disposition. John likened it to a seed that is able and designed to grow and bear fruit. This is the intent of every divine gift, especially the greatest of them all: the manifestation of God's grace to us. It wants our lives, not merely our thoughts; it wants us with all that we are, not merely with what we say.

But now we clearly see that the divine word does not praise or strengthen what we are. Rather, it does away with the old and creates something new. Natural desire opposes it and militates against love, treating others as if they existed for us and were obligated to serve us; it attempts to make God subservient to us on account of what we do for him. Precisely for this reason we need forgiveness of sin, and precisely for this reason we gain access to God through our repentance.

Yet our selfish craving, which prevents us from believing as well as loving, is incited through natural desires and gains strength from them by seizing us with compelling force. Is forgoing these desires, then, advisable? Does it make us happy? It does not cost us any energy to persist in what nature has placed inside us. If we remain arrogant people who cultivate our natural existence despite having heard the word spoken to us and bearing it in ourselves, then the movement into which the word has launched us remains fruitless. But then we have not really received the forgiveness of sins. For the result of forgiveness is not persistence in sin but rather its abandonment, and only when repentance sets us free from our selfish desire has it borne the fruit that it is destined to bear in us.

Acknowledging God as God
January 16

Do not take pleasure in saying, "We have Abraham as our father." For I tell you, God is able to raise up children of Abraham from these stones.
—MATTHEW 3:9

Religious communities have always been particularly unwilling to repent. Sweeping change is more likely to occur in the secular realm; castles turn into ruins, and dynasties disappear. In churches, on the other hand, God's name is tied to the things people say and do, so that everything they inherited from their forefathers—even when it is afflicted with error and sin—continues unabated. They use the truth given them to bolster their communal pride, which inoculates them even against their ailments.

Such was also the dilemma of Judaism. Its national and religious pride were just as strong as its national ties. By virtue of its descent from Abraham, the nation possessed a promise addressed to it and a divine law granted to it and thus an assured claim to God's grace. What was able to induce the people to desire something new beyond what they had already been given? They could assuredly rest in what they already were. The children of Abraham were shielded from every danger and equipped with the great hope that could expect all of God's gifts. Even when this was not coupled with an arrogant contempt for the rest of humanity, this complacent faith, anchored in the present, rejected any call to repentance.

What was necessary and helpful in this situation? The only thing that could make a difference was the undiluted acknowledgment of God as God. It was neither John's nor Jesus' desire to depreciate what the Jews had been given. God's word had, indeed, been issued to Abraham, and the establishment of the Israelite community was God's work. But did the Jew still know who God was? In effect, he claimed that God's word to Abraham and God's work for Israel were his final and greatest revelation. This is the voice of human pride, which claims God exclusively for itself and seeks to confine God's activity to the boundaries of one's own existence. This is why John proclaimed the majesty of God to the Jews. The coming of his kingdom did not require the Jews. The word God spoke to the Jews does not waver, but his royal will determines whom he wants to make a son of Abraham. And he will manifest his kingdom and accomplish the intention of his grace, even if he must create children of Abraham out of these stones.

God's grace originates from outside nature. It enters the natural process and uses it as desired but never becomes part of the natural process. The beginning of eternal life is not birth; it is spiritual rebirth.

The Elimination of All That Does Not Bear Fruit
January 17

*Every tree that does not bear good fruit is
cut down and thrown into the fire.*
—Matthew 3:10

Unfruitful trees resist the one who planted them; they frustrate his intention and nullify his work. Are there unfruitful trees, too, in God's field? No doubt there are people who confess God but dishonor his name. Although concerned for his law, they become its transgressors. They are the recipients of manifold grace without becoming the people that God's grace intended to make them.

Are these unfruitful trees to remain standing when God's rule is revealed? This rule comes about as his will is done. Yet the unfruitful person is subject to God's wrath because he refuses to do his will, and thus the proclamation of God's rule announces his judgment. According to this proclamation, all those who announced God's message desired nothing less than to experience divine kindness.

What about this message? Is a contradiction introduced into it? Is it divided into the announcement of judgment and the offer of grace? If so, this would not provide us with a firm foundation but rather would compel us to waver between fear and confidence. But whoever beholds God's grace knows that it is perfect and reveals to us the One who alone is good, and good in his entirety. How then should he accommodate unfruitful trees in his kingdom? Because he is gracious, every tree flourishes in his kingdom, and everything that is godless is removed from the realm of life.

But does the judgment rejecting unfruitful trees not apply to all? Isaiah once likened all of Jerusalem to an unfruitful vineyard, and Jesus used similar imagery, calling the entire nation an unfruitful fig tree. The Baptist spoke of the destiny of unfruitful trees to those who excelled in their religious sincerity and ritualistic industry. Beside them stood those who cared solely for natural concerns, be it because they wrestled with poverty and obtained sufficient food only with difficulty, or because they strove eagerly for wealth and prided themselves on their abundant possessions. If even the righteous could be likened to unfruitful trees for whom the ax is ready, how much more did this verdict apply to the rest of the people!

To be sure, the Baptist's verdict would have ended in universal judgment had he not been given authority to call everyone to repentance and to proclaim forgiveness to all. Because people can turn and receive forgiveness, there is a field in humanity, entrusted with a seed from which a harvest grows for God. We become fruitful for God when his word frees us from our own ideas, and his grace subjects our will to him.

The Christ Baptizes with the Spirit
January 18

The One who comes after me will baptize you
with the Holy Spirit and with fire.
—MATTHEW 3:11

The promise of forgiveness does not become effective through the one who baptizes with water, nor through its vivid presentation, which, although it testifies to the presence of forgiving grace, has no power, certainly not by what baptism encourages the recipient to do. It alerts him to his sinfulness and readies him to acknowledge the truth and his own guilt and to long for the power that awakens in him the new will. But this hardly enables us to move beyond what we find in ourselves. Even when we are deeply moved by repentance, we can contribute nothing but what a sinful person calls his own, nothing that can undo the Fall or avert calamity. Therefore it is the Christ's calling to render forgiveness effective by baptizing with the Spirit.

Spirit! This is another of Jesus' great words that proclaims his majesty and provides his message with profundity. Through the Spirit he cleanses us internally; through the Spirit he dispels our old thoughts; through the Spirit he teaches us to know God's will; and through the Spirit he produces the desire to do God's will.

What does this mean? It is the Spirit who revives us from within and energizes our ability to think and act. Initially, our body accomplishes this in accordance with our natural constitution, since we encounter the world through our senses and the body awakens our desires through its needs. But is the human being moved solely by nature? Nature only provides us with our selfish desires. In God's kingdom, however, God's relationship with the human being seizes the root of his inner life and brings it about through his divine activity. What is more, the message that proclaims the Spirit also promises that the divine activity will enter our lives, placing the divine word in our minds and the divine commandment in our wills. When the Spirit frees us from sinful desires so that we renounce them, and provides us with faith in God's grace so that we obey him, then we experience the blessed reality that our sins are forgiven and no longer separate us from

God. We rather have him on our side and have been received into his fellowship.

He who baptizes with the Spirit acts upon us in the service of divine grace, which has access to our innermost being, and with the unlimited royal authority that reigns over a person's life. Therefore he has authority to baptize with the Spirit as well as with fire. Effective, definitive forgiveness cannot be separated from effective, definitive judgment; they are entrusted to the same hand. Because the Christ administers them both, he produces the pure humanity that is united in God.

Section 2

THE SON OF GOD APPEARS ON THE SCENE

Even the Christ Was Baptized
January 19

Jesus came from Nazareth in Galilee and was baptized in the Jordan by John.

—MARK 1:9

Baptism divided Judaism into two camps. One group had confessed its guilt, desired forgiveness of sins, and thus had prepared itself for receiving divine grace. The other group were the righteous, who separated themselves from those who were baptized, because as sons of Abraham they were already full members of the divine kingdom and did not need to repent due to their righteous conduct. Into which of these two camps should Jesus be placed? With which of these two groups did he associate? The step he now took, without any reluctance, decided the course of his ministry.

The Christmas story illustrates well the messianic expectation into which Jesus grew. It retained the form given to it by the prophets: a deep longing for the manifestation of God's glory in the sinful nation through the operation of his saving grace. Thus it was out of the question for Jesus to remain solitary and unaffected by what happened among the people. There was no self-centered piety for him, who was led by the prophetic promise depicting the Christ, no interpretation of his commission that made his own greatness and fulfillment his aim.

He could not go to the complacent and proud sons of Abraham, nor could he contradict God's judgment that took away from them the artificial glamour of their own righteousness. Neither was he able to despair in view of the might of sin or shrink back because it was insurmountable and unworthy of divine forgiveness. His place was assigned unambiguously with those who not only heard but also acted upon God's Word, with those who agreed with the divine verdict that declared even the pious to be sinners, who believed in the forgiveness of sins, accepting it as the word spoken by omnipotent grace. His place was the new community of the divine kingdom gathered by the Baptist. He entered it and, by placing himself in its midst and completing his fellowship with it, became its Lord.

Those who deemed themselves pure might say, "He who separates himself from the impure is pure," but they did not know God. He, however, knew the Father's love and was therefore united with those invited into his kingdom by the Father's call.

But will he not vanish in the multitude of repentant sinners when he desires baptism for himself? Had he not now become merely one among many who were hopeful? The hopeful had been a dime a dozen since the time of the fathers; but he can not be merely one of them if he is to take up the word of the Baptist and complete what he has begun, doing so as the one who baptizes with the Spirit and with fire. But he could not publicly lay claim to royalty himself. If he himself announced and fought for it, he would render his claim untrue and incredible. Only God can elevate him; he can only be what God makes of him. While the proud might well sneer that being baptized by the Baptist was humiliating—for Jesus there was no other way to power.

Conceived by the Spirit of God
January 20

The angel answered Mary: "Holy Spirit will come upon you, and the power of the Most High will overshadow you."
—LUKE 1:35

Jesus came to baptism alone, unaccompanied by mother or brothers, not as a member of his clan or village. He came alone. Who were his ancestors? We know he had a mother. None among those who knew him obscured this, even though some penned glorious legends in his praise. Only a later piety, with a very different orientation, eliminated mother and childhood from Jesus' life. When the first worshipers were called to the newly born Christ by the heavenly messenger, that messenger gave them no sign other than that they would find a baby wrapped in swaddling clothes lying in a manger. They found nothing but a baby, one that needed the same care required by every newborn child. His birth placed him into human existence in every way possible, and Jesus confessed this continually and solemnly. His nature and his work are given to him on account of the fact that he is the "Son of Man."

At the same time, Jesus and his messengers always expressly told those who asked about Jesus' ancestors the following: He is not what he is through the inheritance that is his through his father or mother; he is the work of God, the new creature created by God's Spirit, conceived by his mother in amazement and in the kind of obedience that allowed the handmaiden of God to do nothing but receive what she was given.

The same attitude is also reported of Joseph, Jesus' father. Was he the one who could take the mother of the Christ to be his wife? It was clear that he was destined to do so, because Mary was his fiancèe. But he had judged that he must forgo her and sever her attachment to him, and only a divine command enabled him to go through with the marriage.

Thus, from the beginning Jesus' place within his family was marked in two ways: he had been born into its community but was not subjected to it. Rather, he was placed above it and set apart for his own work, in which his clan is unable to help and, even less, to guide him. For the ground and aim of his life and ministry lay not in nature but beyond nature. Therefore he also stood alone before the Baptist when he requested baptism, without family or following.

The Spirit Becomes Visible and God's Call Audible
January 21

When Jesus was baptized, immediately when he came up from the water he saw the heavens opening and the Spirit descending to him like a dove, and a voice came from the heavens: "You are my beloved Son; with you I am well pleased."

—Mark 1:10–11

God is creative will; this was God's characteristic and nature in the world of the Israelites, to whom Moses and the prophets described what God was for them. His will becomes effective through the Spirit and perceptible through the Word. We experience the will of God through the voice of God that addresses us. The God who speaks reveals himself to us. Therefore, in conjunction with the knowledge of God that had been given to his people,

Jesus encountered God's love through an event that manifested for him the arrival of the Spirit and through a word spoken for him.

God addresses him as his "Son"; from God he derives his life, and from him he receives his work. This work is grounded in God's sovereign will and has saving power because God's good pleasure is with him. This was Jesus' secret that eluded perception. In order that he might be completely assured of it (and this assurance gave rise both to his commanding word and to his helping deed), the Spirit's presence was made visible in connection with his baptism, and the divine word addressed to him became audible.

By requesting baptism, he had entered into fellowship with all those who had been roused by the Baptist's call. Now he was set apart from everyone else through the events that had occurred subsequent to his baptism. The outcome of everyone else's baptism was the requirement to believe that they had been given a share in God's kingdom. They had to believe without seeing, but his eyes and ears had been touched by God's effective presence.

Now there was for him no longer any dependence on others. No longer did anyone stand above him before whom he had to bow in obedience: no priest from whom he must seek forgiveness of sins, no teacher of the Law whose teaching showed him God's will, no law book that could serve as mediator to God. God's rule was now manifested through him, and his preaching now consisted in the call "Come to me!" Where Scripture and the temple had stood until then for the Jew, he now stood; what the Law had done for the Jew up to that point, he now did. Now the Son who enjoyed the Father's good pleasure was access to God for others. In him they saw God's will and work, and from him they received his gifts.

The Lamb of God
January 22

John sees Jesus approaching and says, "Look! The Lamb of God, who takes away the sin of the world."
—JOHN 1:29

After Jesus' baptism John saw the Jews' situation in a new light. Until then their hope had been set on the daily sacrifice of a consecrated lamb every morning and evening. This was done to cover the people's sins and to preserve God's grace. But these lambs set apart for God did not prevent the disintegration of the nation. Sinning continued, and its calamitous consequences burdened the people.

But now there was a lamb of God that had the power to take away the guilt of mankind. When Jesus was with John, he did not stand before him as a ruler who could be expected to turn the fortunes of world history, nor even as an expert on the teaching of Scripture who could become mankind's lawgiver. He stood rather as a human being who was a suitable sacrifice, a human yielded to God to be God's own. What it means to be a Son of God, and what God's Spirit makes out of man, could be manifested in him.

While his presence might not lead to any immediate external changes, the fate of mankind was decisively altered. Up to that point humanity's guilt had decided the course and outcome of its history, because God allowed humankind to experience the reprehensible nature of its godlessness. But now the One who brought God's grace to the world was here. What would come of this was not yet plain to the human eye. But one thing was certain: something new would come, a revelation of God's glory in all its splendor. Beside this lamb of God, what were the temple, the priests, and the lambs sacrificed there? All of this was a result of his ministry. When guilt is removed, new praise of God, new adoration, a new kind of service, and a new community will arise. Now those children of Abraham arise who had received the promise and for whom the proclamation of forgiveness will become an effective reality.

But what of Jesus himself; what will be the result of his being the Lamb of God? Lambs were given to God to die. They were sacrificed because they no longer belonged to a person and were no longer to serve him. Will this lamb of God have to die, too, and thereby prove that it does not belong to the world but is consecrated to God? Whatever must come, even if he must fulfill his commission by dying—because the world rejects him as not belonging to it—he will remain God's Holy One and will be willing to make the ultimate sacrifice. John was convinced of this, for he had seen God's Spirit come upon Jesus.

The Freedom Purchased with Blood
January 23

*You were redeemed from your vain conduct that you inherited
from your forefathers not with perishable things, silver or gold,
but with the precious blood as of a lamb without blemish or
stain, even that of the Christ.*
—1 PETER 1:18–19

The activities of those who live only for themselves and wrestle with nature for life's subsistence are vain and without purpose. This kind of life is passed on from one generation to another. It becomes a tradition, an established custom, and presents itself as the only way to live. It is the unconditional obligation that must not be challenged by anyone, since that would be to attack the community in and through which one lives. Nevertheless, this compelling tradition is broken, and the purposelessness of human existence overcome.

Who removed the fetters from mankind? Who set the captives free? This is the work of the Christ. It is he who has redeemed us, as Peter tells the Christians of Asia Minor. Redemption otherwise occurs through gold and silver; property is transferred in exchange for freedom. But these are commodities of nature and are perishable, like our entire natural existence. To redeem mankind, the Christ gave not what he had but rather himself. The price he paid for our freedom was his blood. This unites with him forever all who receive liberty. They no longer have to be what their ancestors were and are no longer compelled to do what their ancestors did; they owe this to him.

Jesus' blood had liberating power because he was like an unblemished lamb suited for sacrifice. When he gave his blood, he did the will of God in perfect obedience. The person who lived a vain life was not suitable for sacrifice; neither his life nor his death served to bring glory to God. His emptiness reveals instead that he exists apart from God. By contrast, Jesus could die in such a way that his blood was precious. People believed it to be the blood of a sinner and shed it in order to destroy it. But this death occurred according to God's good pleasure, because his gracious will was accomplished through it.

Because he has offered his blood, Jesus forgives and has authority to pronounce the acquittal by which he takes away guilt from the world, just as John had told him. This brings an end to the omnipotence of vain, inherited tradition. Guilt that had been forever passed on from generation to generation passes away. His Word, through which he becomes the Lord of a community whose life takes on meaning and power by doing the will of God, is stronger than what has been inherited.

The Difference Between the Two Messengers of God
January 24

John came, neither eating nor drinking, and they said, "He has an evil spirit." The Son of Man came, eating and drinking, and they said, "Look! A glutton and drunkard, a friend of tax collectors and sinners." And wisdom was vindicated by her children.
—Matthew 11:18–19

What Jesus had received was so great that he could not remain in the fellowship of the Baptist. He possessed God's election and good pleasure, and what took place in him internally stood under the guidance of the Spirit. By requesting baptism from the Baptist, Jesus had granted the fellowship he owed him, and it was confirmed by the Baptist's confession of Jesus' commission. It was impossible for Jesus either to replace the Baptist or to subject himself to him. Both had to be what they were, and say and do as they had been commanded. The one did not eat or drink; the other ate and drank.

When these kinds of differences later emerged in Christendom, Paul said, "Let everyone be fully convinced in his own mind." This is the attitude of the free person, who is himself free and sets others free. The liberty Paul possessed was the work of Jesus; Jesus himself exercised it toward the Baptist. He did not elaborate on the reasons that had made the Baptist someone who fasted. Nor did he defend his own right to eat and drink and to be the friend of tax collectors and sinners. Instead, he honored the divine wisdom that speaks precisely to people through the differences in its messengers.

Wisdom exhorts those who are ruled by natural desires to forgo such gratification. The one who fasted reminds them that the narrow path to life is spurned by those who worship wealth and are slaves of fleshly lust. Jesus maintains fellowship with him by being completely poor. But wisdom does not admonish and call any less when it places its messenger freely into nature and does not erect obstacles between people and Jesus. For if he burdened people with the yoke of the Law, he would bar their access to God's kingdom. How, then, would they be able to believe that he brings them acquittal from their guilt?

But the divine wisdom considered even this: the differences in the two messengers confirmed the people in their opposition to the divine call. This opposition had to be—and was—exposed, because the strictness with which John limited his physical cravings reminded them of a demoniac who inflicted suffering on himself. Also, they likened Jesus' liberty to that of sinners who are not afflicted by their own godlessness; this is why they want to know nothing about fasting. The Jew always speaks as one who is knowledgeable, entitled to render judgment and not able to hear the divine voice in the word of his messengers. He always proves that he is unwilling to repent and refuses to judge himself. But by this, divine wisdom is justified, which told them through both messengers, the one who fasted and the One who did not, "Only the one who repents will enter God's kingdom."

Section 3

JESUS GATHERS HIS DISCIPLES

The Nature of Discipleship
January 25

*As he walked along the Sea of Galilee, he saw two brothers,
Simon (called Peter) and Andrew his brother, who cast a net
into the lake, for they were fishermen. And he said to them,
"Come, follow me, and I will make you fishers of men." They
immediately left their nets and followed him. And when he had
walked farther, he saw two other brothers, James the son of
Zebedee and John his brother, in the boat with Zebedee their
father, mending nets, and he called them. Immediately they left
the boat and their father and followed him.*
—MATTHEW 4:18–22

When Jesus left the Baptist, he still lacked one thing he could not do without. He did not need riches, power, or fame, but he needed people to become his disciples, because he gave to them what he himself possessed. He found men with whom he entered into fellowship and drew them to himself in royal authority by his effectual call.

What were they thinking and looking for with him? The disciples made one thing crystal clear: What we imagined or intended was completely irrelevant in our calling. Was our entrance into discipleship the result of a conversation he had with us, in which he described for us the advantages and requirements of discipleship, or did we request admission? None of this happened. Our discipleship arose from his call, and we had to follow without reluctance, without placing conditions on him. We had to follow, resolved to yield everything we had and willing to give up every other community to which we belonged.

The disciples' following him did not create an association of equals, nor a fellowship united by a common cause to which each member made his contribution. Jesus alone was in charge. He talked, and the disciple listened; he acted, and the disciple watched; he suffered, and the disciple stood beside him and perceived his suffering. Again and again the disciples' accounts maintain: We, his disciples, had no share in his word and work. We only listened to him and saw his works. We only believed and obeyed him.

He described to them their vocation as entrance into fellowship with him, analogous to what they had been doing prior to his call: "You will fish for people." Thus they were told what was important to him: he is not grasping for *things*, but his vocation is winning *people* who belong to him, and this will also be the vocation of those he calls to him.

Thus he modeled the disciples' relationship with him after the fellowship he enjoyed with the Father. Just as he completely yields to the Father, discipleship consists in the disciple's complete surrender to Jesus. The Son can do nothing of himself; it is the Father alone who acts and speaks. Likewise, the disciple can do nothing of himself; the master alone is the one who acts and speaks. But the Father loves the Son and shows him all his works. Likewise, the master is open to the disciples and conforms their wills to his and transfers his authority to them.

By constituting discipleship in this way, Jesus determined the constitution of the church. It does not have many heads and does not preserve the traditions of many spirits. It has only the one master.

The Disciples Will Not Lack Anything
January 26

When he had stopped talking, he said to Simon, "Row out onto the lake, and let your nets down for a catch!" And Simon answered, "Master, we tried all night and caught nothing. But at your word I will let down the nets." And when they had done this, they caught a large number of fish. Their nets tore, and they motioned to their associates in the other boat to come and help them, and they came and filled up both boats so that they almost sank. When Simon Peter saw this, he threw himself down at Jesus' knees and said, "Depart from me; for I am a sinful man, Lord." For amazement had seized him and all who were with him on account of the quantity of fish they had caught, including James and John, the sons of Zebedee, who were Simon's partners. And Jesus said to Simon, "Don't be afraid! From now on you will catch people." And when they had brought the boats ashore, they left everything and followed him.
—Luke 5:4–11

Following Jesus as disciple was not a way to make a living. Those who had obeyed his call had left their nets and boats. But neither were hunger and fasting the business they had to learn and practice with Jesus. He called them, convinced that he would be able to ask them at the end of their time together, "Did you ever suffer lack?" and that they would reply joyfully, "No, Lord, never."

Of course, the disciples were not to measure by human standards what they had received by following Jesus. When they relied upon their own ideas, their view of the future quickly darkened, and they wavered between fear and hope. Lasting allegiance to Jesus could not arise unless their openness to what they heard and saw from him was united with a faith that released them from their own thoughts and plans and lent to them the quiet assurance that arises from confidence in the omnipotence of divine grace. This is why in the accounts, the memory of both the beginning of discipleship in Galilee and the beginning of the apostolic office after Jesus' resurrection relates to fishing, which Jesus gave to them in order to protect them from fear and release them from worry.

That they might lack food was the least of their worries, but Jesus did not downplay even this concern. His Father is able to provide them with an abundant catch of fish. What weighed more heavily on them was the closely related question of whether taking Jesus' word to the Jews and then also to the nations would be an enterprise doomed to failure. They were to fish for people; would they catch them through their confession of Jesus? Will they, few as they are, be consigned to a life of loneliness? But he gave them the commission to bring people to him, and he will make sure that they do not cast out their net in vain. This much was clear: their task utterly exceeded their own ability. Without him they can do nothing. What they achieve is not due to their own ingenuity. They can easily labor all night and catch nothing. His word alone grants them the power and duty of discipleship; what they accomplish is his work.

The clearer Jesus' oneness with God became to the disciples, however, the more the contrast separating their entire conduct from what Jesus was and did became apparent to them. Through him they were confronted with God and subjected to his will in such a way that the verdict of guilt spoke to them loud and clear. If he draws them into fellowship with him, he enters into union with the guilty. This realization is indispensable for their entire ministry. Jesus is not surprised when Simon calls himself a sinner, unworthy of fellowship with him. Jesus grants it to him precisely because he is a sinner. For Jesus is the Lamb of God who takes away people's sins.

The Goal of Discipleship
January 27

Seek first God's kingdom and righteousness. Then all these things will be given to you.
—Matthew 6:33

If discipleship was not an association occupied with the acquisition of material goods, it was also not a company of beggars. Food and clothing are not to be the primary concern, but neither are they to be things dispensed with altogether. They are the things the Father gives to them. Does this create a vacuum in the disciples' inner being? Then they would be hurt inside and would harbor the secret longing that thinks wistfully of missed opportunities and craves forbidden goods. From this they are set free, for Jesus awakens a great longing in them that fills their entire hearts and orders their entire conduct. They long for the appearing of God's rule, and this means that they long for the manifestation of his righteousness.

Is it possible for man not to be afraid of God's righteousness? Can he cleanse himself from the wish for God to be unjust and condone his own selfishness? Is it possible for him to think of the appearing of God's glory without being gripped by fear? After all, he is busy making himself comfortable in this world and maximizing his own happiness. When Jesus says that he himself seeks God's kingdom and righteousness, he thus expresses why he is completely different from us. We believe that he, who was poor, who was strong enough to carry the cross, was not overcome by selfish desire. But is the disciple, the product of nature, a child of his people, able to think first of what is God's and desire first the things by which God will show us his greatness and righteousness? But this is why Jesus has taken the disciple into his fellowship: that he may learn to seek what Jesus seeks. If he looks to Jesus, he sees his goal, from which he cannot be distracted or deterred.

God's rule brings us his perfect, renewing grace. Who receives it? Whoever has submitted himself to God. God's righteousness is the end of all godlessness and unrighteousness. Who is acquitted and justified by that righteousness? Whoever submits himself to God. Is there any greater aim? Submitting to God and obeying his righteousness is a calling that never ends. We remain instead the unprofitable servants with whom God can accomplish little.

This is the pain of love that is part of being a Christian and that renders us perennial seekers. Even if we were to do all we ought to do, how little this would be! After all, we are not isolated, solitary people who can strive solely for our own happiness and righteousness. If this were our goal, we would not long for God's kingdom. Our calling is rather to become submitted together to God through our dealings with one another in our community. Because all our strength belongs to him, Jesus gave us this promise: Do not worry about the things you need; they will be given to you.

The Disciples' First Encounters with Jesus
January 28

*The next day John and two of his disciples stood there again, and he looked at Jesus passing by and said, "Look! The Lamb of God." And his two disciples heard him say this and followed Jesus. But Jesus turned around, saw them following, and said to them, "What are you looking for?" But they said to them, "Rabbi," (which, translated, means Teacher) "where are you staying?" He said to them, "Come, and you will see." Then they came and saw where he was staying, and they stayed with him that day; it was about the tenth hour. Andrew, the brother of Simon Peter, was one of the two who had heard John speak and had followed Jesus. He first found his own brother Simon and said to him, "We have found the Messiah" (which, translated, means Christ, the Anointed One). He led him to Jesus. Jesus looked at him and said, "You are Simon son of John; you will be called Cephas" (which, translated, means Peter, "rock").
The next day he decided to leave Galilee and found Philip. And Jesus said to him, "Follow me!" But Philip was from*

JESUS GATHERS HIS DISCIPLES

> *Bethsaida, the city of Andrew and Peter. Philip found Nathanael and said to him, "We have found the one of whom Moses wrote in the Law and of whom the prophets wrote, Jesus son of Joseph, from Nazareth." And Nathanael said to him, "Can anything good come from Nazareth?" Philip said to him, "Come and see!" Jesus saw Nathanael come to him and said about him, "Look! Truly an Israelite in whom there is no deceit." Nathanael said to him, "How do you know me?" Jesus answered him, "Before Philip called you, when you were under the fig tree, I saw you." Nathanael answered him, "Rabbi, you are the Son of God. You are the King of Israel." Jesus replied, "Because I told you that I saw you under the fig tree, you believe. You will see greater things than these." And he said to him, "Truly, truly, I say to you: You will see heaven open and the angels of God ascend and descend on the Son of Man."*
>
> —JOHN 1:35–51

Jesus called those whom he accepted into his fellowship with royal authority, precisely as one who cannot act on his own but is led in everything by God. Because he saw in the disciples those whom God gave to him, he waits until the Father brings them to him. The strongest group within the disciples were the two pairs of brothers, Simon and Andrew, and James and John. They came to Jesus while he was still with John the Baptist. When Jesus left him, John and Andrew followed Jesus, and through them their brothers Simon and James were brought to Jesus. Because they journeyed to the Baptist, they awaited the onset of the divine kingdom and knew that the Baptist had assigned to Jesus the completion of what he himself had begun. Moreover, they knew that the Baptist did this because he saw in him the Lamb of God, the One who would take away human guilt. By appropriating the promise of forgiveness of sins, they were given the opportunity to believe in Jesus. That they were not righteous by Pharisaic standards did not separate them from him.

It followed from John's message regarding the coming rule of God that they could expect nothing but the work of a king from him who was placed above the Baptist. The question with which the disciples approached Jesus was whether he was the Messiah. Thus, whether they were allowed to follow and remain with him depended entirely on his permission. John recounts:

When we followed him and asked him where he was staying, he invited us home with him. This permission, given with royal authority, granted the two disciples fellowship with Jesus.

Their conviction that he acted as the Promised One with royal authority rested primarily on his uncanny insight which revealed their inner selves to him. Were not people's hearts an open book to the One who had the Spirit? This was offset by the offense caused by his origin and home. Was it believable that the son of Joseph, the Nazarene, should become the Christ? By Nathanael's example John depicted how strong this perceived obstacle was for the first disciples. It dissolved, however, because Jesus proved himself to be the knower of hearts through his Spirit-illumined gaze. This also gave credibility to Jesus' promise, which transcended all human boundaries. Moreover, in order that the disciples should not dwell on what they themselves were and what they could do, he promised them the assistance of the heavenly spirits. After all, God's rule is the rule of the heavens and authorizes the heavenly powers to complete what the divine grace prepares for humanity. When the disciples start following Jesus, they come to the One whom the angels serve.

God's Building Gets Underway
January 29

Andrew first finds his own brother Simon and leads him to Jesus. Jesus looked at him and said: "You are Simon son of John; you will be called Cephas" (which, translated, means Peter, "rock").

—JOHN 1:41–42

Jesus acts by the Spirit's guidance, which renders his choice irreversible. Through Jesus' election, God's election had taken place. For this reason the first disciples who came to Jesus after he had separated himself from the Baptist remained with him forever, and two of them, Simon and John, were not only closest to Jesus at his end; they also became pillars of Gentile Christendom.

He issued a particular vocation to one of them immediately upon receiving him. Why did he do this? The disciples did not ask. He is the Lord; they trust him. His decision is valid and not subject to their verdict; it is not measured by the standards human beings use to judge their own actions.

By being given a new name, Simon was told what his share in Christ's work would be. Jesus told Simon by his name what God would use him to do, thereby continually reminding him of his calling. He is placed before all as Cephas, Peter, the stone or rock; and by calling him Peter, all must conform themselves to Jesus' will and honor the Lord's decision.

With this metaphor Jesus expressed why he needs disciples: his work is construction; he is building God's house. It has a firm foundation and is built from solid stones. This construction began when God gave Jesus his first disciples; for God's building is made of living stones. Jesus' illustration remained obscure for no one in Israel; everyone understood that he used this metaphor to describe the greatness of divine grace. Never in Israel had there been individual souls who were lifted out of the human community to receive God's grace for themselves alone. To be sure, there were those who were the particular objects of God's grace, and now Peter was one of them. But the divine word was always given to them so that they might bring it to those who were united with one another in community. "The king" was always the term used for God, because the king makes out of the many one people, whom he unites and protects. The Baptist had just powerfully attested to this because he proclaimed God's rule through which the promised king would come.

Now Jesus gets to work and gathers God's people and establishes the new community, by which God will manifest his grace. This was Jesus' deep joy when his first disciples came to him, and he allowed them to share in it. For they would have an active part in his work. Now the first stones had been laid. Now the building can and will grow. For it is the building of God.

The Son of Man
January 30

You will see the angels of God descending on the Son of Man.
—John 1:51

Jesus had described Peter's vocation to him with a new name. But in his dealings with the disciples and the people, Jesus himself also needed a name by which to express his commission. Which name did he give himself? In common parlance, the people and the disciples called the one who was to come "the Christ," "the Anointed One." This assigned to him the kingly vocation that he had by virtue of the authority given him through divine commission and anointing. Jesus did not accept this name as his self-designation. For the claim he thus would have made to the people would have forced everyone to a final decision. Everyone owed unconditional obedience to the Anointed One: rulers and ordinary people, priests and laypeople, scribes and farmers. They were obligated to entrust him with the destiny of the people and the salvation of all. They were thus commanded to believe with the authoritative power of a divine word. But was this the path God's grace prescribed for its messenger? Can faith be commanded?

Ever since Daniel's prophecy, another name also linked Jesus' commission with prophecy: the Son of Man. This name, too, assigned to him the rule in God's kingdom. For in Daniel the figure resembling a son of man is, in God's name, invested with rule and put in the place of the beasts that prophetically depict earthly rulers. This is how God's royal work took place in Israel. At the same time, however, the name "Son of Man" expressed the contrast between Jesus and those rulers who thus far had influenced the course of human history. The Son of Man had no lethal weapons. In comparison with wild animals, he is weak. His rule is secure, but also concealed, in God because he establishes it not with natural means but by the operation of the Spirit. It is not the world that gives him the kingdom, as by popular vote or military conquest. Rather, he receives it before God's throne out of God's hand.

By calling himself the "Son of Man," Jesus refrained from force, made the Word the tool by which he would accomplish his mission, and adopted as his aim all that the Baptist's declaration "Lamb of God" said of him. The Son of Man receives his manner and his work through the common human lot. He can and must obey and serve. He can and must suffer and die, without diminishing the great things promised by the proclamation of the divine kingdom. For he is not merely a son of man like countless others, but the Son of Man whom mankind has awaited, because it is through him that God's intent in creating man will be revealed.

The Christ in the Midst of Angels
January 31

*You will see heaven open and the angels of God ascending
and descending on the Son of Man.*

—John 1:51

Jesus calls disciples. Will they overcome the world, dispel gods, topple rulers, make swords into plowshares and spears into sickles, and bring God's peace to humanity? Can Jesus reveal God's glory by making these few and insignificant men his own? They who share their lives with him, receive his Word, and appropriate his image are indispensable to him, but if they were merely his companions and helpers, he would not be able to accomplish his ministry. But the angels accompany him, ascending and descending as mediators of his communion with the Father. The extent to which this happens right now remains invisible, but when his mission is revealed, his own will see him surrounded by angels.

This was the vision for the future overarching the entire ministry of Jesus, pristinely human yet humanly limited as it was. The Son of the Father is at the same time the Lord of the angels, and the revelation of the Son also reveals his communion with the heavenly spirits. Are we apprehensive in light of such a hope? Did his hope make him the author of a myth whose glossy depiction portrayed not only human beings and natural elements as his servants but also heavenly powers? But the message of God's kingdom was not a myth. Its proclamation was history, and it did not merely speak of God's gift to us in our present state of life but also included a promise that was as lofty as God's glory.

Even for Jesus, this vision of the future was not visible as present existence is visible. It is solely through what already exists that we receive the means of naming what is still future and of longing for it. But it is clear and universally true that it was impossible for Jesus to speak of God in small terms. Because he spoke of the aim of his government and of the manifestation of his glory, he could not equate God's kingdom with the realm of natural events or look for it solely among those ready to serve him. Those who do God's will in heaven stand above nature, and because the Father has sent Jesus into the world, the world also becomes the heavenly spirits' place of operation. And their association with him will become visible when he is lifted out of the obscurity of human existence and stands before mankind in the light of God.

The Angels of the Little Ones
February 1

Watch out that you do not despise any of these little ones. For I tell you: Their angels continually behold in the heavens the face of my Father, who is in the heavens.

—Matthew 18:10

How is Jesus' greatness to be revealed in those whom he has won and will yet win? Those whom he draws to him are little ones. The words of the psalmist apply to them in full measure: "What is man that you remember him, and the son of man that you visit him?" They are easily despised; what is more, they are easily confused and shaken. They easily stumble when they suffer a blow. Jesus, however, is not concerned for his little ones; his urgent warning is directed toward those who despise them. For the human and the divine verdicts do not agree.

Those little ones who believe in him are loved by God and thus also guarded by him. Because Jesus knew that the heavenly powers had a part in his work, he also includes his disciples in his assurance. The heavenly spirits are his helpers in that they provide divine guidance and protection for those who belong to him. He does not impart to them directly the power to perform the will of God and to avoid stumbling or sinning. They quickly tire and are easily overcome. Yet God's grace comes to their aid, and Jesus celebrated the greatness of his grace with a brilliant metaphor when he said that the angels commissioned to serve them continually have free access to God. To see God's face at all times means that their concerns are continually God's concerns as well. Their prayer rises to God and is certain to be answered, and their path is always made smooth and subjected to God's will. They are not refused what they need in order to act rightly.

Jesus lent such an enormous dimension to his promise in order to strengthen the community he instituted among those who believed in him. He does not permit them to honor only the great ones who excel in word and deed but expels from their midst any indifference that fails to be concerned for the well-being of the little ones. He expels harshness that allows them to err or sin without coming to their aid. He fashions out of them the brotherhood in which one bears another's burden and one person's gift fills another's lack. How can they allow a separation between great and small in their midst now that he has opened their eyes to the grace in which those stand whom he has taken into his community?

Small the Beginning, Great the Outcome
February 2

His master told him, "You were faithful with little; I will put you in charge over much."
—Matthew 25:21, 23

Can we ever thank Jesus enough for all that we have received from him? All his words, (but not only these) and his existence and his coming into the world remove any limits from the divine grace. In that the divine grace appears to us in him and ties our life to its operation and introduces us to the fellowship of God's Spirit, we are given the one thing necessary, for which the church continually gives thanks.

Yet when Jesus prepared his disciples for their apostolic ministry prior to his departure, he spoke with them in detail about his difficult and sacrificial service, which is why he now calls their attention to what will follow after he has gone. How much greater is what is to come in comparison with what can now be fulfilled! What is to come is the new man, a new people of God, a new holy community, a new temple, a new city of God.

Whatever the disciples will be able to accomplish on the hard soil of Judaism will pale by comparison. To be sure, they will proclaim the message of life; but they will proclaim it to the dying in order that they may have hope, because life will be theirs only through the resurrection. The person who lives forever neither arises in the church nor comes about through evangelism, nor even in the apostolic fellowship through apostolic proclamation. Moreover, the reign of death ensues in the inevitability of sinning, the ever-present possibility of falling, the continual breaking of fellowship that can survive only by practicing forgiveness. There is also the downcast mood that considers faith to be a burdensome obligation that often lacks strength, so that the word remains poor and powerless. "Blessed are the poor in spirit" remains the promise that the disciples—those little and poor ones—must claim.

Yet all these difficulties must not lead them into despair. They must serve the divine grace with whatever little is theirs and proclaim God's Word with whatever little insight they have. For the small and few things they now must administer will be followed by things that are great and manifold, things that Jesus will bring about one day: humanity united in God, consecrated to him by the Spirit, those to whom the living God has revealed eternal life. In this renewed world there will be a new community, one that is perfect and fruitful; not merely one's own life that selfishness can overcome, but service; not egocentrism, but stewardship of the things that belong to the master. And all that will be the effect of Jesus' royal reign. For then Jesus will entrust to his faithful ones, not a few things, but many.

Section 4

JESUS RENOUNCES HIS HOME

Separated from His Mother, United with His Father
February 3

*On the third day a wedding took place in Cana of Galilee,
and Jesus' mother was there. Jesus and his disciples
had also been invited to the wedding. When the wine ran out,
Jesus' mother said to him, "They have no wine." Jesus
responded, "What do you and I have in common, woman? My
hour has not yet come." His mother told the servants, "Do
what he tells you." There were six stone water jars for Jewish
purification, each containing two or three measures. Jesus told
them, "Fill the jars with water." And they filled them to the
brim. And he said to them, "Draw now and take it to the
master of the banquet." They took it to him. But when the
master of the banquet tasted what had become wine and did not
know where it had come from (though the servants who had
drawn the water knew), the master of the banquet called the
bridegroom and said to him, "Everyone first brings out the
good wine and then, when it has been drunk, that of lesser
quality. But you saved the good wine until now."*
—JOHN 2:1–10

In the two centuries before Jesus, when a man became prince or king in Jerusalem, the royal family was also immediately there. The man elevated himself with his entire clan over the people in accordance to the prevalent custom that constituted the clan as a close-knit unit. If one of its members rose to prominence, this meant the elevation of the entire house; the mother in particular reflected the glory of her son.

When Jesus returned to Galilee, his family's expectations were high. The clan was ready to celebrate with Jesus. But what about him? Was he prepared to step before the public as the head of his clan? Had a royal dynasty been born through him? How foreign is Jesus to us once more—a foreign species, one might say. For it was not only ancient Jewish but is also presently German custom that the clan participates in the good fortune and fame of its member. Why then is Jesus foreign to us? John provides a brilliant description and explanation of the way in which Jesus ordered his relationship to his clan.

The decision was made immediately after Jesus' return to Galilee at a wedding in which both Jesus and his mother took part. The more joyful the jubilation at the celebration became, the more guests arrived and the more wine was needed, so that the scope of the feast exceeded the provision made by the bridegroom. This is when the mother took charge and approached Jesus: he must prevent a disturbance of the feast. She is rebuffed; her place is that of the woman. She respects his decision and remains unperturbed. If she has to stay out of this, he will make the arrangements himself. Thus she exhorts the servants to obey promptly. Perhaps he commands the incredible, demands what seems impossible; but this must not keep the servants from carrying out Jesus' orders. The necessary thing now is that any resistance be precluded. Then Jesus ensures the smooth continuation of the feast and elevates it above the natural realm, because his good deed did not remain unnoticed.

He acted, trusting in God's creative power. This is the foreign element in him, and this is also the reason why his own could not reign together with him and why he did not institute a new royal family. He distanced himself from them, not because he despised natural relations or disenfranchised his mother, but because what is God's is not subject to human beings but remains in God's discretion. When he called upon God's creative work, no other voice could enter in, and human desires lost all jurisdiction.

By calling upon God's creative activity, Jesus signaled to the disciples that they not ask how Jesus' work came to be. There is no creative process to be dissected; his creative powers did not consist of a matrix of circumstances that all played a role in the final result. Rather, it was exclusively the will of him who alone is able to create.

In this narrative, as in all similar accounts, the question arises, To what extent are we told what really happened rather than merely the disciples' attitude? The narrative has important historical significance, introducing us to a deeper knowledge of Jesus, because it illustrates how the question of miracles confronted Jesus immediately and in a variety of ways. The way he ordered his activity in keeping with his confession of the creative glory of God thus became an essential and particularly profound component of his ministry.

God Removes John the Baptist
February 4

When Jesus heard that John had been handed over,
he withdrew to Galilee.
—MATTHEW 4:12

Similar to Jesus' ordering of his relationship to his clan was the way he arranged his dealings with Jerusalem. He went to seek out his people, and for this Jerusalem was indispensable to him. This is where it was determined what would become of Judaism. To be sure, Jews abroad, who lived in the large Greek cities, and particularly those who had settled beyond the boundaries of the empire under the rule of the Parthians, possessed independent status. Yet even in their extensive dispersion, the Jewish people had remained a unity. What they had in common was the temple in the holy city, the priesthood and its teaching office that watched over the interpretation of the Law and everywhere monitored its observance.

But was Jerusalem Jesus' sphere of operation? The holy city was at the same time the headquarters of opposition to him. The Baptist had already avoided Jerusalem and gone to the Jordan River to baptize. This was not the place where Jesus could start his ministry. This he could do in Galilee, where Nazareth had provided him with a refuge and a home. There too, he found a united Jewish community with a synagogue in every village— complete with a chest containing the Holy Books—where the Law was read. There also was the pharisaism that hovered over every Jew to see whether he sinned or not. There was no place where Jesus was not opposed. Yet in Galilee those in authority did not assert their power as directly as those in Jerusalem. Jesus still found congregations there on the Sabbath that listened to him, and crowds were drawn to him and could follow him without being prevented from doing so by the rulers.

The defining moment came when the Herod who had been made king and ruler of Galilee and of the Jewish territory east of the Jordan threw John into one of his prisons. The marriage the prince had entered into with his brother's wife was blatant sin according to the Law. For the Law forbade one brother from taking away another brother's wife. The Baptist had represented the Law and repudiated the claim that the royal house was above God's law. Yet he remained alone in his opposition. It was apparent that the community and its leaders were neither willing nor able to resist evil. The Baptist's fate revealed not merely the court's and the people's corruption but also God's verdict. This verdict handed John over to Herod's authority. The spokesman for God's Word was not surrounded by the protection of God's power; rather, the divine verdict saw fit for him to die in the line of duty.

Jesus realized what this meant for him. He will not die as a result of a clash with the totally corrupt royal house. His struggle is not merely with Jewish reffraff such as the Herodians; his confrontation is with all of Judaism, including everything it possessed in priestly sanctity and scribal wisdom. His ministry will end in Jerusalem; this is where the Lamb of God is destined to be sacrificed. He still needed time—to draw his disciples, to manifest himself to the nation, and to demonstrate what it was offered through his message and what it did through its rejection of Jesus—and this time he gained by withdrawing to Galilee.

No Worship of the Ruler of the World
February 5

The Accuser led Jesus to a high place and showed
him all the empires of the world in a single moment.
And he said to him, "All this power and glory I will give to you,
for it has been given to me, and I give it to whomever I wish.
If you fall down and worship me, it will be yours."
Jesus answered him, "It is written:
'You must worship the Lord your God and serve him only.'"
—LUKE 4:5–8 (CF. DEUT. 6:13)

Was there no way for Jesus to attain to power over humanity and its rulers in such a way that would include him among those who rule nations and, moreover, would not merely make him one of them but elevate him above them, so that their power and wealth would be transferred to him? In fact, such a possibility existed, and it was not merely fictional or a figment of human imagination on the part of the Bible's writers. For such flights of fancy and explorations of desirable possibilities are off-limits for those who are led by the Spirit. Rather, this opportunity presented itself to him palpably at a moment when he was in dialogue with the spirit who assigns to the nations their destiny.

This spirit offered his services to him and promised him that he could attain supreme power and utmost fame with his help. This offer, however, had a condition. The spirit who rules humanity wants to be honored as well; he will not allow Jesus to worship God alone. To be sure, he should worship God, but not God alone! Worship is due also to the one who has been given power over the world. If Jesus refuses to comply, he sets himself against the one whom the powerful obey.

Yet it was Jesus' calling to worship God alone. That he had the will and the power to do so elevated him above all and made all others his enemies. For man craves honor for himself, and homage is an existential issue for the powerful, because depriving them of honor shakes the foundations of their authority.

The one who had the most legitimate claim of being honored as king was the prince who ruled Galilee. He was closer to the nation than the other rulers, because he was a Jew. Like the Roman overlords, however, he was not prepared to worship God alone. He eagerly lobbied in Rome for his honor and by force compelled those who were subject to him to honor him. When he unscrupulously broke the Law at the occasion of his second marriage, he did so publicly. There could be no rapprochement between Jesus and this regional ruler, because Jesus worshiped God alone and not also the ruler of the world. Jesus' path did not lead to Tiberias, the king's headquarters, and he set foot in his court only when he was on his way to Golgotha. Nor did this king's way lead him to Jesus. For he had no interest in anyone who worshiped no one but God alone.

The Healing Power of the Word
February 6

And he came to Nazareth, where he had grown up, and, as was his custom, went to the synagogue on the Sabbath and stood up in order to read, and he was given the scroll of Isaiah.

JESUS RENOUNCES HIS HOME

*And when he opened the book, he found the passage where it is
written: "The Spirit of the Lord is upon me; he anointed me to
bring the good news of salvation to the poor and to the blind so
that their eyes might be opened, to set the captives free and to
proclaim the favorable year of the Lord." And when he had
rolled up the scroll and returned it to the synagogue attendant,
he sat down, and the eyes of everyone in the congregation were
fixed on him. But he began to tell them, "Today this statement
has been fulfilled in your hearing."*

—LUKE 4:16–21 (CF. ISA. 61:1–2)

What was the significance of the Isaianic prophecy that Jesus read to the congregation at Nazareth? Did it pertain to the present, or could it only be fulfilled at a later time? After Jesus had not merely read the prophecy but also interpreted its significance, he told them: Now what the prophet predicted has happened; what the prophecy predicted would be heard one day, you have heard.

The prophet described the servant of God who has been given authority to proclaim the favorable year of God through the Spirit of God. Now the servant of God who has been given his message by the Spirit has spoken to them and announced the beginning of the year of salvation. According to the prophet, this is when the misery of the poor, captive, shattered nation will come to an end, and this is what Jesus told those in Nazareth: poverty had come to an end, slavery was over, blindness was removed, and hardships and oppression were things of the past. This was the message Jesus delivered, and because they heard it, they experienced what the prophet had called them to expect.

Were they not poor? Their daily struggle was to strain to make ends meet. They were not among the rulers and felt the existential pressures that weighed them down. They did not belong to the wise but rather were disconsolate. Yet now Jesus has come to assist them in all their misery.

Yet were they not just as poor, oppressed, and blind as before? How had their load been lifted? He proclaimed the rule of God, and their share in it is the possession that brings an end to poverty. Whoever is called to God's kingdom has been set free from his crippling guilt. By receiving God's grace, the captive became a freeman, and whoever has understood this must no longer lament his blindness. Or were these mere words? To be sure, they were words, but they were words given by the Spirit, spoken by Jesus by virtue of his sending as God's servant. Thus they were words of God, whose Word becomes reality.

Jesus demonstrated to his listeners his confidence in God's Word. What were the means at his disposal? What had he been given to redress the calamitous condition of the people? He had been given the Word. Nothing but the Word? Only the one who does not trust God because he does not know him can ask this. For the Son of God it suffices that he has been given the Word, and now it has become his calling not to doubt the power of the Word but to proclaim it without fear.

Giving Thanks for God's Word
February 7

It so happened that when he had said this, a woman in the crowd raised her voice and said to him, "Blessed is the body that bore you and the breast you sucked." But he replied, "Indeed, blessed are those who hear and keep God's word."
—Luke 11:27–28

A woman honors Jesus by her utterance because she has felt the impact of his word. The way she sees it, she honors him in a manner he can approve, for she celebrates his mother. The greatness of the mother's son lends her incomparable glory. Is it not also Jesus' joy and pride that his honor is his mother's as well? Jesus does not contradict her, but he expands the horizons of the woman who marveled at him. There are indeed those who are blessed, who ought to be exceedingly praised, who have attained the greatest, incomparable honor and inexhaustible riches. These are the ones who hear God's Word.

God's Word! Jesus had told the Nazarenes that it ended poverty and the shame that issues from sin, and that it liberated those who suffer from external bondage. Hearing God's Word places us in the presence of God, produces fellowship between God and man, and causes us to encounter the gracious God. Hearing God's Word is the call to faith and the grounding of our life in God's work.

Yet God's Word does not constitute a mere onetime event. It enters us and becomes our possession, and precisely because it becomes our possession, it instills in us an obligation that commands our continual attention and energy. "Blessed are those who hear and keep God's word." We can lose it after we have received it. Our selfish desires can militate against the Word until it loses its power over us, and our own thoughts can become more powerful than the Word that has entered us. Alternatively, we may yield to the opinions of others and order our lives in keeping with their counsel. When the Word is lost, however, the one who has spoken the Word to us is lost as well. Whoever obeys it, on the other hand, ought to do what Jesus told that woman, and praise God with thanksgiving and jubilation that his Word has come to him.

The End of Poverty
February 8

*Blessed are those who are poor in spirit,
for theirs is the kingdom of heaven.*
—Matthew 5:3

It was to the poor Nazarenes that Jesus brought his good news, in order to make them rich. He displays the same attitude here in the Sermon on the Mount, because the first Beatitude is addressed to the poor, in order to assure them of their share in God's kingdom. Should it surprise us that Jesus assigned great significance in his ministry to the question of how to help the poor? Did—and does—the question of how to help the poor not possess great weight for everyone desiring to govern and unify his nation? Does it not haunt us at every encounter with the poor? And does not the manner in which the poor person assesses his own condition possess decisive importance for him? Should one feel sorry for the poor because they are poor? Is poverty a calamity? Jesus says, Yes! Does one care for them by making them monetarily rich? Jesus says, No!

He said with strong assurance, "Make the poor well," and thus identified himself as the one who helps them. Yet he did not conceive of helping the poor by a transformation of the national economy. Is it truly just that there is not enough food to go around? God feeds the birds and clothes the lilies. Is it then his fault when someone dies of hunger or spends a lifetime struggling to buy enough food? This is not the cause of the affliction of poverty. It arises in part in the poor person, in part in the community of which he is a member. When a person has nothing but what nature gives him, he is driven by sensual desires and accumulates both essential and luxury items. When natural selfishness is the rule of the day in the community to which he belongs, the poor person lacks the support owed him by the community and is driven into a struggle with it. For it does not support him but robs him. It does not give him space but oppresses him. Without God, poverty becomes unbearable misery. If anyone is not even able to purchase the most essential goods, his existence is futile; he is indeed miserable.

Yet he ought to be considered blessed on account of the rule of God, because God's work occurs for him and upon him. God's grace is present through his Word. Jesus told this also to the poor, and that person is ready to receive his Word because he is poor and does not have anything that strengthens and encourages him. This is his advantage over the rich, whose ear is closed to the divine word by his pursuit of wealth.

Did Jesus thus transform poverty into a merit that he will reward in the new world? Whoever injects the notion of merit into Jesus' promise has not yet grasped why Jesus proclaimed God's kingdom. He called the poor "blessed," just as he eulogized those who mourn and those who are persecuted, because God is the one who has mercy and because his kingdom is the work of his grace. This grace, in turn, is available for everyone who needs it, because he needs it and his lack calls for the divine gift.

Perhaps it is for this reason that the poor person is called "poor in spirit," in order to put the devastating weight of this misery into perspective. He suffers a lack in the spirit that awakens our inner lives, and this is why he is made rich by Jesus' gift of the Word. We all know how poverty with its existential pressures can starve inner vitality. Yet this misery comes to an end when God's works are done for the poor and when God's Word comes to them.

Perhaps this version of the promise stirred in the disciples the memory of those who were expelled from their villages for Jesus' sake and driven to abject poverty. Yet it is the one led by the Spirit who becomes Jesus' disciple, and when someone is cast into poverty because he is a disciple, he has become a poor person in the power of the Spirit and is therefore blessed, because God's grace is with him.

Those in Bondage Are Set Free
February 9

And there was in their congregation a man with an unclean spirit, and he shouted and said, "What do we have to do with you, Jesus of Nazareth? You are coming in order to destroy us. I know you, who you are: the Holy One of God." And Jesus reproved him and said, "Be quiet and come out of him!" And the unclean spirit jolted him, called out in a loud voice, and came out of him.
—Mark 1:23–26

Jesus' message is the call to freedom. Those in bondage need grace and receive it. The call *Set us free!* had the strongest urgency among those whose spiritual lives were held in bondage by destructive powers. At that time many Jews knew they had lost control over themselves. The pagan fear of demons that accompanied their veneration had spread even among Jews, producing calamitous results in many who were spiritually weak or sick. This deterioration was engendered in part by the belief that spirits enabled one to perform magic. It seemed potentially advantageous to engage with demons, because doing so helped one acquire a certain reputation and even a profit. Through an encounter with those who were compelled by a hostile spirit to speak and act, Jesus was asked if he was able to issue also to them the liberating Word in the name of God. Did the spirits possess the power to resist the rule of God? Or were they, too, subject to God's creative power, and the demon-oppressed subject to his grace? God's Word is heard by all his creatures. Even natural forces obey him; supernatural spirits likewise are subject to him. Here as well, Jesus did not waver. "Be quiet and come out of him," he told the spirit.

Thus he subjected his conduct to the assurance of God that does not tolerate any limitations. The statements grounded in such assurance take on general validity. Everything has been entrusted to the Father by the Son. His commission leads him to all, including those who are in the power of spirits. Because he possesses authority to speak God's Word, he addresses all: Jews and Gentiles, righteous and sinners, storm and spirits. God's forgiveness is never ineffective; it extends also to a demon-possessed man. The Lamb of God has the authority to command a demon, "Go!"

Can One Who Is Like Us Be Believed?
February 10

And he arrived in his hometown and taught them in their synagogue, so that they were amazed and said, "Where did he get this wisdom and the miracles? Is this not the carpenter's son? Isn't his mother's name Mary, and are not his brothers' names James, Joseph, Simon, and Judas? Aren't his sisters with us as well? Where did he get all these things?" And they took offense at him. But Jesus said to them, "A prophet is not without honor except in his hometown and his own house."
—MATTHEW 13:54–57

Whoever can manifest his will solely by speaking demands faith. The Nazarenes, too, related to each other by believing one another. They gladly extended trust to one another as long as they believed that the other person spoke and acted uprightly. Yet Jesus desired a different kind of trust. He had described God's activity to them and maintained that it took place through him. When offered to him, the faith he desired for himself was at the same time faith in God.

The Nazarenes, however, decided that they could not do this, because his family was part of their village community. His father had been their carpenter; everyone knew his mother. He also had brothers and sisters, all of whom belonged to their community without in any way differing from their fellow Nazarenes. Believing in Jesus means subjecting oneself to him, surrendering to him, and making him Lord. How can they do this, since he is one of their own? It is deeply written into our inner makeup that we do not bow before one who is like us. This would amount to humiliation, a violation of our rights. Only when we are confronted with one stronger than us, one who displays a superior power, may we decide to obey him. Was Jesus' offer to the Nazarenes not exceedingly great? Or did they not need it? Were they not poor, in bondage, and blind? His wealth consisted of his Word, and his liberating power lay in his Word. They saw only his fellowship with them, not his fellowship with God.

Thus Jesus addressed those in his own village in vain. Yet this did not surprise him. A prophet's supernatural commission was never recognized in his own house. The closer he is to those he addresses, the less credible his word becomes. They measure him by their own standard and do not allow him to have a relationship with God that is different from theirs. Yet their conscience testifies to them that they know nothing about God, do not hear any word of God, and do not stand in his service but accomplish their own will. How can it be any different in Jesus' case?

This also applies to the historical knowledge that acquaints us with Jesus' surroundings and the course of his life. This brings him closer to us, yet how often did he become precisely by this means the remote one who cannot be believed! Jesus cannot remove this offense. For the truth of his humanity is an essential characteristic of his commission. He is the Savior and Lord of mankind not by accentuating the transcendence of God's grace and glory but by showing that these are present in a human being even in his natural state and that they made a human individual their recipient and instrument.

Selfish Desires Are Not from God
February 11

You will quote the proverb to me, "Doctor, heal yourself! Do here in your hometown what we have heard happened in Capernaum."
—Luke 4:23

Is it not an assault on Jesus' honor when he must speak in vain because he desires faith but does not find it? In Capernaum, Jesus had called on the omnipotence of God's grace for others. Those whose spiritual lives had disintegrated had evoked his mercy, and his mercy gave him the right to draw upon God's creative power. The news of this had spread also to Nazareth, and the Nazarenes had marveled at this. He was like a doctor who was able to cure others. Yet now he was in a dilemma, because his own village refused to follow him. Was he not like a doctor whose powers fail him when he himself requires healing, so that his fame collapses, leaving him without the trust of others? "Doctor, heal yourself!" Why does he not use his power for himself, if he really possesses it?

Every Jew thought along the lines of this proverb and thus revealed what separated them from Jesus, which is why Jesus called them unbelieving. Jesus knew that God manifested his grace mightily and gloriously through him; but did this prevent him from drawing other people to him and subjecting them to his wishes? In order that a person might believe in God, Jesus told him in word and deed, "Nothing is impossible with God." Did this mean, however, that a person was authorized to commit every daring act and allowed to transcend all limitations? God reveals himself through Jesus; did he do this because Jesus was God's favorite, who can do whatever he pleases? What the Nazarenes desired, Jesus called an impossibility. The selfish exploitation of God's gift separates the one who attempts it from his grace. To be sure, it extends to the one whom it chooses and enables, freely extending to him in order that he may live in power and greatness. The Father glorifies his Son, but precisely this ties him to God and puts to death any form of selfishness.

The Jew was confounded by such a veneration of God. Because he thought that God's grace would be given to him so that he could become secure, rich, and powerful, there was no possibility of a rapprochement with Jesus.

Jesus' Renunciation of the Wisdom of the World and Its Rulers
February 12

Then Jesus was led by the Spirit into the wilderness, in order that he may be tempted by the Accuser.
—MATTHEW 4:1

When Jesus' fellow villagers told him, "Physician, heal yourself," they were not merely quoting Nazarene wisdom. They considered the truth of this saying to be beyond dispute, because, according to the wisdom enshrined in it, the Lord of mankind himself directs their thoughts and desires. Before Jesus had to contend with this proverb in his dealings with his people, he had rejected it in his discourse with the prince of the world. The disciples revealed Jesus' righteousness by providing us with an account of what Jesus considered to be a satanic temptation and how he overcame it.

The Spirit of God had made it Jesus' obligation to listen to the ruler of mankind and to invalidate his counsel before entering his struggle with Judaism. His adversary had this power, because God's holy law renders mankind sinful and subject to death. For this reason an accuser is placed over it who, as its accuser, is also its tempter. As tempter, he furnishes proof that man sins and destroys any pious pretense in order to expose that man speaks of God but does not believe in him, that he prays but only does his own will, and that he loves himself. If he induces man to sin, it accuses him as well and renders effective God's verdict against him, which denies life to the sinner. The rabbis called him "the messenger of death"; the apostles described his activity as "having power over death" and as "the last enemy" of God's grace. Now Jesus proclaims the end of sin and the end of death and thus appears as Satan's adversary. Yet he does this as the Son of Man, who stands accused like all others who are rejected on account of their unrighteousness. Will he invalidate this charge when he must answer the tempter who examines him?

What is faith? What is obedience? What is love? This is what the tempter seeks for himself: faith, that expects life from God and not from one's own abilities; obedience, that forgoes one's own planning and enterprise and waits for God's direction and carries it out; love of God, that worships him alone and renounces power over the world for the sake of God. Faith, obedience, love—this would be piety and homage of God. Did Jesus really possess these? The Spirit gave them to him. Will he now abuse them and blend them with false, selfish ambition? This is what the Accuser wanted to find out. It was the Spirit's command to Jesus to show the Accuser that he kept what the Spirit had given him. Just as he once had resisted the Accuser, he now stands before his fellow villagers when they refuse their allegiance because he did not subscribe to the world's wisdom that a physician must first use his skill to help himself.

Faith Liberates from Self-Will
February 13

*Then Jesus was led by the Spirit into the wilderness, in order
that he might be tempted by the Accuser. And after fasting for
forty days and forty nights, he was hungry. So the tempter
approached him and said to him, "If you are God's Son, tell
these stones to turn into bread." But he answered, "It is
written: 'Man does not live from bread alone, but by every word
that proceeds from God's mouth.'"*
—MATTHEW 4:1–4 (CF. DEUT. 8:3)

Through whom does man live? Man does not believe that he lives through
God. Is life not his own property, which he acquires by virtue of nature,
defends by his own power, and fashions according to his own desires? If
Jesus, too, believes that he preserves his life by his own power, he belongs to
those who are ruled by the Accuser.

He was tempted in solitude, where he was set apart from natural
conditions of life away from human assistance. Yet this did not happen
because natural laws to which our body is subject did not apply to him.
Now he senses them again with their compelling force; now he hungers.
Must the Son of God suffer hunger? The answer seems clear as day: This
can never be! Hunger is an assault on life—everything is subject to the Son
of God. He can command everything to nurture him. Stones must turn
into bread in order that hunger be taken from him.

Jesus did not use his own new insights to counter Satan's address to him
as the Son of God. Man had long been told what God is for him and how
he ought to believe him. *Bread!* To be sure, bread preserves life—the natural
order of our lives is not in question. Jesus' divine sonship is not contradicted
by his eating bread, but does the natural process include divine power?
Once, God's pronouncement had told Israel that its life did not depend
solely on bread. For only one thing is indispensable for its preservation:
God's pronouncement that calls it to live. Whoever is given life from God
does not die. Has God's life-giving Word died because Jesus has no bread?

In his hunger he saw occasion to believe in God rather than to act on his
own. The one from whom he expects and receives his life is God, the Lord of
heaven and earth, who uses nature in the execution of his will, but who is greater

than nature. He is not separated from him in any situation. His faith in God set Jesus free from self-effort, ended all worry, and made continual thanksgiving possible, which drowns out any opposition to God's rule.

As painful as hunger was, it was also painful to see his own people and, first, even his own village refuse to believe in him. Yet even this was not an attack upon his life. The fact and purpose of his life as well as the nature of his commission are grounded in the divine word that was addressed to him.

Faith Waits for God's Command
February 14

Then the Accuser led him to the holy city and had him stand at the pinnacle of the temple and said to him, "If you are God's Son, cast yourself down. For it is written: 'He will give his angels charge concerning you, and they will carry you in their arms, in order that you may not strike your foot against a stone.'" Jesus said to him, "Again, it is written: 'You must not tempt the Lord your God.'"
—MATTHEW 4:5–7 (CF. PS. 91:11–12; DEUT. 6:16)

Is faith's only effect that it frees us from self-will? Does it not prove its healing power by activating our volition and making God's will ours? For this reason Jesus' interchange with the Accuser issued in a resolution of the question of what faith is. This resolution occurred on the pinnacle of the outermost temple wall above the deep valley beneath. This is where jumping down is fatal. Yet is there any danger for the Son of God, who has received his life from God's decree addressed to him? A Son of God who must be afraid is as much a contradiction in terms as is a Son of God who must hunger. His jump would not be arbitrary presumption. To the contrary, his action would proceed from faith. In this way he would give assent to the promise of God that assures him of the angels' assistance. Above all others he is the recipient of this promise. It tells him that he must not fear the leap, because angels bear him up.

What was still lacking that would give Jesus full assurance and inner compulsion to act? It was the divine command. Such a command alone keeps action from being presumptuous and renders it believing. If someone tempts God or puts him to the test to see whether he chooses to help, this amounts to questioning the deity of God. Jesus did not desire the help of angels; he remained within the realm of nature. It is the way of humans, but not of Jesus, to see how much one can extract from God.

Yet is Jesus therefore without a will? Does he desire that faith provide him with rest and relief from obligation and action? Precisely by not being able to exert any claims upon God, he makes clear when it is that he directs his entire will to action: when he is the recipient of a command of God, when his action is obedience. He will not get ahead of God with the godless presumption that God must follow suit. If God initiates, however, he will follow him without hesitation or contradiction, even when his command calls him to leap into the abyss or to carry the cross. When at one point in Nazareth he was unable to provide the congregation with a spectacular demonstration of his power, it was not therefore allowed to conclude that he was unable or unwilling to achieve something great. For this, however, one thing is indispensable: the command of God.

God Does Not Reveal Himself Solely to the Jews
February 15

"There were many widows in Israel in the days of Elijah, when heaven was shut for three years and six months because a great famine came over the entire earth. Yet Elijah was not sent to any of them, except to Zarephath in the region of Sidon. And there were many lepers in Israel in the days of the prophet Elisha. Yet only Naaman the Syrian was made well." When they heard this, the entire congregation was outraged, and they rose up, expelled him from the city, and led him to the cliff of a mountain on which their city was built, in order to cast him down. Yet he went right through the midst of them and went away.

—Luke 4:25–30

Doesn't every city praise the one who rises from it to greatness? Is his fame not the joy and honor of all who made a home for him? This natural sentiment does not apply to the servant of God. To be sure, what he brings is saving grace; but it is God's grace, and it is dangerous to enter God's service. The individual has reason to fear him, because he desires for himself everything that a person is and has. He is a consuming fire.

If Jesus is God's servant, it is clear that rule over the holy congregation is due him. He is the King of Israel. This renders him even more dangerous. The Christ has the world against him, not merely those who have power beyond the boundaries of his own territory but also those who rule Israel. Does he provide assurances that he will carry out what he promises? He refused any guarantees that had to be required from him. Instead, he demands blind faith. For this reason it is safer for his village to renounce him and to clear itself at the very outset from the suspicion that it was on his side.

Thus the bond that had tied Jesus to his home was severed. This hurt. Yet it did not matter if it did. What must take place must be done without contradiction. Does man have any claims on God? Are the Nazarenes entitled to God's kingdom, possibly because they are Jews? To whom was Elijah sent? He was sent to the Sidonian woman at Zarephath. Whose leprosy did Elisha cleanse? That of Naaman the Syrian. Jesus' loyalty as a Jew did not render him a prisoner of Judaism. For Judaism does not keep God's work a prisoner, so that God would have to obey its constraints.

Just as Jesus was authorized to belong entirely to the Jews and to live solely for them so that he did not move beyond the boundaries of their habitat, he also was authorized to go past them. This did not result in any wavering. For both—preserving or breaking fellowship—are grounded in the same commitment. He performs God's will by being tied to them with a holy obligation and by being a Jew as they are. He performs God's will by being their judge and by refusing them God's help.

Yet a Jewish community practices harsh and prompt justice. Whoever touches the privilege of a holy congregation and claims divine prerogative without providing justification must die, and his fellow villagers are first of all obligated to rise up against him and judge him. Yet they do not succeed: Jesus leaves.

God Has No Favorites
February 16

Peter . . . said: "Truly, I realize that God does not favor certain people, but that he accepts in every nation those who fear him and do what is right."
—ACTS 10:34–35

God does not tolerate contempt in anyone, the kind of stubbornness by which man avoids God and claims ignorance of him, thus denying what he does know about him. Such a person does not fear God. Yet there is also a second condition that God does not tolerate in anyone: injustice. For it infringes on an essential condition of life, which he receives through the community and which falls apart when he perpetrates it. People are different in a thousand ways. They are formed in ever different ways through nature and the communities of which they are a part. Yet one thing remains the same: their creatureliness, which provides them with their existence, and their capacity to do right, which lends their community stability and prosperity. Both make a person the recipient of a divine gift, and his relationship with God depends on whether he keeps or violates these.

If he fears God and does what is right, he possesses God's favor, which assigns to him what he does not yet possess and cannot procure for himself. Now God's call can extend to him. Now the shepherd can set out to look for his sheep, no matter how far it has strayed. Apart from knowledge of this principle of God's work, Luke claims, there would not have been any Christian mission. It was the condition for Peter's acceptance of Gentiles into the Christian community. For the Jew this meant a big adjustment, because he claimed God's favor for himself and excluded others from it. He imagined that God was obligated to extend his favor to him, a favor to which he was entitled because he was a Jew. Yet what Cornelius had experienced made clear that God's work did not subject itself to this claim.

Now the gate was thrust open that led Jesus' messengers to all people. He could find something that was pleasing to God in everyone. The fear of God could be stirred in anyone who longed for his knowledge and grace, and all could be moved by the desire to escape calamity and to exchange strife for community with others. Nowhere did he still encounter any obstacle that barred his access to man, as if God were partial in his dealings with man and thereby determined their destiny. Partiality was never the ground of God's election or rule. Jesus' messenger acted in keeping with the will of his master—the One who renounced his fellowship with the Nazarenes and proclaimed Jerusalem's demise—when he made it clear that God does not play favorites.

God's Love Is Free from Selfishness
February 17

Glory, honor, and peace for everyone who does what is good, first for the Jew and also for the Greek. For there is no partiality with God.
—ROMANS 2:10–11

Our fellowship with God is based upon his free choice. Why was the Jew still not entitled to say that he was the recipient of God's special favor? After all, he had been set apart from the world by God's Word and had been made God's chosen one. To be sure, people obtain a share in God's grace solely by his will, and it is God's work that procures it. Yet it is not partisan favor, for it contributes to God's glory, not man's. It does not accommodate God to man nor adjust itself to man's self-made achievements and longings but is man's union with God's will, God's good pleasure in what he himself works in man.

Favor is love corrupted by selfishness. This is why it is opposed to the deity of God; and when the Jews demanded it from God, or when Christians expected it from him, they replaced who God is with who they themselves were. Divisions and corrupting partiality are found among them, because it is not love that rules over natural communities; rather, selfishness determines what takes place in them, arbitrarily assigning honor or shame, advantage or disadvantage. If it were the same with God's kingdom, people would be able to obligate God on the basis of their own achievements and would exist as self-created beings by virtue of their own value in God's world at a place they had carved out for themselves. These are dark dreams; Jesus shattered them by revealing that God's election is love, nothing but love, perfect love, love free from selfishness.

When Jesus thought of that love, he said that the Father was perfect. His love provides us with the power to make our own choices, to take action. Because his Word enters us, we can think truth, and because his command is addressed to us, we are enabled to do what is just. Because he lets us take part in his work, he honors us with allowing us to serve him. This is the way love is: it gives and makes its recipient rich. Yet for this reason its recipient is unable to elevate himself above others and boast of God in such a way that he is really talking about himself. Because God's election is a function of his love, his power as the Creator and as the sovereign Ruler remains God's sole possession.

Section 5

JESUS STIRS FAITH

Faith Receives an Answer
February 18

Look! A leper approached him, kneeled down before him, and exclaimed, "Lord, if it is your will, you can cleanse me." And Jesus stretched out his hand and touched him, and said, "It is my will, be cleansed!" And immediately his leprosy was cleansed. And Jesus said to him, "Listen carefully! Don't tell anyone, but go and show yourself to the priest, and bring the sacrifice commanded by Moses, as a testimony for them."
—Matthew 8:2–4

The picture the disciples received of Jesus through their dealings with him is particularly well illustrated through the narrative of Jesus' encounter with a leper. A solitary man approaches him. He has a fatal disease and must continually cry out, "I am unclean!" because he poses a danger for others. This is why the Law has expelled him from the holy congregation. What does he represent in relation to Jesus' sky-high aims? Only God's creative power can help him. Will Jesus call on it for this one who is subject to death, for him who is condemned by the Law?

It was the leper's behavior that determined Jesus' actions. He believed that Jesus had the ability to heal him. He also believed that he was able to act toward him with God's power. This removed any presumption from his request. He could not make any attempt to exploit Jesus' power for himself. Because he believes, he must yield to him without reservations. His destiny depends solely on Jesus' will, nothing else: "If it is your will, you are able to do this."

Was Jesus' commission properly described by this statement? Was God's greatness revealed by Jesus' setting a leper free from what corrupted his body? Yes, God's glory was revealed in that Jesus did not send this believer away but attested to God's will that man ought to believe in God, because he hears and responds to his faith. It was, in fact, Jesus' aim to proclaim this message and to engender faith—not man's faith in himself, nor faith in others or in his own natural abilities, but faith in God that lets go of all other things, yields to his will, and asks for his omnipotent grace. According to Jesus, such faith was required to enter God's kingdom.

Since the leper required the ruling of the priest in order to resume normal public life, Jesus sent him to Jerusalem. In this way he made him his witness before the priests. They, who refused to believe in him, now saw in the leper what faith is. Yet did the Jews indeed recognize true faith in his experience? Did they see in it more than a powerful work of God? Perhaps they did not even see this but merely marveled at the power of Jesus. If so, they elevated him to a miracle creature who was helpful in every situation. This made him what the prince of the world wanted him to be: one who can turn stones into bread and can leap into the depths without fearing danger. For this reason Jesus did not permit healed individuals to accompany him. They would have diverted people's attention away from what constituted God's revelation in Jesus' conduct.

Faith in God Is Born
February 19

Through him you believe in God, who raised him from the dead and gave him glory, so that your faith and your hope are directed toward God.

—1 Peter 1:21

Jesus' encounter with the leper (see February 18 above) belongs to his early ministry and provides us with a picture of what faith looked like at that particular time. Peter, on the other hand, wrote to Christians dispersed all over Asia Minor. He tells us the huge impact that Jesus had by his coming and his ministry, an impact that will repeat itself elsewhere as long as people's present needy state exists: in every region of Asia Minor there were people who placed their faith in God.

They were brought to faith by God's raising and glorifying the Christ. Wherever this message entered a person, he became a believer. Through it he obtained the knowledge of God, which was able to lead him to a believing stance toward God. Now was this something great and new? Man acts in faith from the beginning; for by his birth he is subjected to the law that he can live only when he acts in faith, and he is subjected to this law until the end. How could he speak or work without faith? To what end does he speak when he does not encounter faith, and how can he expect to accomplish anything if no one assists him? Yet believing conduct is not the only thing that life gives us. There is faith that is quickly disappointed; there are distrust and suspicion, well- and ill-founded, true and false; fear of nature and of people; crippling insecurity; gnawing doubt and uncertainty. Moreover, when the memory of God is stirred in us, how far it is from being able to help us believe! We cannot believe as long as he remains silent for us. In order for us to be able to believe, a word must come from him to us, a word that speaks to us directly, one that pertains to our lives, a word that reveals to us his grace. Until this word reaches us, we have not yet found the place assigned to us, because we are God's creatures and cannot escape the internal wavering that intermingles faith and unbelief, community and strife, fear and hope.

Yet now he who speaks with us in the name of God is telling us his message, he whose word is relevant for us because he came *for us,* died *for us,* and was raised and exalted to God *for us.* Now we know the gracious God and receive the kind of faith that keeps God's Word, lives by God's grace, and longs for God's work. That is also why we are given a believing stance toward nature and others, because they belong to the One in whom we believe. Now we finally have true "religion," true worship of God, not merely an empty show that ends in deception, nor trust that is weighed down by unbelief, but a faith that is certainty because it is rooted in truth and issues in obedience to the truth.

Yet where there is faith directed toward God, there also has been awakened the hope that is grounded in him. For Christ's work has not yet been completed, and the message of his grace also entails his promise, which transforms believers into those who hope.

Faith Is Righteousness
February 20

God's righteousness is revealed by the message about Jesus from faith to faith.
—Romans 1:17

Paul said that he proclaimed the message about Jesus because it gave a person faith. This faith, in turn, was his righteousness. This is how he was brought into a normal relationship with God. Righteous is what he ought to become and what God makes him to be. We commit an injustice when we deny God honor, knowing that we are his creatures, and when we criticize his government, calling it a hard destiny even though we have received everything we own. We commit an injustice when we subject what we have been given to our own selfish longing and exploit it for ourselves. This constant committing of injustice—with all the theories and myths we use to justify it, claiming to be wise when we are not and never can become wise—is rejected, recognized as reprehensible, and judged when we are granted a believing stance toward God through the message of Jesus.

Yet this righteousness of ours is entirely God's righteousness. It arises from what he, in his righteousness, has done for us and in us. It does not consist in our accomplishments, either in merits we have acquired as part of our ethnic community or in our worship, as though we could purify or deepen our thoughts about God by way of pure doctrine. It consists neither in what we know about God nor in what we do for God but in putting our trust in God and acting toward him in faith. Yet this is God's work by which he reveals his grace.

We also must not attain righteousness by viewing our faith as a particularly meritorious type of conduct, as though through our faith we could persuade God to acquit us and to take us into his kingdom. The effective power of faith does not attach to the inner procedure that takes place in us when Jesus' Word makes us believe. Faith rather is rendered effective through the One in whom we believe, because he gives us everything he promises us.

Faith has the power to extinguish our guilt and to bring an end to our performance of unrighteousness because God's Word has become our property through faith and has become operative in us. Our sinful nature does not permit us to sustain a righteousness of our own. We attain to righteousness only by God's acting toward us in his own righteousness. His rejection of sin leads him to grant us forgiveness in Christ, and his pleasure in what is good and in community causes him to accept us into fellowship with him and to call us to himself. Because righteousness is a characteristic of his will, he shapes our lives through faith in a way that pleases him, and by faith he brings us to the goal that he has ordained for us.

Faith Brings Security
February 21

By God's power you are guarded for salvation by faith.
—I Peter 1:5

The leper was healed because he believed in Jesus. He had become a healthy man once again. Yet did he thereby also receive what Jesus called the gracious gift of God? Did his faith also make him a fellow citizen of the kingdom? And did his faith bring him eternal life? Jesus' aim lay sky-high above the knowledge and ability of the healed man. Was his faith sufficient for him to attain it?

Yet was it any different with those to whom the disciples brought the whole gospel, which portrayed for them the One who not merely had mercy on a dying person in the power of God, but also showed them the One who had died and risen on their behalf? This was the one in whom they now believed, and in him they were set free from their doubt, fear, and unbelief. Just as the leper, they had placed their destiny in his will and his work and no longer sought to achieve their goals by themselves. Indeed, it lay entirely beyond their own ability; for it transcends anything that can be brought about by one's own effort. What ought to bring them to their goal is their faith. Is it able to do so?

God's power is able. This was the apostolic reply when this question assailed believers; and God's power not merely is able but also does it, because you believe. God's power is at work in the lives of those who believe in God. They call upon it and are enabled by Jesus and therefore do not labor in vain. For this reason a guardian stands by their sides who accompanies them to the goal to which they are called. After all, do they believe in one who is dead or absent? Jesus' call places them before God, and their union with Jesus renders him present with them, so that the Spirit gives them their thoughts and moves their wills. They are thus not left to themselves; they are not a flock without a shepherd, not a community without a Lord, but stand under the protection of the One whose grace is omnipotent. They are united with him precisely by virtue of the fact that they believe.

To be sure, apart from his protection, which wards off what would corrupt them, they would not arrive at their destiny. Eternal life has not yet arrived. The believer has nothing yet but a mortal existence, and the flesh and the world incite in him a selfish longing that resists God's will. Nature still conceals for him the heavenly realm and renders Christ invisible. Yet God's power is superior to all that subjects him to danger. His lot is therefore to act in faith toward it. So why is it that faith brought to the one who had been healed by Jesus not merely physical restoration but also eternal life? It is because the One in whom he believed is the giver of eternal life.

Jesus' Commitment to the Jews
February 22

The centurion's servant, who was dear to him, was sick and close to death. Yet because he heard about Jesus, he sent elders of the Jews to him and asked him to come and to save his servant. They came to Jesus, entreated him urgently, and said, "He is worthy of being granted this request. For he loves our people and has built this synagogue for us." So Jesus went with them. When he was already close to the house, the centurion sent friends to tell him, "Lord, do not concern yourself! For I am not worthy for you to enter under my roof."
—LUKE 7:2–6

Because Capernaum was at the Jewish border and therefore under occupation, in Capernaum was also a house set apart by the Law from the holy community, and the guardians of tradition watched closely to ensure that this prohibition was heeded by all. Everyone in the village knew that even Jesus obeyed this custom. If he went in to the foreigner, he would lose his communion with his own people, and there still remained so many "lost sheep of the house of Israel" to whom he must bring God's call, because they had deteriorated to being merely natural and knew nothing but natural desires. Yet when the centurion believed that Jesus could heal his sick servant, the Jews thought this case warranted Jesus' violating custom. Their relationship with the commander at their village was for them an important matter. He had the power to afflict them because he also had police powers. But now, not only had he not afflicted them; he had adopted a friendly stance toward them and had even helped them to build their synagogue. The elders gladly proved their gratitude and took it upon themselves to support his request with Jesus. In this case, they thought, Jesus should condescend and be willing to enter the pagan house. They did not know how Jesus judged the Jews' relationship with God. Because the Jews did not raise any objections, Jesus was indeed prepared to enter the centurion's house.

Yet it was the centurion himself who objected. How can he, who asks Jesus for help, expect him to do what no Jew is allowed to do? Precisely because he adopted a friendly stance toward the Jews and believed that Jesus the Jew possessed healing powers, he dared not transgress the boundary separating him from the Jews. For him, the Gentile, there was no fellowship with Jesus. Now even Jesus did not enter his house. Because the Gentile respected his Jewishness, he also affirmed his ethnic allegiance. He did not correct the Gentile and did not enter his house against his will.

So was he weak in this hour? Did he yield to Jewish pride, after the centurion had bowed to him? Even then he acted in the assurance that the harvest of his seed was ripening, not among the Jews but the Gentiles. To be sure, the Gentile was separated from the Jew—but not from God's kingdom. And precisely now, when he accepted the centurion's faith, granted his request, and allowed him to experience the healing power of God, he stood in the struggle against Jewish pride. In this struggle, however, he always took care so that the truth was not violated. Nothing that was sacred—and the boundary between Judaism and the Gentiles had been created by God's law—could be dishonored by his struggle with Judaism. He could not avoid becoming an offense to Judaism; but he did not create offense by his own action. Yet we misperceive Jesus' fidelity to the Jewish community if we think of it as something that was borne reluctantly and against his will. Love was the bond that united him with the Jews, and this love was completely one with that by which he called God his Father, and this love of his was his joy and honor and strength.

The Message Is Believed
February 23

Now when he entered Capernaum, a centurion approached him and asked of him, "Lord, my servant lies in the house crippled and heavily afflicted." He said to him, "I will come and heal him." The centurion answered, "Lord, I am not worthy for you to come under my roof. Just say the word, and my servant will be healed. For I too am a man under authority and have soldiers under me and say to one, 'Go!' and he goes, and to another, 'Come!' and he comes, and to my servant, 'Do this!' and he does it." When Jesus heard this, he was amazed and said to those who were following him, "Truly, I say to you: I have not found such great faith anywhere in Israel."

—MATTHEW 8:5–10

Ethnic origin and religion separate the centurion from Jesus. Must his request therefore go unanswered? Is Jesus' helping power therefore not available to him? If this were his verdict, he would treat Jesus' word as null and void. When he depreciates his word, he denies his commission that made him Lord. Doesn't the one called to rule possess a powerful word? Even the centurion speaks in the confidence that his word will be accomplished. Whether he addresses a soldier or the servant who obeys him, he is certain that his word will be carried out. He expects the same of Jesus. If he wants to help and expresses his will through his word, help will be given. By not doubting his word, he believes in him.

No Jew has such faith; Jesus' word is not sufficient for him. He wants to see before he believes. Only the Gentile, who is denied Jesus' presence and who is given merely his assistance, will extend to him such faith. And thus his right to rule is manifested: he will grant them salvation by his word. He does not forgo this when he wholeheartedly enters the hour that calls him to service and by living and dying with his whole love and his whole strength for the Jews. The Greek city at the eastern shore of the lake was continually in his view, and the large cities at the ocean—Tyre, Sidon, Beirut—were easily accessible. Yet the path there was closed to him. The Lamb of God cannot abandon Jerusalem and wander into the distance. Yet this did not amount to a forsaking of God's great aim, to a limitation of God's dominion merely to the Jews, or to a renunciation of the world. For his word is grounded in God's power and does not lose it when it reaches the Gentile and is believed by him. This is how the church will come into being alongside the old community. He will bring it into being by extending his word to the Gentiles and by bringing the divine gifts to the one who believes that word.

What Makes Righteous Is Faith, Not Works
February 24

We judge that a man is justified through faith apart from works of the Law.
—Romans 3:28

The Gentile centurion did not approach Jesus by way of any work that was done in order to fulfill the Law. The Jews sought Jesus' favor by praising a work of the Law that he had taken upon himself, that is, the construction of the synagogue. Yet what drove the centurion to Jesus was not his accomplishments for the Jews but confidence in his messianic power. The Law had come to Capernaum long before Jesus went there, and the centurion appears to have respected the fidelity with which the Jew practiced his religion. Yet the Law was not addressed to him but rather separated him from the holy community. But now Jesus had come, and he was no representative of the Law like the rabbi. What he spoke of was no legislation but an announcement of divine action and grace, and what he did made no claim on human willingness to sacrifice or to serve. It was first and foremost effective mercy and willingness to help by virtue of divine power. Because the centurion saw this in him and heard this about him, he believed in him as the one who was good, the one who wants to help, and the Lord whose word is accomplished. He called upon him in this confidence and brought nothing to Jesus but this faith.

"Nothing but faith!" This is how those spoke who saw nothing above them but God's law. God's commandment had seized them and had obligated them to honor and obey God. It made them proud, glad, and despondent: proud, when they hoped that the Law commended what they had done; despondent, when it convicted them of transgression. Yet always they dealt with nothing but works. God was distant. One day he will reveal to them his verdict, be it praise in validating their works, or condemnation in scolding their transgressions. Where was faith beside the weight accorded to works? It was no work, no achievement, no merit. It did not accomplish anything that a person could point to before God as his contribution that he had achieved for the glorification of God. It arose from need, and by it a person expressed his powerlessness. "Nothing but faith!" they say. But Jesus did not say: He has nothing but faith; he can do nothing but believe!

For he himself is the ground of faith as well as the one who brings it about. How could he despise what he himself brings about? The believer has entrusted himself to him, the Lord who can issue commands—to him, the gracious one who is able to help. How could he despise the one he has won for himself? He has what the believer thinks he has. It is true that he can help, and it is true that he is gracious. This is why he shows him what he is and does. Faith unites the one who believes with the One who is believed. This renders faith more than a wish, more than hope. For the community that is brought about by faith issues in a share in the saving power of the One to whom the believer has entrusted himself.

Thus, because he stood above the Law, Jesus acted in complete liberty from the Law, in the authority of the one who can forgive, and with the wealth of the one who can give. Nothing is said about what the centurion once was or now is, and the shame and guilt of Gentile existence is not placed upon him—not because Jesus tolerated it but because he does away with it. He does away with it by offering himself to the believer now as the One who has revealed God to him and has shown him his will.

Jesus, the Atypical Jew
February 25

*Then the Samaritan woman said, "How is it that you, who are
a Jew, ask me, a Samaritan woman, for a drink?" For Jews do
not associate with Samaritans. Jesus answered her, "If you
knew God's gift and who it is that is asking you for a drink,
you would ask him and he would give you living water."*

—JOHN 4:9–10

You are a Jew; what do you want from me?" said a Samaritan woman when
Jesus asked her to give him a drink from her jar. Jew, stay with your Jews.
You have nothing to say to us who are not Jews. Doesn't every nation possess
its own distinctive characteristics, its own interpretation and evaluation of
the world, its own way of entering into communion and of using the fruit
of its own soil? This also includes its own religious customs. In this, no one
ought to disturb the other. Everyone should be what he is by virtue of his
race, a member of his own ethnic community. In your arrogance, however,
you Jews impose your will on others and want to rule them.

Jesus silenced—and silences—this objection that called him a Jew. He
asked the woman for a small favor, and she rejected him. "If you asked me,
I would give to you," he answered, and what he can give, she does not have
and cannot obtain for herself. Because he had asked her for water, he called
his gift "living water." For his message is the promise of life. Will he prevail?
Yes! But he will not do so in the way the Samaritan suspects, who thinks he
wants to make her a Jew and demand that she travel to Jerusalem and
abandon her village community. What he gives is God's gift, and everyone
who sees what he gives asks him and receives. He could not give this if he
were not a Jew; but he possess his messianic power not because he has the
blood of his mother or grandmother flowing in his veins or because he
depends on his ancestors but because God has entrusted him with his word
and has commissioned him to do his work. If he withheld his gift from the
woman because she is a Samaritan, he would be a Jew in the sense she
means it, a Jew who wants to reign over all and who despises everyone who
does not belong to his community. Such a Jew fashions for himself a God
who is available only for him. Yet this is nothing but dark presumption that
vanishes where Jesus is. God is the God of all. This makes Jesus the giver *to*

all. And Jesus gives according to the principle "Whoever asks receives," and what he gives heals a person. For the "living water" he gives to that person imparts eternal life.

Kindness Has Appeared
February 26

The kindness and goodness of God, our Savior, has appeared.
—Titus 3:4

In Paul's experience, kindness and goodness were not human traits. He exhorted his coworkers not to forget how people treat one another. They live in malice and envy, and despise and hate one another. Do those qualities apply only to those who are on the outside, such as haughty Jews or dissolute Greeks? Paul answers that we were the same way. But there is one who is good, who values people precisely because they are people and helps them because they are people—not because another resembles him in race or character and thus pleases him, not because he is of value to him as fellow citizen or united with him in friendship. If one lacks all these, he still has one thing: he is human. But of what value is a human being? There are plenty of people, even more than enough. It is not part of our self-interest to help a human being because he is a human being.

God showed us through Jesus that he does not think this way. He was a friend of humanity because he saw in every human being, regardless of the way he looked, a creature of God. This is the inseparable bond that unites everyone's existence with the divine activity, even when he defiles himself or enters into bondage. He still remains part of God's creation and a member of humanity, which was given life by God. Thus, all are given access to Jesus. Are they worthy or unworthy? This is not the question with which Jesus approaches humanity. Nor does he ask, "What can or can you not do?" Because they are God's creatures, they can and ought to hear what God says to his creatures, and they ought to do what God commands his creatures to do. They all are subject to the same law that judges their godless conduct, and they all are under the same grace that allows them to experience God's kindness.

The Jews said, "We must not enter a pagan house." But in a pagan's house lives a human being, one of God's creatures surrounded by God's kindness. "The Gentiles are our enemies," they say. But they are still human beings, even when they present obstacles to fellowship. God's kindness has appeared! This marks the beginning of a new era. This provides Jesus' community with a constitution that is different from any other law.

Section 6

ALL ARE GIVEN ACCESS TO JESUS

Revelation or Blasphemy?
February 27

And they came and brought a lame man to him, carried by
four men. And because they could not bring him to Jesus on
account of the great number of people, they took off the roof
where he was, made a hole, and lowered the bed on which the
lame man lay. And when Jesus saw their faith, he said to the
lame man, "My son, your sins are forgiven." Yet some of the
scribes sat there who thought in their hearts,
"Why does he speak in such a way? He is blaspheming!
Who can forgive sins except for one: God?"
—MARK 2:3–7

If only the one in need of help could be brought to Jesus! Everything is gained as long as there is free access to him. This is what the men thought who lowered the lame man through the roof to Jesus. He heals him because being lame is an affliction; a person is burdened by misery, and lack is met by gift. But how could he do this without also forgiving sins? If they are not forgiven, his conduct would be subject to the principle "Don't grant requests. Deny aid to those who suffer. Use guilt as the power that decides their fate." Thus the guilty would be left without access to God or a share in his grace. Now what good would be access gained to Jesus if access to God's grace remains closed?

True, trust such as was placed in Jesus at that time is well-founded and effective only when Jesus is sought out, not *apart* from God but *because* of his communion with God. Jesus directs the thoughts of the sick man and of those who carry him to what they request—request from God. They thought like everybody else: Healing can be obtained, but to attain forgiveness is not possible. Sickness can end, but sins are forever. For sicknesses are disturbances in natural processes; sins, on the other hand, constitute a breaking of the Law. Yet the Law is holy, and there is no cure for the one who has broken it. Thus a contradiction is injected into the request to Jesus for help, and his gift is not fully effective. This is why, before uttering the healing word, Jesus told the sick man, "Your sins are forgiven," and this is how he differed from rabbinic Judaism.

Is it beneficial to listen to the rabbis' objection? It certainly is! The discussion between them and Jesus pertains to our deepest concern: Who is God? The one who is revealed, or the one who is concealed? The one who is silent, or the one who speaks? The one who is gracious, or the one who is irreconcilable toward those who have incurred guilt? And who is man? Is he condemned to uncertainty, or called to faith? Incurably guilty, or able to be lifted up? Subject to death, or chosen to life? The common point of departure of both was that Jesus' word had meaning only when it was God's word. God alone is the judge of mankind, and God alone is the one who is able to forgive. The Lawgiver is also the Judge, and the One who convicts our hearts is the One who can forgive. Yet it is the rabbis' duty and obligation to defend God's honor against anyone who presumes upon anything that is due only to God, and Jesus' opponents were sincere men who did not pursue their religion as a game but were tied with a holy bond to what they considered to be their knowledge of God.

When, in the name of God, Jesus forgave the sick man his sins, this was a revelation of God. What was the converse? Blasphemy. His opponents, however, saw in Jesus nothing but the human being, solely the one who was equal to them. He was not allowed to do more than what they themselves were able to do. They were not able to forgive; they could only ask for forgiveness. Because God's judgment is inscrutable, the only counsel they had for those who incurred guilt was this: Humble yourselves before God with fasting and prayers, and get busy with good works. Perhaps God will accept them as compensation for your sins. *Perhaps!* This is not the way Jesus spoke. Rather, he announced God's forgiveness. Now what was this: revelation or blasphemy?

It Is Easier to Forgive than to Heal
February 28

And immediately Jesus realized in his spirit that they thought this way within themselves, and he said to them: "Why do you think this way in your hearts? What is easier: to say to the lame man, 'Your sins are forgiven,' or to say, 'Get up, take your bed, and walk'? But in order that you may know that the Son of Man has authority to forgive sins on earth"— he said

> *to the lame man — "I tell you: Get up, take your bed, and go*
> *home." And he stood up, immediately took his bed, and went*
> *before all of their eyes, so that all were amazed, praising God*
> *and saying, "Never have we seen anything like this."*
>
> —MARK 2:8–12

Is what Jesus said God's word? God's word is one with God's work. He speaks the forgiving word of God, for he does God's healing work. This is why he commands the lame man, "Get up!" and thus proves that the Son of Man has authority to forgive sins on earth. By sins being forgiven—not merely in heaven but also on earth—forgiveness becomes a present experience, and God's grace is revealed in our history.

Forgiveness is not an empty word. It expresses the most real, immeasurably great transformation in a person's existence, for our relationship with God determines the content of our entire existence. It is, therefore, a complete transformation when a person's sinning has been rendered inoperative and inconsequential by divine forgiving. The rabbis' attack was directed against the unity with God's will out of which Jesus acted. They did not accept his divine sonship. Jesus did not speak about this with them, however; this remained his secret. On the other hand, by allowing his word to control the natural process, he revealed to them that he expresses the will of the Father through his word.

We learn why healing power was, for Jesus, an indispensable part of his activity. He desires the miracle not because he takes offense at nature. He does not desire anything unnatural. He does not fight against nature but honors it as the mediator of divine operations. Neither does he desire the miracle because it elevates him above others; he did not soil it by selfish ambition. Yet he could not demonstrate God's grace solely by way of words. This would have contradicted the deity of God. To be sure, reception of God's grace consists precisely in the fact that God speaks to the human being. A silent God leaves a person to his own devices. If he speaks to him, God's love visits him and introduces him to communion with God. Love arises through God's word. God's word, in turn, proves its divine nature in that nature obeys him, too.

According to the rabbi, it is all right for Jesus to heal. For man has been given power in the natural realm. But man has no power over righteousness and unrighteousness, God's grace and God's wrath. Is it really easier, Jesus asks, to change a person's natural condition? Is it not easier to set someone free from the shame and torment of his evil conscience? The natural condition has power over the person. He is what nature makes him to be. Only the Creator is more powerful. When he reveals his grace, what hurts a person or keeps him in bondage is done away with. Yet this takes place when he manifests his sin-forgiving grace.

People have always fantasized about improving their lot. They consider it possible that the evils plaguing them can be overcome—if not now, at least in a better future. But it is always judged impossible for a person to become in his inner being someone other than who he is. Jesus alone contradicted this universal human verdict and said: It is easier for God's grace to renew a person's inner condition than to take away from him what nature oppresses him with. This verdict has been vindicated by the course of history. In vain we resist the deadly power of nature, and the acquisition of life's necessities is for many a harsh business. But to cleanse the soul within through God's Word and to receive great joy from it and to transform life into a fruitful event—this is Jesus' gift to Christendom.

Open Access to Jesus
February 29

It so happened that when he reclined inside the house for a meal, many tax collectors and sinners came and reclined with Jesus and his disciples for the meal. And the Pharisees saw this and said to his disciples, "Why does your teacher eat with tax collectors and sinners?"
—Matthew 9:10–11

When the representatives of the Law undertook to make every Jew subject to God in every action, a deep rupture arose in the Jewish nation. For it was not possible to keep many fellow Jews from violating their obligation toward God. For this reason the population everywhere divided itself into the righteous and the guilty, and this rupture did away with any kind of community, even dealings in the natural realm, such as table fellowship. The sinner's bread could not be enjoyed by the righteous, and his house could not be entered. Any contact with sinners rendered the righteous person unclean.

Yet didn't John proclaim the forgiveness of sins? Didn't forgiveness make one unified people out of those who believed John's message? The righteous, however, did not have any confidence in this message. Didn't it ultimately stand in irreconcilable opposition to the Law? The Law pronounced the sinner guilty; didn't this mean his expulsion from God's people, and didn't this expulsion of evildoers from God's people require the active participation of everyone who knew himself obligated by the Law and considered it his calling to enforce the Law in his own life and in the lives of all others?

For Jesus, this condition of the community that constituted a necessary consequence of the rule of the Law had vanished, because he was the messenger and bringer of the rule of God. Its foundation was the forgiveness of sins, and Jesus granted the guilty this forgiveness by not excluding them from his fellowship. He also gave his bread to them. They, too, found a place at the table beside him.

The attack on custom and the party that defended it was apparent. Thus, the objection against the One who ate with sinners was immediately evident and accompanied Jesus during his entire ministry. This makes Jesus' verdict that there was no place for him in Jerusalem intelligible to us. If he grounded his dealings with all others in the fact that their sins did not separate them from him, he inexorably met with Pharisaic condemnation in Jerusalem. In Capernaum the opposition to him from those representing the Law lay in an effort to play off Jesus' disciples against him. Was it not the aim of every truly pious individual to belong to a pure community, in which all were concerned for their own perfection? What was the inexorable outcome for the community Jesus was gathering around him if it incorporated both righteous and sinners? Whoever honors even the dishonorable as his brothers is himself dishonored, and whoever does not drive from himself the one who despises God and transgresses his commandment is himself godless. They were terrified by the notion that Jesus was to give the community an entirely new constitution.

The New Thing Tax Collectors Learned from Jesus
March 1

Tax collectors also came to be baptized and said to him,
"Teacher, what should we do?" But he said to them,
"Don't ask for more than is due you." Soldiers asked him as
well, "What should we do?" And he said to them,
"Don't exploit anyone, and don't falsely accuse anyone.
And be content with your wages."
—Luke 3:12–14

Those who were zealous for the Law warned against certain occupations, because they necessarily led to sin. At the time of Jesus, those people were especially despised who allowed themselves to be recruited by the governing authorities to levy taxes. The zealous despised a life that, continually showing contempt for the Law, was solely oriented toward the acquisition of money. The same attitude could, of course, be found among all classes of people. It was considered to be particularly contemptible, however, in the case of the tax collector because he stood in the service of the occupying forces and, through his extortionist activity, further exacerbated the national oppression of his people. But the soldier, too, stood in the service of the occupying forces, and during the operation of the police, there were often occasions when those who bore arms incurred guilt through reprehensible acts of violence, earning the hatred of the people and the curse of the pious.

Now there were also tax collectors and soldiers who desired baptism from John, and he promised the forgiveness of sins to them, too. Forgiveness was not merely offered to special segments of the population. The one who announced it sincerely had to grant it to all who were ready for repentance. But what was the sin from which they must refrain and the new behavior to which their repentance now led them? Did the Baptist command, "Leave the customs booth, lay down your arms"? He did not but considered it possible to carry out the duties of a tax collector and of a soldier without sinning. The tax collector does this when he limits himself to the stipulated tariffs, and the soldier when he forgoes greedy extortion and acts of violence and lives by his rightful pay. Both ought to be able to make a living by carrying out their profession, but it must not be a means to amass riches. The Baptist could not say anything beyond this when they asked him, "What shall we do?" He could not revolutionize the national economy; this was a matter for the One who had the royal commission. John himself was one who waited, and he made those whom he baptized to be ones who waited. The tax collectors and soldiers ought to perform justice in their service so that they, too, might wait with confidence for the One who will make all things new and who will accept them, too, into his kingdom.

But now that Jesus has come, there was a different answer for the tax collector who no longer wanted to sin but desired the forgiveness of his sins and asked what he should do, an answer other than what the Baptist was able to give him. "Come to me," Jesus said to him. This lent an unsuspected reinforcement to the repentance by which he renounced his old thinking and willing. What he saw and heard with Jesus did not contradict merely thievery and violence but also the honorable tax collector's day-to-day business. Jesus' opposition to any perspective on life that knows only our natural existence and therefore pours all its strength into the acquisition of natural goods could be perceived by all who came to him. Jesus had neither money nor arms. He stood before the nation in abject poverty and without power, armed solely with God's riches and God's strength. Thus, a tax collector who went to Jesus was drawn away from everything he previously had been and done. If he ordered his conduct in keeping with Jesus' word, it became completely new.

Jesus' Will Is Love
March 2

It is not the healthy who need a doctor, but the sick.
—MATTHEW 9:12

Birds of a feather flock together—sinners with sinners, and the righteous with the righteous. This was public opinion and customary procedure. For anyone whose thinking followed this principle, Jesus had lost all credibility through his table fellowship with the tax collectors. How is a pious person supposed to entrust himself and the people to one who fellowshipped with tax collectors? Yet even this principle knows only self-centered longing. By associating with others like him, everyone confirms himself in his own verdict and his own righteousness. Is there also another aim that can motivate a person?

Jesus illustrates this for the self-centered righteous person with the example of the doctor. Does the doctor go to the sick person because he would like to be sick? He goes to him for the sake of the sick person, not for his own sake; he goes because he wants to help. What are we to call the willingness that arises from another person's need? This is love, and when another person's lack and suffering are the cause for action, love becomes mercy. Does Jesus' love present an obstacle to trust? Doesn't it rather awaken it in us? If love is not able to establish faith, what is? Because Jesus' conduct was motivated by love, the tax collectors found more with him than with the Baptist, who confronted their boundless egotism with his prohibitions: Don't become thieves and robbers! Jesus, on the other hand, did not impose any prohibitions but instead revealed to them the mystery of love.

But Jesus' aim also provided him with the limitation of his ministry. The doctor is there for the sick, not for the healthy. The giver goes to the one who suffers lack, the bearer to the one who cannot move by himself; the forgiver looks for the one who is guilty; the one who acts in God's service turns to the one who does not care for God. None of these turns to the latter to indulge their own desire, particularly not the desire to revel in one's own superiority. Rather, they desire in truth and integrity the well-being and life of the other person.

But does this even exist? Is love not rendered impossible by the natural constitution of our soul? Did anyone ever act without being motivated by his selfish desire? Would anyone ever have become a doctor if his profession were not lucrative? If a person knows nothing but himself and is motivated solely by the incentives that are his by nature, these verdicts are indeed correct. They do not, however, apply to the One through whom God reveals himself. Proclaiming God's kingdom and acting out of love were one and the same reality for Jesus. God's rule makes it clear that God values a person, brings an end to his need, and uses his power for the person's well-being. Whoever speaks of God's kingdom proclaims that God is love. Yet only that person can speak of God's love who has received it and is motivated by it to act. Love was the reason that the tax collectors and sinners were the guests with whom Jesus sought to share.

The Commandment's Goal
March 3

The goal of the commandment is love from a pure heart and from sincere faith.

—I Timothy 1:5

Everyone who lives in the Christian community is continually and strongly called to exert all his strength to hear, to learn, to make every effort to see clearly and to judge correctly, to become strong, to subdue his body, and to subdue his possessions—such are the means for his worship and the weapons for his battle—and to put on the armor of God. What is the purpose of these exhortations? Their purpose is love—not our perfection, not our greatness, not the gratification of our selfish desires, but that kind of disposition that makes us turn to others: to Jesus, that he may be our Lord, and to those with whom we live, that they may become rich in God's gifts and be kept from danger and falling into sin. To make room in us for love and to provide it with the means by which it can work—this is the ultimate goal of all those admonitions that call us to be occupied with ourselves and to make the accumulation of our own wealth our first duty.

It has become crystal clear to all who have been confronted with God that love stands above all our own concerns. Faced with him, all selfish longing loses its compelling power. This is the place where Jesus puts us; led by his hand, we walk before God. By this we are set free from our loneliness. We are no longer the greatest, no longer the only thing we know. Now we love.

Yet are we capable of loving? Love has prerequisites. When will it find room in us? It lives in a pure heart and presupposes a good conscience and accompanies pure—not merely purported—faith, the kind of faith through which our conduct becomes believing. The internal pollution that comes through longings that we must condemn as reprehensible tears community apart. We cannot live for others when we must condemn ourselves. And how are we to transcend ourselves and believe others when we are not even able to yield to God in faith? Thus the plethora of exhortations reaches us: Watch yourself, and become strong and rich in everything. Precisely because what God gives to us is love, what we are in ourselves takes on serious importance, yet in such a way that all growth in wealth and perfection does not become an end in itself but is transcended by something greater. For love is the goal of the commandment.

God Is Not Pleased with Sacrifice
March 4

Go and learn what this means: "I desire mercy, not sacrifice."
—MATTHEW 9:13

God's commandment separates us from sinners," Jesus' opponents claimed and thereby appealed to God's law. "God's commandment leads us *to* sinners," Jesus answered them, and he said this not by his own word but by the word of the prophet (Hos. 6:6), to which they could not object, because they venerated the prophet as the speaker of the divine word. All they could say was this: "We don't understand this statement," which is why Jesus told them, "Go and learn what this statement means."

Why didn't they understand it? Is it, then, mercy that brings God honor? Sacrifices are the means by which a person acknowledges God's deity and venerates it. By offering sacrifices from the fruit of the field and of the flock, he bears witness to the fact that he is situated on the ground that belongs to God, that he has life through God's creative power, and that he receives from God's grace that which sustains his life. When he sets the seventh day of the week apart as God's day, which he must not use for himself, he acknowledges that his time has been assigned to him by God. When he brings a sacrifice after transgressing the Law, he bears witness to the fact that God's commandment is holy and its transgressor guilty, and that there is for him no covering unless God in his mercy forgives his sin. These are human works by which a person demonstrates that he knows and honors God and wants to live according to his will. But what is the outcome of this mercy for God? God's verdict has judged the guilty and has expelled him from the community, and God's hand has stricken the sick, and God's counsel has denied the poor person the goods of this age. Should man be more merciful than God?

This may remain unintelligible to the one who looks at God merely through the Law, but the saying of the prophet and the message of Jesus say: It is not the sacrifice God wants from you; what you can and should do according to God's will is the merciful deed. In our human dealings, of course, the rule applies, "If you want to receive, you must give." The gift given and the gift received ought to be equivalent. This is the principle of law, without which there can be no fellowship between us. But God's relationship with us does not come into being in this way. We do not both give. He alone is the giver, for his communion with us is based solely on *our* need, not his.

Nevertheless, we have been given control over our abilities and possessions. To what end have they been given to us? God has made it our defining characteristic that we live a life in community, and within this community differences arise. The one who does not have stands beside the one who does, which provides us with the opportunity to participate effectively in God's work by bringing his gifts to those who lack them. It is his arrangement that everything good—material as well as spiritual—be continually redistributed from one to the other. Our self-interest, however, resists this and closes us up into ourselves. For this reason God's commandment comes to us and says: Give what you have—not to me but to the person beside you, to the one who needs it.

Jerusalem's Sacrifices Are Futile
March 5

"What shall I do with the multitude of your sacrifices?" says the LORD. *"I am tired of the burnt offerings of rams and of the fat of bulls, and I do not rejoice in the blood of the sheep, lambs, and goats. When you enter in order to appear before me, who asks you to trample down my courtyard? Stop bringing your food offerings in vain. The burnt offering is an abomination to me. New moons and Sabbaths, joint*

assemblies—I cannot bear injustice together with the festive assembly. My soul hates your new moons and celebrations. They are a burden to me. I am tired of bearing it. And when you spread your hands, I still hide my eyes from you, and when you make long prayers, I still do not hear you. For your hands are full of blood. Wash, purify yourselves, remove the evil of your deeds from my eyes. Desist from evil. Learn to do good. Strive for justice, restrain the violent, do justice to the orphan, help the widow."

—ISAIAH 1:11–17

It was no vain exercise when Jesus pointed the righteous to the prophet in order that they might be free from sacrifices and willing to act in mercy. He thus did not isolate an individual saying from the prophetic proclamation, but reminded his contemporaries of the verdict regarding sacrifices that the bearers of the prophetic word repeated again and again with utmost sincerity.

At a time when everyone in Jerusalem took part with burning zeal in what happened in the temple, Isaiah rejected the entire worshiplike operation in God's name, declaring it entirely futile. Jerusalem is like sons who have stopped obeying their father and have broken off their relationship with him. Yet their sacrifices do not remove the alienation but only expose it. Political circumstances drove them to the temple. War had left the land impoverished and had reduced the population to a remnant. Now God was to help, and so that he may help, people offer in the temple that which will render worship effective. But it is precisely here that they show they do not know God and resemble sons who have left the paternal communion. The son who tells the father, "Give me what is mine," and goes his own way, cries in the time of need, "Now help me!"

Their worship is futile, because violence and injustice are perpetrated in the city. The son may no longer recognize the father, but he still cannot deny the brother. He may no longer live in communion with God, but he still lives in and through communion with others. Yet he breaks even this community through his uncontrolled lusts. The national community is founded on justice. Therefore it is righteousness that God demands.

Hosea said: He demands mercy. Isaiah said: He demands righteousness. These two statements are not contradictory. Without righteousness, community degenerates into slavery, humiliation of those who are weaker, exploitation of the inferior, not peace but strife. To be sure, the pressure of natural needs keeps us together. Still, this does not guarantee that our community is genuine and wholesome. It is not when our self-interest uses other people's dependence on us to fulfill our own lusts. "I want righteousness," says this commandment: You act against my will if you attack and injure the lives of others. "I want mercy," says the other commandment: You act according to my will if you make up for another's hurt and need.

"I desire not sacrifices but justice." Thus, we are reminded of the relationship between the community called to serve God and the national community. When we do not attain to a national community that is united by justice, there is among us no holy community, no people of God, no church. Whoever is alienated from God is also alienated from other people. If, on the other hand, a person has yielded himself to God, he is no longer one who destroys community but a member of it; no longer one who resists justice but one who fights for justice; no longer one who despises other people but one who loves them.

God's Creative Mercy
March 6

He displays the riches of his glory in vessels of mercy, which he has prepared beforehand for glory.
—Romans 9:23

God requires mercy, Jesus says. Thus, his opponents charge that he, too, is guilty of the errant delusion that invented the sympathetic God. By this it is no longer the sight of those who suffer that pulls at our heartstrings but the one who cannot be said to suffer. The sentiments that unite us with those who suffer may be wholesome and valuable for us, because they extend our community to all, so that it does not merely comprise the strong and rich and does not merely exist in times of good fortune and success. But this is still no reason to call God merciful.

When we do this with Scripture, we do not presume to portray what God is in himself. Such imaginative meandering is prohibited to the one who has given serious consideration to his innate consciousness that he is a creature and God is the Creator. Thus it is clear that we cannot compare God with ourselves; for the Creator is a person other than the creature.

Yet it is equally certain that we have eliminated any real relationship between God and us if we do not speak of God's mercy. Any divine intervention in our lives tackles what corrupts us. Our behavior toward God would become entirely devoid of truth if we were to present ourselves to him as without weaknesses, as without being helplessness, as without guilt. Man stands before God just as he is: not as the hero who is capable of anything; not as the wise man who never entertains a dark thought; not as the pure one who shines honorably in everything he thinks and does; not as the one who loves, whose lack of self-centeredness renders him dangerous for no one. How can such vain fantasies have any place in our dealings with God? Yet when we turn to him with the truth and are able to do this because he is gracious, with the result that he is on our side and we become his work and he becomes our God, then we have no other word for what he is for us than that he is the one who has mercy. Thus we proclaim his immeasurable greatness and all-encompassing glory.

That we must not compare God with ourselves is manifest also by his mercy, because it reveals God's glory through us. Our mercy makes us people who weep with those who weep. Perhaps we can make their burdens a little more bearable. God's mercy makes misery and shame disappear entirely from human existence. For this purpose God's glory is revealed by his mercy.

The Call Is Issued to Sinners
March 7

I did not come to call the righteous, but sinners.
—Matthew 9:13

There were righteous people among the Jews. The gate through which they attained righteousness was the Law. When a boy's parents were themselves true to the Law and introduced the boy to the knowledge of Scripture and trained him in the observance of tradition, and when he, as a man, zealously and courageously set about to observe the Law, he was righteous and became willing to serve as an example for all who, like him, strove to fulfill the Law. Is there a more glorious name than "righteous one"? This means "My will obeys the divine will, and my activity is part of God's activity."

Did Jesus dispute the righteousness of the righteous? How could he contradict God's law? If there were no righteous persons, the Law would be an empty, useless word. Yet it manifests its power by rendering the one who transgresses it guilty and does not leave him unpunished. But this does not exhaust the intention of the Law; rather, it announces God's pleasure to the one who performs the Law. What then remains for Jesus to do with the righteous? Does the righteous person need to repent? No. Does he have any reason to fear God's wrath? No. God does not reject any righteous person. Anyone who expected God to shower his wrath on the righteous committed a severe injustice. Thus Jesus did not come for them, and they could not complain that he did not make them his guests and did not call them among his disciples. They should thank God that they are subject to him and obedient to him.

Yet the people do not consist solely of the righteous; beside them stand the guilty. What becomes of these if there is no word of God other than the Law? The righteous cannot help them; their righteousness demands that they avoid and judge the sinner. But this is not God's will, not the revelation of his righteousness, not the presence of the divine kingdom. God's righteousness brings an end to injustice by manifesting his grace, and God's rule is realized as he subjects sinners to himself, which issues in the commission given to Jesus. His word therefore differs from the Law that produces righteous persons. The Law prescribes what a person must do in order not to sin and die. Jesus' message tells a person what God does for him in order that he might not sin and not die. The Law stipulates what man's achievement is; Jesus' message stipulates what God's gracious gift is. This is the reason Jesus' call is issued to sinners and not to the righteous. He does not call the righteous, because he calls sinners. If he called the righteous as well, it would become uncertain whether or not he truly brought sinners the call of God. But now this has been manifested to all, sinners and righteous alike.

The Greater Righteousness
March 8

Unless your righteousness exceeds that of the scribes and
Pharisees, you will not enter the kingdom of heaven.
—Matthew 5:20

It was their righteousness, not their sinning, that separated rabbinic Judaism and its adherents from Jesus. To be sure, Jesus confronted them with their abuses in fierce wrath. But the rabbi, too, considered everything sinful to be reprehensible, and Jesus could forgive him if he confessed his blameworthiness. Because he wanted to be a righteous person, however, his righteousness separated him from Jesus and from God's kingdom. Possessing righteousness already, he strove for nothing but what he already was. His verdict regarding Jesus was firm as soon as he realized that Jesus said something different than he did and that the rabbi's righteousness was not Jesus'.

For the disciples, it was nothing short of astonishing, indeed presumptuous, that they ought to possess a greater righteousness than the one that had earned the nation's leaders their proud reputation. Everyone looked up with admiration to the experts in the Law and their observance of the Law. Is the requirement greater than that stipulated in the Law? Is it possible to attain to more than being impeccable according to the Law? Yes! There is something greater than what a person fashions himself to be by learning to keep the Law. There is also another word of God beside the one taught by the rabbi sitting on Moses' seat, binding up heavy loads that must be borne by those who seek to honor God. By doing this, they are not yet at the place where God wants to take them. The disciples stand under God's rule because they *receive* what Jesus gives them in the service of divine grace. Thus they receive the kind of righteousness that accomplishes not the will of man but the will of God, and that manifests not the glory of man but the greatness of God.

The righteousness a disciple received from Jesus had a more profound basis and greater power than that of the Law. Man can never be completely one with the Law. There remains an internal resistance toward the Law. He limits it and determines where his obligation ends. Yet when Jesus draws someone to himself, this awakens love in his heart, and love does not tolerate halfheartedness. The movement inaugurated by Jesus alters not merely a few ideas. It occupies him not merely on certain days and lays claim not to merely a part of his possessions and his energy. No—he, the disciple, just as he is, with all that he has, is moved by what Jesus gives him. Now he has no more enemies and no possession of which he is unwilling to let go. He no longer listens to many voices or lives for many purposes. He listens to Jesus' word and lives for him. For in Jesus' word he hears the word of God and lives for God.

God's Greater Word
March 9

You have heard that it was said to the elders. . . .
But I say to you. . . .
—MATTHEW 5:21–22

According to Paul, Israel's glory is that God's words are entrusted to it (Rom. 3:1). He had in mind the same words mentioned here by Jesus, with reference to the things that had been said to the elders. The speaker of these words was God. This is why it is Israel's glory that these words were unforgettable and repeated from generation to generation and remembered day by day at every moment of decision.

Can God's words fade? This is as little possible as God's will wavering. However, what is possible, worthy of God, and a demonstration of his grace is that he prepares new listeners for his Word and speaks to those who are living now, just as he spoke to the elders. This was what the disciples experienced when they gathered around Jesus in the Galilean mountains and he "opened his mouth" to tell them, "But I say to you."

It was precisely then that Jesus, too, acknowledged the truth of these words, which Paul called the precious possession entrusted to Israel. But the time has passed, and Israel's time has come to an end. It is no longer Moses or a prophet who represents God's truth and righteousness before his own people; now it is the Son of God who calls humanity to God. Now hope turns into history: what was anticipated is fulfilled; what had been begun is accomplished. Now God receives a new name, not merely "God of Abraham, Isaac, and Jacob," not merely "God of the fathers and the prophets," but "God and Father of Jesus Christ." What is more, those who receive his Word receive a new name. Now they are no longer the righteous ones whose crown of honor consists of the commandments they have kept. Now it is their distinctive mark and designation of honor that they are believers. If God's Word had not come to the elders in the way it did, it would not now be possible for the new Word of God to be spoken. Thus all that was spoken to the elders is preserved and rendered effective. But it proclaims a new truth, for it describes the Son of God. What is more, it creates a new righteousness, for it introduces one to love and makes it complete. It also has a new sphere of influence, for it is the Word of the Father, who is perfect and who completes what he has begun and does what he has promised. For this reason the community, too, which has been entrusted with this word and keeps it, is a new creation—not merely the continuation of Judaism or its reconfiguration but the work of the One who has authority to speak God's Word to it in such a way that it is indeed his Word. "But I say to you"—this makes him alone Lord over Judaism.

God's Indestructible Scriptures
March 10

Until heaven and earth pass away, not a single jot or tittle will perish from the Law.
—MATTHEW 5:18

It is impossible to live in God's kingdom and dissolve God's law. In God's kingdom any talk of a hidden, absent, or useless God who can be manipulated by man is muted. It is there that God's majesty is seen and God's glory proclaimed. It is there that omnipotent grace accomplishes its work and all godless and unjust deeds vanish in the omnipotent fire of his wrath. How then can God's commandments lose their holiness and power? If a person's eye is opened to God's work, his nature and will are also confronted with his commandment in such a way that it is indestructible.

This is the reason Jesus framed his commitment to the Law in as powerful and unconditional terms as possible, attributing to every letter that served to make God's commandment known to his people the same imperishable nature as heaven and earth. Only when the present form of man is past and eternal life revealed will Scripture—through which the community currently learns about the divine law—have served its purpose.

By this he told his disciples and his opponents that they would never be able to convict him of any transgression. He will do many things that will astonish, outrage, or provoke them; but one thing they will never be able to charge him with is sin. His answer to all who ask him what they must do to enter the kingdom will be "Keep the commandments." And when the questioner thinks he must have yet another or better commandment able to lead him with even greater certainty into God's kingdom, he will refuse to be the good teacher who can exempt people from the divine commandment. When God's rule is revealed, he will apportion honor or blame according to the smallest commandments that regulate our dealings and subject them to God's law. Then the only one who will be great will be the one who did not dissolve the small commandments but taught and did them. The lament of Isaiah, who once opposed those in Jerusalem who practiced the art of transforming good into evil and evil into good, will not apply to him.

Yet God's first word is neither his only nor his most powerful one. The king in God's kingdom is not merely a lawgiver who tells a person what he ought to do. The One who was sent by grace transcends the Law and is free from it—although his liberty does not consist in transgressing it but in fulfilling it. He destroys the temple, for he builds the living temple. He subordinates the Sabbath to the commandment of love and thus renders it holy. He removes impurity from people, for he purifies their hearts. He does not take vengeance but forgives, for he gives man the gift of love. He breaks down the fence that surrounds Israel, for he gathers into his community all whom God calls. So there are now two words of God, the second of which transcends the first. The first proclaims God's commandment, and the second announces God's grace: the Law and the gospel. This is how Jesus separated Judaism from Christianity.

Hating Only One's Enemy
March 11

*You have heard that it was said, "You should love your
neighbor and hate your enemy."*
—Matthew 5:43

Who helps us with our selfishness, which issues in malice? Nature does not provide us any help in dealing with it. But God comes to our aid and opposes it in his law. You must not hate your neighbor; you shall love him. The only one against whom you ought to direct your hatred is your enemy.

By making Israel God's possession, the Law also assigned to the nation its nature as an ethnic community, which it lost whenever it forgot its God and despised his law. Yet in this community there arise not only ties that provide us with joint activity but also enmity. The ethnic community is inevitably also a place of strife. Israel had enemies and was often endangered in the midst of the tumult of the peoples of Asia Minor. This is why it was told, "Hate your enemies." Yet even within the community, enmity constantly erupts. Injustice dispels peace. Whoever harms another is hated by him. The sinner hates the righteous, and the righteous the sinner.

Thus the Law protected the neighbor's life but did not extract wrath from the soul. It guarded marriages against external interference but did not keep male selfishness from divorcing a wife. It bound the speaker to the truth as long as he invoked God to affirm the truthfulness of his speech. When oaths become indispensable for our dealings with one another, it is evident that we do not trust one another, because we consider distortion and lies to be inevitable. The committing of injustice leads to a struggle for justice, which never issues in peace but completely disrupts community. To be sure, it must be clarified against whom hatred may be directed: not against all, so that everyone loves only himself; not against the neighbor, so that hatred tears apart the existing community. It must not forsake love; if that were abandoned, the people would die. You must hate no one but the enemy; your neighbor, however, you must love and honor as yourself and do to him as you would have him do to you.

As long as it is only the Law that addresses a person, commanding him to do his works, it cannot tell him more. "Love your enemy" is not a stipulation of law; it is part of the gospel. It is not a work of nature but a work of Jesus. As long as man is the agent, he concludes that, when his possessions, honor, and life are attacked, he must defend himself and resist and overcome the enemy. Why did Jesus reach a different conclusion? Because the new word of God is not another law that tells people what they should do, but a word that tells them what God's grace is able to accomplish.

Love Has No End
March 12

But I tell you: Love your enemies and pray for those who persecute you.
—MATTHEW 5:44

Paul described the difference between the Law and the gospel in the following terms. The Law demands works, while the gospel grants faith. In the Protestant church it is customary to depict the difference between the two divine words by way of the contrast existing between works and faith. When Jesus united his disciples' will with his own in the Galilean hills, he described the difference between the old and the new word as follows: The Law allows room for hatred; my message brings you perfect love.

There is no conflict between those two messages. You who are my disciples, Jesus said, can no longer be angry, no longer lie, no longer fight, no longer hate. You have been given love, and love never ends. Others lack love, and they become your enemies and expel you from their village community. But when they cry, "Traitors, apostates, enemies of our people and of God," do not answer them with a curse, but remain those who pray for them, and acknowledge before God in your prayers that you continue to be committed to your enemies.

Why is it that love cannot end? Look at what your Father does! He is perfect and does good to all, unjust as well as just, righteous as well as unrighteous. God's free benevolence, his unmitigated, complete goodness, provides you, his sons, with your nature.

We come to faith the same way we come to love. Consider, Paul says, what God has done for you; then you know that you may believe in him. He has called you and declared you righteous; thus he has transformed your conduct toward him into faith. Consider what God is doing! This will lead to both: faith *and* love. God's power and grace, however, know no end, because the Father is perfect. This is why faith has no end, and this is also why love does not end. Yet this is what Jesus' message tells us and what the Law alone falls short of conveying.

Whenever God appears and acts, all boundaries disappear. "If God is for us, who can be against us?"—this is the word of faith. "If God is for us, against whom can we be?"—this is the statement of love. All are subject to God's government: just and unjust, righteous and unrighteous. This is how the One who knows our hearts views people, the One who alone can judge and who judges righteously. Our view does not penetrate as deeply into others; we do not grasp their relationship with God. We view them as near or distant to us, friend or enemy. We thus evaluate the way in which they affect us and intersect with our lives. For all of these, however, their share relationship to God transcends this. They are all partakers of God's gifts, and as a result our love cannot end.

The Heart Cannot Change
March 13

Moses permitted you to divorce your wives because of the hardness of your hearts.
—MATTHEW 19:8

The divine Word comes to us from above. It does not arise like a blossom from the lifeblood of our own soul. It is brought to us by way of a messenger, and we receive it through hearing. In this way it coincides with the inheritance we already carry in ourselves, which is no formless mass but has contours that cannot be blurred.

The human heart is hard and unbending. It cannot be shaped. This is why we say that we are an individual. The human heart is narrow and not receptive to the greatness of the divine will. This is why we say we are autonomous. Our internal experience is closely intertwined with what takes place in the body. This connection cannot be dissolved. This is why we say that only what can be perceived by our senses is real. Time reigns omnipotent and forms what exists today from what existed yesterday. This is why we say in all stages of our lives that we are one and the same person. It is as Paul says, "The heart is unwilling to repent"; and as Jesus says, "The heart is hard," so that it resists even the divine Word.

Doesn't this Word have God's power, apart from which the Word cannot enter us or become lord over us? Yet it does not come to a person to destroy him but respects his innate faculties. This injects great complexity into our dealings with God. The part of the divine Word that enters into us varies from time to time and from person to person. Moses first told the Jews: Do not abuse another's wife. Then Jesus told his church: Purify your souls from lust that degrades women. One thing is good; another is better. There are things that are in the beginning stages and others that are complete. There is weaker and stronger law, and there is a smaller and a greater element of truth. For we come to know step-by-step. Also, there is small and great faith, for our believing conduct depends on the measure of faith assigned to us. There are also lesser and greater gifts of the Spirit, for the Spirit distributes his gifts as he chooses. There is prayer that goes no farther than sighing because we do not know what we should ask, and there is prayer that calls on divine wisdom without wavering and asks with assurance. This is why, in view of what his first disciples had become through him, Jesus likened it to a master who had given five talents to one servant and two to another. This is why there are innumerable differences and changes in Christendom. They show God's patience with our unrepentant hearts and reveal his goodness, which respects and preserves what each of us has and is able to do.

Jesus' Mercy Toward the Righteous
March 14

Come to me, you who are weary and heavy laden.
I will give you rest.
—Matthew 11:28

The rabbis' reputation withered in the light of Jesus, and the honorific title "Pharisee, separated one" took on a negative connotation. At one time the reputation of those who had earned the privilege of being called by that title was lofty and by no means easily acquired. Whoever decided to be a righteous man engaged in serious business that was accomplished only with great effort. This is why Jesus likens them to hired hands who must do a hard day's work and to those who must carry heavy loads.

The outcome of this kind of worship, however, was that their souls became restless, in continual uproar, for their piety lacked faith. It was their work, which is why it did not bring them assurance. It remained uncertain whether they had attained their desired aim, the paradise of God. Added to this was fear, because there were numerous opportunities to sin, and although the spirit was willing, the flesh was weak. There was also bitter pain, for the state of the people was corrupt; and what was the use of a few turning to righteousness while the majority sinned and became objects of God's wrath? Hardly anyone steered clear of envy and misgivings. For each looked at the others and measured his achievements by theirs. Yet it was bothersome when a rival's righteousness exceeded one's own.

Jesus had mercy on them and told them: Come to me and obey me; I will instill rest in your souls. With me you will cease from your hard labor.

We are to rest—but we must believe! Does not faith inject the most profound unrest into our souls? Who believes properly? Who has enough faith? No! This is the question of the one who believes in his faith and transforms it into an achievement by which he seeks to placate God. Jesus, however, gives us faith by speaking God's Word into us in such a way that it becomes effective in us. Where there is no divine Word for us, there is neither occasion nor opportunity for us to act in a believing manner. Only when Jesus' message is once again transformed into a commandment that we must fulfill, has our obligation to honor God through faith been turned into torturing unrest, bitter despair, and passionate strife.

With Jesus, however, we receive love in addition to faith. Yet is love not a very restless thing, continually disturbing our peace? After all, it is never satisfied and rejoices at any opportunity to serve. In fact, love entails pain. How seldom it is able to produce what it aims at producing! We know that we are useless servants, even when we have done what we are obligated to do. Yet if we do not inject our selfishness into our love, it will not be compromised by bitterness or rebellion against what we are called to do. For in our loving and serving we are completely dependent on what God does for us. If love succeeds in its work, it gives thanks. If we love in vain without being loved, or give in vain without our gift taking effect, love mourns; but it is only our self-interest that can mourn, not love. For it can give only what it has received and does not itself lead but is led.

The Light Load
March 15

My yoke is easy and my load is light.
—Matthew 11:30

A *yoke!* Does Jesus' offer of a yoke not terrify us? The yoke rendered the ox subservient to the plowman, and Jesus' yoke is taken up by the one who subjects himself to his rule. Are these not unreasonable, scandalous requirements he makes of us: to truthfulness without limit; to confession in every situation; to separation from any relationship, be it father or child or ethnicities, even from life? The call to have faith in every time of distress; to respond to any kind of evil with love; to subject all our conduct to the future aim, the revelation of God's glory—this is scandalous.

Did not the things mandated for the Jew dwarf by comparison—circumcising his male infants, setting apart the seventh day for God, embarking on a pilgrimage to the holy city, avoiding unclean things, and the like? And yet, Jesus praises his yoke as easy and his load as light, and John reiterated this pronouncement: "His commandments are not burdensome."

If they were nothing but commandments, they would indeed be difficult, even crushing, and, if not leading to despair, would lead to vain playacting and hypocritical pretense. To be sure, they are commandments; they order our conduct, awaken our thinking and willing, and exert an obligating force. The yoke that Jesus makes the badge of his royal activity earnestly desires to call us to obedience. Yet his primary message is "Come to me and entrust yourself to me," for only then do we participate in his work through his commandments. First comes "I am the shepherd"; then follows "Listen to my voice and follow me." First comes "I am the vine and you are a branch in me"; this leads to the commandment "Bear fruit." He calls us to himself by telling us: Don't be afraid but believe—your sins are forgiven. And now that he has removed fear from us and has restored us to faith, he warns us:

Be afraid to lose or abuse what you have been given. Because he is active among us in the Spirit of truth, he commands us to obey the truth and forbids us to blaspheme the Spirit. And because he subjects us to the promise, he expects us not to fear death. The first thing he does for us is to make God our Father and to place us with him in God's grace. This is why he commands: Now don't be afraid of anyone, for God is for you. And hate no one now, for you have received God's love.

Because Jesus' commandments arise from what he is for us, they are not difficult. If they approach us solely from the outside, they are not merely difficult; they are impossible. For they run counter to our nature. Yet now they are commandments of the One who moves us from within by his Word and Spirit, and therefore they are easy.

The End of Selfishness
March 16

Lord, I knew you, that you are a harsh person, that you reap where you did not sow and gather where you did not plant.
—Matthew 25:24

Nothing results for us from an active Christian existence that labors together with the church. It is always different in the administration of natural abilities. There, fruit grows for the one who administers them. The proper treatment of the body results in health and long life. Serious work secures for us life's necessities and procures for us a carefree existence. This is no different when we do the work assigned to us for the well-being of the people. For the national well-being is our own well-being, its honor our pride, and its safety our protection.

Yet it is different with serving Jesus; this is a selfless service in the strictest sense. And if it does glorify the one who zealously exercises it, it has gone wrong. It has succeeded when it issues in glory for God. But surely it provides one with a large circle of friends, a following perhaps. No! What results from serving Jesus is that people become God's subjects and his possession. To be sure, it is an uplifting thing when our convictions prevail and win others. But this is not a service commanded by Jesus. His work consists in

God's Word coming to man. Yet is it not a benefit when we are trusted by many? Again, we act in an anti-Christian and anti-churchly manner if we bind others' faith to us. It is Jesus' glorious aim and great gift that he shows us God as the one to whom our faith is due. If we incite others to ground their lives on believing us, we arrogate to ourselves what is due only to God. In fellowship with Jesus, one does not commit robbery against God.

Thus it seems reasonable for us to aspire only to what we need for ourselves. This results in the secret, private Christian existence that Jesus portrayed by way of the servant who safely kept the talent entrusted to him but did not work with it. He does not want to sow when he himself cannot harvest, because the master is the one who harvests. Because he expects him to work for him, he charges him with harshness.

Jesus' verdict entirely rejects this disciple, for he has nothing but selfish longing and does not have love. Thereby he has rendered Jesus' word ineffective and has despised his gift. What has Jesus given him? He has confronted him with God. How can he now still serve his selfish desire alone? Only by a false choice and a reprehensible decision could he prevent love from driving him.

And how might this love be created? When we find the One who is greater than us. He is the one whom Jesus has shown us; he shows him to all who listen to him. The one who is greater than us is God. The person who knows him is set free from the omnipotence of his selfishness, which desires only his own well-being. Now he has been welcomed into the divine kingdom, in which no one lives for himself and everyone lives for others. That person therefore calls Jesus the one in whom God's grace has appeared, and not a harsh master.

Forbearing Love
March 17

But I say to you, "Do not resist the evil person."
—Matthew 5:39

Healthy life does not want to die. Whoever possesses it resists the attacker with harsh words and defends himself with every weapon at his disposal. But is there a more dangerous attacker than the evil person? Evil corrupts everything. Nevertheless, Jesus' commandment is "Do not resist the evil person."

By this he has always and everywhere provoked vehement opposition. Does he not amply deserve to be mocked by every healthy German? The weakling who is willing to endure and declares himself prepared to tolerate with surplus, overflowing patience even more than what his evil adversary inflicts upon him—does he deserve anything but mockery? Selfishness is an enemy to love, too, yet mostly in secret; for the gifts of love are precious, and it is not honorable to mock them publicly. Yet when love also learns to be forbearing, battle is waged against it with sheer outrage.

How then could Jesus be God's witness and revealer, unless he also revealed his patience? What, after all, are we—with our healthy lives, glorious race, and heroism—apart from God's patience, apart from him who bears and nurtures not only the good ones in his world but also the evil ones? What are we apart from the One whom we may ask, "Forgive us our debts," and who opens his kingdom to us by forgiving us our sins? God is patient; this fact is as indispensable for our existence as God's life-giving creative power and his wisdom, which ordered the course of the world in its immensity and extent. To be sure, it is a mysterious statement that God is patient, just as it is a mystery that he is merciful. We may actively express our displeasure with this and despise patience as meaningless, unpractical, or counterproductive, but it still remains a fact that we live by God's patience.

Yet because God is patient, Jesus is too; and because Jesus is patient, his disciple is as well. Moreover, because Jesus does not want any grudging, unwilling disciples, he demands from them not the kind of grudging patience that collapses in a moment and turns into hot wrath but the kind that cannot be overcome. He can expect from them more than weak, forced patience, for he makes them strong.

They prove their strength in suffering. For they hold to their confession of God and his law against all evil opposition and do not allow it to exercise authority or power over them. The evil person may do whatever he wants: he cannot corrupt the disciple, for he does not separate him from Jesus. In love's struggle with hate, love remains the victor by its persistence, because patience prevents hatred from subjecting the disciple to it.

Fellowship with Jesus Brings Joy and Suffering
March 18

Then John's disciples approached him and said, "Why do we and the Pharisees fast, but not your disciples?" And Jesus said to them, "Can the friends of the bridegroom mourn while the bridegroom is in their midst? But the days will come when the bridegroom is taken away from them; then they will fast."
—MATTHEW 9:14–15

Those whom the Baptist had constituted as a community remained aloof from Jesus and his disciples. They lacked the confidence that Jesus could indeed turn out to be the Christ. Did he really consider the fulfillment of the promise to be the work he was called to carry out? Thus, two circles coexisted, both of which prepared for the dawning of God's rule. It was inevitable that the disciples of the Baptist should observe Jesus' followers with a critical eye and notice with amazement that he instilled in his disciples an attitude different from what the Baptist passed on to them. They felt the difference between themselves and Jesus' disciples particularly keenly when they fasted. In the Baptist's community, fasting had been practiced, while in Jesus' community fasting had not been observed. By this, however, Jesus' disciples did not depart only from the practice of the Baptist but also from that of the entire pious segment of the community, because the Pharisees made two days of every week days of fasting.

Why, then, did common custom no longer apply to Jesus' disciples? Because the disciples are not mourners, while fasting is the stance of mourners. They are like the friends of the bridegroom who cannot fast on his special day. For his celebration brings joy both to him and to them, and joy dispels mourning. If they mourned on his day of celebration, they would break fellowship with him.

Yet their share in Jesus' joy is not the only thing that the disciples gain from their association with Jesus; it also entails sharing in his suffering. The bridegroom is taken away; thus his wedding celebration also ends for his followers. They cannot continue to celebrate without him. Now they must mourn.

What Jesus prepares for his own is neither unmitigated joy nor sheer suffering. Both proceed from him to them, and both do so with an intensity that sets their joy and suffering profoundly apart from that good or ill fortune that arises for us from natural events. "The bridegroom is in their midst"—what does this mean in our text? Christ has come and, from those he calls, fashions his community by which God demonstrates his grace and to which he grants eternal life. They must rejoice. They cannot remember their sins and implore God for something greater; they cannot fast. "The bridegroom is taken away"—what does this mean? The Christ is expelled from Israel and put on the cross. Thus they are given the realization of human sin, and now they must implore, "Come, Lord Jesus!" Now they fast. Just as Christ's coming into the world results in irrepressible joy, his departure from the world issues in unspeakable suffering. Neither the former nor the latter could be lost on the disciple, because from Jesus he has received them both.

Tears of Joy
March 19

Look! A woman, a sinner, who was in the city and had learned that Jesus was reclining in the house of the Pharisee, brought a flask with oil, stood behind his feet, wept, and began to wet his feet with her tears. She wiped them with the hair of her head and kissed his feet and anointed them with the oil.
—Luke 7:37–38

We are celebrating a wedding, Jesus told his disciples. This is what we see: Joy swelled up mightily; it overwhelms custom; it fills the soul to such an extent that it cannot contain it; it expresses itself in tears and kisses. A stream of tears of joy reveals its intensity, and Jesus' figure is enveloped by the sublime aroma of the oil that entirely fills the room. Everyone perceives by this that a wedding is being celebrated here. The bridegroom accepts the gifts offered. He understands the language of these tears and the purpose of this pleasant aroma, for he perceives in these gifts the love that brings gifts to him. Is it not a festive hour? Is it not the wedding, when love takes shape and exults?

Therefore he rebuffed the one who sought to disturb his celebration. Why this jubilation? A guilty woman is cleared. One brought down by shame is lifted up. One who had been trampled on by the community is restored to it. One who had been pursued by death has regained life. One who could no longer pray learned to give thanks. Is this not a festive hour? The angels rejoice in heaven.

But—the *but* of unbelief was heard already at that hour and has not lost its voice in the church ever since, whose art has depicted its unbelief in resplendent images: the repentant Magdalene, tortured by her remorse with her bitter tears. But—what does this *but* request? It asks for what it once was. It is indeed rather entertaining when one can look at a person disfigured by folly, dirt, and godlessness, and it is an uplifting spectacle when one can witness how she is pained and perishing. "If Jesus knew who she is!" his host said, and by this he thought himself to be illumined by the Spirit and to be the speaker of the divine Word. He considered it a major flaw afflicting Jesus that he apparently did not know who the woman was.

But the gift Jesus receives from the Spirit does not consist in being able to expose what is sinful. He knows what sin is and does not learn this by a person spreading it out in front of him. On the contrary, he brings an end to the compulsion that forces a person to look at his sin continually. He covers sin. His eye searches probingly for something entirely different: Was he able to show her God's grace? Did she hear God's gracious word in his word and see God's saving activity in his activity? Was his word for her more than the word of all who condemned her, more than the verdict of her own conscience, which drove her away from God? Jesus never let God's grace shine without also revealing his holiness. And what was the result? Does she fear him and run away from him, or does she trust him and come to him? If she trusts him, she is set free from her past and liberated from her guilt. If she believes this, she loves him. But now it is out in the open: she loves, and she loves much, and therefore Jesus transforms her bringing to him her gifts into a festive occasion for himself and for her.

The Joy That Is Always Available
March 20

Rejoice in the Lord always.
—Philippians 4:4

Once in Galilee, when Jesus was with the disciples, a wedding was celebrated (see March 19 exposition above). Was this continued in the newer congregations on Greek soil? No, for they lack the Lord's presence. Yet they, too, have become friends of the bridegroom, who will celebrate his wedding with him. Therefore it can be said also of them that the friends of the bridegroom cannot mourn. Joy filled the soul of the one who is united with the Christ of God—a lasting joy whose foundation is continually available.

Everything that Jesus' gift is for us has wholeness, because there are no impediments or limitations to God's gracious activity. God's gifts are always "good and perfect." Faith receives wholeness through Jesus. For we are not authorized to rely on God in only isolated instances; rather, we trust his counsel and intervention in whatever grieves our hearts, in whatever our love is concerned with, in all we do. Likewise, love has been given to us not merely for individual cases, for this person or that one, as for those with whom fellowship can easily be established. Love, too, is given wholeness by Jesus, so that it leads the Samaritan even to the Jew and the traveler to the one who lies half dead on the road. Joy accompanies faith and love and, like them, becomes whole "in the Lord."

If we are "in the Lord" and think "in the Lord" and act "in the Lord," this also issues in the sense of being borne along by our communion with the Lord. This, however, is not a changing state of affairs but has been given to us once for all.

This is the reason Paul can urge joy even though feelings can take hold of us gratuitously, whether we want them or not. Yet the One who gives rise to feeling, the One who awakens joy, is always present, and the believer can and should turn to him, open his ears to his Word, and devote his will to his commandment, and joy will enter his soul.

This is why Paul can command joy from prison even though he does not know the outcome of his imprisonment; and why he can expect it from the congregation, whatever may happen there. Prior to the command that calls them to continual joy is a section written by Paul with tears because he describes the opposition against his message in the church. But the ups and downs of the congregations and their members do not separate them from Christ, and this is why joy accompanies them in everything they experience.

Ready to Suffer
March 21

We are God's heirs, fellow heirs with Christ, if we suffer with him so that we also may be glorified with him.
—Romans 8:17

The bridegroom celebrates the wedding with his friends, but it is cut short by force. The bridegroom is killed, and his friends are alone and mourn. This lends essential shape to the Christian existence of those who are called to Christ by his messengers. They are offered salvation; they are called to blessedness, and their joy in the Lord is the strength that regulates their dealings with one another. Whoever demands happiness to the extent that he refuses to suffer cannot align himself with Jesus; and if he had aligned himself with Jesus, he would again forfeit this relationship if he were not prepared to suffer with him. He would thereby attempt to change who Jesus is, showing that Jesus does not please him with the commission God has given Jesus, nor with the work Jesus has obediently accomplished. By refusing to suffer, he would reject Jesus' love.

Because love has appeared in Jesus, he allows those who believe in him to share in all that he has. It is his desire to reveal God in glory. For this reason it is the goal of believers to be glorified together with him, because his greatness will be their greatness and his righteousness their righteousness. In this way they will become his heirs, who receive from him what he has. But they receive it from the One whom the world opposed, not in times past but continually, the One against whom man rebels by virtue of his sinful nature. And this did not merely make him a sufferer but also makes sufferers out of those who believe in him by virtue of his love, which provides them with access to his life and his will. This is why he is the source not merely of joy but also of suffering for all those who are subject to his rule.

There is no distinction made in the case of those who want to allow one thing into their lives but not another. Whoever does not want to suffer as a consequence of people's rejection of Jesus breaks fellowship with him. That person is like the friend of the bridegroom who wants to celebrate even though the bridegroom has been taken away. In this case he can no longer rejoice with him, for it is of no concern to him whether or not the Christ is glorified. On the other hand, it is inconceivable that we should set ourselves apart from the world and take our place at his cross without sharing in his blessedness. How could we stand by his side but remain unshaken by people's rejection of him? It is because he places us at God's side, where joy, honor, and a song of praise are injected into our lives.

Does our attitude thus turn into wavering? To be sure, changing circumstances evoke in us different responses, be they joy or suffering. But both sentiments have their source in the same consciousness, and both transfer from the Christ to us. And the Word that reveals him to us and procures for us our faith in him is the sure vantage point that keeps us from sinking into the depths of our emotions.

The Liberty of Jesus' Followers
March 22

No one pours new wine into old wineskins; otherwise, the new wine bursts the wineskins, and the wine is lost and the wineskins wasted. No, new wine ought to be poured into new wineskins.
—Luke 5:37–38

Whom does our love esteem? Everyone, even the one who attacks us and wrongs us. Does it esteem even the one who has another faith, another hope, another way of life? Does this apply even to the one who fasts while we ourselves do not fast but celebrate? Yes, it does.

Jesus protected those who lived by the teaching of John from abandoning their own form of discipleship and becoming like his own disciples. This would be like pouring new wine into old wineskins: the wineskins would burst and the wine be wasted.

The call to liberty lures everyone, and everyone considers the obligation to fast to be hard, not only because it constrains natural desires but also because it fastens our view to our shortcomings and to the ills prevailing among our people. But if the disciples' mere example were to move fasters to cease their mourning, they would lose what they currently possess. They would abandon their resistance toward sinful desires and no longer confront the prevailing ills of the people with repentant seriousness. They would no longer wait for the Helper, who is able to turn things around because he comes from above. Nevertheless, they would not possess that which brought Jesus' followers great joy and liberty, and thus they would not yet be one with the bridegroom and his associates nor be ready to celebrate with them.

One does not attain to the liberty of a disciple of Jesus by an arbitrary act. If this liberty consisted in denying one's obligation and guilt and in breaking faith with those with whom it is inextricably linked, it would be nothing but anarchy. But Jesus liberated them by tying them to himself through what he gave them. What gave them the liberty to control their own selfishness? What rendered them free and independent of any person who wanted to chain them to himself and abuse them for his own purposes, no matter how powerful that person may be? What freed them from an evil conscience when they thought about what had happened, and from doubt when they thought about what was going to happen? What made them more powerful than their natural destiny—that is, ultimately, death? In every respect Jesus was the ground of their liberty. All this arose from who Jesus was and what he brought about in them. Because he established their lives in God's grace, they are free.

This is why he cannot transfer this liberty to those who do not find their way to him. Compulsion could not be the means by which he drew them to himself. He would not be free, and the one who frees, if he acquired his power by way of compulsion. His liberty, too, is one with his dependence on God's activity. Whoever the Father brings to him, he takes in. As long as John's followers still viewed him with doubts and skepticism, he confirmed them in their conventional form of religion. If they are what they have become and act according to the insights given to them and faithfully guard what they have received, they have in this way done Jesus' will and have fulfilled what he asks of them.

Guard What You Have Received
March 23

No one who has drunk old wine wants new wine, for he says,
"The old wine is good enough."
—Luke 5:39

Love understands the other person. Whoever esteems no one but himself is under the curse of continually having to misunderstand. To be sure, he is soft and deferent toward himself. Toward others, however, he is hard. Yet when our eyes are illumined by love and our judgments are shaped by it, we become patient, because we understand others, give them time, are able to wait, and can cope with the difficulties they cause us.

The new wine Jesus gave to those who listened to him presented obstacles for some, not only the scribes and the "righteous" but even the followers of John. This was not the old wine to which they had grown so well accustomed. Jesus did not rebuke them for this; for he knew what the old wine meant for them and why the new wine was not palatable to them. To be sure, burning and yearning love could transform his message into the warning "Jerusalem, Jerusalem, you walk on the broad path that will become your destruction." He regards those who praise the old wine as keeping what, up to that point, had been God's word for them, and to those people he says, "I will not disturb you."

This was the verdict of the One who was elevated above the Law, because he had been made the spokesman of divine grace. It is the mark of the free person that he also allows others to be free. What is more, not only does he respect their freedom; he also affirms them and does not demean them. Whoever serves the Law—whether a law of works that tells us what our performance for God ought to be or a law of teaching that assigns to us the ideas by which we grasp divine truth—tolerates no way other than his own. He wants equality and wants it in such a way that it supplants liberty. Those who drank the old wine may not remain with him; there is only one drink for all. They do not ask whether it is burdensome. "What else could we do?" they ask. "We represent God's law." Is God not one and the same for all? This is why there is only one truth, and it is the same for all and is ours. And there is only one righteousness that determines the boundary between what is good and what is evil, and this boundary is fixed at the same place for all. This righteousness, which all must heed, is the one we obey. Is this logic not compelling? Who can oppose it? All of rabbinic Judaism pledged unanimous support.

Why then did Jesus say the exact opposite? Does he not love the truth? Of course he does! He *is* the truth. Did he then not bend right and wrong? No, he is unbending in his judgment of all lawlessness and unrighteousness. But he did not allow man to usurp God's place and to exchange his thoughts for God's thoughts and his righteousness for God's righteousness. Because he is the representative of God's truth and of God's righteousness, he makes us recipients rather than rulers. What is revealed to us is what we ought to accept, nothing more. And what we are told to do, this we ought to do, nothing more. And what we were made to be, this we ought to be, nothing else. Thus, our authority over others comes to an end. For God is not merely our God, but the God of all.

Freedom That Turns into Calamity
March 24

Whoever abolishes a single one of these commandments, even the smallest one, and teaches others to do so will be called the least in the kingdom of heaven.
—Matthew 5:19

This statement of Jesus rises before the Jews as a mighty, flaming sign and warns them against their calamitous ways. They erect the Talmud and make it the ruler of the people, but the Talmud will be their ruin.

By "small commandments" Jesus meant those he lists in the passage immediately following, the second part of the Ten Commandments, which addresses the relations given to us by nature. Was there any leader in Jerusalem who wanted to do away with them? There was no propaganda of godlessness in Palestinian Judaism. Whoever denies God is expelled from the community. Or did anyone want to do away with the Bible? No one thought of doing that; everyone praised the Law as the pride and privilege of the Jewish people. Rather, the commandments were done away with by those who fought for the rule of that very same law.

The rabbi meditated in light of the Law's commandments and pondered, "Am I bound or am I loosed?" If what he intended to do was forbidden, then he was bound. Then he must obey, and then he did obey. But was his case in fact covered by the injunctions of the Law? No law encompasses every conceivable aspect of life. Our actions are constantly reshaped by the movement of history. Perhaps, then, what our rabbi intends to do is not covered by the wording of a given statute. If so, he was loosed, "free" to do what he wanted, released from God's service. He was his own master, and now his internal struggle, evoked within him by the Law, became apparent.

The Law did not address him in his own intention and did not subject his selfish desire. As far as the commandment opposes it, it must remain silent; but when there is no commandment, it comes to the fore and goes to work. For the chains that had restrained it thus far fell off, and thus the person is free once again. He is not free when he does the will of God; he is free when no commandment applies to him and he can dissolve the obligation that binds him. Who is victorious in this struggle between obedience and selfish desire? It is the person's own will, which he does not allow the Law to take away from him. Not that he abandoned the statute; he holds onto it as his glory, his merit, his protection against God's wrath and punishment, as his righteousness guaranteed to him by the good act of God. But his service of God only masks his godlessness. This is why Jesus called him a hypocrite, "an actor," and told him that he had already received his reward. God's grace passes him by. If it comes to us, it subjects us entirely through believing and loving.

The Free Slaves of God
March 25

Live as free persons and not as those who use freedom as a cover for evil, but as God's slaves.
—1 PETER 2:16

The proclamation of freedom results in tyranny if the free person, in order to be free, takes freedom away from others. The proclamation of freedom results in sin if the free person uses his freedom to liberate his own evil desire. As far as Roman military power was concerned, all were subjects of the caesar and subject to the law he created. Only those who were driven by criminal impulses, "the antisocial ones," eluded his coercion. But now Jesus' message spread throughout the Roman Empire and made free persons out of all who received it.

Were they "antisocial" as well? Freedom to do evil? No! This was not what they wanted, not what they had attained through the Christ. "We are free to do evil"—no one who was truly a Christian said that; it would have amounted to an open denial of Jesus.

There was, however, still another way in which freedom issued in sinful desire. "I have authority to do whatever I want": this statement, in fact, was made by some of the early Christians, not as a contradiction against the gospel but as its appropriation and complete application. What an incredibly great and blessed change it was that the believer was no longer under a law that stood between him and God! Now he stood before God with joy, grounded in his grace by his faith, sharing in Christ's kingly work, himself a kingly protagonist. Where was there still a limit that applied to him? What he did was pure and just, because he did it; he acted from faith and was led by the Spirit. No one had the right to judge him if he did what lay within the scope of his freedom. "If the tree is good," Jesus had said, "its fruit is good as well." Now the tree was good; thus its fruit was good as well.

But can evil, unloving, domineering behavior be justified by appeal to a Christian's liberty? This would make freedom a cover for evil, which is impossible, for the free person became free by becoming God's slave. This was the message of those who had been called by Jesus. They freely admitted this with the same gratitude that made them proclaim how he had set them free in the first place. But the slave calls nothing his own; all that he has belongs to his master. And the slave does nothing on his own, but he is told what to do by his master and carries out his work for him. Is there a stronger and more complete tie than the one given to the slave of God? This tie excludes all evil or selfish desire. This is what Peter and Paul attested in complete unanimity to all whom they set free, thus proving that their freedom was not the child of their own selfishness but the gift given to them by Jesus.

God Does Nothing Halfway
March 26

Be perfect, as your heavenly Father is perfect.
—Matthew 5:48

In this case I am bound, and in this case I am loosed. Now I must obey God, and now I can do whatever I want," the Jew said. Jesus tells him, "No!" The heavenly Father is perfect. He does nothing piecemeal, and he does not tolerate anything done halfway. But you dissect God's commandment into many small fragments. It does not seize all of you, does not control your thoughts and volition in their entirety, and does not subject your life in its entirety. This results in your doing things halfway. With your "half" life you are your own master. One moment you fear God; the next you are godless.

Jesus set his disciples free from this kind of "religion." He was able to do this because God through him becomes their Father, who is perfect in everything he says and whose love is perfect love. If you love one moment and hate the next, if you love one person because he did something nice for you but hate another because he is your enemy, you make yourself into a divided, "half" people. You want what is good but also what is evil. You want to give but also receive, help but also destroy. But this is neither the manner of your Father, nor is it what he gives to you. For he is light, and there is no darkness in him.

This is the wall Jesus erected against the Talmud in order to protect his church from it. If it sees its Christianity as a sum of religious duties beside which there were also many other duties, and if it issues a series of ecclesiastical commandments that leave room for unauthorized desire, then such a patchwork may reveal our human nature, but it also makes clear that it is not the work of God.

If we were to protest that to be perfect as God is perfect is an exaggerated claim, a deluded aspiration—how can anyone be perfect like God?—this would not be a valid objection against Jesus' statement. For this argument thinks only of what man can make of his life by exerting his own will, but not of the one whom Jesus praised on account of the perfection of his goodness. This protest renders Jesus' proclamation meaningless. Why does he tell us: You must make a decision that separates you once and for all from evil; there arises in you a faith that places you once and for all under God's grace, a kind of love that renders you unable to hate? Jesus did not offer us this because he thought we could make ourselves perfect people but because he could attest that our heavenly Father does nothing halfway. He is perfect.

Section 7

THE LAW DOES NOT PLACE ANY CONSTRAINTS ON JESUS

Imaginary Sin That Is No Sin
March 27

At that time Jesus passed through a grainfield on the Sabbath.
His disciples were hungry and began to tear off heads of grain
and eat them. The Pharisees saw this and said to him, "Look!
Your disciples are violating the Sabbath." But he told them,
"Didn't you read what David did when he was hungry, and
those with him? How he went into God's house and ate the
showbread, which neither he nor those with him were allowed to
eat, but only the priests?"
—MATTHEW 12:1–4

In the sanctuary there was a table with twelve pieces of bread that were replaced every week. These were considered to be uniquely God's and were forbidden from human use. Once they had been removed from the table in the sanctuary, it was part of the priests' duties to eat them. But the book of Chronicles, which records David's ascendancy to the kingship, narrates an incident where David, when fleeing from Saul, asked the high priest for some food for the journey. And since there was no other food in the sanctuary, he received the holy pieces of bread.

Was this not sin? In the Pharisees' view this was doubtless an infraction, and the lives of all those who had a part in it—those of the priest and of David and of his companions—were forfeit. In Jesus' day, every priest who gave pieces of showbread to laypersons and every Jew who dared to take and eat them would have been executed without mercy. But David did not forfeit God's favor by eating the showbread. He did not forfeit his anointing to become king, and his ascendancy to the kingship was not hindered by this act.

This constituted a blatant discrepancy between Scripture and the oral law. What was the cause for this discrepancy? This is the question Jesus asks when his disciples tore off heads of grain while passing through a field on the Sabbath and were accused by the representatives of the Law as transgressors of the Sabbath commandment. Thus they used the Law against the disciples in the same way they would have had to in David's case. But their stewardship of the Law in the disciples' situation was just as devoid of being truly in keeping with the Scriptures as it was in the case of David.

The teacher of the Law issued a verdict only concerning a certain action but did not ask any questions regarding who committed it. He failed to consider that it was David to whom the priests gave the showbread, and he likewise failed to consider that it was the disciples of Jesus who tore off and ate the heads of grain. It is inconsequential *who* perpetrates a certain action; only the action itself is either sinful or righteous. But is there an action without a perpetrator? And does the action not receive its legitimacy or illegitimacy from the one who performs it? It met with God's approval that David eluded Saul, and it likewise met with God's approval that the disciples accompanied Jesus and ate from the grain when they were hungry.

The difference in the evaluation of the action derives from the difference in their views of God. The God of the teachers of the Law watches over his possessions. Once the pieces of bread have been given to him, no one is allowed to eat from them, and since the Sabbath is his day, no one is permitted to do anything on the Sabbath. The meaning of the Law was considered to be that of man giving God what he required. And this must be done on time and completely as God required it.

According to Jesus, God did not need holy things. Rather, he sets people apart for him by calling them to carry out a particular commission—formerly David, who readied himself to assume the role of king, and now the disciples, who were to accompany Jesus. What these people require and what sustains their lives is not directed against God and does not constitute a violation of his law.

In his effort to evaluate people's actions, the teacher of the Law consulted the Holy Book. For he knew no other expression of the divine will than the written statutes. But this does not enable him to sit in judgment over Jesus' disciples. For they are subject to the new Word of God and are led by the One who perceives God's will in him because he knows the Father. His verdict is just, because it takes into account what is inside a man, not merely what meets the eye.

Jesus' Followers Don't Sin
March 28

*Have you not read in the Law that the priests do not keep the
Sabbath in the temple and yet are not guilty of breaking the
Sabbath?*
—MATTHEW 12:5

In the entire country no work was performed on the Sabbath in any house.
One place alone was exempt: the temple. There, a vast amount of work was
done on the Sabbath, since sacrifices on the Sabbath were greater than on
the other days of the week. Why were the priests not subject to the Sabbath
laws? Because they were priests. And why were the disciples not subject to
the statute? Because they were followers of Jesus. The priests' highest
obligation is to be priests, and the disciples' highest obligation is to be
disciples. Whatever else their duties—which they must obey or else suffer
the consequences for disobedience—they result from their being followers
of Jesus. As long as this is what they are, they do not sin, just as the priests
do not sin on the Sabbath as long as their work is carried out in the temple
and belongs to their priestly service.

Why, then, did this pronouncement provide the disciples with a principle
that continually guided their conduct, even when he sent them out and put
them by themselves into Jewish villages, or when the wedding feast that they
currently celebrated with him came to an end and the bridegroom was taken
away? Once again, what is apparent is the all-encompassing totality of man's
being that Jesus brought out in his dealings with his disciples. They are not his
disciples merely on a temporary basis, nor do they depend on him and his
commandment only now and then, when he expected some particular act of
service. They are always his disciples. He is at the root of their thinking and
aspirations and remains at the root of their thinking when he sends them out
and when he leaves the world once again.

To be sure, this would be different if he were like a lawgiver who imposed
regulations on his people or a teacher of the Law who interpreted the Law
and rendered individual judgments. In this case the disciples would be
induced to right conduct only when there was a statute that revealed to
them his will in a particular instance. In the absence of a pertinent

pronouncement by Jesus, they would remain without guidance as to what they should do. Yet the disciples quickly realized that their relationship with Jesus did not resemble that of a nation to its law book or of a disciple to his master's instruction. The disciple left the rabbi once he was fully trained. But they could not cease being his disciples, just as a priest could not stop being a priest. Because they believed in him, they continued to depend on him. His word had become their own, and his will had become theirs. And he was not distant for them, but they heard his voice and received his instruction, even when he was not visible to them.

For this reason his messengers did not bequeath to the new congregations a book of law in which Jesus' commandments were gathered together in order to instruct them how to do his will. They made believers of those to whom they showed Jesus. If you act out of faith in him, Paul told them, you will not sin; and John told his followers: If you remain in him, you cannot sin but will perform righteousness. This confirmed Jesus' statement, by which he rebuffed those who accused his disciples: Because and as long as they are my disciples, they do not sin.

It Is Impossible to Sin While Being in the Presence of Jesus
March 29

He was revealed to take away sins, and there is no sin in him.
Whoever remains in him does not sin.
—1 JOHN 3:5–6

Jesus does not lead into sin those who live in his presence and are guided by his Word, but rather liberates them from sin. What caused him to enter the world? The eternal Son of God injected himself in human form into world history and thus made it possible for everyone to listen to him and know him. Why did he do this? It was the sins of mankind that moved him to come into the world.

When John speaks of sin, he thinks of our having no law in us to which our volition and our thoughts are subject. Our thoughts are not tied to the truth, and our desire is selfishness, which wants to remain independent. Jesus takes this life, for which there is no valid, divine law, away from us. He removes the compulsion to sin. He sets us free from the guilt that comes from sinning. He puts an end to the misery and the death that issue from sin.

He has the authority to do this because in him there is no sin, no self-seeking exercise of power, no selfishness that commits injustice, no blindness that knows nothing of God's will. In him was the obedience that did God's will. This determined what became of those who remained in him. What they received from him is not opposed to the overarching purpose of his commission and introduces them to nothing other than what constitutes his own nature, power, and honor. Where he is, and where his Word holds sway and his will is done—there also the inability to sin prevails. It is impossible to lie and hate while living in fellowship with Jesus. In his community one can only believe and love.

There is no word here of those ideals by which we engage in wishful thinking about attaining perfection; the fact that believers' natural way of life vanishes is even less a topic of discussion. Had they already been transformed, they would not need to be warned that they must not separate themselves from Jesus but remain in him. John addresses these words to those for whom it has not yet been made known what they will be but who lived in the hope that Jesus' image would become theirs. Here it is rather said that Jesus subjects to God's will all those who have come under his impact. This, in turn, becomes a reality in that we are able to believe and live because we know Jesus.

For this reason the church is not in the dark regarding when it falls into sin and when it escapes from sin. When it distances itself from Jesus, it slides into untruth and into arrogant self-centeredness. If it remains united to Jesus, it does what God commanded it to do and is on its way to God's aim.

Where Does God Live?
March 30

I tell you, something greater than the temple is here.
—Matthew 12:6

Jesus compared his disciples to the priests. Was there any similarity between the priesthood and being a disciple? The priest was given the right and the duty to perform sacrificial service in the temple on the Sabbath. But did Jesus have the authority to assign certain duties to his disciples on the Sabbath because he was like the temple? How absurd this thought appeared to his opponents! Yet he told them, "Something greater than the temple is here." He does not merely provide the same thing as the temple; he gives something much greater. He towers above it, replaces it, and severs his community from the temple.

Whoever wanted to understand this had to realize why he said that the Jerusalem sanctuary was the "temple"—not one among many temples but the only temple that existed for the people. He claimed that God lived in the temple. He referred to God's presence in such a way that he was present there for the people, accessible in prayer, ready to receive their sacrifice, prepared to forgive their sins as the one who extends a blessing and provides peace and protection by directing his face toward them.

But all the things for which the Jew praised the temple were present in Jesus, because he had been given the sonship of God. It lent his call, "Come to me, follow me," an entirely different profundity than those of the regulations of the Law, which commanded the people to embark on a pilgrimage to the Jerusalem sanctuary. There was no living unity and effective community between this house and God. There, everything was nothing but a symbol, a sign of what had not yet become a reality, a shadow of what was yet to come. But in the case of the Son of God, unity and fellowship with God were not a mere picture but life, not a mere thought but an effective reality. This is why he opened up the possibility for a kind of worship that exceeded everything that took place in the temple, a revelation of God that effectively brought glory to God because it brought into being a faith directed toward God. Jesus opened up the possibility of the reception of a divine word that did not merely impart knowledge to the listener but made him a person taught by God in such a way that he yielded himself to God. This cleansed that person from all guilt, so that he was effectively set apart, because through Jesus he became a doer of his Word. This, in turn, resulted in God's praise, which exalted him not only because of individual gifts he had bestowed but also because of the glory of his kingdom.

The newness of Jesus' gift illumined the difference between the two words of God, the Law and the message announcing God's grace. This difference must reveal itself also with regard to the temple. Through the Law, first the tent and then the house came into being, in whose courts the multitude rendered its worship and at whose altar the priests fulfilled their duties. Through grace, on the other hand, the Son arose, who received his word and his deed from God's Spirit.

When he referred to something greater than the temple, he did not merely think of his own presence in the world but also of the house he was to build, the community that was to come into being through him and that was to become a house of God because he gave it a share in God's grace. And this house, too, would be greater than the temple at Zion.

The Lord of the Sabbath
March 31

The Son of Man is Lord of the Sabbath.
—MATTHEW 12:8

Did Jesus want the Jew to give up the Sabbath? Did Jesus do away with the Sabbath? He did not. How could he dispute God's law? There is one God, and even though his ways are inscrutably rich, he does not have intentions that stand in conflict with one another. He is able to render old something that exists and replace it with something new. He is able to surprise everyone by the newness of his work and announce that his goal remained an inscrutable mystery for all. Nevertheless, in everything he does, he is the one God who rules over everything that has come into being through him.

What the Sabbath revealed to Israel is an eternal truth. All who honor God must acknowledge that he gives the time and prepares the hour. By setting every seventh day apart as God's day, the true Israelite testifies that his days are God's gift. But Jesus did not receive his instruction of how he ought to spend his days and honor the Sabbath merely from the statute that prohibited any work on the Sabbath. This was not determined by an external commandment but resulted with great clarity from who he was, and was prescribed for him by his dealings with the Father. The foremost commandment to which Jesus was subjected and that issued from his actions was that he be in everything the Son of his Father. This set him free from the Sabbath in the same way he was free from the temple. When the hungry disciples accompany him on the Sabbath, setting apart the Sabbath consists in helping them get some food; and when an invalid asks him for help on a Sabbath, he honors the Sabbath by healing that person. When his ministry brings him to a given village on the Sabbath, and the congregation is gathered in the house of prayer, he is there as well and joins all the others in hearing the Law read and interpreted by the teacher. When afterward a Pharisee wants to pay his respects and makes him the guest of honor at a meal on the Sabbath, Jesus sets apart the Sabbath by allowing himself to be honored and by sharing the festive meal with him.

It was always impossible for him to cause the Jews to stumble, to confirm them in their rebellion against the Law and to incite them to desecrate the Sabbath. Was he indeed an enemy of the Sabbath? He was its Lord, not its enemy. Nevertheless, he did not allow anyone to forbid him to show to all his freedom from those regulations when he could expect them to perceive the holy origin of his works with a clear eye and with undiluted judgment. The works he did on the Sabbath were holy because they were motivated by love.

The mystery that unfolds for us is profound and reveals to us a problem that confronts all of us. Will the free person enter the community without giving up his freedom, and will he preserve his freedom without violating the community? We often stumble at this point. But Jesus celebrated the Sabbath with Israel and at the same time transgressed the regulations concerning the Sabbath. For he was Lord of the Sabbath.

Doing What Is Right Can Never Be Sin
April 1

Jesus came into their congregation, and there was a man with a disfigured arm. And they asked him, "Is it permissible to heal on the Sabbath?" so they could accuse him. But he told them, "Where among you is there a man who has even just one sheep, and if it falls into a hole on the Sabbath, he does not try to get it out and take care of it? How much more is a person worth than a sheep? For this reason it is permissible to perform a good deed on the Sabbath." Then he said to the man, "Stretch out your arm!" And he stretched it out, and it was made well like the other one.

—MATTHEW 12:9–13

The Sabbath brought honor to God. On it, man's selfish desire should cease; on it, he must not do anything. This severed people's dealings with one another and also precluded doing good deeds. But was this type of Sabbath observance indeed honoring to God? The Son was forbidden to testify to the divinity of God in only this way. His commission made everything he did the revelation of God. It was realized not by severing fellowship but by bringing it about, not by ceasing his activity but by performing good deeds. His disciples report that he methodically revealed this to all by refusing to be told not to heal on the Sabbath.

The way in which Sabbath observance was regulated revealed the petty, self-centered nature of human thinking. No Jew thought of letting one of his domesticated animals die on account of the Sabbath. If it had an accident on the Sabbath, he rescued it, and even on the Sabbath he loosed the rope by which it was tied, so that he could lead it to the drinking trough. He did not consider this an act of work. But healing a person on the Sabbath was viewed as sin by the regulations regarding the Sabbath. Everyone was concerned with preserving his property; another's well-being was a matter of indifference. It did not occur to the Jews that *failing* to do something constitutes an act as well.

A given action represents either a good or an evil deed. Either another's life is preserved, or he perishes. Jesus urged the Jew not to oscillate between performing good or evil deeds, between preserving or destroying life. He must know which of these God commanded him to do and that the Sabbath constitutes neither an authorization to do evil nor a liberation from doing good.

But when Jesus called upon people's ethical judgments, he put their Sabbath assembly in an awkward position. They did not dare to defend harshness or malice. But the regulation "Don't do any work!" could not be ignored, and it spoke against Jesus. Only those who believed in Jesus knew a way out of this predicament. In Jesus' authority to help people on the Sabbath, as on all the other days of the week, they found God's gracious will, and they respected his lordship. The leaders of the people who defended the Law, however, had no reasonable explanation of the regulation, no matter how illuminating, and no ethical judgment carried any weight, no matter how opposed it was to the regulation. Everything, including Jesus' appeal to the Father who is at work through him, must be silent; the Law reigns. The only divine word they knew was the old one.

Once again we are confronted with a profound dilemma. In Worms, Luther appealed to God's Word and his own conscience. But what if one's own judgment contradicts the Law? "Suppress your conscience!" was the rabbi's response. But in this way he made the Law man's enemy and severed it from God's grace.

Jesus Must Die on Account of the Sanctity of the Sabbath
April 2

The Pharisees plotted how they could kill him.
—MATTHEW 12:14

Can we make sense of the Pharisees' action here, or does it rather call forth from us the disparaging verdict: "The wrangling of theologians! Religious fanaticism that will go to any length even over trivialities!" This verdict would apply to both sides: not merely to those who upheld the Law but also to Jesus, who through the healings he performed made them deadly enemies.

How strange what happens here! A healing had occurred. True, the man had not been in mortal danger, but he had been severely afflicted, since his crippled arm kept him from any kind of work. And this becomes a crime by which Jesus forfeits his right to live. Now there is no more possibility of rapprochement between the representatives of the Law and Jesus. They have made up their minds: He must die. But this did not take Jesus by surprise. He performed the healing fully aware of the consequences that would inevitably follow. Did it make sense to escalate the conflict between him and his opponents to such a lethal level on account of one crippled arm or some other sickness of just one individual?

It is immediately clear what motivated his opponents. Without wavering, they staked their lives on God's law, to which their lives were totally committed. Was it irrelevant that Jesus invalidated the unambiguous sense of the commandment? What was Israel without the Law? Not only people's well-being and glory, but their very existence depended on it. If a Jew surrendered the Law and no longer observed the Sabbath, he would disappear into the mass of other nations. Not only the Jew's false sense of identity—which craved eternal existence and glorious greatness for his nation—militated against this, but also everything that constituted true piety and dependence on God and his Word among the Jews. If the Law perished, all of Israel's sanctuaries perished with it. It was therefore the duty of everyone who feared and honored God and who cherished his people to oppose the one who knowingly and deliberately broke the Sabbath. And when Jesus—who proved by the healing that he acted on the basis of God's commission—broke it, he could not be opposed merely by calling him a godless person. He must die.

Equally clear are the reasons why Jesus could not give in at this point. The Law existed to reveal the contrast between God's and man's wills, and the Sabbath commandment, too, showed the people that they could not truly honor God. Because all of their activity serves selfish desire, they must honor him on his day by doing nothing.

But this is not how the Son honors the Father. The commandment "Don't do anything today, so that this day may be holy" applies to the one who wants nothing but to serve his own interests, the unreconciled person who is against God and God against him. But this misery had now come to an end precisely because the Son of God had come to be with the people. But if the regulation stood even between him and God, then there was no divine sonship. How could he elicit faith within people if he was powerless on the

Sabbath, or how could he show perfect love if performing good deeds on the Sabbath constituted sin? He could do no other; on God's day he was the one who worked and who healed, and he accepted the verdict that condemned him to die.

Is Jesus Dangerous?
April 3

Then they brought to him a demon-possessed man who was blind and dumb, and he healed him, so that the dumb man talked and saw. And all the people were astonished and said, "Isn't this the Son of David?" But when the Pharisees heard of it, they said, "He drives out the spirits only through Beelzebub, the ruler of spirits."
—MATTHEW 12:22–24

Israel has an enemy! The intentional distortion of his name—they called him "Beelzebub"—proves that they feared him. He is one of the powerful spirits who have access to heaven. He envies the promise given to Israel, disputes her righteousness, casts aspersions on her worship, demands that God's righteousness look upon Israel in wrath, and brings death to the guilty and severe predicaments on the nation that impede its growth and give it its pitiable, repulsive form. Everyone who leads Israel into sin and danger is his instrument, and this is what Jesus does.

This is the reason Jesus represents the gravest danger for the Jewish people. What a catastrophe it would be if the people were to make him their leader, which they would do if they came to believe that he was the Christ. His opponents' fear of him intensified even further because the people marveled at him on account of his healing a demon-possessed individual and suspected that he could be the Christ. He would take away everything that separated the Jewish people from the other nations. He is against the temple, against the Sabbath, and against tradition. He knows Scripture only as a layman would, since he did not learn it from a rabbi. He preached poverty, disrupted the economy, and rendered sensible politics impossible by failing to accept the caesar's authority and replacing it with the rule of God. Since he destroys the Jewish nation, doesn't that make him an instrument of the Enemy?

"But he drives out the spirits!" was the response of those who admired Jesus. But this does nothing to assuage his opponents' fears. To the contrary, it intensifies them. For demons belong to the army that obeys Israel's accuser and serves as his instrument. Because Jesus is himself an instrument of the Enemy, he has power over the spirits. For it is by their obedience and submission to Jesus that the Enemy provides him with the power to seduce and corrupt the nation.

But the Jewish leaders were not the only ones who feared Jesus. In other nations, too, it is feared that everything will be thrown into disarray if he is allowed to rule. Allowing Jesus to establish his community, they fear, will tear apart the fabric of the nation, and it will be rendered defenseless and impoverished by the influence of his word. Is it really in people's best interest to entrust themselves to Jesus?

This fear is rooted in Jesus' revealing the divinity of God, which unites us beyond what is visible with what is invisible, beyond what is natural with another world, and beyond our own lifetimes with another time. Would life not be simpler if it received its basis and aim solely through what is natural? Now we are supposed to see not only what our senses show us but also to hear what God's Word tells us. We ought not to trust what we find in ourselves but to trust him and obey a higher will than the one that calls for our self-preservation. Is not the One who elevates us above nature an enemy of nature and thus also an enemy of reason and of our happiness? Jesus' answer for those who fearfully warned the people against him, saying, "The Enemy is trying to seduce you!" was this: Don't be afraid! Be glad that I do what I am doing!

Be Glad Now!
April 4

If Satan drives out Satan, he is divided against himself. How can his rule be sustained? But if I drive out spirits through God's Spirit, then God's rule has come upon you.

—Matthew 12:26, 28

THE LAW DOES NOT PLACE ANY CONSTRAINTS ON JESUS 175

If someone beset by spiritual afflictions is set free, this ought to be reason for joy, no matter how this is done. Whoever is unable to rejoice in this has not received love. He has not yet learned how to value another person. Even if Jesus' opponents were right in thinking that he had received his power to drive out hostile spirits from the Enemy, they ought to rejoice. For just as a house disintegrates if its members fight one another, and just as a nation falls apart if it dissolves in various parties that seek to destroy one another, so also Satan's power would be gone if he himself were driving out the spirits who served him.

Owing to their hostility, Jesus' opponents do not face up to what is taking place and do not allow it to have an impact on them. What they saw and had to acknowledge was that an afflicted individual had been set free, and whoever sees this in an unbiased fashion will rejoice. But the liberation of the afflicted person did not take place the way they claim. Their interpretation of what they saw is erroneous. It was by the Spirit of God that Jesus healed the man and freed him from his misery. What does this mean? It means the royal work of God, the emergence of God's grace in the midst of human misery, the demise of all that opposes God: For this reason be glad that I do what I'm doing!

But were there not many others who required help besides the one who had been set free? Did this one event suffice to reveal God's reign? Jesus rejected this objection. God is at work in the present. He is the helper now. He revealed his grace upon this individual. See now what God does. Now open your minds for what you have been shown, and use the moment you have been given. Do not say, "We still need to wait until we can form an opinion. One instance is not enough to convince us. We will make up our minds only later, only later will we decide whether or not we can believe." The missed opportunity will not return. Every moment that reveals to us God's work brings us an irretrievable gift, a glimpse of eternity, a realization of the One who was and is and will be, a share in his grace, which is eternal and grants eternal life. The moment in which Jesus confronts us with God decides the outcome of our lives. It introduces us to God's kingdom.

Section 8

JESUS' WORD CREATES THE NEW PERSON

Jesus Speaks in Vain
April 5

*The sower went out to sow, and as he sowed, some seed
fell beside the path, and the birds came and ate it.
Whenever someone hears the word of the kingdom and fails
to understand it, the Evil One comes and takes away
what was sown into his heart. This is the one in whose case
the seed was sown beside the path.*

—MATTHEW 13:3–4, 19

With this story Jesus gave an account of his success to the people and the disciples. He was like a sower who sowed beside the path. Will any sensible farmer do this? That is a foolish question. Jesus did not use the sower as his example, as if he wanted to appeal to farming experience as a precedent for what he did. He had been given his word for all. For it is the word regarding the kingdom of God, and this cannot be turned into some secret teaching. This message is addressed to all. It shows everyone what constitutes their salvation, and it tells everyone what causes their deaths. But if he proclaims his message to all, it is like the seed that fell beside the path.

For there are people who do not understand even though they hear. The message does not make an impact on them. It does not seem relevant to what they do, and for this reason the message is barred from entering their souls.

But are there really people, even Jews, who have nothing in themselves that attracts them to the message? They all know that they are creatures. Should the creature not pay attention when the Creator addresses it? Do they not know what is good and evil, and is this not true particularly of the Jew? He was told what the Lord his God required of him, and he knew that his desire for what is good found fulfillment in God's kingdom and that it brought an end to all evil.

Yet all of this can be repressed in a person's inner being, even if he is a Jew. In that case he is concerned only with what he himself needs, and he lives a self-centered life and desires nothing but natural possessions. What use does he have for Jesus' word? To be sure, he hears the word, the living Word, which speaks to him in the power of truth. Now that it has entered his inner being, will it not throw him into turmoil? After all, it clashes with everything he has thought and wanted up to that point, and in judgment it contradicts everything he does.

But Jesus' word still has an adversary other than the people's natural way of life and their reasonableness (or lack thereof). The enemy of Israel and mankind is also the enemy of the Good News. He is Jesus' enemy and therefore the destroyer of his word. He causes it to vanish again from the soul without having its proper effect.

For he makes the pressure that our ordinary lives exert upon us so strong that individuals intuitively succumb to it without even realizing what they are doing. This results in a general mood, a kind of spiritual turbulence, that pushes the Word out of the soul.

Only by not simply hearing the Word but by understanding it could a person resist this pressure and fight the fight of faith by keeping the Word and obeying it. But since he did not understand it, it vanishes without a trace, and Jesus' listeners remain what they were before: willing and compliant members and subjects of this world. With this, Jesus explained to us how it can be that he speaks to us people in vain.

The New and Greater Repentance
April 6

Something greater than Jonah is here.
—MATTHEW 12:41

Was it Jesus' fault that he spoke to the Jews in vain? He proclaimed a new message; in the light of his message the old one disintegrated. This required his listeners to adjust and alter their thoughts and volition. Everyone who hears his word is called to repentance. Does this cast a shadow on Jesus' word? Does this make it a deterrent?

To prove that a message does not necessarily lose its power because it is a call to repentance and that this does not justify Jewish unbelief, Jesus adduces the story of Jonah. He called the Ninevites to repentance, and they listened to his message. Didn't an Israelite possess greater knowledge of God than a Ninevite? Is not the one who heeds God's law close to God's kingdom?

Whatever that tells us about the Jews as compared with the Ninevites, it is clear that one greater than Jonah is here. Jonah confronted Nineveh with divine wrath, which it had to fear in order not to perish. Jesus, on the other hand, speaks not only of human godlessness and of divine judgment; his word is the message of salvation and a word of repentance because it calls us to faith. It is a word of judgment because it announces God's gracious act. It takes away from a person only what corrupts him. It takes away his self-righteous presumption and humbles him, since his greatness ought to consist in the revelation of God's greatness upon him. It takes away his righteousness and calls him to plead, "God, have mercy on me, a sinner!" so that he is set free from his guilt and justified by God, possessing a righteousness that is valid before God. It takes away the self-centeredness that makes him lonely and an enemy of others and does not allow him to find peace, and places him into the community of those who received love from Jesus. And precisely through this, God gives that person a life that is distinctly his, one full of incomparable wealth, though also full of inexhaustible obligation. God gives that person an honor that no solitary individual, no matter how proud, can acquire for himself. God bestows a security and a peace that are unattainable for a person whose godlessness makes God his enemy, and whose unrighteousness tempts even other people to work against him. He only takes away what we have so that he can give us what he has, and he judges for the purpose of healing us. Jonah, who instilled fear in the king of the Ninevites, could not yet do this.

The New and Greater Wisdom
April 7

Something greater than Solomon is here.
—Matthew 12:42

When the remembrance of God awakens in us, we are reminded that we need to be wise. We are responsible for our actions and accountable for what we give to others and what we deny them. If we are careless, we may cause irreversible harm. We are also told to use our eyes, to form an opinion, and to be aware of what we are doing. The more we have been given, the greater our responsibility is, and the more indispensable wisdom becomes.

The Jews knew all of this. Because we are given our knowledge of God through the Law, they said, we must be wise in order to act rightly. Hence the great zeal by which they appropriated Scripture. Those who had become experts in the Scriptures were venerated by all as "the sages." Did they not come to Jesus because they thought him unwise? This was not the reason his word remained ineffectual. He gave them something greater than did Solomon.

Solomon was famous among the ancients for his wisdom, and his reputation for wisdom drew the Arabian queen to Jerusalem. Her receptivity to Solomon's wisdom served as an indictment of the Jews' lack of receptivity to Jesus' wisdom. Solomon's wisdom was still available to later generations, because the Holy Scriptures included a book of sayings that bore Solomon's name and provided instructions regarding wisdom. But this wisdom did not transcend the natural sphere. It spoke of the gain or loss of natural possessions and of the disruption or establishment of natural ties.

Jesus' disciples also required instruction in wisdom. They, too, had to learn how to deal with other people and their possessions by virtue of their discipleship. Hence Jesus' message concerning God's kingdom issues in a body of teaching that portrays the kind of righteousness that characterizes the conduct of a disciple who has been united with Jesus in faith. But this is no longer just the wisdom of Solomon, which guards us against suffering loss in body or possessions or against losing our reputation or others' friendship. Jesus' teaching has an incomparably greater aim, for in God's kingdom God's will is done. Whoever is a fellow citizen of the kingdom becomes a fellow soldier for God's righteousness. How will he conduct this battle in keeping with the will of the one whom he serves? The gain desired by wisdom here is eternal life, and the loss it seeks to prevent is the kind of death that separates from God's kingdom. Who can teach us this kind of wisdom? The One through whom God's word comes to us. He offered his wisdom to the Jewish people, but they did not want to listen. For, in truth, they were not interested in God's kingdom. This is why Jesus, when he spoke to them, was like the sower who sowed his seed beside the path.

Insurmountable Resistance
April 8

*And you, Capernaum, will you be lifted up to the skies? No,
you will descend to hades. For if the miracles that were done in
you had been done in Sodom, it would still stand until this day.
But I tell you: It will be more tolerable on the day of judgment
for Sodom than it will be for you.*

—MATTHEW 11:23–24

Seeds along the path, where nothing can grow—did this happen solely
when Jesus entered a house for but a few hours or granted a village only a
short visit? No. The hard soil that could not receive any seed and preserve it
was also the community of Capernaum and the adjacent villages, even
though Jesus had given them his word and his help more richly there than
anywhere else. He had avoided Jerusalem, for there his seed could not take
root. But it was not only the priesthood and the rabbinate that rejected
him; Capernaum, too, which he had made his city, kept its distance.

Was the soil hard only where there were no believers at all but where the
entire community rejected him in united unbelief, condemning him to die—
as had happened in Nazareth? No. The centurion had believed in him in
Capernaum. The ruler of the synagogue had summoned him to help his
dying daughter. The lame man had received forgiveness of sin from him.
When Jesus boarded a boat to leave the village, there was no lack of men
who asked to accompany him. But here, too, the outcome of his ministry
was that his seed did not bear fruit. Each act of faith and each experience of
divine help has the potential of leading others to faith in Jesus. Nonetheless
Capernaum, too, heard Jesus' word in vain. Jesus' lament diagnoses this
result with pained astonishment. How great were the deeds he had granted
the village! He had lifted it up to heaven; but the height of its elevation is
now equaled by the depth of its fall.

What did this reveal? The Jewish heart is unrepentant, even less repentant
than a Gentile heart. Judaism is pleased with its godless condition. It is
afraid to encounter God more closely. It does not consider the rule of the
sinful nature to be tyranny from which it wants to be released. It does not
desire anything better than what it has. If someone keeps his distance from
Jesus, he may hope that soon the heavens will open and, like long ago during

the people's sojourn through the desert, the manna will come down like rain and procure for all a carefree existence. In comparison to this, what was Jesus' promise of the kingdom to those who were willing to take their cross upon themselves? The way Jesus described it and assigned it to his followers, discipleship was a very sober and real matter, and Jesus looked quite entirely like any other man. Was he not something of a loner? Could Capernaum risk following him before the entire nation and, especially, the leaders had made their decision for him? Did any of the rulers believe in him? Capernaum will convert when the others have converted—and thus it never did convert. It was not the soil from which the harvest grew.

The Word Is One with God
April 9

In the beginning was the Word, and the Word was with God, and the Word was God.
—John 1:1

Why does Jesus liken himself to the sower? Why does he trust in his word? Is his ministry not doomed to fail because he has nothing but his word? Since he must sow on hard soil, doesn't this prove right the prince of this world, who advised him to go the path of all great men—to subjugate the people as they do to others? No. To neglect the word would be ignorance of God and apostasy from him.

For in the beginning was the Word. It is the most real thing, the most powerful thing. To what does everything owe its existence? Everything that came into being, came into being through the Word. Where is that which was in the beginning? It is with God. It has its origin in God, and it has its power in God. For the Word was God. His Word does not leave him but remains one with him. Where the Word is, God is, and what the Word does, God does. Where the Word remains ineffectual, God is not present.

How could Jesus desire anything other than the Word, and how could he fulfill his kingly mission in any way other than by the Word? This alone could be Jesus' aim and desire: to be the Word, nothing but the Word that God speaks to mankind. And he desires to be the Word in his entire being: not merely through what he proclaims and teaches but through what he is;

not merely through what he did but no less through what he suffered. Even when the soil does not receive the seed, he is the Word of God who speaks to man. Then the divine Word tells people that they are against God and God against them.

For this reason, the greatest honor his disciples could pay him was to say, "He is the Word, for in him the Word has become flesh." His humanity is what the Word wanted and created, because this is how it speaks to mankind. "Jesus the human being, who is God's Word"—this is the same confession as "Jesus the human being, who is God's Son."

With the divine Word, grace and truth come near to man. The ground out of which the Word springs forth is love. This is why the one who is the Word is full of grace. By speaking the word, he becomes the giver of divine gifts. Where the Word is not, there is no community. There also is no more room for the truth. The one who is the Word, however, is true; and because he speaks not only the word, but because he always is the Word, he is full of truth and without deceit, the shining light that is never overcome.

This is why the sower covers the *entire* field—the soil that is hard, stony, and overgrown with thorns, as well as the good soil. For the Word was God, and God is the God of all. All of them came into being through the Word, and they all are his possession: those who do not receive him and those who do: those for whom the Christ has a word of judgment and those whom he can make children of God. To all alike he states what God has to say to them.

No Root, No Fruit
April 10

Other seed fell on rocky ground, where there was not much soil. It shot up immediately, because the soil was not deep. But when the sun shone, it was burned, and because it had no roots, it withered. The one in whose case the seed fell on rocky ground is the one who hears the word and at once accepts it with joy. But he has no root in himself and his response is fleeting. When there is pressure or persecution on account of the word, he immediately falls away.

—Matthew 13:5–6, 20–21

There were also some who joyfully listened to Jesus and quickly counted themselves among those who confessed him. When a scribe displayed his scriptural expertise in front of the congregation, they might say, "This is not for us." And when someone preached repentance and scolded and warned the congregation, they only reluctantly listened to him. When a person with an apocalyptic outlook told them how wonderful he imagined God's kingdom to be, they wondered whether these were mere dreams. But Jesus was entirely different. He talked to people about what they were and what they could become through their encounter with Jesus. And the vantage point from which he saw his relationship with God and the resulting consequences had been given to him by God's grace. How could there not be some who agreed with Jesus when he called his message "the good news of God"?

But this agreement did not yet provide the certainty that here someone had arisen in whom the Word had brought about the life that originates in God. This will be evident only when it comes to light what following Jesus necessarily entails: contempt and mistreatment, which diminish one's possessions and one's honor; and finally ostracism from one's village; flight from those who want to bring one before the judge; forgoing one's national community and home. Was the value of following Jesus not diminished if it required such kinds of sacrifice? Was it worth belonging to the brotherhood that was rooted in faith in Jesus when this entails expulsion from the nation, separation from one's community, and the loss of one's home?

There were some who confessed Jesus in a fleeting manner, namely for however long there remained peace between them and the Jewish people, during which confessing him did not involve forfeiting any of the privileges that Judaism offered its members. But they considered it self-evident that their allegiance to Jesus would not ensue in being uprooted from their soil, being separated from their kin, or being rejected by their people.

But whoever conceived of being a Christian in this way met disappointment. Since in Judaism the national and the religious community fully coincided, the separation between Jesus' disciples and the Jews already had begun during his ministry. It escalated more and more and culminated in the complete removal of Christians from the Jewish community and the total separation of the two religions. This is why Jesus told those who came to him with these kinds of reservations that they would leave him again unless their faith was prepared to sacrifice everything. The seed he sows into a person's heart must take deep root if the heads of grain are to ripen all the way to the harvest.

Only the integrity that completely agrees with Jesus' verdict concerning man and what he is able to accomplish with the Law provides the proper foundation for a lasting faith. Only a complete victory over natural desires makes possible the kind of faithfulness that cannot forsake Jesus.

The Word Prepares Us for the Time to Come
April 11

But the one in whose case the seed fell into the thorns is the one who hears the word; but the cares of this present time and the deceitfulness of riches choke the word, and it becomes unfruitful.
—Matthew 13:22

The fear of loss and the craving for profit grow from the same root, and both render the Word ineffective. Fruit comes about through the external pressure applied on the disciples. Craving for profit, on the other hand, comes from the inside. For this reason Jesus creates two images: heads of grain that wither in the heat, and those that are choked by thorns.

The disciples' craving is stirred from two sides. "This present time" stirs it, and riches make it strong. By "this present time" Jesus means mankind's current condition, in distinction from what is to come. Present history and our current nature give humanity the shape to which Jesus pointed when he spoke of "this present time."

It drives the disciple to "cares." For nature not only feeds us; it also destroys us, and our dealings with others also bring us sorrow and affliction because they inject not only goodness but also malice into our lives. But when Jesus warns of "cares," he does not merely think of the misery and sorrows that come to us through the world's present condition. For the disciples' attitude is threatened both by hopes incited by the world and also by anxious fears. Valuable possessions are to be gained from it, but not without considerable effort. They require work, industry, resourcefulness, and persistent efforts that consume our entire energy. But how does this pursuit of the things of this world affect the disciples? It has the same effect on them as thorns on grain. It sways the will that Jesus' word created in them and renders what Jesus gave them unimportant. For God's kingdom brings about the time to come and the new world.

But how strong and varied are the temptations that approach us from this world! The challenges with which it confronts us present us with clearly defined goals. Do they not seem more important than what is merely are prophesied about the future? Are we not foolish when we neglect the present for the future? We are certainly fools, but we are equally fools if we forfeit the future for the sake of the present. To be sure, God's kingdom will come at the time and in the manner in which it will come, whether or not we speak of it now. But it is no less certain that the outcome of our lives is decisively affected by whether we are ready for the future. Certainly, there is enough work for us in our nation and in our church. This work will fill our days, and we should not neglect it simply because it is fraught with sorrows. But it is equally certain that the reception and the preservation of the divine Word are the most important experiences facing us, and that they provide us with a source of energy for every task that we must complete in this present time.

Either the World or God
April 12

You adulteresses, don't you know that friendship with the world is enmity with God? Whoever therefore wants to be a friend of the world presents himself as an enemy of God.

—JAMES 4:4

This is what James, the brother of Jesus, told the Jews who had settled in Greek-speaking regions. There, they busily sought to obtain the nations' favor. They pressed into the royal court, and when they were unable to get to the caesar, they made contact with the queen. They established themselves in all centers of trade, accumulated wealth by all means, and thus acquired influence and power. This is what Jesus called "the cares of this world," which oppose and drive out God's word.

But at that time the Jews did not intend to intensify their rapprochement with the world by abandoning their Law and by forfeiting the privilege of being God's people. This has taken place only in the past two centuries. At that time they still derived their claim to a noble position in the world from the privilege given to them by their superior knowledge of God. As the friends of God they also courted the friendship of the world. Should those whom God honors and loves not be honored by all?

This conclusion is erroneous. This is how arrogant egotism thinks, not pure love. It is like the lustful fantasies of a woman who is married and at the same time longs for a second man. What she wants is impossible, because by longing for a second man she has destroyed her marriage. One relationship excludes the other. Likewise, friendship with God binds a person exclusively to God. The one who receives it seeks to please him, makes God's glory his glory, and calls God his mighty fortress, sun, and shield. For he receives from him his joy and his security. But if he is at the same time a friend of the world, he makes its verdict the rule for his conduct and aims for the honor it grants him. He counts on its support and derives his security from its assistance.

And still it is evident that this person does not think or do what God wants. God opposes godlessness and injustice. Everyone who enjoys God's friendship knows about this opposition. For we gain God's friendship by God's revealing his will to us and making it precious to us.

How does one become God's friend? He sends that person his word, through which God's grace speaks to him and does its work in him. It sets that person free from his godless thoughts and selfish desires and gives him its good gifts— that he can believe, hope, and love. But in this way God binds us entirely to himself. Now our ears are deaf to the praises or rebukes of others. And when they present to us their opinions or theories and demand our assent, they no longer blur the lines dictated by our conduct. When they invite us to take part in their activities, they do not pull us away from our service, to which we have been enlisted through God's friendship. This grants us an undivided heart that worships God alone. Whoever forsakes this tie, however, revokes friendship with God and becomes God's enemy.

Wealth Is Deceitful
April 13

But the one in whose case the seed fell into the thorns is the one
who hears the word; but the cares of this world and the
deceitfulness of riches choke the word, and it becomes
unfruitful.
—MATTHEW 13:22

The disciple's most dangerous opponent who attacks him in the world is wealth, the deceiver whose radiance blinds all. Whoever falls for its deceit loses the Word and what the Word has given him. We attach the greatest of hopes to increasing our possessions. This is how we secure our livelihood and attain to much more: we transform our existence into happiness. Wealth also grants us unlimited access to enjoying life, and in the competition for the goods of this age it is our most effective support and the surest way to power.

Yet the Jews did not think that this esteem for wealth amounted to deceit, and all others shared—and still share—the Jews' opinion in this regard. A deep rift opened up between the disciples and the Jews, and in the course of history, between believers in Jesus and the world; some venerated and pursued wealth, and others feared and avoided it.

Why did Jesus set his disciples apart from their nation and from the entire world in this way? By being very poor, he made following him more difficult for all. Our natural lives are God's gift; thus our acquisition of worldly goods, too, is given to us by God. Should the one who is able to acquire these goods in abundance see God's goodness in this and be grateful for them? Jesus instilled this conviction firmly in his disciples. For the first thing we know about God is that he is our Creator. This is why Jesus gave thanks every time before he distributed bread to his disciples. He hated neither life, nor the body through which we have life, nor the earth that bears and feeds us. He hated one thing: what man produces in his inner being, in "his heart."

Our desires are not grounded in God's will and commandment. What makes our selfish longings so strong that we forget God and become his adversaries? Is it not our possessions, our treasures, that which we call "wealth," and everything for which wealth can be used, together with the burning lust with which we now fill our souls? How was it possible to truly subject the Jews to God when they did not give up their pursuit of wealth?

God is king. God is the ruler of lives. God is the master of your wills. God is the one through whom and for whom you all live. From these premises Jesus drew for his disciples the following conclusions: Be poor. Sell what you have. Believe and testify this to the entire world: God is alive. God is at work. God cares. God rules. And we are living in God's kingdom.

God Is the Owner, We Are His Administrators
April 14

But he also told his disciples: "There was a certain rich man who had a manager. And he was accused by others of squandering his wealth. So the man called the manager and said to him, 'Why do I hear these kinds of things about you? Give an account of your administration. For you can no longer be my manager.'"

—Luke 16:1–2

Jesus did not praise anyone for faithfully administering his property. Everyone is like the manager whose master Jesus says demoted him because he failed to be faithful in taking care of his possessions. How right he was in this assessment is proved by our astonishment when we hear the story.

Who has a more compelling claim on our property than we ourselves, who acquired and possess it? To be sure, property can exist only because of the state, and it does not come into being without the work of others. But if the community were to extend its right so far that there were no longer any personal property, it would destroy itself. But here Jesus is not talking about the government's right to oversee our wealth and the use we make of it. The landowner, who in the story is defrauded by his manager, does not represent the landlord. He represents God himself.

If we were to ask, "Why does God's claim extend also to our property?" Jesus' response would be, "You do not yet know God's divinity but still fashion him after your own image. You, a mere man, are motivated by your will to life and to power. From the things that your minds and your hands are able to grab, you create possessions that you claim are yours alone. But because you know that you did not create yourself, you put God somewhere in the transcendent realm, a god whom you make in your image, except that he is an infinitely expanded version of your own selfishness. You let him be in charge of his own affairs, but you take care of your possessions as you see fit. And only when your energy wanes and you get to your wit's end do you remember him and think it is his role to do for you what you cannot do for yourself.

But he is the Creator—do we think his creature eludes his grasp?" He is the Ruler—what does it mean for him to "rule"? Where one is the ruler, all others are servants; no one remains will-less or lacks employment. God's creatures are alive, for he sustains their lives. They exercise their wills and acts, for his commandment reveals his will to them. They have a goal because he has a goal. We people arise from the omnipotent being of the Creator-King with all our abilities, works, gaining, and losing.

If we know how our possessions came into being, we also know what will become of them. The person who is self-sufficient is ignorant of this. For the only criteria he employs in using his property are his need and his lust. In this he is like the manager who used his master's property for his own advantage. Should he not serve the one who has entrusted these things to him? And what an abundance of opportunities is given to us by our possessions, whether many or few! But our self-love is blind to this abundance, because it makes us shortsighted and lonely. No injustice is done to you, Jesus reasoned, if you are removed from your managerial position; and the complaint is pointless that people acquire their possessions with great effort only to have to leave them behind in the end. You can be trusted with eternal possessions only when you have learned to remain faithful to God and to be obedient to him in all things.

Must Wealth Be People's Ruin?
April 15

*Surely, I tell you: It is difficult for a rich person to enter
the kingdom of heaven. Again I say to you:
It is easier for a camel to go through the eye of a needle than
for a rich person to enter God's kingdom.*

—MATTHEW 19:23–24

A camel in front of the eye of a needle! This is how clearly Jesus perceived the abyss that separated him from mankind. This is how far people are removed from God! Jesus could not get through to people, not only because a caesar who demanded divine worship for himself got in the way, and the Pharisees blocked people's way to God, and the teachers of the Law by their scholarship choked out life. No, his word also appears unbelievable and his offer without value if nature comes to man's aid and his natural cravings take their proper course, so that he calls a large piece of property his own and accumulates worldly goods and takes full control of his life.

Has there ever been a clever, healthy individual who did not at one time or another sense a longing to imagine what it would be like to be rich? He would be free of distress or concern and would no longer need to work against his own will. He would be independent of the mercy of others and in charge of his own time. He would control all his energies and be in full disposal of his own powers. He would be master of his own destiny, finally able to live life truly to the fullest.

The bottom line is this: The more he becomes himself, the farther he is from God. Once he is insulated from his destiny—against whose treachery his wealth protects him—independent of people he does not need, no longer limited by his bodily appetites, which he can effortlessly satisfy, then he is totally secure, fully satisfied—and completely severed from God. Is Jesus proven wrong because nature contradicts him? To place a camel in front of the eye of a needle seems absurd. But all this freedom, supposedly the result of wealth, is only an illusion. Instead of setting us free from our bodies, it increases their appetites and makes them even more demanding, and it renders other people truly indispensable. A rich person cannot live without a large number of servants. He is supposed to be in charge of his own time, but it gets away from him and leaves him empty-handed. He is in charge of his own life—but for what? His wealth has increased and grown stronger, but this is due to worldly forces that are not of the Father and will therefore pass away.

So even if our natural cravings exert total control over us so that we cannot stop the movement they unleash, we are far from God and beyond Jesus' grasp only because of what is in us. We are not too far removed to be the recipients of what God did for us. The illusion that blinds us passes away when God's light shines on us. Above the impossibilities of our own making stands the omnipotence of grace, and there is no "impossible" that precludes its saving work.

How Does God Reward the One Who Honors Him?
April 16

People who are corrupt in their understanding and devoid of truth think that the worship of God is a means of income. Yet in fact worshiping God is great gain together with contentment.
—1 Timothy 6:5–6

The strongest commandment most of our men know is "More!" They spend their youth getting an education, and then the major pursuit of their prime years becomes holding down a lucrative job. This is their duty as both citizens and church members. When the state lacks funds to procure what is needed, self-interest has made fools out of their compatriots, and when a church does not have the means to do its work, it fails to fulfill its duty.

But what is the relationship between work and the Christian aim—that our lives ought to bring honor to God and that his will be done? Are both aspirations related, resulting in a kind of trade, where man remembers God, observes his Word, and performs his commandments, while God, for his part, ensures man's well-being and allows his work to prosper? This kind of trade-off seems fair enough, but as Paul rightly contends, it is utter folly. To act in such a way is possible only when man is devoid of truth. Who does he imagine God to be? Has he ever been touched by a thought of the divinity of God, or has any message of the glory of his grace ever reached him? Here the human being thinks of himself as great and important before God and considers his own worship to be worth so much that it procures him God's attention and assistance.

To be sure, it is great gain when we do not have God against us, since his care also extends to the natural realm of our lives. But his providence does not yield to us our natural desires, and it assigns to us no special place within natural events. We operate under the same natural conditions as all others and contend with the same obstacles they do. We do not claim any special fortune, since we would not give God the honor due him if we failed to acknowledge that God is greater than nature and that his grace makes our aim not the acquisition of worldly goods but a share in God's kingdom.

For this reason it is a mark of God's blessing in our work when we become independent of the amount of our possessions. The meaning and the power of our lives no longer depend on whether we incur profit or loss. Paul said that he and his coworkers needed nothing but the most basic necessities: food, shelter, and clothing. This is how rich they were, and this is how fully equipped they were for their ministry. No harm was done if they lacked anything that might have supported it, and precisely in this way they amply experienced that honoring God is a great reward. For those who had nothing made many rich.

The Word Gives Birth to the Congregation
April 17

The one in whose case the seed fell on good soil is the one who hears and understands the word. He yields fruit, whether a hundredfold, sixtyfold, or thirtyfold.
—Matthew 13:23

In Jesus' story the sower sowed not merely beside the path and on rocky soil and into the thorns; he also has good soil, and his seed is destined for it. What kind of claim does Jesus make regarding man when he calls him "good soil"? He characterizes him by one thing only: he hears the Word and understands it. He does not state any conditions that predispose him toward the Word. To be sure, those do exist. For our present conduct depends on how we previously acted. There is a strong connection between various events in our lives. This is why we call what we experience "history." But whatever a person previously was disappears in light of what he experiences when the Word reaches him. Now all depends on whether or not he wants to hear and if he is able to hear in such a way that he understands. If he perceives what the Word tells him and gives him, he is good soil, and now the Word unfolds its characteristic life-giving power.

Now it becomes evident that it is like the seed that includes a germ that must sprout and bring forth the stalk and the heads of grain filled with new seeds, so that one seed turns into thirty, sixty, or a hundred heads of grain. Now the Word transforms that person's thinking and says *no* to his self-centeredness and is the living bond that connects him with God and his grace.

For this reason the sower goes about his work without misgivings, even though he partly sows in vain. For he produces a large crop. The Word does not remain closed up in the one who has received it. It moves from person to person, for it has persuasive powers. This power is the justification of Jesus and his faith in the power of the divine Word—that by making one disciple he actually makes many. If the disciple betrayed his calling to give the Word to others after receiving it, he would be unfaithful to his master. This can happen only when the disciple yields to the power of his own desires or to external pressures, similar to the seeds that sprouted on rocky soil or among thorns.

There is no legal stipulation that assigns to every disciple the same duty and promises him equal success. Every disciple will share in Jesus' work to the extent assigned to him. Disciples' abilities vary, and so does the performance of each. But no one fails to bear fruit; no one receives the Word merely for himself. No one stands idle beside his active master. God's rule puts everyone to work and is realized in that all who receive his Word serve as messengers to others.

Jesus' Legacy
April 18

*It will be like a man who went on a journey, called his
servants, and entrusted them with his possessions. He gave five
talents to one, two to the other, and one to the third—to each
one in keeping with his abilities. Then he went on his journey.*
—MATTHEW 25:14–15

As Jesus illustrated by the sower, what he did could be described as placing his word into a person. The disciples received words from him, and for the rest of their lives, they were to pass on these words to others, even when he is taken away from them. *Words!* Are they the products of their own fertile minds? To be sure, there is no word unless they think and speak. But their message does not originate in their own mental processes set in motion by their senses. It has its origin in who Jesus is.

By the story in which the master entrusts his possessions to his servants, he explains to them what kind of word they have and what makes them capable of speaking it. They receive a share in what he himself owns. They have become his students. This is what they called themselves: disciples, students, learners. But they are more than this; they are his slaves. By comparing them with slaves, he places them in a permanent relationship with him. The slave is always his master's. Neither the master nor the slave thinks of dissolving their relationship. It is dissolved only by the slave's misdeeds, which issue not in his freedom but in his being thrown into prison. Precisely because their relationship cannot be dissolved and because they are closely related to him, he can entrust to them what is his own.

With his word he gave them insights and wisdom that was greater than Solomon's. Also, reminiscences were tied to his word, unforgettable memories of great experiences. But the talents he gives them do not consist merely of knowledge and memories. For Jesus' word speaks of who he is and what the disciples have become through him, and their memories show them not merely what they experienced in the past but what he is now and always will be for them and what they become through him. The disciple possesses the life produced in him by Jesus, and for this reason Jesus likens him to the slave who was entrusted by his master with the talents he owned.

Yet can all that Jesus was truly be transferred to others and to succeeding generations? After all, he was a Jew, and his body and soul received their form from his race. His scope was limited by his historical location and is therefore very different from ours. But Jesus did not talk about his natural condition when he gave talents to the disciples. His possessions are what he has on account of his fellowship with the Father, and his word arose from it. God's omnipotent grace gave him the word by which he calls people to repentance, forgives their sins so that they can believe, and judges their self-centeredness so that they can love. And this is what he did not take with him when he departed from the earth but distributed to his disciples and continues to distribute wherever his Word is heard and understood.

Jesus' Possessions Are Increasing
April 19

So the one who had received five talents went and gained five more. The one who had received two likewise gained two more.
—Matthew 25:16–17

Talents that are merely hoarded, not invested—no! Jesus will have none of it, just as it is impossible for the seed he sows not to grow. The disciples understood at once that, by entrusting them with what belonged to him, Jesus made their discipleship a never-ending task. Had they not grasped this, they would not have received his love.

They will not all do the same work. He does not impose uniformity upon them. Once more he tells them this in the present story, similar to the one about the sower. The master is rich and thus chooses more than just one slave to be the administrator of his possessions. His riches are for many, and he knows his servants and is aware of what he can expect from them. In this way he assigns to every disciple his own share in his work. No one must be idle. All are to make a profit.

What can anyone gain with the things he receives from Jesus? Material possessions? If the disciples' work pursued these, they would deny their master. The One who was very poor did not bequeath to them any material possessions or natural goods. The Word wants to gain listeners; people who hear and understand it are its profit. The disciples must increase Jesus' possessions, and his possessions—with which he is inextricably linked—are those who do God's will.

This is a joyful ministry. For their word is gospel, the message that proclaims salvation. They announce God's rule. Because Jesus has been sent by God's grace, their work, too, is done in the service of divine grace. Nevertheless, their work requires much effort and exertion. It amounts to military service and gives them a part in Jesus' struggle, by which he wages combat with the world and the world with him. To win those who are Jesus' own possession, they must contradict what people think and want, and they must establish communion between themselves and those people.

What a difficult and strenuous enterprise it is to unite people in one purpose! This is already apparent in the national sphere. It is a great task to unite the many in the same goal. The disciples' task is greater still: uniting the many in God, uniting them in faith in Jesus, uniting them to be ready to serve him.

Will the work of his servants be profitable? Just as it is not merely said that the sower labored in vain but also that his word produced a large community, so in the present story the slaves approach the returning master with joyful confidence. Not only have they been faithful to him and kept what he had entrusted to them, but they also have increased their master's property. They present him with the fruit of their labors. Jesus' confidence in God's Word also comprised the effectiveness of his disciples. Their ministry succeeds, for they are what he made them to be, and work with what he gave them.

The Invisible Church
April 20

The one who had received the one talent departed, dug a hole in the ground, and hid his master's money there.
—Matthew 25:18

Jesus enlists into military service those to whom he entrusts his word. But in the line of duty there are also casualties. Jesus always told his disciples this with the utmost seriousness. They belong to the group whose head and leader he is, and he gives them his promise, which he invests with the

JESUS' WORD CREATES THE NEW PERSON

glory and firmness it possesses because he utters it in the name of God. Are they not secure? Who, when he has been granted and has believed Jesus' promise, is not able to say, "What do I still lack? I am at peace with myself"?

"At peace with myself"—in Jesus' eyes this is a fatal step that completely separates his disciples from him. For this contentment arises from one's selfish desires. Only one who is without love can conceive of himself and of his Christianity in this manner. But if he does not have love, he is Jesus' adversary and not his subject.

In order to instill this truth into his disciples, he juxtaposed in his story the servants who administered their master's money with industry and success to the servant who buried it. He does not want to lose the money; he makes sure it is safe. It would be dangerous for him if he were to lose it. Yet he does not want to use it or increase it. Having it is enough for him.

The Christian whom Jesus has in mind here neither abandons his Christianity nor leaves the church. For Jesus' word has seized him and does not let him go. Because he has heard from Jesus the message about the kingdom and eternal life, he joins those who long for the kingdom. But why be concerned for others? He is a Christian for himself.

How did his love die? Was he afraid? Can he not bear the heat of the sun, having been planted on rocky ground without deep soil? In the place where Jesus put his disciples, they had to endure much pressure if they wanted to confess him. Only those who were motivated by strong love were able to be a Christian openly and without secrecy among the Jews and to act consistently as a Christian. How little resistance and contempt it takes to silence us!

But it is not merely the external pressures that produce the inactive, unfruitful type of Christian. The pressures we put on ourselves are even more dangerous. No one can lead another person to faith if he himself does not act in a believing manner. But what is the condition of our own faith? If we tell others Jesus' word, we encounter their objections. Are we able to deal with these, and can we talk about Jesus correctly and effectively? Whoever enters another person's life assumes a serious responsibility. Is this not too difficult for us? Since people's natural way of thinking and the divine Word are incompatible, we must always be ready for misrepresentations that put our self-love to the test. It is not easy to be a sinner as well as a believer, not only secretly but also before others. For this reason we content ourselves with fulfilling our obligation to testify where we are secure and no one can attack us, in the sacred realm of the church and in the printed Word. Can we not be content with that?

Those who were motivated by the love of Jesus were never satisfied with that. His Word looks for listeners, leads people to others, and brings grace to those who need it. Whoever understands this does not make unfruitful the things from Jesus that are in him but increases Jesus' possessions.

Jesus Remains Incomprehensible to the Jews
April 21

And the disciples came and said to him, "Why do you speak to them in parables?" But he answered, "To you it is given to understand the mysteries of the kingdom of heaven; but to them it is not given. For the one who has will be given more, and he will have abundance; but whoever does not have—even what he has will be taken away from him. This is why I speak to them in parables. For although they see, they do not perceive. And although they hear, they do not understand. They do not realize that Isaiah's prophecy is fulfilled, which says: 'You will hear and not understand. You will see and not perceive. For the heart of this people has become hard, and they have trouble hearing with their ears. They have closed their eyes so that they neither see with their eyes nor hear with their ears nor understand with their hearts and turn that I might heal them.'"
—Matthew 13:10–15 (cf. Isa. 6:9–10)

When Jesus illustrated to his disciples their rule of conduct by the servants whose master had made them the administrators of his money, his story was transparent and unforgettable for them, even though Jesus did not add an explanation. When he showed by the example of the sower what he did and accomplished, the disciples complained that he did this merely by a parable and thus rendered his word useless for most. But it was an essential characteristic of Jesus that he remained incomprehensible to the Jews so that he could illustrate merely by parables what took place through him.

The attentive listener will notice, of course, that in the sower he was portraying himself, and in the outcome of the sowing, he was depicting the success of his own ministry. After all, there was no one else who could be compared with one who sowed in a field. Thus, that listener could suspect that the seed was sown when Jesus gave his word to his hearers.

But by this alone the parable took on such mystery that Jewish insights were insufficient to understand it. What did Jesus' word have to do with God's kingdom? To be sure, the Jews acknowledged that, according to Scripture, everything was created when God spoke. But that word was something entirely different from what came out of the mouth of the Nazarene. Thus everything Jesus said regarding the outcome of the sowing process was incomprehensible and incredible to the Jew.

He never acknowledged that his own conduct was depicted by what happened to the seed sown beside the path. When Jesus told the inhabitants of Jerusalem, without a parable, that they had been called to God's kingdom in vain and that they remained subject to the ruler of the world, his words infuriated them so much that they looked for stones in order to stone him. At the Sea of Galilee they listened to Jesus calmly only because they did not understand him.

And when he now spoke about the pressures and the persecution to be endured by those to whom Jesus' word had given life, this remained an entirely incomprehensible statement to all those who did not understand what set Jesus apart from those who fought for the rule of the Law. What rendered the contrast between Jesus' disciples and the Pharisees so profound? The righteous ones ruled the community and rendered their verdict in the name of the Law. How could it be that anyone would have to suffer condemnation or persecution for the sake of God's will in order to preserve God's Word?

Jesus' disciples have set their sights on the world to come and therefore do not grasp for what this world has to offer. But for the Jews the world to come was merely the continuation of the present world, which the Christ will beautify and liberate from the ills that now plague mankind. The Jews saw no danger in what Jesus called thorns and thistles that choked the seed. Why should one who longs for God's kingdom call wealth a deceiver?

And the final sentence—that those who had been gripped by Jesus' word were God's people, having received nothing from him but the word, were without any means of power and nonetheless invincible, a steadily growing community, because one turns into thirty, sixty, or a hundred—how could Galilee's youth, who took up the sword in order to establish God's kingdom, understand this? And how could an inhabitant of Jerusalem who believed in the eternal existence of the temple understand this?

What Jesus illustrated in his parables were "the mysteries of the kingdom of God." Indeed, these were realities and developments that unfolded before his listeners' very eyes. But they were visible only for those to whom Jesus' word had disclosed who he was.

Everyone Must Be Told the Word
April 22

This is why I speak to them in parables. For although they see, they do not perceive. And although they hear, they do not understand. They do not realize that Isaiah's prophecy is fulfilled, which says: 'You will hear and not understand. You will see and not perceive. For the heart of this people has become hard, and they have trouble hearing with their ears. They have closed their eyes so that they neither see with their eyes nor hear with their ears nor understand with their hearts and turn that I might heal them.'

—MATTHEW 13:13–15 (CF. ISA. 6:9–10)

Should God's Word be told to all, even to those who do not want to hear it? Everyone who has been given a divine commission has had to deal with this question. God's Word calls people to a decision that determines the course and outcome of their lives. The other side of the Word's saving effect is the destruction that ensues when a person hears the divine Word but resists and rejects it. Should he still be told the message? And if calamity is to be avoided, what standard should the proclaimer of the divine Word use to distinguish between those to whom he may extend the call of God and those to whom he ought to refuse it? He has not been appointed as the people's judge and is not the one who knows their hearts.

When Isaiah's ears heard God's call, "Whom shall I send?" and he responded, "Lord, send me!" the question regarding to whom he ought to go was answered by a particular instruction that set Isaiah free from any uncertainty or doubt. God made him the spokesman of his Word to Jerusalem not because it would listen to him. Rather, he was installed as God's messenger because it would *not* listen to him. But for this reason God's Word is not taken away from it; it is told the message precisely for this reason. Success therefore does not consist in the people's conversion but in their guilt, so that their exceeding guilt would lead to the demise of the holy city. For the tree God had planted must not remain standing the way it has grown. It must be cut down in order that a new tree may grow from its root.

The same question to which Isaiah received an answer carried even more weight for Jesus. He did not save Jerusalem; it did not acknowledge him and sinned against him. Would he act in keeping with God's gracious will if he kept silent? No! He must tell the entire nation the message of God's kingdom. Its failure to listen does not render him speechless. So he must act the way he depicted in the sower who cast his seed over the entire field. This resulted in guilt, and this guilt resulted in the judgment on account of which Jerusalem fell. If this had been to the detriment of the divine rule and a diminishment of the divine grace, then, of course, Jesus would have had to remain silent. But Jerusalem's coming will reveal both the height and the depth of God's grace.

The Pure Community
Is Not Yet Called into Being
April 23

Again, the kingdom of heaven is like a net that is cast
into the lake and catches all kinds of fish. When it is full,
it is drawn to the shore, and the fishermen sit down and gather
the good fish into containers; but the rotten ones are thrown
out. This is how it will be at the end of time. The angels will go
out and separate the wicked from the righteous and cast
them into the fiery furnace. In that place there will be
weeping and gnashing of teeth.
—MATTHEW 13:47–50

Will the disciple be greater than the master? To be sure, Jesus promised his disciples that they would do greater works than he did. But this would not be the result of any ability on their parts to help everyone to whom they proclaim the word. Nor would it consist in their being able to distinguish between those listeners who would be saved by their word and those who would sin against it.

For the period during which they were to administer what they had received from him, Jesus gave his followers the principle used by fishermen, who bring ashore in their net everything that has been caught in the net. Then, on the shore, they screen and throw out everything that is useless.

Thus they bring God's word to everyone. Their duty of confessing Jesus and realizing what they have become through him encompasses all of their dealings, regardless of who enters their community. So they act in good conscience, which they would not have done if they had denied God's righteousness or removed God's right to judge all people and transferred it to themselves. Because Jesus turned their faith toward God, they expected the execution of judgment from God's kingdom, and they served it by telling the message even to those who did not believe and to those who accepted it but then rendered it ineffective by following their own desires. They thus prove to be the servants who wait for their master; he will reveal God's judgment when he acts regally in God's power and glory.

In this way burning hopes were pushed aside and, in humble submission to God's sovereignty, replaced with patient expectation. "He will separate the wheat from the tares," John the Baptist had promised and thus expressed the longing of those who were concerned for the well-being of the community. These people were moved passionately by a longing for the pure community that did not comprise internal contradictions but rather included only those chosen and set apart by God, and had the authority to promise salvation to all those who joined it. But as long as humanity's present condition continues, this pure community is not what Jesus brings into being.

Didn't he rob the community of its peace by failing to give it the authority to assure its members of their salvation? Does it still possess such assurance? Don't fear and uncertainty descend upon it until the judge's verdict is revealed one day in the future? He had promised eternal life to those who believed in him. He stood ready to accept and not to disregard any kind of faith. But this does not differ from the marching orders he gave to the apostles or from the constitution he gave to the community. Rather, it is precisely by these instructions that he constitutes his community as the community of believers—not as the community of those who believe in their faith and in their church but of those who believe in him, submit to his judgment, wait for his verdict, and find their salvation in what his grace has accomplished—and will accomplish—in them.

As Long as Jesus Is in the World, He Does Not Judge
April 24

God did not send his Son into the world to judge the world, but that the world might be saved through him.
—JOHN 3:17

When Jesus explained his commission to a rabbi, the conversation turned inevitably to the subject of how Jesus intended to reveal God's juridical verdict. This was the first act a righteous person like Nicodemus expected from the one who was able to act royally by God's commission. He would do away with those who broke the peace, perpetrated injustice in godlessness, and cast the community into confusion; and he would establish the pure community that would no longer have to suffer from the guilt of the godless people among it. The righteous person is not concerned for himself. What causes him consternation is that God still allows the godless to acquire fame and power. For this reason he considers the day of salvation to be the day that visits judgment on the godless. And for this reason he was exceedingly astonished when Jesus told him that his commission did not send him into the world as judge.

Who can still speak of God's kingdom when God's judgment is not executed? What then does he still want? He wants to save; he is supposed to save, not to judge! Does he want to save the righteous person, the teacher of Israel, as well? Yes, for he is supposed to save the world, and even the righteous person is not more than a part of the world. His life has the same form as that of all others, and his thoughts and actions are woven into the fabric of the pervasive commonality that is provided to all in this community and that assigns to them all the same destiny.

Because he belongs to the world, he, too, is an object of God's love, by which he loves the world and gives to it his Son. But he, too, needs salvation, because he cannot remove the obstacles or do away with the dangers that come with living in this world. As a citizen of this world, he is subject to the law of sin and death. He performs the will of this world rather than the will of God, and he blossoms like the flower of grass and withers away. For this reason his salvation comes through the One who came not to judge but to save.

From his commission now emerges the commission of his messengers and his church. Because they do not judge but help, they are like the fishermen who bring ashore everything caught in their net; they are also like the sower, who traverses the entire field and everywhere sows his seed. If it were their role to judge, they could not proclaim the word to everyone. To help, not to judge; to help the world, to assist all its inhabitants—that is the revelation of love that divine might conceals within itself. This love gave to Jesus, and to all who serve him, their principle of thought and action.

Only a Few Are Called
April 25

*Enter through the narrow gate! For the gate is wide and the
path broad that leads to destruction, and those who enter
through it are many. For the gate is narrow and the path
narrow that leads to life, and those who find it are few.*
—MATTHEW 7:13–14

Save the world!" These are incredibly ambitious words that we reiterate
when we proclaim what Jesus told us. Do we, as a result, conceal what really
happened? No, we part ways with Jesus not only when we limit his grand
statements as if they were fantasy but also when we are too cowardly to see
and confess what we truly are.

Few indeed follow the Savior of the world. The picture here is not of a
surging mass passing through a wide gate onto a broad road. It is rather of
individuals entering a small gate to follow a narrow walkway. Jesus refuses
to pull punches here. For he utters them in the name of God, who is the
God of all and gives the world its Savior because the world is precious to
him. And for the same reason—because he speaks in the name of God—he
makes it clear to those who follow him that they have entered a small path
through a narrow door. For God's glory in grace and judgment is revealed
not through big words but through what actually takes place.

Thus he presents his disciples with both: the riches of God, who is rich
for all, and their poverty, which can help only a few. He points to God's
omnipotent grace, which sends to the world the one who can save it, and
their inability, which makes them his useless servants. This severs their faith
from their own power and ties it to God alone.

Yet the renunciation that was required of the disciples demanded from
them a committed and unwavering resolve. Truly, it is not only people today
who sense that they are deeply rooted in their national identity. It was already
very difficult for those who joined Jesus to belong to a small minority that
their nation rejected with complete unanimity. But still, they could not
afford to waver. For the end of the road traveled by those who neglected
Jesus' call is death.

Life is brought about only by the living God. In his kingdom he creates
people who live forever. The one who is excluded from the kingdom is thus

handed over to death. Jesus even judged that the immediate future, which this generation brought upon itself through its rejection of Jesus, would be calamitous. Jerusalem's demise would result in a large number of deaths for the Jews. Because the leaders of the nation will reject him, those who rise to power will incite the nation to rebellion against the caesar and thus bring about Jerusalem's demise. Yet when Jesus pitted life and death against each other, he thought not merely of the misery that would come to the nation through war and persecution. He also thought of what would occur at the place he called by its rabbinic name, "Gehenna" (Luther: "hell"). This is the place where God's judgment excludes from his people those who will be barred from eternal life. When Jesus speaks of death, he does not merely think of the natural process that brings an end to our existence. For when he promises life, he thinks of the beginning of a new world and the establishment of the new community. If the disciple believes him, he directs his view to the same goal and bravely bears every burden, even that of seeing only a few who travel the same way, the way of life, with him.

The Number Is Small and the End Regal
April 26

Do not be afraid, little flock, because your Father
has chosen to give you the kingdom.
—Luke 12:32

Those who travel on the way that leads to life are led there by Jesus. They are the ones who have been won and acquired by him, his flock. But there are only a few, a small flock. Can they hold their own against all the powers that assail them? Not only are they assaulted by acts of violence; it is also a powerful affliction when they are reminded of their small number. This puts spiritual pressure on them. Do they keep their confidence? To be sure, no one has to fight alone. Jesus has brought them together and made them into a flock. They are strengthened and encouraged by one another. But this support is negligible. For in their own strength they cannot compete with the resources of the Jews, much less with what the world throws at them.

Is this a reason to be afraid? No! Why are they collectively Jesus' flock? How did they come to faith in him? Why was it given to them to be set apart from the great multitude in order to commence their course to eternal life, which leads through the narrow gate? This came about through God's will. It was his decree that led them to Jesus. It was not their natural way of life, not "flesh and blood," as people said then, that enabled them to recognize Jesus' kingly commission.

But the divine decree that brought them to Jesus did not merely assign to them a temporary gift but rather granted them a share in the Christ's entire work. Now they have a part in his teaching and healing ministry, in his patience and suffering. But he will act regally, and his fellowship with them remains intact even when he is able to act victoriously and gloriously. He promised them eternal life, but by this he means not merely an endless existence or an undisturbed rest or undiluted blessedness. His Father is at work, and because the Father is at work, the Son is also at work. Now he is the Word, through whom God speaks to humanity. He also is the life that brings them to life for God. And what a regal work it will be when he unites humanity in God and overcomes every hostile resistance against God! Those who have received his word and are now his flock will have a part in this work of his.

This is how he explains to them the meaning of the call that was extended to them, and thus he removes the fear from their hearts. His call provides them with a regal attitude. This attitude is not grounded in their number, nor in who they are in and of themselves. It is rather based on God's election and work, which are irreversible and indestructible and grant not merely ephemeral, earthly gifts, but take people into God's eternal fellowship.

God Shows Those
Who Are Lowly What He Does
April 27

At that time Jesus answered and said, "I praise you, Father,
Lord of heaven and earth, that you hid this from the wise and
understanding and revealed it to those who are lowly. Yes,
Father, for this was well pleasing to you."

—MATTHEW 11:25–26

The small flock was small not merely in number but also in its nature. Time and again Jesus emphatically called his disciples "little ones" and forestalled any proud hardening of their own self-perception. They must not think that they are the great, perhaps the greatest, among men. They are small, not merely because they are poor and without material possessions. They are small also in their mental abilities. If they were great, they would be wise people, but they are not. And their judgment is weak. If it were strong, they would be understanding; but they are not.

For this reason they are useless; so it is a catastrophe that Jesus reaches only these lowly individuals—or is it? No! Jesus praises God for this, and all of mankind ought to agree with him in this praise of God.

Naturally, Jesus' attitude is regularly misunderstood. Anyone who accepts as real only what is given to all of us by nature will sharply reject Jesus' words. Does he want to deny the value of our spiritual abilities? Does he elevate stupidity and pronounce intelligence sinful? Such interpretations are nothing but misunderstandings. Jesus views our natural abilities precisely the way we do. Anyone who is lowly, who cannot judge and thus cannot speak because he is inexperienced, is at a disadvantage, and the privilege belongs to those who are wise and understanding. This is precisely what leads to Jesus' jubilant prayer—that God nonetheless reveals his work to those who are lowly, while concealing it from those who are wise.

His prayer springs from his most profound concern: Man, find your place before God. Where do you place yourself? Beside God? Over God in self-centered arrogance? Then you pit yourself against God. Yet you are not your own creature and not your own master; place yourself below God. Listen when he talks to you. Obey when he commands. Receive what he gives. Submit yourself to him!

But for this reason it becomes a matter of utmost importance how God deals with those who are lowly. Can he offer a word that everyone is able to hear? Does he have a commandment that everyone can fulfill? Does he enlist those lowly persons in his service as well? Or does he reveal himself only to a privileged few, such as those whom he has equipped with a particularly religious disposition, or those who are so wealthy that they can afford to spend years acquiring wisdom at the feet of a master teacher? Or does God reveal himself only to those whose leadership abilities have been tested, so that they can be molded into an elite unit marching at the head of humanity? The arrogance of the wise severely distorts what they said about God, for they tied his grace to their own insights and accomplishments. This presumption must be destroyed and is destroyed by God's closing the ears of the wise and his opening the ears of the lowly. In this way it becomes evident that his grace is so rich and strong that it can come to all, and for this Jesus thanked his Father.

Great Things Come from Small Things
April 28

"The kingdom of heaven is like a mustard seed that a man took and sowed in his field. It is the smallest seed of all, but fully grown it is taller than all the plants in the garden and becomes a tree in whose branches the birds of the air can live." He told them another parable: *"The kingdom of heaven is like yeast that a woman took and put into three satas [1/2 bushel] of flour, until it had pervaded the entire dough."*

—MATTHEW 13:31–33

The flock that gathered around Jesus is small and made up of people of low social status. Why doesn't this bother Jesus? Why doesn't this represent an obstacle to God's work? What is small? What is large? Jesus points to natural processes in which great things happen only because small things take place. This tracing of the greatest of effects to the tiniest of causes has been demonstrated by contemporary physics and biology even more clearly than was apparent to the eyes of previous generations.

Jesus acknowledges the limited extent of the effects granted to him by comparing himself to a man who planted a mustard seed in his garden and a woman who put yeast into her dough. The overall appearance of a garden is not altered merely by a mustard seed being placed into its soil. Neither can one detect an immediate change in the dough. But something very great has occurred as a consequence of an infinitely minute event. The mustard seed turns into a large tree, and the yeast ends up pervading the entire dough.

The introductory sentence explains why these two illustrations accurately depict Jesus' ministry, why great things must take their point of departure from small things, and how small things turn into great things. What Jesus does as the one who is lonely, unknown, and controversial is rooted in God's kingdom and has its source in God's grace. From it he draws that which he gives to his small band of disciples, whose thoughts are as human as they are Jewish. In the processes used as illustrations, he refers to natural dynamics that do not rest until great results have been achieved. In the results of Jesus' dealings with the world and with his disciples, God's power is revealed. It does not require any visible manifestation.

Man thinks the success of this power depends on his understanding, his consent, and his cooperation. If so, it would be helpful for Jesus if his work were sufficiently large for all to see. But it is part of his office to destroy this delusion and honor God alone.

Yet his ministry is not diminished by a lack of numbers. God's Word is realized because it is God's Word, and his grace prevails because it is God's grace, and his Spirit is more powerful than human sinfulness and brings about the new man because he is God's Spirit. His promise provides protection and shields people against death because it is an expression of God's will. Because he is his Son, God will exalt Jesus, who is poor and can gather only a small flock. It is then that a small event will have turned into something truly great, because it is then that God's greatness and glory will have been manifested.

So when Jesus calls the disciples little people and does not permit them any form of pride because their abilities are in fact modest, this does not mean that they may consider what they have become through him to be small and insignificant. Nothing is truly great in comparison with what they have received. It is to the little flock that God has been pleased to give the kingdom.

Unable to Pray
April 29

*And it happened that, when he was praying at a certain place,
one of his disciples asked him after he was done, "Lord, teach
us how to pray, just as John also taught his disciples to pray."*

—LUKE 11:1

Strange! Here we encounter Jews who were unable to pray. Didn't they have a hall of prayer in every place, where someone regularly stepped onto the podium and recited the prayer to the congregation, after which the members of the congregation affirmed his prayer with their "Amen"? Were they not at home in the temple courts? Did they not know how people there knelt down to pray, touched the ground with their foreheads, and worshiped? Did they not know the righteous ones who prayed even on the street, undisturbed by the traffic squeezing past them, undisturbed even when a ruler passed by who must be greeted by everyone? Had Jesus' disciples not had ample opportunity to learn how to pray? But even the disciples of John did not know how to pray by themselves. They chose to get baptized and were prepared to fast—but pray? This they could not do unless John taught them.

But no! This is not strange. Everyone who is a part of the church experiences in himself and sees in others this inability to pray. Jesus' disciples saw that he knew how to pray, and this awakened in them the desire to learn how to pray as well. Hence the request "Teach us how to pray"—give us a word that provides us with a clear and strong resolve with which we can turn to God and to which we may hold fast when we stand in God's light. Indeed, this is no small gift. It is a gift for which we must ask.

Why had Jesus not given them this gift until now? The disciples thought it strange that he had not taught them how to pray a long time ago. But prayer cannot be compared to a foreign body that is injected into us. There must be room in us for prayer, and Jesus made room in his disciples by setting them free from the overwhelming power of their own desires, which arises from the natural sphere of our lives and entirely consumes our souls, and by revealing God to them in such a way that they believed in his grace, which gave them access to God. This made room in them for prayer. Through this they knew when they were facing a crisis or danger and which obstacles they had to protect themselves against by way of prayer. Through this they saw what they needed for redemption and what they could find only in God. For now they realized what God's intention was for them, which is why now they could pray and receive what they had requested from God.

Jesus' disciples' request for Jesus to teach them how to pray was not in vain. He taught his church how to pray. He gave his followers a word that constrained their desires in such a way that these desires could be the subject of a prayer through which his followers became one with the will of God. When we become one with the will of God, we are also united with one another. For this reason the early church was right in making Jesus' prayer a model by which we indicate that we belong to the church, whose founder and Lord is Jesus.

The Prayer God Desires
April 30

The hour will come, and is now here, when the true worshipers will worship the Father in Spirit and in truth.
—John 4:23

God is looking for worshipers! If the ultimate thing that we can say about God was not that God is love, this statement would remain utterly mysterious. Is it not insulting to God's divinity to say that God is looking for people who will worship him? But the truth that love is the nature and glory of God illumines this statement of Jesus regarding God. God's love sends his Word to us and addresses us. Is it only he who wants to speak? When he speaks to us, he wants us to speak as well. A word without a response is not a perfect gift.

We are supposed to speak to him, but about whom? About ourselves? Yes! About ourselves, about our childish little concerns and about our hurts, about everything that is so important to us because it stirs our longings. But not only about this but also about our work, on which our salvation depends. God, too, speaks to us about us. He talks to people about their godlessness, their fear of death, and the ministry they must carry out in God's world. His Word indicates to us what we ought to do and what we ought not to do. Yet his Word does not speak to us about ourselves but allows us to understand his will and reveals to us his grace. Through this we learn that we should talk to God not merely about ourselves but also about him.

But whoever talks to God about the things of God, worships. Now God is looking for worshipers who will worship him in Spirit and in truth. Apart from the Spirit, our prayer remains the child of our own desires, which intermingles its dreams into our prayers and also clothes God in the garb of our wishes. Without the Spirit, the storyteller prays, fashioning for himself a world of his own making and dreaming up for himself a world that consists of nothing but figments of his own imagination. This is not what God desires. We cannot worship him with what is foreign and repugnant to his nature or with what we fabricate ourselves.

Yet God is well pleased with all that he gives us. He is well pleased with whatever he introduces into our lives, and this is what transforms our adoration into worship of God. Because we can serve him only with the ability we have received from him, we are able to pray in a God-honoring way only because his gracious gifts are in us. The Spirit and the truth are his gracious gifts. We are "flesh"; that is, we are steeped in nature and thus good for nothing other than what suits our egos. If anything turns our thoughts or desires toward God, this comes from God, constitutes a gracious gift, and is induced by the Spirit. And in this way our eyes are opened so that we can perceive what God signifies for us and what we as humans are before him. Thus we are given the ability to pray in such a way that we fulfill what God requires of us, and the love that spoke to us through his Word now finds in us a response that truly honors God.

God Works in Secret
May 1

And when you pray, do not be like the hypocrites.
For they love to stand and pray in the halls of prayer and
at street corners to display their spirituality before others.
I tell you, they have their reward. But when you pray, go into
your room, lock the door, and pray to your Father, who is
in the secret places; and your Father, who sees what is
in the secret places, will reward you.
—MATTHEW 6:5–6

It takes two people to have a conversation. This seems to contradict the notion of prayer, because it looks as if it is nothing more than a conversation with ourselves. Therefore, those whose perspective is no larger than the world should not be faulted if they find prayer unreasonable; for indeed, the human eye can perceive only one person at prayer. But because Jesus said that the other Person whom we address in prayer is also there, in the secret place where we address him, he prayed and taught us how to pray.

What conceals God from us? His work makes him invisible to us. Nature is the work of his creative powers, and yet it conceals God from us. Because everything holds securely together in it, we find no place for God's activity in what nature reveals to us about itself.

At the same time it is our own sense of sight that conceals God from us, even though it is one of the most wonderful of God's gifts and well worth marveling at every morning when we once again open our eyes. But all that comes to us through our visual perception is the awareness of what takes place in us; yet this is by no means all that exists and takes place. The more our observations penetrate nature, the more astonishing and far-reaching becomes the mystery of its infinity. Our consciousness grasps only a small portion even of what we are and of what takes place in us.

Within the scope of our inner lives, it is particularly the divine activity that we do not see. Whether we look outside or within, it takes place in secret. But it is nonetheless real, powerful, and decisive. Everything that happens depends on it. Everything comes into being through it. Everyone who wants to live must long for it. And this is why we pray.

To be sure, our prayer would remain nothing but blind intuition, carried along by our wildest speculations, if humanity had not been given the Word through which the One who operates in secret speaks to us. But now that we have heard the call of God that brings us into a relationship with him, we have understood with certainty that he is with us in such a way that we can speak with him. This is why it is Jesus alone—the Word of God spoken to us—who can make praying people out of us.

It takes two to have a conversation, not three. In a true prayer we stand before God and not before a third person as well, to whom we display our piety in our prayer. If the third person is able to pray with us, we ought to welcome him. Whatever we do in community is strengthened by it. But prayer is not a means to increase one's reputation with others. This would be a misuse of prayer, thoroughly distorting it. The purpose of prayer is that we might worship God. But only what we do for God's sake constitutes worship of God.

There Is Such a Thing as Sinful Prayer
May 2

Those who devour widows' houses and show off by their lengthy prayers will be judged more severely.
—Mark 12:40

For the crafty businessman in Jerusalem, the house of a widow was a prey that he was unlikely to pass up. The widow lacked male protection, and she found it hard to make a living. If it was not possible for her to avoid going into debt, the occasion arose to seize her property, and a person could purchase her house. Jesus did not deny the success of the buyer. He acknowledged freely that he "gulped the house down." But he said this with considerable indignation. For this businessman is at the same time one who prays and is known by everyone as such. He is known to spend many hours in prayer. The outcome for him is that his judgment will be particularly severe.

Jesus thus told the Jews that their teaching, their "Talmud," was the cause of their demise. Didn't the one whom Jesus described in such terms know God's law? After all, he was one who prayed and thus confessed the Law.

The Law made the Jews into the holy nation called to worship God. But this protects others against all injustice and enhances this protection even more for the defenseless. Widows were placed under God's particular protection. The person who prays knows this, and he knows better than to dispute it. How, then, can he still crave the widow's house? It was clear that the Law forbade any harshness toward widows. But the Law by itself is not sufficient for one to learn how to act. The Law requires interpretation, and the teachers of the Law accomplished this by becoming lawgivers themselves who stipulated through the most numerous statutes possible how the Law ought to be applied to every conceivable case. Was there, then, a regulation for the present instance that incited the greed of the person who prayed? If one such prohibition existed, then, of course, such a transaction was forbidden. But if such a regulation that applied specifically to such a case did not exist, then nothing kept him from satisfying his greed. Now it is never possible to weave the kind of net of regulations that is able to deny sinful desires every opportunity to be acted on. To the contrary, the vast number of regulations stirred the desire to take the opportunity to escape detection. To be sure, the Law protected widows, but not this widow in this particular instance, since it was permissible to take her house from her.

And when the conscience nonetheless was stirred, what then was the purpose of the Jews' prayers? Was prayer not the highly esteemed means of placating God? Whoever venerates God and wins him over with his prayer enters boldly and freely into transactions with other people and takes from them whatever he desires. In this way prayer imparts guilt to the person who prays, and the Law becomes the downfall of its teachers and their students. This is how Jesus showed the Jews the danger to which they had succumbed.

Section 9

JESUS BRINGS PURITY

Human Traditions Are in Conflict with the Divine Commandment
May 3

Then Pharisees and scribes from Jerusalem approached Jesus and said, "Why do your disciples transgress the tradition of the elders? For they do not wash their hands when they eat bread." But he answered them, "And why do you transgress God's commandment for the sake of your tradition? For God said, 'Honor your father and your mother' and 'Whoever shows contempt toward his father or his mother shall die.' But you say, 'Whoever says to his father or mother, "Whatever I could give you is set aside for a sacrifice," does not have to honor his father or mother.' So you have invalidated the word of God for the sake of your tradition."

—Matthew 15:1–6 (cf. Ex. 20:12; 21:17)

We have a mediator with God," the Jewish establishment claimed. What does a mediator with God do? He is the one who proclaims his will, testifies to his omnipresent government, gives his salvific gifts, and carries out his judgment. "The Law," the Jews said, "does all of this to us. It is our master." And in order that the Law might control everyone at every step and not permit anyone to deviate from it, the rulers surrounded the people with their system of regulations. These regulations were justified by the reputation the patriarchs had earned. Their conduct was presented as exemplary for all. Thus the prevailing customs were declared unchangeable and every deviation was regarded as sinful.

When Jesus replaced the Law as the new mediator with God, a new path had to be forged with regard to these regulations. Together with these regulations, the rule over the community of all ages was assigned to the elders, a rule that was incompatible with the rule of God. The question of what constituted God's will was replaced by another: how the elders acted in this particular case. Man made himself the guide (*Führer*) of others and bound them to his own practice. Many of the things prescribed by these regulations made sense and could be commended without reservation. One case in point is the regulation that became the bone of contention between Jesus and the representatives of tradition. This regulation stipulated the washing of hands before a meal, because it entailed the giving of thanks, and only clean hands were supposed to be lifted up at prayer. In the case of this regulation, Jesus' disagreement was directed not at what the regulation stipulated but at its claim to obligate everyone and at the argument that every transgression of this regulation constituted sin.

Such regulations had to be opposed because many went counter to the will of God, which is inevitable when man makes himself the lawgiver and relies upon his own reasoning ability and upon his own logical deductions.

As an example of the conflict that had arisen between tradition and the divine law, Jesus cited the regulation that regarded the formula "Sacrifice, Corban" to be inviolable without exception. What was assigned to God by virtue of this formula was considered to be taboo for any human use. But what happened when a son called what he must give to his father a "sacrifice"? The Pharisees claimed that in this case the decision was crystal clear. The choice between honoring God and honoring one's father was an easy one. Honoring one's father was sin when it involved dishonoring God. Never, not even in order to support one's father, must there be an instance where God is robbed. Jesus referred to this regulation—which appealed to the sanctity of the sacrifice as the means of depriving one's father of the support due him—as the setting aside of the divine commandment. Here, honoring God did not avoid evil but actually made evil one's duty.

Jesus' attack on these regulations takes its point of departure from the same place as his opposition to the statutes that stipulated the Sabbath rest. These statutes monitored only visible acts. They paid no attention to underlying motives. Evil had free reign. God's grace, in whose service Jesus stood even when he did battle, is interested in the person, not in his gifts. This put an end to the kind of evil that becomes entirely reprehensible when it seeks to legitimate a practice by appealing to God's commandment.

Tradition Separates People from Jesus
May 4

They produced false witnesses who claimed, "This man never
ceases to speak out against the holy place and against the Law.
For we heard him say, 'This Jesus the Nazarene will remove
this place and change the customs Moses handed down to us.'"

—Acts 6:13–14

Everything Jesus did stood under the shadow of the cross. By refusing to be set free from regulations, the Jewish establishment never truly renounced sinful desires. They never achieved a faith that was truly directed toward God. They never entered into a relationship with Jesus by which he became the Lord of those who believed in him. He could not share his authority with that of the elders. Yet their statutes continued to intervene in everyone's life. They provided people with the standard according to which they acted. They were the means of their righteousness and pride. No one was allowed to take the Jew's statutes away from him. Thus Jesus was rejected by the Jewish establishment, and his disciples were unable to be integrated into the Jewish community in any way.

Now the disciples affirmed the sanctity of the Law just as earnestly as the Pharisees did. Likewise, they accorded the Scriptures the same believing veneration as the Pharisees. Yet none of this sufficed to gain the Pharisees' approval. For in their view what must regulate people's actions was not the Law and the Scriptures but rather the regulations interpreting them. This became apparent immediately after the formation of the Christian community in Jerusalem. One of its leaders, Stephen, carried the message about Jesus to the halls of prayer where Greek-speaking Jews gathered. And because they asked him what the community would be like once it had received its perfect form through Christ's presence, he told them that, according to the Lord's word, the temple and the customs handed down from Moses would be no more; Christ's rule would put an end to them. For this reason the Greek-speaking Jews demanded from the Sanhedrin that Stephen be stoned, and the entire Council concurred. To them it appeared as if nothing would remain of Judaism once the temple and the regulations were taken away. Yet Stephen had never disputed that the temple had been built in obedience to God's commandment and that God's word had come to them through the Law. Christian freedom *from* the Law never resulted in a wholesale rejection *of* the Law.

But the old word of God had accomplished what it was designed to accomplish by the time the new word of God made its appearance. And the Law was no longer needed to mediate between the community and God, because the Christ was its mediator with God. Regulations were no longer the power that enslaved all, because those who received the word from the Christ also were given by him their own faith and their own love. And only *now*—after the regulations have been overcome—is a veneration of God possible that worships him in Spirit and truth; only *now* can there be a ministry that carries out his will. Yet this now takes place at a new location, no longer in the area fenced in by the Jewish establishment's regulations.

Are There Christian Rabbinic Regulations?
May 5

*Some have turned to empty chatter, because they like to think
of themselves as teachers of the Law.*
—1 TIMOTHY 1:6–7

In speaking out against the rabbinic regulations, Jesus came into conflict with the entire world. How can any community come into existence and prosper if it does not produce a system of law that is binding for all? And will it not necessarily strive to perfect its law through a system of regulations? Jerusalem's scholars, who since Ezra had been led to study the Law to develop such a system, maintained that the people were not helped by regulations that soared above real-life situations. The only one who can compel obedience is the one who clearly and authoritatively adjudicates a particular case. In the Roman Empire, likewise, the law that assured the empire's unity had developed into a system of regulations and a jurisprudence that refined these regulations further and further. Soon after the apostolic period, a holy law arose in the church by which the church bound together those who pledged allegiance to it. Who then proved victorious in the battle over regulations: the Jews or Jesus?

Jesus freed his disciples' conscience from arbitrary human regulations and instituted a community of love, which came into being out of a pure heart, a clear conscience, and genuine faith. Thus, Jewish regulations disappeared from their congregations. Their Jewish members were free to observe them, but they lost their value even for them, since they could not retain their full national identity. As for those Greeks who believed in Jesus, Paul told them not to adopt Jewish regulations.

For this reason new customs were needed that could provide the foundation for a common conduct in Greek-speaking congregations. Was this sufficient? Paul's opponents said, "No! We need legislation. How can the community's unity be achieved unless everyone is obligated by way of a clear regulation that states what the community requires of him? And how can purity be safeguarded unless valid regulations stipulate for everyone what is forbidden in the church?" In this way they presented themselves to the church as teachers of the Law.

Paul contradicted them, because they crowded out both the old and the new word of God with their regulations. Their human traditions obscure the majesty of the divine law, which reveals to people the reprehensible nature of their desires and which renders sin culpable. These new regulations were no less harmful to comprehending God's good news. For this message does not consist in God's stipulating articles of conduct but in his giving us grace to hear what Christ says and to do what he has commanded.

For this reason no one is placed above another as lawgiver in the church, but everyone is placed before God so that he may believe in him and thus be united with all those who likewise have received the same word. This makes the community established by Jesus something other than a collection of individuals who must be kept together by the compulsion of jurisprudence and legislation—for its Lord is Christ, who has united its members with him and with one another so that they may serve God in unity in keeping with his Word.

What Nature Brings Forth Is Pure
May 6

"It is not what enters through the mouth that corrupts a person; what comes out of his mouth is what corrupts a person." But Peter answered and said to him, "Explain this illustration to us." And he said,

JESUS BRINGS PURITY

"Do you fail to understand this as well? Don't you realize that whatever enters through the mouth goes into the stomach and then is digested? But the things that come out of the mouth proceed from the heart, and this is what corrupts a person. For from the heart proceed evil thoughts, murder, adultery, sexual immorality, theft, false witness, and blasphemy. That is what corrupts a person. But to eat without washing one's hands—that does not corrupt a person."
—MATTHEW 15:11, 15–20

According to Scripture, there were righteous people and unrighteous people. But according to the same Scripture, there were also pure people and impure people, and this contrast did not coincide precisely with the former one. For righteousness and guilt arise through a person's conduct. Impurity, on the other hand, is imposed upon him from the outside, because there are impure objects that defile a person and because the defiled person defiles yet others through contact with them.

So, then, did impurity remain after Jesus extended forgiveness? Yes! There are impure things in a person, and there are impure people, who have been defiled by impure things in their hearts and have been excluded from fellowship with God and others. But impurity is not simply a matter of prohibitions against impure things exposing people as impure. Impurity is not a function of natural processes, entering a person through the mouth or attaching to his skin. The place where impurity arises is "the heart." It arises where our thoughts and desires have their source, and it becomes evident through the words uttered by our mouths. Because of this impurity, which originates and is preserved in the heart, one person becomes a danger to another, for he transfers his impurity through his words.

How the pure is to be distinguished from the impure cannot remain a mystery for anyone who is serious about God's law. As always, Jesus referred his disciples on that occasion to the second half of the Ten Commandments. There are not, then, two different series of events by which a person becomes guilty before God—what is sinful in addition to what is impure—but what is sinful *is* what is impure. Hence, people do not need two separate avenues to obtain God's grace: one remedy against guilt and another against impurity. By removing the dilemma that renders them evil, the source of their impurity is taken away, too.

Jesus' recasting the people's entire religious conduct and cultic apparatus had immeasurable consequences. How can anyone act in a believing manner toward God when he must always fear that he is impure before God? And how can true fellowship between people be established when one person is to avoid another as impure? As long as the verdict "unclean" remained on the Gentiles, it was inconceivable that Jesus' message could be carried beyond the boundaries of Judaism. The prerequisite for this liberating act, which freed the disciples of concern in their dealings with nature in all of its processes, was the removal of certain regulations; the prerequisite for this, in turn, was elevation beyond the Law, which took place as "grace and truth came through Jesus Christ."

Jesus Calls the Pure in Heart
May 7

Blessed are the pure in heart, for they will see God.
—Matthew 5:8

If there is a heavenly kingdom, there is also a community God regards as "pure." For through the heavenly kingdom, God is revealed to man and his glory can be perceived by him. When Jesus told his disciples who the recipients of his saving mission were, God's presence and glory came into their view, because he himself was with them. And when he is glorified, they will be able to see God in a new way. However his ministry is revealed within the scope of God's kingdom, it is certain that the value of all experiences that bring us grace consists in that they reveal to us God's effective will. If our view is not turned upward, to God, we have not experienced grace. Everything that, owing to the promise, is an object of our hope is comprised by the one phrase "revelation of God."

Yet when Jesus asked the community regarding who would see God, they responded with one voice and without hesitation: Those who were pure—only the pure. No one who was impure or common would see God, no one who is defiled. This was instilled into everyone who wanted to enter the temple; no one was allowed access to the inner court unless he had purified himself through a ritual washing, and Jesus agrees. He promises God's presence to those who are pure. In the parable of the wedding feast, he says that only the person who wears a festive robe will take part in God's feast.

But now Jesus departs from legal regulations and from the purification rites they stipulated for the people. His call to salvation was issued to those who are pure *in heart*. They are graced with God's presence, and it is to them that his glory will be revealed. He was not concerned with what nature brought to a person. It cannot disqualify anyone from contact with God; it rather mediates God's activity to him. In contrast, there is much in a person's heart that defiles him and renders him incapable of belonging to the community that is set apart for God. If self-centeredness grows, it fills the heart with terrible things—with lustful pictures that arise from desires for women, with sinister plans in which hate delights. Blessed are those who know nothing of this, which distorts their faces into a grimace and poisons their hearts. Jesus unites himself with them and will lead them where the pure ones are headed—where they feel the touch of God's hand and where they see him at work.

But will he find anyone who has not merely been baptized many times but has become pure in heart? His promise would have been the idealistic dream of a child who does not know people and has not yet experienced the world, had it not been given to him by omnipotent grace. For this reason he does not inquire how it comes about that their hearts shut out that which defiles. Perhaps it was the Old Testament word and the grace at work in the old covenant that guarded them; perhaps it was their contact with him and the forgiveness they received from him that freed them from what defiles. One thing is certain: if they are pure, then they belong to him and will stand with him where God is revealed.

God Also Created What Is Within Man
May 8

Now as he spoke, a Pharisee asked him to join him for lunch. He entered his house and reclined for the meal. Yet the Pharisee saw this and wondered why he had not washed prior to the meal. And the Lord said to him, "You Pharisees! You clean the outside of the cup and the bowl, but inside you are full of robbery and malice. You fools! Did not the Creator of what is

outside also create what is inside? But give what is within as
alms, and everything will be clean for you.”
—LUKE 11:37–41

With whom is Jesus allowed to have table fellowship? If he extends it to the outcast, the righteous object and ostracize him. If he grants it to the righteous, they still object and are offended. For when they observe their Sabbath meal, they want to be a pure fellowship, which is why they washed themselves prior to the meal, as the regulation commanded. Jesus, for his part, does not concede that he is unclean and does not submit to the regulation, and when he now explains to them why their washings are useless, he deprives them of a great deal of their righteousness, and the joint, festive meal is turned into combat.

Where does impurity come from? It comes to people, they suppose, from the outside. At a meal it attaches to a person when the cup or the bowl is unclean, and the cup is unclean when it spills over and its outside becomes wet. Now it requires continual alertness and ceaseless effort to avoid impurity. But is this fine art ever crowned with success? It only takes care of the outside, but what use is it for a person to clean the outside of a cup when he is impure on the inside? If he is impure in his heart because his desires render him unclean, then what is put into his cups and bowls is likewise not clean. Then greed and malice have a part in what the righteous possess and in what motivates them to observe their Sabbath meal. But when impure desires, which render their hearts impure, produce what fills cups and bowls, all of their external washing is pointless.

Why is it folly to ensure the purity of the outside while evil renders the inside ugly? Did God only create the outside? Is not the inside his work as well? Did Jesus say anything new that surprised the righteous? Yes, he did! This pronouncement clashes hard with their views—and not merely with the views of the Jews. Once again, Jesus does battle with the whole world’s way of thinking. To be sure, no one thinks he has given life to himself by the same wonderful ability with which the heart does its work. Nevertheless, the righteous person considers what is inside to be the realm over which he has control. This is why he is arrogant. He is unaware of God’s work and gift in this area. Here he obeys the dictates of his desires and carelessly defiles what God has made without realizing that he has thus compromised purity despite his washings. But because God made not merely the outside but also the inside, there are those who are pure in heart, and it is they whom Jesus takes unto himself and leads into God's kingdom.

All Are Sinners; No One Is Unclean
May 9

God showed me that I should not call any man unholy or unclean.
—Acts 10:28

This was the conviction created by Jesus in his disciples: they considered everyone sinful and no one unclean. Both facts were prerequisites for Jesus' aim of uniting humanity in God. There is no one righteous before God, and there is no one who is despised by God as unclean.

This unites Jesus' messengers with all people. If we are divided into clean and unclean, there is no fellowship between us, for then we have become untouchable for one another. For the verdict "You are unclean and unholy" pertains to the nature and state of a man. How can these be changed? The verdict "You are sinful," on the other hand, is directed toward what a man desires and does, and this is what can be changed and cured. "You are unclean" is a statement made by pride, which elevates itself above the other person; beside it there is no room for love. "You are sinful" is a statement made by the truth that heeds God's law and honors God's verdict; and where truth is, love joins in as well. Whoever says, "You are unclean," turns away from the other person and departs, and the one to whom this is addressed refuses to listen and defends himself. For the one who condemns him this way is his enemy. The verdict "You are guilty," on the other hand, entails the corollary judgment "We are guilty." It is not enmity that arises here but fellowship, which internally unites the one who pronounces the judgment with the one who is guilty. He either confirms the sanctity of the divine law to the guilty person by hardening himself to it, or he liberates him from his guilt in the authority of divine grace. They are united with one another for the sake of love.

This was Jesus' perspective; his dealings with his people and his fellowship with his disciples followed this rule. Peter had not found his way to this liberty through his own insight. "God revealed this to me," he claimed. Previously, he had taken care that nothing unclean might enter his mouth, whereby every Gentile home was closed to him. Now God warned him in a vision, "Do not consider unclean what God has made clean." Without Jesus' help there was no advancement beyond the Law for his disciples. When Jesus took away the power to defile from all that entered man from the outside, Peter recoiled from the wrath that Jesus had evoked from the Jewish teachers. Jesus thereby liberated him entirely from his dependence on the rabbinate. But was it merely the rabbinate that erected the boundary between clean and unclean things and between pure and impure people? Was the rabbinate not obeying the injunction of the Law by doing this? Peter must no longer measure God's verdict regarding man by Jewish regulations. He now is subject to the law of God's kingdom, according to which there are people whom Peter considers unclean, but whom God in his royal grace has made clean.

Truth Purifies the Soul
May 10

You have purified your souls through obedience to the truth.
—1 Peter 1:22

What did those who believed Jesus' messengers in Asia Minor gain from their knowledge of Jesus? They expelled from their souls that which was impure, their profane thoughts and polluting passions. Is that not incredible? That which is impure disappeared from their souls—not merely from their conduct, not merely from their words, not only when they participate in the community's celebration and their high spirits draw them away from what they find in themselves—no! Their souls, into which the world carries its image through the wondrous vehicle of the senses, which are set into perennial motion through the push exerted upon them through the world, and which are filled up with wishes and intentions—their souls are what they purified.

Through this, many things have changed in them. Their previous view about nature was profane and made them impure. They might have learned from a philosopher that they were a heap of small, whirring bodies. When we do not look through nature to its Creator, we are deaf to its miracles, and the beast tempts us to become like it; in our attempt to exploit nature for ourselves, we become its slaves. If our greed and thirst for power control how we view others, they, too, are rendered impure figures whom we shamelessly exploit, and thus we become impure ourselves. Even our picture of ourselves, when painted by our pride, renders our soul impure.

Is there any safeguard against this? The truth guards us against what is impure, and it does so when we heed and fulfill its claim to obedience. When we stop resisting the truth, the result is a pure soul, chaste thinking, sensible judgment, clean speech, and praiseworthy deeds. Whoever has obeyed the truth does not separate natural processes from the divine power that produces them, and he thereby is made clean. Now such a person can praise God with his body and in his earthly occupation, and his use of natural energies issues in thanksgiving that praises God for his goodness.

In his dealings with others, too, which provide him with an active, suffering share in human history, he perceives God's sovereign providence and no longer regards people as impure. Whether they stand in the service of divine wrath or divine grace, he honors every person whom God has given life.

And even when he looks at himself, the divine Word that judges and pardons him is with him and does not allow him to vacillate between self-contempt and self-deification. His admission of his own sinfulness is no longer a sentimental remorse that renders him impure but an acknowledgment of the truth of God's righteousness and grace. And his enjoyment of his job and his work is no longer the noisy clanging of a dreamer who inflates himself with lies but the worship of God, from whom he received the mandate and the energy to do his work. Our tales and lies render us impure; the nobility we are able to arrive at comes from obeying the truth.

The Free Person Can Enjoy or Abstain
May 11

I know and am certain in the Lord that nothing is impure in itself. It is impure only for the one who believes it to be so. Everything is pure, but it becomes impure for the one who eats and causes offense by it.
—ROMANS 14:14, 20

Good! It is a wonderful message that impure animals and things that are dead or sick do not render us impure. But what about the unclean spirits? Don't the things that proceed from them have the power of rendering us impure? For those who lived in a pagan environment as servants of the one God, the question *How do we avoid uncleanness?* took on a greater sense of urgency. Religions had created not merely human legends but also dark powers that controlled everyone around them and subjected them to demonic forces. Were not the things that had been dedicated to them—meat consecrated to them, wine poured out for them, a house set apart for them, priests dedicated to them, images depicting them—impure and strong enough to render people impure?

Even in the ancient world where impure spirits enslaved people, Paul upheld Jesus' statement that nothing that enters through our mouths renders us impure. At the same time, he conceded that only the person who possessed strong faith could act accordingly. The strength of his faith must reveal itself in that he does not plunge into doubt and in that his conscience is not divided in his judgment regarding pagan objects. For anyone who considers his food impure and eats it despite his scruples and the warnings of his conscience, such food is in fact unclean; and since he is defiled by it, he sins. Only the one who trusts Christ's presence to protect him from everything demonic can eat what comes from a pagan temple without fear or doubt. And because he acts as a believer, he does not sin but honors Christ's grace and submits to him as his Lord. But whatever takes place for his glory and with thanksgiving does not defile.

But is this strong faith attainable by everyone? Paul was not surprised that there were people in his congregations who meticulously avoided sacrificial meat because they were afraid of any contact with the demonic. He concluded that they were lacking in strength, but he did not consider their faith to be inferior to his own. He did not doubt that they were Christians. Just as there is nothing in nature the use of which renders us impure and separates us from God, so there is nothing in nature the use of which renders us holy and unites us with God. If such things existed, it would be our Christian duty to make use of them, and it would be an act of unbelief to refuse them. But now the one whom Christ has reached stands in the world as a free person—free to use and free to abstain—and this freedom is neither arbitrariness nor lawlessness. For whether he partakes or abstains, his conduct is motivated by his faith in Christ.

Faith Purifies
May 12

*God does not distinguish between us (Jewish Christians)
and them (the Gentiles), because he purified
their hearts through faith.*
—Acts 15:9

The pure in heart will see God. Did Peter remain obedient to this maxim from Jesus when he baptized a Roman official and his servants and friends? By baptizing them he acknowledged that they received what Jesus had promised. But what was pure in these people? Their private lives and their public service were subject to their natural desires, and when they slipped in their thoughts or actions, they were even more severely defiled. What about them was *not* profane? What part of them, when exposed by God's light, was *not* put to shame?

Human assistance is insufficient to bring about change here. Peter did not think he had a way of rendering these unclean people clean, as if he could have "de-sinned" them by baptizing them, purified their thoughts through his teaching, or ennobled their desires by his own example. Even less can a pagan person invent a process by which he is able to remove his own uncleanness. The pagan depended entirely on God's favor and God's work, and God did what man could not do and purified the heart of the pagan.

Was it different with the Jews? They rejoiced in Jesus' promise that the pure in heart would enjoy God's presence. But like pagans, they were unable to purify themselves. God is the one who purified Peter and the brethren once and for all.

Why is there something clean in them that is able to purify them? God has given them faith through his Word. A person who believes in God is not impure. He is impure as long as all he can say is *I*. If he says to God, "You—I trust you," he is no longer an impure person. If faith were his own work, it would be unable to purify him. But now it is received through God's Word coming to the person and subordinating him to it. This makes faith God's gracious gift, and thus it is pure and purifying. Now what is motivated by it is not sin.

Does this mean that all of the believer's thoughts are now pure insight and undiluted knowledge? It is readily apparent that they are the thoughts of an immature person. Or is that person promised that his actions, because they are motivated by love, are nothing but pure love and good deeds, no longer lessened by selfishness? Rather, his experience will frequently show that his conduct is negatively affected by much blind self-interest, which bothers and afflicts others.

Nevertheless, the heart is pure; for faith is now the root from which the thoughts and desires of the heart grow, and God has planted this root in the heart. His heart has received its ultimate impetus from God. For this reason faith creates a relational bond able to surmount the obstacles separating us. Our thoughts and accomplishments are of varying merit, but none of these is impure. What is pure is what takes place in faith, for faith is the gift of God.

Either Everything Is Pure, or Everything Is Impure
May 13

For the pure, everything is pure; but for those who are defiled and unbelieving, nothing is pure, but both their reason and their conscience are defiled.

—Titus 1:15

The clearer one's understanding of God's grace becomes, the heavier is the weight of the verdict that calls our desires reprehensible. Beside the statement that for the pure there is nothing impure stands the statement that has equal validity: for those who are defiled and unbelieving, there is nothing pure—there is nothing that can make them holy, nothing that is not corrupt. For everything they say and do is impure, and everything they draw into their sphere becomes contaminated.

Is there a marriage that does not lessen the honor of a man or woman? Is there a kind of wealth that does not defile, and a kind of poverty that does not bring shame? Is there any participation in governmental authority that does not distort by vain pride the one who serves? Is there any form of subservience or obedience that can be exercised with dignity? Yes, all this is possible for the one who is pure. But who is pure? According to Jesus' messengers, it is God who purifies our hearts through faith.

This is why purity exists for them even where impurity is particularly defiling: pure searching that penetrates into nature, pure gazing that directs one's view toward God's work, pure praying that does not usurp God's sovereignty, pure mercy that is not intermingled with arrogance, a pure pastoral office that is undefiled by the lust for power. Now God is honored by the spirit and body, and love can use everything in order to accomplish its work.

If, on the other hand, one's heart lacks the purity it receives through faith, imperfections surface in one's ability to think and in one's conscience. The former is characterized by ugly, dark figures; the latter by restlessness, self-accusations, and a dulling of one's ethical judgment. And when impurity has taken control of a person, how can the things he touches remain pure? He transfers his impurity to everything he says and does. He transfers his own image to everyone with whom he comes into contact, and he decreases the value of all things by the way in which he deals with them.

Paul told this to those who sought to make the church a community of pure people by way of legislation and who thus used the same method as the rabbis. Like them, they purified the outside while the inside remained impure. Physical actions were subjected to strict discipline, and religious gestures were covered by rules and regulations by claiming that this legislation was binding for the entire church. But in all these efforts they remained captive to the principle that nothing is pure for the one who is impure in himself. As long as he is incapable of acting from faith and worships according to his own ideas, as long he wants to set himself free from evil by his own power and makes his own perfection his life's aspiration—as long as he does any of these things, he remains impure. We may be able to come up with methods of sanctification for these kinds of purposes, but we do not thereby deal with the evil inside. But God can remedy this, and he does so by purifying our hearts through faith.

Honor for Everyone!
May 14

Honor everyone; love the brotherhood!
—1 Peter 2:17

A prohibition by itself is useless. We are helped only when it is coupled with the positive commandment that tells us what we must do. "Don't consider anyone impure; don't despise anyone"—how does one do that? "Honor everyone"—this is how the prohibition is observed.

But is every person worthy of honor? If we wanted to honor even those who are unworthy of honor, the result would be the kind of politeness that masks our contempt for others behind the facade of our friendly words. But Jesus places us in the light and obligates us to tell the truth. The admonition *Honor everyone* does not tell us to examine everyone to see whether and (if so) to what extent he is deserving of honor. This would be to rebel against the maxim under which Jesus subsumed all of our dealings with others, namely, that we were not appointed as judges of others. If we wanted to examine everyone to see who is deserving of honor, everyone would make himself judge over everyone else, and thus we would get entangled in a matter that would destroy any possibility of fellowship.

Hence a condition must prevail in which it is unequivocally clear that we must give honor to everyone both willingly and sincerely. This condition does not come about through what man does but through a person's submitting himself to God's rule and plan in everything he is and undertakes. Wherever our lives may lead us, they will never lead us away from the sphere of God's activity. We are confronted with it in every person and in every destiny, and this is the reason everyone is deserving of honor. As long as one partakes of life, he has a share in the divine benefits and together with us enjoys God's gifts, which are mediated to us through nature. How could we fail to honor a fellow recipient of God's gifts?

Yet we would still miss out on the very best if we merely stood in the kind of fellowship that we have by virtue of our creatureliness and that renders everyone worthy of everyone else's honor. Our fellowship is dignified by something even greater than honor: love. Honor keeps us from hating one another or from treating one another in a hostile manner. It respects the other person as he is and acknowledges his rights. It does not, however, unite us. To the contrary, it keeps a distance and stresses that the other person is different from us and therefore must be protected in his individuality. In this way every type of relationship is different from that of brotherhood. Brotherhood gives us the same goal and the same obligation, confronts us with the same dangers and places us in the same struggle, and makes the will of the Father, through whom we have become a brotherhood, our common desire. Yet this special relationship does not remove the common bond we have with all and does not prevent us from esteeming in everyone what God has given them. For the same God and Father has given us natural life and made us his children through his Word.

When Do We Enjoy Our Possessions the Most?
May 15

All the tax collectors and sinners came to him to listen to him. But the Pharisees and scribes complained vigorously and said, "He welcomes sinners and eats with them." But he told them this parable: "Who among you, if he has a hundred sheep and loses one of them, will not leave the ninety-nine in the desert and go after the lost one until he finds it? And when he finds it, he puts it over his shoulder and rejoices. When he has come into his house, he calls his friends and neighbors and tells them, 'Rejoice with me! For I have found my sheep, which was lost.' I tell you, this is how much joy there will be in heaven over a single sinner who repents — more than over ninety-nine righteous persons who do not need to repent.
Or which woman, if she has ten drachmas and loses one of them, will not light her lamp, sweep her house, and diligently look for it until she has found it? And when she has found it, she calls her friends and neighbors and says, 'Rejoice with me! For I have found the drachma I had lost.' I tell you, this is how the angels of God rejoice over a single sinner who repents."
—Luke 15:1–10

Jesus stood joyfully before those who complained about him and who pitied him. They considered his dealings with sinners and outcasts to be a great calamity—for him, because he commits sin; for his disciples, because he leads them into sin; for the people, because he confuses them by challenging the validity of the Law. But what causes them anxiety and annoys them is reason for Jesus to rejoice. If they do not understand his joy, they act as if they did not realize when people most appreciate what they have. Don't they know that people cherish their possessions? Don't they know what they do when they lose them, and what they do once they have averted the loss? Does a shepherd give up on a single sheep because it has lost its way? Does a woman fail to look for a single silver coin when she cannot find it? And what is the outcome of their efforts? Joy—and not only theirs. No, they call upon all others to rejoice with them.

Yet, to rejoice with him, those who complain must understand his royal commission, which is the basis of his actions and the source of his joy. His royal commission made people his possession. They belong to his Father, and by virtue of his sonship they are his. But he loses them when they are forever controlled by their godless thoughts and desires. To prevent this, he calls them to himself, and his efforts are successful; and what has been lost is found when those who had strayed come to him and desire his fellowship. In so doing, they cast away what they have valued and done up to this point. This is their repentance, the turning of their thoughts and desires. No longer do they treat God with contempt; instead, they long for his kingdom. No longer do they serve the slavery of their own desires; instead, they obey God's Word and become subject to his will. No longer do they indulge in proud rebellion against their accusers; instead, they act in the courage that honors the truth.

Some complained that the loss was greater than the gain, for in this way he was making enemies out of the righteous. They complained; but those in heaven rejoiced with him. They said that he gained only few: he runs after one who is lost and deserts the ninety-nine! But the righteous have no reason to complain and to exclude themselves from the joy that fills him, together with the angels. They, who have no need to return but only need to keep what they have received and to fulfill what they have become, are his possession as well. His royal commission extends also to them. But it is not they who bring him great joy. The glory of his commission that brings him great joy is revealed by his recovery of the guilty. Now that his saving power proves to be stronger than the world's seductive power, he can praise the Father for handing over everything to the Son.

Away from God
May 16

And he said, "A certain man had two sons, and the
younger of them said to his father, 'Father, give me the
share of the estate that falls to me.' And he divided his wealth
between them. And not many days later, the younger son
gathered everything together and went on a journey into a
distant country, and there he squandered his estate with loose
living. Now when he had spent everything, a severe famine
occurred in that country, and he began to be in need. And he
went and attached himself to one of the citizens of that country,
and he sent him into his fields to feed swine. And he was
longing to fill his stomach with the pods that the swine were
eating, and no one gave them to him."
—LUKE 15:11–16

If we participate in the national tasks eagerly and energetically while at the same time living in the church, we readily understand why Jesus depicted the Jews' condition by the story in which the father has two different sons. The soul of the nation was strongly moved from two different directions. Since the days of the patriarchs, it had been the nation's calling to be the people of God. The Law instilled this notion in the people, and the temple reminded them of it as well. This drove part of the nation to practice the Law with all their might; on the other hand, their dealings with the nations and the strong incentives of their culture lent power to the impulses that long for what can be gained in the natural realm. The former part of the nation placed allegiance to God's law above all else; in the case of the latter, the memory of God paled and vanished. It was only natural goods that they still valued, and solely natural desires that they heeded.

Therefore, in Jesus' story the one son stays in the house and service of the father while the other left for a foreign country with his share of the father's possessions. He, too, was the father's son. Even when the Jew yielded himself entirely to sensual enticements, he could not remove the two facts to which he owed his existence: he was God's creature, and he was a member of his nation and therefore obligated to the Law. Even far from home he lived in dependence on what belonged to the Father. How could he suppose that his own possessions were solely his own? Not even apostasy removes us from our dependence on God.

Jesus describes how the creature is alienated from the Creator and how the Israelite is alienated from his God by recounting what one son demands of the father: "Give me what belongs to me." The self-centered will claims for itself what is God's and subjects this to its own desire. The result is the waste of divine gifts and the impoverishment of the one who misuses them.

This is Jesus' verdict regarding the things we call culture. If desire is given free reign, it inflames all the more, and the hotter it becomes, the less it attains true value. The realization becomes all the more powerful that what nurtures man cannot be found in the natural realm. He cannot deceive himself regarding his life's emptiness; he knows that he is starving. Thus he succumbs to pessimism, deplores the insignificance of our existence, and accuses life of being a treacherous delusion.

The natural communities into which we are placed appear to be able to make us prosper and to instill meaning and value into our lives. But they are powerless when inner need awakens. Therefore Jesus recounts that the starving man turned to the citizens of the city where he had moved but received no help from them. They were concerned that their pig herds be fed; they could not care less about the starving man's fate.

Does Jesus give up the son who left his father? Is his counsel for the starving man merely, "Die! Whoever failed must perish"? No. Jesus called no one impure or despicable or damned, no matter how polluted or corrupted he might have become. For the father does not give up on the son, and even the son cannot forget that he is the son of his father.

Back to God
May 17

But he came to his senses and said, "How many of my father's servants have enough bread—but I am dying of hunger. I will get up and go to my father and say to him: 'Father, I have sinned against heaven and against you. I am no longer worthy of being your son. Treat me like one of your servants.'" And he got up and went to his father. But when he was still far

JESUS BRINGS PURITY

off, his father saw him and had mercy on him and ran and
hugged him and kissed him. But the son said to him,
"Father, I have sinned against heaven and against you. I am
no longer worthy of being your son."
—LUKE 15:17–21

How does the misery of a desperate person come to an end? How can a life devastated by natural desires be made right? The memory of the father and of the benefits of fellowship with him must be awakened. This took place as the tax collectors and sinners came to Jesus and fellowshipped with him at the table. The encounter with Jesus reawakened the memory of God in them in a powerful way.

Did they desire the impossible? Did the father remain inaccessible to the one who was looking for him again? Jesus proclaimed the purpose of his mission. The father comes to meet the one who returns and kisses him.

Does he impose any conditions that must be met before he can return to the paternal house? Jesus knows of no work that the penitent would have to—or could—do to conciliate God. To be sure, when Jesus reawakened the memory of God in an apostate Jew, this had consequences, and when these consequences did not ensue, the longing for the father's house was not genuine, and one could not speak of a return that ended in the reunion of the son and father.

When a person once again remembers God, he must first of all acknowledge his guilt: "I have sinned against heaven and against you." As his consciousness of God is awakened, so too does his consciousness of guilt awake. When this happens, his conscience takes on particular force because he not only regards as reprehensible the unfaithfulness that ended his fellowship with other people but also acknowledges the sacredness of his duty because it is rooted in God. By rebelling against the father, the son has rejected God. The self-seeking individual, who cares only about fulfilling his own desires, denies God. This constitutes guilt and is now recognized and acknowledged as such.

But once this happens, all claims to the love and possessions of the father are canceled: "I am not worthy to be called your son. Make me one of your servants." He no longer has a filial privilege. What the father extends to him is free grace. When Jesus calls people back to the Father, he makes them into believers, not demanders.

But in this way the returning prodigal meets all the requirements of repentance. Jesus did not uncover the deeds of those who came to him, and he did not expose in the light what had been done in the darkness. Only the older brother, who speaks of the prostitutes with whom the prodigal had squandered his father's possessions, is interested in this. Surely the burden of these memories will weigh heavily on the prodigal. But precisely because this burden was heavy, Jesus did not make it heavier still. He covered with his forgiveness the things that had happened. For his part, the prodigal acknowledged his guilt and affirmed God's righteousness. This lays the foundation for the new fellowship with God enjoyed by those who come to Jesus.

What Happens with the One Who Comes to Jesus?
May 18

But the father said to his servants, "Quick, bring the best clothes and put them on him, and put a ring in his hand and shoes on his feet, and bring the fattened calf and kill it, and we will eat and be merry. For this son of mine was dead and has come back to life; he was lost and has been found." And they began to be merry.
—Luke 15:22–24

According to Jesus, the Father is perfect. When he pardons, his pardon grants freedom without limits. His forgiveness does not merely appease wrath and cancel the punishment; it also extends his grace and grants righteousness. When he loves, his love has creative power and renders God's riches effective for the one who has been pardoned. For this reason access to Jesus brings great joy to those who come to him and are witnesses of the meal he holds with sinners. And no qualms over what is past or fear of what is to come must diminish this joy.

In this way he explained and confirmed what he had said when he compared himself to the rejoicing shepherd. Because he brings people back to the Father, he renders his service with joy and gives to all who have regard for his work occasion for great joy that unites those on earth with those in heaven.

But could he speak in such a way already at a time when his work had not yet been completed and his cross had not yet been borne? Did he forget that he was able to remove sin and make sinners his guests because he was the Lamb of God? Precisely when he uttered the parable, it became evident that the cross issued from the things he did. He showed those who complained—and called *him* a sinner—what his fellowship brought to sinners. To be sure, those who were introduced to joy in this way gratefully praised him as their Savior. But he was opposed by those who denied that they had a right to participate in God's festive meal. They called the One who promised them such a part a sinner. This festive meal with his great joy could take place only because he was prepared to be condemned. Only for this reason could he attest to his guests that, by having come to Jesus, they had returned to the Father and had once again received the privilege of being called God's children. This is why Jesus' parable does not amount to a renunciation of his commission to receive authority through his death and to be the one who forgives. To the contrary, here he made clear the reason he accepted his own death freely and joyfully. He did this because he thereby made possible a new encounter with God on the part of those who had abandoned him.

The reason for his great joy was that death had been turned into life. Jesus did not call alive those who lived apart from God. The person who refuses to be God's possession makes of himself a dead person. Conversely, if restored to communion with God, a dead person has come to life. Now the one who had been lost has been found. Now he lives once again in God's presence. Like everything Jesus says, this was uttered with a view toward the new era and the eternal state. Jesus takes with him into eternal life the community he has gathered, and he provides it access to that life by removing its guilt.

Jesus Invites the Loveless Righteous Ones in Vain
May 19

But the older son was in the field, and when he came near the house, he heard music and dancing. And he called

one of the servants and asked what this was about.
And he told him, "Your brother has returned, and your father
has killed the fattened calf, because he has received him back
safe and sound." But he became angry and did not want to go
inside. So his father came out and begged him. But he replied
to the father, "Look! For so many years I have served you and
never transgressed your commandment, and you never gave me
even a goat so that I could celebrate with my friends.
But when this son of yours comes, who squandered your
possessions with prostitutes, you kill the fattened calf for him."
But he said to him, "Son, you are always with me, and
everything that is mine is yours. You should be glad and
rejoice, because this brother of yours was dead and has come to
life, and was lost and has been found."
—Luke 15:25–32

Acceptance in one place means rejection at another. By pardoning those who lived apart from God because they came to him, Jesus parted ways with the righteous. The son who had remained in the house and service of the father refused to participate in the feast. He showed himself to be the one who honors God by refusing fellowship to the one who was godless. His relationship with the father is not like what his brother now shares with the father. It is not a gift of mercy, which forgives the rebellion in free grace. He can rely on God's righteousness, which owes him his wages because of his long service and unfailing obedience. Yet this claim remained unmet. His religion brings him no festive joy. He is one of those who are compelled to work but whose souls do not allow them to rest, because they are hard-pressed on account of the obligations they lay on themselves for God's sake. Precisely for this reason, Jesus calls them to himself, and he does this also in his story by saying that the father went out to his older son.

This took place through Jesus' offer of participation in his joy to those who complained. He has come not merely for those who had strayed far off but also for those who were tied to the Law. In him the Father seeks to meet them both. For both, he is the one who is merciful and forgiving. We do not hear at this point how he refuted the righteous but how he sought to attract them. To be sure, he directed words against them that wounded them deeply, because these words ruthlessly exposed what they carefully concealed. But here he does not judge them, just as he did not judge the tax collector and expose his unrighteous deeds. Rather, he showed them, too, the Father who seeks to attract the love of his sons.

For this reason he tells the righteous person what he is given as the son: "You are always with me." God is on his side—is this not the most glorious possession, the greatest honor, the highest joy? And also this: "All that is mine is yours." This is how Jesus conceived of the sonship of God. Once again we hear what it meant for him that "the Father is perfect." All good gifts come from him, and they show their origin by being perfect.

"All that is mine is yours." This also means that "my son is your brother," "my joy ought to be your joy," and "my will that made him, a dead person, alive, must be your will as well." How can he be with the father when he does not want to be with the brother, and how can he honor the father when he shames the brother?

But now the contradiction between the divine will and human self-will becomes evident. To rejoice about the brother—and to do so because he has been pardoned even though he did the opposite of what the righteous person did—is impossible for the self-seeking person. He can rejoice only in what he himself is and in what he gains for himself. In order to rejoice with his forgiven brother, the righteous person would need to have love, and love is what he does not have. Rather, his righteousness only intensified his self-centeredness. Thus it happens that Jesus cannot have his meal with him but only with the one who has returned from afar.

Jesus Fulfills Isaiah's Declaration
May 20

Hear, O heavens, and give ear, O earth! I have raised up and elevated sons, and they fell away from me. An ox knows his master, and a donkey the food trough of his master; but Israel does not know, and my people do not understand.

—Isaiah 1:2–3

What is Jesus' aim? To make children of God out of those who are God's children but do not want to be, and in such a way that they know they are—and want to be—God's children. Could those who venerated the ancients rail against this as a novelty? No! Salvation history, the history in which God seeks to cause us to know him, had never had another aim. In the story that reveals his inner being to us, Jesus, too, took his cue from Old Testament prophecy. Isaiah had told the Jerusalem of his day: What would you be without God? Jerusalem came into being through God. The relationship to God of the community that resided there resembled that of sons to their father. They experienced not only God's power but also God's love. Every father desires his sons to grow and rise up, and this was also what God desired for Jerusalem. Jerusalem rose up; it was borne up by a rich history. It experienced many things, acquired riches and fame, and exceeded all other cities in the land. This was not its own work. The father raised the sons. They rebelled against him, rejected him, and acted against him. Isaiah thought particularly of the disruption of fellowship that resulted from the breaking of the Law and from violent acts. These reveal Jerusalem's rebellion against God's will, and the contrast becomes all the more profound the stronger the Father's benevolence and the richer his benefits are.

Is this not unnatural? The human world, too, certainly knows of divided houses, in which sons rebel against their fathers. But the animal responds favorably to a kind act. The ox and the donkey know the master who feeds them. The son who rebels against his father has acted alien to nature, and this is still more true for the creature who resists its Creator and for the Israelite who rebels against his God.

The consequence of this apostasy is this: "My people do not know me." For Jerusalem, too, God has become the unknown. To be sure, tradition, which reached every member of the nation, conveyed God's name to all. No one could reside in Jerusalem and overlook the temple, on which the name of God was placed. And no one who took part in the life of the nation could fail to hear the reports regarding the origin of the nation, which included accounts of God's activity. Everyone also knew that they had with them a man whom God had called to be his spokesperson. But in all of this they had not yet received the ability to perceive God's present activity. They did not realize that God was speaking to them when his word was brought to them; they did not realize what God's intentions were when he assigned them their destiny in judgment or grace. How could they pay attention to God's activity as long as they denied that they were the sons of God?

Jesus said that Isaiah's prophecy was fulfilled in him, and it is evident that his verdict regarding the sons of God confirms Isaiah's. But it is equally clear that we must not speak of an imitation or repetition of Isaiah. Isaiah brings God's demand to Jerusalem, and what he demands is this: "Do what is just." He lays God's law before the nation. This is the old word of God. But now Jesus prepares a festive meal for those whom Isaiah threatened, and he does so not merely as the one who threatened but also as the one who offers help. And he shows those who were zealous for the Law that they were resisting God's will.

Jerusalem Resembles the Son Who Only Appears to Be Obedient
May 21

What do you think? A man had two sons. He went to the first and said to him, "My son, go today and work in the vineyard." He answered and said, "Yes, sir," but then did not go. And he went to the second and spoke likewise. And he answered, "I don't want to." But later he relented and went. Which of the two did the will of his father? They said, "The second one." Jesus said to them, "Indeed, I tell you, the tax collectors and prostitutes will enter God's kingdom ahead of you. For John came to you on the path of righteousness, and you did not believe him. But the tax collectors and prostitutes believed him. But you, even though you saw all this, did not even relent afterward or believe him."

—Matthew 21:28–32

Jesus explained to Jerusalem's leaders that what rendered the dispute between him and them was irreconcilable; inevitably, the dispute would be resolved when they put him on the cross and he allowed himself to be crucified. As he explained this, he once again depicted the situation to them with the image of the two sons—one who appeared to be obedient but who ended up disobedient, and a disobedient one who became obedient.

In his interaction with Jerusalem, he spoke from the vantage point of the righteous and represented the relationship between the two sons and their father by showing how the father confronted them with a single command. He spoke to those who received their teaching about God from the Law. When a word of God comes to them, it is a commandment requiring action. For this reason, in this version of the story the father asks the sons to work in his vineyard on a given day. The righteous know that a command from God requires their obedience. This is why the one son indicates his readiness to do the will of his father without hesitation. But this is nothing more than a promise; he does not actually go to work in the vineyard.

When did this take place? The occasion for the earlier version of the parable was the festive meal Jesus shared with sinners while the righteous complained and stayed away. In the Jerusalem of that day, there was no room for such a meal. There, the Jews shone in their religious glory, and everyone prepared the Passover meal. All who participated in the feast were exuberant; all were zealously occupied with serving God—the tax collectors and sinners did not come to the fore. In this Jerusalem, when the Father called someone to serve him, everyone said eagerly, *Yes!*

But if Jerusalem dismissed Jesus and did not allow him to disturb it, the Baptist had made it impossible for them to ignore him. His message of repentance and the baptism he administered had confronted even Jerusalem's leaders with a decision. This is when the son who was ready to obey received the command of his father: "Work in my vineyard." And this is when the son's assurance that he was always obedient turned out to be a lie. The forgiveness offered by the Baptist to the righteous was refused by them, and the call to alter their religious conduct was rejected.

But those who were busy serving God were only a part of the people. In addition to them there stood another part that remained unconcerned with God. Jesus represented this part by the one son who tells the father he would not obey, declaring he would not go to work. But within this segment of the people there were some who did what God asked of them. They listened to the Baptist when he called them to God's kingdom and believed him despite their godlessness and evil deeds. Thus the tax collectors and the prostitutes showed the righteous that people enter God's kingdom through the forgiveness of sins. But the older brother does not desire what the father gave to his younger brother, and in the same way Jerusalem's righteous did not understand what took place in the other part of the nation. Their example did not move them to follow through on the *yes* they gave to God. In reality, their *yes* amounted to a *no*. They rejected the Baptist, and they rejected Jesus as well.

Section 10

THE CHRIST
CALLS HIS MESSENGERS

Jesus the Christ
May 22

*Jesus entered the area of Caesarea, the city of Philippi, and
asked his disciples, "Who do people say the Son of Man is?"
They said, "Some say he is John the Baptist, others Elijah,
others Jeremiah or one of the prophets." He asked them, "But
who do you think I am?" Simon Peter answered, "You are the
Christ, the Son of the living God."*
—MATTHEW 16:13–16

If Jesus had proclaimed a general, timeless truth, he would have been able
to continue his teaching activity until he died of natural causes. This was,
in fact, the occupation of the rabbis, of whom there were many, who in
their teachings took the holy teaching from the Holy Book and taught their
disciples and the entire nation without altering anything in the real
condition of people's lives. Selfishness reigned supreme, and all of the
nation's pressing issues were left unaddressed. This was not Jesus'
commission; this is not how his God and Father was manifested. With every
word, he proclaimed the divine will that must be done now and made
himself the doer of that will. All that he asked of others was resolve and
action. Thus his activity was given an aim and also an end, and this end
could not come in Galilee. The place for this was Jerusalem.

But in order to start on his journey to Jerusalem, he must provide
complete clarity for the disciples. The end to which he must bring his work
was his expulsion from Judaism. Were the disciples ready for this? They
were if they acknowledged him to be the Christ and described his
commission by the regal name. Then they would be prepared to face even
death with him. Then they would entrust themselves and their destiny to
him without reservation. The One who has received his regal commission
from God speaks and works in union with God and is the victor even when
the nation rejects him, and is the bringer of life even when he dies.

The vital importance of the confession *You are the Christ* is made clear,
too, by what others who followed Jesus said about him. What is listed here
is not opponents' judgments, not objections by those who fought against
him. Rather, we read what those who considered Jesus to be a spokesman
of the divine Word and a proclaimer of the heavenly kingdom expected

him to be able to accomplish. What the rabbis told the people regarding the coming time of salvation supplied them with several names by which they incorporated Jesus into their picture of the future. The nearest person through whom they could clarify Jesus' intentions for them was John the Baptist. Was he not continuing the Baptist's ministry, but now with new power superior to that of the Baptist because he had been raised from the dead? A prophecy by Malachi had made the expectation of Elijah a firm part of people's future expectations. He will go ahead of the Christ and ensure that the nation is worthy of Christ's benefits. And those who disagreed that Jesus resembled Elijah were reminded of one of the prophets of old, such as Jeremiah, by his words of warning to Israel. The prophets had spoken to the nation in God's name and had possessed the power to confirm their word through signs. Were the people not given once again in Jesus that which had not been experienced for a long time?

Yet with all these thoughts that expressed admiration for Jesus—thoughts that sensed the mystery surrounding him—they interpreted his aim according to their own ideas and evaded what he claimed about himself and showed them through his ministry. Their hopes circumvented him as they longed for one who was greater still, who would bring the community into the state God desired for it. Was Jesus not too small, too weak, too human to reveal God's glory? Must they not wait for someone else? Jesus' disciples decisively parted ways with these hopes and dreams when they confessed of Jesus what he expected them to confess and called him the king who had been installed by God. There is no one else above the king; in him God's kingdom is present.

Peter Speaks God's Word
May 23

Then Jesus answered him, "Blessed are you, son of Jonah, for it was not flesh and blood that revealed this to you, but my Father in heaven."

—Matthew 16:17

After Peter's confession, Jesus' resolve was firm: he would go to Jerusalem. But was Peter the one on whom Jesus relied for support? Subsequent to his baptism, he had parted ways with the Baptist and did not enlist his collaboration, because he could not appeal to the witness of a human being but depended entirely upon what took place on his behalf from God. Yet when Peter recognizes his royal commission, this is not the judgment of a mere human being. How could flesh and blood arrive at the conclusion that Jesus was the king in God's power? What is "flesh and blood"? This is the human being as he proceeds from the activity of nature, the human being who perceives what his senses show him, thinks what the world teaches him, and desires that which preserves his life. Jesus' kingdom stands in total contrast to all of this. In the One who must die, no power can be seen that enables him to rule, and the One who is determined to take up the cross promises no gratification to his natural self-interest. Jesus is nothing apart from his divine sonship; but God is the one who is invisible. Do flesh and blood perceive God's presence and effects? These become apparent only to the one to whom God reveals them.

This is how Peter ought to view his confession: God revealed to him what Jesus is by the commission of God and what his work will be. This binds Peter inextricably to his confession. He can never again revoke it but must consider himself sinful whenever he wavers in his confession. But because he has understood what God showed him and has proclaimed what God told him, his confession binds him forever in complete communion to Jesus. By it he is his servant, his instrument, his messenger, and united with him in his regal work.

For this reason Peter's confession of Jesus is followed by Jesus' "confession of Peter," by which he appoints him to the apostolic ministry. What Jesus promised him when he called him "the rock" can now be fulfilled. This is Jesus' response to those who confess him: he enlists them in his service. Just as his royal will is entirely separated from ambitious self-interest, whoever confesses him is given the divine revelation not in order to know and be righteous and blessed but to serve the Christ who places him in God's kingdom together with himself and makes him dependent upon God's will so that he can bring the gifts of God's grace to others. The seed has within itself the living germ so that it might multiply.

Peter's Mother-in-Law Also Served Jesus
May 24

And Jesus entered Peter's house and saw his mother-in-law lying there with a fever. And he took her hand, and her fever left her. And she got up and served him.

—MATTHEW 8:14–15

When Jesus entered Peter's house, he took away his mother-in-law's fever. She had experienced Jesus' helping power. What happened next? Was she the object of amazement and jubilation? Was the purpose of the penetration of divine power into natural events to enliven the view of the glories of the coming age? What we see is the healed person preparing the meal and rendering the customary service at table.

The truth of the received healing thus becomes visible. One moment she is still sick; the next moment she performs the customary work of women. The One who brings divine help is honored with believing subordination. The strength granted by him is used for him. The One who receives the service is honored; once recognized for his messianic act, he becomes the object of service. Everyone who has been shown God's grace has been brought under his rule and has become his subject. The grace that has been received does not remain bottled up in the sphere of one's own life. It becomes an incentive to get to work.

It was a woman's service that was rendered by the one who had been healed. But is it the woman's destiny to begin serving only when she is placed before God? To be sure, it was the Palestinian custom to place the mother before the men who recline around the table as the one who served. But it is not only by experiencing the divine power as it raises a woman to new life that one is prompted to serve; encountering Christ results in nothing but service, willing service. One is the ruler; one is the commander; one is the giver. One is worshiped; one is believed; one is loved. He is the One who is served by all—by Peter, who must testify to the things revealed to him by God; by his mother-in-law, who baked the loaves of bread and filled the bowl for Jesus' meal with his disciples; by the spiritual infant who praises God; by the spiritually mature person who knows and keeps the ancient words of God.

The fact that the woman's service produces what nature requires for the body does not diminish its value. For Jesus does not establish his community beyond nature. Because acts of service demanded by nature are indispensable, women, too, belonged to the group of people traveling with Jesus. He did not think of sending them out; this was precluded by custom. But he most certainly did not exclude women from his community, following the same principle according to which he included children in God's kingdom, promised it to the poor, and announced it to the guilty. God's rule is God's own work and takes place neither through a man's energy nor through a woman's care. Their life is to serve him; yet the Creator of their lives is God.

Jesus Will Establish His Community
May 25

And I tell you: You are Peter, and on this rock I will build my community.
—Matthew 16:18

A king cannot exist without a community that trusts and obeys him, and the Christ, who rules by the power of divine grace, cannot be like those rulers who reign by placing all others in bondage. All who become his subjects are free persons. They are all related to him through faith and love, all resolved to live for him. Thus they resemble a gathering of people who come together for the sake of rendering a unanimous decision and engaging in joint action. He calls this community a building that he will establish.

Those who live together with the head of a household have always been called his "house," and God's people were always God's "house." This house had not yet been built. It had not yet come into being, even though the Baptist had brought out of the nation those he baptized, and it had not yet been built, even though Jesus had gone across the entire field and had sown his seed—even when it fell on barren soil. This had not yet resulted in the separation of those who believed in him from those who rejected him. But now it is decision time for Jerusalem owing to Jesus' crucifixion, which once and for all sets apart those who are for him from those who are against him. The former are thereby separated from the nation and united to form a community of their own, which has no other Lord but Jesus.

He himself will establish his community. For his Word unites them, and his commandment gives them their duty, and his promise shows them their goal. What they have is given by him; and what they do, they do in keeping with his will and by his strength.

Because the Crucified One will establish his community as his own, it does not correspond to what flesh and blood imagines or desires for itself. It cannot lure people by such kinds of goods. But they will hear from Peter and see by his example that God glorified his Son. And they will gain faith by Peter's faith, and in communion with him they will grow together to form the community of Jesus, through which Jesus will reveal that he is the Christ.

Jesus Predicts the Resurrection
May 26

The gates of hades will not overcome it [Jesus' community].
—Matthew 16:18

Whoever proclaims God's kingdom proclaims eternal life. Jesus proclaims it on his way to the cross. Can he now guarantee his community that they will live? No! Whoever follows him leaves everything behind. Whoever trusts in Jesus readies himself, along with him, to die. For the love received from him puts no limits on sacrifice and cancels out any claims toward God. Did the name *rock*, which Jesus gave to Peter, mean that no one would take away his life from him? To the contrary, he, too, becomes a bearer of the cross in communion with Jesus, and the flock called by him to the Christ enters through the gates of hades into the realm of the dead. These are the gates that close behind a person forever. No one who has gone through them has ever opened them again. Everyone is powerless against them.

But the message of life remains intact, even when Jesus chooses death for himself and obligates his own to die. It could be silenced only if the message of God's kingdom had to be abandoned. While this message prepares his community to die with him, it nonetheless also promises them life. The gates that are stronger than any assault will not overcome those who belong to Jesus. They will open for them and not have the power to keep in death those whom Jesus calls. They will rise. The message regarding

God's kingdom will become the message concerning the resurrection of the dead.

God's regal activity cancels the judgment of death, which lies on all of humanity and, by virtue of his granting eternal life, reveals God as the one who lives. This is the glory and joy of those who may call themselves the community of the Christ: that they are the community of those who live forever. In the Christ they have found the one who has overcome death, and to all who exercise the role of messenger passed on by Jesus, this reveals the glory of the vocation they are called to exercise: they offer eternal life to those whom they call to the Christ.

The Gatekeeper of God's Kingdom
May 27

To you I will give the keys of the kingdom of heaven.
—Matthew 16:19

Did Jesus believe he had found in Peter a successor and replacement? No! The Lord is one. There is no successor for the Christ, no one who can take his place. Only the Son can say, "With my presence God's kingdom is among you." But people do not lose access to God's kingdom because Jesus no longer speaks personally to Jerusalem and instead sends it Peter as his messenger. What Jesus has said remains valid and provides Peter with his message, and what Jesus has accomplished has been done for all time and gives Peter the power by which he will act. In order that Peter might recognize the greatness of the ministry he has been granted, Jesus described it with the powerful phrase that he was placing the keys to God's kingdom into his hand.

God's coming revelation in grace and judgment; Jesus' royal activity, whose scope encompasses all of mankind; the emergence of eternal life—these are aims to which Jesus lifts the view of his messenger; this is what provides his ministry with its ground and goal. What he is called to do takes on its significance not from his own person but from God's accomplishing his glorious work, in which those to whom Peter brings the divine Word have a share. The community that Peter will gather likewise will receive power and glory, but not through what its members will contribute; its greatness and worth derive from its share in God's grace as the community of the Christ.

This removes from the apostolic ministry all concerns arising from one's natural life and its needs. Peter is not made the head of a company out to make a profit. He must make sure, of course, that the necessities of daily life are available for the community. But this is not the great possession that he administers but rather that "which is added unto those who long for God's kingdom and righteousness." He also is not charged with building a political party that, in competition with other parties, seeks to control the destiny of his nation. Certainly, Jerusalem's destiny will have consequences for the destiny of Peter and his community. Their own weal or woe depends upon the prosperity or demise of Jerusalem. But what the apostle must do does not place him beside the reigning priests or the Roman rulers. For he has been entrusted not merely with the care of his national community, nor does he derive his authority from it. The One through whom God's rule is realized gave him his apostolic commission. And this commission is exercised not primarily so that our natural community will become more complete. Rather, it takes place when righteousness is brought to sinners and eternal life to those who die, because it shows them how God's grace comes to them.

Peter Chooses for Himself the Ministry of the Word
May 28

But we want to continue in prayer and in the ministry of the word.
—Acts 6:4

To where in Jerusalem should those widows flee who had experienced the collapse of their houses and, thereby, of their livelihood? To alms? This might be appropriate for a blind or lame person. He could sit at the temple gate, where visitors to the temple would give him a gift. But the woman could not sit in the street without losing her honor, and there was no steady stream of alms given in secret. This aid involved continual concern. It was no wonder that widows took refuge in the apostolic community. Here they found love, not merely temporary pity. Here they found community, which brought an end to their loneliness. Here they found more than bread: they found the Bread of Life; the cleansing of the soul from nagging anxiety and burning need, through faith that yielded to God; love that never lacked opportunities for service; hope that always burned brightly.

Thus, from the beginning there was a group of widows that formed within the brotherhood led by Peter, and Peter could know from this that he was obeying the Lord's command. But this also created work. Food had to be bought and distributed. Was there enough food on a daily basis—for everyone, not merely for those who were compatriots in the more narrow sense (in language and provenance), but also for the Greek women, who spoke only Greek? How should Peter now spend his time and energy? Apart from economic concerns there were also prayer and the administration of the Word. He represented the community before God as the one who prayed for it and with it and was charged with speaking "the Word," a word different from all other words because it is the Word of God spoken by the Christ.

Peter did not relinquish the keys to the kingdom of God. Other brothers could take care of providing for the widows, and the community did not lack members who were capable of doing so. The Word, however, could be administered by no one quite in the same way as Peter, because this required fellowship with Jesus from his baptism to his resurrection, and an intimate knowledge of his Word. Caring for those in need must not be neglected; but what must remain in the church as well is the testimony of Jesus, so that people learn to believe in God through him. For this is how people enter God's kingdom.

The Apostle Speaks the Liberating Word
May 29

Whatever you release on earth will be released in heaven.
—Matthew 16:19

Is Peter not attempting something entirely nonsensical by urging people to enter God's kingdom? After all, they are like those who have been bound and shackled. In fact, it is evident that they *are* bound and shackled. Thus, Jesus' command to Peter is this: Release them! Does he know how he is supposed to do this, or must he himself now invent an art, or even some kind of magic, that will provide him with the power to break the chains with which humanity is bound?

Peter heard how John announced baptism for the forgiveness of sins and saw how Jesus made the forgiveness of sins a part of his healing ministry. He was with Jesus at the table when Jesus described to his guilty guests the meal the father prepares for his prodigal son. Now he also will accompany Jesus to Jerusalem and see Jesus overcome all injustice directed toward him and acquire the authority of being the One who grants forgiveness to the sinful world. And at Jesus' tomb he will see how the unbreakable chains of death are broken. Because Peter himself is one who has been released, he knows how he must release those who are bound.

They cannot release themselves. If they were to justify themselves and dispute their guilt, they would sin, and they would not find eternal life in their own strength. Yet Peter frees them from their bonds, because he is the Christ's messenger, stands in the service of divine grace, and speaks the Word that reveals the gracious will of God.

If he were speaking in the name of the Law, he would not be able to release anyone. In this way he could announce to people only that they were, and must remain, prisoners. But Jesus gave him not the keys to the book of the Law but the keys to God's kingdom, and the Word of God that he has learned and is supposed to speak into the world is the one that the Christ has spoken and himself is.

For this reason the apostle's entire ministry requires that he not attribute the truth and power of his message to himself. To be sure, he must testify to what he himself saw and heard, and his own faith opens his mouth, and his own love leads him to other people. But if he were to bring them nothing but his memories of Jesus and his faith by which he preserved them, he would bind his listeners to him and make them his own community. Yet he was not to build a house for himself but to remain the servant of the Christ, who builds his house through him. He is sent not to recruit people who are Peter's; his goal is rather to locate people who will be Christ's. Therefore his entire ministry is contingent upon his own faith and on his ability to help others believe that his word proclaims the divine will and is therefore confirmed in heaven.

The Apostle Speaks the Word That Binds
May 30

What you bind on earth will be bound in heaven.
—MATTHEW 16:19

Will the disciple become greater than the master? The disciple was told to release those who are bound, to set the guilty free, and to tell the dying that they are alive. By doing this, he renewed Jesus' word. But didn't Jesus frequently offer God's grace in vain? Will Peter's experience be any different? Not at all. The disciple must be like his master, but he is not supposed to aspire to being greater than his master. This is why Jesus' command to Peter was not merely "Release!" but also "Bind!" He cannot do only one or the other. He can bind only if he also releases and release only if he also binds. Both make up his apostolic ministry, and in both instances he ought to believe that he is acting according to God's will, because God's righteousness is revealed when the sinner dies on account of his unbelief and when the believer lives on account of his faith.

Jerusalem, which is where Jesus will send Peter, is completely determined to resist, and when he brings his message to the nations, which stand under the rule of the emperor, he will have the entire world against him. Is Peter to shrink back in fear and call the opposition insurmountable? Yet he sees in Jesus not merely the divine grace but also the sanctity of the divine verdict, which opposes all godlessness and unrighteousness. And Peter, too, experiences both, because his message is met with both faith and unbelief, salvation as well as condemnation. While pronouncing forgiveness on one person because he believes, he must refuse it to another because he rejects Jesus. And just as he administers baptism to one person and introduces him into the community, he must refuse it to another and send him away from the community. Both take place by Jesus' mandate, to the praise of his messianic office.

By doing this, does Peter dissolve the commonality that exists among us? Have we not grown from the same root, and are we not borne by the same tree? Can one man deny that he is the same kin as another? The apostle is not told to do this—he is called to do the very opposite. Neither is this the work of the church, if Jesus' message indeed comes to us through it. The church acknowledges the commonality of our lives, which makes of us one world. Jesus did not suddenly introduce a dichotomy into his Word. His God and Father is the God of all and is the same for all. We are released because we are bound—just as all people are—and we are bound because we despise the redemption that is available to all. The bondage to the law of sin and death does not merely affect the one or the other—we all are affected, and the redemption that was made possible for us through the existence, ministry, and death of the Christ occurred for us all.

Peter would have turned into a ruler who acquires subjects according to his own whim if it had been his skill that moved people to faith or unbelief. But he does not instill faith in people by his eloquence or his intrinsic authority, nor does he produce unbelief by virtue of who he is as a human being. God's Word brings about its own results and releases or binds through what takes place in the person himself. Depending on how he acts, the Word reveals to him either its saving or its judging power.

There Are Hearers of the Word Who Die and Hearers Who Are Raised to Life
May 31

To those who are perishing, we are an aroma of death to death. And to those who are saved, we are an aroma of life to life.
—2 CORINTHIANS 2:16

Christ's messenger brings to people the gift of freedom; he brings them life. These two depictions of the apostolic ministry are congruous with one another. The divine pronouncement that removes a person's chains is one with the creative call that raises him to life. But just as the apostle does not merely release but also binds, so, too, his ministry does not reveal only life but also death.

Paul's statement indicates that in his ministry he consistently experiences what Jesus' commission announced to Peter. In every city to which Paul came, the same thing happened. Nowhere was he able to win the entire city, or even all of the Jews. Everywhere his audience was divided. Vehement objections and jubilant thanksgiving were intermingled in the responses to Paul's offer to his listeners.

Even within the congregations he established, the same situation arose. Those who were granted baptism because they believed—or at least *appeared* to believe, so that Paul's Spirit-trained eyes could not detect any untruthfulness in them—were not all truly taken possession of by Christ in their desires and activities. There were in these congregations some who had been liberated but also others who were in bondage, some who were alive but also others who were dead. What the Lord had said, happened: the net cast out by the fishermen caught a variety of things; the seed of the enemy grew up together with the seed of the Christ.

The only thing that is new in Paul's statement is its specific imagery. In Jesus' saying, that which the apostle was called to do was likened to what the judge must do who either clears a defendant or throws him into prison. The interpreters of the Law used the same terms, *release* and *bind,* for what they did. The one on whom they imposed a prohibition was bound; whoever was given permission was released. Paul, on the other hand, compared the knowledge of God that came about through him with an aroma, because this knowledge, like an aroma, enters into a person without his being able to defend himself against it. For God, this is an aroma brought about by Christ. Similarly, an aroma is transferred from Paul to those who listen to his message. Where there is death, the aroma is one of death; where there is life, the aroma indicates life. It becomes evident what has taken place in a person as a result of the divine Word proclaimed to him. Either it brought him death, or it made him alive. A dead person emits an aroma of decay; a living person emits an aroma of life. This dual outcome of the apostolic ministry cannot fail to come about, since both results glorify the Christ, just as Peter, by both binding and by releasing, carried out the commission Christ had given to him.

The Disciple Is Not Allowed to Judge
June 1

Do not judge, so that you might not be judged.
—Matthew 7:1

The apostolic office was similar to that of the judge and yet highly elevated above it. For when a legal dispute to be decided by a judge arises, regarding a certain matter in a household or in the larger population, only natural and temporal issues are at stake. But the apostolic word issues in a decision that has eternal consequences. The release it brings us frees us for eternal life, and the bonds it puts on us separate us from God's kingdom.

But didn't Jesus tell his disciples not to judge? Did he lift the prohibition when he commanded Peter to bind and to release? If so, it would have been invalidated also for the church, and the church would have the authority to pronounce a valid judgment regarding a given person's worth (or lack thereof) and to decide about his destiny.

How welcome this lifting of that prohibition would be, for we resist it vehemently! Is our life not severely jeopardized, and is utter chaos not introduced into our community, if we cease to judge? If we consult nothing but our natural points of view, we must conclude that our honor, our possessions, and our lives, too, are rendered vulnerable if we are devoid of legal protection. "Fight for your rights; hold the transgressor of the Law accountable!" This is nature's desire and at the same time the intent of the Law. Is this not also the voice of God?

Yes, it is! For God's Word proclaims to us his judgment, and Jesus confirmed this to his disciples at the time he told them not to judge. "So that you might not be judged": this is why they ought to refrain from judging—not so that it might disappear from the way God governs the world, but so that it might not turn against them and they might not incur the loss of their lives. They ought not to announce to the world that they are its judges. Rather, their message ought to be, "God is the one who is your judge. Vengeance is his; it has not been entrusted to you. Righteousness is his; no one among you has his own righteousness that he has acquired himself."

Only because Peter and Paul were completely obedient to the prohibition against judging were they able to carry out their apostolic ministries. It was their calling to justify the godless and to awaken to life those who were destined to die. How were they able to do this if they engaged in judging others? Their message was the announcement of divine grace. This message gave them authority to offer life and freedom to people, and this is the consequence of its truth and validity: those who accept their message are saved, and those who reject it belong to those who are dying. Yet if they ignored the grace that sent them and deemed it insufficient for their security and their ministry—for this they also needed the authority to judge—then they would have denied their apostolic commission.

Forgiveness Knows No Bounds
June 2

Then Peter came and said to him, "Lord, how often may my brother sin against me and I must forgive him? Up to seven times?" Jesus said to him, "Not up to seven times, I tell you, but up to seventy-seven times. For this reason the kingdom of heaven is like a human king who wanted to settle accounts with his servants. But as he started, they brought to him someone who owed him ten thousand talents. Since he could not pay the amount, the master ordered that he and his wife and his children and everything he had be sold and returned to him. Then the servant fell to the ground, prostrated himself in front of him and said, 'Please be patient. I will repay everything.' And the servant's master had mercy on him, set him free, and forgave him the debt."
—Matthew 18:21–27

Forgiveness must not be boundless, Peter said, and we understand all too well what he meant. In every case it requires of us a serious effort. It is not the first impulse of our soul, but only a secondary resolve by which we overcome our desire to take revenge. But in this we imagine that forgiveness must have a limit. Does not constant, never-ending forgiveness constitute the demise of what is right? Whoever exercises it, Peter thought, became an enemy of righteousness, and everyone who loves righteousness must oppose such boundless forgiveness.

This was the verdict of Peter, the rock, the gatekeeper of God's kingdom, to whom Jesus had entrusted the ministry of binding and releasing. Was it not his duty to arrive at this judgment precisely because he had been given this ministry by Jesus? If he prevents those who resist him from entering God's kingdom and binds them, how then can forgiveness be without limits? Indeed, this is possible, Jesus says. Your commission is grounded in boundless forgiveness. For boundless forgiveness is what you need and what you have received. This is what you ought to bring to others, and Jesus explains this to him with the story in which the king settled accounts with his servants.

Large sums had passed through the hands of the servant with the result that he had incurred an enormous debt. Hence the burden of an immeasurable guilt rests on the servant, for which he is accountable with both his own freedom and that of his family. Consequently, the king declares that he should be dealt with according to the law. Is the man not now doomed? The only thing he has left is to plead for mercy, and his requests are heard. The king forgives him his entire debt.

This is boundless forgiveness. Who grants it? God, and Jesus in his service. Who is on the receiving end? Peter, when he was made Jesus' disciple. How is this guilt incurred? When the king's property is administered in such a way that it is misused and lost. Peter lived in a commonly human fashion. Did he give to God what was God's? His own desires told him what to do, and thus he used up what God's creative grace had given him. Not even what the Law told him about God's will kept him from doing so. Is there any way to make up for this? To be sure, people talk about how they want to make up for their mistakes. But these are dreams that do not conceal their powerlessness and desperation. When in Jesus' story the servant says he wants to make restitution for the ten thousand talents that he lost, it is evident that he cannot do this.

And still, there is a way for his debt to be relieved. The king forgives it, and his forgiveness is boundless. The servant's entire debt is forgiven, not just part of it; this is not owing to any action on his part but arises from free mercy that does not want him to die. Because God acted toward Peter in boundless mercy, he is Jesus' disciple, and for this reason he is the rock who has apostolic authority. If he were to say that there was no complete forgiveness, he would break fellowship with Jesus and rescind his apostolic commission. For then he would reject the very thing that made him Jesus' disciple and his messenger.

The Limits of Forgiveness
June 3

But when that servant had departed, he found one of his fellow servants who owed him one hundred denarii, and he grabbed him, choked him, and said, "Give me back what you owe me." Then his fellow servant fell down and pleaded with him, "Please be patient, and I will pay you back." But he was unwilling to do so, and left and put him in prison until he had paid the debt. His fellow servants saw what had taken place and were very grieved because of this. They went and told their master everything that had happened. Then the master summoned him and said to him, "Wicked servant! I forgave you your entire debt because you begged me. Shouldn't you also have been merciful toward your fellow servant, just as I was merciful toward you?" And his master was angry and handed him over to the torturers until he had paid his entire debt. This is also how my heavenly Father will treat you if you don't forgive your brothers from the heart.

—MATTHEW 18:28–35

God's forgiveness knows no bounds; but the consequence Peter feared did not ensue. God's unlimited forgiveness did not result in the demise of right and wrong. This indeed would have been the case if Peter had been right that others were no longer protected from him once he had been unconditionally forgiven. Jesus showed him in the second part of his story what he would have done if he had thought this way. Now the servant is the creditor, and his fellow servant his debtor. The sum that is at stake is small. Only in the royal household, before God, do boundless, unforgivable debts arise. The injustices incurred in people's dealings with one another, conversely, only cause small damage, which corresponds to the small measure of the life given to us. But the servant does not acknowledge this. He considers it inconceivable that he might lose his silver coins, and he insists on his rights. Because the debtor is unable to pay, the man is angry and goes to court in order to get justice. Doesn't this have any consequences for God's boundless forgiveness? Will it be Peter's even if he acts toward his brothers as the servant does toward his fellow servant? Jesus provides the answer by showing in his story how the king reinstates his servant's debt, so that he now must go to prison after all.

Thus Peter is told in what respect forgiveness is not boundless. There is indeed a limit where it ends. It ends when the disciple who has received forgiveness refuses it to the one who has sinned against him. At that point it ends precisely because it is limitless. Because it is without bounds, it applies not only to the one but also to the other servant and makes people not merely the recipients but also the agents of forgiveness. It does not simply reconcile a person to God; it also reconciles one person to another. If it is lacking in the dealings of one disciple with another, it has disappeared also from that disciple's relationship with God. For it is not the intention of forgiveness to grant the disciple a right to harm or torture others with impunity.

So then, does God change his mind? Can he condemn the one he has set free without being untrue to himself? No—it is not God who is untrue to himself but the person who is untrue to his grace. The change takes place inside the person, because at one time he asks for grace and at another rejects it. When he asks for grace, he receives it; when he rejects it, he loses it.

Now Peter knows whom he ought to release and whom he ought to bind. He ought to release all those who are guilty, because they are unable to free themselves from their own guilt. He ought to bind all those who use grace to pursue their own advantage and to judge others. In this way Peter's conduct is fortified against any wavering. Whether he releases or binds, he always serves the perfect grace that forgives unconditionally, the grace in the face of which the debts of all those who desire it have disappeared, and the debts of all those who reject it remain.

Section 11

JESUS' DEMISE BECOMES EVIDENT

Jesus Must Go to Jerusalem
June 4

From that time on, Jesus Christ began to show his disciples
that he must go to Jerusalem.
—Matthew 16:21

What has been begun must be completed; what has been commanded must be carried out; what has been promised must take place. The word is not true if it remains a mere word; compelling necessity requires that word be accompanied by deed. Love is not love when it eludes company; it cannot evade the dynamic that leads it to those who need it.

"Your Father in heaven is perfect," Jesus had said: what he does, he does completely. As long as Jesus made sure he stayed in Galilee, however, everything remained unfinished. All the things that had taken place there were but a beginning that still awaited its completion. The final word had not yet been spoken; the last ounce of energy had not yet been spent; and the total sacrifice had not yet been brought. Galilee could have served as his home only if he had had a self-seeking aim. If he had wanted to enjoy his divine sonship only for himself and had been content to make himself glorious and blessed in relation to God, that locale would have sufficed to grant him peace and security. If his goal had been merely to gather a group of disciples, no different from the other teachers who gathered a flock of disciples around them, a Galilean village would probably have been suitable. There he could attract Peter, John, and the others through continual instruction and mold them together into a small but close-knit group.

But it was not his work to establish a church, an organization filled with collective self-interest that cultivated its own views and customs in the opinion that it was thereby pleasing God. His commission led him to all, not just to some; to his nation, not merely to individuals. For this reason he had to go to Jerusalem. For the Jews' unification into one nation had come about through Jerusalem's becoming the city in which every Jew had his right as a citizen.

Could he not have gone to foreign lands? A short trip led Jesus to the Greek cities on the east side of the Sea of Galilee, and trade often brought Galileans to the centers of commerce at the shore of the Mediterranean. Did he not have an obligation to go to those people, since he spoke to all, not merely to some, and since he had come into the world, not merely to the Jews? Yet it was impossible that he should go to the world while bypassing Jerusalem. God's sonship meant that he must complete the work of the Father. Now it is not characteristic of the Son to have little esteem for the work of the Father. But Jerusalem was the place where God's kingdom had been present in its initial form. Jesus could not speak to the world as if he were the first and only one whom God had made his witness. He had to acknowledge the Word of God that had gone out prior to his coming. Yet he would have invalidated it had he bypassed Jerusalem. But now that he obeyed the necessity that led him to Jerusalem, he acknowledged God's work that had taken place prior to his coming and thus cleared the way for his Word to go out into the entire world.

Trust in Jerusalem Is Misplaced
June 5

And after this, Jesus traveled through Galilee. For he did not want to travel through Judea, because the Jews were trying to kill him. Yet the Jewish feast of Tabernacles was near. So his brothers told him, "Depart from here and go to Judea so that your disciples may see the works you are doing. For no one who seeks public attention does anything in secret. If you do these things, reveal yourself to the world." For even his brothers did not believe in him.

—JOHN 7:1–5

If Jesus had told his disciples no more than "I must go to Jerusalem," they joyfully would have concurred. This is what they had always hoped and waited for, and with them Jesus' brothers, too, had waited for him finally to resolve to end his itinerant ministry in Galilee. It had become offensive to them, since it was for this reason that Jesus failed to go to Jerusalem and did not join the pilgrims who left for the autumn festival in Jerusalem. They concur: he must go to Jerusalem, for he wants to be noticed by all. How can he remain in hiding? He speaks with firm assurance; how can he maintain it when he shies away from Jerusalem? There he encounters all those who had become his disciples. How can he elude them? Yet they thought like Jesus only in that they, too, realized the all-important significance of Jerusalem. Internally, though, they remained separated from Jesus. For they did not realize what, of necessity, had to take place when their hopes were realized and Jesus addressed Jerusalem.

Jerusalem! For Jesus' brothers, this meant the definitive answer to the question that was still to be decided: "Are you the one who is to come, or are we to look for someone else?" In the past, the Baptist had derived his right to ask Jesus this question from Jesus' prophetic activity. But the answer Jesus gave to him had not yet proved decisive. He had told the Baptist's disciples to report to him the saving power Jesus was given. It revealed his communion with the Father, and the Baptist was able to realize that the commission granted to Jesus was superior to his own. But this was not yet the final answer. It was strong enough to establish faith in Jesus, but it did not yet reveal how God's kingdom would manifest itself through him. The one who was to come must do still greater things than Jesus did as the doctor of the sick and the comforter of the poor. And these greater things, his brothers thought, were what Jesus would do in Jerusalem, greater precisely because it would take place before the eyes of the rulers and of the people gathered there. Jesus would achieve there his final victory, his absolute triumph over all. How could he do without it? It was his, as soon as he did his work in Jerusalem. "Let them see your works"; then they will believe in you.

John reports that the expectations of Jesus' brothers were indeed fulfilled and that the inhabitants of Jerusalem did, indeed, see Jesus' works. They saw the blind man who gained his vision and the dead man who rose from his grave. But the success Jesus' brothers expected did not materialize. Jesus' works did not make believers of Jerusalem's leaders. Rather, they confirmed them in their opposition to him. For the works by themselves remain silent. They require the Word in order to effect faith, and only when the Word enters people are they given faith. For this reason the decision did, indeed, come about in Jerusalem, just as Jesus' brothers suspected. But it occurred counter to their own self-centered hopes. The outcome and the goal of his ministry were his death.

Jesus Must Suffer Many Things
June 6

He must suffer many things from the elders, high priests, and teachers of the Law.
—MATTHEW 16:21

Jesus' brothers said that he could do great things in Jerusalem. To this, Jesus replied that he must suffer many things there. The glory of his sonship indeed infuses him with great joy. But he cannot seek only joy with the Father nor preserve it by seeking to elude suffering. His commission results in not merely the blessedness that puts the beatitude in his mouth, "Blessed are you." It also leads to the self-denial that readies him to suffer.

This will be especially painful because of those who cause him to suffer. It is not just a given person who had been so struck by Jesus' word that he rose up to yield fanatical resistance. Nor is it merely a local community that sought to obtain the reputation of extraordinary righteousness by condemning Jesus. Nor is it a Roman official who was incited against Jesus by false accusations. No! The elders of the people, who governed the entire nation from Jerusalem; the ruling priests, who were active on behalf of Israel's holiness through the administration of the temple; the teachers of the Law, who ensured the rule of the Law; all those who possessed the divine commission to govern the nation, to whom everyone owed complete obedience—they were the ones who caused him great suffering. In order for this to take place, Jesus had to go to Jerusalem. For this is the seat of those called to govern, and what they do there takes place by virtue of their offices.

This truly results in the decision—not a misstep that can be remedied, not a temporary lapse on the part of those who are charged with leading the nation, but the final turn, the completion of the work that Jesus must accomplish. Yet this also means the demise of the city, the temple, and the divine calling entrusted to the Jews. Will this also constitute the demise of Jesus' disciples? In order to remove this fear and doubt from them, he required them to confess that he was the Christ. God's rule does not end, and the One whom the disciples know to be the agent of God's kingdom has bound them to himself forever. Yet through what takes place there, they are completely liberated from those who rule Jerusalem. Now it is no longer the priest who stands between them and God but only the Christ; and God's will is proclaimed to them no longer by the teacher of the Law but by God's new word, which they received from Jesus. And the community Jesus has established for them can no longer be merely a part of the Jewish nation, such as a Jewish sect. It is God's newly built house.

All of this will be made unambiguously clear through the unrestrained anger by which Jesus' judges cause him great suffering. It is they who condemn him, and this lends considerable gravity to the verdict imposed upon him, because it was reached by the entire Jewish nation with an appeal to God's law. Yet they will not kill him themselves. For they think his destruction will be all the more complete if he is crucified by the Romans. As long as he is in their hands, they will show him how fierce their hatred is. They will not deplore killing him, and they will not mourn at his grave. Rather, they will show him that he moved their innermost being and that everything in them militates against him, so that they defend their right against him with unbridled passion. And he, by suffering everything they do to him, will show them that he has no part in their rebellion against God but lives in communion with the Father and offers him homage in complete obedience.

Jesus Must Be Killed
June 7

He must be killed.
—Matthew 16:21

Death! This was the heaviest blow Jesus had to face, the great temptation in which he must prove his righteousness. It far surpassed those hours in which he overcame hunger through his trust in God or confronted a danger he had to avoid, mindful of his own weakness. Because of the prospect of being killed, the ultimate is required of him. Thus, the temptation that the prince of this world had instigated when he offered his support had become a powerful incentive. Could he not direct every person in authority—whether priest or Roman, layman or teacher of the Law—to refrain from attacking him? But Jesus was able to worship no one but God alone. He had his life from him, and he had to offer it to him when he required it of him. The same impossibility preventing him from turning to the king in Galilee also precluded any attempt to enter into a truce with the rulers in Jerusalem. Because he had no legitimate means of winning over his enemies, he had to die.

His death was not caused by nature, which brings about our death because it assigns us only a mortal life. None of Jesus' sayings suggests that he saw in natural mortality an obstacle to God's eternal gift of grace. There is no evidence that he viewed nature as God's adversary; it obeys God's will. He will live forever if God's creative will removes natural mortality from him.

The assault on his life comes from another direction—not from the decay of his body but from the wrath of man, and not the wrath of just any man but that of the Jew. Here again, it was not the wrath of tax collectors or sinners but of the priests and the teachers of the Law. God does not protect him from this assault. To the contrary, Jesus knows that he must be killed.

This is why he maintained that his death took place according to God's will and therefore must be suffered by him knowingly and willingly. This necessity is grounded in the fundamental opposition between the divine and the human will. This contrast must not be concealed. It must come out into the open and manifest itself, and it does come out into the open as the Christ is killed. This is how man's claim to know God is destroyed. He is shown his blindness, and his claim to honor God is done away with. He does not honor God but himself, and he does not obey God but fulfills his own desire, and his own self-made religion is a lie. By contrast, the Christ shows him that he glorifies not himself, nor the Jews, nor men, but God. He desires not his own greatness and his own life but rather obeys the will of God. He is true to his commission not merely in words—with presumptuous ideas and fabrications—but earnestly trusts in God's grace and fulfills his ministry toward God with everything that he is, with his body and his blood. This is truth's victory over all human opposition, and its victory makes room for grace. As it becomes clear what man is before God, it also becomes apparent what God is for man.

Jesus Must Rise
June 8

He must be raised on the third day.
—MATTHEW 16:21

God's command was, "You must be killed." Was this God's final and entire will? If so, this would mean the rescinding of the commission given to Jesus, the revocation of the word spoken by him, the destruction of Israel that now became the monument of the divine wrath, and the handing over of man to his own godlessness. But Jesus did not yield to death; he yielded to God and therefore not to death. Had he excluded God in anticipation of his demise and thought only of Jerusalem's hostility, whose hatred he cannot appease, then, of course, being killed would have been the last thing he could have expected. But now by his death he carries out what he was commanded to do. Thus his death does not distract him from his aim. Through it, too, God's rule is manifested, and this rule suspends the law of death to which nature subjects us, and reveals life.

As the witness of God's rule, Jesus had carried the message of life into a dying world. He had received the authority to do this from the living God, the Creator of all life. By virtue of this authority, he had obligated those who believed in him to die and had promised that the gates of hades would not be able to keep them. He issued this obligation and promise to his disciples because he first had overcome the fear of death himself in the knowledge of the Father. He had eluded death's power and had become one who lived, and as one who lived he faced death, and as one who lives he will rise from death. He will rise. This is the proof of his divine sonship once he has been judged by God and has been counted among the lawless, who must be expelled from the holy community.

The entire picture that the disciples had fashioned for themselves regarding the one who was to come, all their expectations, were thus completely altered. How will he deal with them once he has risen, and how will he manifest to Jerusalem that he has risen? Jesus was not one of the Greeks who in their poverty esteemed only knowledge and thought things had value for them only once they had understood them. He proclaimed the active God, whose works are available for us only when they have taken place. Just as the disciples did not receive any instruction from Jesus about how miracles took place and no directions on how to perform them, they also did not receive any description of the life that now reemerges out of death.

Only one statement continually appears in the disciples' reminiscences of Jesus' prediction and of Easter Sunday: that he will rise on the third day. The period between his death and the beginning of his new life is short; only a single day separates them. This day, on which he is dead, reveals the reality of his death. Jesus did not expect a transformation or glorification of his natural being. It suffered decay and belonged in a grave by the divine verdict. But the new beginning does not do away with what took place during his natural existence. The one who rose is the same as the one who died—the master of his disciples, the King of the Jews, the Savior of the world.

Peter Thinks He Knows Better than God
June 9

Peter took Jesus aside and began to admonish him:
"Lord, as sure as God is gracious toward you,
this will never happen to you."
—Matthew 16:22

When Jesus told Peter, "You are the rock," Peter did not contradict him. At that time he did not say that this was impossible. God can exalt; God can send. And when he issues an order, he also supplies the power. But when Jesus predicted his death, Peter spoke up against him. He considered this impossible. Why will this never take place? Because for God all things are possible. God can protect Jesus; God can prevent Jerusalem's demise; God can convert the leaders of the nation and overcome their unbelief. And because God is able to do this, Jesus cannot be killed, and his prediction cannot be fulfilled.

"God cannot." When do people say this? Whenever they consider their own aims to be enormously important, indubitably correct, and wonderfully wholesome and hence transfer these to God in the conviction that he, too, is bound to them. For this reason the declaration "God cannot; God can!" is quickly coupled with the assertion "God must not; God must!" Why must he? If he did this, he would be harsh and would act as my enemy.

Jesus must live. What disciple can desire anything else? Jerusalem must submit to Jesus. Who could not long for this with all his heart? Peter was promised a share in the work of the One who acts in God's power. How can he forgo this aim? This is world history constructed from a human point of view. Here, a person's desire makes plans for what he will experience.

Did anyone ever call a worldview his own that came about in a different manner?

Our worldview always expresses what we perceive and desire. No matter how industriously our minds are at work, our worldview is and remains a mirror image of our own self. Jesus did not dispute that the disciples' contradictions against him represented what *they* desired for themselves as his disciples and what *they* considered to be necessary. He did not call it sinful that they wanted to keep him with them because they loved him. Nor did he fault them for desiring Jerusalem's salvation rather than its demise. Nevertheless, their ideas are fundamentally mistaken and must be forsaken by them. For they assume that human interest determines what takes place in God's kingdom. Our worldview is true because, and to the extent to which, it arises from our experience. At the same time, however, it is completely certain that we are not at the center of the universe and are not its architects or rulers. For this reason our ideas about this world do not yet tell us what will take place or what ought to take place. Those ideas are partly confirmed, yet partly contradicted, by what the creative will of God brings about. That the disciple mourns when he thinks of Jesus' demise is in keeping with what he is as a disciple. But he must not forget that Jesus is the Lord, and he only his disciple; otherwise, he forsakes his discipleship.

Likewise, a person must ponder how he ought to go out into the world and how to arrange his relationship with it in such a way that he does not put himself in the place of God. He must resist the notion that he is the one who guides history and that his worldview is the final, definitive word. No one, including the disciple, should say, "God cannot." It is solely through what God says and does that the disciple finds out what God is able to do, and when the disciple contradicts this, he does the work of Satan, no matter how well intentioned he may be.

Renouncing Human Plans
June 10

You are not concerned for the interests of God,
but for the interests of man.
—MATTHEW 16:23

Was Jerusalem not right when it expected Jesus to exalt it? Was the disciple not entitled to desire that Jesus not forsake him? Can his community not legitimately expect that he be present with it? But now they all think of nothing but their rights, those things that concern them and threaten or strengthen their lives. But their right is one that is derived and given to them. In God's kingdom it is *God's* righteousness that is the all-controlling power. And God's righteousness is Jesus' concern—that God's verdict, which condemns all godlessness and unrighteousness, be carried out; that his forgiveness, which receives the guilty into his grace, be preserved pure from all contamination with sin; that the royal greatness of his grace be revealed, against which human enmity, though able to kill, cannot prevail. For this reason, so that the first and true righteousness—*God's* righteousness—might be accomplished, Jesus bore the cross.

Yet is God's righteousness not one with his love? Is love not the power through which everything in God's kingdom takes place? Are trials and suffering its gifts? Does it require blood? Does it kill? Again, those who speak in this way think only about what they themselves consider easy or difficult, sweet or bitter. They esteem the gifts of love. But Jesus does not merely crave God's gifts; he honors God's love, which is the source of these gifts and makes them redemptive. His love is not revealed through human self-interest's receiving what it desires. When our self-interest obtains what pleases it, this is grounded not in the love of God but in God's opposition toward us. God's love is realized in man when he does God's will. Jesus bore the cross in order to remain in God's love and so that people might see what God's love desires and accomplishes.

Jesus confronted Peter with the following choice: Who ought to be praised? Who ought to rule? Whose will ought to be done, God's or man's? When he did this, he pulled him toward himself with a strong grasp and made the choice easy for him. Even if Peter was terribly tormented and frightened by the prospect of Jesus' crucifixion, even if his future appeared to him completely dark and he did not understand the necessity mentioned by Jesus, there was no wavering between concern for his own well-being and submission to God's rule. Peter held fast to his confession that Jesus was the Christ, and he went with him to Jerusalem.

The Disciple's Sole Duty
June 11

Another one of his disciples said to him, "Lord, permit me first to leave and bury my father." But Jesus said to him, "Follow me, and let the dead bury their own dead."

—Matthew 8:21–22

If the sights of Jesus and of his disciples turned toward the future now that his demise was imminent, one thing was clear: the disciple was tied only and entirely to Jesus. If next to their allegiance to Jesus there was still another dependence that bound them, they must now give up their association with Jesus. If the Crucified was their Lord, the Jewish leaders were no longer their masters, the Jewish priests no longer their mediators with God, and those who kept the Law no longer the righteous ones whose praise they sought to obtain. Their destiny was no longer that of the Jews, and the national community was no longer the ground in which they were rooted. Now everyone was against them, and now, in the strictest sense of the word, they had no one left but Jesus.

In many of his actions and words, Jesus made sure from the very beginning that the exclusive nature of his association with his disciples became clear to all. In Judaism there was no holier obligation than that which required the son to assist the father. Among those obligations there was none more important than the son's duty to take care of his father's body when he died. It would have been inconceivable for a son not to ensure that the father was buried in an honorable manner. The man who offered Jesus his discipleship and asked only to be allowed to bury his father was considered by all to be ready to perform the greatest possible service. In everyone's opinion there was nothing more Jesus could legitimately demand. But he did what no one deemed thinkable. Everything that the disciple previously had been, must be shed. Every tie that makes him dependent on others must be cut, and nothing must be placed above his duty to follow Jesus.

Why must this be the case? Why does following Jesus entail the radical renunciation of every other kind of relationship? Jesus explained this by the contrast between the realms of the dead and the living. Whoever is accepted by Jesus as being among his disciples has received from him the promise of life. Whoever remains aloof, on the other hand, belongs to the multitude that chooses the wide road ending in death. There is no wavering here. Burying one's father is one of the many tasks that are part of the natural course of our lives. These can also be taken care of by the dead. On the other hand, the aim to which the disciple has turned by aligning himself with Jesus lies beyond the natural sphere. He wants to gain life in God's kingdom and gains it only if he devotes himself to it completely. The One who demanded this of the disciples himself surrendered everything when confronted with the cross. For he was the Living One; through his total surrender he won the crown of life.

Who Is Worthy of Him?
June 12

Whoever does not take up his cross, and does not follow me, is not worthy of me.
—Matthew 10:38

Had that which Jesus offered to his disciples been diminished because he now stood before them as the one who would end up on the cross? This would have been the case only if his decision to allow himself to be killed had indicated a rejection of his commission or a lessening of his divine sonship. But he went to Jerusalem precisely because his regal commission enjoined him to do so, and he was unable to reconcile with Jerusalem's leaders only because he lived in unity with the Father. For this reason the things he gave to his disciples through his fellowship were not obscured but rather revealed.

What he gave them were gifts that could not be separated from his person; the disciple did not receive from him anything material. He himself is the gift of God, and he himself is what he gives to the disciple. Jesus makes what he is before God effective for the disciple. His righteousness covers the disciple's guilt. His word opens the disciple's eyes to God's work. His death introduces the disciple to God's grace. And his resurrection is the disciple's rebirth to eternal life.

But is the disciple worthy of Jesus? What does he give him as a gift that is equivalent to Jesus' gift? How does he thank him for what he does for him? Jesus does not come to the disciple as the one who makes requests. Rather, it is the disciple's task to see what he can offer Jesus that is commensurate to the grace shown to him. Only the one who takes up his cross and subsequently follows him is worthy of him. Conversely, whoever does not take up his cross lacks what makes him worthy of Jesus' forgiveness and love. He does not acquire this worthiness through his own achievements or power. He obtains it by something entirely different, namely, that he does not refuse to accept the cross assigned to him as his own and to bear it.

The divine verdict that placed the cross upon Jesus also applies to the disciple. He, too, is subject to God's verdict, which calls him guilty and refuses him life, not in order to condemn him—no!—but so that he may receive the pardon that grants him righteousness. All this occurs, not to condemn him to death, but that he may enter eternal life as a risen one, yet in such a way that the divine verdict, which rejects all godlessness, remains valid and is acknowledged and honored by the disciple.

This is now the question that decides his relationship with Jesus: Does he accept the divine verdict, or does he defend himself against God? Does he want to have a righteousness of his own, or does he honor the righteousness of God? How will he receive life: as a gracious gift of God, or because God owes it to him? Does he want to live forever in his natural state, or does he expect life from the resurrection that will be given to him?

Whoever accepts God's verdict against him aligns himself with Jesus, because he, too, accepted his cross from the Father. He declares God right; everything that man is, he declares wrong. This is the renunciation of selfish desires, the forgoing of all claims that man directs toward God. In this way too, all of his obligations cease, just as the One—who has been condemned by a human judge and now takes up the tree on which he must die—leaves everything behind and turns his back to the entire world. And now Jesus says to the one who is condemned and dead before him and the entire world: "You are worthy of me. You have understood why I bore my cross, and you can be my follower."

Self-Denial
June 13

If anyone wants to follow me, let him deny himself,
take up his cross, and follow me.
—MATTHEW 16:24

When Jesus' call, "Come to me!" reaches us, a conversation begins inside us: Depending on the outcome, do we really want to come to him? A voice is audible within us that warns us, "Don't do it! He is the Crucified One, and he has prepared a cross also for you. This is what you will find with him, and you must bear it if you want to remain with him. With him you will become a sinner, lose all greatness and your entire reputation, and learn to pray, 'God, be gracious to me, a sinner.' Watch out and preserve your dignity! And the world will perish with him. You will experience what Paul went through for Jesus' sake. You will be a crucified one to the world, despised and mocked, and the world will be crucified to you. It will lose its glitter for you. You will no longer be able to celebrate with it; you will lose the ability to mingle with it. Watch out and pursue your own happiness!"

Because this conversation takes place within us, Jesus says this to us: Deny yourselves. Do not serve as your own counselors and do not look within yourselves for the instructions you obey. Tell yourselves, "I do not know you and do not listen to you," just as one says that he does not know someone he has denied, and has nothing to do with him.

But who in the entire world should we believe, then, if not our own eyes? And who is capable of directing our actions if not our own judgments and consciences? Does Jesus want to kill our reason and take away our individuality? Does he keep us from developing ourselves? Will this be replaced with slavish obedience?

All of these objections are foolish, because this conversation does not take place in a dark corner in solitude but in Jesus' presence in us, because we know Jesus and ponder whether we want to belong to him and to live our lives under his direction. For this reason self-denial does not introduce into us dull thoughtlessness, nor do we fall into some empty existence. To be sure, when we listen to Jesus and deny ourselves, we do not think our own thoughts and do not insist upon our own wishes. We do not speak our own words and do not live for ourselves. Yet this is not because we do not think or want anything or because we do not say or do anything. Rather, it is because we think Jesus' thoughts and want Jesus' will and speak Jesus' word and stand in his service.

Is self-denial, then, another word for *repentance?* Indeed, through it we do free ourselves from our own opinions and desires. Yet our denials do not merely pertain to what is reprehensible in us. On the contrary, it frequently pertains precisely to what we have thought up in our ingenuity and have seized with noble excitement. "Deny yourself"—this command is addressed not merely to the pagan but also to the Christian thinker.

Self-denial is greater than repentance. For it requires faith. "Do not listen to yourself" means "Listen to me." "Do not trust in yourself" means "Trust me." "Take up your cross" means "Look at my cross, where God has judged and pardoned you, O man."

The Battle Is Fought with Unequal Weapons
June 14

Look! I am sending you out as lambs among wolves.
—LUKE 10:3

In everything Jesus did, he was watched and attacked from all sides. The situation was like that of a flock being attacked from all sides by wolves. Yet the battle fought by Jesus takes on its irreconcilable acrimony through his crucifixion. The goal for which his opponents contend is the destruction of his followers. Nevertheless, "I am sending you." It would be inconceivable for them to remain silent. They have heard the glorious message about God's kingdom and grace in order to proclaim it. It would be impossible for them to go their separate ways and leave the people to their own devices. God's message is directed to the Jewish people and must not be taken away from them, not even by engaging in ministry to the Samaritans or in the Greek-speaking towns where Jews lived. They must wrestle for Jerusalem, as Jesus himself did.

They are not unprepared for this battle. Jesus does not send them out without equipping them. They no longer have the same nature as those to whom he sends them, just as lambs do not possess the same nature as wolves. For Jesus gave them what he himself possesses, so that they resemble servants to whom their master has given his talents to administer. After all, it is not merely ideas that they must spread; he has taken them into his own relationship with God and thus shaped their inner lives. He has made them those who believe and those who love. For this reason his word cannot end with his death, which leads him out of the earthly community. He lives in those he has called, and the first aim that bids them work is Jewish need—the sin of those who live under the Law and the unbelief of those who waited for the Christ.

But by comparing the situation into which his commission places them with that of lambs among wolves, he gives them the guideline for their conduct. The rabbi worked with the scourge and the ban, and he called upon the Roman judge—who did not spare the crosses—for support. But these are not the disciples' weapons. Jesus made it impossible for them to use their enemies' tactics. They must not return curse for curse or violence for violence. They can no more do this than a lamb can defend itself as if it were a wolf.

Will they lose in this unequal battle, which must be conducted with different kinds of weapons? "I am sending you"—that is enough to vanquish any such fear. Just as Jesus is not overcome by his crucifixion, so they, too, will not speak or minister in vain. When a person rejects God's rule, the outcome of this battle is clear: God's rule is carried out, and whoever resists it falls.

The One Who Is Good Is the Victor
June 15

Do not be overcome by evil, but overcome evil with good.
—Romans 12:21

Either we are overcome, or we prevail. There is no third option for us. Can we not avoid this and go someplace where we watch from a neutral vantage point as evil clashes with evil? This would be a place where we would not be afflicted by enemies but where we would be surrounded only by love. But such a place does not exist for us; for we are a part of the world and, because we believe in Christ, have the world set against us. Thus evil continually confronts us.

But does it also enter us? Then we have been overcome. It is no small endeavor to steer clear of the contagious power of evil. All evil exerts powerful impulses. If another person breaks fellowship with us, we also break it with him. If he destroys our reputation, we destroy his. After all, we experience in ourselves how deeply wounded we are when we suffer evil. If we resort to the same weapon, it will also wound the other person. Our invective hits no less hard than his hits us. If we aim well, our blow will meet its target, and we can enjoy the proud feeling of being the victor.

"No," Paul will say, "you have been overcome!"

He says this to those who are in Christ and live under the influence of Christ, because they are recipients of his grace. They cannot desire evil. Evil is not part of their calling and is not what Christ produces in them. If they reply, "Then should we be defenseless and suffer all evil?" he tells them, "It is not the manner of Christ that he merely endures evil, but that he overcomes it. This is his work. You are called to be victorious, not to be overcome. And what is worst about your defeat is that you were defeated when you could have been victorious. You can desire what is good and do what is good. But you consider what is good to be null and void, and yet it is stronger than all evil. It is the power that overcomes evil."

Is this only a so-called faith, wishful thinking of how we imagine the world as we would like it to be rather than as it really is? To be sure, Paul is able to say this only because he is a believer. But the superiority of good over evil is no longer a mere figment of the imagination for those who found God's grace in Christ. Of course, there are blatant lies that shamelessly misrepresent the truth. There is hatred that fills the entire heart, and hardened godlessness that is no longer able to hear. Paul's advice, "Overcome evil with what is good," does not promise us that we will not have to suffer. Humanity is still subject to God's dual manner of operation: his opposition, which renders them sinful, and his grace, which produces what is good in people. But this is not God's final word or work. And the superiority of good over evil is made part of our experience also when we are allowed nothing other than to preserve the good gift given to us. And when we respond with good to the evil that confronts us in the world, we experience that it is no empty saying that all things serve for the good of those who love God.

Jesus Does Not Derive His Power from the World
June 16

My kingdom is not of this world. If my kingdom were of this world, my servants would fight for me, so that I not be handed over to the Jews. But now my kingdom is not from here.

—JOHN 18:36

The young men of Galilee considered it self-evident that a true disciple fought for his master. Was it not part of a king's commission that he lead his nation's army? Was royal service not military service? In the past, Moses, the judges, and the kings led their armies into battle in the name of God. And when Jerusalem celebrated the rededication of the temple after its desecration through Greek kings, it also remembered the heroes who had overcome Gentile tyranny in armed combat. But this is not how Christ's rule is established! His disciples would need to fight for him if his rule were grounded in the world. Then he would draw on human power, and then he would have expected his disciples to make every effort to be ready for combat.

But how would this be able to reveal God's rule? This would result in the victorious person who in battle with others proved to be more ingenious or strong and from this derived his right to be greater than them. The wisdom that devises such plans is not from God and does not provide humanity with a constitution through which God's righteousness is realized. God subjects humanity through the One who obtained his rule solely through his communion with God. For this reason it is only the defenseless person who can proclaim the message about his rule; only the one who serves, not the one who subjugates others; only the one who is free and who frees others, not the one who enslaves them; only the one who leads them into life, not the one who takes it from them.

The disciples would not have understood Jesus if they had deplored their defenselessness as weakness. Jesus is the King precisely because they cannot fight for him. If they were to bring him a crown they had won for him, it would not be his crown, not one he could wear. For people could not obtain the rule for him, because he has received it from the Father. And he did not forsake what God gave him for what people were able to conquer for him.

While his rule does not come *through* people, it is *for* people. His love draws him to people; he established his community out of people; and it is people he subjects to God. Yet the one to whom he subjects them is God. This is the aim his disciples must serve, and this is the reason the service they must render is different from that which rulers require from their followers, just as the lamb is different from the wolf.

Jesus' Disciples Are Not Like the Prophets
June 17

And he sent out messengers ahead of him, and they went and came to a Samaritan village to find lodging. And they did not receive him, because his face was set toward Jerusalem. But when his disciples James and John saw this, they said, "Lord, do you want us to call down fire from heaven to destroy them?" But he turned and admonished them. And they went to another village.
—Luke 9:52–56

The disciples defenseless? No! They are not. True, they have no weapons and do not resemble the bodyguards of a ruler who instills fear in all. They also could not admonish or put adversaries in their places with harsh words. In fact, malicious rage is forbidden to them. Yet, instead, they have an ability that surpasses all of these: they can call to the One who judges righteously, the One who is able to protect the honor of his Christ with his peals of wrath. Which weapon protects more surely than this one? God is a good shield and weapon.

To be sure, the disciples are not able to do this by virtue of their own righteousness. But then, they do not fight for themselves but for the honor of their Lord, and they want to call upon the judging work of God only when Jesus authorizes them to do so. They do not doubt his effectiveness in prayer, nor are they in doubt regarding God's willingness to punish those who insult his Son. If they pronounce their verdict in his name according to the instructions given to them, it will be valid in heaven. After all, he gave them the authority to bind those who resist his word in such a way that they are bound in heaven. And who must be bound if not proud, Jew-hating Samaritans who refused Jesus lodging at night, for no other reason than because they knew he was headed for Jerusalem?

Yet Jesus admonished his disciples and thus at an important juncture established a boundary between the old and the new word of God. The two disciples were emboldened to ask for God's judging intervention, not merely by the authorization Jesus was supposed to give them but also by the memory of Elijah. Jesus himself had placed them alongside the prophets. Admittedly, he was speaking of the suffering prophet, who remained God's messenger even though the people did not listen to him, the one who, not deterred by constant danger of death, fulfilled his commission and remained true until death. Yet the prophet who lived in the memory of the people and who spoke to them through Scripture was not merely the one who suffered but also the one who was powerful through God. Yes, Moses patiently endured people's complaints, but he also called God's judgment upon Pharaoh and upon those who rebelled against him. And Elijah had not merely provided sustenance for the starving widow; he also defended the honor of his God—and thus also the honor of his role as his messenger—through the lightning that struck the emissaries of the rebellious king. These were holy memories by which those who lived in God's old word were all too willing to be moved. Now Jesus replaced these memories by his cross, and they paled in comparison with its brilliance. Precisely when he traveled to Jerusalem to be crucified, he erected a boundary between those who once had been God's spokesmen and those to whom he passed on his word.

There Is Only One Danger
June 18

Do not fear those who kill the body but are unable to kill the soul. Rather, fear the One who has the power to destroy both soul and body in hell.

—MATTHEW 10:28

What can enemies do? They can kill the body! Is that not the end of it all? Should they not therefore be feared? Yet the destruction of the body does not also entail the destruction of the soul and thus does not yet determine whether a person has lost his life. That depends on what happens with his soul, and judges and executioners have no power over this. They received their existence from God's creative power and their lives from his paternal will. For this reason man cannot destroy them as well.

Thus the disciples' view is directed toward the One who alone is to be feared. God's verdict alone decides their existence or nonexistence, their living or dying, their salvation or destruction. And this verdict is to be feared because it pertains to everything a person represents. The entire person—not merely his body but also his soul—is in God's hands, and he is able to separate people—in their totality, not merely their bodies but also their souls—from life in his kingdom. Jesus says that this final verdict is suffered in "hell" (Gehenna). This was the name for the place where those were brought who were excluded from God's people and who were not given eternal life.

Does Jesus thereby instill in his disciples' souls the fear of hell? No! He taught them to honor God by believing in him, and faith in God and fear of hell have no place in one and the same soul. But when their opponents threaten them and they fear death, they ought to remember that there is still another danger to which they succumb when God is against them. And compared with this danger, every other loss, every kind of suffering, even death, loses its terror.

This is how Jesus rendered his disciples unafraid and elevated them above every fear. The fear of what God's judgment would impose upon them if they forsook Jesus overcomes every other type of fear that might afflict them. Through this they are, as the next passage indicates, safe in God's care, from which no power can extricate them. Thus they can truly say regarding themselves, "We fear no one but God alone."

Love Is the End of Fear
June 19

There is no fear in love, but perfect love drives out fear. This is because fear has to do with punishment; but the one who is afraid has not yet been made perfect in love.

—1 John 4:18

Jesus on the cross! There was no prospect that could frighten the disciples more than this. Such then was the destiny of the One who honored God, of the One who acted in love and from it received a right to rule that did not make him similar to a predatory animal. And now Jesus predicted the same destiny for his disciples. Was it not inevitable that continually new waves of fear would flood through mankind from his cross? Not so—the opposite was true. Jesus seized the cross fearlessly, and when he assigned the disciples their crosses, he simultaneously liberated them from fear and doubt. He did not set the Passion in contrast to the Christmas story. The latter depicted Christ's arrival as the end of fear and the rise of peace, and "Fear not!" is the message that penetrates mankind from Jesus' cross with increased intensity.

This happened because "there is no fear in love." Fear does not arise from love but is driven out by it. Fear is born from our desire for self-preservation and self-promotion. For this desire is confronted with powers that are completely superior. Nature surrounds our existence with a series of dangers, and our activity is frequently threatened or hindered by what we call our "fate." Fear arises from these opposing forces, which often hurt us badly. But when our self-centeredness is dethroned in our lives, fear loses the soil from which it grows. The dethroning of selfishness, in turn, takes place by tying our lives to God's Word and work, by which we are granted love.

There were always people seeking to drive out fear by strengthening their egos. Is fear not weakness that puts one to shame? The strong person asserts himself by locking out fear. Yet in this wrestling match, fear still remains the victor in the end. This only results in the tragic hero who finally gives up his resistance against hostile powers because it is futile.

Love, on the other hand, is not concerned with what we gain for ourselves but desires that the other person's will be done. And this other person, who provides love with its will and its joy, is the One who is not deterred by any obstacle or rendered powerless by any need, the One whose gifts are all good and perfect. This brings an end to fear. This does not change the nature of events. They retain their painful harshness, and their destructive consequences are not concealed. But above them love recognizes love and allies itself with its creative power and its all-encompassing rule.

This, of course, provides us with not merely an initial, provisional love but with perfect love, which has mastered our selfishness. This was the meaning of the demand directed toward Jesus: he had to preserve his assurance and joy while he headed for Jerusalem. This required him to complete his love and show a frightened humanity that love drives out fear.

Save Yourselves!
June 20

What would a man gain if he were to win the entire world but lose his soul? Or what can a man give in exchange for his soul?
—MATTHEW 16:26

The Christ lives and dies for humanity, and it is to humanity that he sends his messengers. They must win the world. They are bound to this, their calling, through everything Jesus gave to them. They believed that the Christ would reveal himself to the world. They believed that his call would reach everyone and that his work would be completed when humanity is united in God. This lends incomparable significance to their lives. Should they not spare their lives and wisely avoid any danger?

Yet one danger exists for them, which they must fear: that they might not pass Christ's judgment. Whoever is rejected by him loses his soul and does no longer belong to those who live forever. What good is it, then, if they save others and perish themselves, if they bring God's grace to others but are themselves rejected by God? What they were for others cannot justify or protect them if they become sinners in their own Christian lives.

They are the chosen ones. How easily this could make them proud! They are given the promise. Can they not be fully assured that they will reach their goal? They administer God's Word and are other people's teachers and leaders. Will they steer clear of an arrogant abuse of power? But if they lose God's favor for themselves, they have lost everything. This is why it is their foremost duty, which precedes all others, that they themselves remain in the faith, that they not let go of their confession even when confronted with death, and that they remain true and obedient to Jesus' word in their dealings with the Jews.

Is this at odds with the love commandment, by which Jesus told the disciples that they live for others? Here he tells them to take care of themselves; their foremost concern must be that they be saved. Yet in no way is there a contradiction here. Both ought to obtain life, the apostle and the world, I and the one with whose well-being I am charged. Whoever corrupts himself has not acted in love. It establishes fellowship between me and others. But this fellowship is corrupted if I myself become a dead person who is condemned by his conscience, enslaved by his selfish desires, and rejected by God's verdict. We are only deceiving ourselves if we think that we will be able to gain the world while corrupting ourselves with untruth and selfishness. We may indeed win others for ourselves through such means. But for Christ the world is won only through those who serve him faithfully.

Free of Charge
June 21

Freely you received; freely give!
—Matthew 10:8

What takes place for God's sake is not a business in which we seek our own advantage. It was one of Jesus' greatest concerns that the Jewish establishment understand this, for this was one of the most important conditions for their salvation. Does a person ever do anything without thinking of his own tangible profit? Jesus' response to this kind of thinking was to send out his disciples as those who were poor. He sent them into Jewish villages without any possessions and commanded them to take no compensation for their services, even when they healed the sick.

In this, too, he acted completely counter to Jewish conventional wisdom and practice. Why should a pious person not expect to be made rich by God's blessing? Did faith rendered to God not entail that God would protect his property against harm and prosper his dealings with others? And was this not true now more than ever, because God did not treat people according to the Law but offered to everyone gracious gifts from the riches of his divine kingdom? How then can poverty be the mark of those who proclaim the kingdom?

But precisely because they come by God's commission, the disciples are completely poor when they enter the villages and no less so when they leave them again. This is their pledge to God, their rejection of human selfishness, the visible expression of their believing conduct, which they received from Jesus. Thus what they do for others corresponds to what Jesus did for them. He gave to them freely, without requiring of them compensation or gifts. He took them into his fellowship for their sakes, not according to the Law—which provided for only one service in exchange for an equivalent one—but in obedience to love, which did not allow him to remain alone.

This is why the disciples' poverty has nothing in common with the renunciation of the weak person who is too tired or too lazy to acquire property. Rather, the disciples are poor because they are rich on account of the treasure they have in heaven. By not having any other riches, they prove that their share in God's grace is truly a treasure.

The disciples' poverty also has nothing in common with the renunciation of the penitent. Such a person hates the lust that exudes from his body, because it provides the impulse for evil deeds, and so he deprives his body of anything that feeds or strengthens him. But the disciple of Jesus does not make a virtue out of his lack, the way the penitent do in order to gain a favorable verdict from God. He does not deny the message of forgiveness—on account of which he aligned himself with Jesus—through his poverty. He is poor because he has been forgiven and because he has freely received. *Freely!* That means that everything he has is a free and gracious gift of God. This gift, in turn, does not ensue in the renunciation of the self-deprived, but rather in the kind of love that surrenders everything it has to the Lord to whom it belongs.

Jesus Does Not Make Beggars Out of His Disciples
June 22

Remain in the same house, and eat and drink what they give you. For the worker is worthy of his wages. Do not move from house to house. And when you enter a city and they receive you, eat what they put in front of you, and heal their sick and tell them, "The kingdom of God is near you." But when you come into a city and they do not receive you, proclaim in its streets, "We are wiping off even the dust of your city that has attached itself to our feet. But know this: God's kingdom is near." I tell

> *you, it will be better for Sodom on that day than it will be for that city.*
> —Luke 10:7–12

Did Jesus make beggars out of his poor disciples? Those who stand in the king's service and who come as his emissaries are no beggars. They make those to whom they are sent rich and thus are like the worker who does not work free of charge but receives wages for his labor, or the farmer who must not be kept from enjoying the fruit of his harvest. The freedom and joy that are the disciple's, owing to his faith in Jesus, are expressed by unhesitatingly accepting food from those whose house he enters. At the same time, he must not bother his hosts with improper requests or select a house that is especially comfortable. His freedom from natural desires must be evident in all situations. This is why he remains in the house he has entered.

But if people refuse to listen to him because the village is opposed to him, this cannot create a predicament for the disciple. He is not under compulsion to persist in this village and to expose himself continually to its hostility. If they do not listen, he leaves. In this case he must underscore the importance of his commission by uniting it with the proclamation of divine judgment. He is to remind the obstinate village of the fate of Sodom, because Sodom did receive the visit of angels, albeit in a way that resulted not in the city's rescue but in its demise. Jesus' messengers render an angel's service to those to whom they come, and they do so to a far greater extent than those heavenly messengers who paid a visit to Sodom. For this reason their rejection ensues in even more severe judgment.

These were the guiding principles for the relationship between Jesus' community and the economy. The community that comes into being through his message does not itself engage in business dealings but lives from the available food in the general population at large. It does so in such a way that it is not open to the dishonorable charge of being an idle parasite. For it does not merely receive but also gives and receives in order to be able to give. The disciples give to a much greater extent than those who produce natural products, and consequently their rejection results in a loss for those who reject them, a loss that cannot be compared with what the presence of Jesus' messengers requires of people.

Jesus Rewards Every Good Deed
June 23

Whoever gives one of these little ones even a cup of cold water in his name because he is a disciple, let me assure you: he will not go unrewarded.

—MATTHEW 10:42

The poverty of Jesus' disciples did not place them among those who depended upon the mercy of others. They are their benefactors, not merely when these people receive God's gracious Word but already when they receive from them any kind of service or help. Every service they perform will be rewarded if it is performed because they are Jesus' disciples.

For it will be no small thing if a Jew in the heat of combat—by which his people seek to destroy the disciples—retains so much respect for a disciple that he is prepared to give him a gift. The disciples will no longer be under the protection of the custom that requires granting hospitality to every fellow countryman. They must expect that houses will be closed to them and that they will be refused nourishment. Jesus speaks of the smallest service. On the one hand, it is nonetheless refreshing for the one who is on the receiving end. On the other hand, the gift requires no effort for the giver, and he incurs no loss. Rather than turning away from the disciple in hatred and disgust, he gives to the thirsty disciple a cup of water, which he draws from his well or pours from the water pitcher in his house. When Jesus speaks of cold water, he thinks of the custom of warming up water in order to mix it with wine. In that case the service rendered would entail a certain amount of work.

Those whom Jesus sends lack that which otherwise rendered a man honorable in people's eyes, in which case people were glad to offer service or help. They are neither prophets nor righteous ones; they are "little ones." The only thing that elevates them above others is their discipleship. Through it, however, they are aligned with Jesus in such a way that he will reward that which is done for them. No good deed is rendered to them in vain. If anyone is kind toward them because he knows and honors them as Jesus' disciples, Jesus becomes Savior for the villager, who distributes to him the divine gifts. He sends his disciples on their renunciation-rich way as those who are the richest of the rich, the ones who administer the divine gifts. No one honors them in vain. There is no one who helps his disciples whom he does not notice. The gravest sin can arise in people's dealings with the disciples. But there is also room for a good deed, which has abundant consequences. This reveals the perfect union Jesus established between himself and his disciples. What is done for them is done for him. And he makes gratitude for what was done for them his own business, which he dispenses with royal grace.

What Does the Disciple See in Nature?
June 24

Look at the birds in the sky. They do not sow,
they do not reap, and they do not gather their harvest into
barns. And yet your heavenly Father feeds them. Are you not
worth more than they are?
—Matthew 6:26

Nature tells us unmistakably, "You, O man, are a part of me. You are a part of the flow of life, which gives existence and life to everything you see. Regard the animal as your brother and ancestor. You grew from the same root as the bird, and the same ray of light that shows you the world also shows it to the bird, and the same air that quickens his blood also gives strength to yours." This insight issues in a sense of our insignificance, which cuts at the root of our lives. "What are you, O man? The powers accumulated in your race brought you into being and now play with you just as they do with the mosquito or the frog."

Jesus, likewise, bids us not to forget our kinship with the animals. The One who sustains both the birds and us is the same. The same hand gives them and us the opportunity to live. Both of us are dependent on God's provision. Yet he keeps us from sinking into a feeling of powerlessness. The sentiment is valid: "What is man, that you think of him, and the son of man, that you visit him?" What we find in ourselves gives us no greater confidence than that with which the young bird flies into the world. Yet we are remembered, and we are visited, and the One who visits us is the One who lives forever. By visiting us, he elevates us above the birds, whom he feeds just as he feeds us, and above the lilies, which he adorns just as he clothes us. Moreover, he assigns to us a service in this world that he does not give to them and provides us with a purpose that they are not given.

Jesus said, "You," and he meant his disciples, whom he called to himself and whom he has given a part in his work. They know that God remembered them and visited them in his grace. For they hear the One who speaks to them as the living Word of God and are able to receive his Word within themselves and to preserve it. Yet whoever bears God's Word within himself no longer stands solely in the kind of relationship with God that the birds do. He has received something that does not rise from the flow of natural forces, and thus has an obligation that is not exhausted in allowing these natural forces to act upon him according to their law. When God speaks to man, this results in more than a bird; this is a new act of creation. But Jesus does not lead us into the kind of thinking by which people despise nature or deem themselves sufficient in themselves. He does not allow us to treat God's work with contempt. We ought to believe in the One who feeds the birds. For the same God also feeds those whom he makes to be his children.

Those of Little Faith
June 25

If God clothes the grass of the field, which is here today and tomorrow is thrown into the fire, will he not much more clothe you, O you of little faith?
—Matthew 6:30

The disciples are believers. Their God is no longer one who is unknown. God has spoken to them. The fear of God no longer drives them away from him. They have found the Christ, the witness of divine grace, and have received from him the ability to believe in God. But this is not the only thing that they are. Their faith often fails them. One moment their faith controls their conduct; the next it does not. They are "short of faith" and cannot judge out of faith or act out of faith when their predicament calls them to faith most urgently.

What makes them partly believers and partly unbelievers? They are not only dealing with God. They are confronted with nature, whose effects they cannot control, and other people obstruct their paths, and not only individuals—no!—the world, the close-knit totality of all, on which they are dependent. Thus faith is separated from seeing. They believe that just as God clothes the lilies, he also clothes us, and just as God feeds the birds, he also feeds us—yet the disciples do suffer lack. They believe that God has given them his grace, yet they experience much bitter suffering. They believe that life has appeared, but they are those commanded to die. Christ is the source of the word that makes them believers; but what happens contradicts that word, and the promise announces what has not yet occurred but will do so only in the future. So the disciple is moved from two different directions: by virtue of his knowledge of God, he is a believer; yet his experience in the world makes him fearful, one who mourns and grows tired, one who remains silent, fails to engage in ministry, and is primarily concerned about himself.

Is this the way it is supposed to be? Jesus warns, "O you of little faith!" Wavering steps do not lead to one's destination, and our will becomes unfruitful when it is torn apart by internal contradictions. This confronts us with the danger of incurring serious guilt. "If I rebuild what I tore down," Paul had said, "I prove to be a transgressor." If I revoke my faith at one time and at another admonish and overcome my unbelief, I have not yet been made perfect. This is an incomplete beginning, with which I must not remain content. For our Father is perfect and does not make double-minded individuals out of us but wholly subjects us to himself.

Yet Jesus does not break fellowship with the disciples simply because they have only little faith. What has been begun in them, even though it is still incomplete, is nonetheless his work, to which he is committed and which he will complete. For it is not merely the disciple and his faith that are still imperfect; Jesus' work and God's revelation are also imperfect—that is, not yet brought to completion. On the day when his work is completed, the dilemma of those who only have little faith will come to an end as well. For then they will see.

Cares Are Cast on God
June 26

Cast all your cares on God, for he cares for you.
—1 PETER 5:7

The newly planted congregations in Asia Minor had a variety of concerns. For they were attempting something unheard of. They banded together to form a community that was grounded not—as other associations were—in natural self-interest but in a common faith and love. And Jews and Greeks were united in this community. Who had previously considered this possible? What is more, slave and free were united as well—a social problem that had previously defeated all political attempts to solve it. They endeavored to remove the entire glamorous business of idol worship and did not fear the world's opposition, even though the state authorities had already risen to combat them. How much they had to ponder here! How many obstacles lay in the path of these congregations that had to be overcome! Time and again it required the most profound reflection and the use of all the strength given to them in order to choose the right course of action.

But this does not make being a Christian into a burdensome enterprise. Peter says: Release what concerns you, makes you anxious, and weighs you down with cares. Cast it away! Where should we cast the things that strain our thoughts and desires with mounting intensity? Into a corner where we can no longer see them? No! "Cast your cares upon God," Peter says. We cast them away, not so that nothing will happen, nor to allow ourselves to be driven—without reflection, plan, or our own work—by whatever comes our way. This would be fatalism and a rejection of our duty to serve and a desertion of our service in Jesus' army. We cast upon God everything that moves us, so that his will might be done and his activity might make a way for us. "Cast away what afflicts you, and close your eyes" is the counsel of the cowardly and the desperate. "Cast your cares upon God" is the attitude of the believer; it brings an end to restlessness, but not to sensible reflection and action. Now the challenge is to pay attention to what God does, so that we unite our wills with his will and integrate our services into his work.

It is not that we receive from our faith either peace or courage and energy. Both are the effects of faith. The believer knows that his own wishes and his own efforts are futile. Now our souls quiet down, and we shed our impatience. Yet the believer also knows that God's Word is with him so that he will obey it, and that his grace has come to him so that through him it will also be effective for others. This makes a person attentive to God's call and ready to follow his leading. Thus is fulfilled Jesus' promise to us that we will find rest for our souls with him, the rest that we possess by bearing the yoke and the burden that he assigns to us.

The Believer Calls upon the Almighty
June 27

Then the disciples approached Jesus privately and said,
"Why were we unable to drive it out?" But he said to them,
"Because of your little faith. For I assure you:
If you have faith like a mustard seed, you will say to this
mountain, 'Go from here to there!' and it will go there,
and nothing will be impossible for you."
—MATTHEW 17:19–20

Jesus elevates his disciples to rulers in this world. They command mountains, and they obey. Nothing is impossible for them. Is this really true? Does he think the disciples will be omnipotent? No! They have this promise because they have faith, and faith is the total opposite of a self-understanding that views oneself as having unlimited power. When Jesus talks about faith, he does not think of the confidence that is ours on account of our consciousness of our own strength. Rather, the believer looks away from his own ability to the One in whom he believes. He depends on the One to whom he calls and seeks the power he needs from him rather than from himself. Now the one to whom the believer turns is God, and this is what the disciples forget. This is why they are powerless and incapable of faith. For this reason Jesus uses his powerful statement to impress upon them what they do when they believe. They turn to the One, who in truth possesses omnipotence, moves mountains, and for whom nothing is impossible. The believer can speak to him only the way the leper spoke to Jesus: "If you want to, you can!" If he thought differently, he would say to God, "If you can," and would be a doubter.

This is what Jesus said regarding every believing action. The disciples must not object that he speaks only of those who possess a faith that is particularly strong, because they received a gracious gift of faith that is their special privilege. But they, average disciples, could not have such great faith. Such ideas reveal what would render the disciples incapable of faith. They measure their faith and can only find something that is weak and imperfect. Then they ask what they can do with their weak faith. Jesus' reply is that this shows they have no faith at all—not only one that is smaller than they would like, not even one that resembles a mustard seed (and Jesus used the mustard seed to designate that which is the very smallest). If they expect their faith to grant what they desire, they have fallen into the trap of "little faith," believing in their own power to believe.

What happens when they act in a believing manner? If they think as believers, they think what God has told them. If they act as believers, they do what God has commanded them. If they pray as believers, they pass on their concerns to God. *God!* Don't they know what this name implies? Even mountains obey his word. If they believe, they have the Almighty on their side.

So, then, are the disciples world rulers after all, free and subject to no other authority, victorious over every obstacle? Yes, they are—but only when and to the extent to which they believe. They are not victorious in their own power and not for the sake of their own honor. There is no room for an arbitrary use of power or high-handedness—the believer has renounced these. He finishes his course unhindered and unconquered, because he has God on his side, and he has him on his side because he trusts in him.

For this reason there is no contradiction between Jesus' statement that highly elevates the disciple and his other statement that makes him the bearer of a cross. Because he, as a believer, agrees with God's verdict that pronounces him guilty and grants him God's grace, he is no longer subject to any other power. Because he has been *set* free, he *is* free.

Section 12

JESUS ALONE IS THE JUDGE

Jesus Will Pronounce the Verdict upon the Disciples
June 28

The Son of Man will come in the glory of his Father
and of his angels, and then he will repay everyone according
to what he has done.

—MATTHEW 16:27

The disciples are to become his messengers. This is why he had predicted his resurrection to them. Speak as the messengers of a dead person—no! This was absurd. Only someone who is alive needs people who represent him. But they also needed a statement regarding the outcome of their ministry. By promising them that he would be their judge at his new revelation, Jesus gave them this statement. Only he himself, who sent them, can complete their work. They were not able themselves to pronounce the verdict on what they had done. He alone can determine whether their work was done according to his will and whether it will be accepted by him as the fulfillment of his intentions.

But when he comes to them, he will have a different form than what he has now. At that time God's glory will be visible in him, and then the heavenly spirits will accompany and serve him. By this he confirms the testimony of his messengers regarding his regal commission. They proclaim the One who, in a human manner, spoke of God's glory and who, as one who suffered and died, promised the world the kingdom of God. Thus it will be his task to reveal the truthfulness of their message and to remove from it the dark mystery that his end attached to them. Because at that time he in regal glory will pronounce the verdict on the disciples, the verdict will with final authority determine their participation in God's kingdom.

What he subjects to his verdict is their work. For he commissioned them to do a work, just as he, who performs God's works, has come and will come. Whether or not they did what he wanted them to do, and whether or not what they brought about meets with his approval—this they will learn from him when he is once again with them, and every disciple will passionately long for this verdict. They were commissioned to this service because they believed in Jesus. Their faith provided them with the impetus and the guiding principle of everything they did. And precisely because they believed, they long for Jesus' verdict regarding what they do. For because they believe, they live for him, speak his word, and teach people his commandment. All of this receives eternal value only when their work is confirmed by his verdict.

Does he thereby instill fear into their souls? To be sure, his role as judge assumes that the disciple may act on his own and deviate from Jesus' commandment. Time and again he sought to impress this upon them. Yet he speaks to them not only as their judge when they were unfaithful to him. He does so because he has enlisted them in his service and because this service reaches its fulfillment when he recognizes their obedience and honors their faithfulness. We do not understand Jesus and his disciples if we place the proclamation of the coming judgment beside his gospel as if it were an addition that essentially contradicts the message in praise of God's grace. Rather, the proclamation of God's judgment was part of his gospel.

The Coming Settling of Accounts
June 29

*After a long time the master of these servants
comes and settles accounts with them.*
—MATTHEW 25:19

The master entrusted his possessions to his servants. Everything belonged to the master—the servants and the talents he gave them—and everything remained his property, even when he moved to a distant land. Even if his separation from them lasted a long time, this did not alter that they were his in everything they did and that nothing of what they had acquired was theirs—everything had been acquired for the master. Can a faithful servant fear the arrival of his master? Will he not long for the day when he can show his master what he has accomplished on his behalf?

Equally as firm as the bond uniting the servants with their master is the fellowship with himself into which Jesus introduced his disciples. His death does not remove it; his distance from them does not weaken it. Into his call that led them to him, he placed the mystery of the divine will that brings about what is eternal. For this reason a faith was born in the disciples that yielded itself completely to him. They have no one other than him, and he has placed within them all the desires and knowledge that they bear. Even during their separation from him, they remain his. What they tell others is his word, and what they give is his gift. They do not proclaim an insight they themselves acquired; do not speak in their own name; do not possess significance or power in and of themselves; do not gather a church as their own possession. Everyone they win over, they make Jesus' possession, and they pass on to them what they received from him.

When, therefore, the separation from their Lord comes to an end, the fellowship that unites them will become effective not merely because Jesus will take them to himself and put his glory upon them but also because he will pronounce his verdict on their work. At that time they may hand over to him what they have acquired. At that time they no longer will stand before him by themselves but with those to whom they brought his Word, and they will bring the community to him. It was their intention that those whom they instructed be his possession, and this must become evident when he is present once again.

Can this be a joyful expectation? This will depend on how they carry out their service. The joyful administration of their role as messengers also results in the joyful expectation of the judgment. Likewise, unwilling service and fear of judgment belong together. Believers serve joyfully; for this reason, the believer longs for Christ's verdict. Conversely, unwilling service indicates lack of faith, and where faith is lacking, people shrink back from Christ's verdict and forget Jesus' promise by which he told his disciples about his coming judgment.

Paul Brings to the Lord What He Has Acquired
June 30

Hold fast to the word of life, which will be my ground of boasting on the day of Christ, because I neither ran in vain nor labored for nothing.

—PHILIPPIANS 2:16

What Jesus showed the Twelve by the faithful servants who bring what they had acquired to the master once he is back with them, Paul appropriated for himself and seized with intense longing. To be sure, everything will become new when the Christ reveals the glory of God. The Risen One will even call the dead to himself. For believers, this will result not merely in a spiritual transformation. Rather, the natural conditions of their lives will be changed as well. They no longer will be tied to the bodies they now have been given, so that they no longer will be controlled by the flesh, and mortality will be removed from them. There are no words that can express this, no prophecy that is able to depict it.

But as inconceivably great as this transformation will be, it is equally certain that the apostle's work will be made completely visible in Christ's presence. Then the Philippians will stand before the Lord, united as a community, and Paul will stand with them. They will acknowledge him as their apostle, from whom they received the knowledge of Jesus, and he will acknowledge them as those whom he brought to the Christ and instructed regarding his will. They are the talents he will have acquired with his master's possessions and that he now will present to him so that he may recognize them as his own. When they receive from the Lord the verdict allowing them to enter his kingdom, blessed honor will be brought to Paul, just as it will be the Philippians' glory when Christ confirms Paul's work with his verdict and renders it of eternal value. Just as in his fellowship with the disciples, Jesus saw the divine will become effective with eternal validity, so Paul, too, praised as the work of eternal grace his fellowship with those he had won and the union of those who grew together to form a community.

Very strong powers and mighty impulses issued from this hope. It was not a perishable, death-bound community that united Paul with those who accepted his message and that united those who confessed Christ with one another. Because it was the work of the Christ, it was destined to an eternal existence and an unimaginable kind of life. This gave their love profundity and power. Paul's concern for "his" believers is thus indefatigable, and the community's efforts intensify to appropriate his message with all of its implications and to remain obedient to it in all of their actions.

That Which Is Hidden Will Be Judged
July 1

On that day when God will judge that which is hidden in men
according to my gospel through Christ Jesus.
—ROMANS 2:16

Jesus promised his disciples that he would come to them again and announce his verdict over what they had done. But he does not come only for his disciples. The Christ is sent to mankind. And since in Christ's sending the greatness of God and the wealth of his grace will become evident, he is the judge for all mankind and not only for his disciples. That is what Paul reckons to be "his gospel," the restorative message of God that Paul, by God's command, must proclaim. In just the same way, Jesus promised his disciples that he would be their judge, the means by which God's assessment of what they had done would be enforced.

That God's lordship truly comes about through the Christ becomes clear by the fact that his judgment will be based on what men hide. A human judge must restrict himself to what can be arrived at on the basis of human testimony. Therefore, human judgment never has the absolute last word. In the light of the divine presence, however, there is no longer anything in the dark. Through it the internal process from which every deed grows comes to light in keeping with its entire existence and is judged by the divine verdict.

That which man carefully guards can be secret evil that is clung to right along with confession learned by rote, or morality that is piously exercised. But since all is now revealed, all untrue appearance dissipates. It is an essential part of the gospel that lies and untruth remain entirely separate from the divine kingdom. This transforms the revelation of the Christ into the victory of the truth and brings the divine righteousness into full view.

What remains hidden in man, however, can also be that which God's grace works in him, that through which he is prepared to do the divine will. In addition, there is secret obedience to divine truth and to secret faith placed in God that no one else witnesses. Stirrings of conscience are given to man that withstand his self-seeking greed. These things, too, will become visible in Christ's judgment and will then receive the divine confirmation. For Jesus' sending encompasses this as well: all the good that God has put into mankind will be united in his kingdom and perfected.

Each must await this verdict. No one can anticipate it for himself or for others. It marks a divide down the middle of all human associations; it makes the last out of the first and the first out of the last; it excludes from the kingdom of the Christ even certain people who worshiped him as their Lord, and it accepts other people into that kingdom who did not know him personally—all this, so that God's deity might be revealed.

The Pure Church Arises Only After Judgment
July 2

He spoke to them another parable and said, "The dominion of heaven is like a man who sowed good seed in his field. But while the people slept, his enemy came, sowed weeds among the wheat, and went away. Now when the seed sprouted and the heads of grain appeared, the weeds were also evident. So the owner's servants came to him and said, 'Lord, did you not sow good seed in your field? Where then did the weeds come from?' But he said to them, 'An enemy has done this.'"
—Matthew 13:24–28

If through the disciples' doctrine and care a church had arisen in which nothing was at work other than what stemmed from the Christ, then the church would have to be a religious institution guaranteeing people's spiritual safety. This assessment of their fellowship suggested itself to the disciples when they compared it to the Pharisaic expression of Judaism. Was Judaism not separated from the nations by an unchangeable divine decree? Was every son of Abraham not also an heir of the promise? Was God not building his kingdom for all of Israel? Now it was no longer Jews as such but the disciples of Jesus who were called to the kingdom. Was not the logical implication of this that everyone who belongs to the church participates in its salvation?

With many stern words, Jesus renounced this notion. For the thought rendered anyone who embraced it faithless. An assurance would, indeed, be granted to every person, but it would make trust in Jesus unnecessary—

Jesus, who will one day pronounce judgment and give life to the one who believes on him. This person's security would be his very own possession.

In order to keep the disciples from falling into such false security, Jesus described to them the battle that would rage within the fellowship he creates. In the field that is sown with his seed, another also sows. This is the enemy of Jesus, because Jesus establishes God's lordship in mankind. For that reason he does not sow his seed beside the fellowship that believes on Jesus but rather right in the middle of it. Can Jesus not build a wall around it so that the enemy cannot penetrate? But not even a mighty lock avails against the spirit of the world. Since that spirit is active even in the fellowship of those who confess faith in Jesus, such people, who look like Christians, also belong to that fellowship. As in Jesus' story here, the weeds resemble the wheat until the heads of grain appear. But there are events that make it evident that it is not the word of Jesus that gives them their thinking and their willing. Then they conduct themselves in the same way as those who bow to the pressure of the forces that rule the world. Is there also in Christendom godless self-seeking and evil callousness? "Yes," Jesus says: These things are present in it because Christians must live in the world and not beyond the world. Because the world is Jesus' field and his call goes out to all, there are various forms of Christianity. There are those who stem from Jesus and those who remain mired in the natural way of human thinking.

In his story Jesus places this question in the mouth of the servants: "Did you not sow good seed?" This has the effect of dramatizing the offense that always arises out of the mixed composition of the church. Now suspicion falls on the One for whom the church is named and for whom it does its work. Is his message not refuted by there being also powerless, indeed damaging, Christianity? This offense remains in existence until Jesus, by the power of judgment, purifies from everything that defiles it the church he has built. But Jesus warns his disciples against ascribing to him that which the state of being Christian causes them to regard as deficiency and others to regard as temptation. He sows the good seed. What he gives comes from above, and from above come only the good and perfect gifts.

It Is Not the Disciples
Who Produce the Pure Church
July 3

The servants said to him, "Do you want us to go and
to pull out the weeds?" But he said, "No, otherwise you
will tear out the wheat at the same time you try to remove the
weeds. Let both grow until harvest, and when harvest comes
I will say to the reapers, 'First gather together the weeds and tie
them in bundles so that they can be incinerated.
But gather the wheat into my barns.'"
—MATTHEW 13:28–30

When Jesus described to the disciples the healing power of the word that he had given to them, he removed every restriction from his promise. They are the ones who loose with God's grace and bind with God's judgment. Can they now lack the fullness of power necessary to establish peace and unity in the church? Even if what is within man is hidden at first, there are moments when it comes to expression. And then it is subject to their judgment, and they must reject it. When a weed is full grown, no one can confuse it with wheat. Jesus demanded that his disciples make clear and definite judgments between what stems from Jesus and what opposes him because it reeks of the sinful ways of man. Even when, with treacherous appeal to the Spirit, alleged prophetic words confront his disciples, they are not defenseless. For they will know by the fruits of those who testify that they speak to them in the name of God, and they will know what sort of a will moves them. A wolf never resembles a sheep, even if it wears a sheepskin, and one can never harvest grapes from thorns.

Nevertheless, Jesus does not entrust to the disciples the fullness of power to purge the church of those who are internally hostile to it. This would endanger the wheat too. They would pull out not only the weeds but also what Jesus had sown. They would judge the faith of others by their own faith, which would be to apply an unusable standard. Based on their own capacity, they would measure the behavior of others, and their verdict would often err. A Jewish-Christian congregation observing the Mosaic worship pattern would have trouble granting fellowship to Greeks who do not make use of this pattern. In the same way a Gentile-Christian fellowship free from the Law would too readily conclude that those who cling to the old law have something less than the full value of Christianity.

Jesus' mercy was greater than the disciples'. John was surprised when Jesus said to him, "He who is not against us is for us" while John wanted to withhold the call of Jesus from those who did not wish to enter the disciples' ranks. The disciples' mental capacity was exceeded when Jesus promised the poor in spirit that God's grace was effective for them and when he thanked God that his revelation came to mere children and not to the wise. Where the spirit that rules the world is manifest, the disciples have to set themselves against it and protect what they have received from Jesus. On the other hand, they do not have the fullness of power to delimit the effectiveness of Jesus according to their own knowledge. In this sense, the edifice the disciples erect remains unfinished. This does not mean that those not belonging to his fellowship will not be expelled. The perfecting of the church, however, which gives it its unity and purity, will occur at the time the Christ is revealed.

Why Are We Called to Render a Verdict?
July 4

You will know them by their fruits. You do not gather grapes from thistles, do you, or figs from thorn bushes? In the same way every good tree produces good fruit, but every rotten tree produces bad fruit. Nor can a good tree bring forth bad fruit, any more than a rotten tree can bring forth good fruit. Every tree that does not produce good fruit is cut down and thrown into the fire. Thus you will know them by their fruits.
—Matthew 7:16–20

We speak of the verdict of history that falls upon those who strongly influence its course. By this we mean that the consequences of their actions show whether and to what extent they received their goals from the truth and from justice. It was also Jesus' concern that the disciples not doubt the close connection between what we ourselves are and how we influence others. The ways we affect others reveal what we are.

He brought this home to the disciples using a botanical observation. Every plant yields its own fruit. The good tree brings forth good fruit and the unhealthy tree unhealthy fruit. Applied to the human sphere, this makes it possible for us to arrive at a secure verdict and a healthy ordering of our relationships. We are not handed over defenseless to anyone who wants to lead us. We are not obligated to obey every call to embark on a divine mission. In the case of that person who makes great claims for himself with great words, it will become clear what sort of power moves him. For where the Spirit of God is absent, that Spirit can never be imitated in such a way that the contradiction between raw human ambition and the divine will does not make its presence felt.

As indispensable, however, as is our capacity to render verdicts, we are not called to render judgment. Therefore, judgment is not something that happens through history, and the pronouncement of subsequent ages is not the ultimate truth. The fruit of a tree, to be sure, does permit its species to be recognized. But how it is that the tree produces this and not some other fruit is a deep mystery. We see the principle that is at work and its all-pervasive effectiveness, but we cannot explain it. In the same way, human history takes place under a veil through which we cannot see. Beneath the visible lies infinitely more that is hidden, and never is that which occurs brought into being through one individual alone, even if he has elevated himself high above all the others. Always, we are dealing with one member of the community in commonality with unnumbered others without whom that person could do nothing. No one has the capacity to calculate how much of the responsibility is rightly attributed only to him.

What history reveals to us is shown so that we will recognize where we are placed today and what our situation now demands from us. On the other hand, it is always arrogance to speak of those who do their work in front of or alongside us as if we were their judges, just as we also do not have the right to pronounce a verdict upon ourselves. It is not the so-called verdict of history that matters. What confers seriousness on human actions, rather, is this: above them stands a divine verdict that is born out of the totality of the truth, and that reveals the divine righteousness.

The Christian Honors
Even the Unjust Ruler
July 5

It is written: "You shall not revile the ruler of your people."
—Acts 23:5

As long as natural urges rule our will, hate generates hate, and injustice generates opposition. There was no restriction on the Jews' hate, which made them desire the annihilation of Christianity. Would hate also make Jesus' disciples the judges and enemies of their people? Would they despise the orders of civic life and resist their leaders? But the person who stands in fellowship with Jesus cannot do evil. The disciples were separated from their fellow Jewish citizens solely for Jesus' sake, but he had made hatred impossible for them, because he taught them to trust in God, and bound them to every person in a relationship of love. The disciples no longer stood before God as the Jew stood, and yet they did not give up their participation in Jewish political life.

Paul proved this in a situation that would have justified him in heated objection against the Jewish leadership. On the order of the Roman officer in command in Jerusalem, the Jewish council, under the jurisdiction of the high priest, had come together for legal negotiation regarding Paul's case. But the high priest immediately ordered Paul to silence in the crassest manner, because Paul had asserted that he was aware of no guilt but rather served God with a clean conscience. For this, one of the guards was ordered to strike him on the mouth. Paul was filled with indignation at this hypocrisy, with which the high priest elevated himself to the status of judge but actually deprived him of justice. And he confronted him with the contradiction of his action vis-à-vis the Law. But when questioned whether he was reviling the high priest, he conceded without hesitation or second thought the truth of the command of Scripture that forbade the reviling of the person to whom political leadership is given. Aspersions must not be cast on the honor of the high priest. Had this been Paul's intent, he would have had to confess his guilt.

Yes, breach of justice and hypocrisy must not be treated lightly. But by the same token the power of a ruling figure may not be attacked in such a way that his honor is taken from him. The path upon which Christianity was placed was narrow indeed. It could not refrain from speaking words of rebuke, for such words were a part of the message entrusted to it. But it could also not destroy the fellowship that was intrinsic to the natural conditions of life.

When Does the Bible Unite Us?
July 6

Every plant that was not planted by my heavenly Father must be pulled out.
—MATTHEW 15:13

The rabbinate reacted angrily when Jesus set aside the ordinances forbidding physical contact with unclean things. In this the disciples had to recognize that peace between them and the rabbinate was impossible. Their fellowship with Jesus was analogous to the grapevine that belongs to the owner of the vineyard and brings forth the vintage. In the same way, the disciples bring forth fruit for him. In contrast to this, Jesus called the rabbinate a plant that had not been planted on Jewish soil by his Father. The human arrogance and self-seeking will to power gave the rabbinate its existence and conferred upon it its stature.

How peculiar! Both groups, the rabbinate and the disciples, had the same Holy Scripture. How could it separate them from each other? Both heard God's word in the Scripture. To take the Bible from the rabbinate would be to eliminate its existence. In the same way, the message of the disciples was refuted if it became doubtful that this message agreed with Scripture. Was it, then, possible that an irreconcilable hostility would arise between them? The offense that issued from this situation was not easily healed. Doubt gets the upper hand when two parties have the same Bible yet wage war against each other.

The Bible unites us only when we not merely subordinate our thinking to it and use it to construct sound doctrine, but even more so when we make our wills subservient to the good will of God. Only in unification with the will of God do we as people become one. (In contrast, the selfish ambition of one person necessarily calls forth the selfish ambition of the other.) Two become one in a third party. But this third party is not a holy book, not a law stipulating doctrine and custom. If we study and defend such a law, we remain isolated to ourselves and place our intellectual capacity at center stage. The third party, in whom we find unity, can only be that person who is greater than any two contending parties because he is the creator and Lord of both.

The rabbi found his praise when he deciphered and interpreted Holy Writ in his sermon to the synagogue congregation. When he explained the Law through his ordinances and supplemented and kept watch everywhere over their observance, this appealed to his sense of power. For in this way the leadership of the people fell under his own hand. That was not an outworking of divine grace. In contrast, Jesus had put space between himself and his disciples and equipped them to have faith in him. For this reason they were a plant tended by the Father, as Jesus himself was the grapevine belonging to the Father.

Christianity Is More than Correct Doctrine
July 7

The scribes and Pharisees have placed themselves in the seat of Moses. Therefore, do and observe everything that they say to you. However, do not behave according to their works. For they just talk and do not act.
—MATTHEW 23:2–3

The disciples of Jesus could never become the enemies of their people, and yet they were separated from the teachers of the Law, the leaders of their people. They did not have a legal mandate that would have made it their calling to topple the rabbinate. Thus in the villages where they lived, they always operated alongside the scribes. How were they to relate to them? What sort of respect did they owe them? The scribes expected people to obey and honor them, for the chair they occupied to exercise the teaching office was the chair of Moses. They interpreted Moses' writings. Moses' commands were the Word of God. Both the people's and their own salvation were tied to that Word. If they decreed new ordinances, they did it with the intention of securing compliance with Moses' commands. But Jesus did not live in conflict with Moses. Rather, to all who asked him, he told what they should do in terms of the laws of Moses. These commandments told them what is good in God's eyes and what brings them to eternal life. Yet Jesus' disciples also could not deny honor and obedience to the rabbi. Jesus' disciple obeys the rabbi because he interprets Moses' law.

This does not remove the separation that exists between the disciples and the rabbinate. This separation arises not only through what the rabbis say but also through what they do. Their conduct is no example for the disciples; rather, it shows them how a person can go wrong. They see this in the conduct of the scribes over against Jesus. If they had followed the Law seriously, they would have been willing to attach themselves to Jesus. A true Israelite, who has no guile in him, will become Jesus' disciple. But those who proudly call themselves disciples of Moses combine opposition to God's kingdom with the doctrine that proclaims to the people God's grace and righteousness. The same contradiction against the Law becomes visible in how they give free rein to their self-seeking greed. In spite of their knowledge of the Scriptures, they crave honor and affluence. Only their thinking is conformed to the Law, not their willing. Therefore there is no place for the scribes among the disciples of Jesus.

The goal of Jesus was not some kind of orthodoxy that covered over the godless essence and activity of man with the help of a supply of religious ideas. He not only transformed a person's words and thoughts but became Savior of the whole person. The righteousness into which he leads us through his fellowship with us frees us not only from erroneous doctrine and bogus viewpoints; rather, it liberates us from our despicable lusts. In this it becomes clear what separates the message of Jesus from God's Word as formerly understood. Jesus' word is not a Law that subordinates us from the outside. It is rather the word of grace that gives us life.

Without Rights of Citizenship for Jesus' Sake
July 8

Peter to the chosen sojourners,
who are dispersed in the lands of Asia Minor.
—I Peter 1:1

When Jesus called his disciples, all other ties fell away. But how was it when his messengers brought his word to the Gentiles? It is true that Palestinian Judaism had made the ethnic fellowship much stronger than those ties that bound the inhabitants of the Greek cities with each other; therefore, the pressure under which the Jewish Christians in Judea and Galilee had to suffer was especially severe. The Jew's religious zeal fueled his desire to eradicate the Christians. In Hellenistic regions too, however, those who were subject to the lordship of Jesus were immediately separated from their local peers by a constantly visible contrast.

God's election had reached out and claimed them. We experience this election in such a way that Jesus' message comes to us and enters us to make us believers. Thus, Greeks were brought into a connection with God, which was something totally new to them. All their religious notions were thereby done away with. But God's election did not give rise to isolated worshipers and servants of God. An election came to them through the Christ, who makes of them the fellowship united in him. This gave their life a goal that was quite different from the one that had occupied them previously.

But those who were won to the word of Jesus were everywhere only a small number. They were chosen out of their former ethnic fellowship and existed alongside it. Now they resembled those who, because they have emigrated from a foreign country, do not possess the rights of citizenship but only the prerogatives of guests. The leadership of the people did not lie in their hands. Public prestige was not bestowed upon them but rather upon the advocates of the old tradition. Soon misunderstanding and suspicion of Christian aims made the relations between the traditional citizenry and Christian assemblies difficult. These assemblies had to dispense with the rights and privileges enjoyed by citizens who exerted political leadership, and they must do this because of the wonderful grace that came to them through their divine choosing. They had to do without the security of public law and common opinion. They could answer their detractors only by not responding to their insults with insult and not paying back their hatred with hatred; rather, they must be ready for every good work.

There is nothing else they can do as long as they are the dispersed ones who wait for the royal work of the Christ. Until he reveals himself, they cannot form their own commonwealth that would have its own homeland under its own ruler. The only one who can provide that for them through his presence is he in whose royal mission they believe and from whom they cannot be separated by curtailment of rights and lethal danger.

Everybody Agrees: It's Good to Do Good
July 9

Keep your behavior among the Gentiles excellent so that, although they blaspheme you as evildoers, they will become eyewitnesses because of your praiseworthy deeds and praise God on the day of visitation.
—1 Peter 2:12

Is there any common ground between those who confess Jesus and those who remain pagan? They no longer come together in the pagan temple. Greco Roman myths no longer bind them together. For the Christians, those tales are no longer true at all. The Christians no longer participate in the public festivals that draw everybody else into a raucous tumult. For the festivals excite fleshly desires that believers work hard to suppress and subdue. Christians also no longer strive for the honors that the state confers upon warriors or athletes or the rich. It appears as if there is no longer any middle ground, no avenue of mutual understanding. Only hostility remains.

Yet there is one tie that does not rupture: that which is good, is good in the judgment of all, and that which is bad, is bad in the judgment of all. This gives Christendom the possibility to uphold its legitimacy in the public square and, indeed, to find common ground with everyone. Peter put no stock or hope in controversy. Even if Christians prove to have superior intellectual capability over others, this alone will not win them over. But when Christians perform deeds that are clearly exemplary, others will side with them over against wrongdoers. For every person has a high regard for his life; whoever attacks it is an enemy, and whoever enhances it is a friend. Every person affirms the social decency essential to civic life. The person who creates peace has his praise, even when he himself defends his so-called rights in a spiteful way.

The pagan expects something bad from Christians. Since he abuses Christians verbally, he anticipates that the Christian will abuse him because of his paganism and dishonor him because of the wrong he does. Instead, the Christian honors every person for God's sake. When he speaks with a non-Christian about his sins, he does it with a merciful willingness to be of assistance. The pagan expects the Christian, who has rejected the culture's myths, to be intent on pulling down the naturally grounded societal structures. But now the pagan sees that Christians are willing at every time to make natural associations fruitful. Anyone who needs help is apt to let himself be helped, even if he himself is quite unmerciful.

In this way believers protect from abuse that which is private and unique to Christians. They cannot openly exhibit to others what they say about the divine grace that has come to them, what they recount about Jesus, and what they expect at his appearing. Nevertheless, excellent works arise out of the state of being Christian. These speak directly to detractors and make them eyewitnesses to what God's grace works in Christians.

An effective weapon is thereby given to them. Yet even with this weapon they are not given power over the human heart and prerogative over human fate. Only God's visitation, his gaze turned toward persons, his word spoken to them, brings people into a relationship with God.

And what about success? Does it consist in the veneration of Christian achievement, in being regarded a hero by the church, in the praise of the apostles as the benefactors of humanity? That is not the success longed for by Christendom. What it longs for is that God be praised and his glorious grace extolled. It is said of the apostolic work, just as Jesus said of himself, that no one comes to him unless that person is taught by God. When God accepts a person, however, and opens his eyes and reveals Christ to him, then God is the one who is praised—God alone.

The Christian Honors the Emperor
July 10

Fear God; honor the king.
—1 Peter 2:17

Those whom Jesus rules may have become strangers to their people, but they are not their enemies. They remain dependent on what their ethnic ties give to them, for they are not yet liberated from the natural conditions of life. For this reason their obedience to God is not revolution against the emperor. It is true that the king is not the one whom they fear. They are bound without reservation to God's will alone. To despise his command and to deny his Word is impossible for them, for this would be death. Even in their interaction with others, they keep before their eyes the inviolability of the divine will. They assess the demands others place on them based on whether they separate them from that divine will. If a contradiction arises between the divine commandment and that of the king, their behavior is clearly prescribed to them. That fear of the king, which would subordinate them to him without reserve, is forbidden to them. A royal command is null and void when it arises from the sinful desire of man or even reaches the point, under satanic influence, of being an attack on the work of the Christ.

And yet Christians' glorious freedom, which they cannot surrender under any circumstances, does not hinder them from honoring the king. This means that the royal command is valid for them, just as that which is commanded is grounded in the office entrusted to the king. Civil society requires someone to be in charge, and since society is the medium in which every person's life unfolds, the rule of the king rests on a divine order against which in Christendom there can never arise revolution, rather only willing and grateful appreciation. When Christendom places itself alongside or over the king and places demands on him that bind him to its will, it forsakes the place God's choice has assigned to it. This is a place that, in God's grace, has made them "sojourners" and "those who live scattered in the world." They cannot themselves attempt to bring about what the Christ has reserved for himself and for his new revelation. Rather, they wait for him.

When Does Condemnation by the State Become an Honor?
July 11

Let none of you suffer as a murderer or thief or evildoer or meddler. But if someone suffers as a Christian, let him not be ashamed but rather praise God in this name.

—1 Peter 4:15–16

Human convictions can vary so widely that what one person calls a crime and seeks to punish with fire and sword is for someone else the means of bringing to God an offering of thanks, an offering that exalts God's grace above all else, and that bears witness to God's wonderful will more clearly than any miracle of nature could do. "Are you a Christian?" the Roman magistrate would ask, and that meant "Do you confess that you are a criminal who must be put to death?" "I am a Christian," answered the believer, and thereby expressed his greatest happiness and his most blessed hope.

What is the source of this discrepancy? The magistrate is forming his opinion according to what is accessible and visible to everyone. The Roman state was there for all to see, with its binding ordinances that recognized no religions other than those passed along for centuries. The goal of the fellowship created by these religions lay in the concerns of natural life. In the sphere of these concerns, however, the Christ had no place. The Christ does not look to the caesar's imperial command to confer validity on his Word. He does not inquire of general opinion what the majority recognizes as the truth. Nor from the desires that move everyone does he deduce what things are considered to be permissible. Accordingly, whoever confesses allegiance to the Christ disturbs the peace. In acknowledging the Christ, the believer encountered God not as someone who was unapproachable but as the one who gives grace; not as the one who judges him but as the one who calls him into fellowship; not as the one who simplifies and adorns his short, natural life but as the creator of eternal life. Does that mean that the interests defended by the civil magistrate disappear? No! Those interests remain in their place. The Christ, however, stands above them, and so does what the believer has received from him, which he can no longer cast aside. And so does what the Christ has promised to him, which now is the goal of the believer's life.

So a highly implausible situation arises: it is an honor when the Christian stands before the imperial magistrate as a criminal defendant. The manner in which a Roman judge dealt with an accused person was frightening. The torture was awful and the execution gruesome. Natural instinct would be to avoid any encounter with the imperial judge, regarding it as a most unpleasant disaster. Nevertheless, it is an honor when the magistrate justifies condemnation by using the name "Christian." The praise of God does not fall silent because of this, and the praise offering presented to the Christ is in no way minimized.

It is, however, the praise of believers that nothing other than their name (Christian), with which they praise Jesus' lordship, gives rise to the state's hostility. No other cause is to bring the judge's disciplinary authority upon the believer. If the judge persecutes him for some other infraction, then the believer has not brought honor to his status as Christian. Fellowship with Jesus can bring about nothing else the judge would have to persecute. Only his name can incite the magistrate to opposition. That name shines so brightly that its light illuminates even the prison cell and the judgment chamber.

God Appoints Those Who Rule
July 12

Submit to every authority instituted among men
for the Lord's sake.
—1 Peter 2:13

Community comes into existence among us through there being those who rule and those who obey. Peter sets out three of these relationships alongside each other:
1. The king, along with the imperial officials he sends out and the populace subject to them;
2. The employer, whose command must be followed by all who belong to him;
3. The husband, whose will the wife fulfills.

How do Christians place themselves into proper submission in all these cases that make them subject to those who rule, and with an obedience they render as unto God?

They do this by recognizing God's creation in those whom they obey. The rulers and the ruled together produce a community of will and action. Obedience rendered unto the creature occurs according to the will of the Creator. One cannot in obedience to the Creator attack the creature. The pride of the Jews deduced, from the divine calling that made them a people, the right to revolt. How can those whose Lord is God be subject to a human? That is the way someone talks who is in conflict with God; such a person thereby also becomes a contradictor of his creation. In contrast, whoever has become subject to God does not make out of his relatedness to God a basis for enmity against man. Rather, he obeys those who rule, precisely because they are human. For they are what they are by God's direct action.

The pagan disfiguring of the imperial office, which idolized the ruler and reduced those who were ruled into a body of slaves, is thereby done away with. The ruler is obeyed, not because he is more than human but because he is human. Both the one who rules and the one who obeys have in common that they have their lives, including the place in which they are placed, by means of God's prerogative. Out of this there arises, with perfectly legitimate justification, the reserve with which the Christian combines all veneration of fellow humans. The citizen who renders honor to the king, or the slave to his master, or the wife to her husband—none of these can ever put the one whose honor consists in his creatureliness in the place that belongs solely to the Creator. If one who is in authority undertakes to occupy such a place, then he no longer does what is fitting for him as a human. He rather obeys impulses that are hostile to God and satanic. As long as a person does not violate, however, that for which he is created, the person who believes in Christ is not compromised by doing his will.

"For the Lord's sake," in the power of his fellowship with Jesus, he obeys him. He would be withholding fellowship from Jesus if he set himself against what has been established by God in the natural sphere. It is the glorious gift of the Christ to those who hearken to him that they honor God in all they do. Their faith in God makes them subject to God, even when God makes persons with the authority to rule to be head of the human community. Christians obey them precisely because they are obedient to the Christ.

The Divine Mandate of Rulers
July 13

*The governors appointed by the king are given for
the punishment of evildoers and for the praise of
those who do what is good.*

—1 Peter 2:14

Peter demanded that the church obey the caesar's governors, because they have been appointed by God as leaders. They therefore have a divine mandate. What are they commanded to do? How is it that God's will comes about through what they do as civil officeholders? The reason God appoints regents is because the natural community encompasses both those who do good and those who do evil. Through those who do good, the community is enriched. By contrast, the evildoer is the community's enemy, who brings it down. If there were no administrator of justice who could give the evildoer what he deserves, then that trust, without which there can be no community, would vanish. Avoidance of the danger that threatens every naturally grounded association is not, however, the only thing entrusted to the one who rules. Rulers can strengthen community in important ways by honoring those who do what is good. It is true that they are not in a position to create goodwill through their honor. Voluntary, proactive goodwill has its worth in itself, and its roots reach to the depths of the soul. But it is made more difficult for us when the judgment of those with whom we live and for whom we act turns against what is good, and doubts or even denies its worth. But as those who possess governing authority, no one has as much ability to strengthen or confirm what is good by acknowledging it. The consent of all conforms to that authority's judgment. In its presence, the opposition that glorifies what is evil falls silent.

Resistance against evil, the demand for what is good—both of these are also characteristic of Christendom. Its fellowship with those who rule is therefore grounded on a substantial foundation and is irrevocable. Such a community does not arise through ephemeral, temporal, and self-seeking purposes but rather from what Christianity has become through the grace conferred upon it. From the divine grace, it has received its striving against evil and its willingness to do what is right. Out of this grows its joyous, ready participation in the work of the state.

To be sure, for Christendom the knowledge of good and evil has received a depth that far transcends the norms according to which the caesar's governors acted. But Peter gives no further specifications for recognizing the opposing realities of evil and good. He ascribes to them a sense that is clear to all, since our sensibilities instruct us directly regarding the value of what happens to us. Whoever does not recognize this general human conception of the commandment that calls for the good and rejects the evil, obviously cannot speak of Christian service to the state as a duty to be joyfully exercised by the Christian. For the good that the ruler of the state honors and the evil that the ruler punishes do not transgress the natural sphere of life. But for those who stand near Jesus, it is abundantly clear that both natural community and the community created by Christ are creations of God. Therefore it is also clear to the Christian eye that God's will is fulfilled through the condemnation of evil and the honoring of what is good, both of which are exercised by those who rule the community as a whole.

The Worker Obeys His Master
July 14

You servants, submit yourselves with all due respect to your masters, not only to those who are good and considerate, but also to those who are perverse.

—1 Peter 2:18

What would become of workers? As soon as Jesus' word was carried out beyond the borders of Judea and Galilee, within which there were only occasionally slaves in large numbers, this question received the very greatest urgency. Workers were overwhelmingly slaves with respect to their legal situation. With respect to their economic importance, they were the pillars of the state. The welfare of the population depended on their labor. It was impossible for Jesus' messengers to ignore workers. It was a basic truth of the Christian proclamation that God's Word was spoken to all and that God's grace appeared for all. From the very beginning, the basis on which the church was built was the principle "Here there is neither slave nor free."

The same rule that gave to the church its active interface with the activities of the political entities around it was binding also on the involvement of workers in the church. This gave it its place in the community at large. Christian workers adopted the will of their Lord and made it their own will. This did away with the total dependence that granted no personal worth to the slave and robbed him of all personal rights. Such abject servility was no more consistent with the Christian status of the slave than would have been total complicity of Christians with the leadership of the government. The slave was the free man of the Lord. He belonged to the Lord entirely, no less than the free person.

But this did not result in the disappearance of naturally given communities with the designation of some people who were part of them to lead and others to follow. These orderings were preserved even when a given master misused his rights as master in selfish ways and for evil purposes. It was not the goodness of a master that gave him the right to demand obedience, but the simple fact that he was a master. That meant, of course, that suffering became a Christian duty for Christian slaves far beyond the point of what their difficult situation already called for. Now the plight of Christians was made yet more difficult by the opposition that divided the pagan master from the Christian slave. The saving message that came from Jesus had, however, nothing in common with those promises that place happiness in the satisfaction of natural desire. In Jesus' name workers could not be lured by promising them the improvement of their situation. They could only gain entrance and abiding citizenship in the church if they laid hold of the high courage and unstoppable strength to suffer. But this was given to them by the fact that grace had appeared to them in the Crucified One of God. In the sign of the cross, Gentile workers streamed into the church, not as a revolutionary band but as persons willing to suffer. But they were therefore also willing with honest labor to render those services without which the welfare of the general populace would have been imperiled.

Roman Judgment in Keeping with God's Command

July 15

Jesus answered Pilate, "You would have no power over me if this were not given to you from above; therefore, he who has handed me over to you has even greater guilt."

—JOHN 19:11

Pilate will pronounce the verdict over Jesus. What an absurdity! The pagan will determine whether Jesus' statement about his relationship to God is truth or deception, and the Romans arrogate to themselves the right to decide whether Jesus' claim on the Jews—that they should obey him and recognize in him their king—is justified or seditious. Was it, then, necessary that Jesus subject himself to Pilate's judgment? True, if Pilate were the only one rendering the decision, the whole affair would have been irrelevant to Jesus. He could have defended himself before Pilate, not just by being silent but by eluding his grasp and going someplace where Pilate's might did not extend. The authority of pronouncing judgment on Jesus is, however, given to Pilate by God. Jesus' sidestepping this would amount to flight from God.

Pilate will execute the commission given to him only by sinning, but this does not take away from his commission its divine validity. Jesus cannot prevent Pilate from sinning, just as he also could not prevent the leaders of Israel from sinning against him in an even greater sense than Pilate did. When Jesus submits himself to Pilate, he is not honoring man but God. He is not exalting the behavior of the man; rather, he is stepping forward to accept God's verdict.

If we ask how it is evident that Pilate received authority from God, we will first think of the fact that it is not Pilate who steers the course of things in such a way that the verdict falls to him to make. He does not bring about the fact that earlier the Jews, in their rage, could not lay hands upon Jesus as they wished. Pilate could not control or change the fact that Jesus had repeatedly left the temple without a hurled stone or a thrust dagger injuring him. Nor did Pilate contrive so that now, while he is resident in Jerusalem, the Jewish leaders would be gathering their energies for the deed they were contemplating. It was God's prerogative that led Jesus to Pilate as his judge.

But we will also not yet understand Jesus' attitude if we find in it only agreement to the course of events that occur just as they unfold under the divine leading. An inner certainty leads him. It is God's will that the Jews fulfill their opposition to Jesus, but this comes to pass by the Roman governor's having him crucified. The man who rules is the bearer of divine authority not only when he is intent on justice and brings about security for the peoples he rules. He is also that bearer when he serves as a tool for the divine wrath, that wrath that gives people over to perform the sin they desire. The service of the emperor does not protect the Jews' hatred from taking place nor the will of Satan from coming about through that service. It is not Caesar who is the shield of justice and the creator of peace. The one who knows nothing besides the will of the emperor hangs the Son of God on the cross. That must take place. That is God's command, and the Son of God must suffer the judicial decree of the Roman. And his followers must bear it in patience and faith when the caesar becomes an antichrist.

The Disciples Are Ready for Victory
July 16

James and John said to Jesus, "Grant to us that we may sit, one at your right and another at your left, in your glory."
—Mark 10:37

The disciples know that Jesus' goal is Jerusalem. What will be the outcome of Jesus' entry into Jerusalem? It could only be the triumph that reveals to Jerusalem its king and submits all to that king's judgment. The leaders among the disciples augmented this expectation with overactive imaginations. Since Jesus had proclaimed to them his coming crucifixion, it was obvious that judgment would have to take place. Those who persisted in opposition to Jesus must be removed from the holy people even if they were priests and teachers. The throne on which the judge is seated will mark the beginning of his glory. But this was precisely what the disciples were demanding. They had by now suffered in silence for a long time. They had borne opposition silently. They had forgiven insults. But when the Christ seizes power, this patient waiting and forbearance will be a thing of the past. The disciples take heart in this expectation, and they are ready to take part in Christ's judging. It would be their highest honor to be given their place beside his throne.

Do these disciples show us an accurate picture of Jesus? Are they thinking here as a disciple thinks? Are they preserving here what they received from Jesus? Certainly! Even in this hour they were his disciples, and they have the attitude he gave them. He did not involve them in his battle without giving them the certainty of his victory. They should go to Jerusalem not as those who doubt or even despair, as those who have lost hope that he would prevail. The one with no hope of winning is in no position to fight. Jesus himself went to Jerusalem as the conqueror. The disciples would have been able to sink into doubt only if they had forgotten that Jesus had called them in the name of God. If they stand in God's service, they are victors. If they uphold God's justice, their judgment has ultimate validity and will come to pass. The one who acts in keeping with God's commission stands upright and fears nothing.

But when they turned to Jesus with this request, the disciples had not yet understood all of what Jesus had said to them. With their certainty of victory, they are not entirely and fully in conformity with Jesus. They do not render him entire obedience with their willingness to proclaim his judgment. In Jesus the certainty of victory and the will to give his life and to bear his cross were inseparably one. Only when their union with Jesus' will, which demands the cross, is just as strong as their desire to share in his glory will the confidence of the disciples have become identical to Jesus' confidence. The disciples do not come to that conviction by their own means. They did not grasp that Jesus' death will be his victory. We are told the request of the two disciples because through that incident Jesus assisted them in conforming their will to his with its goal of the cross.

Jesus Extends the Cup to His Disciples
July 17

But Jesus said to them, "You do not know what
you are requesting. Can you drink the cup that I drink or be
baptized with the baptism with which I will be baptized?"
They said to him, "We can."
—Mark 10:38–39

Jesus must show in his own life what it means to be the Son of God. He was prohibited from taking as his model the tragic heroes, who close off their inner selves against suffering even when they succumb to the superior power of those who attack them from the outside. By claiming to be the Son of God, Jesus is what he is through God, even when his life ends with the cross.

Therefore he compares what he will experience at his death to a drink he willingly partakes of because the Father extends to him this cup. It follows from his fellowship with the disciples that his suffering includes them, too, and becomes a part of their discipleship. They, too, are to drink the cup that he will drink. Can they do this? That is the question he puts to them. And he puts it first to those who expect him to honor them above the others.

They would have declined to share his cup if his drive to the cross had remained incomprehensible or even offensive to them. They would drink it if they, in his cross, recognized God's will as Jesus did. This was a will that reveals his righteousness, a righteousness that judges the godless ambition of man and thereby creates space for grace. This grace does not reckon sins but frees man from the chains that bind him. The disciples had come a long way when they came to be unified with Jesus' will, intent as it was on the cross. They could not drink it if they were not freed from the pious self-seeking that hankers after distinction, power, and well-being. They could not drink it if they still believed in the righteousness the Jew attained for himself through his legal performance, and if they expected that righteousness to secure infallibly for them God's favor. But they could also not drink it if the visible world was for them the only one that possessed reality, and if the message of the Resurrection remained for them a dim, meaningless bunch of words. Yet they would participate in the suffering of Jesus and would drink his cup if they agreed with God's verdict upon man, gave up the righteousness of the Jew, and trusted grace to provide the full measure of strength needed to lead from death into life.

Jesus helped the disciples share his understanding by comparing his demise with baptism. Baptism puts an end to the old, not in such a way that the old is annihilated but in such a way that life is renewed. Baptism testifies to man that he is condemned, and yet in such a way that this condemnation is forgiven him. By taking from man that which cannot enter into fellowship with God, it leads him into fellowship with God. The disciples could understand that Jesus yearned for the baptism that would dedicate him to the reception of God's glory when they realized that man, as nature has made him, does not have life in himself. A new creation must come about so that he can arrive at God's glory.

Paul would later rub shoulders with these two disciples, whom Jesus credited with experiencing his demise as their own suffering and as the baptism that makes new. They all joined together in the fellowship that confessed itself faithful to the Crucified One. Extending their insight, Paul recognized in Jesus' death the death of all. In his crucifixion was the crucifixion of the old man, and in his resurrection the creation of something new.

God Has Ordained What Lies Ahead
July 18

Jesus said to them, "You will drink the cup that I drink, and you will be baptized with the baptism with which I will be baptized. But to sit at my right and left is not mine to grant but is reserved for those for whom it has been prepared."
—Mark 10:39–40

Jesus gives no special promise to James and John. He does not because he cannot. This is another royal pronouncement that effectively determined the attitude of the disciples and the earliest church. The fanciful depiction of heaven with Peter as the keeper of the heavenly key, with Jesus' mother as the queen of heaven, with the many saints from all ages of the church vested with special power of intercession—all this is a later representation of Jesus' promise and is foreign to it. Paul departed this life without referring to a special promise that had been given to him. He was certain of receiving that which will be given to those who long for the appearing of the Lord. When John prophesied in Revelation, he did not mark out a single figure of the early church as one to whom a special promise had been given.

In this there appears in the disciples what Jesus was. It was not because of uncertainty about the outcome of human history that he was incapable of showing to the two disciples the place they would receive in the fellowship he would perfect. "The Father knows." Under this certainty stood all that Jesus said and did. Just as the present world is known by God, so also its final form is not hidden. Those who in the coming kingdom will be united with Jesus in the most intimate way now stand squarely visible in God's field of vision, which sees all in advance. But because the Father knows what he will do and ordains what will take place, Jesus can give no such prophecy. That would be an intrusion into what belongs to God.

But doesn't his status as God's Son give him the privilege of partnership in all that belongs to the Father? Pious, selfish ambition would think this way of being God's Son. But that is not what Jesus revealed his sonship to be. It does not make him into someone who pries into what is God's. He is not one who arrogates God's Word to himself and makes demands of God because he wants to learn what will come to pass. In his status as God's Son, as Jesus shows it to us, God is the one who speaks, and the Son is the one who listens. His calling is to say what he hears, and this is not description of the future but revelation of what is and is taking place. God's grace grants a "today" that is illumined by divine light, and it grants to us a "now" that is filled with God's gifts. To this Jesus looks, and to this he directs the gaze of the disciples. They should see what is present and what must now occur. The future does not become a darkness that plagues us with uncertainty because of this. Rather, God's present working, his will to which we continually respond, brings light into what may look like darkness.

All expressions of genuine hope have their basis in what is given to us. That fact is offensive to all who want only to gain knowledge and to whom the restrictions placed on our knowledge appear unbearable. But it is an essential attitude trait of those whom Jesus brings into God's presence. Every rabbi could tell you infinitely more about the future than Jesus could. Compared with their discourses, he had little to say. But precisely this, his silence, marks him out as the Son who obeys the Father, because he knows him.

The Disciples Become Like a Child
July 19

In that hour the disciples approached Jesus and said, "Who then is the greatest in the kingdom of heaven?" And he called a child to himself and placed the child in their midst and said, "Truly I say to you: If you do not convert and become like children, you will not enter the glory of heaven. Therefore, the

person who makes himself little like this child will be greatest
in the kingdom of heaven."
—MATTHEW 18:1–4

When we commit ourselves to Jesus, we have entered into a small world. Even including all who lived in dependence on it, Jerusalem, over whose fate the verdict would soon be pronounced, was only a small part of mankind. The Twelve with whom Jesus shared his life were only a tiny number. The natural circumstances in which Jesus lived were insignificant when we compare them with all that is open to our powers of perception. Jesus' view of history is limited when compared with our historical vision as we gaze back over the millennia. But those who speak to us in the Gospels by no means suppress or deny all this. They say to us that if we count ourselves as their fellows, we find ourselves in a society of people whose goal is to become like a child. They tell us that they obey this directive as a holy necessity.

Every greatness has become unbearable for them, because God's kingdom is offered to them and God's glory visits them. Now he who is truly great has entered their field of vision: the great God. Next to him no others have greatness. There is no place for a greater Jesus or a great apostle or a great church. Through the wonder of his creative power and through the glory of his grace, he is the Unique One. By comparison, no one has any authority, justice, or possessions. In his presence every person and thing possesses the mark that also characterizes the child: neediness.

And by this neediness children become something truly great. What truly makes greatness is guilt that has been covered by God, weakness that has been strengthened through God's power, toil that has been accomplished in accordance with God's will, dying that has been suffered in fellowship with God. The disciples felt strongly that their lives had received a greatness that far transcended all that nature offered to them. They did not ponder whether they might be the great ones in the kingdom of God. They were assured of that. It seemed to them that the only decision Jesus needed to make was which of them was greater than all the others. But with this manner of thinking, they stand no longer in God's kingdom but alongside it, and in such a way that entrance into it remains closed, and fellowship with Jesus is lost. By avoiding this outlook they achieve true greatness. This takes place as they are loved by God, as they receive of his grace, as they follow his lead, as they are placed by God into life by him. They are not great in themselves.

Jesus planted two seeds in their minds. One describes what they are, the other what God is for them. They must not let either of these apparently contrasting truths extinguish the other. If they do not forget what they themselves are, they remain children, but if they forget what God is for them, then they become childish—useless, pitiful children. If they remain in that truth, which accords to man what is man's and to God what is God's, then they live as God's children in God's house.

Those Who Serve Are Great
July 20

Jesus called them to himself and said to them, "You know that among the nations those who rule suppress others with their power, and the great ones use their force against others. Among you, however, it is not to be so. Rather, whoever of you wishes to be great will be the servant of the others, and whoever among you wishes to be first will become the slave of all."

—Mark 10:42–44

The disciple thinks and behaves like a child after God's grace appears to him. Can a child exercise lordship? No! He cannot be a master; rather, a child serves. He cannot be in charge. What he can be is a servant to all. The child does not have his own wisdom, but neither is wisdom demanded from the one who is to serve. A child carries out the mandate given to him and complies with what the hour demands. He does not have jurisdiction over his own means, and in that way he is like a servant. And the child should also behave like a servant who maximizes his master's property.

In all of this, do the thrones vanish about which the disciples had earlier spoken? Do those thrones turn out to be dreams? Are the disciples now the leaders to whom the greatness of God appears? Are they the peers of the Lord of Glory if their business is service, and again service, and then more service without end? To serve, says Jesus, is the way to power. And being a slave gives the status of being first.

It is completely proper that this instruction regarding the acquisition of power give rise to revulsion and contradiction from all who only know the natural way of looking at things. It does not require much cleverness and spirit to reject Jesus' rule, which makes us humble and willing to serve. We easily join the side of those who make themselves rich by robbing others and who make themselves masters through the forcible submission of others. Jesus also admits that everywhere in the structure of human societies, things proceed in a way that the disciples would regard as normal. His rule gives to the church he is building a new and different form from that which previously has come into being in the course of world history.

If God vanishes from our field of vision, then admittedly it is completely enigmatic how greatness should come out of childlikeness, and power from service, and lordship from submission. The disciple does not act on the basis of his own wisdom; does he therefore act foolishly? No, God's Word leads him. He does not have prerogative over his own goods; is he therefore without means? No, he administers God's gifts. Doesn't that, then, make him one who is strong, one who leads, one who is able to bring about that which lasts?

Whatever successes the disciple may achieve by his service, he can do nothing other than serve. For only when he serves does he obey the law that stands over everything that takes place in God's kingdom. Only thereby does he act and live in love. And only in that way does his action lead him and those he serves to the place where the Christ brings mankind. Only thereby does he bring about peace, and only in this way does he confess himself as loyal to the Son of Man. When Jesus answered those who asked him who he was by saying that he is the Son of Man, he called to mind what Daniel had said about the course of human history. There is in Daniel a sequence of wild animals that with their murderous weapons acquire for themselves lordship over others until all power is given to the Son of Man. But he has no weapons and does not make use of the methods of the predatory beast. He creates the fellowship in which the great ones are the ones who serve.

Jesus' Path into Death Is Service
July 21

For even the Son of Man did not come to be served, but rather to serve and to give his life as a ransom for many.

—Mark 10:45

Does serving make a person great? In order to show his disciples that it does, Jesus makes clear to them what he will attain by giving his soul over unto death. That is not some useless self-sacrifice. It is service, a rich, strong service. For it takes place for many and procures for many God's gift of grace, God's acquittal that confers upon them life. If his death were a useless self-offering, how then would God's will occur through it? Pain for the sake of pain, death for the sake of dying, is alien to love. Such death would not be God's revelation showing forth his glory. But Jesus' death is not useless, for it grows out of his royal sending. This obligates him to call people to him who are his own and who obey him. He gathers his people, whom he intends to elevate along with himself into eternal life. He cannot yet reach them, however. There is a hindrance between him and them that does not allow those he seeks to come to him. They are bound. Upon them lies the divine verdict that says that they sin and will die. An acquittal must take place that permits him to take them to him and permits them to come to him. The chains must break that hold them far from him. That is God's work.

It is solely God's affair to declare the godless innocent and to give life to the dying. Jesus had to beg from the Father the authority to bring about his saving work. Beg? No. The fellowship of the Son with the Father does not take place merely through words. He makes of himself a ransom and makes his own death the deed that frees the condemned. Out of his royal sending comes service, and out of his service, which makes him the last and humbles him beneath everyone else, arises his glory. In this the disciples can recognize how one becomes great in God's kingdom. For the disciple can see in this what love does.

Thus his death attaches in a unified way to what Jesus had been doing all along. He did not come in order to be served. He did not demand that others care for him and extend nourishment to him. Instead, he served them and cared for their lives. It is not he who is nourished by them; rather, he nourishes them. And now he does not let others die while he protects his own life. He rather chooses death for himself so that they, through him, will live.

The Disciples Are Invulnerable
July 22

I have given you power to tread on snakes and
scorpions and over the entire army of the adversary,
and nothing will hurt you.

—LUKE 10:19

The disciples, too, must drink the cup that Jesus drinks. Does this prospect make them cowardly and weak? Does the fact that they experience with Jesus the depth of the divine verdict he bears cause them anxiety? Jesus is led solely into death through his royal sending, and he bears God's verdict because he reveals grace. Because he is the one who saves, he will be the one who dies. If the disciples view his demise not only from the outside, and if they accompany him to Golgotha, not because they are being forced but because they recognize what he suffers and suffer with him as he suffers, then the cup that Jesus drinks will not make them weak. They will draw from it strength that will make them unconquerable.

Granted: those who do not understand what moves Jesus, and therefore also what gives the disciples their outlook, see only garish distortion here. What the disciples do and say falls to pieces in apparent contradictions. First, at Jesus' arrest and crucifixion, the disciples appear to be victims of circumstances, who simply give up. They dispense with all resistance. Without a word they resign themselves as best they can to retain some loyalty to him who is given over to death. Yet later on they once more take heart as those who are untouchable, who defiantly challenge the adversary and confront him with a bravery reminiscent of the jaunty confidence of a Siegfried, the legendary Teutonic hero who knows that he is invincible. The Foe has an army that he can deploy against the disciples. Spiritual powers obey him, and he also commands nature in ways that can injure them and terminate their effectiveness. Snakes and scorpions in this foe's service can assault their lives. "Tread on them," Jesus commands them. "Nothing will hurt you."

In all this, however, Jesus does not make out of his followers wavering people who flee one minute and fight the next, who feel their impotence and fall away one minute and perform like heroes the next. Their deportment now changes because they stand before God and the world and its ruler in an altered state. The army of the Enemy is not an opponent whom they must fear. They are hidden in God's protection, since they trust in him. Moreover, the cup Jesus drinks is not given to him by the Enemy. The cross is not placed upon the disciples by their adversary. The cup comes from the Father, and Jesus' cross has its ground in the righteousness and grace of God. Flee from the presence of God? Protest God's verdict? Fear God's grace? No! The disciple can do none of these as long as he looks to Jesus. Then he submits himself, is silent, and is prepared to suffer. And because these things are true, he remains invincible against the army of an enemy who attacks in vain.

Abiding Joy
July 23

Do not rejoice that the spirits are subject to you, but rejoice that your names are written in heaven.

—Luke 10:20

What a joy to be able to help! How rewarding to be able to render assistance where it appears to be impossible, where life has become agony because hostile powers have disrupted the internal life of man. And not only that: to be able to help through the name of Jesus and to experience his saving power that is superior to all that brings man to ruin—should not every person rejoice who is full of the knowledge of how Jesus comes to the rescue? "Even the spirits are subject to us through your name," reported Jesus' disciples after their return, full of joy.

No question about it: to be able to help is joy. To be permitted to serve others is a privilege. To be active in the work of the Lord and in service, and to be able to fight together in the service of Jesus, brings great reward. Yet how often are we unable to help? How often does love bring pain because people we would like to help do not permit themselves to be loved? In Jesus' service one receives wounds. Those who are active in his work also take part in his suffering.

Jesus ensures an abiding presence of joy for his disciples by not locating it in what they experience and accomplish. Instead, he centers their joy upon that with which the eternal will of God has graced them. Their name stands in the Book of Life. God knows those who are his, and they know they belong to him. For Jesus has extended to them a fellowship that he makes eternally effective.

The carrying out of their service brings to them varying kinds of experiences. They see how God's grace purifies man and uplifts him. But they also see how God's wrath hands man over to sin and death. They truly apprehend the effectiveness of the Christ, but they also apprehend the effectiveness of his adversary. Among those to whom they are sent, they encounter receptivity from some, yet hostility from others. They rejoice with those who rejoice, but they also weep with those who weep. Their participation in the things of God is always certain and independent of the success of their work and untouched by their shifting fortunes, because it is by God's choice that they are graced with participation in him. That is the basis of all the gifts that grace grants. These are gifts that make life fruitful, and joys that give life rich depth. Jesus says here to his disciples the same thing that he later said to Paul: "It is sufficient that I give you my grace."

Section 13

JESUS REVEALS HIMSELF TO JERUSALEM

The Disciples Want to Die with Jesus
July 24

Now Thomas said to the other disciples,
"We should go too, in order to die with him."
—JOHN 11:16

The more Jesus' travels took him toward Jerusalem, the more the disciples became conscious that the loyalty they expressed toward Jesus would have to be loyalty unto death. When had a single revolutionary ever been executed without this persecution also affecting his followers? Just as little as Jesus hid himself, so little could the disciples hide themselves or flee. As he approached Jerusalem so that the entire people would see him and all in Jerusalem might hear his word, so it was also the disciples' clear duty to stand with him and expose themselves to the attack that would come upon him there. If stones fly at Jesus in Jerusalem, these stones will strike his disciples, too. Even if they did not die in the same hour at his side, Jesus' execution would jeopardize their own lives. And if Jesus' prophecy was fulfilled and the power brokers of Jerusalem delegated Jesus' killing to the Romans, then the future of the disciples was completely in doubt. The person who was politically guilty knew that along with the demise of the leader of a revolt would come the annihilation of that leader's followers. "Do you want to die with Jesus?" That was the question directed with unmistakable gravity to the disciples.

How they responded to that question arose inexorably from what being with Jesus had made them. "We have left all and followed you." Whoever has left all for his sake cannot change his mind when he now, also with him, must lay down his life. The promise that whoever would lose his soul would win it helped them not to present their sacrifice with complaint and not to dampen the joyfulness of Jesus with their misgivings. Nevertheless, their resolve to stick with Jesus was fraught with great seriousness.

But with that resolve alone, had they yet accomplished entirely what Jesus wanted? Was the response of those two disciples sufficient when Jesus asked them, "Can you drink my cup?" To want to die with Jesus—this was not yet full oneness with that will of Jesus which was intent on the cross. It was not the complete overcoming of that objection to his demise which was silenced only when the service Jesus accomplished in dying was also visible to the disciples. Jesus accomplished this work all alone. His death was the ransom for those he wished to save. That was not a calling shared by the disciples. They had need, as all did, of the one who laid down his life in their stead. He, not they, presented the ransom for others to the Father.

Therefore, what was in the cup that Jesus had to drink was also this: that he alone, deserted by the disciples, must die. He makes them to be his witnesses, not through their death but through their lives. They are thereby entrusted with his word so that they might bring it to mankind. But that could only happen if he was able to protect them. Could he do this, he who was not able to protect himself? Here the disciples' unbelief and faith could only wrestle mightily.

Hosanna!
July 25

Those who went before him and those who followed cried out, "Hosanna! Blessed is he who comes in the name of the Lord. Blessed is the kingship of our father David, which is coming. Hosanna in the highest!"
—Mark 11:9–10

The festive jubilation is intensified when a great multitude joins together in it. A multivoiced choir offered up the cry of "Hosanna!" Isolated voices could not carry the festive shout into Jerusalem. But here we should think not only of the easy excitability of the multitude that quickly arises when someone appears who wants to be its leader. *Hosanna!* No one could make that cry—whether he belonged to the narrower or to the broader circle of disciples—who was not certain, perhaps after lengthy reflection, that Jesus was coming in the name of God and that the sending in whose strength he acted he had received from God. But if this was the case, then the jubilant hosanna was fitting, whether unstated in the heart, expressed quietly in hidden prayer and guarded conversation, or as now, under Jesus' leadership, in loud celebration.

It required no artificial means to elicit this outcry. Was there, then, anything that could stir up in a mightier and stronger way than someone's coming now, sent from God to the people? If astonished joy and gratitude had already arisen on the basis of the individual deeds through which Jesus had shown to the people the saving mercy and creative grace of God, then this would break out more clearly and strongly when he made his appearance in Jerusalem. He appears in the strength of the commission given to him, and by appearing in Jerusalem he comes to the notice of the entire people. Here was a revelation from God. What should the reaction be except to bless the one who revealed God? For that he reveals himself is grace, and where the grace of God becomes effective, the gratitude praising that grace will not be long in following.

Were the groups that clustered around Jesus the only ones able to praise God for this? They could not remain alone if the hosanna was also in evidence *in the highest,* that is, among the heavenly beings. Those who know God's will and behold his work with heavenly eyes celebrate Jesus too.

Those who praised Jesus as he entered Jerusalem did not yet see what would arise as a result of his arrival. But it is certain that his sending was grounded in the promise given to the people. The kingship of David is now granted to the people once more. What they expected from the future was grounded in what had once taken place in their midst. Because they were Israelites, they drew near Jerusalem, and for the same reason Jesus drew near, too. They were Israelites, heirs of a promise that made them God's people and granted to them an eternal existence. To this first promise a second one was added: the gift to the people of a king. This was bound up with the establishment of the kingship through David. How many generations by now had no king? How long had the people had no one to lead them with divine authority, no one who established justice in their midst and secured their peace as its protector? Now, however, Jerusalem, and with Jerusalem the entire people, again had a master who, like David, could say that he would administer the kingship as the one anointed by God according to God's will. Whoever grasped what that meant longed with ardent desire for God's blessing to be upon that one who now took up his rule.

What Was Promised to Jerusalem?
July 26

At the end of days the mountain of the house of the LORD will be placed on the peak of the mountains and will be elevated above

Jesus Reveals Himself to Jerusalem

*the hills, and all peoples will stream to it. Great nations will go
and say, "Come, let us go up to the mountain of the Lord, to
the house of the God of Jacob, and he will instruct us in his
ways, and we will walk in his paths." For out of Zion the law
will go forth, the word of the Lord from Jerusalem.*

—Isaiah 2:2–3

A towering mountain peak draws the eyes of all to it. Is there such a place
to which everyone's eyes are currently turned? If God's Word were to become audible, would that not create a sight to which everyone would pilgrimage? Actually, no. That is not what Isaiah is talking about. He does not
speak about a possibility of hearing God's audible voice. And his hope is
not merely that all peoples will listen to him, for he knows a mountain on
which God's Word can be heard. At the time, to be sure, it was still a small
hill, not a towering peak and certainly not the place to which the gaze of all
was directed. It is certain, however, that God speaks on this hill. It is also
certain that he will speak there in the future. Here the peoples will be instructed regarding his will and will be shown his way. So it is also certain
that all peoples will experience the will of God. Then the humble height
that rises only a little bit above their surroundings will become higher than
every other mountain.

The event that transpired within the prophet at the impulse of the Spirit
when he turned his gaze to what is to come was misunderstood when later
interpreters inferred from it the doctrinal teaching that in the place of the
temple on Mount Zion there will one day rise the highest of all mountains.
Rather, when the longing of the prophet gazed forward to what would come,
he was moved to draw from the realm of nature a concept that could be
related to the goal toward which he saw things moving. Isaiah's longing
goes forth and takes up the new word that will go forth beyond Jerusalem
to the peoples. The new and inexhaustible thing that will come to pass received its clarity for him as he saw the small elevation transformed into the
highest of all mountains.

Zion experiences this transformation not because the temple stands there,
the temple that can be proudly adorned, nor does the transformation take
place because an altar can be found there on which sacrificial animals are
brought for ceaseless offerings. The transformation also does not take place
because the holy courts of the festive gatherings provide space through which

the multitudes of the worshipers are spiritually stirred up. Isaiah does not speak about that which men place upon Zion or will one day place upon it. In that sense nothing distinguishes Zion from other holy sites. But Zion has one thing that no other place shares with it: someone stands there who is able to speak in the name of God. An answer comes to the person who seeks after God's will. That is an advantage of incomparable weight. Will Jerusalem participate in it? Will not God's Word come to all? In that case, there is no site that would tower as high as the one upon which God's Word comes to the nations.

Out of Zion Comes Peace
July 27

And he will judge between the peoples and mediate between great nations. And they will beat their swords into plowshares and their spears into pruning hooks. No longer will one people raise a sword against another people. And they will no longer wage war against each other.

—Isaiah 2:4

The peoples are divided. How will their dispute be mediated? By sword and spear? That is an insufficient means of bringing about righteousness. People will die and countries will be desolated. But other than by force, there appears to be no means of grounding justice. Is it not the case that the stronger must rule? Indeed it is, but the strong one who must rule is God, and he rules through his Word. From the place at which his wisdom will be heard, peace goes forth. When the peoples turn to him so that he speaks justice to them, when they are willing to obey his wisdom, weapons will become superfluous. Then they can be transformed into peaceful tools to bring forth the earth's bounty.

Isaiah knows no other way to peace, and this judgment is the way that not only he sees things: it is the collective wisdom of the entire Scriptures, both New and Old Testament. That is the message of the Christmas story, which promises peace on earth because the Christ is born. That is the message of the book of Romans, which says that God's righteousness is revealed by God's healing Word as it makes of us people who believe in him.

It is the basis of eternal controversy when man seeks to rule over man and when a master race seeks to subjugate slaves. What God has created remains his possession. Man is God's work, and therefore no man is given up to another who makes of him a slave. As long as man makes himself lord and judge, and makes his self-seeking will to be the law for others, the lawgiver carries the sword. Force alone prevents the retaliation of those who are victimized. When two dispute with one another without a third standing over them, the end can only be that one of the two succumbs and is annihilated. But when God's Word can be heard, a place is provided in which two persons in dispute are able to become one.

They become one in honoring him who is greater than all persons. They become one in obedience to him. Who alone is the just and the good one? In him they find that strength whose work and fruit is righteousness, namely love. Christ is the Word and Christ is our peace. Those are not two different messages. That is the one truth, the inseparable gift that God's grace has conferred upon the world. Jesus offered that grace to Jerusalem when he entered the city to the hosannas of his followers.

The Words About Jerusalem Are Fulfilled
July 28

Jerusalem, Jerusalem, who kills the prophets and stones those sent to you. How often I wanted to gather your children, as a hen gathers its chicks under its wings! But you were not willing.
—Matthew 23:37

Was the prophecy that called Zion the place where the peoples received the divine Word extinguished for Jesus when he went to Jerusalem to die? On the contrary, a divine necessity led him to Jerusalem precisely because of the promise that his coming fulfilled. As the speaker of the divine Word, he entered the holy city. From there his Word would go forth to all Israel and the nations. The resistance of the city against him came from its killing those who spoke God's Word to it. It repelled with hurled stones those bearing God's commission. Of this, too, the Scripture spoke. It described not only the gloriousness of the Word that would be spoken to Zion and heard from there by the nations, but also of the pride of the holy city that suffered no master to rule over it and strove against the divine Word addressed to it. Jesus points to both truths: the promise of the coming divine Word that will instruct the nations and teach them peace, and the witness that judges Jerusalem and reckons as guilt its striving against God.

Was it possible to believe in both prophecies and to make a place for both in history? That Jesus accomplished precisely this is the doing of the Son who perfected his obedience. He obeyed the Scripture when it proclaimed the praise of Zion. He brings to Jerusalem what gives it glory—namely, the Word of God. By the same token he obeys the Scripture when it unmasks Judaism's godlessness, and he pronounces over it a scathing judgment.

Therefore, at the time of Jesus' entry into Jerusalem, the disciples' jubilation and Jesus' lament stand in close proximity. The sacredness and the profanity of the city become evident. Its election and its rejection are made effective. The city is chosen so that it might hear God's word, and it is rejected in that it kills the Christ. Its holiness lies in its being the city of the Christ and belonging to him. Its profanity lies in that it cannot bear the Christ in its midst. Therefore, with the entrance of the Messiah into the city, peace comes into the world. For God reconciles the world to himself. And at the same moment, the war begins in which Jerusalem meets its demise.

God's Word Remains in Force
July 29

It is not as if God's word has failed.
—Romans 9:6

Jesus' rejection and its implications for the fate of Judaism could appear to indicate that God's word had become invalid. This would have been an unmitigated disaster. Not only Judaism but also Christianity would have become worthless if God's word had turned out to be void. When Paul was asked what the value of Judaism consisted in, he answered that the words of God had been entrusted to it. That these words were spoken to Israel and were to be preserved by it made it a great advantage to be a Jew and not a pagan. But now the outcome of Jewish history was taking a calamitous turn.

Paul had no illusions about the bitter brew the Jews had concocted for themselves. Paul's insight into what now must take place caused his soul great pain. The ultimate high value of the divine gift to them did not, however, attach to the Jewish people, to their civic organization, or to their ethnicity. These lay in the realm of the flesh and remained within the aspect of life grounded in nature. It did not upset Paul that sin and blindness and, repeatedly, a tendency toward death permeated the sphere of natural life. That is the verdict God spoke regarding all flesh, and Paul is fully reconciled to this even when the verdict affects his "brothers according to the flesh."

But if the word of God were to fall to pieces, then not only Israel's praise but also the message of Jesus would sink into oblivion. Then justice would vanish from the world and life would be swallowed up by death. Where would mankind be without God's word? Mankind received God's word, however, and it is being fulfilled. This is not contradicted by the conduct of Judaism. For God's word always stands in opposition to what man thinks and pursues. It is spoken to man as formed by nature and enables him to take part in God, but it does not confer justice on his desiring and does not make eternal his natural existence. The divine word proclaims the righteousness of God, not of man, and praises God alone as the creator of life. Through the calamity of the Jews, it became obvious that the divine word is not bound to their natural existence. In this way it demonstrated its origin from above and testified to God's supreme divinity.

Jesus Suffers
July 30

And as he approached, he looked upon the city and wept over it.
—Luke 19:41

At Jesus' entry into Jerusalem, the celebration of the disciples sought to elicit his joyous participation. Yet his view of the city compelled him to reflect on its lamentable end. Not only on that day, however, were great joy and painful lament intermingled in his soul. They were constantly present together, each an integral part of his divine sending. He had the fervent lament in him when he spoke of the seed he sowed on hard ground, and he had a sense of bright celebration when he thought of the seeds he entrusted to the good ground. It was a word filled with pain when he turned aside even from his mother and his brothers, and it was a word of celebration when he, at the same time, found himself in inextinguishable fellowship with those who do God's will. It was perfect joy when he praised God that he had revealed himself to infants. This joy, however, contained within itself a suffering, since God withheld his revelation from the wise to whose opinion the people listened. It is at the sight of Jerusalem, however, that his joy and suffering receive an especially strong quality.

He had to have room in himself for both, because he was bound to both God and man. To bring about God's work is blessedness. The disciples saw this lived out in him even in the last night, when he prepared for them the festive meal of departure. But God's work was effective in him also in that he drew men to himself. That made of him the Suffering One. That he was able to call them is perfect joy; that they do not permit themselves to be called is his agony. He is able to love them and show them how God loves the world; they do not let themselves be loved, however, and this causes pain. He is peace for all, and for this the hosanna of the disciples praises him with a loud voice. His peace, however, is rejected. For this reason, from his encounter with Jerusalem, there arises Jerusalem's demise.

With this encounter both components make their presence felt. They bring death to Jesus and to Jerusalem. He dies like the grain of wheat dies, which only becomes fruitful through its dying. Jerusalem dies because man is not able to stand against God. In light of all Jesus faced, the glorious and the evil, how could he not rejoice? Yet how could he not also lament? The hosanna unto Jesus praised the work of divine grace. Yet the obligation of love is to weep with those who weep and to mourn over those who die.

God Gives Up His Vineyard
July 31

My beloved had a vineyard on a fertile height. And he dug around it and removed the stones from it and planted it with choice vines. He built a tower in its midst and also dug out a wine vat in it. And he expected it to bring forth grapes, but it yielded wild grapes. And now, you inhabitants of Jerusalem and you men of Judah, judge between me and my vineyard. What more was there to do for my vineyard that I did not do for

JESUS REVEALS HIMSELF TO JERUSALEM

> *it? Why did I expect it to bring forth grapes, and it brought
> forth wild grapes? And now I make known to you what I will do
> to my vineyard. Its hedge will be removed and it will be laid
> waste; its wall will be torn down and it will be trampled under
> foot. I will make it a waste place. It will not be pruned nor will
> it be hoed, and thorns and thistles will proliferate in it, and I
> will command the clouds so that they do not rain on it. For the
> vineyard of the LORD of Hosts is the house of Israel, and the
> men of Judah are his pleasant planting. He looked for justice,
> but behold, bloodshed! And he looked for righteousness, and
> behold, a cry of lament!*
>
> —ISAIAH 5:1–7

The vineyard frustrated all expectations. It brought to naught all attempts to salvage it. It bore no usable grapes. What is to be done? It would be senseless for the vineyard to continue to exist and be maintained. It will be given up and laid waste by him who had planted it and sustained it as his possession. That is the picture of Jerusalem and the indication of its fate. The citizens of Jerusalem—whose moral sensitivity Isaiah, as the friend of the one who built the vineyard, addresses—must agree with this judgment.

Did a Jew actually write what Isaiah 5 says? Yes, definitely! He who spoke this verdict to his people ascribed to Jerusalem the incomparable value its election had given to it. He speaks to God's people, who are his possession in a deeper sense than can be said of any other people, and whom he honored with special care. In the realm of its existence lay numerous and clear proofs of the divine goodness. The prophet concedes all that the Jews could claim for themselves by appeal to the divine word they had received. The great hopes with which they gazed into the future of the holy city are not dismissed as groundless.

Nevertheless, the verdict of the prophet is completely different from the verdict of his contemporaries, and the point at which their opinions differ comes clearly into view. Do the calling and care God vouchsafed to the people confirm its selfish will, or put it to flight? Does Jerusalem want merely to receive that which works to its advantage, or is it also willing to give to God what it owes him? In Jerusalem people found in God's revelation to them no cause to set limits to self-seeking desire. Even the most elementary restriction of personal ambition—that justice without which there can be no common life—is cast aside as a burdensome chain. If breach of justice furthers personal power and multiplies one's own possession, every act of violence is attempted.

But with this, God's relation to his people is disfigured, and the effective working of the divine grace is nullified. Isaiah's parable underscores with graphic clarity the impossibility of this state of affairs. The Jew desires God to act redemptively for him, but he does not acknowledge that he must in turn do what God desires from him. Through the way he proceeds with God's Word and God's work, he intensifies his wicked desire. In this way he transforms the revelation of God into hostility. That revelation, now, does not set forth the reconciliation of God with man but rather makes a parting of the ways unavoidable.

So the prophet points to the spectacle of God destroying what he had built. No worldly power can destroy God's vineyard if he himself does not surrender it. The same will that built the vineyard as an act of grace for the sake of gathering its harvest now, in fact, destroys it as an act of wrath for the sake of punishing its barrenness. God's will is not divided, nor is his action fickle. The fault lies rather in man, who sets his will against God's. There is the cause of the alteration that makes the conferring of a gift into the withdrawal of that gift, and the implantation of life into a death sentence. If the Jew paid attention to Isaiah, he could understand why Jesus, for the sake of the divine grace and as its witness, spoke against the godless desire of man with an unshakable *no!* and remained true to this verdict even unto death.

Who Should Be Honored: the Jew or God?
August 1

There was a landowner who planted a vineyard. He placed a fence around it, dug a winepress and built a tower in it, leased it to some tenant farmers, and went off on a journey. But when it came time to harvest, he sent his servants to the tenants to gather his crop. The tenants took his servants and beat one, stabbed another, and stoned a third. Again he sent servants—

JESUS REVEALS HIMSELF TO JERUSALEM

this time in greater numbers than before—and they treated them the same way. After this he sent his son to them, because he thought, They will fear my son. But when the tenants saw his son, they said to each other, "This is the heir. Come on, let's kill him and claim the inheritance for ourselves." So they took him, cast him out of the vineyard, and killed him.

—MATTHEW 21:33–39

In the form Isaiah gave to the parable of the vineyard (Isa. 5:3–7), it already said to the leaders of Jerusalem why Jesus had come to them, what he sought from them, and why his presence with them must end with his being killed. But now Jesus made the parable far more applicable by relating the owner of the vineyard not only to the sickly vines but also to those who tended the vineyard. He depicted those tenants of the vineyard as ones whose actions and speech were a picture to Jerusalem of its true nature. This means that the story also became a vehicle for revealing a picture of Jesus. In the form of the Son, he could show Jerusalem what separated him from them and why they were intent on killing him.

At the forefront stands the powerful testimony of his fellowship with them. He speaks to them as the King of the Jews. Judaism is God's own planting. It is therefore the possession of the Son of God that he cannot forsake. He is fully engaged and gives up his life for its preservation. His confession of loyalty to his people is at the same time a declaration of loyalty to its Scriptures. What he desires from Jerusalem is nothing other than what the ancient messengers of God demanded from it—and still demand at the present time. For their word did not pass into oblivion but speaks constantly to God's people as Holy Scripture.

Yet what now takes place is not merely a repetition of what had occurred earlier. It is rather an incomparably greater process. Those prophets were servants. He is the son, and the son is the heir to whom falls lordship over the people. This is what deepens the guilt of the treacherous act of the tenants. Earlier, they robbed their master of the fruit of his vineyard; now they forcibly seize the vineyard itself. The Jewish rejection of God becomes total in that they toss Jesus aside. Judaism is what it wants to be: Jewish greatness, Jewish power, Jewish kingdom. God's role now is to fulfill the selfish will of man. Is that why God was revealed to the Jew? Is that the instruction that Jews received from the Scriptures, and is this the goal served by the sending of Jesus?

God, in the glory of his creation and mighty grace, gave testimony to Israel in order that it might honor him. Israel was summoned to this through the Scriptures given to it, and for this purpose the Christ is placed into its midst. Jesus went to Jerusalem to honor God, and what he demands from the people is that it recognize that he gives honor to God. In turn, Jerusalem must honor God as he does. The people honor God by believing in the One whom God has sent to them. Instead, the Jew holds fast to his personal ambition and casts out from his fellowship the One who honors God.

The Outcome of the Battle
August 2

"So when the owner of the vineyard comes, what will he do to these tenants?" They said to him, "He will deal horribly with those horrible people and lease the vineyard to other tenants, who will present him with the harvest when it is ready."
—Matthew 21:40–41

The Son is put to death. But that is not the end of this story. He dies defenseless, for he comes to Jerusalem armed only with a plea. He comes to them because God called them to his service, and he comes with the word that is directed to them because he has set them apart for himself. He comes to them as their king, who is their Lord because they are the people of God. He cannot come to them as their enemy; he rather comes as their deliverer. Their deliverance would lie in heeding his call. If they believe him, they will bring forth the fruit he demands. But that would signify a complete conversion, a new priesthood, a new Bible, a new commandment, a new righteousness. They remain what they are. They remain the sole chosen ones, the righteous ones, the ones called to rule the world. And he dies.

Now what will the owner of the vineyard do? This question carries great weight. Jesus did not end his tale by querying about the fate of the murdered son. That eludes the view of the Jew. The mystery is that the murdered Son is resurrected; it is the miracle that takes place on the far side of the human field of vision. What will become of the tenants is a different matter. Even to the Jews they occupy center stage. That is why Jesus directs this question to them. They are to furnish the ending to his story. No teacher of the Law could entertain the kind of conclusion that it called for: the crime of the rebels is avenged; their rebellion does not succeed; the master of the vineyard intervenes and brings them to justice. The rulers of Jerusalem should ponder that. They pronounce the death sentence on Jerusalem if they condemn Jesus.

But what about the vineyard? It remains in the hands of the owner. He will give it to others, who will not plunder it but give to the owner what belongs to him. Jesus confirms this to them. He dies, but this is not the end of his mission. Jerusalem meets its end, but this is not the revocation of the divine grace that makes people into God's possession. Jesus dies as the one who lives, who will rise again. His Father gave him the disciples, the beginning of the new community, the first stones of the new temple, the first whom the new righteousness brings together to form the holy community, the first to worship God in spirit and in truth. Now the new Israel arises, the people of the Christ, who receive the grace from him to honor God aright. This is the fruit of his death.

The Proud Boast of the Jew
August 3

If you, however, call yourself a Jew, and take comfort in the Law, and praise yourself as near to God, and acknowledge the divine will, and uphold what is excellent, since you are instructed by the Law; and if you have confidence that you are the leader of the blind, a light for those who are in darkness, a corrector of the foolish, a teacher of the immature, since you in the Law have the form of knowledge and of the truth....
—Romans 2:17–20

Is Paul making fun of the Jew when he paints his picture with these striking colors? How could he for a moment be insulting him when he discusses with him the most serious of all questions: What should he expect from God? To be sure, this is not written to give easy confidence to the Jew. It is not written to encourage him to pass by Jesus as if Jesus were of no consequence. With these words Paul summons the Jew to the Messiah and directs his gaze to the plight of the Jewish people. In order to make this visible to him, however, it would be entirely ineffective to trivialize and denigrate his pious achievements. As Isaiah and Jesus praised the status of the vineyard because it contained everything needed to produce a valuable harvest, so Paul reminds the Jew of his rich possession.

Because he has God's law, he prides himself in God. Can more be conferred upon someone than that the recollection of God fills him with joyful confidence? Whoever takes pride in God is convinced that he has God on his side. Is that not faith? Could Paul, in the name of Jesus, give anything more to those who believe in him? The Jew takes pride in God because he knows him, and how could the knowledge of God be insufficient for him? He possesses the Holy Writings. He has their interpreters. He has the Sabbath, which sets all natural concerns to the side and makes the day free for God. He has instruction in the continually recurring Sabbath assembly. And this schooling often extended even to the instruction of children. And it could be said that the Jew, from childhood on, knew the Holy Scriptures.

To this zeal for learning corresponds the compulsion with which the Jew pursued behavior becoming of God. He is not immediately content with his performance. He wrestles to achieve complete fulfillment of the Law. The greater the demand of the Law, the greater is the praise of the one who fulfills it. When in Palestine the Roman authorities desecrated the Law, great multitudes were willing to lay down their lives in response.

Are they here somehow concealing from the pagans what their Judaism involves? On the contrary, they are acutely conscious of their superiority. They quite willingly make their services available to the pagans, to be of service to the blind, to illuminate those who find themselves in darkness, to give instruction to those who do not understand, to teach those who are ignorant. They are the bearers of the divine knowledge and truth to mankind. This position is accorded to them, for they live in and under the Law.

That is God's vineyard, in which all that is necessary for successful production has been provided. Doesn't it look glorious? Its vines grow prolifically. It is resplendent in the glory of its foliage. Rich blooms promise great production. But Paul renders the same judgment as Isaiah and Jesus: You are unfruitful.

The Plight of the Jew
August 4

You, who teach the other, do you not teach yourself? You who proclaim, "Thou shalt not steal," do you steal? You who forbid adultery, do you commit adultery? You who abhor idols, do you commit temple robbery? You who take pride in the Law, do you dishonor God through the transgression of the Law? For the name of God is blasphemed among the nations because of you, just as it is written.

—ROMANS 2:21–24 (CF. ISA. 52:5)

To bear fruit for God—what form can that take? God's love is not self-seeking. He does not desire our gifts. But he has placed us into fellowship with other people. Paul points us away from the veneration with which the Jew approaches God and, instead, points us to the manner in which the Jew interfaces with other people. Are others safe from his greed? It is uncertain that the other's wife is safe. Jewish greed seeks after her. It is uncertain that the other's property is safe. Jewish greed seeks after it. What is dedicated to strange gods should be safe from him, for he separates himself from every foreign god with exquisite pedantry. If, however, anything dedicated has value, it is not safe from the Jew. The name of his God should be safe with him. How could he put up with God being insulted, since he takes pride in God? What is the Jew without his God? The reputation of Judaism, however, casts dark shadows on his God and blocks the nations' way to him.

What becomes visible in this sketch of Judaism? What happens when zeal in service for God and untamed greed lie so close together? Judaism experiences here the weakness of the Law but also the power of the Law. Paul gave both answers to the Jew, and both are in agreement with each other. The weakness of the Law comes from the fact that it becomes powerless because of the flesh. The various types of greed that grow out of the naturally given situation of man do not give way to the Law. The self-seeking will asserts its force and craves the desire that arises for the visible things around it. This will resists the restriction the Law sets for it. Therefore, the holiness of the command is praised with words. And verbal veneration of the Law was exercised by Judaism with, in fact, great earnestness. The confession of the Law was especially zealously expressed, particularly when it was displayed before another person, where it could be used to obligate and to judge him. Open contradiction arises, however, between the word with which man honors the Law and that which he desires and does.

But precisely here, Judaism experiences the power of the Law. "It puts you to death," Paul said to his countrymen. It inserts itself divisively between people and God, for it makes them guilty because of their covetousness and excludes them from life. So the vineyard remains barren. The tenants of the vineyard, who want to appropriate the vineyard for themselves, meet with disaster.

Bear Fruit or Be Cut Down
August 5

He spoke this parable:
"Someone had a fig tree that was planted in his vineyard.
He came and looked for fruit on it. But he found none.
So he said to the caretaker, 'Look, I have been coming and
looking for fruit on this fig tree for three years and have
found none. Cut it down. Why should it take up space?'
But the caretaker answered and said to him,
'Lord, let it stay here one more year. I will dig around it and
fertilize it. And if it then in the future bears fruit, that will be
good; and if not, then have it cut down.'"
—Luke 13:6–9

The fig tree, which stands barren in the vineyard, and the tenants, who exploit the vineyard for themselves, present closely comparable situations. Similarly, the gardener—who pleads for the fig tree to be spared and takes pains to cause it to be fruitful—and the son—who comes to the vineyard tenants in order to make them obedient to their master—present the assessment of what Jesus wills and does. And since the fig tree is to be cut down, if despite the efforts of the gardener it remains unfruitful, Jerusalem is exposed to the same fate as that tree if the Lord of the vineyard comes and brings disaster to the vineyard tenants.

And yet the parable of the fig tree shows with new clarity how Jesus makes a unified will out of polarities that look like a contradiction in him. These include his calm patience and his frenetic labor as well as his forgiving and his judging. Israel's unfruitfulness will come to an end. This is God's will, in which the sending of Jesus is grounded. It ends when that which is barren becomes fruitful, and it also ends when that which is barren is cast aside. On the one hand is the revelation of God's mercy; on the other is the revelation of God's justice. God's lordship occurs through both, and both are Jesus' office. God's glorification occurs not through the one or the other, and Jesus is not free to do just one or the other. God's own will makes a unified work out of his living and his dying.

Jesus stands in the service of mercy and becomes the intercessor for those whom God's verdict judges. He brings to conversion those who are living for themselves. He is sent for their salvation. At the same time, he hallows God's justice and brings to those who oppose him exclusion from God's kingdom. He is the Merciful One in that he bears the cross and confers forgiveness on the guilty, but he does not acquiesce in the godlessness of man. He is himself subservient to God's verdict, which rejects all the godless. He is placed between the divine wrath and the divine grace, obligated to both, obedient to both, a tool of both. He makes it evident that God is for man and that he is against him. He brings to light that the end of godlessness is death and that God declares righteousness to the godless and calls them into life. His intention is that the barren fig tree become a fruitful tree, and his desire is that the barren tree be done away with. In having both intentions and bringing both situations to an appropriate conclusion, he reveals God. That is why the cross is the place in which God is recognized and faith in him arises. For Jesus went to the cross because he was obedient to the entire will of God.

God's Love Becomes Visible in Jesus' Cross
August 6

God loved the world so much that he gave his only Son, so that everyone who believes on him would not perish but have eternal life.

—JOHN 3:16

What Jesus, through the story of the arrogant vineyard tenants, said to the ruling men of Jerusalem is, by the saying with which he interpreted his sending, expressed also to the teacher of Israel who sought him by night. It is only with Nicodemus that Jesus emphasizes not his fellowship with Jerusalem but his mission for the world. The vineyard's owner sets great store by his vineyard. For he constructed it, and it is his possession, and he desires the fruit that ripens in it in the same way that God loves the world he created. The love of the father sends his son to the vineyard tenants, and the love of God shows its greatness in that it sends the only Son into the world. The sending of the son to the tenants leads to his death, and through his sending into the world, God hands over his Son to the verdict that brings death to him. If the tenants accept the son, they will live. Now, however, they fall prey to death. The Son of God is given over to death so that there might be those who do not lose their lives through God's judgment. In the place of the former tenants, the vineyard receives new ones. And these tenants do what the son demands of them, and through the death of the Son, there are those who have eternal life, and these are the ones who believe in him.

Also according to this word, the unified will of God is revealed in the death of Jesus —a will that is gracious and brings about righteousness. The death of Jesus is proof of the divine love in that the world stands under the divine verdict, which debars it from life. He frees those who believe in him from this verdict. In them, God's love becomes effective by their receiving eternal life. In order to separate them from those who must die, Jesus suffers death.

It is an open, although highly surprising fact, upon which darkness cannot be cast, that Jesus' disciples recognized in his demise the perfection of love. How did this singular result come about? It was not the invention of some kind of theological and intellectual labor. It was rather Jesus' doing. His love laid hold of the cross, and in his love the disciples truly apprehended God's love. This is a love whose gloriousness and truth consist in its juxtaposing the verdict, which decrees death, over against the godless will of man. Nevertheless, it also confers upon man entrance into the fellowship of God's love through faith.

The Work of Grace
from the Work of Wrath
August 7

God's righteousness is revealed through the gospel from faith to faith. For God's wrath is revealed from heaven against all godlessness and unrighteousness of men.
—ROMANS 1:17–18

Why does God make his righteousness effective by making people believers through his message? In this way God brings human behavior into conformity with his justice, because he opposes all human godlessness and unrighteousness. Because man runs up against God's opposition when he despises God and withholds fellowship from his neighbor, and because man cannot overcome God's opposition, God has made the Christ into the one through whom righteousness becomes effective in humans. Outside of righteousness, there is no life for them. If there were, it would mean the godless will of man could assert itself and win victory for itself. But the one who does what is wrong is dishonored, and the one who despises and denies God comes to grief. It is certain that man receives death from God through his sinful activity, but it is just as certain that this is not the final fulfillment of God's will. For God did not create man for the purpose of destroying him. His royal work occurs, rather, through his shaping people into the way they need to be so as to arrive at eternal life.

The mediator of this shaping is the Christ, who comes to be among humans so that the verdict pronounced against them might stand and the grace offered to them might be revealed. Thereby the foolishness and folly of man comes to an end—man, who one moment insults God and flees from him when he feels this opposition, and then flatters him and plays the beggar before him because God's gifts, which he needs for life, attract him. Jesus did not flee from God but went with him hand in hand to the cross. He did not lie to or defraud God but administered the gloriousness given to him in such a way that he brought glory to God. For this reason, man receives in Jesus everything that he needs to see God's will and to be made one with him. Now the door of faith is open and the basis for faith extended to him. He honors the wrath of God that rejects him and lays hold of the grace of God that helps him—all through believing in the Christ.

With this, Paul objectively and truthfully repeats what Jesus was and what he did when he went into God's vineyard and was tossed out by those who presided over it. He underwent this because there is no room for godlessness and unrighteousness in God's kingdom. It is his mission to bring the godless and unrighteous into God's kingdom by pronouncing to them the gracious word of God that puts us in the position of being able to believe God.

The Advocate of Those Who Fall
August 8

If anyone sins, we have an advocate with the Father,
Jesus Christ, the Righteous One.
—1 John 2:1

God's Word has entered into the lives of those who believe. Christ now possesses lordship over the believer, and the believer walks in the light of God and his presence. That makes him incapable of hating. Such sin is for him a thing of the past, but that does not mean he is removed from all danger. What happens when he does sin, inasmuch as the will still exerts influence upon him and he is not only exposed to sinful drives but also can succumb to them? If he sins, does the Christ break off fellowship with the believer? It is not possible to deny the reality of guilt. The believer's guilt is greater than it was before, when he sinned without God's Word being in him and without the helpful presence of the Christ having been granted to him. No one who believes can obscure the fact that the opposition of the Christ against everything godless and unjust possesses a full and comprehensive nature. But the Christ was sent into the world with the authority to forgive. This authority, which he had on earth and for the sake of which he bore the cross, is given to him and cannot be taken away. In his heavenly form, he exercises this authority by serving as advocate with the Father for the sinner who sins.

When the believer cries out for the mediation of the Christ, he acknowledges his guilt and for his own sake hallows the divine justice. He does not desire suppression of the divine judgment. He does not think he can remain in fellowship with Jesus if condemned by the divine verdict, as if he could flee from God's verdict to the Christ because the Christ has the grace that frees from divine judgment and exonerates guilt. For the Christ never steps out of his unity with the divine will. The believer can never expect the Christ to despise the pronouncement of the Father for the sake of the believer. There is no grace for the believer to desire from God other than God's grace. And he can remain in fellowship with Christ only as Christ carries out the judgment of God on him. This is emphatically expressed by there being no exoneration for the one who sins other than the exoneration Jesus attains for the sinner before the Father.

But now the believer calls to mind what the life and death of the Christ reveals. The believer calls to mind, that is, that the Christ bound himself with man in order to lead back to the Father those who had forsaken the Father's house, and to proclaim justification in the power of his righteousness to those who know themselves to be guilty. That was and is the work given to him by God because he is the Righteous One, the enemy of unrighteousness and the victor over unrighteousness. He is the judge of godlessness and its conqueror. He is the one who contradicts our lack of faith. Through his Word he brings us to faith. He is the bulwark against our self-seeking. He is the one who heals our lovelessness. When the sinner who has stumbled is enabled to come to a new awareness of faith through the mediation of the Christ, the sinner experiences what the blood of Jesus testifies to him.

The Gift of the Murdered One Is Eternal Life
August 9

As Moses lifted up the snake in the desert, so must the Son of Man be lifted up, so that everyone who believes in him might have eternal life.
—JOHN 3:14

How can a rabbi like Nicodemus be freed from his customary pattern of thinking, unless a word of Scripture be given him to accomplish this? He will always mistrust what his eyes see and his ears hear if a scriptural passage does not help him believe the truth that Jesus testifies to him. But is there a word in the Torah that could make understandable to the rabbi why Jesus bore the opposition of the people, peaceably and conscious of God's presence, and why Jesus had no fear regarding the demise to which his life must lead? And all this without contradicting the proclamation of the lordship of God or dispensing with his royal mission?

There is. Jesus reminds the rabbi of what once took place when some in Israel's camp were bitten by snakes. At that time Moses brought about deliverance by hanging an image of a snake on a pole and admonishing those who were fatally stricken to look upon it with a believing gaze. What helped those who were dying at that time? It was faith. What kind of a faith? It was faith in the One according to whose command Moses acted, faith in the One who promised that he would heal them by having the serpent suspended from the pole.

Didn't this amount to showing the rabbi how Jesus can come to be the Savior by being elevated on the cross? As Moses had commanded: Look in faith to the crucified serpent! so Jesus commanded the people in word and deed: Look in faith to me! Look to me even when I am crucified! I am dying so that you will live!

No one expected help from a serpent. Just as little did the Jews expect deliverance from the one who would be crucified. One who is crucified in this way appeared to be a sinner whom God had judged. Nevertheless, those who believed for the sake of the serpent received life. And in the same way Jesus will have authority to bring those who believe in him into eternal life with him precisely because he will be crucified. With this the cross of Jesus was set into the light of the divine grace. From his condemnation arises the liberation of those who were imprisoned. From his death comes the eternal life of the dying.

Love Does Not Cut and Run
August 10

I am the good shepherd. The good shepherd gives his life for the sheep. However, he who is not a shepherd but a hireling, to whom the sheep do not belong, sees the wolf coming and deserts the sheep and flees. Then the wolf plunders and

*scatters them. For the "shepherd" is a hireling and the sheep
mean nothing to him.*
—JOHN 10:11–13

Why is it that Jesus cannot simply forsake his field of service? Why can he not just be silent and leave his people to the care of its priests and the leadership of its teachers? He could do that if his only goal were to live forever in the glorious presence of God. But that is an impossibility. True, there are shepherds who flee when the wolf attacks the flock. Those are the ones who shepherd for the sake of gain. The flock does not belong to them but to someone else. Such shepherds are not hired to die in the line of duty. They tend the sheep because this is the source of their income. But the shepherd to whom the flock belongs will not conduct himself in this way. He does not flee. He rather risks that which is ultimate for the preservation of what is his.

But how is Jerusalem Jesus' possession, his flock, so to speak? Does he place himself in the line of kings who made the land their own and regarded the people as their servants? Or does he see himself as one of the priests who bind participation of others in God to their arts? Is he like one of the leaders of the rabbinic schools, who obligate their students to their word because they live from the income of what their students give them? In any of these cases, Jesus would be like the lowly servant who plies the trade of the shepherd because he receives money for it and lives from this money. He would be doing what the thieves do who crowd their way into the sheep pen in order to take control of the sheep so that they can slaughter them.

If he is in truth sent to his people with the gracious gifts of God and destined to be that people's Lord, then he must show this by not fleeing and by doing what is necessary to lay hold of the cross. By that cross David's kingship returns to Jerusalem. That is how Jerusalem is Jesus' possession. He is the Son of Man. That is how lordship over God's people is given to him. He proclaims liberty to the captive and life to the dying. God points to him all who are in need. That is the divinely ordained tie that binds him with mankind and mankind with him. It has its basis in the gracious will of God, a will fully shared by the Son. Commonality of will is love. It does not give way or betray. This love in its divine form must now prove itself, since the course upon which love places Jesus leads him to the cross. Any tie that is held together by selfish will tears apart when tested by that which endangers its very life. But the fellowship that love brings about does not come to an end. Love brings about this fellowship, to be sure, only when it is free from every selfish quality. Love possesses this purity when it binds us with other people, because it is the love of God.

The Condemnation of Jesus Is Invalid
August 11

Have you never read in the Scriptures,
"The stone that the builders rejected became the cornerstone.
This is from the Lord, and it is wonderful in our eyes"?
—MATTHEW 21:42

A building is erected; this building is built by and for God. That is Jesus' aim and the meaning of Jewish and all human history. Jesus and the apostles constantly used images borrowed from the building trades to give their goal a clear conception. This is already clear from Jesus' naming the first disciple Peter, which means "rock." Through this there was a constant reminder of the building on which Jesus and the disciples were working. Jesus unifies man. He brings people into fellowship with one another. The basis of their fellowship is the divine working. And their goal is to do the will of God. Inasmuch as Jesus and the disciples created this fellowship, they are builders.

An enigmatic saying of Scripture, Psalm 118:22–23, describes this same building. There, the thought was of that moment in which a building is prepared and decisions are made regarding where, and the material with which, it will be built. Which stone should be the cornerstone? Once the cornerstone is laid, the decision has already been made regarding the place and the size of the building. It has also been decided what sort of material will be used for the building. The stones that now will be added around the cornerstone must fit in with the cornerstone's situation and composition.

Conflict arises, however, concerning the cornerstone. The builders reject the stone that would have been suited to be the corner. The intention of the project leader and the opinion of those who carry out the building operation are not the same. The building should be constructed so as to be pleasing to those who build it. The divine intention and the human desire are in conflict. That is the same situation as when the command of the father displeases the son, the tenders of the vineyard take the harvest for themselves, or the invited guests desecrate the king's feast. The builders insist on having their way. The stone is rejected and has no place in the building. The son who went into the vineyard was cast out from it.

Now, however, the psalm continues and describes what will next take place. Will the building be erected for the builders? Is it their judgment that has validity? What they do has no weight, and their judgment is futile. The rejected stone is, despite them, the cornerstone. And what they judge disparagingly is nevertheless the Christ, the Lord of the eternally living fellowship, the Lord with whom all the redeemed are bound. The builders condemn the Chosen One, but God's choice endures. They kill the one who promises them life, but God revives him. They drive the people away from him, but God leads his fellowship to him. Through his being rejected and remaining the Chosen One and being killed and remaining the one who lives, he becomes the sign of God that reveals God.

Jesus Brings His Word into the Temple
August 12

He entered the temple in Jerusalem and looked all around and then went to Bethany with the Twelve. For it was already late.
—Mark 11:11

When a king in festive procession enters into his own city, he leads his followers into that city's temple. The greater the victory he celebrates, the less likely that the festal procession will lack the necessary offerings. The more brilliant the honor that he, as conqueror, presents to his gods, the brighter his fame shines forth. And now into Jerusalem comes a festive procession that can end only in the temple court. *Jerusalem*—a city the existence of which depends entirely on the temple and which would be little more than a heap of rubble if the temple were destroyed, a city that now possesses great power as the center of the dispersed people, giving that people unity in that place, but only because the temple stands there.

Jesus does, indeed, enter the temple court with the Twelve. But no great festive offering and no worship service of thanksgiving come of this. Jesus took careful note of what was going on in the temple and then left with his disciples. He did nothing different from what any stranger did who visited the temple. Yet Jesus called Jerusalem his possession. Was the temple not also his possession? Yes, it was. He was not going to give up on it.

Yet he brought nothing to the priests and desired nothing from them, neither their anointing oil nor their temple services. What he brought into the temple was his word. In the temple he fought the last battle with Judaism. He said what he had to say, not in the marketplaces of the city and also not merely in their houses of prayer. He did not speak his word against the old word of God or alongside that word in the synagogues but at the place the former word of God had created, where, according to its ordinance, the priestly service took place and where, according to its command, the people came together for festive purposes. Here he offered his word to the priests and to the people, and the newness of his word was clear to everyone in that his word was the only thing that he gave to them.

The word indicates God's lordship. Through the word the Christ creates his regal work. Through the word he gathers his people. Through the word that creates faith, he confers righteousness upon humanity. Through the word that expresses grace, he calls mankind into life. In the same way, the word is the power that brings down the temple, brings death to Judaism, and judges all that is godless. But whoever comes to Jerusalem in such a way that he remains a stranger in its temple must leave it again. The outcome of his entry into the city is his exit, and this exit leads Jesus to Golgotha.

The Temple Is Defiled
August 13

Jesus says to them, "It is written: 'My house shall be called a house of prayer.' But you have made it into a den of thieves."
—Matthew 21:13

Jesus' warning was unmistakable, but the rulers of Jerusalem did not believe it. They were protected: didn't they have the temple, and was this not the guarantee of their security since it indisputably proved that the city was the city of God? The temple did, in fact, belong to that with which the Lord of the vineyard had equipped that city so that it could be his precious possession. For the temple bore witness to the people that they were empowered to pray. That they were able to call on God was grace. But this is not the reason the Jew prizes the temple. He expects from the temple what thieves receive from their lairs.

They draw back into their lairs, which protect them, because they are robbers and want to remain robbers. For this reason, they fear those who administer justice, and they shy away from the light. But they tarry in their hideaways only until another opportunity to rob shows itself.

What the Jew sought in the temple was precisely what the hideaway offered to the robber. He goes to it because he sins and so that he can sin again. That means he seeks protection from God and from his righteous judgment. He seeks forgiveness, but he has in mind the indulgence of evil, not liberation from evil. He wants to perform repentance there, but through this he will not become a changed person. He celebrates there God's greatness, but that strengthens his pride instead of bringing it to an end. He petitions there for God's lordship, but by that he has in mind his own praise.

Can the temple protect him now? It is a fruitless undertaking for man to seek protection from God for his godlessness. Every godless and unrighteous act meets with his opposition, and man's venture to appropriate for himself what belongs to God can never succeed.

Jesus offers to the Jews what temple service, in the way they carry it out, can never grant for them. From Jesus they receive the authority to pray, the forgiveness of their guilt, the consolidation into a harmonious fellowship, and the common celebration that praises the gloriousness of the divine grace. But he cannot give this to them by making himself the Lord of their temple. He calls those who listen to him to come out of the den of thieves. The temple must go under and be built anew in him, and this takes place by his being condemned and killed.

The Temple Worshiper Acceptable to God
August 14

The tax collector stood at a distance and would not even look up toward heaven, but rather beat his breast and said, "O God, be merciful to me, a sinner!" I tell you, this man went

down to his house justified, but not that other person.
For whoever exalts himself will be humiliated, but whoever
humbles himself will be exalted.
—LUKE 18:13–14

W as there no one who went to the temple for legitimate religious reasons? That was not the meaning of Jesus' negative judgment on the people's usual conduct there. Numerous and dramatic differences existed side by side among the Jewish people. The behaviors of those who visited the temple were often starkly divergent. To the temple came not only the righteous person for whom it was bliss to remind himself and God in prayer how great a claim he had on God's blessing. There came also that one whose god had been money. For him, what the temple signified had previously meant nothing. He knew he had little right to be there and was at best only a casual visitor.

He did not come to enjoy an hour of enraptured devotion, nor to fill a religious duty according to the rules and customs. He came because he was personally devastated. Were there really penitent tax collectors? How could there not be? The striving for worldly riches always gives rise to conflict in which one person is unjust to another and uses dishonest means to overcome his adversary. Such a person could not be around Jerusalem long, however, without the temple reminding him constantly that God stands against every godless and unrighteous act. But the temple also pointed to the One who revealed himself to persons in order to come to their aid.

When a greedy tax collector could finally pass by the temple no longer, nor evade its claim with some pious front, he did not need to say much in the temple. But what he did say had great weight. He stands before God, knowing that he is condemned by God and has no claim on him. He is dependent on God's pardon. Dare he ask this of God? One of the truths that the existence of the temple broadcasts to every person was that God is merciful and forgives trespasses and does not reject the one who comes to him. For that reason there were altars and priests and a courtyard into which every civic member could enter—even those who knew that they would find no place of honor there.

Yet the person who entered the temple would find there nothing more than a place to make petition. There was no one with the power to answer his request and pronounce God's gracious word of pardon to the guilty.

That is why Jesus said of himself, "Here is someone greater than the temple." When he told this story, he did what only he could do, and he added to what the tax collector in the temple could not yet experience. Jesus proclaimed the divine verdict, and this said, "Your prayers are answered. God has pardoned you; you have his blessing and stand vindicated before him."

In saying this to the tax collector, Jesus freed from the temple those who believe on him. A result of this for them was that God removed the larcenous tax collector from his iniquitous booth—not a bad thing.

The Law Prescribes the Love of God
August 15

The scribe said to him, "Correct, teacher. You have spoken truly that there is only one and there is none other besides him. And to love him with the whole heart and all understanding and all one's strength and to love one's neighbor as one's self—that is more than all burnt offerings and other offerings." And when Jesus saw that he had answered intelligently, he said to him, "You are not far from the kingdom of God."
—Mark 12:32–34

Were there not also righteous people for whom a visit to the temple had been wholesome? When one man who lived according to God's law tested Jesus by asking him whether the Law spoke to him with illuminating clarity and furnished for him his will, Jesus cited for him the two great commandments that are one in that they show us in love that which is demanded of us. As a result, the teacher of the Law judged that Jesus was right. Here he thought about his own greatest concern. The biggest share of his service to God consisted in presenting certain prescribed offerings. For the greatest share of the Law was the law of offerings. But anything that man lays on the altar as a gift is far less significant to God than what he brings to God when he has love. Now it was Jesus' turn to reveal his judgment to his questioner. Jesus' verdict was, "You are not far from God's kingdom."

If he went to the altar with the consciousness that what he brings there to God is something small because God's grandeur and grace obligated him to love God with all that he is and can do, and if he did not forget that God showed to him in his neighbors those whom he should love, then that which obscured for him the knowledge of the divine work was no longer strong. It might soon be the case that the lordship of God would become visible to him in Jesus.

If he knew that love was what God commanded of him, could he then not understand that Jesus did not serve God at the altar but honored him by accepting the cross from him? And must it then become a stumbling block to him that the love of Jesus drew him to the Crucified One, who would die in ignominy, and not to the high priest, who ruled Jerusalem in pomp and splendor?

Yet even if the teacher of the Law is not far from the kingdom of God, he has not yet become one of its heirs. And if he were to ask, "What do I still lack?" he would receive the same answer Jesus gave to the rich young ruler. The teacher of the Law sensed that love was demanded of him. Did he, however, have love? He is not yet so free from himself that he is able to join himself to Jesus. He looks at what he himself can do and achieve for God.

But he recognized that this service cannot consist in trivialities and does not exhaust itself in words. He realized, rather, that the will of God and the goal of Jesus are that his thinking and acting grow out of love. This knowledge binds him to Jesus. His status under the Law separates him from Jesus. But by hearing in the Law the command of Jesus to love him, the temple became for him a place of prayer, and he did not enter the temple as a robber takes refuge in his cave.

Love with a Whole Heart
August 16

As he sat across from the treasury, he watched as the crowds put copper coins into the treasury. And many rich people put in much. Now a poor widow came and put in two small coins that, taken together, are worth a penny. And he called his disciples to him and said to them, "Truly I say to you, this poor widow put in more than everyone else who has contributed to the cash box. For they all gave from their excess, but she gave from what she does not have. In fact, she gave her entire income."

—MARK 12:41–44

JESUS REVEALS HIMSELF TO JERUSALEM 375

Here another visitor to the temple is described: a woman who receives Jesus' praise. There is a tie here to the teacher of the Law mentioned earlier, whom Jesus said was not far from the kingdom of God because he recognized the great command of the Law in the command to love.

Jesus had placed himself near the treasury so that he could see how those who brought their gifts dealt with the priest of the treasury. Here it became visible how the people understood the command that empowered them to love. Love gives, and the form of their gifts shows their power. What was brought into the treasury was given to God and revealed *that* the giver honored God and *how* he honored God.

Rich people came and gave much. It would have been a scandal for the rich if they had given only a little. But did that mean that the stingy rich man no longer belonged among those who made a robber's den out of the temple? What did they want to receive as God's recompense for their rich contributions? Jesus did not conceal what was in their hearts. One thing is certain: they gave much. But did they give all? No! How senseless it would appear if the people wanted to bring their entire possessions into the treasury of the temple.

But alongside these clever givers, there was one who gave to God everything. She belonged to the poor level of society, for she was a widow. Therefore, she certainly does not stand before God's kingdom as a camel stands before the eye of the needle. She had two of the smallest coins, which were virtually worthless, and she contributed both to God's service. Did the priest accept these worthless gifts? He had to, for the sake of the Law. For whatever a person called corban, or "offering," was an untouchable contribution devoted to God. But the widow was not going to gain much recognition with such a gift. With what the rich brought, the temple could be beautified and the temple service greatly enhanced. But you couldn't do much with these two tiny coins.

However the priest may have looked upon the giving, Jesus ascribed to the widow's gift a value far greater than that of all the other gifts: she gave all that she had. What did she think when she did this? What did she expect from God? Jesus is not her judge, and he leaves unmentioned what may have been lacking in what she gave. He does not go into the clarity of her knowledge or the purity of her love. She gave everything! What she herself had need of did not come into view, since she entered the temple to honor God. What would happen to her was in this moment not a concern that could move her. Everything for God, absolutely everything: Is that not the mark of love? That is how the commandment described love. It said that we must love not halfheartedly but rather only with a whole heart. The person who loves us, loves us entirely. And that which we love, we give ourselves to entirely. "Love endures all things, believes all things, hopes all things, bears all things." Whoever loves his people gives his all to them, and whoever loves God gives himself entirely to God. The clever and rich scoff at this, and therefore Jesus is their adversary. But he gives his praise to those who give everything to God, as he himself did when he went to the cross. What did he do when he did that? He gave everything to God. He gave entirely of himself to God.

The Sons, the Laborers, the Guests of God
August 17

> *Jesus spoke to them again in parables: "The kingdom of heaven is like a king who prepared a wedding for his son. He sent his servants to call those who had been invited to the banquet, but they were not willing to come. Again he sent some more servants and said, 'Tell those who have been invited, "Look, I have prepared my banquet. My oxen and the fattened calf have been butchered, and everything is ready. Come to my wedding banquet."' But they paid no attention to him and went away, one to his field, another to his business. The others, however, seized his servants, mocked them, and killed them. The king became enraged, sent out his soldiers, and killed those murderers and burned their city."*
>
> —Matthew 22:1–7

How can Israel's relationship with God be put into words? Out of the communities that produce natural life around us arise the words that make it possible for Jesus to express what he was doing, despite the hiddenness of the divine activity. Nature binds people to people in three ways. A father begets a son; from him the son receives life. The landowner places workers in his service, for the ground becomes productive when human labor brings about growth. And a people's community spirit recognizes their king; the participation of the king's city is expected for a regal feast. With all three word pictures, Jesus made clear to the Jewish leaders the sort of relationship to God in which they were found, and how they related to him. They are God's children, for Israel is God's work. They are God's laborers, for he had expressed his will to them and they are obligated to do it. They are the invited guests of God, for the King will prepare a wedding celebration for his Son, and he will magnify his grace through the glorification of the Christ. This brings blessing to his people.

Jesus' depiction of the proclamation of the lordship of God was suggestive. Entrance into God's kingdom brings man the sonship of God, which relates closely to sharing with God in his earthly work. Such sharing makes man God's servant. It also results in gifts of grace that take away from man the sometimes dire and even fatal dimensions of human existence.

In this way Jesus reiterated without attenuation Israel's high destiny. No teacher of Israel could say anything greater in praise of the chosen people, and Jesus did this precisely in view of his crucifixion. He is dying not because he was an apostate who did not believe in Israel's vocation. On the contrary, he will die because he affirmed this call and regarded it as true. For in all three depictions it becomes clear how impossible and reprehensible Israel's conduct had been.

In Jesus' parables the sons reject the command of the father. The laborers work only for themselves and not for their master. The citizens reject the king's summons, partly because what they already possessed suited them nicely, and partly because the king's honor is repugnant to them. This unmasks the depth of opposition against Jesus. In rejecting Jesus, the sons declare their independence from the father, while the laborers withhold from the master his due. Likewise, the citizens decline to show honor to their king. The consequences are disastrous.

At the same time it becomes evident what Jesus brought about through the giving of himself to death. He makes obedient sons out of the disobedient. He creates the community that does the will of God with joy. He presents to the king guests who join in the king's celebration with gratitude.

Jerusalem's Politicians Miscalculate
August 18

*Now the high priests and the Pharisees convened the council
and said, "What should we do? This person is performing
many signs. If we let him continue doing this, everyone will
believe in him, and the Romans will come and do away with our
status and our nation."*

—JOHN 11:47–48

The leaders of any ethnic group—East Asian, African tribes, peoples of northern descent—know they are responsible for group vitality and survival. They take steps to uphold and preserve national independence and ancestral customs. That was precisely the goal of those men who, in order to preserve Judaism as they knew it, put Jesus to death. Their goal was the preservation of the temple and of national freedom. Both were in danger, for Rome was their enemy. The Jews' political freedom was an irritant to Roman imperial authority, for it contradicted the unconditional might of the caesar. Jewish independence had its strongest support in the temple. If it came to armed conflict, the temple would be the fortress to which Jewish forces would flee and from which they would fight to the last drop of blood. The outcome would be the annihilation of the temple.

Does Jesus safeguard these two precious possessions of the people? Does he guarantee peace with Rome? What he commands and seeks to make out of the nation and the world stands in sharp contrast to that for which Rome strives. If Jesus comes to power, all Roman deities will vanish. Even "the goddess Roma" will no longer have a site over which to preside. The Roman claim to power that seeks to subjugate all peoples will end. The legions that uphold Roman might will be dissolved. Rome can never tolerate the Jewish people rallying around Jesus. Doesn't loyalty to Jesus lead to war against Rome, and in that case would Jesus protect the temple and the freedom of the people? Sheer delusion! Who could possibly believe that Jesus is stronger than Caesar, or that he could defend against the legions or preserve the temple and its treasures? Jesus must die in order for Jerusalem to remain a free city that enjoys self-rule and the sovereignty of its temple. He must die for the sake of Judaism, die for his people.

When John wrote this, the temple lay in ruins and the Jews' political independence was a thing of the past. Jerusalem's politicians in Jesus' earthly days had miscalculated.

Are they the only politicians who deceived themselves and whose actions brought about the opposite of what they intended? World history shows this happens repeatedly, and German history likewise illustrates this with particular clarity. What is the basis for the bad luck that plagues all politics? It is this: politicians reckon only with what lies visible before them. But the course of history is not subject solely to what people do. It is not determined purely by what nature shows and gives us. But can the politician make plans on any other basis? No! God's governance is not one of the factors the politician has at his disposal or can include in his calculations. We do not bring God's power under our authority. That spells disaster again and again for political shrewdness, as we humans learn constantly that we are not the ultimate masters of our own destinies.

Jerusalem's politicians supposed that the temple's future rested on them and that they must secure the freedom of their people. This was delusion. Whether the temple falls or remains, and whether the Jew is free or subject— the decision lay not with the Jew but with God.

Is Jesus a Freedom Fighter?
August 19

The Pharisees sent their disciples to him, along with the Herodians. They said, "Teacher, we know that you speak the truth and teach God's way accurately and aren't swayed by human opinion, because you don't base your judgment on mere appearance. So tell us what you think: is it permitted to pay taxes to Caesar? Or is this unlawful?"
—Matthew 22:16–17

How could the young band of Galilean men shake the conviction that it was wrong to pay the head tax to Caesar, even though a century had passed since Jerusalem's political independence had vanished? It vanished when the Roman field commander Pompey stormed the temple in 63 B.C. Since that time Palestinian Jewish life had been under the rule of the Roman caesar. The petty kings of the Herodian family were the last to be willing to undermine dependence on Rome. But now, every year the number of people increased whose conscience did not permit them to pay the annual head tax. "We have one king," they said; God is Israel's king and no other. To acknowledge the ruler in Rome as king was to deny God, and this happened every time someone paid the head tax that the Roman ruler demanded. The feeling was, "Since that day when the voice of God proclaimed, 'I am the Lord your God,' we have been God's kingdom; as we belong to and obey him, we are free from every other dominion."

Was Jesus not a suitable leader for those with this conviction? Much about Jesus forced those who were zealous for freedom to pay him heed. They lived under the lordship of God, the sole King; so did Jesus. They gave themselves to God in life and in death; Jesus did the same. They relied on God's almighty intervention; Jesus did too, and not only with words but also in deed. He led his disciples to become believers who trusted God completely.

But Jesus had erected an unbridgeable barrier between himself and the liberation movement. The faith he gave to his disciples was equally characterized by love. And love is patient; indeed, it even endures injustice. Where in Jesus' group was there a sword sharp enough to smite Rome? He has no sword, said the teachers of Jerusalem. But he did hold out hope of freedom; he must, if he is claiming to be the Promised One. If he remains silent on the head-tax question, it must be only because of fear; he knows that he is lost the moment he unveils his political program.

The liberation movement, it seems, projected its own outlook and behavior onto Jesus. It was difficult for Jerusalem's leaders to stand against those zealous for liberation. These leaders agreed with the Zealots' basic principles, but they were terrified at the prospect of applying Zealot teaching to politics. The call to liberation was the call to war, and what a war! It would be war against Rome: Jewish farmers against Roman legions, the tiny population of Palestine arrayed against imperial might. The Jerusalem leaders had rejected the evasion of the tax. But the freedom fighters despised this fearful policy. Must Jesus not despise it too? It was crystal clear that he trusted God without reserve, praised God's lordship as the sum of all heavenly gifts, and rejected all transgression but called for perfect obedience to God's command. Given such commitments, how could he not share in the dream of liberation? If he speaks what he must secretly believe, this will be his ruin. They supposed that Jesus walked in the same darkness as they.

When Is the Jew Loyal to Caesar?
August 20

The high priests answered Pilate, "We have no king but
Caesar."
—JOHN 19:15

Every Jew said, "Oh, if only we had some other king than Caesar!—someone from our own people, not a Roman; someone who reigns in our own midst, not from a far-off throne; someone who judges according to our law, not according to a foreign legal code; someone who venerates our God with us, not someone who worships demons and deifies himself; someone who is a recipient of divine promise, not someone who will be brought down into hell when God judges. It is a great misfortune that we have no other king but Caesar. But we have no other, and we cannot very well do without any king at all, for he provides peace and security for our people and orders its dealings with other nations. The caesar does this, and since we cannot replace him, we must declare our allegiance to him."

"But you have Jesus," Pilate said to them. Jesus? The one born a powerless child? That solitary figure with no army? That penniless figure who lived like he had never seen a silver coin? That religious fanatic who communes with God somewhere out there beyond reality? No! He is no replacement for Caesar! All the Jewish sects disagree with him. Those who are zealous for the Law consider him a sinner. The priests view him as an enemy of the temple. For those intent upon political freedom, the Zealots, he is far too pacifist. So there is no other position for a Jew to hold than this: like everyone else, Jesus must be loyal to Caesar.

What kind of Jew is this? It is a Jew who has assimilated himself to the pagans and has made his Judaism into a degenerate form of paganism. His religion invents a God who somehow, whether beyond or in the world, means nothing to him but merely frees him to shape his own life as he sees fit. This form of Judaism arises when there comes to be only one reality for man, the world; only one reasonable driving passion, the desire for material possessions; only one law, the survival of the fittest; only one arbiter of questions, armed force. Under these conditions the Jew has no choice but to say, "We have no king but Caesar." And even if he succeeded in realizing his desires and putting a Jewish king on the throne, this king would be nothing but a Tiberias—just another Roman emperor.

Jesus Is No Enemy of Caesar
August 21

But Jesus knew their wickedness and said, "Why are you testing me, you hypocrites? Show me the gold coin you use for the tax." They brought him a denarius. He said to them, "Whose image and inscription are these?" They said, "The caesar's." Then he said to them, "So give to the caesar that which belongs to the caesar, and give to God that which belongs to God."

—Matthew 22:18–21

Jewish expectation viewed the Christ as an enemy of Caesar and the caesar as an antichrist. They battle each other, and the Christ emerges as the victor who annihilates Caesar. To view the promise given to Judaism this way was to mistake and reject who Jesus was. Jesus rejected the Jewish concept of kingship not because it expected too much of him; on the contrary, whoever sought to make him an enemy of Caesar demeaned him and disputed his high position. He brought this point home with surpassing assurance to those who attributed anti-Caesar intentions to him. To make his point he pointed to the coin used to pay the head tax.

He was asked his opinion on whether it was lawful for the Jew to give this coin to Caesar. But how could a Jew be in doubt about this? The coin displayed Caesar's image, and it was engraved with Caesar's titles. How could a Jew suppose that this was God's doing and possession? It was obviously minted by order of Caesar and received its value by imperial authority. The question was not, Should God or Caesar receive this coin? It was, rather, whether the Jew must keep it or hand it over. Now how does Jesus regard the Jew's denarius? If it had been Jesus' mission to protect the money of the Jews, then he would certainly be an enemy of Caesar.

Once again, how strangely disfigured was the Jewish outlook! The freedom being fought for in the name of God by the Zealots was liberation from the tax. They were zealous about the prohibition of images. How could they be concerned to amass coins picturing Caesar? The very title "Caesar" was to them a demand to give him divine veneration. Were the Jews not showing zeal against the worship of a man? Why would they want these inscriptions, which they rejected as idolatrous, in their possession? But it was money! Didn't Jesus realize what value money possesses? These coins meant commerce; to possess many of them was to be rich, and to stand before the kingdom of God like a camel before the eye of a needle. God's lordship comes about through the Christ, and therefore he is no enemy of Caesar.

If this coin were the only thing that Caesar sought, no one would have risked battling for political freedom. But the yoke of Caesar pressed down hard. It demanded not only the head tax but a large portion of the harvest. It subjected the people to the judgment of whomever Caesar sent. That was difficult to bear for those who longed for their own self-determination. But did they live solely from what grew from the soil, as essential as that was for them? Was there only flesh and not also Spirit? Did human will establish divine righteousness? Was it the Jew's business to arrive at greatness? Did praise belong to him? Is it not man's sin and shame when he seeks praise and honor for himself? That which governmental order conferred upon him was necessary because he is God's creation; but because of that he also requires something more. Could a Jewish king give this to him? Jesus offered it, and therefore he was no enemy of Caesar but chose the cross and, in his death, buried the dream of the Jew's concept of kingship.

What Happens to That Which Belongs to God?
August 22

Give to God that which belongs to God!
—Matthew 22:21

What man creates is formed in his image and is given his name. Accordingly, the coin bears the image and name of Caesar. Is there nothing that bears God's image? Man was created in the image of God. God is the Living One; therefore, man has life. God is wisdom; therefore, man thinks and wills. And man speaks because God speaks. God is good; therefore, good exists for man to strive after. And man loves because God is love. And man should hate evil because God hates it. God is eternal; therefore, man longs for eternity. God reveals himself in his kingdom; therefore, man can live only in fellowship with others.

How can Jerusalem still be asking what it should do? Those fighting for political freedom consider anyone placidly giving his coin to Caesar as cowardly and subservient. But the goal that exercises the people's entire strength stands before them in complete clarity. If man lives through God, then he lives for God. If he has received his willing and thinking from God, then he is to obey, hear God's Word, do his will. If he receives from God that which is salvific, then he is to shun evil; if he is loved and graced by God, then he should praise him. Let him give to God what is God's and not set himself above what belongs not to him but to God.

Is there any other command besides this one? This is the one command that determines all human behavior and gives life its fullness of meaning. When this command is honored, the temple ceases to be a robbers' den and becomes what God gave it to the people to be. The fig tree no longer stands barren on God's earth, but brings forth fruit for him who planted it. Scripture is no longer an empty word but enters man and guides him. And the dream dissipates of a freedom that seeks to make man the lord of his life but instead turns him into the enemy of all.

"Give to God that which is God's." With this, Jesus showed Jerusalem what can protect it from perdition. He also indicates the holy necessity that leads him to the cross. The Son of God and messenger of God and bearer of his grace is God's possession. Because he belongs to God, he gives himself to God. He gives him everything: body and blood, obedience and love, all praise and honor. How can the Jew arrive at the conclusion that he would be denying God by not fighting against Caesar? Because Jesus gives to God what is God's, God's kingdom comes through him.

The Sign of the Christ Is the Sword
August 23

Do not think that I came to bring peace to earth.
I came, not to bring peace, but the sword.
—Matthew 10:34

Jesus did not let the freedom fighters force a sword into his hand. They said he was lacking in courage and strength, but they were mistaken. He brings the sword. In this he confounds all expectations. Is the Promised One not "the Prince of Peace"? And it is entirely certain that God's reign will usher in righteousness, peace, and joy. Jesus would contradict this, were he to place the sword in his disciples' hands. But he did not give it to them. He did not make death their ally and comrade in arms as a means of subjugating the people. They could not build the body of his followers by force or fear. They proclaim life and are the heralds of freedom. For their word plants the seeds of love.

Yet the sword does come into the world through Jesus, because he is opposed. It is used against his disciples, whose adversaries exert the will to annihilate them. Which is the hero: the one who needs the sword, or the one who does not fear it? The one who vanquishes without the sword, or the one who can prevail only by destroying the lives of the opposition? He who joins battle and prevails without the sword has overcome the world.

Jesus' mission calls on him to elicit this life-and-death struggle. That is why he came. If he did not precipitate this battle, he would remove the truth and the power from God's message. For God's lordship is not a pleasant improvement and desired refinement to the human condition. It repudiates what man is and seeks. It terminates what he creates and disrupts the community by which he makes himself secure. For it brings a new force into human life through God's Word and work, to which every other power must now yield. But the existing authorities do not give way willingly. They put up a stiff defense, as if life hinged on their continued existence.

That is the magnitude of the commission Jesus was given. He is peace, and at the same time he is the cause of a battle that engulfs everyone. He defuses God's hostility toward humanity, yet he makes men his enemies. He pardons the guilty, yet he calls forth opposition that causes serious guilt to arise. He reveals that God's gift is life for us, yet his fellowship with God becomes the cause of death for many. Why must it be this way? The will of man is not the will of God; that is where the conflict arises. God's will, however, is salvation and life. Therefore, the Christ is our peace.

The One Who Overcomes the World
August 24

In the world you have duress. But take heart:
I have overcome the world.
—John 16:33

I will overcome the world"—that would be the proclamation of Jesus' future victory. "I have overcome the world"—with this he proclaims the victory he has attained. He won the victory in the hour he finished his work, because he knew the Jerusalem authorities in that very night would attempt his arrest. At that point his disciples' situation will separate from his own. The world's opposition will focus on them; because he is crucified, they are despised, harried, and driven away. But he is no longer handed over to the ravages of the world. He is no longer subject to its restrictions—not because he flees the world and terminates his dealings with it, for he cannot. For the one who bears the name of the Christ offers an indissoluble fellowship expressive of the steadfastness of the divine will. Just as he does not evade the world's ravages by fleeing them, so he cannot place his disciples beyond their reach. But he fortifies them for opposition to the world as he stands before them as the world's victor. Precisely this is his victory over the world: it put him to death.

That is proof that he was in the world without becoming obedient to it. Without it bringing him to silence, he spoke the word of God to it. He fearlessly testified to it of its godlessness. He revealed to it God's grace, without which his love would have flagged. Nothing beclouded the antithesis in which he stood to the world, and nothing was able to thwart or frustrate his work. He bore the form of a servant and the image of man without losing the form of God. Now he can die, and he can confirm the promise of forgiveness for sins through the shedding of his blood. For while he was in the world, he remained in the house of the Father. Therefore he can now depart the world in such a way that he returns to the Father. But by doing so, he also gave the disciples certainty regarding the outcome of the struggle arising from the world's resistance to them. The outcome of their struggle lies in his hand, and he is the one who has overcome the world.

The Victor over Satan
August 25

How can anyone enter the house of a stronger person and plunder it if he does not first bind the stronger person? Then he can plunder his house.
—Matthew 12:29

Was it only humans who fought against Jesus? There is a kingdom of spirits so closely related to the human world that they are unified. In this kingdom there is one who accuses people and opposes God's grace. He is an enemy who hinders the work of the Christ, a master of death who carries out God's judgment on humanity. The world has not been overcome if he is not overcome.

Jesus stood before the Jews not as someone wrestling with this enemy, and still less as someone subject to him and trying to break free by rising up against him. As a sign that he had overcome him, he acted to serve as the liberator of those who had lost their way and fallen prey to the dominion of hostile spirits. He thus reveals himself as the one over whom the Accuser has no power.

He has the capacity by the Spirit of God to rescue the captives. Through the work of the Spirit in him he is superior to all satanic working. But he has this superiority because he yielded himself, his whole mind and will, to the Spirit. He did not allow the Accuser to dictate to him his behavior when he sought to lure him away from his status and mission as the Son of God. In looking to the Father, no delusion intruded that would have obscured God's presence by some worldly illusion or conception of himself. The enemy plants such conceptions in the human soul to try to convince people that they are unworthy of God's grace and have fallen away from his acceptance. The Son did not permit the Enemy to stir up self-seeking desire that would have made him seek something other than what he knew to be God's will.

The consequences of this decision affected his entire outlook and course of action. It gave him the authority to forgive sins, and the saving power to free those who were inwardly disturbed. It gave him the right to pronounce the verdict on Judaism and to bind his disciples inseparably to him. It made him the victor over the world. Because he conquered the Accuser, he was the impeccable sacrifice, who had the authority to be the Lamb of God.

Peter Saved from the Tempter
August 26

Simon, Simon, look! Satan has sought you out, so that he might sift you like wheat. But I prayed for you, that your faith may not fail. And once you have returned, strengthen your brothers.

—LUKE 22:31–32

Jesus cannot be thwarted by the Accuser. But is this also true for his disciples? Among them it was first of all Peter over whom the Accuser sought to gain control. He was the point at which the attack aimed at Jesus could meet with success. If Peter were pried out of Jesus' hands, Jesus' accomplishment would be marred at a critical juncture.

The Accuser received power over Peter by impugning as untrue and worthless what he had become through Jesus. Peter is not wheat; he is chaff. That will become evident when the Accuser sets to work on him. His confession of faith in Jesus and his relation to him will wither. That will be the end of the career of the man designated the rock and the pillar of the church. The collapse will be total.

Satan's attack on Peter takes place, occurring during the nighttime activities through which the Jewish Sanhedrin sentenced Jesus. Yet the attack goes awry. For Satan is not the only one making a claim on Peter's soul. Jesus enters the list as his advocate in intercession before the Father. Satan's claim remains undisputed. It is true that Peter can deny; it is true that Jesus entrusts his word to a man who is unreliable. But the case that Jesus makes in the Father's presence is no less true: Peter believes in Jesus, and this grants to Peter fellowship with Jesus and makes Jesus into Peter's advocate.

Peter's critical need is that he not forsake his faith, and that is what Jesus prays for from the Father. The danger is very much present. When he made his denial, he broke faith. The guilt he incurred and the regret he must now suffer can easily have the effect of making faith ultimately impossible for him. But the fatherly grace of God works in such a way that Peter cannot doubt the truth of Jesus' forgiveness or question the call Jesus extended to him. With that, the Accuser is overcome. As long as the disciple continues in faith in Jesus, he is not handed over to the Accuser.

Because he has been unfaithful, yet was again freed from his unbelief, he can and must strengthen the others. They are no stronger than Peter. The Accuser calls them chaff too. But to them also the divine verdict applies: if your faith perseveres, then your deliverance is assured. Peter will be of assistance here since, in spite of his unbelief, he himself has been preserved through Jesus in faith.

Jesus Powerfully Transforms Human Lapse
August 27

I thank him who has strengthened me, Christ Jesus our Lord, because he regarded me as faithful by placing me in his service.
—1 Timothy 1:12

Is a man like Peter still usable to Jesus? After all, he could make him his messenger only by forgiving his lapse. Will Peter not always be weakened by inconsolable regret? Must he not always silently suffer as he wears the hair shirt of the penitent? If he were to wear it, the Accuser would have accomplished his purpose and made Jesus' intercession fruitless. For Jesus prayed for Peter's faith, and now he can and should believe Jesus' assurance that the forgiveness granted him is the gift of God and the work of the Christ. That made him into the strong apostle.

The same process repeated itself in the calling of Paul. For he, too, became an apostle in the wake of the serious lapse of becoming an enemy of Jesus and a persecutor of his followers. The pure ones in Ephesus, who praised their own knowledge of God, reproached him as guilty beyond forgiveness. It enraged them that someone who bore such a guilty past could be an apostle. But Paul could give way to them and cease sharing his message only if he disbelieved the Christ. From him he received forgiveness and much more besides: not only release from the punishment he deserved, and not only the failure of the Christ to repay his enmity with enmity or his calumnies with calumnies. Rather, he called Paul into his service and thereby proved his faith in him by affirming: You, Paul, are my loyal follower; I trust you.

If the Christ had not trusted him but had expected him to abuse his commission, the bestowal of his office would have been an act not of grace but of wrath. Anyone who places an unreliable person in office makes failure and guilt inevitable. That is not how grace functions; rather, it is the action of someone who, in the interest of displaying strong displeasure, repays guilt with condemnation by intensifying the sense of failure. But in Paul's office he received a freely given grace, and he was deeply thankful.

But how can a person consider himself reliable, particularly once he has fallen? Whoever falls once might fall again. But it was not his own judgment that elevated him above his regret for past deeds and above the mistrust of his detractors. The Christ had extended trust to him. Now it is his business to trust the Christ. He does this by carrying out his service indefatigably, undeterred by all opposition. He thereby experiences the truth of the verdict with which the Christ placed him in his service. For Christ became for him the source of strength. Christ had made into a stalwart figure someone who would in turn be true to him. It was a matter such as this that Jesus had in mind when he called himself the one who overcomes the Accuser.

Faith Is the Victory
August 28

This is the victory that overcomes the world: our faith.
—1 John 5:4

The disciples professed faith in him who overcame the world; were they victors over it too? Was the imperial power not superior to their defenseless congregations? Were the ideas venerated by the Greeks not stronger than their message? Didn't the cravings of the flesh present an insuperable challenge? Could the disciples transcend their own fleshly weakness? Finally, were the Jewish and pagan heritages not too strong to eliminate from the congregations, with the result that at no time or place would a church rise that was sufficiently removed from the world? Such deliberations undermined the certainty of the disciples: that which overcomes the world is not enough for us to maintain our stand.

But why not? We believe, and this means victory over the world. In passing along what Jesus said of the believer, John did not say, "We will overcome the world. Even if we haven't won yet, we'll arrive at victory later!" No! The later generations of the church will not be stronger than the first ones. The disciples rather expressed concern on the basis of sober observation that subsequent eras in the church would give rise to dire circumstances. The congregation would not meet with victory at some future date. Their conviction was rather "Our faith is the victory that has overcome the world."

Because they believe, they belong to the Christ; they are in the Christ; they are those whom God has set apart for himself. As long as this is who they are, they are more than a match for the world. The world's onslaught is undone, because the world cannot take away the disciples' confidence in Jesus. The numerous impossibilities they face do not demoralize them; the adversities that befall them do not cripple them. In this the word of Jesus proves its strength, and his promise its truth. Jesus' presence becomes evident. Where there is faith, there is Spirit, and where there is Spirit, there is God—and God cannot be overcome.

John speaks of "our faith." He does not speak of himself alone as the overcomer of the world. If he had been crowded into some posture of alienation, he would not have been able to function in a faithful fashion. Participation in the Christ is never to become a private affair. But faith proved its conquering strength and created congregations that confessed a united faith in Jesus and lived harmoniously in love according to his command. For that reason they stood as the victors in the struggle with the world. For they were the people who believed.

Jesus Dies in Peace
August 29

The Lord said to my Lord, "Sit at my right until I place your enemies beneath your feet."
—MATTHEW 22:44 (CF. PS. 110:1)

The king whom the psalmist venerates is invincible. Therefore he is the sure protection of his people. Yes, he has enemies. But that does not mean he must fight. It is not his business to vanquish them. For God places him at his side and makes into his own concern the concern of the one he calls. Now his enemies will be vanquished by God and made subject to him.

With this verse from the Psalms, Jesus expounded for the Jewish mind the calmness with which he regarded their schemes and tolerated their actions. Such aplomb was unfathomable to his opponents. They attributed it to preparations he was presumably making in secret for his followers to rise up in revolt against his opponents. So they paid close attention to whether the mood of the people swung in his direction or turned against him. They took it seriously that his word deeply affected the multitudes who heard him speak. It was unavoidable that he should become an insoluble puzzle to those who saw nothing of his close relationship with God, to those who only looked upon him outwardly, truly apprehending nothing about him except what was visible on the surface.

Those who, like Jerusalem's rulers, do their own will must obviously join battle against Jesus. For this they need the favor of public opinion and the support of the people. Yet that does not suffice, for God is not on the rulers' side. In contrast to them, Jesus is at the Father's side and does his will. He is not deterred by their attacks. He is protected by the peace of God. He is not brought into disgrace, for God honors him. He is not defeated, but rather dies as the one who lives and who will live into the future.

Later the disciples consoled themselves with the same verse from the Psalms, when they found themselves alone, when Jesus was no longer there to step in as their advocate and could no longer reduce their detractors to silence by the force of his presence. Yet that does not rob them of their peace. It does not force them into fights with their opponents. They know where Jesus is; the psalm informs them. His place is with God, and there he holds the place of honor and is exalted over all. He has taken his place at God's right hand. From the beginning his work was God's work, and that is what it remains, forever. His detractors are God's enemies, and by the same token his supporters are God's servants. That puts to flight their fear and gives certainty to hope. For this reason they await the day when God will reveal the lordship of the Christ to all that lives.

Jesus Is David's Lord
August 30

When the Pharisees were gathered together, Jesus inquired of them, "What do you think about the Christ? Whose son is he?" They said to him, "He is David's son." He said to them, "Then

why does David, in the Spirit, call him 'Lord'? If then David calls him 'Lord,' how is he his son?"
—Matthew 22:41–43, 45

To clarify the relation of his aims to the dominion given to David, Jesus also uses the saying of Psalm 110:1, which grants him the place next to God and promises that God will subjugate his enemies. The Promised One is David's son; that was the highest thing the scribes were able to say about him. In their judgment this meant that his royal prerogative was securely founded and comprehensively described. But God's Son? No! The scribes regarded that as a dangerous word. What then: did God have a son? Can the boundary that separates creation from the Creator disappear? But Jesus could not describe his goal with the understanding bequeathed to him by this ancestral wisdom.

David was assigned the task of making a unified people out of the plurality of tribes. He could only attain this by showing himself to have the uppermost hand in the struggle against the enemies of Israel and the opponents of the union he sought to form. But Jesus' assignment was not to win the spoils of war as a battlefield conqueror. The Jew was to learn trust in God; faith is not taught with the sword. The Jew and the Gentile are to become one united people of God; this is not achieved by battle. The sinful ways of humans bring them into dire straits, for out of man's heart come his evil thoughts. But only the creative power of the Spirit can transform the heart. Death has lost its power over God's kingdom; only the life-giving Spirit takes that power from it, and only God's grace silences the Accuser. How then can Jesus' detractors be overcome? By God's placing his enemies under his feet as he reveals his lordship in glory.

This far exceeds what David was commissioned to achieve. David was not the "Lord" in God's kingdom; he was one member in the fellowship called to eternal life, just as all the others who had served the will of God. Therefore only he who is David's "Lord" can be his son, the one who inherits his kingdom and fulfills the Davidic promise. The secret that David's "Lord" is his son arises through God's beginning his eternal work with what took place in Israel. For that reason David's kingdom precedes that of the Christ yet has its basis in that which comes through the Christ.

Nothing Remains of the Temple
August 31

*And Jesus left the temple and went away. His disciples came up
to him to show him the temple buildings. But he said to them in
response, "Do you see all of this? I tell you the truth: Not one
stone here will be left upon another that won't be torn down."*
—MATTHEW 24:1–2

When Jewish forces manned the temple walls to turn back the attack of Roman legions, there had to be partial devastation of the temple. Then a portion of the temple courts was burned down. Such damage to the temple was a bitter blow to Jewish authorities, but it did not leave them without hope. When the battle was over, the people quickly used their resources to restore the temple to its earlier perfection, and the damage was quickly repaired.

Were these events comparable to what would take place after Jesus left the temple? Did he now leave the temple with his followers so as later to lead them back into it? Might they expect, first, judgment to be rendered that would bring woe even to the temple but disrupt it only temporarily, because it would be restored when the day of the Christ comes?

With thoughts like these, did the disciples understand what Jesus was doing when he left the temple? No! He leaves nothing standing; every stone will be ripped out of its setting; all that will remain is a pile of rubble. There is no restoration for the temple and the worship ceremonies it housed and the Jerusalem of old. That sounded incredible. "Look at these stones!" exclaimed the disciples. God's house was built in such a way that its construction alone made a statement: this house will stand for all eternity.

But with this verdict Jesus by no means proclaimed only unrelenting wrath and the absolute validity of the judgment that punishes irredeemable guilt with unending death. He simultaneously sets forth deeply religious testimony to the sanctity of the new covenant. The new covenant truly makes the old one old. The old has passed away, and there is no way back to it.

Christendom later made room for much that had come from Judaism. It concerned itself with some temple ruins, so to speak, with the view that these could be incorporated into the church's own edifice. This outlook was dearest to those who, from childhood, had seen the temple as the guarantee that God is with his people. It seemed to them that heaven would collapse if the temple were destroyed. That is why Jesus used such strong language to disengage the disciples entirely from the temple, so that they would not pour new wine into old wineskins but rather learn from him how God's grace visits them.

Temples Everywhere Fade Away
September 1

God, who made the world and everything in it and is the Lord of heaven and earth, does not live in temples made with hands nor is he ministered to by human hands as if dependent on mankind. For he himself gives to everything life and breath and all that is.
—Acts 17:24–25

Jesus' act of leading his disciples out of the Jerusalem temple meant the fall of many temples. When Paul in Athens addressed the Areopagus, the temple of Athena still possessed its full beauty, situated on the fortress hill of the city. Was Paul a barbarian when he summoned them away from this glorious edifice? It was indisputably a brilliant celebration when the Athenians wended their way up the magnificent stairs to the temple. What did Paul have to offer them as a replacement? He had a truth that was simple and clear enough for all to understand, but also one that overturned the entire outlook of individuals and society alike.

By the construction of their temple, the Athenians sought to induce the goddess to inhabit their fortress hill. For her presence with them was thought to depend on what they did for her, and along with the building came the liturgical service that extended to her what she required. Imagine a deity in need of human ministrations! How completely this inverts the relationship in which man stands to God. Does God require man's blessings and endowments? What foolishness. God is the one who gives. And what does he give? Everything. That you live and breathe is his gift.

But who ever heard of a God who was not a creation of humans? Athens first had to exist before a goddess Athena could arise. Continually man forms his god in his image and for that reason ascribes to him human needs. From this there arose across the classical world the dazzling pomp of myth. Did Paul suppose he could put it to flight? As a matter of fact, myth gave way before a simple, very near, and yet so distant discovery.

Myth dissipates when man discovers that he is a created being; and realizes that, when he speaks of God, he speaks of the Creator; and recognizes that there is no parity between the Creator and the creation. Further, the creation can give nothing to the Creator, because created beings have nothing that is their own in the sense that they have not received it. Temples are superfluous, altars obliterated, and priestly ministrations a thing of the past in light of this quite simple yet quite certain truth. Doesn't God dwell with us? Yes, although in the dwelling not built by us but by him. Are we then not to offer him our service? Yes, we may, but not in such a way that we confer needed resources upon him. It is rather the case that he bestows upon us all we have and need—and not in such a way that he does our will but through our doing his.

The Disciples Exercise Persistent Prayer
September 2

But he told them a parable that they should always pray and not lose heart. He said, "There was in a city a judge who did not fear God or respect men. Now there was a widow in that city, and she came to him and said, 'Give me justice against my opponent!' And he would not for a long while. But eventually he said to himself: Even though I don't fear God or respect men, yet because this widow is making my life difficult, I will give her justice, lest she finally come and strike me in the face." But the Lord said, "Listen to what the unjust judge says. Won't God give justice to his chosen ones, who call to him day and night, even if he remains long-suffering with them? I tell you, he will give them justice quickly."

—Luke 18:1–8

After Jesus left his disciples, their standing orders did not include building temples, erecting altars, and ordaining priests. Did this mean that prayer, too, was now a thing of the past? That cannot happen; on the contrary, prayer now takes on an immeasurably great meaning and becomes even more urgent than before.

What can a widow do if a brutal adversary uses her helpless situation to defraud her? She will make her plight known to the judge. He has an obligation to extend legal protection to her. But what if this last line of defense fails because the judge is an unjust man who could not care less if she must suffer injustice? Is she now defenseless? Not at all—if her plea is continual and unrelenting. Even the unjust judge will bow before the urgency of her entreaty.

The disciples' situation is like that of the widow. For all that they say is disputed, and all that they do is ridiculed. In the judgment of all, they are sinners and deserving of contempt. They are placed in an unfair fight, for they are not allowed to use the same weapons their opponents wield. The only thing that lies in their capacity is to make request. Their protection is God; they must turn to him. No one can reveal justice to them other than their Lord. He alone can offer the proof of the truth of their word. Only he has the ability to give to them what they hope for by leading them into his kingdom. They have received the capability to make request in faith, for they are his chosen ones. Where did the word they received come from? That word brought to light for them the love of God. Where love brought about fellowship, it also planted the seed of prayer.

And yet even the prayer of the disciples appears to be useless. The answers sought are not forthcoming. They appeal to the Christ, and he remains invisible. They put their trust in God's righteous judgment and fall prey to the oppression of their enemy. For God is long-suffering. Next to his thoughts, ours are puny and fleeting. He reckons with long intervals; his disciples do not see things that way. To suffer injustice is bitter. They cannot endure it long. Their strength is soon used up.

So do they wish to give up on prayer? Their pleas have power only if they persist in prayer. It is true that God's patient ways may result in negative answers to their requests. Yet this does not change the love that made them into God's elect. As a result, they cannot cease their prayerful labor. That remains their task even when answers are not forthcoming. When indefatigable persistence becomes the hallmark of their prayer, it will be their shield and the means that brings their deliverance.

The New Prayer Arises
Through the Spirit and the Truth
September 3

You will worship the Father neither on this mountain
[Gerizim] nor in Jerusalem. The hour is coming —
and is now here — when the true worshipers
worship the Father with Spirit and truth.

—JOHN 4:21, 23

Is the only reason that prayer does not vanish from among the disciples because their situation is like that of the defenseless widow, whom no one will help unless her plea succeeds in getting the city's judge on her side? How can prayer fall silent where Jesus is at work, since he erects the new temple and makes those who believe in him into persons who present God with the living sacrifice? In addition to the new temple, the new priesthood, and the new offering, there arises also the new prayer.

Jesus does this through the indwelling of the Spirit and the truth, as these both abide with the disciples. What drew the religious masses to Zion and Gerizim was not the Spirit. The Law set the agenda: on a given day there was a prescribed religious observance. The majestic temple beckoned: you must be present. The corporate mentality placed each individual into the masses who surged toward this or that holy mount. And when the pilgrims had visited the hallowed halls, they could look back on times when prayer had been deeply moving and on celebrations that had stirred the souls of the people. Still, the prayer had not yet arrived at the truth. The temple was redolent of God's presence, but in what took place there, that presence was not fully revealed: the one who prayed assumed the posture of a believer without the capacity to arrive at personal faith and dedicated himself to a hope that was a figment of his own longing.

Our prayer arrives at the truth only when it is our answer to that word that God addresses to us. The initial word is that God speaks to us; on this basis a human discourse can arise that addresses God with truth. Acknowledgment and affirmation of the divine will comes first; then we are united with what God desires. Jesus speaks to us humans this divine word, which renders divine grace intelligible to us. And since this word works in league with the power of God, it enters us and moves our thinking and willing. We are thereby brought under the strength of Spirit.

Now we no longer live "as if" God were with us and we lived in fellowship with him. Rather, we actually have become recipients of his grace. We do not position ourselves to look "as if" we knew God's will and saw his work. Rather, in the Christ we have this before our eyes. We do not merely assume that we take part in God's work. Rather, we are summoned to God's service and want to do his will. We petition for that which is God's so that we might obey and glorify him. Now in all our ways we seek the counsel of the Most High. We commend to him not only our worst troubles but also anything that concerns and moves us. Of course we cite our ills, but we also share with God in prayer what our minds wrestle with and our courage undertakes. Now our prayer is no longer hopeful rhetoric; it is rather a gift bestowed upon us by God. And it has thereby become truth.

We Have the Right to Pray for Every Person
September 4

I urge most of all that requests, prayers, petitions, thanksgiving be made for all persons.
—1 TIMOTHY 2:1

Did Paul wish to lead prayer into boundless expanses? The exhortation to prayer must be given to us by the lives of others becoming intertwined with ours. But then no hindrance to prayer exists, as surely as the one whose fate moves us to pray is human. No prayer can be formulated without the one who prays clearly having before him God, the Perfect One, to whose grace there are no restrictions that might frustrate grace. That elevates the faith that pursues grace above all restrictions and gives it the totality so that it encompasses everything by which life unites us.

It is impossible that congregations would pray only for themselves, somehow appealing to the presumed fact that God's call has come only to them and that they have been severed from the world. It is true that out of the commonality of the faith arrives the fellowship of prayer; for those who pray are bound in a shared task, and therefore they pray with and for one another. But their separation from the world does not commission them to despise other people. It would be wrong if humans, because they are humans, were to become for believers something other than the object of veneration and love, and therefore also of prayer. Believers would be doing violence to God's glory as Creator; they would be descending into a sinful preoccupation with self.

There is admittedly a presupposition here: is it God's will for all to receive his help? We cannot pray against God; we can pray only on the basis of his will. The legitimacy and force of our prayer rests on our becoming one with God in prayer. That is why Paul frames for the congregation the basis for the unbounded breadth of its mandate to pray as follows: God's will is that every person be saved (1 Tim. 2:4). Just as there is no person whom, because that person is a human, God does not want to save, so there is no person for whom the congregation may not pray. Because and as long as someone is a human, God's redeeming will extends to him, and for that reason so does the prayer of believers.

But doesn't the secret that lies hidden in God's future work get in our way? Are we not thereby forbidden to conduct ourselves toward all others in a believing manner? Yes, we have heard the tidings of coming judgment. We worship him who opposes every evil deed as the righteous Judge. In order that we not go astray in that coming mystery but remain united with the will of God, which assigns us our place of service and orders our prayers, Paul tells us what God's saving intention will bestow on all: they are all to come to the knowledge of the truth. That is the manner in which God delivers us. He removes the deception from our eyes and dispels the darkness in which we languish. He leads us into light, which makes the truth visible. This is God's goal with every person. This is the substance of our prayer in interaction with everyone. We simply do not know what takes place subsequently, when the truth gains mastery over man. We do not know whether faith will follow someone's knowledge of the truth, or whether that person will become God's adversary. We do not pray against people but for them. We are to ask that the knowledge of the truth be granted to each person, imploring the divine will as we embrace it with trust.

Jesus Makes the Spirit of Truth His Disciples' Advocate
September 5

I will ask the Father, and he will give you another Advocate,
so that he may be with you forever. This is the Spirit
of truth, whom the world cannot receive, because
it does not see him or know him. You know him,
because he abides with you and will be in you.

—JOHN 14:16–17

The disciples call on the heavenly Judge. They do this tirelessly, even when he is silent. They wait upon their Lord, although they do not know when he is coming. They wait even if he delays a long time. But they also have in their midst that one who intercedes for them, who does for them what Jesus had done until the time of his death. When this one was with them, he was the proof of their privilege and authority. He deflected the objections brought against them and proved by his deeds the truth of their faith. None of the disciples is able to be the advocate of the believing community. The only one with that capacity is he whom the Father sends into the world. It is the Spirit, who steps into the role of Jesus in leading the congregation and defending his Word. By the work of the Spirit, God's grace becomes visible, and through the Spirit-given Word the message of Jesus is continually brought afresh to mankind.

But what is the hallmark of the Spirit? How can he be recognized for sure? He himself is, of course, invisible. His work takes place within the inner lives of believers. But the existence of the Spirit is discernible, because he is the Spirit of truth. For that reason he can represent Jesus, because Jesus, too, is the truth. Where the Spirit is, pretense dissipates. Empty words die away. The following are put to flight: blather about faith in God when a person trusts only in himself, cheap talk of love when a person is driven by personal ambition, deception of the congregation when mutual hostility is avoided only by tiresome repression, religion learned by rote when a person enthusiastically affirms only himself and nature. The Spirit gives the disciples integrity. The Spirit makes them invincible by guiding them in such ways as eliminating deceptive practices and tolerating no false appearances among themselves, being what they say about themselves, and saying about themselves what they really are. The Spirit gives their message persuasive force.

In this manner the Spirit separates the disciples clearly from the world. The world does not inquire about the truth, but only about what is useful to it. Man in his natural state does not reckon with the Spirit but only with purely natural powers. Man sees only the causal links in events, in keeping with natural law. He sees in Jesus a human, no different from any other, and he does not discern the Spirit. Similarly, he sees in the disciples mere men who took up faith only in reaction to a sense of the soul's necessity and who act according to faith's dictates.

That is why the aims of the Spirit are inscrutable to such a person. He cannot understand the Spirit. He declares as impossible what the Spirit seeks. He rejects as fantasy what the Spirit achieves. But to this Spirit-less thinking, which originates only from selfish inner drives, the truth remains locked away. Such thinking produces rulers who are like predators, rich people who are corrupted by their holdings, sexual relations that are defiling, worldviews that distort, and religions that make humans guilty. Against this historical realm stands out clearly what the Spirit gives to man, because he is the Spirit of truth. This contrast establishes the disciple's legitimacy and gives him his strength. In this way the Christ reveals his existence and his mission. For the Spirit of truth is his gift, the gift he prayed the Father would bestow upon those who believe in him.

It Is Not Yet the End
September 6

You will hear of wars and reports of war. Pay attention; do not be distressed. For such things must take place. But that is not yet the end.
—Matthew 24:6

The person who recognizes himself as the work and possession of God has always lived in hope. To see that God reaches into human history is to receive a great expectation that extends beyond all surrounding objects and longs for the end of what currently exists. For that which will begin when the end arrives—God's untiring wisdom and inexhaustible life—will show forth more gloriously than what currently exists and takes place. And because expectation is united with faith and therefore forms not merely an image of what lies ahead but a genuine longing for the consummation, it continually requires the divine exhortation that says, "It is not yet the end."

The first time this took place was when the Baptist stood at the end of his ministry and recognized the Christ. Would he now baptize Israel with the Holy Spirit and with fire? Will the visible lordship of God begin right now? When the Baptist sent a query to Jesus from prison and urged him to declare his royal mission, and instead was referred to Jesus' authority to heal, the message he received was "It is not yet the end."

Again, when Jesus had completed his ministry and the accompanying multitude saw that he was journeying to Jerusalem, the expectation intensified that the end was near. In obedience to Jesus' will, his disciples shared his cup with him. But he spoke only of a single day during which he would become a dead man; by the third day he would again return to life. Will the world not believe the one who has risen from the dead? Can there still be resistance to the one who overcame death? Again those who hope receive the word, "It is not yet the end."

Jesus said it to his disciples by promising them that he would bring them back to Galilee. He described to them the battle into which they were now placed. With this Jesus fixed the disciples' gaze on that which would render their service difficult. Jesus' exaltation to God does not bring peace to mankind; rather, history retains its bloody character. Peoples rise up against each other. Both in Palestine and in the world's far corners, conflicts arise in which cities fall and are razed. Do these horrors not suffice to call forth the deliverer from heaven? Still, it is not yet the end.

The revelation of the Christ is not dependent on the deeds of those who rule the nations. It does not even put a stop to the carnage that people bring upon each other and that is inflicted by natural catastrophes. The end of the divine patience, the end of forces hostile to God, the end of Christendom's persevering and waiting—it is not yet the end.

Should this "not yet" demoralize the disciples? Does it incite them to painful denunciation? The demand addressed to them remains constantly in force: Let your hope be undaunted! Not just faith and love abide (1 Cor. 13:13): so does hope. And hope cannot be extinguished in a person after

God has reconciled that person to him. Then he gazes continually on the rich abundance of God. And his hope endures.

Jesus' Words Do Not Pass Away
September 7

Heaven and earth will pass away,
but my words will not pass away.
—Matthew 24:35

Jesus' thoughts were always directed toward what lay ahead. For God's lordship not only encompasses that which presently exists; it also makes all things new. But when Jesus spoke of his death, particularly in the last days before his departure, he divulged to his disciples in depth what they were about to face. But is there such a thing as predictions that come true and are not belied and rendered void by future events? Previous prophecy had announced to everything in existence that it was transient. Will Jesus' words remain, although heaven and earth pass away?

Inherent in Jesus' mission was the declaration that his word would be everlasting. That was obligatory for him, because he spoke it not as his own word but as the word given to him by God. Through the confession of his word, he confessed the truth of God and his status as God's Son, through which he had been made spokesman of the divine word. But he served this role without any attenuation of his humanity. Our thinking is grounded in what we are, for our seeing and understanding are granted to us for the sake of what we are supposed to do. The task of our worldview is to describe how the world relates to the tasks set for us to confront and complete. The worldview of Jesus and his notion of the future remained fully subordinated to the standards and laws that are set for man. When he prophesied, he spoke of what his actions had accomplished for the future.

He received a royal commission from God, and this remains his own. That he must die is not the revocation of his commission but its fulfillment. But human strength does not suffice to bring God's grace in its perfection to mankind. Jesus accomplishes this when he goes to work, manifesting the Godhead. This was granted to him at that time so that he would become manifest to all in his sending.

Jesus' word carries with it a second prophecy: that his fellowship with his disciples would endure into the future. As they are currently his, so they will remain his own. His death does not separate him from them. Rather, a fellowship now arises through which their life is grounded in him. Because they are bound to him, they remain bound with one another. They comprise a community that continues beyond his death and even then does not cease to grow.

Jesus' struggle against all godlessness and unrighteousness went hard in hand with the gathering of those who believed in him. His unceasing office is to continue and to perfect the repudiation of all that opposes God. The day newly given to him by God, therefore, will be the day of judgment.

In the same way that his connection with the disciples is unalterable, his fellowship with his people is never-ending. He therefore prophesies to the Jews that what they do against him will decide their fate. It is a consequence of his crucifixion that their temple is taken from them and that they face the duress of homelessness and spiritual desolation.

But the Jewish nation was ordained as God's people, not for their sake but for the sake of the world. For that reason, what will happen to Jerusalem is a part of world history. The fall of institutional Judaism results in the proclamation of divine grace to all peoples. The new revelation of this grace will make Jesus both Savior and Judge, not only of his disciples but for the whole of humanity. Those were the statements made by Jesus regarding what was to come, and regarding these remarks he said that his words will never pass away.

Jesus Prophesies for This Generation
September 8

Truly I say to you, this generation will not pass away until this all takes place.
—Matthew 24:34

Jesus sent his disciples to this generation, and for their service to this generation he strengthened them, and this strengthening was necessary for them, because what Jesus charged them to do was difficult. Jesus thought in merciful terms about the burden that he placed upon them. For that reason Jesus spoke with them about their generation, not about the centuries yet to come; not about mankind that would live in other places and at other eras; not about the church, which he, through his Word, would establish and rule over in distant times.

It has often been said that the above saying and others related to it diminish Jesus' fame. In this view, such sayings make it evident that the course of world history was hidden from him. Jesus didn't know everything. Now, it must be admitted that people who demand from Jesus primarily knowledge will be frustrated here. If you expect Jesus to reflect the omniscience of God by being an infallible teacher, this saying will understandably produce disappointment. But for those who inquire only about ideas, Jesus' word is unusable not only here but everywhere. It is not our business to master Jesus like a concept or to prescribe to him what he should have said, so that we can put ourselves in the place of the ones whom he addressed. Our task is truly to apprehend what he was and to hear what he said.

Regarding this generation of Judaism—which had known and heard him; in whose midst he placed his disciples; which had sought with passionate hatred to destroy him and yet would not reach its goal—Jesus said, to proclaim to it his prophecy, what would happen to it and be fulfilled in its midst.

His prophecy encompassed a great deal. It spoke of the Jews' plight and of the temple's ruins, the same temple that was widely regarded as indestructible. It spoke of the perplexed, intense longing that gave birth to wild dreams, yet also of the unshakable loyalty of his followers and their unflagging hope by which they awaited him. It spoke of his undiminished right of lordship that even now, while he dwells in heavenly realms, makes them his servants. And it spoke also of what terminates this waiting, suffering, and serving: his new coming, which will signal the ingathering of the community of the elect from among the entirety of humanity.

This generation had as yet no place for this conclusion to his prophecy. But what he said to it about the unwholesome outcome of the Jews' sin and the unconquerable power of his message did take place. Jesus' prophecy shows that he knew his generation. He was not deceived, either about the strength of Jewish opposition or about the power of the faith he had created in his disciples.

There Are Disciples Who Will Not Die
September 9

I tell you the truth: Among those standing here are a few who will not taste death until they see the Son of Man coming in his glory.
—MATTHEW 16:28

Jesus connected the work of his disciples with this generation among whom he lived and because of which he died. This generation is to enjoy the fruit of his work through the service that his disciples will render to it. In the struggle against the Jews' opposition, however, many of his disciples will fall. Many will realize that they are not to hold their own lives dear: they will find their lives by losing them. But this generation will not achieve its aim of silencing the word of Jesus in its midst and killing all Jesus' messengers. The word that calls Judaism and punishes it will not be withdrawn from it. Jesus' messengers will be sent to it until he comes.

Since eternal life begins with his new and glorious sending, those disciples who fill their office as heralds until he returns are exempt from dying. They set aside the naturally given form of their lives, not by being destroyed by death, but by the transforming power of the Spirit making them similar to those whom the Christ will awaken from the dead. In this word reverberating between Jesus' end and his glorification, all that is clear is that a generation has been raised up whose members are Jesus and his cohorts. That miracle that Jesus promised them was not that God would wonderfully prolong their lives but that the creative might of God, which will make the dead body of Jesus into a vessel of eternal life, would be revealed to his disciples, including those still living in the world.

Jesus spoke this promise in the power of his royal sending. He sets a limit to the opposition of the world against his disciples, sees to the preservation of his word, assumes control over the life and death of those whom he sends forth, and makes his fellowship with them eternal, whether by raising them from the dead or by translating them directly.

But Jesus placed the end of mankind as we know it at the end of that generation. This shows that knowing and not knowing coexist in him in the same manner that they are present side by side in us in every faith judgment. Every act of faith is based on a certainty that has been disclosed to us, and every such act is inherently less than fully informed. Jesus knew when he made this promise that his gospel would remain victorious. The work of his messengers cannot be thwarted. Hidden from him was the fact that at the end of this generation, the divine decree would once more sound forth: "It is not yet the end." For a long series of generations would follow the present one. Generations in this sequence will be in the same position as those in Jesus' day; they will be sinful and mortal, and they will be in need of the divine Word, through which God's grace speaks to them.

The first generation of Christians later appropriated the promise that Jesus gave here to a few of his first disciples. For they expected that at his return the Christ would bring them to him and transform their natural existence into conformity with himself. In this posture, knowing and not knowing were again closely intertwined. This interrelationship remains our own distinguishing feature as long as we are bound together with God, not through sight but through faith.

God Has Promised a New Heaven and a New Earth
September 10

Heaven and earth will pass away.
—Matthew 24:35

Paul said that God's steadfast, never-failing power becomes accessible to our understanding through nature. Nature grants us this understanding all the more as it discloses to us the depths of what exists and takes place. Nevertheless, in the prophecies of Israel there arose not only the sense that God intended a new heaven and a new earth, or, again, simply the wish that what exists might be renewed through a creative act of God. Rather, there arose the certainty that the current form and state of nature is not the final manifestation of what God has in mind for humans. Rather, they face the sure prospect of a completely new world.

This prophecy was made because in the dialogue between God and mankind, by which the prophet became the receiver of his word, the wealth of the divine grace had been revealed. Now there could be no more languishing in what had come to pass. There could be no suppressing that which was occurring. The life being infused into nature streamed forward to new formations. If a discontinuity arose, a new construction arose to replace it. It is true that the peoples often succumbed to widespread dying. Yet the end was never annihilation. Out of death arose new life once more. That was also the experience of Jerusalem and of those who in Jerusalem administered the divine word. "The remnant will return," Isaiah had said. In light of such experiences, one could not be complacent with the way things currently stood. The view was opened up ahead, elevated beyond all that was already in existence. God was greater than all his works; none of his works revealed him entirely, and none marked the end of his power. Thus there arose the powerful message of the end of this heaven and this earth, both of which must pass because God would create new ones.

With this, hope was pried free of all that exists. Not even that which is most secure and important has unalterable existence. Only God is above and beyond change. But this meant that all attempts to experience and describe "right now" what lay in the future were forbidden and rendered impossible. Who could assemble the new heaven and the new earth in his thoughts? Every prophecy became partial, less than comprehensive. Each was a parable, for every prophecy can present what is to come only by means of what the natural world around us makes visible. In contrast, our gaze does not penetrate far into the wealth of the divine creation. God's work is accessible to us only after it occurs. We stand before God not as those who know but as those who wait. This was the posture that Jesus commended to his disciples by his prophesying.

Section 14

JESUS RECEIVES THE CROSS

Jesus Celebrates Easter by His Death
September 11

*Jesus said to his disciples, "You know that in
two days it will be the Passover. Then the Son of Man will be
handed over to be crucified."*
—MATTHEW 26:2

Jesus traveled to Jerusalem to observe the Passover meal. Would the celebratory aspect of the feast be destroyed when he was crucified while it took place? Not in Jesus' opinion. He celebrated the Passover feast precisely by his death. True, as a result of his observance of Passover, the Passover of the Old Testament people of God came to an end, that Passover that was prescribed to them by the Law. But what they had long celebrated—that God is the Redeemer of his people—was revealed in a new way through the Passover celebration of Jesus.

"I brought you forth out of Egypt, out of the house of bondage." That was the reality that gave the feast its substance. But that statement expressed the will of God out of which the work of Jesus grew. Pharaoh wanted to rule Israel. His lordship was rooted in the nobility of his lineage, the military strength of those who served him, the vastness of his land holdings, the support of the priests who assured him of the blessing of his gods. All this combined to give a sense of one man being exalted above many others. Pharaoh had the awareness of being in control. But what this meant for Israel was slavery. For man's will to power elevates him by humiliating others. Man effects his lordship by putting others in bondage. Now Moses as God's representative came before Pharaoh. God claims the people as his people. Pharaoh must acknowledge that, and because he does not, his fate is death. That was a redemption, the end of bondage, the reception of freedom through submission to God's leading and command. That was a revelation of God. For it was a visible manifestation of his saving and liberating grace.

Not only the grateful nation celebrated that grace. Jesus, in truth and power, affirmed the God who redeemed. The nation celebrated the Redeemer and remained in the house of bondage. Whoever breaks the Law is subject to its condemnation, and the nation in its sinful hankerings and godless ways broke the Law—the consequence of which was death. But Jesus, by his death, brought forgiveness to the guilty and life to the dead. He received the capability for this from the same will of God that the people praised at Passover as they recalled what had taken place through Moses.

In Jesus' day, God once again embraced his people, brought the oppression of man to an end, and made those who believed Jesus into his own possession. Once again this took place through an exodus. Jesus led his followers out of their former social location, out of the temple, out of the synagogue school, out of the Law. That had to be. For they would not escape the lordship of man by their own self-interest, which works injustice, nor by their disdain for God, as by their hypocrisy they thought they could fool him. But also in Jesus' day, the opposition to an exodus was once again strong. For that reason Jesus bore the cross. But the redeeming will of God is the will that prevails. It was impossible for Jesus not to celebrate it.

Jesus Is Honored Beyond Measure
September 12

While he was in Bethany, in the house of Simon the leper, a woman came to him as he was eating. She had a vial full of genuine, expensive nard oil. She broke open the vial and poured it upon his head. But some of the people there spoke angrily to one another: "Why this waste of anointing oil? For it could have been sold for more than three hundred denarii, which could have been given to the poor." And they berated her.
—Mark 14:3–5

Three hundred pieces of silver were squandered when an overzealous woman dumped an entire vial of nard on Jesus. Or so it appeared to the eyes of "reason," which here raises its voice in the disciples' circle. Jesus was the object of an act of veneration; of what relevance are dollars and cents when Jesus should be shown gratitude and praise? He calls forth maximum engagement from those of us who recognize him as well as from those who reject him. Jesus becomes the object of immeasurable honor—and of immeasurable loathing. The woman in Bethany committed everything in order to honor Jesus, and Jesus' detractors, in keeping with their condemnation of him and eventually by executing him, did all they could to profane his reputation. Through many centuries Jewish thinkers derided him who hung on the cross, and through many centuries the magnificent edifice of a heavenly city built to his honor has taken shape.

How does that come about? He transforms our encounter with him into an encounter with God, and now there is no more evasion, no more hair-splitting, no more partial responses by which we equate our interests with his will. The person whom Jesus summons to God has been gripped at the deepest point of that person's existence. This evokes a never-ending gratitude, a party of indefatigable followers, a trust that gives itself wholly to him. The woman in Bethany honored Jesus as the Messiah, the one whom God "anointed" so he might rule. Should she not render to the King all that she possessed? She honored him as God's Lamb, strong and willing unto death. Should she not honor the one whom God had ordained to be the genuine sacrifice?

Yet what does man possess that suffices to show God honor? Even if the scent of nard was pungent through the whole house, in a short time it dissipated. So what did it accomplish? Jesus likened the ointment poured onto him to those elements that would be applied to his corpse later on. But what good are acts of veneration to a person who is dead?

Such musings arise from the same rotten roots as the calculations of those who figured out the selling price of the nard. That is how self-seeking desire thinks. It takes into account only sensual values. Grateful love, from which respect for the dead arises, is not something to despise or to dispense with. And this is all the more true of the honor shown to the Messiah, not to his corpse but to the now-existing Christ. He is worthy of honor and faith and thanks because he went to the cross. No one could have given him a gift that would have helped him with that. But he calls on us to take full and true account of what he does and gives. That is our way of showing him the esteem he deserves.

Jesus Is Always Ready to Forgive
September 13

Peter said to Jesus, "Never shall you wash my feet." Jesus answered him, "If I don't wash you, you have no part with me."
—JOHN 13:8

When the disciple walks through the country or over village streets, his feet require washing. Foot washing is an ongoing need. Jesus turned it into a parable of what happens to the disciple through his relation to Jesus. Jesus effects a purification that the disciple repeatedly needs and that Jesus confers in an ongoing way. That is how the disciple takes part in what Jesus does and is placed by God in the location where Jesus stands.

Can he not excuse himself from this awkward ordeal? The purity that man awards to himself is arrogance and falsehood. The cleansing that disciples receive in Jesus' fellowship is the gift of Jesus; it has its basis in his patience, his loyalty. It would not have come to the disciples if Jesus had been intent on displaying his majesty and lording over the disciples his right to rule and his power to judge. His fellowship with the disciples is always characterized by the distinctive truth that it is grounded in his death. He dies in order to free them from their indebtedness. His blood grants them acquittal despite their guilt. With this, Jesus dispenses with power and honor for himself, and he does this willingly with the energy of love, so that the disciples stand with him in God's kingdom.

But this sets the course of his dealing with them for the whole of their lives, because the human condition is such that we cannot fulfill our service to God without standing in continual need of his forgiveness. He promises it to them by washing their feet. By taking this position before them, he generates the strength that makes the disciples' fellowship with each other possible and persistent. But when Peter wants to play the hero, in no need of Jesus' cleansing and not conceding that his office and work are entirely the gift of Jesus' grace, his fellowship with the Christ is threatened.

Jesus performed this action in his final interactions with the disciples because it was of highest importance for the continuance of his work and the stability of future congregations that all disciples, most of all Peter, be protected from the sense of security that would ascribe infallibility to them. That would have invited domineering management of the power given to them. It would have brought them into a dire contradiction with the divine will that Jesus had divulged to them by his demise. They must remain truthful in their judgment of themselves. They can accomplish this only if they remain conscious of their sinful tendency. They must not forget that they possess their authority only because Jesus removes their impurity from them.

Jesus Cleanses the Clean
September 14

Simon Peter said to him, "Lord, not only my feet, but also my hands and my head." Jesus said to him, "Whoever has bathed needs only to have his feet washed, for he is clean. And you are clean—albeit not all of you." For he knew the one who would hand him over; that is why he said, "Not all of you are clean."

—JOHN 13:9–10

If Peter's fellowship with Jesus—which is to say, his entrance into God's kingdom—depends on the washing by which Jesus cleanses his feet, why does Jesus not grant him a washing that would also cleanse his head and hands? How is Jesus supposed to entrust his message to Peter if he is an unclean person? Jesus made him his messenger by cleansing him. But if it is inevitable that he will sin, and if he possesses nothing besides a bad conscience that rejects his conduct and regret that laments it, he will not be able to speak God's saving message. Who will believe that message if it does not even free from impurity those who proclaim it? "You are clean"—that was no less Jesus' parting word to his disciples than when he said: You will always stand in need of ongoing cleansing.

How did Jesus bring together these two seemingly disparate claims? Did they cast his disciples in some wobbly state, so that one minute they felt like sinners and the next like saints, one minute confessing their indebtedness and the next claiming forgiveness and rejoicing in their justification? Were they to live making contrasting confessions, the one contradicting and refuting the other? That was not where Jesus left his disciples. Why are they clean? "Because of the word that I have spoken to you" (John 15:3). His word has entered into them; they have heard and believed it. That his word has become their possession—that is their purity. Because of his word they are the object of not only his mercy but also of his love. Through his word they are not separated from him, as the "unclean" cannot be touched by the "clean"; rather, they are united with him. Their privilege before God is the possession of his word, for it is God's word; the rightness of their actions arises from his word's furnishing them their will.

But the word with which Jesus graced them is not the only thing they bear within them. He spoke a word into the existence of persons who retain their human nature, who hanker for what man in the grip of nature desires for himself. This results not only in limitations to their effectiveness, not only in weaknesses and being unsuited for certain tasks, not only in states of distress that must be borne. No, it is also possible that sins can arise out of all this, just as the person who is clean cannot get away from the dust and filth of the street simply because he is clean.

Therefore they are in need of Jesus' pledge that he will cleanse them. But he grants this to them because they are clean, as the vinedresser tends the vines because they have grown from his own nursery stock. There would no longer be daily forgiveness for them if they were to reject that which makes them clean, or if the word that promises them God's grace and makes them believing were no longer with them. We continually receive renewed forgiveness for our ministry as we believe that Jesus' word has made us clean.

Sinners Become Righteous Through Faith
September 15

If Christ is in you, though the body is dead due to sin, yet the Spirit is life because of righteousness.
—ROMANS 8:10

Did the disciples preserve the attitude that Jesus prescribed for them when he washed their feet on that last evening? He testified to them: My word is in you and leads you; therefore you require and receive cleansing. When Paul later described what happens to believers through the message of Jesus, he ascribed to them simultaneously the status of being dead and the status of being alive. They live, yet in such a way that death stands alongside them; and they are subject to death, yet in such a way that life dwells in them. For they participate in both: in that which brings us into life, and in that which results in death. The condition of life is justification, and the event from which death results is sinning. Both—justification and sinning—lie in the sphere of their experience. For they receive what they are and do from two different authorities. Fellowship with Christ brings them under the sway of the Spirit, through whom they receive their thinking and willing from God. But where the Spirit is at work, there arises righteousness, and therefore it is the mark of the Spirit, who is given to them, that he is life. But they are animated not only by the Spirit but also by the flesh, and from this arises self-seeking desire and the mortality that accompanies it. They have not yet received a body that can live eternally; rather, they are flesh and blood. They can perform what the flesh desires.

"My word is in you," Jesus told his disciples. "Jesus' Spirit is in you," Paul told the believers. "Because my word is in you, you are clean," Jesus said. "Because Jesus' Spirit is in you, you are righteous and have attained life," Paul said. What is clean and divinely given in their being is this: that Jesus' word is in them. It is not what they think and will that makes the disciples clean. That is why they are in need of cleansing. It is not what believers are by nature that makes them righteous; it is not from their bodily existence that eternal life arises. Rather, they are righteous because the Spirit is in them. For that is the means by which they are believers, people acting in faith. Jesus' word, however, is the word of sovereign grace. It is stronger than what the disciples find in themselves. The Spirit who moves them is the Spirit of Christ and of God. He gives the believer the strength to withstand the demands of natural desire and obey the impulse of the Spirit.

The twofold essence of those who believe makes it clear that God's call has gone out to sinful beings and that the gift of grace has been implanted in their natural existence. If they knew nothing of sin, they would know nothing of the human state and plight. If they knew nothing of righteousness, they would know nothing of the Christ, nothing of his word and his Spirit. If they were Christians yet knew nothing of sin and nothing of righteousness, they would be at best just hopeful people, bereft of love and duty. If they no longer knew of sin and had only righteousness, they would no longer need to hope. But through the foot washing, Jesus informed his disciples that they had not yet arrived at their goal. Yet he would bring them there eventually, because he had prepared it for them.

Did Jesus Make His Disciples Perfect?
September 16

Therefore you are to be perfect, as your heavenly Father is perfect.
—Matthew 5:48

On the night he was betrayed, did what Jesus testified to his disciples fall short of what he had described as his gift when he called them together for the Sermon on the Mount? In that sermon he distanced himself from the Jews' dissonance and hypocrisy by testifying to them of the unity and wholeness of the fatherly love of God, a love that frees them from their biased, divided wills. But are the disciples, whose feet Jesus must still wash, perfect? Are they, when they have both a spirit that gives them life and a body destined for death, a body in which the Spirit wars against the flesh and the flesh against the Spirit? This duality, in which our being and willing remain split, is not wholeness and entirety.

But when Jesus spoke of the perfection of God and of his disciples, he was not thinking of the outcomes invented by our self-seeking desire, which is intent upon the glamour and the strengths that ego longs for. These amount to dreams that falsely attribute a perfection to us by which our hankerings are fully satiated, our thinking flawlessly successful, and our inner self overwhelmed with bliss. Such illusions are contradicted by the fact that God is perfect. Because God wills what he wills entirely, does what he does comprehensively, and does nothing by half measures, there is no peace between Spirit and flesh, no unification of love and raw ambition, no reconciliation between obedience and high-handed self-will. Therefore, there is no eternal life in the natural sphere, no righteousness as the reward for human virtue, and no genuine fellowship that can be manufactured by the skill of a politician or church leader. Therefore, opposition of God's will to our will has unalterable validity, and the godless person remains condemned until he is declared righteous by God himself.

The comprehensiveness of the divine grace does not become effective by annihilating what the creative word of God has brought into being, as if God's perfection grew out of the flesh disintegrating into dust and the world descending into a state of nothingness. The commission that the sun has to fulfill involves casting light on both the good and the wicked. The clouds obey the command given to them by sending rain to both the righteous and the unrighteous. In that way they are witnesses to God's perfection. In the same way, the believer experiences the totality of the divine grace when faith in God awakens in him in spite of self-seeking desire, when that grace draws him into its service despite his lovelessness, and when grace keeps him in fellowship with the Christ along with his true and bogus thoughts, his spiritual and natural desires, and brings him to eternal life.

In all this, the one who believes is not thrust back into the crowd of Jewish "righteous ones" who conceal their inner godlessness by donning the garb of a righteous person. The believer has nothing to hide, nothing to minimize by artifice. He fully acknowledges the verdict that renders him guilty, while entirely affirming the word that transforms him into someone beloved by God. In this way he is subject to the entire will of God. He has become what the Spirit of truth makes us to be.

The Apostolic Prince Is Judged
September 17

Who is the faithful and wise servant, whom the master places over his household servants so that he can give them their food at the right time? Blessed is the servant whose master finds him doing this upon his return. I tell you the truth: He will place him over all he owns. But if that wicked servant says to himself, "My master is a forgiving man," and begins to beat his fellow servants and eats and drinks with the drunkards, his master will return on a day when he is not expecting him and at an hour that he does not know. He will cleave him in two and place him among the hypocrites. In that place there will be weeping and gnashing of teeth.

—Matthew 24:45–51

Jesus promised his forgiveness to his disciples. But with no less resolve he declared to them when that forgiveness would be denied them. They are in danger not only when mobs rage and judges condemn them as heretics or some Roman official falsely accuses them of sedition against Caesar. By transferring his mission to them, Jesus elevated them above others; but to be elevated is dangerous for a human. Prior to this the disciples had Jesus over them, and even after his departure they are nothing but his servants, belonging to him along with all that they have. But now in the place of the departed Lord, they have care of his servants, in the power of the authority he delegated to them.

How will they now regard this Lord who is no longer physically present? Are they not yet fully up to their task? Why is it necessary that he return? If they disregard dependence on the Lord, the fellowship into which Jesus has brought his disciples with each other will disintegrate. Should he who has received ruling power not use it? He will be tempted to lord it over others, and they must bow to his rule—if not willingly, then by force.

And with the selfish will to power grows also the lust of the senses. A spiritual prince is no less inclined to display festive pomp than a worldly one. For this he makes use of the same means that the rulers of the people use to procure praise and pleasure for themselves. What good is having power if it does not fulfill every desire? An apostolate that degenerates into the use of force and the pursuit of enjoyment is a drastic fall. To strike a fellow servant and get drunk with others who imbibe is to distance oneself from the name of the One we serve, without whom we are nothing.

The servant of Jesus cannot dissolve his dependence on his Lord. He stands under his judgment, and Jesus pronounces to him the death sentence with these words from Matthew's gospel, which pungently depict his rage over this form of "spirituality." That person's place is with the hypocrites, for he has placed himself among the "righteous" who honor God with their words but shut off their hearts. He has chosen the same path as the rabbi who forced followers to submit and acquired riches by means of his spiritual advantage. Jesus did not send his messengers into the world to replicate the proclamation that laid low Judaism. Rather, they should heed the message of the enraged vineyard owner. New vinedressers will bring forth the fruit that God desires and deserves.

Those Who Get Drunk on Hope Lose Hope
September 18

Then the dominion of heaven will be like ten virgins who took their lamps and went out to fetch the bridegroom. But five of them were foolish and five wise: the foolish ones remembered their lamps but did not take along any extra oil; the wise ones, however, took containers of oil along with their lamps. When the bridegroom delayed, they all fell asleep. At midnight there came the call "Look, the bridegroom! Go out to meet him!" All the virgins arose and got their lamps ready.

But the foolish virgins spoke to the wise ones,
"Give us some of your oil, because our lamps are going out."
The wise virgins answered, "There isn't enough for us and you.
Go instead to the oil merchant and buy some for yourselves."
But once they had left for the market, the bridegroom came.
The virgins who were prepared went with him to the wedding
reception, and the doors were locked shut. Presently, the other
virgins arrived and said, "Sir, sir, open up for us!" But he
answered, "I tell you truly: I don't know you." Therefore be
alert, for you do not know the day and the hour.
—MATTHEW 25:1–13

The surrounding world confronts disciples with the danger that they will accommodate themselves to it. But the prospect of the age to come also constitutes a danger for them. The brilliant light of God's glorious promise renders them comparable to people eagerly awaiting the beginning of a wedding reception. The party begins when the bridegroom arrives. It is his celebration that all await, but they will celebrate it with him.

Alongside the promise, Jesus places a warning. If a living hope lays hold of that promise, will it not become the congregation's sole concern? By comparison, everything else they are and do fades into the background. They have crossed over into life, although they still stand under the law that brings them death. They are pronounced free from their guilt by divine decree, although they still carry in themselves the conflict that sets the desire of the Spirit against that of the flesh. They are a brotherhood and experience the reality of love, although their closeness also means common suffering endures only because they exercise forbearance toward each other. They proclaim the gloriousness of the Christ, which means they also bear the heavy sorrow caused by the unbelief of others. They believe in the one they have not seen, yet how entirely different their fellowship with him will be when he again comes to them! How much more jubilant will the wedding day be than the present! When the Christ in full divine splendor again unites with his people, the immortal will swallow up the mortal, the body will be subject to the Spirit, and the congregation will swell to an incalculable throng and take its place of worship before God's throne.

Just how important is the disciples' daily life? What is the use of their toiling day after day? If this kind of thinking takes hold of the disciples, they become like the virgins in the parable above who await the bridegroom so they can accompany him into the wedding hall, but whose lamps go out as they wait because they did not think of getting enough oil to keep their lamps lit. That is to say: there is burning hope and joy in the promised one, but they lack what they need for the reception. The promise does not bring about watchful attention that centers on keeping alive a close fellowship with Christ. There is rather the fanatical kind of hope that despises and looks past the present. This kills the redemptive drive within, because it thinks little of what needs to happen here and now. The result is an illusory certainty that forgets this: What is to come is closely attached to what currently takes place.

The attitude of those who hope in such a way that they lose sight of present reality is different from those who become dazzled with power (cf. the reading for Sept. 17). They will not struggle violently for their esteem and become preoccupied with their own glory and gratification; they live in the light of what is to come. But since they neglect what must now occur in order to honor Jesus and do his will, he withdraws his fellowship from them, just as he did from the power hungry. He says, "I don't know you" to those who despise the gift given to them in the present, who neglect the ministry that the present day demands from them.

Jesus Establishes the New Covenant
September 19

This is my blood, the blood of the covenant, poured out for many for the forgiveness of sins.
—Matthew 26:28

A new word was added to the old word, and in place of the Law to which the people were subject came the Christ, and instead of the old people of God there arose the new. How was this possible? What happened, on God's side of things, to cause the old to pass away and the new to come into being? The relation of humans to God is not determined by them but by God. His disposition sets the stage for how man finds him and what man receives from him. It is nonsense for man to fancy that he can order his relation to God according to his own discretion. If now we find the new Lord and the new fellowship and the new temple and the new righteousness and the new life—this must be because God is determining the place of humans in his sight according to a new order. He establishes "the new covenant." Israel was made ready for this contingency by prior promise. This proclamation was part of Jeremiah's message. It was made known to all through Scripture.

Not only God, however, through whose directive the covenant arises, but also man is part of the agreement. Man assumes the rights and obligations of the covenant. What happened, on man's side of things, to cause the new covenant to take effect? In earlier times the covenant was sealed by sacrifice: the covenant was validated by the people presenting the covenant offering. The new quality of the covenant, however, ruled out Jesus' calling the church to the altar, as if they could testify, like in former times, to the reception of the new covenant with a sacrificial offering. The disciples were in no further need of instruction on this point once Jesus departed. The ineffectiveness of the old sacrifices had made it obvious that the old covenant was not the enduring one.

But now something could happen to make the existence and the validity of the new covenant visible. That was Jesus' death. By the giving of his blood, God's fellowship with mankind was made manifest in a completely new way. Here is a new will of God, a new grace, a new union of man with God, a life of man from God by the Spirit for the accomplishing of his will. In the old covenant God was not so close to humans, and by the same token they were not so close to God. Previously, humans had never been so much one with God. Now, because Jesus ended his life in free obedience, God made new his relation to mankind.

Jesus Gives to His Disciples His Body and His Blood
September 20

As they were eating, Jesus took a loaf of bread, spoke the blessing, broke it, gave it to his disciples, and said, "Take and eat; this is my body." And he took a cup, gave thanks, gave it to them, and said, "All of you, drink from it, for this is my blood,

> *the blood of the covenant, poured out for many for the
> forgiveness of sins."*
> —Matthew 26:26–28

One time Jesus asked the disciples nearest him: Can you drink the cup that I drink? Or do you oppose God's decision that requires me to die? Do you recognize that I honor God by my death—that I thereby bring you his grace and establish his lordship? But now on the last evening, he expected all his disciples to fulfill their discipleship by recognizing in his departure the saving act that would be performed for them. He demanded this of them by making the bread they ate and the wine they drank into the gift of his body and blood, received from his hand. What he accomplishes in dying occurs for them. It signifies no break with the promise given to them but is rather its fulfillment. It signifies no basis for deserting him but is the perfecting of his fellowship with them.

In order to depict what his death would accomplish for them, he uses the nutritional power of the bread and the inviting, joyously festive image of the wine. This completely excluded the notion that he would be lost to the disciples through the sacrifice of his body and the shedding of his blood. His body, put to death, would be for them life, and from his blood arises for them the celebration of divine grace.

Their participation in his gift is again, as at the beginning of their discipleship, completely removed from what they themselves achieve. In regal fullness of power, he is the one who bestows favor upon them. As it was their task to take up his call "Follow me!" with a faith that surrendered to him, so too now, in perfecting his fellowship with them by his death, Jesus laid no claim on their understanding and gave them no explanatory lecture. Nor did he seek to rally their bravery so that they might accompany him to the cross. They are to receive what he offers them, eat what he feeds them, drink what he pours for their refreshment. He makes them into persons for whom his body is put to death and his blood poured out. They become persons whose sins are forgiven. Their sins do not hinder God from being on their side and placing them under his grace by his new covenant.

All this also indicates to them the ministry that is placed upon them by their commission. Jesus' blood is shed not only for them but also for many. The forgiveness of sins has been accomplished for humanity. Jesus' death cannot disappear from their message; on the contrary, their message is precisely the proclamation of the Crucified One. The meal he established strengthens them not only for the dark night and the arduous day of his suffering; it is also given to them forever and becomes known to all who believe, so that their stake in the slain body and shed blood of the Christ is their praise before God and the basis of their eternal life. In the wake of this act of Jesus, it was fully justified that this meal of departure did not close with sighs and lament but in expression of thanks lifted up to the praise of God.

Jesus' Flesh Nourishes, Jesus' Blood Quenches
September 21

Whoever eats my flesh and drinks my blood has eternal life, and I will raise him up on the last day. For my flesh is true food and my blood true drink.

—JOHN 6:54–55

A certain horror attaches to the destruction of life and to death. Jesus overcame it by saying to those who walked with him: That which is put to death gives nourishment. How does flesh become nutrition? Precisely by being killed. And how does blood become a drink? Precisely by being shed. Does Jesus' body needlessly succumb to death, and is his blood wasted by being poured out? Absolutely not. This is precisely how Jesus makes bread out of his body and a drink out of his blood. That is how he plants life in mankind and gains authority: at that time when mortal life ends and eternal life begins to awaken those who believe on him.

By this evaluation of his flesh and blood, Jesus, first in Capernaum, lifted his followers above the frightfulness of death. That was when his departure from Galilee and his final appearance in Jerusalem were at hand. He did the same later, when dying was no longer in the future and as the night began when he became a prisoner, after which came the day that saw him go to the cross. He presented to the disciples, through the bread they ate and the wine they drank, the meaning that his body (because he was killed) and his blood (because it was poured out) had for them.

He himself goes to the Father. The life mediated to him by flesh and blood ends. But he did not receive his body for nothing; he did not live in vain in that flesh whose veins coursed with blood. Not only his Spirit and not only his word—no!—but also his flesh and his blood are effective with eternal outworking as the tool of the divine grace. For in the power of his death—which is to say, by means of his body and blood—he becomes the giver of eternal life.

In this way the utter horror associated with the destruction of the body was taken away from his crucifixion. The disciples saw that Jesus was not tormented by the notion that his bodily life would end by a senseless devastation. Yet in their souls, the horror of death still lay deep and uneradicated. In Capernaum, when he commended his flesh as the bread of life that they must eat, many said it was a hard saying that would not bear listening to.

The secret consisted in the binding together of the divine outworking and bodily mode of living. It consisted in fulfilling with eternal force what took place at that time: the unifying of the verdict that took Jesus' body from him with the grace that through him creates life. But this unifying of what is conditioned by nature with what is effected by the divine—a unifying by which the verdict that rejects man and the grace that calls him become visible and effective at the same time—was the fundamental assurance that gave Jesus the authority by which he called himself the Son of God.

Jesus' Saving Power Stems from the Spirit
September 22

It is the Spirit that gives life; the flesh does nothing.
—JOHN 6:63

How can flesh be healing? Its highest achievement is to bring forth flesh in its wake. Flesh begets flesh, and what it conceives is just as mortal as its forebears. But when Jesus spoke of his flesh as yielding nourishment and his blood as slaking thirst, he spoke of eternal life. This requires a working different from flesh and blood, especially flesh that has been slain and blood that has flowed forth from wounds. Such working is performed by the Spirit, who brings divine transformation into the inner being of persons. His power is present and active when Jesus suffers in his flesh from that with which death confronts him. At work here are not only those who sentenced him to die: he himself is also the active party, exercising discretion over himself in the freedom of his royal might.

But where does this will come from that makes him willing to face death? Does it arise from the flesh? Does a natural urge desire this demise? His will is to honor the divine verdict that declares man guilty. The flesh strives against this verdict, for it wishes to be free from guilt and to be right in the end. For Jesus to lay hold of the cross is obedience that does the will of the Father, but the natural urge of the flesh is self-seeking. Jesus acts in the power of that saving will which liberates the guilty from guilt and the dying from death.

But what does the flesh know of love? Flesh is selfish, even when it loves. Jesus acts in the confidence that his saving will is at work. He is convinced that he will free many by his death, procuring them as his own possession and bringing them into fellowship with God. How does faith arise? The flesh is moved by that which is visible. What gives the Crucified One the upper hand over souls? What creates fellowship between persons and the One who was put to death? All this lies entirely beyond what the flesh desires, comprehends, and is competent to attain. It is rather the work of the Spirit.

The decisiveness that made Jesus the bearer of the cross was confidence in the Spirit. He dies because he honors the Spirit and trusts that he is the power that creates life. In this confidence he relinquishes the flesh, because in itself it does not possess the power of eternal salvation. Yet he does not despise his flesh but proclaims the power of the Savior conferred upon flesh, because what he does with the flesh and suffers in the flesh fulfills the will of the Spirit.

Jesus Invokes the Omnipotence of Grace
September 23

> Jesus went a little farther, fell upon the ground, and prayed that, if possible, the hour might pass him by. And he said, "*Abba*, Father, everything is possible for you. Let this cup pass from me! But not what I will, but rather what you will!"
>
> —Mark 14:35–36

For the one who sees God at work in what happens, the hour that he expresses his will in the completed act takes on great weight. This weight remains completely incomprehensible to the person who is moved only by the mechanism of his natural feelings. Of the suffering that meant the end for him, Jesus said that the Father had made him drink this drink. For this reason he cannot evade it. That created in him the rock-hard will that did not collapse even under the load of his cross. But if God's working is experienced in what happens, then we simultaneously receive, with the connection to what happens, the liberation from the constraint of history.

Above the causal chain of things in the worldly sphere stands the One for whom all things are possible. No situation forces his hand. No power of man hinders him. Over against the world, he remains at all times completely free, the God who does wonders.

Judas left Jesus in order to summon the high priests. They are, no doubt, ready to exploit the hour. There is no human might that would stand in their way and save Jesus. But nothing of what they plan will happen if the Father does not will it.

For this reason this question arises in every carefully regarded reality and every closely regarded necessity: Is it God's will? Every resolve is qualified by the proviso, If it be God's will. Here there can arise no resignation that lets itself merely be carried along. Life lived in God's fellowship makes one wakeful and brings forth the constant willingness to follow the divine command as it makes itself known.

Jesus was not exempt from this watchfulness that listens closely to God's will precisely because he had come to Jerusalem and had prepared his disciples for his death, all of which he did on the basis of a clearly recognized certainty that Scripture itself confirmed. For no divine word expresses God's will exhaustively and without remainder: this will stands in creative power even over the divine word.

For that reason, even in his last night, Jesus appealed to the omnipotence of the divine grace. "With God nothing is impossible," he had said when he was able to break neither the enchanting power of riches nor free men from the burden of their possessions. "With God nothing is impossible," he said also when those who would kill him arrived. He remained certain that God, if he let this cup pass by him, would reveal his glory with a new word and a new work. He would glorify his grace.

It is evident that the intensity with which his suffering assaulted his life called forth Jesus' prayer to be freed from this cup. But the prayer arose not only from natural desire seeking to avoid suffering, although Jesus never denied this. Rather, he acted here also as the Son, who even now remained in fellowship with the Father. This barred him from devaluing what was happening by regarding it as meaningless. It did not permit him to gloss over death as mere appearance, nor to reduce the force of the divine verdict as if it did not, in fact, carry a life-destroying power. The truth of his divine sonship forced him to plead for liberation from this cup. For dying is forsakenness from God, and suffering separates from his presence, a presence whose character is to make blessed. Just as it is certain that all rule is in God's hands, not in the hands of human rulers or some spiritual force, so it is clear that Jesus could give himself into the hands of men if and only if this was, at this particular time, the will of the Father. His request did not receive an immediate divine answer, and for that reason Jesus repeated it. The repetition made it certain that God's will lay behind the unfolding circumstances and made him the prisoner of the Jews.

The Disciples Can Bear No Temptation
September 24

Be alert and pray that you may not fall into temptation. The spirit is willing enough, but the flesh is weak.
—Matthew 26:41

Jesus did not desire to save himself. But he was concerned to save the disciples. They are in danger. They do not yet realize this but, shortly, it will become clear. Then their comrade Judas will appear in the driver's seat with those who arrest Jesus. Which way will they go? Will they cast the same vote that Judas did? Or will they remain true to Jesus? The flesh is weak. Its desire is bound to what is visible. And on this night, what is still visible of Jesus' mission? Those who condemn Jesus are the disciples' fellow countrymen. The flesh draws us to those who share our blood lineage. The flesh abhors death, and shame is bitter to it. What are the disciples, viewed as companions of the despised Jesus? Don't the events of this night refute their faith? Are the disciples not robbed of their honor, their happiness dashed to pieces?

To be sure, the spirit is willing. The disciples wish to remain with Jesus.

They do not want to reckon him among the transgressors or to regard him as a dead man. Rather, they want to retain and uphold his word. The Spirit keeps them close to the word of Jesus. But the Spirit-given desire is not all that is at work in them. For they are flesh, and the outlook natural to them, as humans and Jews, sets itself against the desire of the Spirit.

They are in need of strength to fulfill what the Spirit bids them do, and they do not find this in themselves. They cannot rely on their willingness, which of itself will not keep them close to Jesus. It is a gift of grace not to fall prey to the opposition of the flesh, and this gift must be prayed for. Only divine enabling can confer upon them the ability to remain at Jesus' side.

When the disciples do not place themselves under the protection of divine grace through prayer, they are exposed to temptation. Then, without foreseeing it, they are brought into situations that confront them with well-aimed blows. This reveals what is in them—their natural incapacity, which is incapable, too, of fulfilling the will of the Sprit. The disciples acknowledged the truth of this assessment when the plea "lead us not into temptation" was made an enduring feature of their prayer. They owe it to a merciful protection that they remain in faith and love, even though their natural hankering cannot submit itself to the will of the Spirit.

Jesus Protects the Disciples
September 25

Jesus asked them again, "Whom are you seeking?" And they said, "Jesus of Nazareth." Jesus replied, "I told you that I am he. If you are looking for me, let these others go."
—John 18:7–8

Jesus' desire was to protect the disciples when he stood before those who arrested him. In the same way that in Gethsemane he woke the disciples and admonished them to prayer so that nothing would befall them due to their lethargy, so during his arrest he takes measures to ensure that none of the disciples would be seized along with him. It is true that he was not crucified alone. But those between whom he had to die were not two disciples but two revolutionaries. It was purely Jesus' will and work that none of his disciples was led away to trial with him and crucified as a partner in crime with him.

When the disciples seriously pondered Jesus' end, they felt their obligation as disciples was to accompany him into prison and into death. But this was to offer him a service that he declined because he desired a different and greater service from them. The preservation of his message and the inauguration of his church hinged on the disciples. For that reason Jesus applied to his disciples the same rule that he cited to Peter when he rejected Peter's contradiction of Jesus' prophecy that he must die: they must set their thoughts on what is of God, not on what appears to their human judgment as the obligation of loyal supporters.

The disciples have often been derided because they permitted Jesus to go alone in the way of suffering. They took flight after he was arrested, and this would not have become part of the church's Passion narrative if the recollection of this behavior had not felt burdensome. But Jesus was not led into suffering so that the disciples might have opportunity to attain to the fame of loyalists faithful until death. What Jesus' departure established was not the greatness of the man who can become a hero but rather this: the fact and reason that God forgives the man whose faith fails and whose human weakness makes him unfit for God's service. To bring this about was Jesus' sole mission. The disciples grasped this and took great pains that the narrative of Jesus' demise not become a presentation of how the disciples proved to be heroes. It was impressed on the church from the start that the one to whom faith is due is Jesus alone. The word of the disciple is believed not because he had a hand in Jesus' last great work but because he received Jesus' word and has become the witness of his suffering and his life.

The Rulers of the World Prepare Death for Jesus
September 26

If the rulers of this age had known the wisdom of God, they would not have crucified the Lord of Glory.
—1 Corinthians 2:8

God is the one who becomes manifest in the death of Jesus. That is the premise that explains Jesus' conduct and the entire activity of the apostles.

In this way they preserved what they had received from Jesus. For Jesus called his suffering the cup that his Father gave to him, and he was willing to die because God would thereby be illumined. Compared to the divine will and work, those who were active in Jesus' final condemnation have no real power. Jesus was not done in by the blindness and evil of this or that Jew, nor was it the will of Satan that erected Jesus' cross. Rather, God pronounced this sentence upon him, and it was God's action that translated this pronouncement into accomplished fact.

But the consequence was not that those who actively carried out God's sentence became merely passive instruments. They acted according to what they regarded as their knowledge and truth, and they obeyed their desire. That point was brought home forcefully in Jerusalem in Peter's initial proclamation of the Christ. He stated categorically to the Jews: You crucified the Christ and have thereby incurred guilt. But what took place among men was the result of not only natural forces and usual human decisions. It was also determined by spiritual powers active in the world.

These powers, created by God and bestowed with spiritual authority, are circumscribed by the omnipotence of God no less than nature itself is limited by him. They have no might independent of God. Paul did not give thanks to the sun for the bread that nourished him; he rather saw in it the gift of God. Likewise, he did not offer honor and prayer to a heavenly prince and sovereign of the people. But he assessed the magnitude of what happened at Jesus' death as involving the powers that steer history, that take spiritual form and work in an invisible manner. They had no place for the Lord of Glory in the world where they exercised sway. Those subservient to their will rejected and killed him. In this appears the newness of what took place with Jesus' saving act. Not even those who preside over mankind as spiritual rulers recognized the Christ. They were unable to apprehend the truth that God reveals his greatness in this way and prepares for mankind the glory that his grace decrees for it.

This demarcates the message of Jesus from all that humans regard and pass along as wisdom. Paul insists on this point because in Hellenistic congregations the conventional wisdom was immediately combined with what Jesus gave them. The powers who move human history also possess, of course, wisdom. But Jesus' cross makes evident that their wisdom is entirely different from the wisdom of God, which manifests its goal by making Jesus the Lord of Glory. The spirits at work in the world keep man far from God and set themselves against the divine grace. They keep man in his sinful condition and make of mankind—since these spirits know of no resurrection—death's sphere of power. Therefore the Christ, through his cross, renders the person of this age obsolete and the present world fleeting. He becomes the creator of a new humanity and the Lord of another world.

Where Did the Jews Seek Jesus' Guilt?
September 27

We heard him say, "I will tear down this temple, which is made with hands, and build another, not made with hands, within three days."
—Mark 14:58

How could a person arrive at the notion of destroying the temple and replacing it with another one? The temple was built in accordance with the Law. Its splendor expressed the people's willingness to honor God with their wealth. Jesus' detractors felt that his opposition did not apply to broadminded Judaism, which regarded the cult as useless and dispensed with the temple. It was clear that Jesus called for a temple, yet for a different one than currently stood in Jerusalem. How could he find fault with it?

In the Jewish outlook, there was only one way of rejecting the temple without doing so in a godless fashion. The Old Testament prophets had declared: Those objects made with human hands are not gods; do not worship the works of your hands. Could it be that the temple, in Jesus' judgment, fell under this condemnation? It was made with hands, a work of human art and piety. A temple not produced by human hands would be a miraculous work of divine creation, obviously superior to the temple of first-century Jerusalem. For such a temple would testify more eloquently than could the Jerusalem temple to the fellowship of God with his people.

But Jesus' accusers distorted his word grotesquely by the explanation they used to try to render it understandable. Jesus ascribed to himself authority to work in God's manner. Did he suppose he was a Lord of heavenly sanctuaries? Already in this attempt to condemn Jesus one sees the ultimate motive for opposition to Jesus' unity with God, from which flowed everything he said and did.

The attempt to make his proclamation against the temple into the basis for his condemnation failed, but only on formal grounds, because the relation between the statements of the two witnesses could not satisfy the requirements placed upon the testimony of witnesses by the rabbinate. The suspicion remained on Jesus that his intention was the destruction of the temple. For that reason he was reproached, as he hung on the cross, with taunts that the hollowness of his antitemple utterances was now clearly unmasked. The esteemed visible token of Israel's fellowship with God stands firm, and he who wanted to replace it with a more worthy temple ends up forsaken by God.

The High Priest Expresses Horror
September 28

Then the high priest rent his clothes and said, "He has committed blasphemy."
—Matthew 26:65

Both the high priest's question and Jesus' answer were phrased in purely biblical terms. "Christ" and "the Son of God" are the names that Psalm 2 gave to the Promised One. The psalmist (Ps. 110:1) and the prophet (Dan. 7:13) speak of the one who sits at the right hand of God and who will come down to earth in the clouds. These were all familiar words to the high priest. What was so horrifying that he felt obligated to rend his tunic? "Are you this person?" Caiaphas had asked, and in reply Jesus gave him confirmation.

But why was this such a blatant blasphemy that no one thought proof was necessary for this judgment? Was there need for proof that Jesus stood before him in chains and that his condemnation was certain, so that at the break of day he would come under Pilate's jurisdiction, and this would lead inevitably to his crucifixion? And he himself confesses his royal sending and his status as God's Son and describes his goal with the highest messianic expressions. Was it not visible to all that the most glorious words of Scripture are being used blasphemously by this one, who suffers defenselessly and dies ignominiously?

The high priest did, in fact, have reason to fear because of the confession to be God contained in Jesus' answer. For what he said was completely incompatible with what the Jew affirmed. This contradiction, it could be supposed, touched on everything that Jewish belief defended as true and holy. A dying Son of God! Was that not the denial of God's exalted rule and almighty grace? The God of the high council was a God of power, who does not let his Son die. The rejection of a Christ by Judaism was only possible if that Judaism was blinded and fallen. This would be to deny the righteousness of the Jew, which he attained by fulfilling the Law. Was this not clearly the denial of the Law, which was given by God's revelation to the people? What still remains of Judaism if there is removal of the hope rooted in its Law and the accomplishments performed to please God? And this denial of all teachings and commandments that defined Israel's identity occurred in the name of God and presented itself as the fulfillment of the promise given to Israel.

It was blatantly evident: the God and Father of Jesus was not also the God on whom Judaism called. Either Jesus was guilty, or Judaism was. But the outcome of this question could not be in doubt. Caiaphas had the power, and Jesus suffered. The one who has power is right, and the one who must suffer is the guilty party. For this reason alone Jesus is condemned, because he suffered. Of course it was according to God's will, but was not precisely this a blasphemy?

The High Priest Finally Recognizes What Jesus Was
September 29

See! Now you have heard the blasphemy.
—Matthew 26:65

What the Jerusalem rulers had agonized over for so long was finally out in the open. When those around Jesus had ascribed David's kingship to him, he remained silent, and when they had questioned him regarding his authority, he declined to furnish an answer, because they were not able to tell him where John the Baptist got his authority to baptize. And when they had pressed him and demanded that he put an end to their perplexity, he told them that his statements about himself were clear enough. He called himself the Son of Man; but what did this mean for the relationship of the people to him? Did he seek to make himself Lord of the people with this enigmatic name? Or was he still leaving room for the Christ?

But now, at his trial, the perplexity that until then had hampered the rulers was over. Jesus finally spoke clearly and fully uncovered his purpose. Now, since he had arrogated to himself the status of being sent as a king and had appealed to God to make this point, it was no longer necessary to seek another ground for his condemnation.

For the rulers it was just as incomprehensible why Jesus had not proclaimed his royal name as it was incomprehensible that he suffered. Was he not obligated to testify to his divine commission if he really had received it? Should he not have clearly summoned the people to obedience if he had the right to demand it from them? Can the Son of God conceal himself? Can the one born to rule demean himself and, instead of fighting for his lordship, wait inactively until someone comes to him? "I can receive nothing unless it is granted to me from above"—that contradicted Judaism. "Whoever exalts himself will be humiliated; whoever humbles himself will be exalted"—by Jewish standards that was not wisdom and strength but weakness. To be unable to summon others to oneself; to wait for God to lead someone to you and to accept him because God draws that person—that was, in the opinion of others, not to exercise power but to dispense with it.

To the person who placed himself in God's hands so that God's rule might work through him, this was the only possible way to function. But it was based upon the presence and effectiveness of God. The Jew knew nothing of this, since for him, even in his relationship with God, everything depended on the performance of man.

Why didn't Jesus step before his interrogators and clearly declare his kingship? Why didn't he confess his identity until ordered to by the high priest? Why didn't he take his disciples with him so they could testify to his deeds? Why did he accept his death sentence when he was supposed to rule, liberate, and bless? These were puzzles with which none, so far, was able to come to grips. How could they put faith in him? Now, however, his confession before the high priest required that they place themselves and the entire fate of the people under his control. It appeared to them that they had sufficient grounds for skepticism. For this dispute there was only one solution: Jesus' death.

Jesus Confesses Peter
September 30

And the Lord turned and looked at Peter, and Peter remembered the word that the Lord had spoken.
—Luke 22:61

Everywhere he stood and went, Peter could find opportunities to conceal his relation to Jesus. When this or that acquaintance asked him whether he had perhaps heard if Jesus was arrested or not, the discussion could take a turn that gave Peter cause to conceal his status as a disciple. But now, through the intervention of John, who knew the high priest, Peter was in the courtyard. He had managed to sit unrecognized among the servants until Jesus' cross-examination was over and Jesus, too, was brought back out into the courtyard. It happened that way—Jesus remained in custody—because he had not renounced his claims, his mission, or his disciples. He had not renounced Peter.

And now he helped Peter with his look. How did he look at him? Furiously? Sadly? Plaintively? We must not yield to the inclination to embellish. In the circle of those who formed these recollections, it was said only that Jesus looked at him. Jesus' look was his confession of loyalty to the disciple who had renounced him. And because the Lord kept his communion with Peter in force, Peter was not lost to him. With Jesus' look, Jesus' word to Peter revived, and with that, Peter's attempt to protect himself by remaining unrecognized was over. Now the name of Jesus stuck to him forever, and he could be nothing other than the one whom Jesus had chosen personally to be the rock in the structure he was erecting. In council chambers it had been disputed that Jesus had the capacity to build the eternal temple. The same claim of Jesus was being tested through what took place simultaneously in the courtyard, where Peter fell into temptation and it was established whether the pressure of the cross would rip "the rock" out of Jesus' hands.

In their report about Jesus' last earthly hours, the disciples proclaimed with great gratitude that Jesus remained the victor in this battle. He showed himself to be the builder of the new temple of God.

Jesus Receives
Peter's Confession of His Love
October 1

When they had eaten, Jesus said to Simon Peter,
"Simon son of John, do you love me more than these?"
He said to him, "Yes, Lord. You know that I love you."
He said to him, "Feed my little lambs." A second time he said
to him, "Simon son of John, do you love me?"
He said to him, "Yes, Lord. You know that I love you."
He said to him, "Feed my little sheep." A third time he said to
him, "Simon son of John, do you love me?" Peter was sad that
he had asked him a third time, "Do you love me?" And he said
to him, "Lord, you know everything. You know that I love you."
Jesus said to him, "Feed my little sheep."

—JOHN 21:15–17

What occurred the night of Jesus' suffering did not separate Peter from Jesus. It did not nullify the commission that gave him the office of herald. John made this clear to the church; that is why he closes his report with the exchange in which Jesus put Peter's will to the test. In the night of suffering, Jesus was quiet; at that time it was his gaze that said to Peter, "The Lord knows you." Now Jesus' resurrection had renewed his fellowship with the disciples. They receive a new word from him. Those who tested Peter on the night of suffering asked him whether he knew Jesus. Jesus tests him by asking whether he loved him.

That Peter knows Jesus is obvious, but that does not make him suited to the office of herald. He can only accomplish this if he loves Jesus. When he denied Jesus, he was saving his own neck and following his own agenda. It would have been the end of his apostolate and discipleship if his love were set on himself. He can only remain a follower of Jesus if he is freed from his selfish ambition. He must also value what Jesus did for him, and he must have within himself the one for whom he now lived.

This test of Peter is extremely serious, because it is being conducted by one who knows hearts and sees all things. He must love Jesus more than the others do, for he received more than the others and sinned more gravely.

But by loving much, Peter, who had received much, demonstrated that forgiveness had freed him from his sinful will.

Also, Jesus now conferred more on him than on the others. For Peter's commission placed him above them. That is only possible if Peter (as well as the others) is freed from his selfish ambition. They must all receive the love that sets affection on Jesus and not on their own lives. Then there is neither pride nor envy among them, neither pushy self-promotion nor selfish competition, but one common will shared by all, which is in turn the will of Jesus himself.

Whoever loves Jesus loves the shepherd and is ready to care for his flock. The unity of Peter's will with Jesus gives him a hand in Jesus' work. But for this he needs Jesus' commission. He does not become an apostle by his own scheming and self-glorifying labor. Jesus gives his commission only to the one who loves him. But if Peter loves Jesus, he values his commission as the gift of his great grace and pours his strength intensely into his cause.

Those whom Peter is to lead and care for are the people who belong to Jesus. They are not in Peter's possession; he is not the shepherd who owns the flock. But neither is he just a hired hand who watches them merely to earn a paycheck. Peter's love for the shepherd makes the flock dear to Peter. In this connection the very experience Jesus had will be reflected repeatedly in his dealings with the Jews and the Greeks: the call of God reaches out to "the least of these." But these "little sheep" belong to the Christ, and this places on Peter the duty and furnishes him with the will for total devotion on their behalf.

Paul Cannot Deny Jesus
October 2

If we died with him, we will also live with him. If we persevere, we will also reign with him. If we deny him, he will also deny us. If we are unfaithful, he will remain true. For he cannot deny himself.

—2 Timothy 2:11–13

In the courtyard of the high priestly palace, Peter bowed under the pressure laid on him by the enmity of Jewish circles against Jesus. And in a

Roman prison Paul strengthened himself and his friend and coworkers in the face of the pressure placed on them by Roman imperial power. The Roman threat was even greater than the Jewish. Did it make sense to cling to a confession of loyalty to Jesus rather than to Caesar? But it is not possible for Paul and his companions to deny Jesus.

If the disciples no longer know Jesus, then the Lord likewise no longer knows the disciples. He withholds fellowship from those who withdraw fellowship from him. Denial would be the revocation of faith. To deny Jesus is to break faith with him. But the result of this is not that Jesus would become faithless. The disciple can deny Jesus, but Jesus cannot deny himself: he is the truth. But precisely this fact—that he is the truth and does not forsake his mission and stands behind his word—renders lack of faith a sin that has become impossible for the person who knows Jesus. The result is that those who know Jesus persevere, even though the pressure they face is great. They are not silenced when Caesar orders them not to speak, and they continue their labor even though it brings death to them. They do not turn away from the church on account of Caesar's determination to destroy it.

For because they believe in Jesus, they long for what Jesus promised them. They died with Jesus and acknowledge the decision through which God consigned Jesus to face death. For they know that through their fellowship with Christ's death, life is bestowed on them. If the Roman magistrate takes Paul's life, this is the same thing that happened to Jesus. Like Jesus, Paul must die because man thinks godlessly. But at work here is not only God's decision, which declares man sinful, but also his grace. This transforms the condemnation of the Christ into the vindication of man; it makes the giver of life out of the one who was put to death. What the Roman magistrate does to Paul will not separate him from the one through whom and with whom he will live.

But when the Christ reveals himself as the Living One, he will act in a royal manner. Those with whom he shares his life also take part in his royal activity. Although they may currently be dishonored and powerless, they are nevertheless persons called to a royal task. Meanwhile, all rulers who fight against the Christ will be divested of power. That sets the agenda for Paul and his colleagues: they endure; they do the heavy lifting; they persevere in their confession of the one who cannot deny himself and therefore also will not deny them.

Jesus Dies as the King of the Jews
October 3

Jesus stood before the governor, and the governor asked him,
"Are you the king of the Jews?" Jesus said, "You have said it."
—MATTHEW 27:11

With a measured and succinct statement, Jesus affirmed that the demise of Jerusalem would follow from his condemnation. The tenant farmers who lay violent hands on the son will lose their lives. The guests who are invited to the king's feast, but say no and mishandle the king's messengers, are slain. The temple collapses, and the city is destroyed.

But Jesus by no means said that his fellowship with Jews had ceased. Those pronouncements that proclaimed to Jerusalem its end were not spoken because he was dispensing with his Jewish kingship. Rather, he attributes divine validity and power to that kingship. His lordship over his people was no less a part of his sending than was his ability to unite to himself every person who would believe in him. Nothing is detracted from the truth of his kingdom by the fact that he cannot effect his kingdom by exalting himself but must rather be lifted up by God. This does not reduce his kingship to a mere concept or futuristic fantasy. In reality there is no other Lord than the one to whom God gives the power and the glory.

Jesus' sentence ended up being pronounced by Pilate. This excluded negotiation over the theological correctness of Jesus' statements. The content of the charge against Jesus and the basis of the condemnation lay solely in his claim to own his people's loyalty. The Jews did not err in concluding that it would be impossible for Pilate to acquit the king of the Jews. By affirming Pilate's question as to whether he was that king, Jesus ensured that he would bear the cross.

At no time has the holy dignity of Jerusalem as the home of the people of God been so powerfully attested as when Jesus was not ashamed of his people but upheld his Jewish kingship in Pilate's presence and thereby took upon himself the cross. He cannot dispense with this kingship, because he refuses to negate God's promise. Therefore the Jewish people are his people and are subject to him, even if they mock his leading and opt rather for those who attempt to break Rome's rule by means of the sword. Yet for God's sake Jesus remains loyal to his people. He conducts himself in a royal manner toward them by suffering what they deal out to him and by placing them under God's judgment and grace.

No Roman Puts Up with a Jewish King
October 4

Then the governor's soldiers took Jesus into the citadel and assembled the entire company against him. And they stripped him and placed a scarlet robe on him, wove thorn branches into a crown that they placed on his head, and put a rod in his hand. They knelt before him, mocked him, and said, "Hail, king of the Jews!" And they spit on him and struck him on the head.
—MATTHEW 27:27–30

The king of the Jews was condemned by the governor and thereby deprived of any rights. Now he learns what kind of fate is intended for him—and, by extension, for all the Jews—by those in the imperial army, the upholders of Rome's interests. He receives a royal robe that is a grim mockery and royal accolade that is pure insult. That is Rome's response to Judaism's claim to power. For the Jews' self-seeking twists the promise given to them, and they misappropriate it for their own promotion. Through this sacrilege, the Jew incites against himself the hatred of the world and goads the Roman powers so they oppose him. Jesus must suffer for the people's guilt and misdeed.

The crown of thorns, a mockery and repudiation of Jewish arrogance, was borne by the Jews through the centuries. Jesus wore it for their sake. But by wearing it, he made manifest the absolute distinction between his lordship, on the one hand, and both Jewish and Roman dreams of power, on the other. He is the king of the Jews and the Lord of the world both in wearing the crown of thorns and also because of it. For his right to rule does not vanish because he wears it; on the contrary, that right is thereby established. He transforms the scornful royal attire into the highest honor. The same crown intended to proclaim his powerlessness becomes a testimony to his overcoming might. For mock robe and crown are signs visible to all of his unconquerable loyalty; of his forgiveness, which is stronger than any injustice; and of his grace, which no rage can supplant and which he upholds even in his function as judge.

The king with the crown of thorns and with the reed scepter is the Lord of the world not because he crowns himself or because men crown him but because God crowns him. But for that reason it is blindness when those who fight on Caesar's side hate and mistreat him. They are the ones who drape the red officer's cape around him; this is not attire he chose for himself. The one who allows himself to be crowned with thorns is not their enemy, for his power does not have the same basis or the same goal as theirs.

Behold the Man!
October 5

Pilate came out again and said to them,
"Look, I'm bringing him out to you so that you
may know that I do not find him guilty of anything."
Then Jesus came out, wearing the crown of thorns and the
crimson robe. And he said to them, "Behold the man!"
—John 19:4–5

The Jews fought against the Son of God. They were angry about Jesus and reproached him because he arrogated to himself what belongs to God and made himself equal with God. For that reason they demanded his crucifixion. Now he was in the hands of the Roman soldiers. Now how great was he? "Behold the man!" said Pilate. Nothing enigmatic, nothing supernatural about him now. The majesty of a "Lord" exalted over all others, before whom the Jews and even the whole world must bow, was stripped from him. No trace of godlikeness remained. He was a mere man, his words rapidly fading into oblivion—for human words are fleeting—and his plans dashed. For the wishes of man do not fulfill themselves when the man is stripped of power, when those around him withhold recognition and assistance from him, when fate smashes him and death snatches him away. Why are Jewish authorities so worked up against this person? They themselves are just a band of men. Why do they find no place for this man in their midst?

For John this exclamation of Pilate had unforgettable significance, because it expressed what Jesus revealed by his dying. What is man before God? That is the question that received a divine answer when Jesus was condemned to the cross. That answer was reinforced by the crown of thorns, the soldier's scarlet cloak, and the reed scepter, all tokens of his dignity. Look at the person who seeks to be Lord over himself and his life and even over others, who exalts himself and seeks only his own interests: God's judgment renders him shamed and dead! God grants to him the cross.

But that is not the only thing revealed by Jesus' dying. "Behold the man!" indeed: that was the astonishing responsibility that God's grace entrusted to Jesus. He is a human, one of us, but not merely a product of nature, a specimen of the animal kingdom; he is, rather, a human who is one with God and does his will, a human who is not bound to sin or cut off from God's life. Instead, he can reveal God's love and has life within himself. "Behold the man" who stands in fellowship with sinners and therefore dies and thus fulfills the commission given to him by divine grace. In this way John expressed why he was concerned to show every person how Jesus bore death.

Jesus Was Reckoned Among the Transgressors
October 6

Two thieves were crucified with him,
one on his right, the other on his left.
—MATTHEW 27:38

Man condemns Jesus' attempts to subject us to God as sedition threatening to the state. Jesus' movement represents a particularly dangerous uprising, since it constitutes an especially harsh attack on the interests of those in power. That is why Jesus' cross was placed between two other crosses on which men were sentenced to die who had run afoul of the rule of law. By this procedure, what had taken place in Jesus' work and passion once more came to light. Since man defends his self-seeking desire against Jesus, he calls Jesus the destroyer of the peace. He is vermin who poisons the people's ties with one another. He is the enemy of the state. As a matter of fact, Jesus *is* the strongest imaginable opponent of our self-seeking desire. Since we regard as right what brings us benefit, the objection to Jesus—that he robs us of peace and attacks our rights—never really dies away, not only in the public sphere but also in the secret counsels of the soul.

But precisely this objection proves that Jesus' sending has its basis in God's grace. Can self-serving desire bring forth justice? Can it create peace? Does Pilate create peace by setting up crosses? Did the rulers of Israel produce a harmonious social order by appointing themselves everywhere guardians of the Law? Man is at odds with God and also with one another, for he is at odds with himself.

But now God's grace comes to us and brings us the call that makes us believe in God, because in this way our life receives its basis in what God gives to us. Here, our self-seeking encounters an effective antagonist, one who will put that self-seeking in its place. How can I turn my will against God's will? When he speaks to us in such a way that we trust him, our self-seeking desire is soundly defeated. We are ready to be what he has designed us for and to do what he prescribes. But this clears away the cause for division between us, and we can live at peace with one another. Therefore, precisely the one who has been reckoned among the transgressors is the one who secures our natural associations, family and society, rendering them beneficial to us.

Jesus Suffered Guiltlessly
October 7

At the ninth hour Jesus called out with a loud voice: "Eli, Eli, lama sabachthani?" That means, "My God, my God, why have you forsaken me?"
—Matthew 27:46

"Now the Scripture is fulfilled," said Jesus when he offered God's grace to those from Nazareth (cf. Luke 4:21). "Now the Scripture is fulfilled," he said also on the night he suffered. Which of the psalmists' words describing the suffering of the Righteous One were the gloomiest? Which, when applied to the Christ, seemed the most implausible? That would be Psalm 22:1. For there the psalmist laments that God has forsaken him. And he cannot make out the reason God would have withdrawn his protective presence from him.

When God forsakes someone who breaks his law and who for that reason receives God's judgment, that person, if he knows God, raises no objection. Every godly person knows God's displeasure is justified and praises God's righteousness. But to be forsaken by God and to have to ask *why?* That is the grimmest of circumstances. Now darkness obscures God's will, and inner union with him becomes impossible. Was even this most foreboding utterance written for the Christ, or does this prophecy go beyond what the Christ had to suffer?

Matthew and Mark praised the suffering Christ by stating: This was Jesus' prayerful outcry on the cross; he was entirely engulfed by the depth of the suffering that the prophecy prescribed for him. Would it have been possible, then, for what Jesus suffered to be described with softer words? He had lived in fellowship with the living God, and in the end he succumbed to the dominion of death. Why? In obedience to God's command he had testified to his royal mission before the Jews and the Romans, and the recompense for this was the cross. Why? Only a godless person could suppose that this took place apart from or without God. Rather, the cross accomplished God's will, and it was publicly visible that God withdrew his protection from him and placed the death sentence upon him. But why?

That is the very question of the one who suffered guiltlessly. This is truly a mystery, indeed a troubling mystery. Free from guilt, yet sentenced to suffer—this violates our deepest sense of justice. Yet Jesus suffered in this very way. Why? The just suffered for the guilty. "Why have you forsaken me?" Because man has forsaken God.

Jesus Does Not Call for Elijah
October 8

Some of those who were standing there heard this and said,
"He's calling for Elijah."
—MATTHEW 27:47

In the area around the foot of the crosses one could hear all those great statements rooted in God's great promises to Israel. There was talk of God's temple and its inviolability, of the coming King and his conquering might, of the Son of God, who was invincible under God's protection—and of

Elijah, who would descend from heaven and lead the purified and unified people to the Christ. All these holy words were cited as the basis for the righteous necessity of relieving Jesus of his life.

Even the invective that demanded him to call on Elijah damaged Jesus in the eyes of the Jews. From the beginning of his ministry there were warnings that, according to prophecy, the first thing required for the time of redemption to begin was the arrival of Elijah. Even the Baptist had been asked if he was Elijah, and the rabbis demonstrated to the disciples that Jesus could not be the Christ, because Elijah had not yet come.

Jesus called these notions into question by seeing in John the Baptist's announcement of the divine lordship the preparation for his ministry. Jesus trusted the divine word and ascribed to it power to show the people God's grace, to create the new man, and to gather God's people, who would receive eternal life.

For the Jews, Jesus' cross refuted his confidence in the divine word. Some other means would be necessary to bring mankind what Jesus sought and promised them. The person who possesses only the word falls victim to the authority that opposes him. The bringer of the divine word must suffer and die. Only the appearing of a heavenly figure renders humans subject to God. If this figure did not materialize at the moment of highest need, then the Jews figured Jesus was lost.

Once more we see that two outlooks fundamentally diverge. "Listen! God speaks," was Jesus' approach. The Jews' response was, "We cannot believe; we wish to see; we will exalt the one who becomes our leader in heavenly might." Precisely this demand upon God by man, made by people set against God and seeking their own goals and aggrandizement, was the sin on account of which Jesus died.

Jesus Promises Paradise
October 9

The other thief, who hung crucified beside Jesus, said, "Jesus, think of me when you come into your kingdom." And he said to him, "I tell you the truth: Today you will be with me in paradise."

—LUKE 23:42–43

He suffered guiltlessly. The Righteous One was reckoned among the transgressors. The place of the righteous, when they are removed from the earth, is paradise. For there stands the tree of life. Jesus is going there. There he has not only citizenship but lordship, after Jerusalem has driven him out. Is he going there alone? No! He is taking with him the person who is dying next to him.

Shared fates create a close bond. Can Jesus forget the person who has been crucified at his side? Therefore this man requests, "Remember me when you come in the power of your royal mission." For those who crucified and derided him, his coming will be a horror. But the one who suffered next to him has hope that Jesus will think of him. And then he will not judge him; rather, he will bring him into God's kingdom.

Once more Jesus deals with a person as one who responds to faith placed in him. The man who makes the request will not only be resurrected by Jesus some day. He today will be among the righteous to whom Jesus goes. And yet Jesus endured death as the end of life; death was not transfigured by hopes. For the reason he died was that God forsook him.

Do we have to choose between the two gospel writers: one who says the Crucified One suffered the misery of death with no amelioration of agony, and the other according to whom Jesus while dying promised life to the one dying next to him? When the Evangelists use Psalm 22:1 to describe for us what Jesus suffered, they are saying, "The Guiltless One suffered." Why did he suffer? He suffered for the guilty. That establishes the certainty, in all the pain and injury of the cross, that his dying will be fruitful for many—even for the one who suffered at his side and whose tie to Jesus was simply that he called upon him.

Again the turn of the times, the new era, is visible. Even if a righteous person could assure himself with good reason that he stands in the front ranks of the righteous, it remained unknown to him whether his soul would arrive in paradise. For God's judgments are unsearchable. Who can know where the soul that leaves the body will end up: in the realm of the righteous, or in the place of judgment? If people assess their own works, the result of their self-assessment is inconclusive. But the one who bore God's judgment and suffered for the guilty has authority even in dying to promise life to the one who believes in him. He has this authority because he suffered for those who are guilty.

The Just One Suffers for the Unjust
October 10

Christ, too, suffered because of sins, the righteous for the unrighteous, so that he might bring us to God.
—1 Peter 3:18

Humans made the Christ into the Sufferer. What kind of humans were they? Righteous people, people who knew God and obeyed his will? True, they said they fought for God's honor and acted according to his law when they killed Jesus. And it was also true that God's supreme authority led them to carry out their deeds. But they did not know what they were doing. In their proud piety they obeyed the spirit of this world and defended, against Jesus, their godlessness and unrighteousness. Those who killed him were sinners. The Righteous One suffered through the unrighteous. He died for the sake of sin.

The result was what Jesus had to do when he took such suffering upon himself. He suffered because of sins; did he turn away from them with revulsion? Were those sins able to work the calamity that sin always sets in motion? He suffered because of unrighteous people; did he break off fellowship with them to force them to confess their faults? He suffered for the unrighteous so that their injustice would not despoil them and their sins not cut them off from God. Rather, God's grace will come to them, and they will receive forgiveness.

His suffering makes those in the church into suffering people. The cause of his suffering shows them why they must suffer. The goal of his suffering makes clear to them why they should suffer willingly and why they cannot evade suffering. They, too, suffer because of sins for the sake of righteousness through those who are unrighteous. Objections raised against them are lies, and the opposition they face is unjust. Their persecutors hate them because they are unrighteous. Can they withdraw, hide themselves, and suspend performance of their duties? Christ suffered for the unrighteous. Because they speak his word, proclaim his lordship, and bring people his grace, they suffer, too.

The Christ is not only, however, the Suffering One. The church places faith in the Living One, the one who is present with them, the one who rules over all. Through their fellowship with him they are called not only to suffering but also to life. But the Christ did suffer once, decisively. His suffering cannot be expunged from his history or separated from his ministry.

With inexorable force it determines the relation of the Christ to God and to the world, and therefore also the relation into which Christendom is brought to God and to the world. Because the church is graced with faith in God through him, it enjoys the fruit of his death.

To bring unjust people to God in such a way that they live in his presence and take part in his love—that was the wonderfully ambitious goal for which the Christ suffered. That is why Christendom has the ground of its existence and its calling in the suffering of the Christ. For that reason the church, too, cannot break off its fellowship with those who cause it to suffer. For the church possesses for its detractors that word that leads men to God, takes away their sinfulness, and makes just persons out of the unjust.

Jesus Becomes the Church's Example
October 11

You servants, if you do good and suffer and persevere, you have God's favor. For Christ, too, suffered for you and left you an example so that you might follow in his steps.
—1 Peter 2:20–21

Jesus' message must be declared to all. It was impossible for his messengers not to take the message to the working classes. Indeed, in Hellenistic areas they were the greater part of the population. But by incorporating the vast slave class, the church laid hold of a huge task. The slave succumbed easily to bitterness in view of the privileges of those who were free. Was the slave not forced to suffer injustice? And does this not necessarily beget rage? To avoid this required that no revolutionary, restive crowds take shape in the church because of the participation of those in bondage. Such unease would direct itself first against slave owners and employers, but it would unavoidably spread to infect the entire atmosphere in the churches.

The situation of Christian slaves was made even more difficult by their having two burdens to bear: first, the miseries that reigning custom and imperial law laid upon them, and second, the new and bitter suffering that frequently grew out of their confession of faith in Jesus. How could slaves be moved to enter the congregations in great numbers if God's grace was not discernible to them even in the painful outcomes of their Christian stance? Without the proclamation of the death of Jesus this could never have been attained.

But because the Christ had suffered, from whom believers have received all the gifts of grace, the notion carried convincing force that it is grace when man can suffer for God's sake. At the start of Jesus' ministry, discipleship meant that his followers accompany him, and what he did was normative for their own actions. So also now, Jesus' own comportment is the example to follow for those who confess his name. If they follow the trail he blazed, they accept suffering, neither intimidated nor embittered by it.

This distinguished the courageous freedom that Christianity enabled working classes to assume before their masters from the defiance with which slaves often enough carried out their secret battle against masters, resulting in harsh penalties when they failed to display due subservience. For the saving power of Jesus' death lay in the Guiltless One's suffering for the guilty. In the same way, the suffering of the slave was only an indicator of divine grace, assuming he did not deserve it because of disloyalty and insubordination.

A relationship with Christ also weakened the notion that resistance to injustice was obligatory and willingness to suffer, cowardice. For when Christ suffered, he did not deny God's justice. He rather appealed to God's verdict and honored him as the sole and final judge. And through the suffering of the Christ it was completely certain that believers' suffering borne with Christ did not curtail the gift of grace from God. For through his suffering the Christ had taken away believers' sins. He had united them as the people of God by becoming their shepherd.

Jesus Affirms His Mother
October 12

At Jesus' cross stood his mother, his mother's sisters, Mary the wife of Clopas, and Mary Magdalene. Because Jesus saw his mother and the disciple whom he loved standing nearby, he said to his mother, "Woman, behold your son!" Then he said to his disciple, "Behold your mother!" And from that moment on, the disciple took her into his home.

—JOHN 19:25–27

What happened among the Jews to the mother of someone who had been crucified? She shared in the curse that lay on her son. His death means for her an abiding indictment, an ongoing disgrace. For that reason Mary needs a home where she has refuge, where unbelief does not besiege her or doubt afflict her, a place amenable to Jesus' word. She needs a son who honors her as the Christ's mother and gives her a part to play in his work, by which he will gather his congregation. Jesus' last act in dying was to give his mother this son.

This one, to whom he passed on his duty as a son, did not fail him. At the cross alongside Mary stood John, the disciple for whom he cared deeply. He will honor the gift entrusted to him and loyally will carry out Jesus' will.

Jesus did not proclaim to his mother the Father from the cross; he did not divulge the secret of his demise, the saving power of his death. If she had not apprehended his unity with the Father during her days of earthly association with him, he could not show it to her now, at his hour of death. Now he can only commend her to the disciple who, she sees, receives Jesus' saving power by Jesus' handing over his word and work to him.

During his ministry it could often appear that Jesus separated himself entirely from his mother and brothers, that he had laid aside all natural ties for God's sake and lived solely for the world to come. But this was a false appearance. It arose only because self-seeking desire cannot break free from what is intrinsic to man. In fact he was always the son of his mother, just as he was always a member of his people and always saw his call to be the Son of Man. For him God's work was always not only that which would be but also that which is. He saw God's gift not only in the time to come but also in the present day. True, only what God will create is pure, glorious, eternal, and separated from death. But how could the One who will take part in the future work of God rise in rebellion against what God is presently doing and despise what God bestows upon man in the present time? Where had Jesus gotten the life that he was now offering God as a holy sacrifice? From his mother. Therefore he did not waver from his course when he now, in the hour of his death, expressed loyalty to his mother and spoke to her as her son. In this way he connected the beginning and the end of his life into a unity. It had begun with his mother, and he brought it to a close with his declaration of gratitude to her.

The Mother of the Christ Must Suffer
October 13

And Simeon blessed Mary, his mother, and said to her,
"See, this one has come to Israel to cause many to fall and
many to rise up, and to be a sign that will be contradicted.
The sword will pierce your very soul so that the thoughts of
many hearts might be exposed."

—LUKE 2:34–35

When a sword passes through the soul, is the result only an injury? Indeed, it was a death that the mother of Jesus had to endure—not a death that slew her body, but certainly a death that snatched away that which filled her soul. To be the mother of the Christ: what depth her life received from this! Will inconceivable bliss not stream into her life? But what stress also comes upon her with this maternity, since the one to whom she becomes mother is the Christ. All her expectations and claims, all her hope and jubilation, all her care and fretting are refuted and die away. She must wait, obey, keep silent, suffer—she must believe. This restraint reached its peak when she stood by Jesus' cross. There, the sword thrust itself through her soul.

Yet this does not contradict the promise that had been given to her with her child. For part of the Christ's office is to be a sign spoken against. Of course there will also be those who believe in him; if he were unable to awaken faith, his word would be spoken in vain and his work done for nothing. For many, he will be the sign through which God reveals himself to them. But since man does not think what God thinks—he rather demands that God be pleased with what pleases man—the Christ is embattled. Mary's path is not a serene and sunny detour around this struggle. That does not prevent her from having a believing relationship with Jesus. She, too, like the disciples, must drink the cup Jesus drinks. And the baptism that does away with what was earthly in Jesus immerses her hopes and motherly love in death, too. Out of his cross, a cross is provided for her, and since his soul is troubled to the point of death, her soul likewise is exposed to a sword thrust that assaults her being. Her maternal connection with Jesus makes this particularly painful for her. When the Crucified One is resurrected, it will become clear to her that this is a passage into life. Then the secret of his suffering will become clear, and the goal of his royal mission will become visible. He creates the pure and abiding faith community, and he equips it by putting up with opposition and accepting the verdict that rejects him.

For all this lays bare what people long for in their hearts. The shape and nature of their inner desire is not truly and completely visible from the way they express themselves outwardly. Over the Jews reigns the Law, and this makes everybody equal. Everyone speaks the same language and conforms to common usage. What the individual really thinks and truly pursues as his genuinely desired goal is often unclear even to the individual himself. But what is internally diverse cannot remain together. There comes a parting of the ways between those who set their affection upon God and those whose affection is set on themselves—between those who trust God and those who do their own will. The Christ builds up the new faith community by coming to man as light and leading him into the truth.

Mary's share in Jesus' suffering brought testing to her, too, and exposed what was in her heart. This came to light when she set out on the path, along with John, to Jesus' cross. She acknowledged the crucified Christ as her son. Because she acknowledged him, he also acknowledged her.

A Grave Is Found for Jesus' Body
October 14

And when evening came (it was the day of preparation, the day before the Sabbath), Joseph of Arimathea came, a distinguished member of the council, who was waiting for the dominion of God too. He dared to go before Pilate and ask for Jesus' body. Pilate was surprised that he should have died already and summoned a soldier. He asked him if he knew whether Jesus had been dead a long time. After being informed by the soldier, he gave the corpse over to Joseph. He bought some linen, took him down from the cross, wrapped him in the linen, laid him in a tomb carved out of the rock, and rolled a stone over the mouth of the tomb. Now Mary Magdalene and Mary the mother of Joses saw where he had been laid.
—Mark 15:42–47

Both love and lament drive the disciples to care for Jesus' corpse. But at first they could not do anything. Pilate's permission was required for Jesus' burial, and a grave had to be found in which he could immediately be placed. Otherwise the onset of the Sabbath would make any burial preparations impossible. A favorable outcome for these circumstances was beyond the disciples' power to engineer. Yet things worked out. For Jesus' mission had not yet been accomplished, and in order to carry it out completely, he would need his body again.

He had testified that God's judgment was upon every lie and evil deed. He had fulfilled this witness by his cross; he bore God's judgment against sinners. He had testified to God's grace, a grace available to all, and fulfilled this testimony, for he had loved his own until the end. But he had yet another message to proclaim to the world, the message of life. His death was part of this message. But it was not the entire message.

His message of life did not speak of an endless continuance of present existence, perhaps in some improved form without the adversities that now beset us. He spoke of eternal life under the divine lordship, which makes it clear that God is our God. For this to come, the body that nature gives us must come to an end. In this connection, part of Jesus' mission still remained to be fulfilled: his death as equipping for his life, and the rise of life out of this death, a death that reveals God's judgment regarding man. To proclaim his life-bestowing message, Jesus would require once again the slain but resurrected body.

Accordingly, his body was the object not only of human but also of divine care. His body did not hang for days on the cross decaying, nor did it disappear as useless remains in the immensity of physical matter. It was protected, as an instrument of the divine grace made useful for its ordained service. With its burial all could see that it was now a corpse. For life to come from this through resurrection would surely mean the suspension and overcoming of death.

This could also be seen from a day of rest being interposed between the day he bore God's judgment and the day he became the herald of life. This day separates the new mission from the former one now fulfilled. He did not descend from the cross and step directly into life but rather brought to an end the natural life appointed to him. A grave received his corpse.

Section 15

JESUS REVEALS ETERNAL LIFE

The Slain Christ Is the One Who Lives Eternally
October 15

As they were discussing this, he himself stood in their midst and said to them, "Peace be with you." But they were startled and were filled with fear, thinking they were seeing a ghost. And he said to them, "Why are you confused? Why are your hearts doubtful? Look at my hands and feet; you can tell that it's me. Take hold of me; a ghost doesn't have flesh and bone, as you can see I have."
—Luke 24:36–39

The point of Jesus' appearance after his death was not to show us that spirits exist. Faith in spirits was and is common in the world. But Jesus' message was not that God has also created spirits and made Jesus to be one of them. His message pertains to us, creatures of the natural world, persons who die. He promises life to us; he brings divine grace to persons like us, who sin. For sinfulness and mortality exist side by side. Both are hallmarks of being human, the essence of which is expressed with the saying "What you are, you have through your flesh and blood." Our wistfulness and the fleeting nature of our lives arise from this.

When Jesus showed himself again to his disciples, he said to them: It is I— I, the Crucified One. The capstone of his fellowship with them was not an event of the inner soul but an encounter that united him, who now possessed the glory of eternal life, with those still living in the natural human state. That is the overcoming of death, the exaltation of the temporal into eternal existence. That is not the rejection of earthly life but rather its transformation.

Therefore, the new presence of Jesus was also not the weakening and laying aside of his earthly effectiveness but rather its confirmation. This was not the commencement of a new message to take the place of the old. Rather, the old message receives the seal that makes its truth public. A new congregation is not being founded; rather, the fellowship that Jesus established through his word is being made permanent, never to pass away. The resurrected Christ is the one who has come into the world, and this one is now revealed as the eternal Christ. His proclamation of forgiveness is thereby rendered eternal forgiveness; the righteousness he secured for his disciples is made into eternal righteousness. Now his word possesses immortality, and his command announces publicly the eternal will of God. Now the disciples receive the mission, because they have recognized that their connection with Jesus, whom they followed during his earthly life, bound them to the eternal Christ.

John Believes in the Empty Grave of Jesus
October 16

They did not yet know the Scripture that he had to rise from the dead.
—JOHN 20:9

John relates when it was that he became convinced of Jesus' resurrection. When he stood with Peter in the carved-out tomb that no longer contained Jesus' body, just the grave clothes—it was just then, he says, that he believed. It was certainly not earlier, but only then that he inwardly said yes to Jesus' promise, which proclaimed his resurrection. Earlier his faith and that of all the disciples was impeded by something that forbade faith in the Resurrection. This impediment was the Scripture. It was not until the course of Easter events that they recognized that Scripture itself unquestionably spoke of the resurrected Christ.

John tells us this after his report about the instruction Jesus gave to his disciples prior to his departure. Had his teaching made them messengers of a deceased person? Did he tell of a withered vine, from which the disciples hang like grapes? The vine of which Jesus spoke lives and nourishes the grapes it bears, and those who abide in him do not cling to the memory of a dead person; rather, the Living One receives them into his fellowship and demands their love and service for him. But was this not a completely new life, one that began with Jesus' return to the Father? Did this promise include the renewal of his body? Did this also promise to the disciples a new interaction with Jesus after his death? He would have believed all this of Jesus, John says, based on Jesus' word and not for the first time in view of the empty grave, if he had known the Scripture.

The Scripture! Unshaken by the death of Jesus, its validity stands firm. The expectation of the disciples was thwarted; in contrast, the prophetic word does not waver. To doubt what God says is unthinkable. But the Scripture speaks of this world. It knows an abiding people of God, yet not abiding persons: it is appointed to each to die. To God's people living in earthly associations, Scripture promised a king who brings the people under the lordship of God. But did Scripture know the slain Christ, the one whom Israel rejected and who rose again? Did it know a kingdom of God in which man is graced with eternal life? Between faith in the Scripture and faith in Jesus, a full unity must exist, for both have the same basis. Both bring faith face-to-face with God, whose word comes to pass and whose will does not waver.

Because Scripture did not yet suffice for him, John had to wait until the resurrection of Jesus had taken place. Then, when he saw the empty grave, John received strength from the Resurrection, which guided his mind and will—not only from the unquestionable reality of Jesus' death, nor merely from his proximity to Jesus in the fullness of his divine nature. After he witnessed God's working at the tomb, the words of Scripture that spoke of the Coming One said more to him than they had previously. Now he heard in them, too, the will of God that exalted the Christ to glory through his death. From now on his confession of faith in Scripture and his confession of faith in the Resurrected One were one harmonious word.

The Resurrected One Is the One Promised by Scripture
October 17

Jesus said to them, "O you of little faith, whose hearts are slow to believe because of all that the prophets have said. Didn't the Christ have to suffer this and enter into his glory?" And he began with Moses and all the prophets, explaining to them what was said about him.
—Luke 24:25–27

The appearances of Jesus in the days after his resurrection had the effect of eliciting from the disciples a steadfast commitment to the Resurrected One. In order for that to happen, what nature teaches us had to be debunked, for nature knows nothing of the rise of mankind to eternal glory. It knows of no suspension of the necessity and effect of death. But the disciples were accustomed, through Scripture and through interaction with Jesus, to hope in God's creative strength, which brings about what nature cannot. Yet greater than the hindrance of nature to the disciples' eventual Easter message was their faith in Scripture. Even John alluded to this, and it becomes still clearer to us in the report of the two disciples walking to Emmaus on the very first Easter day. By being executed by the leaders of the people, had Jesus not forfeited any claim to a divine mission? That was the judgment of the Jewish hierarchy, and the disciples were in no position to repudiate that judgment from Scripture. In Jesus' resurrection something came about that was entirely different from what they and Jewish leaders had expected. In the days after Easter there arose for the first time the question of whether Jesus' message could still be placed alongside the Old Testament so that both were true. Could one still come to the conclusion with which Paul begins Romans—that God promised in advance his saving message through his prophets by the Holy Scriptures—if this message proclaimed to the world the resurrected Christ?

But a break with Scripture was impossible. And it did not happen, first of all, because Jesus had freed the disciples from the Law and temple and bound them solely to his will. For Jesus did not attack the holiness of the Law. His command, where it touched upon what had been said to the elders, was not the dissolving but the fulfilling of the old command. But now, in place of one ruling as king in Jerusalem (as many expected) stood the Resurrected One. Could this still be regarded as what Scripture had promised?

In the report of Jesus' interaction with his disciples, we never find that he read Scripture with them and interpreted it for them. Their faith arose from what their eyes saw and their ears heard. When his opponents contradicted Jesus, they adduced Scripture against him; but even then his discussion with them did not become a discourse over the meaning of Scripture. Rather, his answer made clear how his will grew out of Scripture.

But now, as the disciples on the way to Emmaus must transition from faith in the One who tarried visibly with them to faith in the One who was resurrected, Jesus caused the Scripture to speak to them before they were able to recognize him. They must not lose the previous divine word just because the glory of the new life in God's fellowship appeared to them. Presumably, the interpretation of the Old Testament contained in the apostolic portion of the New Testament shows us how, during the days following the first Easter, the Old Testament promise grew to be intertwined with faith in the Resurrected One through the Emmaus glimpse of Jesus.

Jesus Quiets Mary's Longing for His Bodily Presence
October 18

Mary stood outside the tomb and wept. As she was weeping, she leaned into the tomb and saw two angels sitting, dressed in white, where Jesus' body had been, one at the head and the other at the feet. And they said to her, "Woman, why are you weeping?" She said to them, "They took my Lord away, and I don't know where they have put him." When she had said this, she turned around and saw Jesus standing there; but she did not know it was Jesus. Jesus said to her, "Woman, why are you weeping? Who are you looking for?" She thought he was the gardener and said to him, "Sir, if you have taken him away, tell me where you have put him, and I will go get him." Jesus said to her, "Mary!" She turned and said to him in Hebrew, "Rabboni!" (that means Teacher). Jesus said to her, "Don't take hold of me, for I have not yet ascended to the Father. But go to my brothers and tell them, 'I am ascending to my Father and to your Father, to my God and your God.'"

—JOHN 20:11–17

The disciples sought Jesus in the tomb, for that is where his body was. A person without a body—that is not how people conceive of someone. If you say "person," you say "body." That is why Mary's great grief intensified on that first Easter morning. Now her heart was completely broken, for his body had vanished. She reported to the disciples that his body was no longer there when she found the tomb open at daybreak. She lamented to the angels who appeared at the tomb that she did not know were Jesus' body was.

And when Jesus stood near her, she did not recognize him but requested that he help her retrieve his body.

But was it really his body that constituted her fellowship with Jesus? By his body Jesus made himself visible to her, but Mary most certainly would not have recognized him through that means alone. What revealed Jesus' presence to her was his voice, which spoke her name, his call, which said to her, "I know who you are." Right at the beginning of the report of Jesus' appearances, John indicates that Christ was not resurrected to furnish the disciples once more with a presence mediated to them through his body. His body is a necessity to show them that he lives and is the one who had been with them and was slain. But his body is not a necessity in the sense of being intrinsic to their fellowship with him. That is why Mary is not permitted to tarry with him indefinitely. He sends her to the disciples with the message that he is alive. For his final destination is the place the Father has prepared for him. By entering into the divine mode of existence and ministry, he from now on exercises his royal commission. He fulfills the promise given to the disciples: he is their Lord and will remain so in a never-ending relationship.

When Mary heard Jesus' call, it took away all her anguish. As he called her by name, so she calls him by his, expressing her stake in him: he is her Lord. Yet she cannot cling to him. It is not bodily contact that mediates her fellowship with him. It is rather his word, which is the witness of his love and the bearer of his grace.

The church should see in this that the Resurrected One was with her in that present time and was also active in her. What she receives is not just a glimpse of him but the message from him. Through this message he speaks to her, and his word becomes powerful within her through his Spirit. Through this she is placed into fellowship with him, and this confers immortality upon her. In subsequent times, followers of Christ will not consist of those for whom Jesus emerges from his heavenly glory to make himself bodily visible. It will rather consist of those who are "called" and who answer the call they receive with the confession that he is their Lord.

Jesus Rescues the Disbelieving Disciple
October 19

*Thomas (called Didymus, "twin"), one of the Twelve,
was not with them when Jesus came. Now the other disciples
said to him, "We have seen the Lord." But he said to them,
"Unless I see the mark of the nails in his hands and put my
finger on the mark of the nails and my hand in his side, I will
not believe it." On the eighth day, his disciples were again in the
house, and Thomas was with them. Jesus came while the doors
were locked, stepped into their midst, and said, "Peace be with
you!" He then said to Thomas, "Put your finger here and look
at my hands; reach here and put your hand in my side. Do not
become unbelieving, but believing." Thomas replied to him,
"My Lord and my God!"*
—JOHN 20:24–28

What had the disciples experienced? Was the person they saw really Jesus, really the one who had been put to death? "Unless I can touch the places where his body was wounded, I will refuse to believe that he has risen from the dead," said Thomas. He appeals to the right of reason. Our senses convey to us the way nature is and functions. Our knowledge of nature is expanded through our senses, and our knowledge expands through broader sensory exposure. Even insight into another person comes to us only insofar as that person discloses himself to us in perceptible ways. Women said they had seen Jesus; Peter and the other disciples said they had seen Jesus. But what good was that for someone who had seen nothing but Jesus' crucifixion?

But Thomas's appeal to reason could lead only one direction. It required him to terminate the fellowship into which Jesus had placed him with the other disciples. With this step Thomas placed himself in the greatest possible danger. Now it was absolutely crucial that Jesus be the Resurrected One, not only for the others but also for him. If Jesus wasn't, then Thomas's role as herald of the message was extinguished. He could not speak in the name of a dead person. He could only serve as herald for one who was still alive. This drove a wedge between him and the other disciples. Already in their circle he was a foreign presence, an outsider: among the believers he was the one who doubted, and among those who rejoiced he remained silent. If this didn't change, he would have to leave. Once more—as in the case of Judas—one of those whom Jesus had chosen was in danger of perishing.

It was Jesus' doing that Thomas remained in fellowship with Jesus until the point of his crucifixion. "I have protected those whom you gave me," said Jesus in his prayer (John 17:12). Therefore he remained now the Son of Man who came to save that which was lost. His new self-disclosure is the salvific act of the one who does not let those he chooses come to ruin.

Could Thomas not have been brought to faith by the internal working of the Spirit? Conceivably; yet Thomas had withdrawn himself from that word through which the Spirit makes himself effective in us. He desired the same plain look at Jesus that the others had been granted. Without this his role as apostolic messenger was incomplete. For that reason Jesus fulfilled his wish: Look at me and touch me, and believe! Even if all your thoughts terminate in the one you see, and all the goals you strove for are finished and your life is moved into a completely new mode, your Lord and your God appears before you. Believe him!

Faith Arises Without Seeing
October 20

Jesus says to him, "You believed because you have seen me. Blessed are those who do not see, yet believe."
—JOHN 20:29

By seeing, Thomas believes. This was also the manner by which faith was preserved for the others in whom Jesus planted it. But things would be different for the mass of persons who would embrace faith in the future. Otherwise, the task of Jesus' messengers would have been to set the stage for the Resurrected One to appear to people at some appointed hour. But according to what Jesus had said about his mission, there could be no prolonged period of Easter appearances following his passion. He stood in the service of God's lordship, whose goal is universal and is reached when all that is created has been made subject to God. That is what the new revelation in Christ will lead to. Upon this revelation was built all that Jesus said and did in the final stages of his earthly days.

But the preparation for this goal occurs through the Word. Therefore there must be believers who do not see at first, and such believers there will be. They are to be praised as blessed, because they receive that faith without seeing. Here is a greater display of the divine grace than what took place with the first disciples and Thomas. For such believers owe to the Word and its creative power the fact that they believe without having seen. What saves those who believe is their confession of the Word. For it is a manifestation of divine grace when the divine Word enters a person and releases within him the power of God. When our objection ends in view of what God visibly brings about, we bow before the divine might, against which we are unable to strive. On the other hand, when his Word wins us for God and draws us to God, God makes his love clear to us. It becomes evident that the gloriousness of the Christ consists in this: he is the Word of God for us.

This does not upset the inner disposition that Thomas reflected when he desired to see Jesus bodily. For the Word comes from those who have seen and leads to seeing. Those who do not see but believe are made into those who see when the one in whom they believed is revealed to them. True, something would be awry if the words that make us believe were nothing but the creation of our mental processes. Such a faith remains foreign to life and is, in fact, inimical to it. Jesus' call to salvation, however, applies to those who believe through his Word. And his Word does its work.

Jesus' Resurrection Is the Rebirth of Man
October 21

Praised is the God and Father of our Lord Jesus Christ, who has given us a new birth in accordance with his great mercy through the resurrection of Jesus the Christ from the dead, so that we have a living hope.
—1 Peter 1:3

When Jesus rose from the dead, the new man was created. For he was not just anybody from among the innumerable horde of the dead. Rather, he was one with a royal mission, because God was his Father. In him eternal life has appeared. Through this we are born anew. This is the end of death for us, too, and the beginning of eternal life—not because we were transformed and no longer bear the features of natural existence. Rather, through

Jesus' resurrection the grand hope arises in us. It is a living hope, because it is not the child of our wishes. Nor is it a feat of our mental ability that somehow arrives at this solution to the riddle of death. Rather, this hope arises out of an act of God that occurred in the sphere of our world. The result is that our hoping is a genuine longing to which assurance gives strength. This longing comes to govern our inner desires, to separate them from what is merely temporal, and to free them from what must die. From this hope our life now receives its structure.

God shows us his great mercy in all this. It is the act of the Merciful One that he accepts those who are dying, removes the destiny of death from them, and gives them a new beginning, a second birth, out of which a new life will arise.

But is there a connection between our lives and Jesus' resurrection, a connection that makes his resurrection effective in us in such a way that it can provide a foundation for hope? Peter's answer was this: The Resurrected One is the Christ, whose mission makes him the Lord of humankind. He makes this lordship effective through his message, by which people come to know him, are called by him, and become connected to him.

This was the manner in which Peter won a following for Jesus out in the marketplace of peoples. He offered life to those who gave him a hearing. For them it was an unshakable certainty that they had to die, and they were right. For the only life they knew was the one they had received via natural birth. But now the thing that was most certain of all is no longer true. Christ brings an end to life-destroying death. He brings eternal life into humankind. He thereby transforms those who had no hope into people filled with hope. And the hope that fills them is no myth. For he did not merely talk about this eternal life: he was raised from the dead.

Our Life Is Guarded for Us in Heaven
October 22

You were born anew to an indestructible and unblemished inheritance, which will not fade and which is being kept for you in heaven.
—1 Peter 1:4

Peter made those who heard him into people of hope. But he did not mean that their hope altered their present circumstance. If it had done this, it would no longer have been hope. Even those who hope stand under that law which applies to all and is at work in all the realm of nature, so that here there is no abiding existence. For the life that we possess as reborn persons is not inherent to us. It is rather our possession, just as an inheritance is our possession, and this inheritance is not entrusted to our bodies in such a way that the body nurtures it until it becomes visible. Nor is it infused into some means of grace, as if there were holy objects in which our life might be concealed. No, this inheritance is in heaven. For Jesus' resurrection is our rebirth, and out of Jesus' life arises our hope. But he is the one who lives in heaven—the one who has been received into full fellowship with God. There is our life: where the Christ is. For his life and the effectiveness of his grace are the power against which death can do nothing. They are stronger than our mortality—stronger, in fact, than all we are as natural creatures. That gives steadfastness to our hope. The inheritance stored up in heaven is not subject to attack. The One who promised life to us, and who will confer it, has entered into heaven. His is the sovereign authority of that grace that cannot be bound by the restrictions placed on nature. For that reason he is the victor and Savior who overcomes our death.

What this inheritance will be transcends our words because it transcends our experience. Peter speaks only of what currently restricts and defiles our lives. This is characteristic of natural life only; it does not pertain to the life we will receive from the hand of the One who rose. That inheritance is indestructible, and this distinguishes it entirely from what we now are and possess. For we decompose, and all that we do passes away. That inheritance is undefiled. In contrast, imperfection attaches to all that pertains to our bodies and our activities, so that truly pure satisfaction in these things is withheld from us. But where there is no corruption and no defilement, there is also no fading away. There is no regret of things done, no hindrance that prevents completion of what we start, no extinguishing of the joy that in this life is threatened by harm and wrong. No corruption, no hindrance, no termination of joy—these three things by no means describe the fullness of our inheritance. Yet they point powerfully to the magnitude of the hope that Christ gave to us mortals by his resurrection.

The Light of Life Has Appeared
October 23

I am the light of the world. Whoever follows me will not walk in darkness but will have the light of life.
—JOHN 8:12

Because the sun illumines the earth, the earth is the land of the living. The sun does not shine on the place of the dead; only darkness is there. This a principle grounded in nature. But a second principle follows: where the Spirit is at work, life arises. But where the Spirit is taken away, there is death. Where the Spirit is at work, there is place for the eye that sees the sun. For the blind there is no light. The secret of the life that is given to man appears to the seeing eye. That life is consciousness. To these two principles a third can be added: when the light that awakens life gleams, that is God's gift of grace. God's absence results in the removal of life and light.

For that reason, the herald of the divine grace is the light of the world. He is the rescuer of the blind who misuse God's gifts without regard for the One who grants them. He is the guide of the immature who do not know the purpose for which their lives are given to them and who learn from his instruction how they can serve God. He is the overcomer of the illusionists who beguile us when we pay attention to our self-seeking desires, who cause us to walk in darkness and not see where we are headed, because what they regard as their fame and happiness is sham and nothingness.

The One entrusted with God's commission in the service of his grace calls into the world: Learn from me! He could not be the messenger of light for us if he did not possess beaming rays of illuminating power. This power floods the world, and every human eye is created for the reception of its beams. For with God there is no partisanship. His light illumines not only noble persons; it does not come to us as reward for our merit. God's light shines for every person who comes into the world. The eye of everyone is awakened by the light; within each person the fountain of knowledge is made accessible.

But this is not given to us so that we can gaze upon ourselves and the world. We are rather to recognize the One from whom light and life come. Jesus summons all to follow him so they may attain to this. We must expose ourselves to the light in order for it to shine upon us. If we turn away from it, our lives will play out in darkness. To follow him is not a venture into the unknown, not baseless thinking, not fruitless striving without a goal. If we listen to him, we listen to the One through whom God speaks to us. And as we do his bidding, we obey the One through whom God has graced the world. In him shines on us the eternal light.

The Word of Life Creates Radiant People
October 24

You shine like stars in the world, for you hold fast to the word of life.
—PHILIPPIANS 2:15–16

The appearance of mankind reminded Paul of the nocturnal skies. The vast vault above is dark. Yet still higher the gleaming stars are strewn. He uses this image to paint a scene similar to another one found in his writings: the "night" that is far gone when a few people rouse themselves to make ready for the dawning day (Rom. 13:12).

The Greek philosopher once compared people to cave dwellers who sit in a dark cavern and see only the images that appear on the walls through the cave entrance. He thought this way because he rebelled against the ties that give form and limits to our intellectual capacity. Paul, however, had regard not only for the crests and troughs of concepts that toss in our consciousness like waves, for he gave man more credit than to picture him as merely one who thinks. Life was what Paul longed for, and man lacks this. He brings forth only fruit for death. Death speaks the last word over all people and over all that they do. They are doomed to pass away, just like all their accomplishments. Is human existence not a dark condition as long as the grave is its destination? Is man not the victim of a cruel joke when he subjects himself to desire that, in turn, propels him into ruin? And it is completely incomprehensible when he sets himself sacred goals—morals that he does not uphold—and institutes religious ordinances, when he has no Word of God that sets him in God's presence. As long as he does not know God, the One who is the first and the last remains hidden from him. Each person remains just one among the numberless masses who appear between the beginning and the end and then fade away, knowing neither their origin nor their destination.

But into this darkness God spoke the Word of life. The resurrected Christ is the one through whom he spoke it. This Word breaks through human darkness as a radiant light. Now there are luminescent persons who are like stars in the night sky. Now there are people awake, who recognize that the night is ending and lead lives that correspond to the day. They are the ones who have heard the Word of life in such a way that they do not leave its message unheeded. Instead, they draw from it the goal and the principles that guide what they do.

But they are not transferred into the light solely for their own sakes. Since they have become children who know the Father and servants who know the will of their master, and they bring forth fruit for God and not for death, they shine forth into the world. The Word that proclaims life to them gives them the strength to attract and win others. Man gives himself over to death only because he has no choice. He is all ears when there is talk of life—as long as it is not just a poet sharing his intuitions and wishes, but rather when the Christ, in whom life has appeared, speaks with him. Yet it is not the stars that bring an end to the night. Therefore, the children of light await the arrival of that One who will bring to the world the light of life.

The New Creation
October 25

When someone is in Christ, that person is a new creation. The old passed away. Look! Something new is here.
—2 Corinthians 5:17

The Resurrection does not promise humans the unending continuance of their present lives. So what does the death of Christ mean? True, through the Resurrection the effect of death is transformed. But this is not so that the old situation can be restored and finally terminate once more in death. Rather, the purpose is that what must die can be laid aside and become something new.

This is why Jesus' resurrection prevented the disciples from attaching the Pharisaic doctrine of the resurrection to the message of Jesus. For this doctrine sought only to remove what is not pleasing to us; it did not call for a new life, new participation in God, a new fellowship of persons with each other, a new righteousness. The death of Jesus pronounced a judgment on man, and this judgment buried the images of the future invented by human self-seeking.

A creation had occurred that brought an end to the old. The newly created one is the Christ. Since he regarded himself as man and related closely to those around him—so that their thinking and willing were ordered by his word and generated through his Spirit—the newness of his life was also effective in them. For them, too, a death separates their current life from their future condition, namely the death of the Christ, which shows them how God relates to them. But the result is not merely renunciation of their earlier condition; rather, because they have met the Resurrected One, it is the beginning of a new life.

This renders fully new Christianity's vision into the future. And in the same way Christians' fellowship with one another receives a new basis and a new regulating principle. No longer do natural desires and interests bring them together. Since they have received from the Christ the gift of God's grace, God's honor has become their shared concern. While rifts arise from natural self-seeking within normal social networks—to say nothing of rifts between different people groups—the fellowship that the Christ generates unites people far beyond anything possible within purely natural boundaries. It unites even those who are separated from each other because of differences in economic level and intellectual ability. It does not do this through the coercion of a legal ordinance and the power of a magistrate; rather, people are subject to Christ and live no longer for themselves but for God. They are capable of fellowship because they have received love. Such love, however, is not the production of natural occurrence but is God's work, creating something that is really new.

Section 16

JESUS BECOMES THE LORD OF THE NEW COMMUNITY

The One Community
October 26

*But you are not to be called "Rabbi," for you have
only one Master; you are all brothers. And you
are not to call anyone on earth "father," for you have one
Father, who is in heaven. Nor are you to be called* Führer, *for
you have one* Führer, *the Christ. The greatest among you is to
be your servant. For whoever
exalts himself will be humbled, and whoever
humbles himself will be exalted.*
—MATTHEW 23:8–12

A king unites his subjects. That is the task he is supposed to fulfill. In the case of the Christ, this task takes on worldwide proportions: his goal is to see mankind united in God. For Jesus' disciples and their office as heralds, this means they are to work to form one unified community, not many fragmented ones. For that community has one Father, from whose grace (available to all) comes the life of all people. Divine blessing comes to it through the Christ, and he is its sole teacher and *Führer*. There is therefore in the community no one who is owed the rights and privileges of a master, no one who may demand that his word and actions be the rule for the others. For this would splinter the community into factions, each obligated to its respective *Führer*.

What arises is not merely a community but a brotherhood. Yet this is not attained by accommodation and cheap conformity. That would have been to reestablish the Law. And that immediately would have led to the renewed dominance of the rabbinic leaders with their lordly demands that made the people dependent on them and subject to their demands. Since access to the Christ is assured from every individual through his Word, each person enjoys his own, personally conferred relationship with God, whose gracious working gives to each a full participation in the life of the community. At the same time he grants to each a freedom and commonality with others for which the natural family creates an example and pattern. Siblings stand together, conceived by the same father and sharing an indissoluble community. None has power over the other; each orders his own life.

Jesus explicitly impressed on the disciples that he was adding to their fellowship a calling that elevated them high above merely natural ties. Even among them, selfish human desire would rage. They would be tempted to suppose that their own elevation to greatness was the goal of blessedness, even if that elevation were reached only by humiliating others. To oppose this temptation, Jesus voiced the threat that God opposes human self-advancement; he calls for its transformation into self-abnegation. The common will, in which all find their meeting place, is the readiness to serve. In the community of Jesus, there is no such thing as a church office that is not bent on serving. Since Jesus had arrived at glory through his crucifixion, it was clear to all who believed that the obligation to serve is of the very essence of Jesus' doctrine and leadership. To twist service into some sort of ruling oversight would be to renounce Jesus.

Whoever Believes in Jesus Remains in Him
October 27

Abide in me and I in you.
—John 15:4

If the shepherd is struck down, the sheep scatter. With this parable Jesus described the disciples as he moved toward Gethsemane. His condemnation would scatter them. If the bridegroom is snatched away, the wedding celebration ceases. But now through his resurrection, he has reestablished his close ties with the disciples. He had made their community complete. Now it was unthinkable for any disciple to distance himself from Jesus. The newness of their community was visible in that he said to them not only, "Abide *with* me," but also, "Abide *in* me."

That was the command he had directed to the disciples when he asked them earlier, "Do you want to leave too?" (John 6:67). In those days their inclusion among his disciples occurred in response to his call, "Follow me!" But now this discipleship in the earlier sense was no longer the distinguishing feature of believers. No more was it like pupils following a rabbi, accompanying him in all his comings and goings. What rather characterizes disciples is not merely remaining *with* him: something far profounder has evolved, an abiding *in* him.

Now Jesus' ministry is freed from human standards and occurs in the manner of the divine activity. That brings the disciples into a dependence on Jesus that subjects their inmost beings to his influence. Not only do their outward fates and fortunes stand under his royal will; even their internal identity—the things that fill their hearts, their faith, their love—becomes his work and springs forth from him. Jesus' godly, strong love is able to bring this about. It is that very love that not only proclaims to the disciples, "You are in me," but commands them, "Abide in me!"

Fellowship with Jesus by no means robbed the disciple of inner mobility, nor did it take from him the prerogative of determining his own behavior. Individuality is not annihilated but created through God's presence in the natural domain of life. Accordingly, the disciple had the capacity to function independently of Jesus, to attach his faith to his own work or to other people, and to make his goal his own personal greatness or that of his church. To discourage him from turning in this direction, Jesus' command forbade him to disengage himself from Jesus to indulge selfish drives and intents. That would be to lose all that God is doing in him. He retains that activity's fruit by abiding, through faith and love, in the sphere of power of the Christ.

Who Are the Ones Who Belong to Jesus?
October 28

While he was still talking to the crowd, his mother and his brothers stood outside and asked to speak with him. Someone said to him, "Look, your mother and your brothers are standing outside and asking to speak with you." But he replied to this person, "Who is my mother, and who are my brothers?" And he motioned to his disciples with his hand and said, "Here you can see my mother and my brothers. For whoever does the will of my Father in heaven, that one is brother, sister, and mother to me."

—Matthew 12:46–50

Everyone said that Jesus' blood relatives have the highest claim on him. When his mother and brothers arrive, he will interrupt what he is doing, regardless of how important it is. The fellowship he establishes between himself and his disciples does not reduce the force of obligation to his blood kin. But Jesus did not leave the room where he was gathered with his disciples; mother and brother called him in vain. For there is a fellowship that is even stronger than the fellowship of blood: namely, the fellowship that unites those who do the will of the Father. Jesus said: They do the will of my Father in heaven—therefore they are brother, sister, and mother to me.

With this Jesus set his community apart from every other kind of close tie, whether familial or national, working class or artist, school or state. These connections help us fulfill our natural drives. But with Jesus there is no fellowship other than the one that makes his will into ours. This means that we exercise and carry out not our own will but God's.

This principle, however, not only explains how Jesus' intent was different from that of natural relations. It also separates, even in the church and at any time, what is alien to Jesus from what belongs to him. Jesus' *no* in this incident affected his mother and brothers. He was not denying an audience to enemies or defending his fellowship with the disciples against evil-minded disturbers of the peace. His family came to him out of concern for him. Were they not justified in seeking to advise him and take him with them, since he had evidently placed himself in the greatest danger? But neither a service performed allegedly for his sake, nor an honor accorded him, moved him to grant his fellowship, as long as doing God's will was not the greatest concern of those who called to him. Churches whose goal is to preserve their existence and their power are churches without the Christ. But those who renounce their own will and muster their energies so that God's will might occur through them—it is they whom Jesus has brought into unbreakable fellowship with him. As mother and child, brother and brother, belong to each other, so he belongs to them and they to him. An eternal bond connects them.

The Firstfruit of the Harvest Is the Spirit
October 29

We who have the firstfruits of the Spirit.
—Romans 8:23

The realm of mankind is a grain field in which the harvest will ripen for

God. Much that grows on this field was not planted by God and therefore dies off. And some of what God plants remains unfruitful and is cast aside. But the field contains not only vegetation planted by an enemy and seed that sprouts and then withers. Since the Christ has come, the harvest for God ripens in his own person. Before harvest day comes for the entire field, the firstfruits become ripe. The firstfruit whose life arrived at its God-intended goal is the Resurrected One. With his revelation to accomplish his royal work, the day of harvest arrives for all.

But to the church, too, a firstfruit was given, an initial ripe fruit, growing out of God's grace. It guarantees the coming greater harvest. This firstfruit is the Spirit. The church confesses with great gratitude and reverence, "We have the firstfruits of the Spirit." The church at the same time confesses here what it does not have but rather awaits. It has only the Spirit, not the eternally living body that will one day be formed by divine grace. Nor does it have a heart that is impervious to suffering and has no cause to sigh. Therefore it also does not possess a visibility that comprehends all and admits no contradiction, rendering every attack impossible. It performs its service in secret and is strong, although weak; indeed, precisely because it is weak, it is strong.

Yet in the church something new has taken shape that is not found in the broad stream of human life surging alongside the church. It has not only what nature confers upon it; rather, through what Jesus has brought to it, there are persons in it who are moved by God in their inner life. They receive their willing and thinking from God. But God's Spirit exists in the midst of humankind—this is a part of the harvest that will ripen for God in the church. Here the divine working attains its initial goal.

To be sure, the church is not so separated from those who live around and alongside it that they alone have contact with God. God's activities also lay hold of those outside the church, for they are creatures, made by God's creative power. Yet their destiny is futility. That is clear from how they are always waiting for something and can never be satisfied with what they are. They themselves do not know what lies ahead, nor are they able to burst the bonds that hold them captive to mortality and prevent them from coming to life. But now, because the Spirit has come to humankind, it is evident what the harvest consists of that ripens in the church. It is ripe when people arrive at the freedom and glory of eternal life. The firstfruit of the harvest, the Spirit, makes this evident.

The Powers That Create the Church
October 30

You have been chosen according to the foreknowledge of God the Father through the cleansing of the Spirit, for obedience and sprinkling with the blood of Jesus the Christ.
—1 PETER 1:2

It is not our natural qualities that grant us participation in the church. Birth and schooling, intellectual ability and enterprising spirit—these do not grant us entrance. What are the powers that do? Their origin is God's fatherly will, from which predestination arises, through which all that occurs in the earthly domain is called forth. Human competence does not suffice to create a church that would be God's possession; rather, that is God's work. For what arises in the church is the new creation, and this new form of being human is a matter of being children of God. Children receive their life from their father.

But how does what God foresees and decides become realized in our history? It occurs through the sanctifying work of the Spirit. The one who brings God's activity into our internal being is the Spirit, and what he effects is sanctification. What belongs to God is sanctified. Sanctification takes place by the Spirit making us God's possession. We belong to him.

But that does not yet fully describe how the church comes into being. What is the destination of the action set in motion by the Father's predestinating and the Spirit's working, which make us holy? This all leads us to Jesus. But why is he the one to whom God's fatherly love brings us through the Holy Spirit? Because of his obedience and because of his blood sacrificed for mankind. For Jesus is the Christ because he rendered obedience to God and granted us partnership in his death.

The Spirit makes us subject to God in the innermost reaches of our personal lives. He gives us a unique mode of thinking and willing, which he transforms to believing and loving. But that cannot take place by his locking us up within ourselves. How could we be united to God and live for him if we knew nothing apart from ourselves?

Therefore, the Spirit moves us in such a way that we come to Jesus. And it is fitting that we come to him, because in the power of his obedience and death, he attained the forgiveness of our transgressions. Without this we would have God against us. We cannot attain it for ourselves but can only receive it from God.

Entrance into the church, therefore, occurs as we come to the knowledge of Jesus by God's wondrous choice and by the leading of the divine Spirit. We put our trust in Jesus because he obeyed God and died for us.

Jesus' Unbounded Authority
October 31

Jesus came up to them and spoke with them, saying, "All power in heaven and on earth has been given to me."
—MATTHEW 28:18

Are there restrictions placed on Jesus' lordship? Many questions can be raised at this point. Are there people for whom Jesus has no significance because his Word is not able to touch them? Are their peoples to whom his Word cannot come because Jesus has no power over them? Are there some eras in which Jesus' message is effective but others in which it loses its power? Might there be opposition against which not only the disciples but even Jesus is powerless, whether in the natural and historical sphere or in the realm of spiritual forces that exist between God and man? Such reflections would have had deep implications for the disciples, depending on what kind of answers they received. All such misgivings were removed from the disciples' souls when the Resurrected One said: My authority to command and to exert influence is unbounded, in heaven and on earth. The actions of angels and men stand under his command and occur according to his direction. He makes everything subservient to his gracious or directing will. He makes all to be his tools, willingly or unwillingly, wittingly or without their knowledge. That is how God's lordship occurs.

In Jesus' interaction with those who called upon his healing power, he insisted that their plea not waver between hope and despair. He repudiated pleas that sought his aid "just in case" he could do something. He responded to requests that affirmed, "You can, if you are willing." But how is this now, since we cannot actually see Jesus? Are there even today no hindrances that he cannot overcome? Or must disciples content themselves with the hope that he will act on their behalf . . . if he is able. Jesus proclaimed to his earliest followers the infinite reach of his ruling power so that they would keep the faith in every situation.

There is, accordingly, no power of sin and of defilement for which the disciples would have to make exceptions, because the authority to pronounce the redeeming word is constantly in the Christ's possession. There is no enemy that can mount up against them without its time and extent being meted out to it by the Christ. With this knowledge Jesus gave the disciples the assurance and fullness of faith, and in this faith they built the church.

Was the disciples' conception of the reigning presence of God obscured by affirming the authority of the Christ? Hardly: who would suspect Jesus of claiming an authority that he arrogated to himself but had not been given to him? Since he had attained glory through the Crucifixion, there was no longer any room among the disciples for a Christ who stood in God's place and wielded some power other than what God gave him. In this power there was no praise of Jesus that was not also praise of God, no faith in Jesus that was not also faith in God, and no proclamation of a message whose beginning and end were not also the confession of that one God who was the Creator of all things. Precisely this confession gave the disciples the confidence that Jesus' will was more powerful than any other.

The Sending of the Disciples to All Peoples
November 1

Therefore go, make all peoples into disciples!
—Matthew 28:19

Jesus' authority is unlimited, and therefore so is the commission that he gives his disciples: Go to all peoples! That is the revelation of the new covenant that came in to replace the old, which had created a people of God by separating Israel from the nations. Now, however, in every place the eye of man is directed toward God, man's will is turned to God, and all hear the offer that they may place their trust in God. God's righteousness is revealed, which knows no partisan favoritism but extends itself to all. God's care for all people is also revealed, a care that does not forget the humans he created. For at the end of the divine Word stands the promise that all will be subject to God. This shining purpose of all that happens is confirmed by proclamation to all peoples of the Christ, who has come into the world.

The goal served by Jesus' messengers as they went out to all peoples was described to them with the directive *Make them into disciples!* They are brought into the same relation to Jesus as experienced by those whom Jesus called to him during his earthly life. By living alongside him, his followers came to know him. Now the disciples bring the knowledge of Jesus to all. His name, which expresses the manner and extent of his sending, is spoken and explained to them. They are informed about his demise, both his death and his resurrection. They become acquainted with him as the one whom the Jewish hierarchy had rejected and whom God had given over to death—but also as the one whom God exalted to his very presence and through whom he will one day reveal his glorious lordship.

But when Jesus is set within a person's field of vision, that person does not receive simply a historical report. When a disciple was able to accompany Jesus, he become not merely cognizant of his doctrine and an observer of his deeds. The word he heard gave him his will, and having a hand in Jesus' activity incorporated him into Jesus' service. It drew him into Jesus' fellowship, for service and for suffering, in this era and in the one to come. In the same fashion, the teaching that Jesus' messengers spread is, from beginning to end, a call that seeks to bring the hearers into connection with Jesus. Those who hear it become linked with Jesus by placing trust in him.

Who is the one doing the calling here? The answer is clear to anyone who has come to know Jesus. When I see what the Christ is, I know that the one who calls me is God. Those who became disciples received a share in God's revelation, and his revelation is the activation of his grace. In the commission and service of this grace the disciples go forth to the nations.

That places their activity under the same principle that governed Jesus' ministry. The disciples could not acquire disciples by any manner or means other than what Jesus himself utilized. He accepted to himself those whom the Father led to him. That is just how the congregations arise that gathered around the disciples. They consist of persons who by God's grace have responded to the apostolic call.

The Presence of the Christ with Even a Few
November 2

Where two or three are gathered in my name, there
I am in their midst.
—MATTHEW 18:20

Is it always huge groups that are bound together by their status as Jesus' disciples? Perhaps there are only two or three that his name attracts, because his name draws them to him and in that way binds them to one another. With this saying Jesus thought first of the situation the disciples would face due to the opposition of the Jewish hierarchy centered in Judea. But what Jesus promised remained valid as his messengers ventured far beyond the borders of Palestine. It came to light repeatedly that the lordship of the Christ is not of this world. His lordship does not accrue to him via the applause and decision of gatherings among the peoples. The newness of the Christ and his message, which renders him the opponent of our natural desire, was repeatedly seen in that his word was spoken to little avail, and the "success" of the apostolic preaching consisted in only a few recognizing what the name of Jesus revealed to them as God's gift and command.

Does Jesus disdain these little enclaves? Are they, in effect, an incomplete church? Does the church acquire sufficient validity to assert its presence only once it has become large? Even if there are only two or three drawn together by his name, he is among them. He promised his presence to all who committed themselves to him.

True, if they are linked solely by their own interests and self-seeking intentions, and if they establish a "discipleship" of their own making, then they would be on their own, not with him. But if their fellowship is grounded in his ownership of them, and if their desire is to do his will, then their modest numbers should not hinder them in their faith.

Still, they are fully conscious of their impotence. They have the world against them. Does their small number not work against them and weaken them? Jesus removes such concerns from them. Those who come to him find not only two or three others there but Jesus himself. They hear not only the views of two or three but Jesus' own call. They meet not only in their own insignificant power, under the jurisdiction of two or three, but

Jesus himself makes available his saving power on their behalf. Because he himself is with them, the drive and ability for growth is latent in every small assembly. For the one who is with them has been given all authority. And even if they remain small in number, they are not permitted to lament their modest size, discouraged and dissatisfied. No! For this little group is not alone. He is with them.

The Apostle Is Obligated to All
November 3

I am indebted both to those who speak Greek and to those who speak foreign languages, to the wise and to those who lack understanding.
—Romans 1:14

It was not commercial interest, research purposes, or even wanderlust that led Jesus' messengers to the nations. They came as their debtors. The nations have a claim on them that obligates them. For the messengers have what the nations lack: the word that saves them. They have received this not merely for themselves but for others, who rightly expect them not to leave them languishing in their sin and lost condition.

But don't they face insuperable obstacles? In the passage above, Paul is not speaking of the grave hindrances that weaken his word, of natural desire and its gripping force, of the foolishness of human thinking about God's being and will. It is not solely the incivility and animosity of man that creates opposition. There are also natural hindrances that appear to make it impossible for the apostle to get his message out to all.

What difficulties we face because of the diversity of human languages! In Greek-speaking regions, Paul could tell all who Jesus was, and thus it was his obligation not to deny the word to any. But he also came in contact with speakers of other languages, whether in the mountainous areas of Asia Minor or, especially, in the large cities. Is his obligation not simply impossible to fulfill when the person he encounters speaks another tongue? But is the message of Jesus to be bound to the vocabulary of the Greeks or any other people? True, every language has a unique tie with the people who speak it and takes shape within that people's history. But the word Jesus and Paul proclaimed to people was not coined through the experience of humans so peculiar as to be virtual aliens. And the substance of what they said was not something trivial, touching only the surface of lived life. When God addresses us, he speaks of what man is in truth. He sheds light on his actual concerns. For such verities every language has the capacity to coin terms that place items from one cultural setting into another's field of vision. That is why Paul was so confident that linguistic boundaries posed no insuperable hindrance for him.

But there is the further obstacle of people's varying intellectual capacities. There are bright people who with ease and eagerness appropriate a great store of knowledge. They readily understand something new that is presented to them. But there are others with much lower levels of mental ability. Should Paul remain silent before the intellectual elite, as if his word were dispensable for them and really beneath the level of their lofty achievements? And should he pass by those who have neither the urge nor the ability to become scholars? He brings to both groups, in fact, not just a doctrine, which the wise might dismiss because it resembles their prior insights, which they prefer to cling to, and which the less intellectually gifted might reject because it is too high and incomprehensible for them. What the apostle shows to both is the work of divine grace, which the wise cannot fabricate and the simple cannot dispense with. And what the apostle demands from his hearers and seeks to effect is trust in God. Faith is the response that every person, intelligent and average, is capable of. Because Paul summons every person to faith, he says that he is indebted to all, to bring them the word that can save them.

What Must a Guest of the King Do?
November 4

The servants went out into the streets to gather everyone they could find, evil and good, and the guests filled the banquet hall, reclining at the tables. Then the king entered to see who was among the guests, and he saw someone who was not wearing festive clothing. He said to him, "Man, how did you get in without banquet attire?" But he was

silent. Then the king said to his servants, "Tie his hands and
feet, and cast him into the darkness outside. That is where there
will be weeping and gnashing of teeth."
—Matthew 22:10–13

The disciples took Jesus' warning with them as they made off for distant destinations, spoke to all they encountered, and shared the great promise with every person. In this they functioned exactly as Jesus had commanded them when he spoke of the coming feast of God. After he has invited Jerusalem to his wedding banquet in vain, his messengers call to seek whomever will come, whether good or evil. But none is permitted to despise the king and disturb his banquet by coming to the king's table without festive dress. That would mark him as not belonging to those celebrating with the king; rather, prison is where that person will end up.

Jesus distributed his gifts in such a way that the purest and greatest that he has and gives will not become our undoing. These things can be a danger to us—pure gifts offered to us without conditions, free grace that does not inquire what we ourselves are, love that commits itself simply because it loves. Doesn't this permit us to remain as we are? Is it not the confirmation of our self-seeking, the much-sought means to undergird us in our wrong-headed striving? Obviously, what Jesus promises is highly desirable. Blessedness, freedom, healing of internal sin, access to eternal life—who does not gladly hear of such things? Who would not want to celebrate with the king? What hinders us, since he calls to each of us and demands nothing in return?

But this misconstrues the intent of the goodness whose goal is to lead us to conversion. It is not shown to us so that we might remain what we are. It rather appeals to us to transcend our base drives and free ourselves from coarse desire. For the king remains the king, even when in his grace he opens his banquet to all. And his banquet serves his glorification, even if it bestows great blessedness upon us. The fellowship of those who celebrate with him is not the place to put our contempt for God on display. Nor is it an occasion to assert our resistance against his command. Without our cooperation, God's grace comes to us and lodges with anyone who places trust in it. But to trust in it is to recognize its greatness and treasure its value. For it is to know that it is God's grace. One can no longer live as though grace no longer claimed him, as if it were some negligible trifle or extra ingredient of only secondary importance. Grace, once received, obligates. "You are guests at God's banquet, through which he glorifies the Christ." That is the goal to which life leads, to which all else is subordinate, if the way we live is to be worthy of our calling.

The Message of Jesus: First to the Jew
November 5

The message is God's power for salvation to everyone who believes, first for the Jew and also for the Greek.
—Romans 1:16

To everyone who believes!" Here Paul praises the unfathomable greatness of divine love and the unbounded glory of Jesus' mission. "To everyone who believes!" Paul's way forward was now clear, and he journeyed with tireless joy to every city and listener as the divinely commissioned herald proclaiming to all the saving word.

It would have enmeshed him in stifling complexities if he had felt compelled to lay upon his listeners preconditions that had to be met before he was allowed to speak to them the gracious word of God. Could he discern human intentions and determine who was worthy of God's gift and who was not? To attempt this would have been to contradict completely the will of Jesus. He did not come in order to spur men onward in becoming effective for God but to testify that God is there for man and is full of grace.

Yet a glimpse into God's radiant light does not blind our eye to the fact that people have particular identities. We do not dissolve their distinctives into a single mass of uniformity that robs them of what they are by virtue of history and heritage. Thus, Paul always dealt with the Jew as a Jew and with the Greek as a Greek. This distinction arose from their respective knowledge of God. The Greek venerated numerous myth-generated gods; the Jew confessed the creator God and his law. This distinction could never be erased, denied, or derided. It remained valid when the message of Jesus was spoken and when his congregation was gathered. Jesus had spoken first to the Jew, and his disciples did likewise. Jesus' first congregation was in Jerusalem. That was a logical consequence of earlier events, including the spiritual heritage of the Jews: they know the Creator, they know the law of God, and they possess a promise that has been proclaimed to their people.

The entire apostolic circle affirmed the principle "first to the Jew." Yet this attracted the bitter enmity of their Jewish countrymen. For this "first" implied "and then likewise to every other person." In contrast, many Jews sought a Christ and a kingdom of God that would be for no one but them alone. That lent strong passion to their self-seeking ambition against God's righteousness and all-sufficient grace. And as in other instances, false prophets arose here, Christians who expanded on Jesus' "salvation for all who believe" with the proviso "assuming they become Jews." But Paul did not go along with this false peace, because it implied that people made themselves blessed and conferred honor on themselves. Paul's rejoinder to all, whether fully Jewish or only partially so, was the same: first to the Jew, but never only to him!

There Is Only One Saving Name
November 6

There is also no other name under heaven given to people by which we must be saved.

—Acts 4:12

At Peter's trial, sacred names stood like an unbreachable wall between Peter and the honorable assembly in which the leading priests and the greatest teachers were gathered. "We are sons of Abraham." "We are Moses' disciples." Divine splendor adorned those who took upon themselves such a privileged heritage. But for their followers, the names of the great teachers served to deflect all criticism of their convictions: there could be no doubt that their ways were correct. Such sacred names are, admittedly, reminders of great divine gifts. But they guarantee no one a share in God's kingdom. There are sons of Abraham who have no access to the eternal people of God. They stand instead under the judgment of Jesus that some sons of the kingdom were created for the revelation of God's glory and will be banished into darkness. There are those who venerate Moses and are guardians of his Law, but whose righteousness does not withstand God's judgment, because they justify themselves. They are therefore incapable of faith, which is why Moses condemns them, since they believe neither him nor Jesus.

Yet there is a name that grants the one who trusts in it a great hope that will put no one to shame. While there are sons of Abraham and disciples of

Moses who stand under God's judgment, there are none who believe in Jesus whom he casts out. No one who keeps Jesus' word will fail to have his sins forgiven. No such person will fail to have God's will written on his heart. That is the sublimity of Jesus' commissioning, elevating him beyond all previous bearers of the divine word and revealing the magnitude of the divine grace. For it is the gift of free grace that this saving name circulates among humankind.

But does his name not express an indictment? It is the name of the Crucified One. Doesn't this point expectation in a future direction? Doesn't Jesus' cross force human longing to the admission that some other kind of Savior was hoped for, some new and different prophet, whose hallmark is not suffering and dying but sovereign victory? But those who turn from Jesus on account of his death do not know what they are doing. For precisely because he suffers the judgment of God, his name is the name that saves. This gives Peter the right and the obligation to demand that the Jewish leaders suspend their opposition to Jesus and let his word go forth freely. For to repress that name is to rob listeners of the one name that shows them how the day of God will be, for them, the day of their redemption.

The Same Blood Gives Life to All
November 7

From a single man he caused all nations of men to live upon the entire earth, as he had previously established specific times and boundaries for their residence.
—Acts 17:26

To proclaim new gods—what a damaging business! The inevitable result is division between persons whose unity is critically important, for they live in the same city. Is not every ethnic consciousness rooted in its own distinct tradition? Here the Athenians shared an even richer heritage than the surrounding cities. Surely it suffices for all who embrace it. Why grant a hearing to some new and strange gospel? This was the mood of Athens' leading citizens as they turned away from Paul.

But that ethnic vanity blinds. It conceals the origin of that people's life. The fountain of blood coursing through the Athenians' veins did not spring up in Athens. Their fellowship did not grow out of its own roots in self-gratification and personal power. It does not survive on its own. For mankind grows out of a common root, and the same blood flows in all its branches. This lies at the base of all ethnic manifestations. None is independent and self-determining in the way it arrives at its distinctive existence; no people has selected its own area to inhabit. Rather, they settled wherever the flow of history took them, often far from where they began, often driven by dire need, as when hunger forced their migration or when a more powerful people robbed them of their former territory. Every people experiences the divine regime in that it cannot create the conditions of its life for itself but simply receives and affirms them. And because it is not wholly self-sovereign but is subject to external leadership, it cannot deny the commonality of being and of destiny that binds it with all other peoples.

Just as ethnic origin is not self-determined, nor a people's fate decided and superintended by that people, so no people have the power to exercise discretion over God's Word. None can demand that his Word become audible first or exclusively for them, nor can any get away with rejecting it because its messengers are outsiders. All the peoples arose from one man, and in one particular human setting God revealed his grace. Growth abounds for all from this one event, so that the word spoken there is spoken to all. The One born in a particular people is made to be Lord of all. By being subject to his lordship, the peoples do not fall under some foreign domination; rather, they obey the principle that governed their origin and development and that gives them their existence as members of the human race. Their ethnic distinctiveness is a subset of an overarching human identity. There is a common goal pertinent to all, that from them all, the human race that is unified in God will take shape.

The Jews and the Pagans Are Called
November 8

Because they recognized the grace given to me, James, Cephas, and John (who are viewed as pillars) extended the hand of fellowship to Barnabas and me, that we might be sent to the nations and they to the circumcised.

—Galatians 2:9

In this text from Galatians, Paul writes of the time when he, Peter, John, James, and Barnabas agreed in Jerusalem on what constituted their common work and how their respective ministries differed. What they had in common was the Lord's commission to them. What differed were the groups to whom they were being sent. Each saw his goal clearly before him. Peter brings the word of Jesus to the Jews; Paul brings it to the Gentiles. None of them is able to say anything different from what they received from Jesus; that produces the fellowship between them that they share. Each speaks his message to a different part of mankind, however, and as a result the ministries of Peter and Paul never precisely overlapped.

Did they damage the unity of the church when they established these two different apostolates? Was the Christ not the same for the Jews and for the pagans? Was his message one thing here and another there? Yet the Jew was no Greek, and the Greek was no Jew, and it was forbidden to Peter to make a Greek of a Jew, since that would have defiled him. For the Jew had a holy inheritance to preserve. In the same way, Paul would have defiled the Greek if he had made a Jew out of him. Both Peter and Paul had to—and wanted to—make neither Jews nor Greeks, but Christians: people who received what Jesus had brought to them; people of God, who believed God and obeyed him; those who were reconciled with God and led by his Spirit; citizens of his kingdom. That made of Jew and Greek the one church. They were unified only in the Christ and not in their own manner of thinking and custom which had been given to them through their ethnic identity.

As far as the naturally grounded ties in which they lived, bitter enmity prevailed. An apostle who lived with Greeks like a sibling, and sacrificed his life for them, was considered by the Jews a betrayer of the Jewish people. The Greeks felt that an apostle who did not forsake the synagogue and the Jewish law was as a stranger to their ways and an enemy of their identity. The men and women whom the apostles had to seek were to be found in various locales. In order to find them, varying methods had to be used. The apostle who lived conscientiously according to the Law came to the Jew; the apostle from whom nothing was to be heard other than Jesus' word came to the Gentile.

And yet one church arose, and how could it be otherwise? What does man possess in comparison with what Jesus gives to him? What were the national unity of the Jews and the cultural achievements of the Greeks in comparison with God's grace and God's Spirit? Whether Jew or Greek, is it man who is first and who creates? God is the first and the last, God the Creator and giver, God who is knowable and present for us in his Son. That gave unity to the church far beyond the distinctives of all natural ties.

Jesus Prayed for the Unity of His Disciples
November 9

I pray not only for them but also for those who will believe on me by their word; I pray that they may all be one. Just as you, Father, are in me and I in you, they, too, should be one in us in order that the world may believe that you sent me. And I have given them the glory you gave me, in order that they might be one as we are one — I in them and you in me — so that they may form a perfect unity from which the world may understand that you have sent me and that you have loved them just as you have loved me.

—John 17:20–23

One condition had to be fulfilled so that the disciples could proclaim the word of Jesus: they had to be unified. John concluded the instruction that Jesus gave to his disciples with this prayer in which Jesus requests from the Father the unification of the believers. Thereby he expresses that it is beyond their capacity to produce unity among themselves. They have unity because Jesus requested it for them in prayer.

Is there still unification for those who are no longer held together through the Law's strong grip? Don't they necessarily become individuals and loners? Everyone is obligated to obey his own conscience. God's grace has said its word to every person in such a way that he possesses it personally, and it has awakened every individual to his own faith. No one is permitted to obey an alien faith; otherwise, that person forsakes his believing posture and trusts in the person to whom he has attached himself as a student. Even the believer retains within himself a hefty measure of self-seeking desire, and this desire does not seek harmony and peace, but self-importance and honor. This desire becomes the enemy of anyone who does not grant these things to it. Believers are commanded to "lay aside evil and envy," but that says to them that they are capable of this. For the desire of the flesh and that of the spirit fight against each other.

And yet the unifying of the disciples is completely indispensable. They want to show the truth to those who listen to them. But these hearers cannot prize their word as truth if their language is ambiguous. They call them to baptism to receive the forgiveness of sins. But how can it be credible that there is such a thing as forgiveness of sins if they are fighting with each other and not forgiving one another? They are supposed to lead the believers to one another so that a single fellowship arises from them. But no fellowship arises from those who are divided against each other. They praise Jesus as their Lord, but when they fight, they do their own will and obey their own opinion.

What is to be done in this situation? One thing that can happen—and which Jesus did—is to appeal to the Father, "Bind us together!" Strong assistance is given to us so that we can pray this prayer with faith, even though it completely transcends our capacity. This help comes from the Father's uniting Jesus with himself. The one who, in his sovereign grace, made the man Jesus one with him is also willing to unify those who are with one another in him. It is they whose task is to bring his word to those who are alienated from each other because they are alienated from God but now are called to peace with God.

The Jews Are Enemies and Beloved at the Same Time
November 10

According to the saving message, the Jews are enemies for your sakes, yet according to election they are beloved on account of the patriarchs.
—ROMANS 11:28

For the church, there could be no unification with Judaism. But it was just as impossible for the church to be silent about its origin in Judaism and to deny what the two communities of faith had in common. The gracious work of God shown to the fathers of Israel could not be forgotten, and the word of God spoken to them was a testimony of God that would never pass away. Didn't this create an impossible relationship? Can Christianity demonstrate to Judaism both enmity and love? Paul said that they are, in fact, enemies and beloved at the same time, and this is by no means a function of capricious mood and unstable disposition. Rather, enmity and love spring up here at the same time from the true apprehension of the divine work. Both are offered to the Jew for God's sake.

The enmity does not arise here out of jealousy. It is not grounded in some competition between Christian and Jewish theology, and it is not ignited by a comparison of the respective organization and successes of the two groups. God's message—and this is the message of salvation, which proclaims the only name that saves—is a message disputed by the Jews. This places on Paul and on all who accepted his message the obligation to be the enemies of the Jews. For the sake of the message, the Jewish Christian left the synagogue. With this he gave up not only participation in the Jewish worship service but also a share in the Jewish people and, not seldom, also membership in his own family. The price for union in this setting would have been giving up confession of faith in Jesus. This was unthinkable.

Yet it was also true that for God's sake the Scriptures remained in the church. Christianity had heard how God led the patriarchs, and it learned how Moses had proclaimed to the people the divine will. Because what is holy and what is sinful, what is received from God and what is made of ambition, coexist side by side in the Jew, he finds in Christianity love and enmity. The Jew finds both affirmation and contradiction of what he says. He finds support that makes it possible for him to serve God in the manner of his forefathers, and an aversion that always hinders his effectiveness in a true connection to God's work. At issue here was not a matter of the greatness of man, whether a person be a Christian or a Jew. The issue was rather the veneration of God, who treasures and protects his gifts and who provides the measure according to which Christianity distributes its enmity and its love.

It was not until the Europeans began to despise Jesus' message that they consequently gave up their enmity against the Jews and reconciled themselves to the existence of Judaism among them as an unpleasant necessity. For the end of enmity was also the end of love. What remained was self-seeking competition between the two groups.

Paul: A Jew Among Jews and a Greek Among Greeks
November 11

*Although I am free from everyone, I have made
myself their slave, in order to win some of them. Thus,
to the Jew I became a Jew, in order to win the Jews.
To those under the Law I became like one under the Law, in
order to win them — although I myself am not under the Law.
To those without the Law I became like one without the Law,
in order to win them — although I am not without
God's law but have the law of Christ.*

—1 CORINTHIANS 9:19–21

Imagine a valiant knight, one without fear or reproach. Or imagine a judge like the one Jesus told about in Luke 18, who feared neither God nor man. Such people might look down on Paul from their lofty vantage points and say to him disparagingly, "Why do you humble yourself around people? Why do you give way to Jewish preferences here and Greek ones there? Why trouble yourself? Why not just follow your own inner tendencies, your own way of doing things, and not worry about conforming to others' expectations?" The proud knight and judge and Paul do not have the same goal in mind. For the noble and powerful, it is enough that they represent themselves. They are not interested in persuading anyone. An exception here could be that the knight might be willing to convince someone to serve him and make himself useful. For this the knight has his trusty sword. Paul, on the other hand, wants to win people, and people of all sorts, Jews and pagans.

Is he trying to win followers, people who think just like him, a band of loyal supporters? No! For him, winning people means bringing them to Christ. A Jew or a Greek is won for Paul's cause when that person believes in Christ. When Paul converses with others, therefore, it is not Paul that he talks about. He speaks rather about who his hearers are and what they ought to become. They are Jews. How can Jews belong to the Christ? Paul portrays for them how one can be a Jew who pays heed to Christ. Or they are Greeks. How does a Greek obey Christ when he is accustomed to adhere to the teachings given to him by nature? Paul portrays for the Greek how one can live rightly in faith in Christ without the Jewish law.

Was Paul contravening the truth by operating this way? Were the objections valid that some made against him? Some charged him with deceiving the Jews by speaking with them as a Jew yet no longer believing that the Law should be the force that gives the Jew his will. Paul was also charged with pulling the wool over the eyes of the Greeks, with whom he interacted as someone who was subject to no guide other than his own reason, when in fact he possessed a will that was completely determined by and bound to the will of Christ. But why should love be rendered inauthentic when it speaks with the other person about what he is and should be? Should Paul rather have spoken as a self-seeking person speaks, only of himself, showcasing his own ego and intention?

Now, it is admittedly possible that some people got the wrong impression about Paul and regarded him as fully a Jew or fully a Greek just as they were. Paul could hardly prevent people from interpreting him according to their own misconception and bringing him down strictly to their own level. That in no way compromises the truth of what he says. Paul acted rightly and reasonably when he showed to Jews and Greeks a form of Christian expression true to both believing communities. Paul was always consistent, always compliant with the law of Christ. This law forbade him to lay his burden upon others. It commanded him to bear others' burdens himself.

The Church Arises Through Baptism
November 12

Make disciples of all nations by baptizing them in the name of the Father and of the Son and of the Holy Spirit and by teaching them to obey everything I have commanded you.
—Matthew 28:19–20

Disciples of Jesus are to be made among all the peoples. How will his disciples do this? Those whom Jesus sends out will baptize and teach. First they will baptize them, then they will teach them. The establishment of Jesus' message preceded baptism. The hearer was made familiar with Jesus; but that is exactly what happened when baptism was offered to him. If a hearer recognizes what Jesus is, then he desires to be baptized. When he receives baptism, he is inducted into the fellowship of the Christ.

So Jesus made the proclamation of the disciples to be a sermon inviting to baptism. By doing this, Jesus assured that their ministry would remain on the same track and continue in the same direction as the ministry he himself had exercised. This ruled out the possibility that his word might be used only to increase knowledge. Preaching, inviting hearers to be baptized, defines Jesus as more than a teacher who assists the hearer in attaining a great and true set of ideas. In baptismal preaching Jesus was present, demanding from the hearer a decision he can make only if he really is able to believe in Jesus. Jesus' right and demand to be regarded as Lord came immediately to the fore. The hearer who was interested only in having his intellectual capacity stirred up was going to decline the act of baptism that he was called on to commit. And with this he was also declining membership among Jesus' disciples.

The meaning of baptism that called hearers to conversion and offered them the forgiveness of sins took on full clarity in Jerusalem through Jesus' crucifixion; its clarity extended beyond the bounds of Judaism through the rejection of worship of the pagan gods. What had to be repudiated in conversion and what forgiveness required were perfectly evident. But through Jesus' death, the divine grace to which baptism testified had also received a much clearer depiction. The meaning of his death went far beyond what had been visible at the beginning of Jesus' ministry, when his efforts were directed to those among the Jews who had been baptized by John.

That is why the disciples felt an essential difference between the baptism they administered and the baptism that John had offered to the Jewish populace who came out to hear him along the Jordan. John's baptism administered hope in the coming kingdom. Now that hope was offered under the auspices of the Christ, so that the baptized person, the initiate, might receive what Christ had brought to the human race. Baptism did not take place in the name of the apostles. It did not obligate the initiate to the one who had invited him to baptism by proclamation and who perhaps also had actually baptized him. Baptism was administered in the name of the Christ. It was the sign that made public to the initiate the gracious will of the Christ and his saving work. That is why more was received through Christian baptism than under John's baptism. The latter only promised purity to the initiate through washing in water. Now the person baptized received the full effect of the work of the Christ, who makes people internally pure, because through his Spirit he makes them into believers in the fullest sense. Now the congregation, with whom the initiates were bound by their baptism, was the communion of those who had received the grace of the Holy Spirit.

Baptism Comes from the Triune God
November 13

Baptize them in the name of the Father and of the Son and of the Holy Spirit.
—Matthew 28:19

There was never such a thing as a silent baptism, and no one who baptized did so in his own authority. It was always obligatory to remind the person being baptized, the initiate, of who had empowered the baptizer to give this promise to him. This was a promise that completely superseded human authority. Because baptism did not mark the conclusion of religious instruction, nor the test of the knowledge that the initiate had acquired; the words that were spoken at baptism did not cover all kinds of concerns. There would be time later for the initiate to arrive at a complete grasp of all that the Christian purpose embraced. For through his entrance into the Christian congregation, he found the apostles to be teachers and leaders. Now the spoken word must show him in whom he had placed faith, before whom he had confessed himself as a sinner, among whom he sought forgiveness, and to whom he devoted himself in abiding subservience.

The name of the Christ was spoken in baptism; through his royal sending, baptism received its content and its force. But that which made the Christ head and Lord of the congregation was his divine sonship. His message was completely emptied if the Father was not recognized in the Son and if the call of Jesus was not received as the call of God summoning hearers into God's grace. Baptism comes from the Father, and for that reason it comes from the Son. The Son, however, has the capacity both to bring about the promised forgiveness through the renewing of people and also to bring about people's entrance into eternal life. He had this capacity because the Christ is everywhere at work by the Spirit of God—everywhere, that is, where his Word awakens faith. That is why the one from whom baptism comes and to which it leads is described by the triune name "the Father and the Son and the Holy Spirit."

With these words, the content of baptismal preaching and the saving power of baptism were expressed with a strong, all-encompassing formula. Even though baptism took place in many places and was performed by various individuals, this formula had the effect of uniting all who were baptized in the same faith and placing them into the one fellowship of believers. It assured that Jesus would not be sought somewhere off to the side from God, nor be honored as something other than God, and it assured that God was affirmed with every recollection of Jesus and that the veneration of Jesus was, without any attenuation, veneration of God. Baptism assured that Jesus would not remain for the congregation some form purely from the past, separated from them by a great historical distance. Baptism assured that the believing community trusted in the Jesus who was present and who is active in them by his Spirit. Therefore, the baptismal formula, when it is not only spoken but understood, expresses the magnitude of the gift of grace offered to us through baptism. The manner in which God makes out of us people who stand cleansed before him is this: in knowing the Son we know the Father and have a share in his Spirit.

The Ethiopian Is Baptized en Route
November 14

As they were traveling along the road, they came to some water, and the eunuch said, "Look, here is water. What prevents me from being baptized?" And he gave orders to stop the chariot. Both Philip and the eunuch went down to the water, and he baptized him.
—Acts 8:36, 38

The Ethiopian received from Philip the report about Jesus; now he desires baptism. It is therefore evident that Philip spoke of baptism in his instruction about Jesus. Perhaps he even mentioned baptism when he spoke of the beginning of Jesus' ministry and related how Jesus proclaimed the glory of God after John had administered baptism to the people and also to him. It is still more likely, however, that he spoke of baptism when he reported how the Holy Spirit transformed the Crucified and Resurrected One before the eyes of Jerusalem, and how in that same city arose the congregation that confessed its loyalty to Jesus. It is clear that the Ethiopian, by affirming within himself what he learned about Jesus, also received the desire to be baptized.

There was no condition that had to be fulfilled for baptism to be conferred upon him except for this: he had to have sufficient knowledge of Jesus to render him believing. When Philip now gives baptism to the Ethiopian, he marks out faith as ranking above all else that is found in our soul and places a value on faith as that experience through which God's grace visits us.

Yet it must be said that the extent and correctness of our thoughts have great importance for our believing comportment. What kind of knowledge did the Ethiopian possess? Because Philip had interpreted for him the fifty-third chapter of Isaiah, he had spoken with him about the cross and the resurrection of Jesus. In addition to this, he possessed some knowledge of the Old Testament. Did this suffice to justify baptizing him? This question was not posed. When at that time an evangelist had indicated how Jesus completed his work, he also knew himself to be empowered to address hearers personally and invite them to receive the gift of Jesus and to count themselves among the band of those who were bound to him by having received baptism. The person summoned by this message desired baptism as soon as he recognized what Jesus brought as God's great gift of grace.

Yet that gift brought with it obligation. The one who devotes himself to Jesus incurs guilt if he is not obedient to him. Will the Ethiopian be capable of fulfilling the obligations that became his with baptism? This was another question that appears not to have been entertained either by the one baptized or the one baptizing. They left no room for fear about the future. How could they at that moment estimate what being a Christian would mean for the Ethiopian once he returned to his homeland, and how he would have to respond there in the power of his faith? For both Philip and the Ethiopian, the one thing that mattered now was that they acted in faith in the presence of Jesus as those who belong to him and are obedient to his Word. The initiate is commended to Jesus' care and leading.

There was no church in the Ethiopian's homeland for him to return to. He will be alone and will have to do without fellowship and its powerful assistance. This baptism was not entrance into a church. The Christ, however, does not receive his saving power from the church. Rather, the church receives it from him. If the person baptized keeps his word, he remains in the fellowship of Jesus. Whether and how a congregation of believers will arise out of the word entrusted to the Ethiopian depends on Jesus.

Those Buried in Baptism Rise Again
November 15

Don't you know that all of us who were baptized in the name of Christ Jesus were baptized into his death? Thus, by baptism we were buried with him in death in order that, just as Christ was raised from the dead by the glory of the Father, we, too, might walk through the new gift of life.

—Romans 6:3–4

How can someone who has been baptized expect God to view him as cleansed and not impute guilt to him? How can the one who baptizes him assure him that he will receive this kind of grace? The magnitude of the promise that was associated with baptism made it a mystery. And yet as Paul rightly stated, everything depended on baptism not being something just endured with silent wonder; rather, it was received with clear knowledge and a good conscience. As a result, it grounded the believing comportment of the early church in an abiding way.

The promise associated with baptism became transparent only when it was recognized what had happened through the death of the Christ. The one baptizing does so on the basis of Christ's death, and the initiate professes faith in the death of Christ. For both recognize in that death how God regards fallen humans. God pronounces a death sentence upon man; therefore the Christ was placed into the grave. The grave makes it visible that life has ceased and nothing remains but what has been slain, which must also pass away. And because on that day the Christ was a corpse and could be nothing different, he was buried. That is why fellowship with him begins with the grave being prepared for those who believe on him. They dip down in the water of baptism. That this grave is prepared for them is not their doing but the work of the Christ. Because he was buried, they are baptized: "They were buried with him."

But the grave of the Christ was the place where life appeared, because God's great glory raised up the Christ. Therefore, baptism also becomes the start of life by serving as the grave of the one who believes. Graced with life, that person rises again out of the baptismal waters. Because he takes part in the death of Christ, he also participates in his resurrection. Not only is this new life the object of his hope; in faith he is united with the One who has eternal life because he died. Therefore he experiences the newness of his life in what Jesus' gift effects in him. Now something abiding—not subject to death—takes form in him, because it does not stand under divine condemnation. His faith, hope, and love remain. For this is God's work in him.

And so an all-encompassing turning point arises in the life of man through baptism. Previously, all he had accomplished stood under the judgment of God, the ruler to whom he must submit; he must bear fruit for him. But now that he belongs to the Christ, he has become a living person whose existence has meaning and force because it stands in the service of the Christ. Neither the baptizer nor the initiate, however, invests baptism with this effectiveness: rather, the death of the believer ends because the Christ died, and his life begins because the Christ rose again.

The Jailer Is Baptized in Prison
November 16

The jailer led them outside and said, "Sirs, what must I do to be saved?" They said, "Believe on the Lord Jesus, and you will be saved along with your household." And they spoke the word of the Lord to him and to all the members of his household. So at that hour of the night he took them and washed their wounds, and he was immediately baptized along with all his household.

—Acts 16:30–33

Because the grace of God is unsearchably deep, that grace shows us in baptism an unsearchable mystery. In order that it not remain a dark enigma, Paul gave those whom he baptized a clear picture of the great act of grace comprised by the death and resurrection of the Christ. Yet this does not mean that baptism became for Paul a laborious trick requiring all sorts of preparations to keep the mysterious deed from failure.

The Philippian jailer saw suddenly in Paul and Silas men whom God protected and attested as his messengers. In that very night Paul baptized him. Previous to this, Paul, as the herald of the Christ, spoke to him "the word of the Lord." He told him who the Christ is, the one crucified and risen, through whom God will reveal his lordship. But with Paul that was never a narration describing only something past. The story always contained a "for us" that riveted the listener, an element that depicted what the Christ did as the saving act on behalf of humankind. This made a believer of the jail keeper.

But he was not told to come back another day. Paul was right there now; there is no way of knowing whether he will be there the next day. The jailer must now receive the answer to his question, the answer Christ gives to the one who believes: Christ accepts you, and therefore you are pure in God's sight. His faith contains within itself a plea, which is not deferred to some later time; it receives now what it seeks. His faith seeks out fellowship; it is not thwarted. The Christ is with those who call upon him.

When baptism was prepared for the head of the household, he was followed by all those who stood in his service or were under his command. It can be asked whether all of these were as strongly moved by what took place as the keeper of the prison was. But Paul did not look for the saving power of baptism in the accomplishments of those to be baptized; he did not bind baptism to exacting expectations that laid claims on human knowledge and ability. When Paul founded a Christian house church in a single night in that Philippian jail, he made a visible statement regarding what should be said to the person who made request of the God who bestows grace. He responded to this question with the answer he had received from Jesus: "Believe, and you will be saved." Jesus turns away no one who comes to him. For that person comes because the Father draws him to Jesus. Those men in Philippi whom Paul baptized had been prepared for baptism by God himself. The mishandling of Paul and Silas, their songs of praise in jail, the earthquake, the terror of the jailer, his rescue by Paul, his willingness to hear the message of Jesus and to believe—all these were the means ordained by God. God awakened the desire for baptism. Without hesitation or delay, Paul responded to the divine leading. He proclaimed to those who still had authority over him as a prisoner the word of acquittal that would deliver them from guilt and death.

Baptism Makes the Conscience Clean
November 17

*Baptism saves you — not the removal of dirt from the body, but
the offer of a good conscience toward God through the
resurrection of Jesus the Christ.*

—1 PETER 3:21

The basic component of baptism, through which it makes visible to us the will of Jesus and renders our behavior pleasing to him, is this: a washing. The baptized person is washed; the congregation of the baptized is the congregation of those who have been cleansed. With this cleansing, it is not the body but the inner person that is freed from what earlier disfigured it and made it useless for fellowship with God and man.

What is washed away? A baptized person is cleansed from the conscience that condemned him. Here we must not think only of the judgment that measures our behavior against others' and rejects the harshness and injustice that destroy our fellowship with others. The most important achievement of our conscience is that it instructs us regarding our relationship to God. Man receives no sure answer from nature to the question of how God regards him. What is more, man suspects that God is against him, since he is bound to reject the evil that we perpetrate against one another. Man apprehends in his godlessness and evil selfish ambition that God stands against him. He experiences this frequently in bitter pain, aware that his life is a shambles.

The transformation of the conscience does not originate with man. Our relationship to God does not depend on our decision; God decides what he is to us. A new conscience presupposes a new relationship with God, and a good conscience before God presupposes that God's righteousness, which itself creates righteousness, places us before him at the place his gracious will has determined us to be. This occurs through our being baptized. That is why man is washed in the name of Jesus, so that he might experience in his relationship to God something different and better than what his evil conscience says to him.

For this, the forgiveness of sins is the condition. If we cannot believe that our sins are forgiven, the condemnation of our consciences will not be silent. But the acquittal from condemnation would not yet bring us the renewing of our life if that condemnation were not combined with the offer that Christ as our Lord reveals to us the will of God and makes us obedient to him. "Do you desire your sins to be forgiven you, and do you desire not to do your own will but the will of God?" Those are two questions that are posed to the person in order to invite him to baptism. The person who makes this offer to him is the Resurrected One. If his word gains force within us by our believing in him, then from his offer we receive a new standing before him.

The Disciples Teach the Commands of Jesus
November 18

Make disciples of all nations by baptizing them in the name of the Father and of the Son and of the Holy Spirit and by teaching them to obey everything I have commanded you.
—MATTHEW 28:19–20

When Jesus' messengers go out among all the nations and testify to all who desire the grace of Jesus that they will baptize them, they have rendered the first service they owe them. But there now follows a second responsibility, which is indispensable for those who become Jesus' disciples: the messengers teach them. And what they have to give them as the teachers of the people are Jesus' commands. They are to give them unabridged, just as he taught them when they accompanied him. When the word of Jesus gains mastery over a person—the mastery that the word gains when someone recognizes its truth—the direction of his thinking and acting now grows out of his faith in Jesus. The one who believes is ready to obey. But that person must learn how to conduct himself in a manner consistent with faith and with what Jesus commands him. It is the ongoing obligation placed upon the messengers of Jesus to teach him this.

Did Jesus in this way make his messengers into lawgivers for the church? The newness of the divine word, which was not a repetition or an improvement of the Law but the promise of God's ministry in Christ, was revealed most clearly in that Jesus' message implied the offer of baptism to every person. Forgiveness does not occur through the Law; rather, it is God's own gracious work. Inasmuch as Jesus invited those who had crucified him to receive his grace through baptism, and inasmuch as baptism was also offered to those whose lack of the Law separated them from the people of God, it was visible to all that he was the end of the Law for those who believe on him. And this took place in such a way that they received from him the righteousness through which God makes us subject to his will.

That is precisely why there does not exist alongside the commandments of the Christ some other will to which the church must be bound. His commands are holy for the church and must be fulfilled in it, because the church wants to arrive at life through him and enter into his kingdom.

Through the teaching office of the apostles, an office that is carried forth in the recognition of the New Testament, a school did not arise through which the new doctrine was pondered and formulated. Nor did an institute arise that was established on the basis of apostolic principles. What arose was rather a fellowship of people bound by common activities, whose goal was Jesus' goal, and whose honor and joy consisted in this: that the will of their Lord occurred through them, and their actions were integrated into his working.

Where the apostles are the teachers, no uncertainty exists regarding what Jesus commanded and which law all must obey. For his demise conferred full clarity upon his commands. Jesus commanded love. The rule that ordered the interaction of all in any changing circumstances was that they love one another. Those who were baptized entered through baptism into the brotherhood ruled over by the Christ, and because by nature they knew only selfish ambition, they responded tirelessly to what Jesus commanded so that it might become clear to them how love thinks and what love does.

Free for Fellowship
November 19

You were called to be free, brothers. But do not use your freedom as a means to ingratiate the flesh; rather, serve each other in love.

—Galatians 5:13

Christ set us free. That was cause for great joy, first for the Jew. For now the demands of the Law did not dog and threaten him at every turn. It was also joy for the Greek. For now he was released from the domination of a sinister tradition and from the judgment of his surroundings that made him aware of the necessity of moral compliance. Yet this was no victory of mere desire, as if it could claim for itself mastery over man. The one who believed recognized that he belonged to the Christ. To belong to him is to be God's servant.

All that the believer possesses belongs to God; he has received it from him. And God's is the grace through which he belongs to the elect and will attain salvation. Because all he is and has comes to him through God, his entire working capacity belongs to God. The goal of his actions now lies beyond his own ego. His goal is drawn from God's will, and the fact that he is a servant of God makes him free.

Accordingly, his freedom does not consist in possibilities that he invents and from which he may arbitrarily select. The possibilities before him receive their content through the ministry of the Christ, who fully determines the actions of those he has freed. Being placed into this freedom does not therefore lead the believer out of the congregation but rather into it. For the congregation is the work of Jesus. He is the one who builds it up, and in this construction project every member of the congregation plays a part. The acquittal that is pronounced over the believer at baptism does not make him into an anarchist. The reversal bringing that acquittal to the free-thinking Jew and Greek was no less momentous than the change brought by the message of Jesus to the one whose conscience had been chained by the Law. This message fully ruled out man being the measure of all things. There was no question of man being self-satisfied, having arrived at a pleasing frame of mind characterized by pride or perhaps self-denial. Rather, the sinfulness of self-will was now recognized, the will that created enmity between God and man, and brought him into danger of losing his life. The Christ became his protection against this. But he would have a share in the saving grace of Christ only as a member of the congregation. His freedom therefore consisted in harnessing his entire strength for the existence and growth of that fellowship.

All of this conferred a lofty goal upon the apostolic labor: it must order the fellowship of believers so as to serve as the shepherd and defender of every person's freedom. The goal was to present to God each person with his own faith and love in such a way that he lived for the fellowship. As the society of the free servants of God, the apostolic congregations stood as a new manifestation of human fellowship in comparison both to Jewish bodies and the organizations of the state. It became clear in the very constitution of the churches that in Christ a new creation had come into being.

The Law Attains Force
November 20

Do we, then, rob the Law of its force through faith? Not at all! Rather, we establish the Law.
—Romans 3:31

Everywhere, not only in Jerusalem but also in Hellenistic regions, Jewish believers brought their nomistic interpretation of religion into their understanding of Christianity. This mentality was likewise not foreign in principle to the Greeks. For they also regarded religion and morals as something dictated to them from the outside. Gospel freedom was a new standing that would first have to be learned, and which in Jesus' cross had an unambiguous foundation. There could no longer be a religion of performance for those who believed on the Crucified One. That was the end of all attempts to make man subject from the outside through habit and compulsion. The Resurrected One made visible how man truly arrives at a life reconciled with God. That is why the apostolic answer to all attempts at intermingling Judaism and Christianity was a decisive, strong *no!*

But did freedom from the Law consist in simply setting it aside? Was it not in fact fulfilled by virtue of Jesus' command having dominion over the congregation? If it was really righteousness that Jesus created in his church, then the Law was not done away with by him but brought into force.

What was the purpose of the Law? It condemned evil as judged by God. In the death of Jesus this judgment was carried out not only with words but also in fact. This judgment was affirmed by each believer, whose expectation for salvation lay in the Crucified One. The Law forbade people to be selfish and bound them to God's will. Through the faith placed in Jesus, the believer united his will with the Lord's and gave himself over to his service. The Law was given that there might be a people of God, who possess a saving fellowship for all in peace and in harmony. The congregation under construction from Jesus was united in love. How can there be room for injustice and wrongdoing where love orders relationships? In this manner the intent of the Law was fulfilled: guilt was acknowledged; evil judged and banished; God's sanctity honored and his will embraced; the fellowship created that united people with one another comprehensively, not just by physical descent and compulsion.

The Law consistently proved insufficient to bring about what it commanded. It always ran up against the opposition of our natural desire. It never arrived at the untrammeled expression of the blessing that it promised. For against it stood the natural human condition. Accordingly, the Law also could not remove from man the sentence of death nor convey to him eternal life. For that reason, law tended to get in the way of faith, for it stood between the guilty person and God. But now, because Christ stood where the Law had formerly loomed, the unholy effect of the Law was abolished. And what it made known as the will of God was fulfilled.

Those Who Believe Are Willing and Active
November 21

Work out your salvation with fear and trembling, for it is God who works in you to will and to act for the sake of his pleasure.
—PHILIPPIANS 2:12–13

By being accepted into the Christian fellowship, the one who believes is added to those who are being saved. He attains redemption when the Christ accepts him by his royal authority into his eternal congregation. But here no one could suppose that he would be allowed to waste his time. There is no life out of which service does not arise. There is no faith that does not shape behavior. Love that consists only of words receives no praise. How can a person carry God's Word in himself without harking to God's command? How can someone abide in the fellowship of God if he denies what God commands him to do?

Salvation or destruction arises out of what the Christian does; this must have complete irrefragable certainty for everyone who believes. It is impossible to regard as immaterial that which the Christian does. The kind of person we are for others cannot possibly be a matter of indifference for the Christian. With the grace that places us into fellowship with those who are saved, Christians at the same time receive the high calling to do that which salvation conferred upon us.

Accordingly, the one who believes has been given faith—yet at the same time has been graced with fear. Paul describes the seriousness of this with his customary formula "fear and trembling." He feared that which might rob him of salvation; the impulse to act against the command of Jesus would have been exactly that.

The one who believes has a resolute will to do what salvation brings to him and to avoid what brings corruption. This is because God works both the willing and the doing in him. When he draws his willing out of himself—which is to say from the flesh, from the drives that are inherent in the body—he does not bring himself into salvation. And when in the power of self-will, he sets about carrying out his plans, the result never causes him joy and honor in the judgment of Christ. Those who believe are not, however, left to themselves, and they do not receive the impetus to act only from the outside, from the human race and from their individual bodies. For they live in the realm of the power of the Christ. They live "in him," and they are moved by him in their thinking and willing. Therefore, they receive their will from the gracious presence of God, and because they do the will that has been given to them, they work out their salvation.

For it is not only their will that God makes courageous and alert. Such a will would do them no good at all if it remained nothing more than a wish and intention. For this reason God also prepares for them the opportunity to convert willing into doing. And he helps them move beyond the inhibitions that easily hinder us from action. It easily appears to us impossible to carry out that which we recognize as just and good. But when we have the capacity to do good and do not do it, it is sin. God protects us from this sin by giving us both the will and the ability to act.

But because both of these, willing and acting, are his gifts, both serve to please him. The measure according to which willing and capacity are given to us is not our wishes and ideals. What we have to bring about is distributed to us by the divine pleasure. But because willing and ministry are given for us to do, the church can and must be admonished, "Now work out your salvation with fear."

Our Willing and Working Are God's Work
November 22

Work out your salvation with fear and trembling, for it is God who works in you to will and to act for the sake of his pleasure.
—Philippians 2:12–13

It is clear to many peoples and likewise to many individuals who reflect about their lives that there is a destiny that exercises control over what they will and what they do. Without this, they can neither will anything nor bring anything to pass. But here they are thinking only about what determines from the outside the form of their actions and the course of their lives. In what happens internally within them, they see the realm of power delegated to them. They suppose there is little room for the divine activity in the interior reaches of the soul. Here is where those who glorify themselves form their intentions and carry them out with their own strength and, as a result, produce ground for their personal esteem.

This estimation of man has often called forth the objection against Paul that he is speaking rubbish here, something that is self-destructive. How can he say both "Work out your salvation" and "God gives you the will and the doing"? Moreover, how can he ground the first clause in the second, and therefore demand fear and action from us because God works the willing and the doing? This objection occurs to every person who is not reconciled with God and is aware only that his willing and doing cannot be pleasing to God. In that case, it is his desire that God remain far from him. Is it not already sufficiently bitter that a fate from outside him has disposal over him, against which he is powerless to resist? Could also that which is the most personal to him, that which he possesses in his soul, be handed over to God? He would indeed lose himself if he must endure God's working there, too. And his willing would no longer be his will, and what he does no longer his deed. Thus the pagans said of the prophet who lost consciousness and no longer knew what he said and did that now some divine power had gone into him. And thus spoke the Greeks, when they raved in wild intoxication, that now the god of wine, Dionysius, was in them. And thus spoke our German ancestors when fury laid hold of them and they swung their swords in all directions. They said that now the god of rage, Woden, was their *Führer*. Man should, however, preserve his sobriety and remain in control of himself. For that to happen, many say it is necessary that man's most inner being remain closed off from God so that he himself may be in control of his will and the master of his actions.

Now there is admittedly good reason for man to fear that God might become active in him. Even Paul warns: Because your will is God's gift, therefore, work out your salvation with fear and trembling. For it is dangerous to despise God's gift and to leave undone the service that is apportioned to us. But when it is granted to us to believe in God, we no longer see in God the destroyer of our lives, and we no longer see in his creative power the defiler of our wills. Through faith in God we have recognized in Christ the love of God. Love gives not just things, not just fate, not just assistance that helps us from the outside, but much more: love gives his Spirit, the one who awakens our thinking and willing, the one through whom his love is poured out into our hearts. In this way we remain in fellowship with God, a fellowship through which God will be the "Savior"—the one who works the salvation he calls us to work out.

Great Purposes
November 23

I pray that your love will grow richer and richer through knowledge and all insight, so that you will concur with what is best.
—Philippians 1:9–10

To "concur with what is best": the person who thinks this way thinks as love thinks. That was Paul's view. Under his leading, it was not some staid, serene Christian existence that arose, which was readily satisfied with what was easily attainable. But what is it that brings into love this state of dissatisfaction that wishes love to become always richer, always greater? Or, to recall a word of Jesus, what moves the person who has done everything that he is obligated to do, to arrive at the judgment that he is still only an unprofitable servant? For there is no Law goading us on; there is no greed driving us forward; there is no anxiety torturing us. Yet we find ourselves placed before unbounded possibilities.

In what way are they unbounded? They would not be unbounded if God's capacity had boundaries and if his grace could be contained by our measure. But he does not give the Spirit according to measure, and this gives free reign to the active power of our love. To be sure, the history of the church reveals much that gives pause. Much that is overwrought has been said and done; there has been much overenthusiasm, overheated misuse of the Bible which read into it fantasized ideas. There has been overenthusiastic willingness to come to the aid of others, a willingness that imposed itself violently into their affairs and sought to overwhelm them. There has been wrongheaded love, which committed vain and foolish self-sacrifice.

Love falls into this trap when it ignores knowledge and experience. It might be tempted to do this because knowledge and experience allegedly make love cold. But the fact is, love can become stronger through increasing knowledge and expanding experience. Knowledge and experience show a person what lies in the realm of his capacity. For none should attempt what he is not able to accomplish. But he should not query his self-love and indolence regarding what he lacks and what he might do; rather, it is divinely generated love that he should allow to instruct him. Even when this love attempts something momentous, it is our protection against religious overenthusiasm. For it cannot sever itself from the faith, nor can it forget that what it risks for God's honor must arise from the faith.

Therefore a limit is set to how far we can reach for lofty goals: the measure of the faith given to us. If our belief is genuine, our thinking and willing remain circumspect. On the other hand, if self-satisfaction in our achievement enters in, then all that we undertake becomes dangerous. There is no place for arbitrariness where action grows out of faith, for divine instruction always precedes genuine faith. There is faith only through the divine Word, and believing behavior consists in following what that Word sets forth.

With the admonition to desire not the easy and comfortable but the great and difficult, Paul touches on an issue of great importance for the life of the church. Fellowship can have a crippling effect on the church's members. A middle-of-the-road Christianity can arise, which makes people comfortable if they just follow custom. The hope that fellowship can be strengthened by the conformity of its members increases the pressure of prevailing usage. In such a setting, the person hindered by inner uncertainty finds no resources to overcome it. Are there assurances that accrue to love when it renders its service with commitment? There can be no certitude here; but after all, there is still faith. Faith places us under God's command and moves us to action through his will, and this is "the path that leads us to the most excellent way of all" (cf. 1 Cor. 13:13).

Powerless Faith Is Good for Nothing
November 24

What good is it if someone says he has faith but has no works? Can that faith save him?

—James 2:14

I have faith!" When the early church began, that was a highly significant confession. It implied weighty experience and bespoke glorious hopes. "I have faith"—that is the expression of someone who is asked to give account of his relationship to Jesus. Because of Jesus, Jewish parties were divided into those who had faith and those who did not. The one who said "I have faith" found a home in the fellowship of Jesus, for this community consisted of those who believed. And he appropriates the great hope: he places himself among the community of the redeemed.

To say "I have faith" meant something more than to say "I believe." The person who "has faith" is not like the one who called out to Jesus, "I believe," and then continued, "Help my unbelief," in other words, "Help me even if I cannot believe." "I have faith" implies a continual posture, such that the word of Jesus has become a secure fixture.

But in the text above, James warns the confessor of faith against the view that the outcome of faith—what faith calls for and what it expects of Jesus—can be taken for granted. On the contrary, it is certain that such faith cannot save that person when he has only faith and no works. But doesn't Jesus make believers out of people? Yes, but he also makes doers out of them, persons who carry out God's will. But isn't the church the fellowship of those who believe? Yes, but the reason it has assembled is so the work of its Lord will occur. But won't the Christ in his glory pronounce his blessing upon those who believe in him? Yes, but he will not recognize those who fail to do the will of his Father. But doesn't faith already lay claim to the promise? Yes, and so James warns those who claim to believe that they dare not hold their faith in such a way that they lose what they were promised. For faith is dead—it is bereft of effect and lacks saving power—if man does not do what he is commanded to do.

But is there such a thing as a person who has no works? Even if we allowed ourselves to be misled, so that we affirmed only pure doctrine and were nothing but Christian thinkers (as opposed to doers), we would still be acting agents, because we cannot dispense with fellowship. But James does not say that the person he warns about does nothing; rather, he does not do what a believer does. He does not act as one who has committed himself to Jesus and carries his Word within himself. For when such a person acts, he does not adhere to the Word. To be sure, he affirms it when it shows him the Christ and promises salvation. But he deflects its force when it shows him how he is to serve God. He has broken the Word into two pieces, and doing so because he has split himself in two. Half is open to the Word and half is closed. He has submitted his thinking to the Word, but he has not repudiated his selfishness. But our selfishness is the irreducible "I." That is why James, with irrefutable truth, says that there is no salvation for the person who believes but at the same time acts in whatever manner his fleshly desire dictates.

Love Determines the Actions of Believers
November 25

In Christ Jesus neither circumcision nor uncircumcision has any considerable force. But faith does have such force, as it becomes effective through love.

—Galatians 5:6

In Christ, in the domain over which he reigns, where he makes the decisions and distributes God's gifts—there Judaism and Hellenism mean nothing. And here Paul had in mind not mainly the ethnic and cultural difference but rather the boundaries set between them by God, which made them into two basically different types of peoples. For he speaks of the absence or presence of circumcision.

We can take this a step further. Compared to the domain of Christ itself the following are meaningless distinctions: Catholic or Lutheran Christendom; the pastoral office or civil service; Christian culture or a worldview dominated by nature and rationality. When Christ renders judgment, the only thing that carries weight is what he himself produces. And what he has produced in us is faith. Can it be of significance to us if we appropriate what the Reformation brought to the church? Certainly, if Luther assists us in coming to faith. Can the administration of a spiritual office be of importance to us? Yes, when it occurs in faith. Can it become meaningful for us when we become completely preoccupied with a worldly calling and the building up of the state? Yes, if as a result we do not come to faith. Can it be of significance to us if we lose ourselves in pursuit of knowledge of purely natural and immanent phenomena? Certainly, if we remain distant from Jesus, and God remains unknown to us.

But why is faith all that matters to God? It is not simply that faith makes us confess true belief, nor is it that faith fills us with great joy and lifts us to praise of God. Rather, faith makes us active. In what way? It turns us aside from what we ourselves are and do. It is the repudiation of our own work and the renunciation of our sinful desire. If faith were any less powerful, it would have no saving force. It makes us active by combining with love, and if love is in us, it governs what we do. James tells us that saving faith produces works and is not saving faith without these. The way he formulates it echoes the Jewish usage of that time. But James basically says nothing different than does Paul, who states that Christ recognizes faith as valid when the believer acts in such a way that it is clear he is being directed by love.

What would confession of faith in God be if we thought only of ourselves? What would renunciation of sinful desire amount to if, as a result, love did not reside in us? Our efforts to serve God would be futile if we were moved merely by coercion and fear. And of what value would be participation in the Christian congregation if we were not bound to others by the tie of love? You cannot have a God and at the same time locate the goal of life in your own ego. For believers there was, therefore, no other instruction or adaptation necessary to make the Christian congregation the place where the law of love ruled. The person graced with faith has also received the gift of love.

Love Arrives at the Proper Resolve
November 26

No one who serves in the military concerns himself in the
affairs of making a living; he serves to please the one who has
recruited him. But if someone takes part in a competition, he
cannot win unless he plays by the rules. The farmer who labors
must be the first to share in the harvest.
—2 TIMOTHY 2:4–6

In writing to Timothy, Paul cites three occupations that serve the welfare of civil society. This was so Timothy could gain perspective on himself and learn how he ought to respond in that hour. All three, the soldier and the athlete and the farmer, are familiar fixtures of everyday life. None of these vocations is lived out in isolation; none is restricted to the acquisition of knowledge and the cultivation of the Word. Each plies an activity that requires full engagement and demands one's full concentration and strength. The soldier does not also run businesses on the side so that he can get rich; he trusts his superior officers that he will receive an adequate wage. When the athlete competes, he is completely subject to the rules of his sport; to diverge from them would be to forfeit the prize. The farmer toils for the landowner, but in such a way that his portion of the harvest will remain intact; it is unthinkable that the one who gathers in the harvest would have no share in it.

That is how God deals with those whose privilege it is to serve him. All three similes confirm that service for Jesus entirely consumes the person who is called to it. There is no place for other interests. That person is claimed entirely by his work. Concern about one's own state becomes secondary. The obligations of ministry are unconditionally binding and admit of no evasion. The work is his means of livelihood and assures that he will not suffer lack.

What stands behind this abandon, this resolute will that brooks no divergence from the task, this assurance that the worker will not be denied what he needs to carry out his task? To pursue a secular vocation with this kind of commitment would be to love one's work. Paul reminds Timothy that he, Paul, who with Timothy carries the word of Jesus throughout the world, acts in love. Timothy will have arrived at the proper resolve when his will is drawn entirely from love. Paul makes clear to Timothy how love moves those who master their secular callings, how they are completely engrossed by them and fruitful in pursuing them. As a result Timothy understands how the person who stands under Jesus' command is to live.

Faith Makes Love Strong
November 27

*Understand what I say. For the Lord will
give you insight into everything.*
—2 Timothy 2:7

Paul's coworker Timothy was faced with a momentous decision. Would he resolve to journey to Rome to the imprisoned Paul and take his stand alongside the apostle in negotiations with the Roman authorities? If he did so, it would be a crowning touch to his fellowship with Paul, a final and decisive affirmation of his apostolic ministry. This would necessarily have great consequences for Timothy's subsequent work as well as for the course of the entire church.

Could the issue not be settled by a command from Paul? No! Timothy was not Paul's servant. He has his own relationship to the Lord, his own rights and his own obligations that he has to recognize, using his own judgment. He possesses the freedom that belongs to all who have learned to serve God. Paul does not disturb this relational state of affairs. He does not insert himself between Timothy and the Lord.

The force that generates the fellowship of ministry and suffering between them is love. But love does not dictate conditions and is not dictated to. It can only make request, admonish, and assist in clear apprehension of the situation and proper appropriation of resolve. Paul brought this about by reminding Timothy of the soldier, the athlete, and the farmer. Now Timothy must ponder what these figures have to teach him in his situation and in what sense he must imitate them. Paul must wait to see which direction Timothy's decision will take.

Is Paul uneasy about this? Will uncertainty plague him until Timothy reaches Rome? Paul has faith. He knows he is dealing not simply with Timothy, as if Timothy would make the decision in complete isolation. Rather, there will be the presence and leading of the Lord. He will give him understanding. This will do more than help apply the images that Paul has set before him. It will enable him clearly to recognize his duty to curtail all other work and sever every tie in order to fulfill his fellowship with Paul with complete fidelity right down to the last hour.

This furnishes the key to understanding how such a fellowship arose between these two men. It was the complete mutual commitment of two free parties. One clearly had the dominant position of leadership but did not wield arrogant authority. The other acted in complete obedience but did not compromise his freedom. These two closely tied individuals were both believers, subservient to the one Lord and led by the same Lord. Their common fellowship with Christ gave them their unity. Love bound them in a common and shared ministry; this was the work of their faith. Love held them together in the darkest of hours, because their faith bore them along.

The New Temple Is Built
November 28

Come to him, the living Stone, rejected by men but chosen by God and precious to him. You also, like living stones, be built into a spiritual house, into a holy priesthood, to offer sacrifices worked by the Spirit, pleasing to God through Jesus Christ.
—1 Peter 2:4–5

The true temple arises because the Word of God does its work among humankind. The new order of worship comes into being, one far removed from all that went before. Was it even thinkable that God could be worshiped without sanctuaries, without altars, without priests, without sacrifices? Yes, the old order was done away with. But this took place so that the Law might be established. The temple vanishes so that the temple might arise, and the priests are disbanded so that the priestly service might begin, and the sacrifices are suspended so that the true sacrifice might be rendered unto God. It is not holy objects that make God's grace known; rather, it is sanctified persons. And those persons exist wherever people are to be found whom the apostle led to Jesus.

In Jesus is found the cornerstone of a new, holy edifice made by God into a place where he reveals his grace. When people come to him, he makes "living stones" of them. They are stones because he receives them into his fellowship and places them into the temple he is erecting. And they are living stones because they are born again through the Word of God unto life, as Jesus himself is the living Stone, and as those who believe on him are united with him because life is given to him.

Believers who are related to the temple in this way are now the true priesthood. For honor accrues to God not through the gifts people present to him but through the gifts that he gives to man. The one who bears these gifts is the Spirit. The house through which Jesus is exalted is of a spiritual nature, because it arises through what man receives from the Spirit of God. With the pronouncement made to a person being baptized—that in baptism God cleanses that person through his Son and his Spirit—the distinguishing features of the Christian fellowship into which baptism places him were named. Persons come to Jesus through the Holy Spirit, who renders them believing with respect to Jesus. And likewise through the Holy Spirit, persons bring offerings to God that are pleasing to him, and are permitted to render priestly ministry through which God's will occurs. It is the Spirit who places God's law in their hearts. And he plants love there, which displaces the natural selfishness.

This sent a message to the congregation regarding what their first and highest priority must be. Their most important concern must be their call to worship God aright. Above all, they must be intent on the fact that God's grace becomes visible, and God's veneration takes place, through them. They do not have the capacity to alter world history or to radically reform civic institutions. Yes, their Lord is King of Kings and Lord of Lords. Yet the revelation of the lordship of God in glory is left in his hands, not delegated to the church. Nor does the church pursue some economic goal or become a society promoting successful material acquisition, even though under the auspices of love it is charged with the responsibility of ensuring that the basic needs of life are met for members. Yet the ground of Christian existence and the goal of the work of the church are shown to it by what the temple once was. It is the place where God's Word is heard and his grace received.

The Congregation Proclaims God's Mighty Acts
November 29

*You are a chosen people, acquired by God as his possession, so
that you might declare the excellencies of him who called you
out of darkness into his wonderful light.*

—I Peter 2:9

When the word that has become resident in the congregation touches merely temporal interests, and when other sources of information and instruction are regarded as more significant than what Christianity offers, the church's word falls silent. But her call is to proclaim the "excellencies" of God. That does not mean speaking of his incommunicable attributes or the like. In that case the message of Jesus would roar past listeners without their even perceiving what was said, much less their being led to faith. God's excellencies are the mighty deeds of God through which he has personally involved himself in human history. Those who believe in these deeds participate in them through what they experience.

Once they lived in darkness; now they live in light. What led them out of that darkness? The call of God came to them; in their benighted state he sought them out. And by the power that freed them the gloom was dispelled. The light that now illumines them is God's light, and his radiance overcomes all apprehensions and transports them forever into astonished wonderment. Gone are the idols; gone is their godlessness and unrighteousness; gone is their hopelessness, which promised them nothing but death. Who would have thought that God is love? Now they have fully apprehended it. Who could suppose that there was a justification for the condemned and a reconciliation for those who were God's enemies, so they could lay aside envy and hate and enter into the fellowship of love? And who had perceived that this age will terminate because God's glory will be made manifest? It is through God's great acts that man will be lifted high out of darkness into light.

In order to proclaim these acts, those who have been transferred into the light must speak of Christ, of his coming into the world, of his authority to bring people the call of God. They must tell of how he consecrated himself to God as a sacrifice and how in him the newness of life has appeared. That is why the tidings came of the founding of the church; of the sending of

Jesus' messengers and the signs that confirmed their word; and of the revelation of the Spirit, who conferred victorious power on the message of Jesus. These were all mighty acts of God. They bestowed upon the word of the congregation a necessity that never diminishes and a force that is always fresh. This word must be spoken at all times and to all persons.

This also made clear the boundaries that established which word must be excluded from the church: any word that trumpets the congregation's own achievements, places the spotlight on its greatness, or directs praise to itself. When such deforming temptations are avoided, the church's word cannot go wrong, as long as it continues to be led out of the darkness and God's wonderful light illumines it.

God's Witnesses Speak
November 30

This is the one who came by water and blood: Jesus Christ. He did not come solely by water, but rather by water and blood. And the Spirit is the one who testifies, because the Spirit is the truth. For there are three that testify: the Spirit, the water, and the blood; and the three are in unity.

—1 John 5:6–8

In Christian assemblies it is not only believers who address one another. Nor is it only the apostles who exercise leadership. For the message of Jesus and the doctrine that serves every believer are confirmed by three witnesses. Through them God speaks to the congregation in such a way that none of the three becomes the sole spokesman. The three are the actions of Jesus by which he made his mission publicly visible.

The first of these witnesses, whose testimony was received at the very onset of Christian experience, is the water. For Jesus came with water. The proclamation of Jesus arose out of a baptismal movement (that of John the Baptist) at work in Judaism. Jesus' baptizing with water and with the Spirit gave him the authority to proclaim deeds befitting a king. And by passing on to his disciples the ordinance of baptism, he united the believers into a unified congregation.

The second witness by which Jesus speaks to the congregation is the blood.

For alongside baptism there is a second action through which the things Jesus did become visible to the congregation: the Lord's Supper, whose testimony is one with that of baptism. Baptism brings forgiveness to sinful man, and the cup that the congregation drinks because Jesus shed his blood for it proclaims forgiveness to it. Baptism brings the beginning of new life, and the cup testifies to believers of Christ's fellowship with them, since in the power of his death he confers life upon them. Baptism unites believers into the congregation of the cleansed, and the cup makes them one body, which serves Christ for the establishing of his will. The testimony of the water and the blood, of baptism and the Lord's Supper, is unanimous. And now comes a third voice in addition: the Spirit, who makes baptism and the Lord's Supper to be true.

The Spirit brings an end to man's battle with God. It makes his will subject to God. The Spirit plants life in those who are sinful flesh. The Spirit gives the congregation harmonious relations and makes out of it the body of the Christ, which does his will. Without the Spirit, ecclesial fellowship would be untrue and the church's hope empty.

These three witnesses and their unanimous testimony add no foreign or novel element to the message of Jesus, as if Jesus' actions, repeated in what we call "the sacraments," were some magic potion to be added to his message. They are the offering up of the gospel, a presentation testifying the spoken Word to us. They have the force of witnesses because they are not only words. They rather grant us in active fashion a share in what the Christ did. In the same way, the Spirit does not stand beside the Word, as if the promise of the Spirit were a supplement and postscript to the gospel. The Spirit is the truth, to the end that sinners are made God's children by the message of life and by the offer of salvation. For through the Spirit there occurs what the Word describes.

The Church Is the Body of Christ
December 1

You are the body of Christ and individually members of it.
—1 Corinthians 12:27

The connection that binds the church with the Christ is fellowship of life.

How is this secret to be described? How can we express what the church is for Christ and what Christ is for the church? When Paul called the congregation of believers the body of Christ, he created for this community a richly suggestive image.

Doesn't man possess in himself a visible duality that exists in the closest possible unity? He is spirit and body and lives through the unity of the two. Through the spirit, man receives the divine impulse, and through the body he is rendered tangible and visible. The spirit is that which reigns, that which sets man in motion, while what man wills is carried out by the parts of the body. The spirit is singular; in contrast, the members are many and various. Yet they are combined as a bodily unity, because the spirit is in the body.

Christianity can recognize in this how Jesus relates to it and vice versa. Jesus lives in the form of God where God dwells; Christianity abides in the natural domain. Therefore, Christ is recognized and has his effect in the world through Christianity. His Word becomes audible through it, and his story is carried forth unceasingly. Through it mankind receives his grace and the gifts that grace brings. Through Christianity he bestows mercy on those who suffer, and he implants his life-giving Word in mortal individuals. But just as the spirit rules a person, so too the Christ exercises his rule. The church cannot animate itself or build itself up by its own strength. Paul noted that all he accomplished was fully the work of the Christ; for the church it is no different.

From the Christ the church receives unity, and the body is a visible image of what form this unity takes. Every body part has its function. None is dispensable for the others, and none is free from others in such a way that it could be dissolved from its interconnectedness. It lives only within that connectedness; what each part receives in return is its very life. This yields a fruitful analogy for Christian community. That community takes from each his self-seeking desire and makes it subject to the others. It establishes each one in the faith, gives him individual responsibility, and shows him his eternal purpose. It simultaneously frees and unites us. It leads us into freedom so that we find community and do not live for ourselves; it furnishes us with community so that we become aware of ourselves and have a life that belongs to us. Christian community attains this when it is nothing through itself but is bound to the Christ—without whom it resembles a body from which the spirit has departed.

The Truth Is Entrusted to the Church
December 2

The church of the living God is the pillar
and foundation of the truth.
—1 Timothy 3:15

When two soldiers fight it out from opposing trenches, there is no room for "truth" in their exchange. All their mental powers are focused on deceiving the other. To insist on truth in this situation would be suicide. But is this the case only when we are dug in, in combat, seeking to defeat one another? Are we not always exposed to an attack that could do us harm? So when can we put aside the lie and ruse by which we protect ourselves? Are we not forced in the end to think only of what strengthens us, is of value to us, and makes us rejoice? These are the standards by which we measure people and things. How can we concern ourselves about the truth, too? It is damaging to us.

But our world has now grown quite dark, for it has now been completely deserted by God. Whoever extinguished the truth put God to flight. Every godless movement is fundamentally a struggle [*Kampf*] against the truth. It is fundamentally indoctrination into lies and the cultivation of false appearance. At the same time it is the death knell to fellowship, the banishment of peace, the transfer of our social interaction into unending war.

For that reason it is the high, holy calling of the Christ to furnish within mankind a place for the truth where it cannot be put to flight, where, rather, it grips all with its riveting force. This place is the community of the living God. For people submitted to God are submitted to the truth, and those bound together in God are a community who contend entirely and passionately for the truth.

Here is how it happens: with mighty strokes the divine Word crushes and dispels all that makes liars out of us. But these are powerful forces that we cannot control by our own might. What is behind our lying? Our strong desires. Who restrains them and gives us a different will in their place? Hate lies; who removes it from the soul? Anxious worry lies; does it not dwell deep within us? Ambition lies; who frees us from living for the acclaim of others? Remorse lies; who heals the bad conscience? Pride lies; who puts to flight the falsifications with which we distort the picture we present to the world and even our picture of the world itself? All these questions receive the same answer: God shatters every compulsion that drives us to lie. To be called by God, to know him and be able to trust him—that is the end of the night in which lies wreak havoc.

But plugging only the source of lies would not solve our problem. We could hardly love and cherish the truth if its function were merely to show us our nothingness, guilt, and transitoriness. But the fellowship entrusted with the truth is the church of the living God. Through him it knows what abides, and is just, and will endure. It has given its entire, undivided yes to his power, which does not waiver, and to his grace, which does not fail. It, therefore, does not need lies to get along with people, for it loves. And it does not need illusions to deal with anxious worry, for it knows that all things work for good. And it has no cause to make a myth out of dying, for it lives. If asked, "What is truth?" it is not at a loss for an answer. Its answer is, Truth is the living God and all that he does.

Mythmakers Are Not Believers
December 3

*Command certain persons not to teach strange
doctrine nor to place value on myths.*
—1 Timothy 1:3–4

The young Greek churches were the site of a lively religious history. People established religion through a powerful vision. This vision answered to the desire to penetrate the secret of nature and the Deity by furnishing a malleably formed and colorful image. Thus, myth arose. The Greek achievement in art shows that many were gifted with a powerfully active imagination. This contributed not only to the shaping of stone into statues and structures; it also made the spoken and written word into its raw material, creating intellectual monuments that shrewdly attempted to interpret the incomprehensible.

Christianity gave new impetus to such attempts. Was the ultimate secret now not disclosed? God was manifest within human life and was at work in the personal experience of believers. But the revelation made the secret of the relation of the world to God all the more visible. In him who had been crucified and resurrected, God's grace appeared. This was enigmatic and drove people to invent solutions to the opaque aspects of God's work. But this only brought out what man finds in himself in the domain of his soul's inner existence. Paul accordingly banned myths from the Christian community. Those who speak the message of Jesus contradict those who compose myths. They tell them to be silent in the gathering of those who believe in Jesus.

What is the difference between myths and the message of Jesus? Myth gives rise to religion, which means this: man speaks about the divine; he attempts to elevate himself to God and form an idea by which he can describe God. He would also like to influence divine power, if possible, so that it might work in favor of his desire.

And Jesus' message? It shows us God's work, which takes place for us, and God's utterance, by which we are addressed and called into his fellowship. We do not appropriate the message of Jesus by an intellectual achievement that fills us with pride because we have grasped the most secret mysteries. Rather, that message demands that we hear it. It does not ground our life on the natural equipping given us by nature; it rather graces us with trust directed toward God, which makes us willing to receive what is given to us. It makes us willing to go where we are led when, through repentance, we are freed from our own desire. Do you want to compose, or are you willing to listen? Do you want to figure out what you think God ought to do, or are you willing to let God have his effect, so that out of you will arise that which God's grace seeks to make of you? Those are two divergent paths; each excludes the other.

What We Do Is Stewardship
December 4

Myths promote speculations rather than the stewardship of God, which occurs by faith.
—1 Timothy 1:4

When a composer of myths and legends enchants people or appeals to a smaller circle of listeners in the church, he discusses problems. This is a way to create astonishment and stimulate thought. For he has no intention of solving the riddle and replacing it with something lucid and comprehensible.

The images he sets forth are intuitions, not experiences, and what he invents are possibilities, not reality. Does God's call go out to people so they can inform themselves about the mysteries of the universe? Is that why Jesus was sent? Is that the reason he secures and builds up his church?

There are those question-lovers who seek to know how worlds arise and fate comes to pass, how Jesus received his divinity and proceeded from the eternal being of God, how the dead look when they are resurrected, and how God's glory will rule his eternal kingdom. Paul contrasts such question-mongers with those who administer the things of God. The church's mandate is stewardship of what belongs to God. The talk of the Christian faith is to speak the Word that is spoken to it. Christians did not invent it but heard it, and they should speak it as they heard it.

Does that Word therefore hover above our time as changeless irrelevancy? Critics of the church object to the rigidity of its teachings. This is a mistake, for the Word addresses even the most personal concern of each person and searches out every aspect of his specific situation. It therefore enters meaningfully into the manifold diversity that characterizes human existence. But the one who speaks to all is the one Lord of all, and he who is his witness is the one God of all. His Word has life-creating power; but this is not implanted into us so that we might have that power at our disposal. Rather, our efforts receive their standard and success through God's will, and our duty is always to make effective use of what is God's.

Because the Word penetrates people and creates faith in them, they become God's possession. Now they belong neither to themselves nor to others: they stand under God's leading. That makes the stewardship that is Christianity immeasurably rich and great. Those alongside whom we live are not made subject to our will—whether we lead them or obey them, teach them or learn from them, carry them or are carried and promoted by them. For by Christ they are made God's possession. All that gives us fellowship is the result of things entrusted to us, exchanged between one another, and producing among us the harmony of life. Our participation in others' life is stewardship. What is God's must remain his. If our selfish desire seeps in domineeringly, forcibly, pressing for recognition, then the Christian vocation is abandoned. But how could we desire something greater and more fruitful than stewardship in God's household?

The Believer's Body Is Offered to God
December 5

I admonish you by God's mercy to present your
bodies as living, holy, God-pleasing sacrifices.
This is your reasonable act of worship.

—ROMANS 12:1

Are we who stand under the word of Jesus forbidden to present sacrifices to God? Was it, then, delusion when peoples built altars and generously brought there what they regarded to be suitable for sacrifice? To be sure, Jesus' directive is clear: "Give to God that which is God's." We will not placate God with silver coins that bear the image of the Roman emperor. When man supposed he could find a gift that furnished God with something he lacked, that was an unreasonable act of worship. But we have, in fact, a possession formed by God's creative hand, yet in the fullest sense it is our own, over which we exercise full disposal: our bodies.

How we use them depends on the orientation of our desires. It can be subject to selfish greed, but it can also be subordinated to God's will. And it must be, as surely as God's gift of grace is life and this works itself out in love and service. For nothing proceeds from us and becomes action without the body having a part in it. True, this sacrifice lacks the perfection it will receive at the completion of life, when spirit and body are united. "The spirit lives," Paul said, "but the body is dead." But even now, because the blood gives us life, the believer makes something out of his life that far outstrips what people earlier presented as their sacrifice.

For this sacrifice is alive. In contrast, that which was formerly presented to God as his possession was removed from human use by being killed. That is how the unreconciled person operated as he lived in contradiction to God and had to keep God at arm's length. But now, because God deals with us as the giver of life, we honor God not by the slaughtered sacrifice but by the living body.

And while what is dead is not holy, this sacrifice is. It is truly God's possession, which he acknowledges as dedicated to him. So are there holy human bodies? Don't evil desires proceed from the flesh, and isn't death resident there? Yet because through Christ there are sins that are forgiven, guilty people who are declared righteous, and dying people who rise, so now there are also human bodies that possess the value inherent in all that belongs to God.

This sacrifice attains what every sacrifice strives for: it pleases God. What good is a sacrifice otherwise? But when we place our body at God's disposal, we do what pleases him.

This sacrifice retains none of the discomfiting aspects that were part of the old objects sacrificed. What good were the scorched meat and the shed blood? Even if the sacrifice was accompanied by prayer and an awareness of God's presence, it frequently involved meaningless words and actions. But now, since the body is dedicated to God so that he can accomplish his gracious and glorious will, the act of worship is freed from all unreasonableness. Now the constant care we must devote to our bodies makes sense and is not something profane. We know why the body has a right to make its demands on us. For it is indispensable for the service set before us.

Through the Body Arises Praise to God
December 6

Glorify God with your bodies!
—1 Corinthians 6:20

When desires overpower the body and subject it to their demands, it sustains a terrible setback. The body becomes the site of agitated passions, through which it is misused and defiled. It loses the honor inherent in the miracle of our divine creation, through which we possess our bodies as a stewardship. How much wisdom has our body encountered, and how often has this been wasted because strong desire overcame it!

Help for the body arrives in that it is made a sacrifice. This is no assault on its existence and capacity to achieve. True, our corruptible side, which hungers for sensual fulfillment, experiences the offering of the body as a harsh, painful deprivation. The hallmark of the Christian condition, rejection of self-seeking, shows forth forcefully in the handing over of the body to God's leading. The body is no longer master of the believer, who has handed himself over to his Lord. He thereby makes his body subject to him. That was expressed in the early church as believers called themselves servants of God. Whatever servants own—and our body is our greatest and most valuable possession—belongs to their master. Yet dispensing with our right to self-determination does not make the offering up of ourselves a bad thing. A sacrifice that we lament and bring only grudgingly is unclean. But how could irritation and resentment creep in here, since we see, by the giving over of our bodily conduct in God's strength, how glorious God's will is, how healing his grace, and how lavish his gifts?

We tend, of course, to limit this great outcome of the Christian condition to individual functions, like musical giftedness that creates praise hymns, or the ability to work and make money so as to be able to help others and maximize the fruits of fellowship. But this trivializes what Paul had in mind. Because the body is part of all we are and do, it renders essential service in all that God's grace brings forth from us. We experience the great truth that God's praise is enhanced through our bodies.

For that reason it is sin for the believer when he weakens and defiles the body. He can, in fact, cherish it and revel in it without turning away from God by caring seriously for it. Rather, this is to agree with his Creator, who gave him life by giving him the body.

Therefore, God's promise does not lead us to long for a bodiless life. Rather, we learn from Jesus' resurrection that resurrection is promised to us. Thereby we will receive for our lives in eternity a body as our possession and tool. It will not trouble and limit us but will reflect the Spirit's reality and be of service to him, to God's honor and praise.

God's Word Is Spoken in the Church
December 7

Serve one another with the gifts of grace, each as he has received, as good stewards of God's manifold grace. If someone speaks, let him speak because the words are God's; if someone serves, let him serve with the power that God furnishes.
—1 Peter 4:10–11

For fellowship to grow, all who are part of it must devote their strengths to the task. But Christianity lives through the constant exercise of two activities: speaking and serving. It lives from the Word, for its unity is not forced from the outside but arises within by the Spirit. Therefore, it constantly needs the Word, so that it might be of one mind, and act in unity. But since love is the force that moves it, its daily concern is also to care for others, through which is extended to all what they stand in need of. If Christianity lives from itself, it will also speak of itself and expand the power it furnishes to itself. But then it would no longer be the work of Christ. For he has made it to be God's people. It proves this by its speech, for what is said in it are God's words. And it proves this by its serving, for what it performs takes place with the strength extended to it from God.

Is this not too much for the church? Dare it offer all that is spoken in it as God's word? Does the ocean of writings surging out of the church bring us nothing but words of God? Natural existence, too, cuts a wide swath in Christian interaction and discourse, and in this domain each has the right to say whatever he wishes. But the work of the church occurs not through intellectual counselors and gifted orators, nor through teachers gifted with remarkable intellectual ability. Rather, it occurs through the divine Word that sounds forth continually in it.

It does not sound forth as one person here and another there receives a new special revelation. Rather, through the Word spoken to all, it becomes possible for not only human speech to be heard in the churches. Admittedly, the divine word is committed to the one, Jesus, who spoke the divine word in the land of the Jews in a narrowly bounded span of time between the ministry of John the Baptist and his own crucifixion. Yet after this word was given, it did not simply die away. That is not Peter's rule; he does not say that in the church nothing may be spoken except the sayings of Jesus, as if the repetition and interpretation of these were the only word given to the church. That would contradict Jesus' message that promises us his living presence and the ministry of the Spirit. His Word is not so tied to those bygone events that it disappears if they are gone. Nor does it float free from those events, as if it were a group of general concepts. Rather, his Word speaks to all at their levels. And in furnishing to all persons their goal and informing their judgment, it does not cease to be the divine Word. The boundary that separates the divine Word from our word is always easily recognizable. Man speaks of man, of what he desires, does, hopes, and suffers; God's Word speaks of God—and then of man, because it tells man why God is against him and what God does for him so that he can be for God.

The work of the church is salvific because it is able to speak God's word. In the same way, the church's work is made possible because God extends to it the strength it needs. The good it brings about occurs in part in its own circles and in part in fellowship with those sharing its common cause.

The Old Testament Is Read Publicly
December 8

*Until I come, make the public reading of Scripture,
encouragement, and doctrine a priority.*
—1 Timothy 4:13

Much could take place in Ephesus that Paul will support when he again comes there with the message of Jesus. Paul said that message was his own message. It had been passed along to him, although not only to him: he was not the only or the first apostle. Yet no other would speak the gospel in just the way it had been commanded to him. Now for Jesus' will to be clear and understandable to hearers, the Old Testament was of importance. Therefore Paul's helper should see that it be read in Christian assemblies.

Did Paul believe that the Old Testament was a validation of Jesus' message? His message can receive its validation only from itself. Jesus' work proves itself simply by taking place. It is true that the Old Testament word derives truth from Jesus' mission, but not that the message of Jesus becomes truth through the Old Testament word.

Or did Paul prescribe the knowledge of the Old Testament in the churches he founded so they could fulfill a part of their religious obligation? Along with knowledge of Jesus, was knowledge of Old Testament history a prerequisite for salvation? That would be an entirely different gospel from the one Paul proclaimed. That would again establish the Law, and it would do it in such a way as to endanger free access to Jesus. That would bring the Jewish scribe into the church as the overseer for believers, who would need to inquire of him regarding the knowledge required to take part in God's grace. But for Paul not even "works of the Law" were sacrosanct, nor did they contribute to justification for those who performed them. Much less did mere knowledge of the Law achieve this purpose.

Reception of the Old Testament in the church was a matter neither of proof for Jesus' word nor of the establishment of an ordinance serving as a prerequisite for salvation. Instead, it assured that God's word would be heard and his work beheld. Paul meant the same thing when he demanded that we perceive and ponder nature as pointing to God's power and divinity. What comes from God has unflagging effectiveness: his gifts do not become obsolete. When the word of God spoken to the Old Testament patriarchs is heard and the work done for them is recognized, the church's capacity to hear Jesus and cling to his word is enhanced. For the place Jesus stands was given to him through what came forth from God in Jewish history. Those to whom he was sent became what they were through the Scriptures. Scripture gave the nexus for Jesus' words and deeds. That is why the public reading of Scripture went hand in hand with the message of Jesus. For Scripture clarifies Jesus' work for us and deepens our knowledge of him. And anything that brings us to him leads us to faith in him.

We Are Admonished and Instructed
December 9

Until I come, make the public reading of Scripture, encouragement, and doctrine a priority.
—1 Timothy 4:13

Read the Bible with the congregation; encourage and teach them!" That is the means by which Paul's coworkers upheld the proclamation of the Christ and made it fruitful. Those who are suffering need encouragement. Those who are able to give comfort must not fail the congregation. Suffering must not have the effect of robbing their joy in Christ from those who suffer. He who encourages, strengthens those who have worry and care so they can bear up. For zeal can flag and love become tepid. The encourager counteracts such downward force. And when habitual sin gives rise to connections that defile the conscience and jeopardize fellowship, the encourager is the one who warns so as to enable a breaking away from these connections. When the awakening call of the encourager does not fail the congregation and all its members, Jesus' message is not spoken to it in vain. It becomes easier for them to remain in the faith. There was a place in the early church for the word of encouragement, because they walked in the light and stood under the lordship of the truth. The darkness of a perfectionism having no need of the word of encouragement did not exist where Jesus' word was heard.

But congregations need not only the willingness to act rightly but also insight into what they must do. This is the concern of doctrine. Even in the beginning stages of the church, many burning questions arose that call for a sober response from us based on clear principles. Such questions include matters of marriage—monogamy, which permits no casual sexual relations; mixed marriage, which protects natural ties beyond the distinctives of religious behavior; celibacy, which forgoes marriage in order to be completely free for service to Christ. And then there are grave questions that arise regarding the lot of the working class, since it could cripple the inner growth of the church if its workers were embittered and suffering from lack of respect. And what about the whole web of tough questions posed by the church's relation to the broader society, and the way the state wars against the church's influence?

Here the separation from earlier Christian ritual's influence on government has created weighty difficulties we can hardly avoid. The Jewish question likewise demands constant reflection; the construction of the conception demands great clarity from everyone. Congregations need to receive an effective mandate and exercise their disciplinary ministries in such a way that the church upholds purity, yet at the same time remains obedient to the saving will of the Christ who came to save the guilty.

Was it not enough when faith took shape out of the knowledge of the Christ? And was it not enough when the preacher announced the encouraging, sweet consolation of forgiveness to the shattered conscience? Was it really necessary, in addition, to undertake the deadly serious business of the formation of doctrine? Yes, for congregations were created to live, not to die. They were created to act, and for that they required clearly stated goals and carefully devised directions. The apostolic letters made it clear, inasmuch as the larger part of their content deals with doctrine, how seriously the leadership of the church at that time took up the doctrinal task.

The Old Testament Leads to Faith in Jesus
December 10

You have known from childhood the Holy Scriptures, which can make you wise unto salvation through believing in Christ Jesus.
—2 Timothy 3:15

There had been sages in Judaism since the time it possessed Holy Scripture. A sage was someone with the skill to interpret those enigmatic written symbols and to preserve what they signified in memory and understanding. When this wisdom consisted in a knowledge of holy letters that sought to elevate itself to domination over the people, Paul banished it from the church. A wisdom that generates corruption rather than redemption is folly, and through Jesus' crucifixion the wisdom of the scribes had become folly.

Yet this debased wisdom had by no means attained to an understanding of the Scriptures. A veil lay over this wisdom. It was as if the scroll had not yet been removed from the container in which it lay rolled up for safekeeping. The wisdom given by Scripture to the one familiar with it since childhood leads him to salvation. This casts light on what moved Paul to commend the Old Testament even to new congregations.

Knowledge of Scripture helps the church reach the goal upon which it sets its sights. The church's concern is for the day of God to be a day of salvation for it. But there are no other means for it to stand in God's judgment than faith, and no other person in whom to find the basis for faith than the Christ. Jesus is the one who empowers the church to hope in God. Knowledge of the Old Testament has precisely this effect: it leads to faith in Jesus and thereby to attaining salvation. The person who possesses this knowledge is like the good soil of the parable—those who hear and understand the Word. This person has learned from Scripture that God's grace comes to us as he speaks to us. He recognizes the contradiction between the divine Word on the one hand and the human outlook and the sin of the Jew on the other. He is prepared to accept that Jesus' mission called him to the cross. The Old Testament word and Jesus' message will grow into a unity for him, the former serving as promise and the latter bringing fulfillment.

But when the message of Jesus comes to the person who is a stranger to Jesus' spiritual homeland, he lacks the standard for assessing the newness of

Jesus' word. He will immediately mistake this newness and exaggerate it. He will mistake it and will not grasp what Paul meant when he said that Jesus has become a servant of the circumcision for the sake of the truth of God. He will not understand why Jesus was a Jew, and what binds Christianity with Judaism. Nor will he be able to assess what it means that Jesus has freed from the Law those who believe in him. Without knowing it, he will think in the same way that the Jew thinks and remain in the place where the Jew stands.

But he can also easily fall into an interpretation of Jesus that exaggerates the newness of his word. For Jesus to come, did there need to be a history preceding him? Why was he not simply able to descend from heaven to Capernaum? That would corrupt the message of Jesus by making it into a speculative myth, as if Jesus' gift consisted in stirring up our thinking and stimulating us to compose fables. The Old Testament asserts that God creates his kingdom in humanity. Since this kingdom consists of those who do his will, the Christ came into the world so that we receive faith and love from him.

The Old and the New Are God's Gift
December 11

Every teacher of Scripture who commits himself to the reign of heaven as a disciple is like the master of the household who brings forth from his treasure both new and old things.
—MATTHEW 13:52

The person who stands under God's leading is placed into a history in motion. What happened in Old Testament times is unforgettable, for God's Word and work do not pass away. The person who knows this cannot free himself from it; he must preserve it. But God's creative act stands behind not only olden days but also current times, and whoever stands under God's leading must also follow that leading when it brings about something new. He cannot simply harden himself against it based on the charge that it did not exist in former times.

The pious Jew praised the elders and appropriated their word and deed as law. The elders had received a special grace because God had spoken to them. The pious Jew no longer heard the voice of God in this way, so he rejected all that was new and passed over Jesus without a second thought.

Jesus showed his disciples how they fulfilled their mission in contradistinction to Judaism, by speaking of the master of the household who made use of both old and new. He does not act wisely when he leaves what he owns unused and seeks to use only what is new. But he also acts wrongly when he tries to get along with only what is on hand and is unwilling to make use of anything at all new. Jesus' parables also gave his disciples strong cause to act in accordance with this principle, because by his parables he showed them what takes place in God's reign and what will take place in the future. They must never lose sight of that. The insight into the divine working that he gave to them by the parables must always lead them, for this prepares them for all that will come upon them—yet not in such a way that it will bring them nothing new, for which they would need new instruction. They will receive that instruction and be able to lead the congregation aright when they neither despise the old nor deny the new.

Does this cause the direction of the disciples to lurch back and forth and their path to become crooked? All their thinking and action were rooted fast in what they had experienced at the beginning, when they were with Jesus. But the course of their work distanced them quite far from this beginning. The start of the church already lay far in the past when Paul preached in Athens and when he spoke before Caesar in Rome, and when John spoke the message of Jesus to the Christians of Ephesus. Had they cut themselves off from their beginnings? Had their initial convictions become worthless for them and obsolete? By no means! What the disciples had received through Jesus' instruction, what his crucifixion had revealed to them, what they had seen on the first Easter day, shone within them in undiminished brilliance. But then came the new. The congregations of believers among the Gentiles arose through the divine Word that sounded forth from them, and the biggest portion of the Jews paid no heed to the words spoken by the disciples. They could not tolerate the apostles remaining in Jerusalem. For their part, the disciples did not shy away from the new and, for the sake of what had taken place earlier, did not leave undone that which now had to be said and achieved. The word remained a united proclamation. The church that arose as a result was the one church of Jesus. For the old and the new came from the same Giver, and whether they received their word from Jesus or from the Spirit, it flowed from the same source. For it was God's gift.

Now admittedly the church later experienced turns and breaks. In some cases, the new annihilated the old and the primordial. In other cases, the insistence on what was already present cast out the new gifts of God. So it goes when the scribes are only overseers and are not also disciples who receive their instructions from the lordship of God. This lordship created the old and out of the old brought the new into being.

We Hope in God's Appearing
December 12

We await the blessed hope and the appearing of the glory of the great God and of Jesus the Christ, our Savior.
—Titus 2:13

All that the church thinks and does is permeated by its great hope. For everything is directed toward the one goal, to which God's royal ministry will lead it. Does the church's heart beat with anticipation at what is to come? Or does its vision of the future rob it of the ability to believe, or transform the church into a band of penitents who think they can reconcile God by their offerings? What we anticipate will bless us, for then God's glory and greatness will become visible to us. This will occur through the Christ's becoming manifest to us in his divine working.

Are we still completely ignorant of God's greatness and gloriousness? Creation is vast and the Creator glorious; grace is vast, as is the work through which God accepted us; mercy is vast as it injects his assistance into all our need; love is vast as it makes us into God's children. All this is true because what we receive from Jesus is vast and glorious. What he accomplished by his human life was vast, and what he extends to us through his abiding presence is vast as well. It is glorious and grand that we may live in him. We could not await the appearing of God's gloriousness if we were bereft of knowledge of it; we could not long for the Christ's arrival had we not recognized the greatness of his first advent.

And yet what a change it will mark when God is no longer invisible to us and Christ no longer hidden! Currently, the form of the world is determined by what is not God. God's presence becomes visible through man's plans being smashed, through man reaping the consequences of the error of his ways. Death has the last word. Now man exalts himself over the nothingness of existence so that he reigns supreme. Whether he does this by violence or by the strength of his words, he makes world history only through what he thinks and craves. Now there is no veneration of God without the pain of remorse, no fellowship that does not also bear others' pain, no love that does not have to battle selfishness and struggle with the urge to hate. No word is spoken that suffices ultimately, no knowledge gained that does not remain provisional and partial and must eventually be set aside. And in this world stands the tiny band of Christ's followers. It is beleaguered. It speaks his word often to no effect; it divides; it stumbles; it sins. It must cling to the word of Jesus and live by faith, not by sight. In what we are and live, the gloriousness of the great God and of his Christ is not yet revealed. We await that glory. We know that this is a blessed hope, since we have before us the miracle of divine grace whose marker is the name *Jesus*.

God Has Patience
December 13

God bore with great patience vessels of wrath,
which have been created for destruction.
—Romans 9:22

We wait for God. For what takes place within human history stands under God's discretion. But this is the offense that makes man the critic of divine sovereignty. If, however, we are critics, we have lost the capacity to trust God.

Obviously, many things happen that cannot possibly be fully in line with God's will, and whose outcome, therefore, can only be destruction. And yet such undertakings are sometimes permitted great success. Does this not present a clear contradiction to the notion of God's sovereign reign? What ought not to be nevertheless has existence, and things attempted in direct rebellion against God take place. And it is not only individuals who succumb to the illusion of their empty thoughts. Rather, vacuous and destructive notions become the normative ideas of their time, and like venerated rulers they determine the fate of their generation. In all of this we see that God has great patience and bears with even those who have fallen prey to death.

Now why do we take offense at this? We are impatient because we are unbelieving. We protest against the hidden God. He should be visible at every turn of the course of events, and since he is not, we have to wait for him and trust him. This is something we do not want to do.

But is God really hidden because of his patience? That was not Paul's conclusion, since he speaks of vessels to which the wrath of God had given existence and form. Even when the Jewish establishment was blinded and separated itself from Jesus, Paul did not lament the hiddenness of God. He rather praised God's richness and his wisdom through which all is ordained. If mankind goes awry and succumbs to death, he experiences God's resistance against himself. And through his opposition to all evil and human selfishness, God's working is present and perceivable. Paul raises no objection to this state of affairs. He is always united with God's will, whether that is wrath or mercy, and he is always willing to desire what God seeks and to be what God makes of him.

This unrestrained willingness to be at God's disposal is the precondition for faith. We cannot believe if we give way to the tendency to criticize and deride God's mode of operation. An acquiescence to God that respects his judgment is, however, not some difficult agony—at least if it is carried out in the fulfillment of faith. For the one who believes "has tasted that the LORD is good" (cf. Ps. 34:8). And he waits "for the appearing of the glory of the great God through the revealing of the Christ" (cf. Titus 2:13), who through his judgment will reveal to the vessels of wrath that God opposes them and to the vessels of mercy how rich the gift of the divine grace is.

How Does Man Become Free from the Workings of the Evil One?
December 14

We know that we are from God, and the world lies entirely in the one who is evil.
—1 JOHN 5:19

We are not equipped for Christian service if we do not allow this apostolic word to address us. It is often cited, but frequently in such a way that it does not result in truth and strength but rather makes people frightened and weak and extinguishes their love. What good is our activity if everything stands under the power of evil? Along this same line, the question is often flung at Christians, "How can you live fruitfully in natural life and take part in civic affairs if all you see around us is the work of the Devil?"

What does it mean that "mankind lies in that which is evil"? That means the human race is so oriented that in all its affairs it stands under the influence of a will that opposes God and that its mightiest representative, called the Evil One, is Satan. The human race occupies a place in which everything that happens in and around it is exposed to the permeating influence of the Evil One.

The one who brought mankind into this situation is God. And that is why with this verse from 1 John 5, not all is said about the world that can be said. Since the world is God's creation, it has life by God's power. What takes place in the world takes place under God's leading. Therefore, this word does not express the final goal of God and does not say what humankind will eternally remain. We have heard, through the message that Christ has come, what will become of it. The will opposed to God, however, makes its presence felt in the world. How far does its influence now extend?

Does it extend only to a certain part of the world? Is it only present in a certain portion of what takes place among humans? In government perhaps, but not also in the church; in the realm of religion, but not in the area of science? Or maybe it is present in places that are dirty, but not where things look fine and tidy. John, however, says "entirely." Everything that takes place in the world is intertwined with and permeated by evil.

There is no situation in the world that can be entirely in keeping with God's being, and no event transpires that actualizes the pure and unadulterated will of God. Nowhere do we find anything that could not possibly put us in danger. Nowhere is there a place where we might not be subject to falling, as if the one part of the world were dangerous, the other, in contrast, not dangerous, so that we, for example, are on the safe side of danger in the church but are near to danger in drinking establishments. Or is it the case that one vocation is dangerous, but the other is free of harm? No, there is no place where satanic ideas are not able to penetrate, and there is no person incapable of bringing us into contact with evil.

Therefore we do not free ourselves from the influence of evil by giving ourselves over to natural urges, trying to imitate some person whom we regard as a wise person, or taking pains to purify ourselves and making ourselves untouchable by any infection of evil. By God acting on us in his fatherly capacity and, by his Spirit, making his Word the basis of our lives, we gain freedom from dependence on that which is of Satan.

The One Who Believes Is Not Judged
December 15

The person who hears my word and believes the One who sent me has eternal life and does not come into judgment, but has passed out of death into life.
—John 5:24

Part of Christianity's mission in the world is to inform the world of God's judgment. The appearing of the glory of the great God occurs precisely as God's judgment extends over the whole of mankind and over every individual. May the church exclude itself from this judgment? Doesn't the church also need to demand that it be placed fully in God's light and receive his judgment? Has Jesus' promise made this demand superfluous for those who believe that they do not come into judgment?

The words "he does not come into judgment" do not mean that this person enters God's kingdom in the authority of his own righteousness. Nor do they mean that he has a different righteousness than the one God gives us through faith. Nor do they mean that he finds eternal life in himself. Jesus' promise is given to those who, because they heard his word, believed in God and recognized in Jesus the one whom God sent. If they believe, they keep his word. They act in such a way as to be responsive to faith, and they have life because they have received it from Christ, and they are freed from judgment through the One to whom God has delegated judgment over us humans.

A believer can never suppose his life has some basis other than God's verdict, which acquitted him, and the grace of the Christ, who received him into his eternal fellowship. Therefore, every believer will always remain in agreement with Paul, who completely repudiated the notion that he had justified himself. His conscience did not accuse him; it rather testified to him the correctness of his behavior. He knows that he acts as a coworker of God. He knows that he speaks not against but for the truth and that he does not tear down but rather builds up. "He knows"—but what difference does it make that he knows? What has eternal validity is not how he judges but how the Lord judges. If he were to depend on his own judgment, how would he still be a believer? Therefore, he must wait for the judgment of the Lord and long for it. For eternal life has its basis in God's judgment, and precisely this is what testifies of that word of Jesus to believers with which he promises that he will not serve as their judge.

With this, Jesus confirms to them the forgiveness of their sins, gives them eternally meaningful existence, and acknowledges the life that his word has conferred on them. This is the true life, the reception of which marks them as born of God. But by praising the truth and authority of his grace, he in no way casts darkness on the sacred majesty, which excludes all evil from its kingdom. He does not cease to be our judge because he is our Savior.

The Unpardonable Sin
December 16

Men will be forgiven of every sin and blasphemy; but blasphemy of the Spirit will not be forgiven. And whoever speaks a word against the Son of Man will be forgiven; but whoever speaks against the Holy Spirit will not be forgiven, neither in this world nor in the one to come.

—Matthew 12:31–32

Everything in our lives, even our sins, takes on deeper dimension when our lives grow out of our relationship to Jesus. What comes to us from him is made effective in us through the Holy Spirit. God becomes present and clear to us in such a way as cannot take place in our natural condition. We are received into the domain of his grace, which gives importance to our behavior, an importance far exceeding that of which we were previously capable. But this opens up to us a new possibility of sinning. God's gift always takes precedence over our sinning; God's work is always the highest element of our lives, and the work that we do always secondary. We can only misuse God's gifts after we have first received them. With the existence of the Spirit, God becomes perceptible to us in a manner that gives new weight to the question of how we behave in opposition to him. We are faced with a new decision. We can honor the Spirit as God's Spirit, or we can insult him. We can desire him, or we can refuse him. We can rejoice in his ministry to us, or we can resist him and, as far as we are able, hinder him and destroy the work he seeks to do.

But forgiveness is withheld from those who find it possible to insult the Spirit. This is the foundation upon which the congregation is built. The Christian message begins with its proclamation, since without it there can be neither faith nor hope. But how will this message become effective in those who wage war against the Spirit, and how will it free them from sinful desire? That is the work of the Holy Spirit. But some wish to know nothing of him, and they insult what he does. If they claim for themselves forgiveness, they make out of it an empty word, void of all meaning. That is why Jesus' mission encompasses both the assurance of forgiveness and its withdrawal. And the message that proclaims him as the Savior indicates at the same time that he is the administrator of judgment. His judgment upon the world and upon those who confess their loyalty to Jesus will take place in holy righteousness.

But when Jesus spoke this word of judgment, he at the same time made public his great mercy. He covers with his forgiveness the fact that men contradict him, insult him, indeed even blaspheme against him and harbor opposition that eventually ripens into hate. Therefore, he does not give up on man, for in the history of Jesus, God's revelation occurs as he takes on the form of humanity. But where God's Spirit is at work, his grace emerges with creative force into the field of vision of man. Through the Spirit, man is now unable to continue the fight against God; now he finds it impossible to hate and slander. Now he must give thanks and believe. Otherwise, he severs the bond with which God draws man to him. And because he is in a position to do this, the divine Word tells us that the day of God will be the day of the judgment.

The World Ceases to Be Worthy of Love
December 17

Do not love the world, not even what is in the world. If anyone loves the world, the love of the Father is not in him. For everything in the world—the desires of one's flesh, the desires of his eyes, and his prideful way of life—does not come from the Father but from the world, and the world and its desires are passing away. But whoever does the will of God will remain forever.

—1 JOHN 2:15–17

We belong to the world. It is necessary for our lives. Excluded from the world, we would be ruined externally and internally. Nonetheless, our relationship to the world is painful. It brings us hurt and woe; life in the world involves agony. It becomes clear in the confessions of those who are active in it with great cleverness, superior strength, and impressive success. This becomes audible through the lament that not seldom arises to this effect: we have acquired all we desired and enjoyed all there is to enjoy, and all was for naught. The end of it was futility.

The forces that move the world forward are easy to recognize. Above all stands the sinful nature with its insatiable desire. The body will be nourished and cared for. If it does not receive what it desires, the result is strife and even murder. If there is lack of food, the peoples attack one another and bomb each other's territories.

Yet there is another power that agitates mankind, who looks out into the immeasurable reaches of the worlds and is unsatisfied. How much there is to see there, and how splendid it is! Here man exercises his capacities of observation with serious intention and gathers knowledge; here he makes it into a tool of pleasure and makes merry.

But there arises from the inmost reach of the soul yet a third desire: man's necessity of making a name for himself. He craves admiration and honor. What would riches be if they could not be displayed to impress others? What would power be if it did not result in widespread acclaim?

That is what is in the world. In these things consists the world's common possession, the dominant feature of all times and among all races. With arrogant claims the world demands for itself and for its accomplishments a full measure of admiration. Only a fool, says the world, despises the good things that are attainable in the higher reaches of culture.

But now God's warning comes to us: Do not love and venerate the world, and do not value what is in it too highly! Why not? What is in the world does not come from the Father. And yet God gives us our lives by means of our bodies, and our eyes are his wondrous work, and he has placed us into the social setting whose acclaim and honor are indispensable to us. But what gives force and direction to all this is fleshly desire, and this is not an echo of the divine will but a construct of our own selfishness, generated by us in opposition to God. Man moves along in a direction that his desires give him, because he directs himself. Things are different when God's Spirit leads him.

Accordingly, we live in the world and take our place in relation to the various aspects of the world that drive it, yet without being able to set our affection on it. This is an uneasy situation that we accept because we know the world is passing away. It is not the abiding lot of man to be dependent on others and to protect himself against the emptiness of his days by letting his gaze sweep off into the distance, and he will not eternally quote those literary dramas that human vanity inspires in him. For worldly desires do not originate with eternal life but are part of that which is passing away. When revealed, the lordship of God will bring about that passing. That lordship will confer eternal life on whoever is not able to set his affection upon the world because the love of the Father is in him. This is a love that does not permit him to give high veneration to what does not come from the Father. More is given to him than what the Creator extends to us through nature alone. That person's life does not end in nothingness, for he does not serve the cravings that are passing away but the will of God, and this grants us eternity.

The New Order of Our Lives
December 18

The time is short. From now on let those who have wives be like those who have none; let those who weep be like those who do not; let those who rejoice be like those who do not rejoice; let those who buy be like those who own nothing; let those who use the world be like those who do not enjoy it to the full. For the form of this world is passing away.
—1 Corinthians 7:29–31

To have a wife or a husband, to have to weep and to be able to rejoice, to buy and to possess, and to make your way in society and to find a place there for yourself—Paul calls all this the form that characterizes the life of mankind in the present age. It repeats itself at every place in every time for every human life. That is what fills the existence of all, the great and the small. But this is not the structure of the coming world. In it humankind has other concerns and will be moved by other forces. At that time there will be an end to what humankind currently seizes with hot desire as the condition of its life and its welfare. What man cares for with endless love will terminate.

Now even at the beginning of the church, and continually since, there arose audacious thinkers who said, "So then, let's get out of the world! Have we not attained the right of citizenship in the world to come?" Therefore, let the congregation consist of people who do not marry. Elevate yourself into a stoic mentality that can no longer cry and no longer rejoice. Organize yourselves as a brotherhood of people without possessions, who no longer buy and sell but give to one another what is required and hold themselves aloof from what binds others to their people and their nation.

Was this the command of Jesus given to those who eagerly desired what he promised? No, that is the revolt of selfish desire against God. We speak against God both when we immerse ourselves in nature and when we want to remove ourselves totally from it. Both courses are self-destructive. But our call is not to destroy; it is, rather, to be that for which God has made us.

And yet, if Jesus' word has entered into our lives, our relationship to the world has become new. To take a wife or a husband, to taste suffering and delight, to acquire, to administer possessions and eke out a place in the world—this is not the only thing we have. All this suffices only for the little person, who seeks quiet pastures for himself, cares for his little heart, and builds a nest for himself, as if there were nothing other than or greater than himself, as if what this little person feels and gains were the most important thing in the world.

We who have listened to Jesus have a God; we have a Creator; we have a Father. For that reason, our lives are no longer circumscribed by the form of this world. To have a wife or a husband, to cry or to rejoice, to multiply possessions, and to grow stronger in the eyes of the world—we have concerns that are greater than these.

"So then," the objection comes, "you are saying that the things currently valued by humans are immaterial, making no difference. But why should we regard them with apathy? What does indifference have to do with the obligation through which God binds us to his will?" Naturally based relations produce no attachments as strong as those that arise from faith in God. There is no marriage more secure, no equally serious entrance into the joy and suffering of others, no use of material values that is as faithful, and no more authentic participation in the fate of the world than what faith in God enables us to experience. Yet this is not the only thing that can fill our field of vision. For our ultimate hope is set on none of it. We must take care so that there remains room in us for what is to come, not only for what is already around us. There must be room for the love of the Father, a love that sets its affection on what is of God—and not room for our sinful desire, which seeks and makes demands only for itself.

The Eyes of the Heart See What Is Promised
December 19

. . . that God would illumine the eyes of your heart, so that you might know the hope promised through his call.
—Ephesians 1:18

What is the object of hope? No eye saw it, and no ear perceived it. It did not enter into a human heart. For what is hoped is not seen; what is visible is no longer future but has attained an effective presence. Nature knows of nothing pertaining to what *promise* denotes. World history gives no clue as to what this promise is. Jesus has no visibility; he does not prepare a day of personal appearance for any of those who believe in him as he did, for example, with Paul. The church cannot set forth, even on the basis of its ministry and the richness of its life, what the Christ will bring about. What the church possesses is no sure indicator of what it hopes for. Yet it has received hope. For it has heard the call, and the call speaks to it not only about the present day. The call comes to earthly man and sanctifies him, but it orders not only his earthly existence. It reconciles us with other people and leads us to our brothers, but it unites us with not only people of like kind and hardship. For the call that has come to us is God's call, through which we are summoned to him, and the bearer of the call is the Christ, through whom the lordship of God occurs. That is what we experience; that is what the believer cannot explain away, because it has happened, and what he cannot forget, because it makes not only yesterday new but also determines all coming days. Therefore, with the call we receive hope, and with hope comes the question of what the object of that hope is.

If we know what we hope for, then the thing we hope for draws us to it. What hinders us is warded off, and we take decisive steps toward the goal. Yet our physical eye cannot tell us what the thing hoped for is. But does only the body have eyes? The heart has eyes too. There is an ability to see within us, and it fills our consciousness with images. This organ dreams and meditates when it lacks illumination, just as the physical eye sees nothing if no rays of light reach it. But there are other light beams besides those that enable the physical eye to make out images of the world: those that illumine the eyes of the heart.

Then the words through which the call comes to us open up their depths and show us the magnitude of what is promised. Then we see the glory of the divine kingdom contained in the name "Christ." Then his cross gleams in the light of a grace that removes all the distress of guilt. In the Resurrected One the power of a life appears that is eternal. The cry of victory goes up out of Jesus' challenge to the world, which informs it that God is against it. The small band of those loyal to him grows into an innumerable multitude gathered from all tribes. Those who wrestle with their sins become those clad with white robes of righteousness. For the message of peace of Christmas is then heard by all who have ears to hear. And so we receive the hope that the apostle called "living" and termed the beginning of the new life. It is bestowed on us when God's light illumines the eyes of the heart.

God Shows the Christ to All
December 20

Therefore God also highly exalted him and gave him the name above every name, so that in the name of Jesus every knee might bow of those in heaven, of those on earth, and of those under the earth, and so that every tongue might confess that Jesus Christ is Lord, to the glory of God the Father.
—Philippians 2:9–11

The sphere of creation encompasses immeasurably great diversity. In the heavenly places there are living beings who have a radiant knowledge of God and are moved by his will. And on earth there are living entities to which nature apportions their measure of life. They are placed before the invisible God and bound to their natural desire. And there are beings situated in depths where not only heavenly but also natural liveliness fails. Yet all these—above, below, and beneath—form a single whole. For there is one God, in whom they all have life and move and have their being. Therefore a shared experience is granted to them all from the will that rules over all.

There is One whom God shows to all, so that all recognize in him the One whom God exalts over all. That is the person who bears the name *Christ*. Through the royal mission given to him with that name, God is revealed to all, and the worship of God is given to all. By confessing their allegiance to the lordship of the Christ, people unite themselves with God's will and praise his glory.

For the Christ reveals and does not darken the glory of God, and his lordship perfects and does not suppress God's kingdom. Jesus has this name, which becomes for all living things a testimony to God's greatness, because in his fellowship with God he incorporates fellowship with man, and in possession of lordship he preserves the posture of a servant, and while possessing life in union with God, he was willing to die on the cross. Therefore he reveals God's glory pristinely and purely. This is not his own work; he has this glory because he was a servant, without his own possessions and not seeking his own will. His glory is not grounded in his insistence on power but in the fact that he was subservient to God. This is not the exaltation of a man who casts a shadow on God's glory because of what he has and does; rather, he personally, first of all, bent the knee to God in perfect obedience and worshiped none but God alone. Therefore God's will appears in him, a will that gives its glory to no other. And by God's power a grace appears that he created, full of glory possessed by nothing else in creation. And all that partakes of life is caught up in the one kingdom of God as it recognizes in the Christ its Lord. Since he becomes Lord of all, all is made subject to God. That is the message when the promise speaks of the revelation of the Christ; the one who reveals him is God, and those to whom he is revealed are the ones to whom God gave existence. They are all to recognize in the Christ the greatness of that One who gave them their being.

The Rulers of This World Pass Away
December 21

When he has done away with every rule and authority, Christ
will hand over the kingdom to God and the Father.
—1 CORINTHIANS 15:24

For Paul the statement that world history consists of merely contingent events would be foolish drivel. For he knew the one who is "sovereign over all things." Yet neither is world history in its entire sweep and in all its events a transparent display of divine activity. The magnificence of the divine power is not yet revealed to our perception, for in the realm of world history there is immensely much that appears impossible in natural terms, although not impossible in God's eyes. True, God's wrath is evident in human blindness and evil and the destruction that arises from these. But the revelation of his wrath is restricted in that man experiences not only that God opposes him but also that God, by his goodness, is patient toward him and calls him to repentance. In Jesus' time, God's righteousness, which gives us the fellowship he intends with him and with each other, remained a mystery. God's Word spoke of it from the beginning, but it first became truly perceptible for believers by the outcome of the history of Jesus. And then the grace of God, which does not hand us over to ourselves but places his love in our hearts, is bestowed on us by the Spirit. But in world history it is not the Spirit who is visible and effective but the flesh. That is the riddle of world history: it stands under God's governance yet plays out in such a way that it does not bring forth God's revelation and glorification.

Spiritual powers exist, therefore, between God and man. He has granted them a certain dominion. They are rulers God has established, but they are not commissioned to carry out his full and entire will. That is why the Christ is placed over mankind in godlike power with the call to rule. And a world history will unfold that is different from the one we presently observe and endure. For that is the destiny of humans placed in the hands of the grace that heals all and the righteousness that sets everything straight.

What a transformation is foretold of all our associations! Currently, God's glory is obscured everywhere we look: on battlefields, in art halls, in academies of science—and still more in seats of political power and most of all in centers of worship. Every great person with the power to steer the destiny of his people confirms how man falls short. Unbridled selfishness disfigures all that takes place as we see at all times how strong passions move the nations to smash existing orders to pieces and attempt to create a new one. This is seen also in the more tranquil pursuits of knowledge and artistic beauty, which are of valuable service to all but also bring forth much that is damaging.

But then the One who will have lordship brings into the world the light that darkness will no longer withstand. He will speak the word that all will obey. He will exercise the judgment that gives mankind purity and create that life over which death no longer possesses power. Yet here Paul falls silent. His commission does not include describing the Christ's royal ministry; he proclaims the Crucified One and shows the world what came into being through him.

Christ Hands over Lordship to God
December 22

When everything has been subjected to him, the Son will also subject himself to the One who placed everything in subjection to him, so that God might be all in all.

—1 Corinthians 15:28

When God shows the Christ to all the world, no enemy will withstand him, none of the power brokers who now make world history—not even death, which presently dictates to all life its form and end. And yet with this, Paul still did not speak the last and most glorious word concerning the destination to which God will bring the world through the Christ. What is even greater than Christ's victory over all opposition, more glorious than the Christ's lordship, which makes its presence felt in all mankind? Greater than victory and lordship is that the one who has become the Lord of the world gives honor to, and submits himself to, the One who gave him lordship.

That is Jesus' goal, because he is the Son of the Father. The Son does not crave his own achievement and fame; his aim is not to rule eternally, even if he does so for the honor of God. The most glorious thing he can show to the world is his divine sonship, and the greatest thing with which he can reveal God is that he submits himself to the Father and hands over to him all he possesses. His goal is attained when nothing besides God's will takes place in the entire fullness of all that happens, and when nothing besides what belongs to God exists in all that lives.

Was it Paul's view that at the end of time God will revert back into himself and suspend life in its varied forms, so that the end will be once again the unmoved, silent stillness of eternal existence, as it was before the beginning? Those who know Jesus, and who learn from the Son what the Father is, do not speculate in this way.

For such explanations deny life and derive life from what lacks it; they devise an empty Being and know nothing of the true unity that creates love. In contrast, Paul received the clear image of Jesus in his inmost self, and this comes to light most transparently when he speaks of his highest, most glorious hope. What was the grand aspect of Jesus' earthly life? Just this: that he submitted himself to God. On earth he had nothing but his own flesh and blood, and he devoted these to God. In times ahead the world will be his own, and what a world that will be: the world that he brought to the knowledge of God and unified in that knowledge; the world that he taught to honor God in truth and to worship in spirit and truth, because he overcame it; the fellowship of those who will live eternally, through the power of his grace. And now he offers himself and all those he has won for himself to the Father, so that he might be present and active in all that exists.

Here, there are no longer words to describe the worship that Paul foresees at the end of Jesus' struggle and victory, his suffering and ministry. This joy is too great for words to capture. Paul exulted in the thought that all that lives will recognize the lordship of the Christ, whether things in heaven or on earth or in the place of the dead. But his jubilation rises still higher because the name of the Christ will fade away and his ministry will be complete, because he will reveal in perfection that he is the Son who is one with the Father. We have before our eyes what it meant when Paul said that love abides and is eternal, and that it is the greatest of all.

The Marvel of Honoring God
December 23

As all confess, the mystery of the glorifying of God is great.
—1 Timothy 3:16

JESUS BECOMES THE LORD OF THE NEW COMMUNITY   555

Everywhere in Christianity we sing, "Glory in the highest be to God alone!" This song arose in Israel. We hear it in the Psalter: "Not to us, O LORD, not to us, but to your name give honor." In the New Testament the refrain intensifies: "To the glory of God the Father." And now this rings out as far as Christianity extends. It is a mark of the Christmas season: "Glory to God in the highest." Yet it is peculiar that we sing this verse. All must feel and admit this. All of us, whether friend or foe, member or opponent, of the church share the conviction that it is a great miracle if this verse becomes truth and we actually give the honor to God—to God alone and not to ourselves.

Honoring God: how does a person make this happen? How do we go about making the presence and outworking of the invisible God so clear that all we are and do in ourselves becomes unimportant? No matter how much has been said to us about God, the soul remains subject to sensory stimuli. In this state how can prayer arise that truly honors God? And how are we to attain mastery over our sinful desires, which reside in the innermost corner of our beings, in such a way that God's will becomes our own will and God's praise the aim of our actions and content of our hopes?

This mystery is not something dreamed up, not a figment of imagination fostered by religious poets. As great a mystery as this is, the veneration of God in man, which truly honors him, is an undeniably present reality that can no longer be expunged from human history. Rendering honor to God is a fixed feature of our human existence. For there is a revelation that shows God to us, and there is a force that moves us toward God, and there is an action that meets God's approval because it is obedient to his will. Through Jesus this secret has been brought into the world.

He was the one who honored God. He is the one who makes us into venerators of God. That is the meaning of his entry into human likeness. That is the sum of his Word. That gives his death saving power. That drove him to his prophecy speaking of God's coming glory. That makes him singular and unique. The burden of the struggle lies on him. For he lives among those who do not honor God as one who does honor him.

But as alien as everything about him is to us, he turns to us with all he is. We banish God into the distance, but by taking on human form he brings us near to God. He makes his Word the call that draws us to God. He makes his death the offer of divine grace, and from his promise comes the message of life. Thereby he works the miracle that veneration of God exists in mankind. Our secure certainty and deeply desired aim becomes "Glory in the highest be to God alone!"

Jesus' Humanity Renders Him Visible
December 24

He was made visible in the flesh.
—1 Timothy 3:16

Jesus brought about the veneration of God in that his flesh—the mode of human existence we all share—served to make him visible. But can our mode of existence make visible anything besides mere human existence and the forces that naturally form it? After all, we speak of our "race" because what is conceived reproduces what conceived it. As Jesus said to Nicodemus, "What is born of the flesh is flesh." But what is new and astounding with Jesus is that, in him, the flesh reveals the One who is not flesh but who was with God and is one with the Father.

So how does his humanity benefit us? It does not, if only his state of being human becomes visible. If we wish to study man, even remarkable and brilliant figures, there is plenty of opportunity. Moreover, it is rightly observed that if we wish to learn what *human* means, then we should inquire of those around us, of our ancestors from whom we have our flesh and blood, and of our contemporaries with whom our lives are intertwined for better or for worse. Why try to learn such things from someone who grew up from other ethnic roots in another culture and who is separated from us by thousands of years?

Yet Jesus' humanity is absolutely irreplaceable if he wishes to show us through it what is divine. Then his history puts us in touch with our God and our Lord. Compared with this story, everything else that happens on earth is meaningless play, just good enough to fill empty days. In contrast, what he accomplished in his humanity through history was the saving act accomplished for all eternity. His birth is then the condescension of the grace of God to mankind, which previously had to go its own way. His word makes audible the voice of love that grants us fellowship with God. The judgment that death inflicted on him is the judgment pronounced on all mankind, which condemns and yet forgives its godlessness. His resurrection is the appearance of eternal life, and his coming revelation the disclosing of the divine glory. Compared to all this, what is the birth of a mere human, in whom ancestors again appear? What are man's deeds and drives by which he preserves and supports himself? What is his dying but the revelation of the nothingness of his existence? Compared to the One whom God has made into his image, no one else even comes close.

But the mode by which Jesus enters our field of vision remains critical. We cannot separate that mode from his person, as if his humanity were only the shell in which the divine hid itself, so that to be freed from the shell would be to arrive at its true appearance. That would be to make of his Word a doctrine valid for itself and a law directed to our will. For that would rob his history of the feature that is essential to it. God deals with us in his Son. His flesh, which makes him visible, inserts him into the domain of our knowledge. What no one can truly apprehend, no one can access. But in his humanity Jesus has a substantial form that draws our gaze to it. Through his humanity we have access to the fact that God is with us.

The Vindication of Jesus Is the Spirit
December 25

He was vindicated by the Spirit.
—1 Timothy 3:16

Jesus was disputed and accused from the time he was born. King Herod declared him an enemy who wished to rob him of his throne and therefore had to be destroyed. He was continually spoken against, and this opposition increased. Offense was taken for two reasons: that Jesus is like us, and that he is not like us; that he was manifest in the flesh, and that he received life not from the flesh but from the fact that he proceeded from the Father.

The one objection takes this form: You, Jesus, are too human for us. To Jesus, a man, we are supposed to go and then become his disciples. But why? There are plenty of men everywhere we look. We are sufficient for ourselves, and if we extend a hand to one another and form a united line, we are strong. He calls us to him, it is said, because in him God is present.

But how is God to be found in one man and in what he did and suffered? The one we call God is unsearchable and fully hidden from our field of vision. And now this tiny slice of ancient history is supposed to be his revelation!

At the same time opposition arises on another front: in our view he is not human enough. Nothing about him is congruent with what we are. When he speaks, he attacks us, and when he acts, he repudiates human desire and insight. He wants to make us different from what we are. So the situation is and remains: Jesus is opposed and hated. We cannot all celebrate Christmas. For those who oppose him, his birth is no occasion for joy. Only those who in Jesus have found God's word and grace praise God on account of him.

Yet Jesus is not only opposed; he is also vindicated. The manner in which this took place again confronts us with a great mystery. The one who reveals his authority is the Spirit. His human nature gives him his fellowship with us but also causes people to take offense. But he also shows us his unity with God, and this takes place by the Spirit. By the flesh he is known to us; by the Spirit he becomes the object of our faith. Through the flesh he was once among us; through the Spirit he is now among us. Because he lived in the flesh, we can reject and forget him; because he is actively present in Spirit, he is our Lord.

But is the Spirit the correct means of proving Jesus' authority and overcoming contradiction to him? Is the Spirit not invisible and his effects inaccessible to our observation? What are we talking about when we speak of the "Spirit"? The Spirit is the one who awakens our inner lives. The Spirit acts so that we will and think, and so that we will what he wills and think what he says to us. Because Jesus is at work in the Spirit, he touches us where no one else can: in the innermost recess of our "I." He moves us at the very point from which life originates. No one can hinder the Spirit from finding us there. And when he enters in, we become those whom Jesus has conquered and who believe and obey him.

In the World There Are Those Who Believe on Jesus
December 26

He was seen by angels, proclaimed among the peoples,
believed on in the world.
—I TIMOTHY 3:16

It is not the vision of Jesus that vindicates him and gives his word convincing force for us, but the Spirit. He was seen by angels, not by us. But he was proclaimed by us, and now comes what is fully unexpected: his message gains a hearing among the peoples of the world. Does something actually exist that is relevant to every human, that every person can grasp regardless of level of education, that no national objective can suppress or replace? Without a doubt the phenomenon of humankind poses a question to which the message of Jesus speaks: Is there a spokesperson for God through whom God addresses all peoples, a mediator with God who leads us to his grace, a Lord who claims us for the will of God? That is a question directed to all and that calls all to attention when they hear it. For they are all created beings and know that they are created, even if they do not know the One who created them but regard themselves as simply having cropped up in the creative flow of nature, without having been informed where they come from and what their lives are for. They know that no one is left totally to himself, nor obligated completely to his neighbor. Rather, everyone is subject to the commandment that divides human action into righteousness and guilt. And the question is, *How is the former found and the latter eradicated?* It is human for man to inquire about God and to desire righteousness.

If man does not do this because nothing but life's natural affairs consume him, he can still awaken when the word of Jesus comes to him, when God speaks with him, and when God queries him about his righteousness. Regardless of the sector of mankind one inhabits, every person can harbor the knowledge that he or she is a solitary figure in the great wide world until the Creator reveals himself to that person. We all know that we are vile when we persist in battling against righteousness.

But the message of Jesus penetrates the world so that it will be proclaimed among all peoples. Can this incursion into the world succeed? The message has great power. The fellowship of life—by which that message gives to all a unified outlook and steers all toward the same destiny—leaves none untouched. That is why the same patterns recur in world history; for millennia it has followed its regular course and has been moved by the same forces. And now Jesus enters into the world, calls people everywhere to him, and takes persons out of the world, for he gives to them what the world does not have.

Can there be such a thing as people who are more than part of the world? Can a fellowship of persons arise who live in the world but are not of the world? This may be considered ludicrous. But what is deemed impossible by those who do not know Jesus happens: he is believed on in the world. By this means, what vindicates him is revealed: the Spirit. And so that notoriously great mystery comes to pass: there are people in the world who truly honor God. Because Jesus is present and actively effective in the Spirit, there are people who believe in him and say of him, "My Lord and my God." And this confession is the manner in which a person living in the world is able to honor God.

Jesus Has Glory
December 27

He was taken up into glory.
—1 Timothy 3:16

He was proclaimed in the world but not merely proclaimed: peoples put their trust in him. And he, whom we do not behold and have only in his Word—what is he? He has glory, for he has entered into the unsearchable richness of the divine life and activity. That gives to the church its peculiar construction. Its head and Lord takes part in God's own glory, while the church itself has all the characteristics of humanity. It is entrusted with the task of honoring God and has received the capacity to do so. To honor God means to worship him and praise his glory. But the church does not achieve this by worshiping itself. This is forbidden to it. It worships God because he took Jesus up to himself in glory.

We sometimes hear the objection, "Your Christian fellowship does extend among all peoples, yet as a whole you are small in number, and you are divided, and you are unable to unify and are therefore weak. You just talk of love while each lives for himself." There is in a sense no reply to this. It is true that in the church we have many disfigured faces, many hearts rent by chaotic thoughts, many enslaved by selfish desire, many whose word is profaned and made powerless by vanity. But the church consists not only of us who believe on Jesus; he who made the church and continually keeps it also belongs to the church. And he was taken up in glory.

The ability truly to honor God is given to us through God's exalting not the glory of the church but the glory of the Christ. There exists for us no honoring of God as long as we abide in the realm of lies. Only in the domain of truth is there worship. But how would we attain the courage to face the truth if we were forced to exalt ourselves? But now, because the glory belongs to Jesus and not to us, we do not seek our help in some empty appearance. We seek it rather by preserving the word of Jesus, which judges our natural desires and saves us from them and from all their devastation. Jesus unites our repentance with our faith in him, and since Jesus' end was his entrance into glory, hope, too, is intertwined with faith in him. Therefore a promise inheres in his message, and what it promises is glory that has become evident. That is the aim of our lives and of human history. For God's power to create and his will to dispense his grace are becoming evident.

The One Who Rejects Jesus Does Not Know What He Is Doing
December 28

Jesus said, "Father, forgive them, for they do not know what they are doing."
—LUKE 23:34

At the moment, our dear Germany reminds us of Golgotha, where Pilate ejected three from civil society as enemies of the people. Two assaulted national existence by their lawbreaking. Jesus was numbered among them due to his proclamation. For he made the claim to be king of his people. In our current setting there are likewise outlooks that are demonized, like French liberalism and Russian communism. Jesus is often placed alongside these deceivers of the people as an utterly foreign figure, the adversary of the nation's greed who breaks the pride of the German male. Do we know what we are doing?

When the high priest and the governor who represented Caesar united in joining forces against brigandage, and crucified all who stepped outside acceptable social boundaries, they were fully aware of their action. For unless they made conditions secure for life and property, civic life would be jeopardized. But when they ruled against Jesus, they acted blindly. They did not know what they were doing when they rejected what he offered. Nor did they know what it was they were defending against him. They protected from him their darkness, which made them adversaries of God and man, and their perverse desire, which nothing could satiate. They also protected their shortsighted plans, bound as they were to purely earthly concerns. They failed to recognize that precisely such policy was the ruin of the nation. They cast aside what they received from Jesus: the strong confidence of the one who can believe God; the freedom of the one whose sins are forgiven; the joyous hope of those who await God's lordship. They did not realize that precisely these things would have been salvation for their people, and that Jesus had come to them with divine authority to bring them God's gifts of grace.

They rejected him because they considered him their enemy. And indeed he was, in the sense that he often made clear enough: he is not entirely just one of us. But they did not recognize what separated him from them. The difference did not lie in his being some new creative variation produced by nature, maybe with some exotic blood type. Rather, God was at work in him and God's love led him, and they did not recognize that this actually bound him to them and rendered his word light—the light that illumines every person who comes into the world. They rejected him in the battle for their honor, because it would have been humiliating for them to subject themselves to him. Nor did they know how empty were the grand words they used to proclaim their own praise. They mistook the way in which Jesus exalts the person to whom he gives a share of his ministry. The authorities' minds were filled with foolishness and blindness. This was reflected in everything they said about the Jews and others, and about God and the Christ. Because they did not know what they were doing, Jesus used the last hour of his prerogative over himself to request forgiveness for them.

Today we must likewise trust the One who will reveal the forgiving mercy of Jesus even in the destiny that lies ahead for Germany. When we cast aside the person who seeks to use his life only for himself, who demands that others serve him; when we recognize those who build up the state with blood and force as obviously our enemies, and that the strength of the state appears to be in its submitting all to its aims, we act with good understanding. But when we also reject Jesus as the destroyer of our people, we know not what we are doing.

Attack or Assistance?
December 29

Learn from me, for I am gentle and humble in heart.
—MATTHEW 11:29

What was Jesus' intention: attack or assistance? Which of these two words objectively describes the meaning of his gospel? It is true to say that it is a call to arms against the world. And one can also say that it strengthens man, comforting him when he suffers and supporting him when he falters.

One view holds that the goal that describes the story of Jesus is attack. The Son of God is sent down into this fallen world as God's witness against the world's godlessness. It is an attack when he faces the rebellious, admittedly without weapon, but precisely thereby excludes every peace agreement and confirms discord as the incurable human condition. He is an attacker when he administers the office of teacher. Is it perhaps his intention to teach us an ethic that blesses us and grants to us a worldview attractive because of its depth? He speaks to this so that we might be silent before God, each confessing himself submissive to God's law and convinced of his inability to do what is good. He was in attack mode when he gave himself into the hands of those who condemned him. For this lent his attack the greatest possible offensive force, because he thereby disclosed mankind's guilt. There can be no vestige of belief in a human righteousness.

Another view says that Jesus brings assistance. This is the goal of his being sent into the world God created: help for our blind eyes, which are unable truly to apprehend God but now become assured of God because of Jesus. He brings help for our deaf ears, which can hear no word of God in the purely natural realm, but now, through Jesus, hear the Father and thereby experience his grace. He brings help for those of troubled conscience, who protest against what they deeply desire and do but cannot help themselves even though they condemn themselves. He brings help to frivolous, philanderous people, who do not know how to use the powers given to them but for whom Jesus now makes God's will the holy object of their desire. He brings help for our constantly threatened social order, into which our selfishness constantly introduces strife but to which Jesus brings healing as we recognize in him what love does.

Depending on the viewpoint from which we interpret the gospel, even what we do in worship can be variously assessed. Preaching is an attack on us, for it declares our thoughts and wishes to be futile and demands that we listen, believe, and do what Jesus tells us. And we are assaulted by Jesus' offering baptism to us, for baptism does not permit self-admiration of human worth. And we receive a strong blow when we share at the Lord's Table, because we find ourselves confronted there by the slain body and shed blood of Jesus, which puts an end to praise of humans.

Or preaching can be joy for us. For it is a redemptive aid that proclaims there is a message of God that calls us to him. And our baptism is a help that never fails us, for it extends the peace of God over our entire lives, and so does the Lord's Table, through which he receives us into his eternal fellowship.

Which of the two viewpoints recognizes the Lord's understanding? Neither of them, as long as one is understood to contradict the other. "Learn from me": by saying this, Jesus not only dismissed all other masters; he also divested us of the self-glorification that is such a common feature of our lives. This is, however, the fruit of his patience, and he exercises this because he seeks to help us. He attacks in order to heal, and he heals by removing from us what would otherwise destroy us.

That Which Abides
December 30

Now there abide faith, hope, love: these three.
—1 Corinthians 13:13

Static uniformity is unthinkable in the church. Paul saw clearly that every congregation takes on its own form; every generation has its peculiar appearance. True, Jesus' message was the same for all, for it instructed all who heard it regarding what Jesus had accomplished. How the message now prevailed over the thinking and willing of the congregations in the various locations and times did not, however, admit of being reduced to a single binding word. If Paul had coined terms that laid claim to being unchangeable, he would have been leading the church back under the Law. But now the passage of time brought diversity into the church, to say nothing of the momentous reversal that turned everything around when the Christ came. Is there anything permanent at all left for the church?

The intellectual accomplishments of the church were certainly not permanent. But we do not receive from Jesus only ideas. Rather, he shapes our inmost being according to his will. And what arises through him in our inner lives never passes away. What is permanent exists so that we may trust God. God in the glory of his grace draws our gaze and desire toward him; through this we believe in him. And this will always be the case. The testimony of the divine grace will no longer vanish from the world. Another constant is how the message of Jesus continually goes forth and appeals to us to place trust in him. And it will always be the case that when his word enters our lives, the fruit and effect will be our believing response to him and devotion to him. No matter how our situation alters, or our knowledge shifts, or our needs change, the empowerment to faith that Jesus gives remains constant and in full force. And on the day when not only the word of Jesus but also the sight of him calls us to him, that same empowerment will be no less active; it will, in fact, be perfected in force. Then all that tempts us to unbelief will dissipate and depart from our souls. We will be certain of his grace.

But all that comes to us from God is greater than our present day and the measure of life we currently experience. Whoever truly believes also truly hopes, and with this hope something immortal has entered into life. The wealth of the divine activity will make an upward movement out of our inner lives, not only now in our temporal being but also in our eternal lives. The new gift will stand continually above the gift we now have. It is this new gift that we long for and for which we ready ourselves.

If we can believe and hope, then God has redeemed us out of the solitude of our own selfishness. He has transferred the goal of our lives out of ourselves by our believing on and hoping in him. Now we love, and this is the third thing we are gifted with that does not pass away. Never again will we sink down into self-love, which seeks to find sufficiency in itself. We will always be placed into the fellowship of those who have become submissive to the gracious will of God.

Can our faith, hope, and love not waver and end? Of course! But the possibility that we may shift does not overturn what God has made to be the foundation of our share in him. Continually valid and true in every situation remains this: his Word makes us into persons who have faith, hope, and love.

What Is Left for Us Without Jesus?
December 31

Now Jesus said to the Twelve, "Do you wish to go away too?"
—John 6:67

What Jesus could achieve in Galilee was complete. What he intended to do with his flesh and blood has also been thoroughly explained. Would he protect it and preserve it for himself? He would have to, if he wanted to serve as king in the normal sense of the term. But he had said that he did not possess his flesh and blood for the sake of his own life. They are destined, rather, to become the food and drink of the world, and through them it, not he, would receive life. In response, the crowd that accompanied Jesus dwindled. The throng coming to him lessened. What would be the point of remaining with him if he was not going to remain with them? And why hope in him if he planned to die?

Now Jesus placed before the Twelve, too, a choice. Did they wish to leave him as well? Was he retracting the call that had established his fellowship with them? No, he did not waver on that point. His will stood firm. He was not releasing them. But their will had to grow out of his. Did his fellowship with them create their fellowship with him? Did his offer to serve as their leader bring about their obedience? If he was the only one to give his flesh and blood while they protected and kept safe their own, then their fellowship with him would have become impossible.

The disciples were alarmed at the void that would open up before them if their fellowship with Jesus were to end. Where would they go if they departed from him? They had no other Lord besides him.

Much about Jesus may remain foreign to us and push us close to turning away from him. We cannot clarify to ourselves the oneness with God that

JESUS BECOMES THE LORD OF THE NEW COMMUNITY   567

he ascribed to himself by analogy with other human experiences. It is a onetime, unparalleled phenomenon, a mystery we cannot penetrate. We can be alarmed by the manner in which he places God's action above the natural order and at the same time makes it visible in nature. For from this the claim could arise that we are free with respect to our natural desires. We cannot arrive at a clear image of the events that took place on the first Easter, and his prophecy does not account for the course of history lying between us and the final end.

But where else could we go? Our situation is still completely that of the disciples when Jesus placed before them the choice of whether they wished to terminate their fellowship with him. Go elsewhere? Where then? A trip without a destination is a senseless undertaking. Backward is not a viable option for us. As it was completely impossible for Peter and John to return to the rabbinate and the Talmud, so it is impossible for us to return with our ancestors to the altars of their warrior gods and to celebrate the festivals of their nature gods. This is forbidden to us, first, by what we have learned about nature since the era of such primitive worship. And then, second, consider what we have received from Jesus. The faith that has turned to God and the love that has been freed from self-promotion—these cannot simply vanish now that Jesus has planted them in mankind. Whoever has received them cannot forsake them. For the most fruitful and blessed hour of that person's life remains that time at which Jesus became for him the giver of faith and of love.

Scripture Index

Exodus

20:12 220
21:17 220

Deuteronomy

6:13 87
6:16 99
8:3 98

Psalms

22:1 .... 446, 449
34:8 541
91:11–12 99
110:1 .... 391, 393, 435
118:22–23 368

Isaiah

1:2–3 245
1:11–17 130–31
2:2–3 346–47
2:4 348
5:1–7 352–53
5:3–7 355
6:9–10 ...... 200, 202
52:5 359
61:1–2 89

Daniel

7:13 435

Hosea

6:6 129

Matthew

3:1–2 34
3:7 50
3:8 53
3:9 54
3:10 55
3:11 .... 44, 57
4:1–4 98
4:1 96
4:5–7 99
4:12 86
4:17 39
4:18–22 70
5:3 91
5:8 226
5:18 137
5:19 156
5:20 135
5:21–22 136
5:39 146
5:43 139
5:44 140
5:48 .... 159, 418
6:5–6 216
6:26 299
6:30 300

6:33 73
7:1 264
7:13–14 207
7:16–20 314
8:2–4 106
8:5–10 113
8:14–15 255
8:21–22 282
9:10–11 123
9:12 126
9:13 .... 129, 133
9:14–15 148
10:8 295
10:28 292
10:34 388
10:38 283
10:42 298
11:18–19 66
11:23–24 182
11:25–26 210
11:25 35
11:28 142
11:29 563
11:30 144
12:1–4 162
12:5 164
12:6 166
12:8 168
12:9–13 170

569

12:14 171	18:1–4 335–36	26:28 . . . . 49, 423
12:22–24 173	18:10 80	26:41 430
12:26, 28 174	18:20 483	26:65 . . . . 435, 436
12:29 387	18:21–27 266	27:11 442
12:31–32 544	18:28–35 268	27:27–30 443
12:34 50	19:8 141	27:38 445
12:41 179	19:23–24 192	27:46 446
12:42 180	21:13 370	27:47 447
12:46–50 476	21:28–32 247	28:18 480
13:3–4, 19 178	21:33–39 354–55	28:19–20 . . . . . 496, 505
13:5–6, 20–21 184	21:40–41 356	28:19 . . . . 481, 498
13:10–15 200	21:42 368	
13:13–15 202	22:1–7 376	**Mark**
13:22 . . . . 186, 189	22:10–13 489–90	1:4 42
13:23 194	22:16–17 379	1:9 60
13:24–28 311	22:18–21 382	1:10–11 62
13:28–30 313	22:21 383	1:14–15 41
13:31–33 211	22:41–43, 45 . . . 392–93	1:23–26 93
13:47–50 204	22:44 391	2:3–7 120
13:52 537	23:2–3 318	2:8–12 121–22
13:54–57 94	23:8–12 474	10:37 331
15:1–6 220	23:37 349	10:38–39 332
15:11, 15–20 . . . 224–25	24:1–2 394	10:39–40 334
15:13 317	24:6 402	10:42–44 337
16:13–16 252	24:34 405	10:45 338
16:17 253	24:35 . . . . 404, 408	11:9–10 345
16:18 . . . . 256, 257	24:45–51 420	11:11 369
16:19 . . . . 258, 260, 262	25:1–13 421–22	12:32–34 373
16:21 272, 275, 276, 278	25:14–15 196	12:40 217
16:22 279	25:16–17 197	12:41–44 374
16:23 281	25:18 198	14:3–5 413
16:24 285	25:19 307	14:35–36 428
16:26 294	25:21, 23 81	14:58 434
16:27 306	25:24 145	15:42–47 455
16:28 407	26:2 412	
17:19–20 303	26:26–28 424–25	

SCRIPTURE INDEX

Luke

1:35 61
2:10–11 37
2:34–35 454
3:10–11 51
3:12–14 125
4:5–8 87
4:16–21 89
4:21 446
4:23 95
4:25–30 100
5:4–11 71
5:37–38 153
5:39 155
7:2–6 111
7:37–38 149
9:52–56 290
10:3 286
10:7–12 296–97
10:19 340
10:20 341
11:1 213
11:27–28 90
11:37–41 227–28
12:32 208
13:6–9 360
15:1–10 237
15:11–16 239
15:17–21 240–41
15:22–24 242
15:25–32 243–44
16:1–2 190
18:1–8 396
18:13–14 371–72
19:41 351
22:31–32 388

22:61 438
23:34 561
23:42–43 448
24:25–27 460
24:36–39 458

John

1:1 183
1:29 63
1:35–51 75
1:41–42 76
1:51 .... 77, 79
2:1–10 84
3:14 365
3:16 361
3:17 205
4:9–10 116
4:21, 23 398
4:23 214
5:24 543
6:54–55 426
6:63 427
6:67 .... 475, 566
7:1–5 273
8:12 469
10:11–13 366–67
11:16 344
11:47–48 378
13:8 414
13:9–10 416
14:16–17 401
15:3 416
15:4 475
16:33 386
17:12 465
17:20–23 492

18:7–8 431
18:36 289
19:4–5 444
19:11 330
19:15 381
19:25–27 452
20:9 459
20:11–17 462
20:24–28 464
20:29 465
21:15–17 439

Acts

4:12 488
6:4 259
6:13–14 222
8:36, 38 499
10:28 229
10:34–35 102
15:9 233
16:30–33 502
17:24–25 395
17:26 489
23:5 316

Romans

1:14 484
1:16 487
1:17–18 363
1:17 108
2:10–11 103
2:16 310
2:17–20 357
2:21–24 359
3:28 114
3:31 508

Philippians

6:3–4 501
8:10 417
8:17 152
8:23 477
9:6 350
9:8 45
9:22 540
9:23 132
11:28 493
12:1 529
12:21 287
13:12 470
14:14, 20 231

1 Corinthians

2:8 432
6:20 530
7:29–31 547
9:19–21 495
12:27 523
13:13 .... 403, 514, 564
15:24 552
15:28 553

2 Corinthians

2:16 263
5:17 471

Galatians

2:9 490
5:6 515
5:13 506

Ephesians

1:18 549

Philippians

1:9–10 512
2:9–11 550
2:12–13 ...... 509, 511
2:15–16 470
2:16 308
4:4 151

1 Timothy

1:3–4 526
1:4 527
1:5 128
1:6–7 223
1:12 389
2:1 399
2:4 400
3:15 525
3:16 .... 554, 556, 557, 559, 560
4:13 .... 533, 534
6:5–6 193

2 Timothy

2:4–6 517
2:7 518
2:11–13 440
3:15 536

Titus

1:15 234
2:13 .... 539, 541
3:4 117

James

2:14 514
4:4 187

1 Peter

1:1 320
1:2 479
1:3 466
1:4 467
1:5 .... 38, 110
1:18–19 65
1:21 107
1:22 230
2:4–5 519
2:9 521
2:12 321
2:13 325
2:14 327
2:16 157
2:17 .... 235, 323
2:18 328
2:20–21 451
3:18 450
3:21 504
4:10–11 531
4:15–16 324
5:7 302

1 John

1:8, 10 46
1:9 48
2:1 364
2:15–17 545–46
3:5–6 165
4:18 292
5:4 390
5:6–8 522
5:19 541